Evidence from neuroanatomy, brain imaging, molecular biology and behavioral studies points to a key role for neurodevelopmental factors in the pathogenesis of the major psychiatric disorders, particularly those within the schizophrenia spectrum. In this important book, the fields of developmental neurobiology, clinical psychiatry and behavioral neuroscience are brought together by an international group of experts, including many of those responsible for the ideas that have come to dominate current thinking.

The first section, "The Developing Brain", reviews neurodevelopment from the molecular to the behavioral level. Section II "Development and Psychopathology", covers clinical applications of the basic principles of developmental neurobiology, including the role of potential etiological factors in the pathogenesis of neuro-psychiatric illness, and examines the continuity between developmental disorders of childhood and adult neuropsychiatric disorders. The third and final section, "Integrative Models", presents approaches towards a synthesis of neuro-developmental and clinical findings.

For students, scientists and clinicians in psychiatry, psychology and neurodevelopment, this is an essential reference.

"A very significant volume . . . that can be read from cover to cover and yet will also provide a comprehensive reference for some time . . . Taken as a whole, the authors collectively make a strong statement for the necessary integration of basic and clinical neuroscience in the emergence of psychopathology." From the foreword by David Kupfer, University of Pittsburgh Medical Center.

D1707919

Neurodevelopment & Adult Psychopathology

Neurodevelopment & Adult Psychopathology

EDITED BY

MATCHERI S. KESHAVAN

Department of Psychiatry, University of Pittsburgh

AND ROBIN M. MURRAY

Department of Psychological Medicine, Kings College School of Medicine and Dentistry
and the Institute of Psychiatry, London

CAMBRIDGE
UNIVERSITY PRESS

PUBLISHED BY THE PRESS SYNDICATE OF THE UNIVERSITY OF CAMBRIDGE
The Pitt Building, Trumpington Street, Cambridge CB2 1RP, United Kingdom

CAMBRIDGE UNIVERSITY PRESS
The Edinburgh Building, Cambridge, CB2 2RU, United Kingdom
40 West 20th Street, New York, NY 10011-4211, USA
10 Stamford Road, Oakleigh, Melbourne 3166, Australia

First published 1997

Printed in the United Kingdom at the University Press, Cambridge

Typeset in Monotype Ehrhardt 9/12 pt by SE

A catalogue record for this book is available from the British Library

Library of Congress Cataloguing in Publication data

Neurodevelopment and adult psychopathology / edited by Matcheri S.
Keshavan and Robin M. Murray.
    p.   cm.
    Includes index.
    ISBN 0 521 48104 X (hardback).   ISBN 0 521 48565 7 (paperback);
jc 06 10 10 96
    1. Schizophrenia   Etiology.   2. Developmental neurobiology.
3. Schizophrenia   Pathophysiology.   I. Murray, Robin, MD, M Phil,
MRCP, MRC Psych.   II. Keshavan, Matcheri S., 1953–
    [DNLM: 1. Schizophrenia   etiology.   2. Brain   growth &
development.   3. Brain abnormalities.   4. Affective Disorders
etiology.   5. Obsessive-Compulsive Disorder   etiology.   WM 203
N49325   1997]
RC514.N4437   1997
616.89′82071   dc21
DNLM/DLC   96–46969   CIP
for Library of Congress

ISBN 0 521 48104 X hardback
ISBN 0 521 48565 7 paperback

Contents

Contributors

Blanes, Tomas, MRCPsych, PhD
Department of Experimental Psychopathology, Institute of Psychiatry, De Crespigny Park, Denmark Hill, London SE5 8AF, UK

Bullmore, Ed T., MRCPsych
Department of Psychological Medicine, Institute of Psychiatry and King's College, De Crespigny Park, Denmark Hill, London SE5 8AF, UK

Castle, David J., MRCPsych
Department of Psychiatry and Behavioral Science, The University of Western Australia, 35 Mills Street, Bentley, WA

Chugani, Diane C., MRCPsych, PhD
Department of Pediatrics and Neurology, Children's Hospital of Michigan, 3901 Beaubien Blvd, Detroit, MI 48201, USA

Chugani, Harry T., MD
Division of Pediatric Neurology/PET Center, Children's Hospital of Michigan, 3901 Beaubien Blvd., Detroit, MI 48201, USA

Done, D. John, PhD
Division of Psychology, University of Hertfordshire, Hatfield, Herts AL10 9AB, UK

Feinberg, Irwin, MD
Psychiatry University of California, Davis, Department of Psychiatry, VA/UCD Sleep Laboratory, Davis, CA 95616-8657, USA

Frangou, Sophia, MRCPsych
Department of Psychological Medicine, Institute of Psychiatry and King's College, De Crespigny Park, Denmark Hill, London SE5 8AF, UK

Harrison, Paul J., MRCPsych
Department of Psychiatry, Warneford Hospital, University of Oxford, UK

Haas, Gretchen L., PhD
Department of Psychiatry, Western Psychiatric Institute and Clinic and the University of Pittsburgh School of Medicine, 3811 O'Hara Street, Pittsburgh, PA 15213, USA

Hollis, Chris, MRCPsych
Institute of Psychiatry, De Crespigny Park, London SE5 8AX, UK

Jernigan, Terry L., PhD
Brain Image Analysis Laboratory 0949, University of California, San Diego School of Medicine, La Jolla, CA 92093-0949, USA

Jones, Peter, MRCPsych
Department of Psychiatry, Mapperley Hospital, Porchester Road, Nottingham NG3 6AA, UK

Kennedy, James L., MD
Section of Neurogenetics, Clarke Institute of Psychiatry, 250 College Street, Toronto, Ontario M5T 1RB, Canada

Kerwin, Robert W., FRCPsych, PhD
Clinical Neuropharmacology, Institute of Psychiatry, De Crespigny Park, London SE5 8AF, UK

Keshavan, Matcheri S., MD, MRCPsych
Department of Psychiatry, Western Psychiatric Institute and Clinic, 3811 O'Hara Street, PA 15213, USA

Klunk, William E., MD, PhD
Department of Psychiatry, Western Psychiatric Institute and Clinic, Neurophysics Laboratory, 3811 O'Hara Street, Pittsburgh, PA 15213, USA

Kotrla, Kathryn J., MD
University of Texas Science Center at Houston, Department of Psychiatry and Behavioral Sciences, Harris County Psychiatric Center, Room 2C01, 2800 South MacGregor Way, Houston, TX 77021, USA

Lewis, David A., MD
Department of Psychiatry and Neuroscience, University of Pittsburgh, Western Psychiatric Institute and Clinic, W1651 BST, 3811 O'Hara Street, Pittsburgh, PA 15213, USA

Lewis, Shôn, MD
School of Psychiatry and Behavioral Sciences, Department of Psychiatry, Withington Hospital, West Didsbury, Manchester M20 8LR, UK

Lund, Jennifer S., PhD
Institute of Ophthalmology, University of London, Bath Street, London, EC1V 9El, UK

McClure, Richard, J., PhD
Senior Research Principal, University of Pittsburgh Medical Center, Western Psychiatric Institute and Clinic, Neurophysics Laboratory, 3811 O'Hara Street, Pittsburgh, PA 15213, USA

McGuire, Philip, MRCPsych
Department of Psychological Medicine, Institute of Psychiatry, London SE5 8AF, UK and Wellcome Department of Cognitive Neurology, Institute of Neurology, London, UK

Minshew, Nancy, J., MD
Department of Psychiatry and Neurology, University of Pittsburgh Medical Center, Western Psychiatric Institute and Clinic, Neurophysics Laboratory, 3811 O'Hara Street, Pittsburgh, PA 15213, USA

Murray, Robin M., FRCPsych, DSc
Department of Psychological Medicine, Institute of Psychiatry and Kings College, De Crespigny Park, Denmark Hill, London SE5 8AF, UK

Nasrallah, Henry A., MD
Department of Psychiatry, The Ohio State University, College of Medicine, 1670 Upham Drive, Columbus, OH 43210, USA

O'Connell, Paul, MD
>   Department of Psychological Medicine, Institute of Psychiatry and King's College, De Crespigny Park, Denmark Hill, London SE5 8AF, UK

Panchalingam, Kanagasabai, PhD
>   Department of Psychiatry, University of Pittsburgh Medical Center, Western Psychiatric Institute and Clinic, Neorophysics Laboratory, 3811 O'Hara Street, Pittsburgh, PA 15213, USA

Pettegrew, Jay W., MD
>   Professor of Psychiatry, Neurology and Health Services Administration, University of Pittsburgh Medical Center, Western Psychiatric Institute and Clinic, Department of Psychiatry; Director, Neurophysics Laboratory, 3811 O'Hara Street, Pittsburgh, PA 15213, USA

Pogue-Geile, Michael F., PhD
>   Department of Psychology, University of Pittsburgh, Pittsburgh, PA 15217, USA

Sater, Amy K., PhD
>   University of Houston, Department of Biology, Houston, TX 77204, USA

Sowell, Elizabeth R., PhD
>   Brain Image Analysis Laboratory 0949, University of California, Diego School of Medicine, La Jolla, CA 92093 0949, USA

Stefanis, Nick, MRCPsych
>   Department of Psychological Medicine, Institute of Psychiatry, De Crespigny Park, London SE5 8AF, UK

Suomi, Stephen J., PhD
>   Laboratory of Comparative Ethology and National Institute of Child Health and Human Development, Building 31, B2B15, 9000 Rockville Pike, Bethesda, MI 20892, USA

Taylor, Eric, FRCP, FRCPsych
>   Institute of Psychiatry, De Crespigny Park, London SE5 8AX, UK

Vicente, Astride M., MSc
>   Neurogenetics Section, Clarke Institute of Psychiatry, 250 College Street, Toronto, Ontario, M5T 1RB, Canada

Weinberger, Daniel R., MD
>   Clinical Brain Disorders Branch, Intramural Research Program, National Institute of Mental Health, NIH, Neurosciences Center at St. Elizabeth's Hospital, Washington, DC 20032, USA

Foreword

While such a book could have been written a decade ago and even then would have represented an important set of contributions, Drs Keshavan and Murray have now capitalized on neuroscience advances in the last ten years and have produced a very significant volume. This is primarily true because our theories have traditionally outpaced the tools in our "toolbox" to test hypotheses. With new neuroscience tools now available, we are actually engaged in a set of iterative investigations generating an acceleration of scientific advances in neurodevelopment relating to psychopathology.

In seeking to provide a background for non-neuroscientists or "clinical consumers," the authors have selected, in the first section, a core group of areas which are well-covered in a comprehensive, but readable fashion. They range from developmental neuroanatomy, particularly the cerebral cortex, to the genetics of neurodevelopment, to selected neurochemical receptors and, finally, to a careful review of neuroimaging (including magnetic resonance imaging, spectroscopy, and position emission tomography). Potential clues to psychopathology are provided by an overview of primate development. The second section is an important key to the reader's ability to be treated successfully to a series of viewpoints on development and schizophrenia, with lesser attention to affective and obsessive compulsive disorders. In short, this section on development and schizophrenia presents a sophisticated update of ongoing investigative efforts. The final section of the volume includes three integrated viewpoints on neurodevelopment and schizophrenia.

This is a volume that can be read cover to cover and yet will also provide a comprehensive reference for some time until a second edition of this book is available. Taken as a whole, the authors collectively make a strong statement for the necessary integration of basic and clinical neuroscience in understanding the emergence of psychopathology. Even if the authors do not prove their specific hypotheses for the development of adult onset schizophrenia, they will have moved our field several steps in the direction of translational research, and provided new knowledge in understanding critical periods, both pre- and postnatal, and over the early life span.

This volume provides a compelling example of why we need to increase our understanding of brain plasticity and critical periods. First, the role of genes and gene expression in determining critical periods need to be addressed in a substantive manner. In improving our understanding of adolescent and adult onset psychopathology, it will still be crucial to emphasize the role of plasticity and development. Among many questions that need to be addressed, the following two are representative. What processes in neurobiological development are crucially time-dependent compared with those that continue to demonstrate plasticity throughout development? Are there critical periods in brain development associated with the emergence of specific cognitive and emotional maturational windows?

Finally, psychopathologies are highly complex phenomena consisting of a variety of biological and behavioral features. Their development within the highly dynamic process of development itself is a "rapidly moving target" that is exceedingly difficult to investigate. Thus, understanding plasticity issues as they relate to the development of psychopathology is no small challenge.

This process has begun with imperfect tools, perhaps as we might have to use a still camera for capturing a dynamic process; however, even still pictures from various parts of the "movie" will serve to give us better clues as to what this film's plot may be all about than no pictures at all. We may feel that we are getting some still pictures from a movie, which we have some information on the beginning and some information on parts much later in the action – which things appear to have settled down and are more stable. We do not have the tools to study development and the onset of psychopathology in real time, but we hope to take as many still pictures with little temporal delay, so that we may then cartoon them in such a way that we "simulate" development in real time.

In summary, the editors and their colleagues are to be congratulated in achieving a first generation synthesis. We look forward to further efforts which continue to explore this important frontier to neurodevelopment and psychopathology.

David J. Kupfer, MD
Thomas Detre Professor and Chair,
Department of Psychiatry,
University of Pittsburgh

Preface

The central goal of this book is to present to the reader the rapidly expanding knowledge in developmental biology, and its consequences for our understanding of major adult psychiatric disorders. The past decade has witnessed a dramatic increase in research activity in the interface between basic developmental biology and clinical neuroscience; in particular, the new knowledge of human brain development has had a growing impact on contemporary views of the origins of adult onset psychopathology.

Section I of this volume contains chapters describing the latest knowledge of normal development of the brain. The development of the cerebral cortex is a particularly complex process, involving a cascade of events in which a disruption in one step leads to a compensatory modification of subsequent steps because of the enormous plasticity of the neural systems. To paraphrase Jennifer Lund who reviews this subject in Chapter 1, it is amazing that in most individuals the brain develops normally!

The fact that disruption of higher order cognitive functions characterizes several major psychiatric disorders has stimulated a great deal of interest in the association cortex, critical for these functions. The development of the prefrontal cortex, which is the last brain region to complete maturation, proceeds through the period of adolescence, the age period when major psychiatric disorders such as schizophrenia typically begin. As David Lewis outlines in Chapter 2, an understanding of the development of this circuitry during the peripubertal period may therefore shed light on disorders characterized by disruption of the integrity of the frontotemporal network.

The mechanisms which underlie the shaping of cortical organization involve both genetic programming and the effects of experience. Molecular genetics has been remarkably successful in localizing and identifying the aberrant genes determining many medical and neuropsychiatric disorders such as Huntington's chorea and Alzheimer's disease. As Astride Vicente and James Kennedy illustrate in Chapter 3, inroads are now being made into understanding the genetic control of brain development, and genes are being identified that can be examined as possible candidates for involvement in neurodevelopmental disorders such as autism and schizophrenia.

Synaptic and axonal survival is driven by the need for selective stabilization of functionally valid connections, shaped by experience. Thus, enriching experiences may potentially facilitate survival of neurons and synapses while, on the other hand, adverse experience may contribute significantly to disordered development. The exuberant growth of neurons and synapses early in development underlies the brain's capacity to compensate in response to early insults. Neuronal growth and synaptic formation involves feedback from the target cells by trophic humoral factors and neurotransmitters including glutamate, and neuronal electrical activity; these and their possible relevance to schizophrenia are described in Chapter 4 by Nick Stefanis, Paul Harrison and Robert Kerwin.

The next three chapters outline the dramatic advances that have stemmed from neuroimaging technology. Terry Jerigan and Elizabeth Sowell (Chapter 5) review data from in vivo structural neuroimaging studies concerning the anatomical development of the brain. Studies showing decline in the volume of the cortex in later childhood and adolescence may be consequent on pruning of redundant connectivity later to increase functional efficiency (which may mediate the development of abstract thinking) albeit at the expense of plasticity. In Chapter 6, Jay Pettegrew and colleagues summarize data compatible with this notion pointing to reductions in membrane phospholipid metabolism during puberty and the adolescent period. These changes have a strikingly similar temporal course, and perhaps reflect synaptic pruning processes. Harry and Diane Chugani (Chapter 7) provide evidence from positron emission tomography (PET) studies of infants and children showing a developmental rise and fall in regional cortical metabolism.

It has been widely held that early experiences can have

important effects on developmental trajectories and in turn on adult functioning. Suomi (Chapter 8) has reviewed recent findings from his own and other laboratories examining effects of early rearing experiences on adult behavior and physiology in nonhuman primates. These findings clearly have important implications for our understanding of the development of normal and abnormal human behavior.

Section II focuses on research findings relevant to adult onset psychiatric disorders. The new neurodevelopmental knowledge has led to a shift in our conceptualization of the pathobiology of major psychiatric disorders beginning in adolescence or early adult life. In particular, recent years have witnessed an impressive expansion of new information pertaining to the neurodevelopmental pathogenesis of schizophrenia. Peter Jones and Michael Done (Chapter 9) and Pogue-Geile (Chapter 10) review the epidemiological data that implicate neurodevelopmentally mediated premorbid deficits in schizophrenia. In Chaper 11, Gretchen Haas and David Castle point to the substantive data that suggest important sex differences in such premorbid deficits as well as in several key aspects of the later illness such as age of onset and course. Shòn Lewis (Chapter 12) distils the crucial ideas about schizophrenia which have emerged from structural neuroimaging studies while Kathryn Kottrla, Amy Sater and Daniel Weinberger (Chapter 13) summarize the neuropathological evidence that points to derailed early brain development. Chris Hollis and Eric Taylor (Chapter 16) have gleaned insights from studies of childhood onset schizophrenia which shed light on the origins of its later onset counterpart.

While much of the research has focused on schizophrenia, our understanding of some other psychiatric disorders such as autism (Jay Pettegrew, Chapter 6; Harry and Diane Chugani, Chapter 7), affective disorders (Henry Nasrallah, Chapter 14) and obsessive compulsive disorders (Philip McGuire, Chapter 15), can also be enhanced by a neurodevelopmental perspective.

Not surprisingly, this wealth of information has led to a search for hypotheses and constructs that can serve to organize complex data sets and generate specific predictions. Several neurodevelopmental models of schizophrenia have been proposed. **Section III** focuses on the contrasting ideas, with Ed Bullmore and colleagues (Chapter 18) ascribing the origins of schizophrenia to dysplasia of critical neural networks in fetal life, and others such as Irwin Feinberg (Chapter 17) primarily implicating postnatal developmental processes. Finally, in Chapter 19, Matcheri Keshavan presents an integrative view, proposing an interaction between early and late developmental deviance.

We anticipate that this book will enable students of psychopathology as well as neuroscience to obtain a fuller understanding of the evolving developmental models of adult onset psychiatric disorders. We also hope that this work will serve as an important resource for researchers in the fields of behavioral neuroscience, developmental biology and biological psychiatry. Finally, we are grateful to Joanne Miller, Mary Newell, Donna Siviy, Erica A. Spokart and Jenny Marchant for their painstaking work in editing and preparation of the manuscripts for publication.

Matcheri S. Keshavan, MD
Pittsburgh, Pennsylvania, USA

Robin M. Murray, MD
London, UK

SECTION I

The developing brain

1

Development of the cerebral cortex: an overview

JENNIFER S. LUND

The cerebral cortex is a feature unique to the mammalian brain. When considering the normal development of the cerebral cortex and the factors which may control that complex process, there appears to be an almost endless list of events requiring specific genetic and environmental controls, and therefore, an equally large set of possibilities of disruption. The remarkable fact is that in most individuals the cerebral cortex develops normally. Like most neural developmental processes, all stages of cortical development have many controlling factors and if one factor fails, others adjust to compensate. This points to the difficulties experienced in identifying single factors required for any of the many steps in the construction of the cerebral cortex. To recognize the nature of defects in cortical construction and function it is essential to understand as much as possible about its normal adult state and its normal developmental history. Human cortical tissue comes available either through biopsy of highly abnormal tissue, or at post-mortem, with the problems of significant delay and consequent deterioration of all aspects of its organization; thus, much of our current knowledge about cortical organization has been obtained from studies on laboratory animals.

Cortical development can be broadly divided into two phases. The first is a genetically determined sequence of events, occurring in utero in most mammals, that can be modified by manipulations of the local environment within the fetal nervous system and which is also modifiable by the maternal environment. The second phase is one that occurs both before and after birth where the connectivity of the cortex becomes acutely sensitive to patterns of activity. This is first driven by spontaneous activity in the sense organs that generates activity in the afferents to the cortex plus spontaneous activity in the cortical neurons them-

selves in utero; after birth, sensory information driven by external events starts to modulate the synaptic connections that are being built. This lability of cortical connectivity wanes as sexual maturation occurs and the cortical synaptic connectivity is pruned to a final stable adult pattern that shows little evidence of change (but see Darian-Smith and Gilbert 1994, for evidence of axonal sprouting) apart from gradual slow attrition of neurons and their connections in normal aging. While the adult cortex does not undergo massive anatomical changes following lesions or disruptions, cortical functional patterns such as topographic maps show considerable changes (for a review see Garraghty *et al.* 1994). All mammals seem to have a similar series of cortical developmental events but the total length of the developmental period, the temporal relationships of different aspects of development, and the time at which birth occurs relative to the maturational stage of the cortex vary widely between species. For instance, primates are born with a cortex rich in synapses and with thalamocortical projections already well connected; in the rat, however, thalamocortical fibers have still to complete their ingrowth and the cortical neuropil has very few synapses within it. These differences in timing can lead to different controls operating on particular developmental events in different species.

The first stage starts with cell proliferation in the ventricular generative zone with subsequent cell migration laying down first a narrow zone of cells that will be split in two by later migrating neurons to become a subplate region below layer VI, and layer I (see Fig. 2.1 in Chapter 2). The later migrating cells build a region called the cortical plate that will become layers VI through II (Angevine and Sidman 1961; Rakic 1974). Once cell generation comes to a halt, no further neurons are added to the cortex at any stage in the animal's life. While much of this migration is radial (Rakic 1972, 1988; O'Rourke *et al.* 1992), there is also significant lateral neural migration (Price and Thurlow 1988; Walsh and Cepko 1988, 1992; Kirkwood *et al.* 1992) so that each cortical area is made up of neurons whose primordia were mainly but not exclusively neighbors in a common generative region. During this proliferative phase it is uncertain if final adult proportions of different types of neurons and glia are generated as there is continual cell death during cortical maturation (Finlay 1992). Indeed, there may be selective loss of particular cell populations to achieve the constant proportions of different cell classes observed in the adult cortex; cell death is particularly marked in the subplate of some species with up to 90% of the cells lost during maturation of the primate cortex.

Cell loss occurs as a gradual attrition in the cortex, unlike other regions of the nervous system where sudden phases of cell death occur as a normal part of development (Williams *et al.* 1987). In the adult, cortical depth and the total cell number per unit column of cortical tissue are fairly uniform across areas and species (Rockel *et al.* 1980); an exception is primary visual cortex of the primate that manages to generate a higher cell density than other regions (see review by Kennedy and DeHay 1993). We do not understand what determines final cell number or the different cell densities in the different cortical layers in adulthood. We know through study of clonal development that early primordial cells must be genetically different as progeny from single primordia seem already to be determined in their fate to become glia or neurons, and perhaps even subclasses within these categories (Luskin *et al.* 1988, 1993; Parnavelas *et al.* 1991; Mione *et al.* 1994; Gotz *et al.* 1995). It remains unclear which mechanism determines the proportions of different cell types generated (for instance in the adult cortex there are about 15–25% of gamma amino butyric acid (GABA) containing neurons in any region or layer of the cortex). One hypothesis is that they may be self-regulating; this could be achieved by each cell type releasing a cell-specific diffusible factor (even their normal neurotransmitter substances), that begins to halt division of primitive cells of like kind (see Anderson 1989; Gao *et al.* 1991).

In the adult the afferent and efferent projections of each cortical layer have a predictable arrangement: layer 6 feeding back to the source of afferents to layer IV, layer V projecting subcortically, and the superficial layers 2–3 projecting to other cortical regions. These relationships seem genetically determined and can be shown to persist in cultures where cortical and subcortical regions are grown as separate tissue islands that then grow cross-connections (Bolz *et al.* 1990; Yamamoto *et al.* 1992); the connections are laminar specific even in initial outgrowths. Thus, efferent projections to different destinations arise from cells in different laminae in cortical depth; even within laminae, different cell populations generally serve different external regions. In the reeler mouse mutant, an autosomal recessive mutation disrupts migration of the cortical cells such that later generated cells cannot pass through earlier generated cells: this results in an inverse laminar relationship in depth compared with normal. Although cells no longer lie in their correct positions, they still make correct extrinsic projections according to their birth date, and therefore according to the laminar position they would have occupied in the normal cortex (Caviness and Sidman 1973; Drager 1981; Lemmon and Pearlman 1981). Even ablation of the cells that would normally migrate to make up the superficial layers cannot persuade the deeper layer cells to alter their normal fate (Yurkewicz *et al.* 1984). The commitment of cells to specific laminae occurs during their final cycle of cell division and is induced by the local environment in the germinal zone. Layer V–VI cells can be induced to become layer II–III cells if they are transplanted during the cell cycle to a host germinal layer producing layer II–III cells; but if transplanted too late in their cycle they will go to layer V–VI of the host (McConnell 1991; McConnell and Kaznowski 1991). In other words, the laminar fate is already determined premigration in the germinal layer. These experiments also show that termination of migration is not determined by contact with the limiting border of layer 1 but by recognition of surface molecules on their matched cohort of cells; in cultures of dissociated embryonic cortical cells, cells of common age of final division (and therefore common laminar commitment) aggregate together (Krushel and van der Kooy 1987).

In the adult, each cortical region relates to many different subcortical centers and other cortical areas, each cortical area having its own unique constellation of connections. In the cat, subplate neurons send out axons to subcortical targets before the neurons of layers VI and V have finished dividing (McConnell *et al.* 1989) and these early axons act as guides to the more permanent projections. In rodents, subplate and layer VI cells send axons to the thalamus much later than the thalamic axon invasion of the cortex; this reflects the different timetable for cortical neurogenesis between different species and the difficulty in determining single factors that act as controls to cortical development (Miller *et al.* 1993). The basic framework of specific laminar connections is built very early in cortical development and even as cells are migrating toward the pia they can already be sending out axons to their appropriate targets (Schwartz and Goldman-Rakic 1991; Schwartz *et al.* 1991). Transplants of an early cerebral wall to abnormal positions in the cortical sheet, at a time when the cells are nearly all still dividing, adopt many connectional patterns of cortex at the new position. With even slightly older grafts the connectional patterns resemble more the region from which the graft was taken. Thus each cortical region develops a regional specificity imprinted upon it by local environmental cues very early in development (Barbe and Levitt 1995).

The different afferents to the cortex are as specific as the efferent projections regarding the area and laminae within which they will terminate. The thalamic fibers are already growing toward the cortex as the cortical cells that will be their targets are dividing; as the migrating cortical cells reach their final laminar positions the thalamic fibers begin to invade their neuropil. The precise timing of target cell migration relative to axon ingrowth in each species varies and seems to determine if the thalamic axons grow immediately into the cortical tissue (Catalano *et al.* 1991; Sheng *et al.* 1991) or wait below the cortex (Lund and Mustari 1977; Rakic 1979; Shatz and Luskin 1986; Shatz *et al.* 1990) in the region of the subplate. The subplate layer of cells below layer six may be the first target of the thalamic axons, and indeed the thalamic axons do provide synapses to this region as well as to layer VI (Herrmann *et al.* 1994). Lesions of the subplate region prevent entry of the thalamic axons (Ghosh and Shatz 1990, 1993) but whether this is due to mechanical disruption of the local environment or specifically to removal of subplate cells is not clear.

The means by which the boundaries of different corti-

cal areas are determined and their match to thalamic fibers from specific nuclei is not understood. As mentioned above, there is evidence that the cortex germinal layer has some innately determined program that helps specify areas independently from the thalamus, and yet there is clearly a role of the thalamic input in shaping the size and internal configuration of each area. Kennedy and DeHay (1993) point out that the different developmental timetable in different species may allow different factors to come into action in specification of areal characteristics. For instance, in nonprimates there is an early uniform distribution of callosal terminals that later undergo refinement to innervate only particular regions of the cortex (Innocenti 1986); in contrast, in the primate the adult pattern of callosal termination is established in the first outgrowth of the pathway (DeHay *et al.* 1988; Schwartz and Goldman-Rakic 1991). In the early outgrowth of thalamic axons there is evidence of a special affinity between appropriate regions of the cortex and the growing thalamic axons (Bolz *et al.* 1990, 1992). None the less, it is possible for thalamic axons to enter an innappropriate cortical region and even to make an appropriate terminal pattern within that foreign region, as has been demonstrated for whisker barrel field afferents persuaded to enter visual cortex transplants in rodents (Schlaggar and O'Leary 1991). Despite this apparent lability of the cortical sheet, experiments have demonstrated that after cortical lesions of sensorimotor cortex, transplantation of cortical regions matched in area to that lesioned produce superior behavioral recovery compared with transplants of nonmatched (e.g., visual) cortical regions, even when they received appropriate thalamic afferents (Barth and Stanfield 1991; Castro *et al.* 1991). It is possible in the primate to change the area of at least the primary visual cortex to less than 30% of normal by removing the majority of the normal thalamic input by fetal enucleation that causes massive loss of lateral geniculate nucleus neurons (Rakic and Williams 1986; Rakic 1988; DeHay *et al.* 1989). The eye removal has to be carried out before the generation of the thalamic recipient cells of layer IV (E70) to produce a significant effect, which suggests that the afferents control the generation of cortical neurons, but the unique cellular architecture and cell packing density of the remaining smaller cortical area looks very close to normal (DeHay *et al.*

1993). In rodents, however, manipulation of the peripheral sensory organs during development has very little effect on the size of cortical areas (see review by Kennedy and Dehay 1993). Molecular markers for specific cortical areas have been found which are expressed before entry of thalamic fibers (Barbe and Levitt 1991; Cohen-Tannoudji *et al.* 1992) which suggests that a template of thalamic independent regional specification is present in the fetal cortex.

Characteristic patterning of thalamic afferents within their layer of termination, which is a feature of many cortical areas, seems to be a product of the interactions between the thalamic fibers and other terminating fibers, both extrinsic and intrinsic, rather than a pattern forced upon the fibers by the cortical environment (Schlagger and O'Leary 1991). Experimental removal of cortical areas can cause significant thalamic degeneration as well as apparent rerouting of thalamic fibers to neighboring areas. Primary sensory afferents can be experimentally induced to innervate thalamic nuclei other than their normal thalamic terminal zone; a cortex driven by the thalamic nucleus with foreign input can reproduce surprisingly well the patterns of activity seen in the cortical area normally devoted to that type of sensory input (Frost and Metin 1985). This suggests that all cerebral cortex may have a similar functional architecture and that afferent and efferent connections can play a major role in determining regional functional differences in the adult.

In comparing the range of cell types seen in different areas of the primate neocortex, the same basic components are clearly present in all areas (Peters and Jones 1984; Lund and Lewis 1993); moreover, these same cell types are present with little variation in all other mammals, even in marsupials that diverged from the eutherians more than 150 million years ago (Lund *et al.* 1994). This suggests that the neocortex has a very conservative anatomical structure and that the basic cell types that we see in the cortex of species alive today do not represent particular features of individual species. The human cortex has the same set of cell types seen in other mammals and so studies on other species have been and will certainly continue to be illuminating. This constancy of morphology does not however mean that the cells also maintain a constant biochemical expression; for instance, cells as clearly identifiable as the GABAergic interneuron known as the chandelier neuron,

differ in expression of the functional modulators corticotropin releasing factor (CRF) and parvalbumin depending on the particular species, age of animal, cortical area, and laminar location within an area (Lewis and Lund 1990; also see Chapter 2 by David Lewis and Fig. 2.7). Thus, generation of a correct morphological set of cortical components need not imply that a particular set of substances, presumed to be important to their function, will be automatically expressed; local environment and developmental history may also play a role.

Within any area of cortex the patterns of interlaminar connections made by both excitatory and inhibitory neurons are highly specific (Lund *et al.* 1977). Again, we are almost completely ignorant of what factors determine this amazing specificity. The intralaminar patterning of termination of both extrinsic and intrinsic afferents is however modifiable and very dependent on patterns of activity within the region. The activity driving the infant cortex can occur spontaneously in utero. For instance, ganglion cells in the fetal retina show waves of activity crossing the retinal sheet (Galli and Maffei 1988; Maffei and Galli-Resti, 1990; Wong *et al.* 1993) and this activity drives input to the thalamus. This activity is in part responsible for the segregation of axon terminals from ganglion cells in the two eyes and the formation of eye-specific layers of the lateral geniculate nucleus of the thalamus (Shatz and Stryker 1988); in turn, early activity in the thalamus prenatally drives cortical activity via the corticothalamic afferents in those animals, including humans, where the thalamic axons make their cortical connections before birth.

The importance of the role of patterns of activity in forming the connections of the cortex cannot be overemphasized. Complete blocks of afferent activity by the voltage gated sodium channel blocker tetradotoxin (TTX) in the cat prevents further development of ocular dominance columns (Stryker and Harris 1986); if two pathways innervate a cortical lamina and activity in only one is blocked or even partially suppressed, the active pathway literally takes over almost the entire available territory causing the retreat of the deprived axons. Many experiments have been carried out, mainly in the early postnatal stages of cortical growth, to examine this plasticity in axon distribution following initial recognition of the phenomenon by Wiesel and Hubel (1965; LeVay *et al.*1980) in kitten and infant monkey visual cortex. While most investigations continue to focus on the visual pathways there is no reason to doubt that the same phenomena are true of other regions of the cortex (e.g., Juliano *et al.* 1994). In the rodent, a different effect is seen where TTX block of afferent activity during formation of the elaborately patterned vibrissa "barrel" field fails to interrupt the vibrissa representation or its reorganization after ablation of vibrissa follicles; however, the application of 2-amino 5-phosphonovaleric acid (APV), an excitatory amino acid receptor antagonist that prevents postsynaptic cell responses, does appear to partially block cortical reorganization. This raises the possibility that it is the coordination of pre- and postsynaptic responses that is important in development of thalamocortical patterning (Chiaia *et al.* 1994; Schlaggar *et al.*1993).

Early work in the kitten visual cortex (Wiesel and Hubel 1965) showed that the afferents compete for postsynaptic targets over a finite period, known as the critical period, in early postnatal development. In the primate, different afferent fiber groups and those innervating different laminae have variable critical periods during which they can proliferate terminal synapses and consolidate their control over postsynaptic neurons (LeVay *et al.* 1980; Lund and Holbach 1991). While maturation of the thalamic inputs to layer four may be complete within a few months after birth, the superficial layers, 2–3, receiving relays from layer four and from other regions of the cortex, may have a critical period that extends through adolescence, waning as sexual maturity is achieved (LeVay *et al.* 1980; Anderson *et al.* 1995) During these critical periods the numbers of synapses increase markedly, often to twice that found in the adult condition (Lund *et al.* 1977; Boothe *et al.* 1979; Rakic *et al.* 1986; Missler *et al.* 1993). There is a constant turnover of these supernumerary contacts until the critical period begins to wane; as the critical period draws to its end many synapses are lost and it is believed that only those terminals that have been most reinforced by use during the critical period survive. In the primate the final synaptic complement of the cortex returns to a level resembling that seen close to birth.

The factors permitting the onset, time course and waning of the critical periods for all the different neural components are yet to be understood. The timing of the critical period varies between areas, between laminae within areas, and between different cellular components within single laminae, so it is likely that the neural components have their own internal "clocks" as well as there being permissive environmental factors such as nerve growth factors available over particular maturational periods (also see Chapter 3 by Vincente and Kennedy). Expression of receptors for growth factors is known to change on neuron surfaces over time (Kokaia *et al.* 1995) and receptors such as the *N*-methyl-*D*-aspartate (NMDA) receptor, which may help consolidate synaptic connections, also change with development and with afferent activity (e.g., Gordon *et al.* 1995; Kumar *et al.* 1994). Neural modulators such as noradrenaline and acetylcholine (Bear and Singer 1986), serotonin (Gu and Singer 1995) and dopamine (Goldman-Rakic and Brown 1982; Rosenberg and Lewis 1995) also show marked changes in cortical development and are known to influence cortical excitability as well as affecting the nature of interactions during critical periods for cortical neuron development. Interaction of many factors of this kind are likely to control these waves of maturation (e.g., Anderson *et al.* 1995).

This overview is not intended to be an exhaustive review of the literature but to illustrate probable developmental causes for cortical malfunction, that may underlie the pathogenesis of neuropsychiatric disorders. The overview makes clear that it is unlikely that malfunctions are caused directly by single abnormalities. There is more likely to be a cascade of effects each nudging the cortical system nearer and nearer the brink of a condition where all its best attempts at self-regulation can be defeated.

ACKNOWLEDGMENTS

Supported by grants NEI-NIH EY10021 and MRC G9203679N.

REFERENCES

Anderson, D.J. 1989. The neural crest cell lineage problem: neuropoiesis? *Neuron* 3:1–12.

Anderson, S.A., Classey, J.D., Cond, F., Lund, J.S. and Lewis, D.A. 1995. Synchronous development of pyramidal neuron dendritic spines and parvalbumin-immunoreactive chandelier neuron axon terminals in layer III of monkey prefrontal cortex. *Neuroscience* **67**:7–22.

Angevine, J.B. Jr and Sidman, R.L. 1961. Autoradiographic study of cell migration during histogenesis of cerebral cortex in the mouse. *Nature* **192**: 766–68.

Barbe, M.F. and Levitt, P. 1991. The early commitment of fetal neurons to the limbic cortex. *J. Neurosci.* **11**:519–33.

Barbe, M.F. and Levitt, P. 1995. Age-dependent specification of the corticocortical connections of cerebral grafts. *J. Neurosci.* **15**:1819–34.

Barth, T.M. and Stanfield, B.B. 1994. Homotopic but not heterotopic, fetal cortical transplants can result in functional sparing following neonatal damage to the frontal cortex in rats. *Cerebral Cortex* **4**:271–8.

Bear, M.F. and Singer, W. 1986. Modulation of visual cortex plasticity by acetylcholine and noradrenaline. *Nature* **320**:172–76.

Bolz, J., Novak, N. and Bonhoeffer, T. 1990. Formation of target specific neuronal projections in organotypic slice cultures from rat visual cortex. *Nature* **346**:359–62.

Bolz, J., Novac, N., and Staiger, V. 1992. Formation of specific afferent connections in organotypic slice cultures from rat visual cortex cocultured with lateral geniculate nucleus. *J. Neurosci.* **12**:3054–70.

Boothe, R.G., Greenough, W.T., Lund, J.S. and Wrege, K. 1979. A quantitative investigation of spine and dendrite development of neurons in visual cortex (area 17) of *Macaca nemestrina* monkeys. *J. Comp. Neurol.* **186**:473–90.

Castro, A.J., Hogan, T.P., Sorensen, J.C., Klausen, B.S., Danielsen, E.H., Zimmer, J. and Neafsey, E.J. 1991. Heterotopic neocortical transplants. An anatomical and electrophysiological analysis of host projections to occipital cortical grafts placed in sensorimotor cortical lesions made in newborn rats. *Dev. Brain Res.* **58**:231–6.

Catalano, S.M., Robertson, R.T. and Killackey, H.P. 1991. Early ingrowth of thalamocortical afferents to the neocortex of the prenatal rat. *Proc. Natl Acad. Sci. USA* **88**:2999–3003.

Caviness, V.S. Jr and Sidman, R.L. 1973. Time of origin of corresponding cell classes in the cerebral cortex of normal and reeler mutant mice: An autoradiographic analysis. *J. Comp. Neurol.* **148**:141–51.

Chiaia, N.L., Fish, S.E., Bauer, W.R., Figley, B.A., Eck, M., Bennett-Clark, C.A., and Rhoades, R.W. 1994. Effects of postnatal blockade of cortical activity with tetrodotoxin upon lesion-induced reorganization of vibrissae-related patterns in the somatosensory cortex of rat. *Develop. Brain Res.* **79**:301–6.

Cohen-Tannoudji, M., Morello, D. and Babinet, C. 1992. Unexpected position-dependent expression of H-2 and bet2-microglobin/lacZ transgenes. *Mol. Reprod. Dev.* **33**:149–59.

Darian-Smith, C. and Gilbert, C.D. 1994. Axonal sprouting accompanies functional reorganization in adult cat striate cortex. *Nature* **368**:737–40.

DeHay, C., Giroud, P., Berland, M., Smart, I. and Kennedy, H. 1993. Modulation of the cell cycle contributes to the parcellation of the primate visual cortex. *Nature* **366**:464–66.

DeHay, C., Horsburgh, G., Berland, M., Killackey, H. and Kennedy, H. 1989. Maturation and connectivity of the visual cortex in monkey is altered by prenatal removal of the retinal input. *Nature* **337**:265–7.

DeHay, C., Kennedy, H., Bullier, J. and Berland, M. 1988. Absence of interhemispheric connections during development in the monkey. *Nature* **331**:348–350.

Drager, U. 1981. Observations on the organisation of the visual cortex in the reeler mouse. *J. Comp. Neurol.* **201**:555–70.

Finlay, B.L. 1992. Cell death and the creation of regional differences in cell numbers. *J. Neurobiol.* **23**:1159–71.

Frost, D.O. and Metin, C. 1985. Induction of functional retinal projections to the somatosensory system. *Nature* **317**:162–4.

Galli, L. and Maffei, I. 1988. Spontaneous impulse activity of rat retinal ganglion cells in prenatal life. *Science* **242**:90–1.

Gao, W.Q., Heinzt, N. and Hatten, M.E. 1991. Cerebellar granule cell neurogenesis is regulated by cell-cell interactions in vitro. *Neuron* **6**:705–15.

Garraghty, P.E., Kaas, J.H. and Florence, S.L. 1994. Plasticity of sensory and motor maps in adult and developing mammals. In *Advances in neural and behavioural development*, vol. 4, ed. V. A. Casagrande and P. G. Shinkman, pp. 1–36. Norwood, NJ: Ablex.

Ghosh, A. and Shatz, C. J. 1990. Pathfinding and target selection by developing geniculocortical axons. *J. Neurosci.* **12**:39–55.

Ghosh, A. and Shatz, C.J. 1993. A role for subplate neurons in the patterning of connections from thalamus to neocortex. *Development* 117:1031–47.

Goldman-Rakic, P.S. and Brown, R.M. 1982. Postnatal development of monoamine content and synthesis in the cerebral cortex of rhesus monkeys. *Dev. Brain Res.* 4:339–49.

Gordon, B., Ying, L., Jaeger, R., Petrovic, A., and Tovar, K. 1995. The development of MK-801, kainate, AMPA, and muscimol binding sites in cat visual cortex. *Visual Neurosci.* 12: 241–52.

Gotz, M., Williams, B.P., Boltz, J. and Price, J. 1995. The specification of neuronal fate: a common precursor for neurotransmitter subtypes in the rat cerebral cortex in vitro. *Eur. J. Neurosci.* 7:889–98.

Gu, Q. and Singer, W. 1995. Involvement of serotonin in developmental plasticity of kitten visual cortex. *Eur. J. Neurosci.* 7:1146–53.

Herrmann, K., Antonini, A. and Shatz, C.J. 1994. Ultrastructural evidence for synaptic interactions between thalamocortical axons and subplate neurons. *Eur. J. Neurosci.* 6:1729–42.

Innocenti, G. 1986. In *Cerebral cortex. vol.5. Sensory- motor areas and aspects of cortical connectivity*, E.G. Jones and A. Peters, eds., pp. 291–353. New York: Plenum Press.

Juliano, S.L., Eslin, D.E. and Tommerdahl, M. 1994. Developmental regulation of plasticity in cat somatosensory cortex. *J.Neurophysiol.* 72:1706–16.

Kennedy, H. and DeHay, C. 1993. Cortical specification of mice and men. *Cerebral Cortex* 3:171–86.

Kirkwood, T.B., Price, J. and Grove, E.A. 1992. The dispersion of neural clones across the cerebral cortex. *Science* 258:317.

Kokaia, Z., Metsis, M., Kokaia, M., Elm, R.E. and Lindvall, O. 1995. Co-expression of TrkB and TrkC receptors in CNS neurones suggests regulation by multiple neurotrophins. *NeuroReport* 6:769–72.

Krushel, L.A. and van der Kooy, D. 1987. Selective *in vitro* reassociation of early versus late postmitotic neurons from the rat forebrain. *Soc. Neurosci. Abtsr.* 13:1114.

Kumar, A., Schlieb, R. and Bigi, V. 1994. Postnatal development of NMDA, AMPA and kainate receptors in individual layers of rat visual cortex and the effect of monocular deprivation. *Int. J. Develop. Neurosci.* 12:31–41.

LeVay, S., Wiesel, T.N. and Hubel, D.H. 1980. The development of ocular dominance columns in normal and visually deprived monkeys. *J. Comp. Neurol.* 191:1–51.

Lemmon, V. and Pearlman, A.L. 1981. Does laminar position determine the receptive field properties of cortical neurons? A study of corticotectal cells in area 17 of the normal mouse and the reeler mutant. *J. Neurosci.* 1:83–93.

Lewis, D.A. and Lund, J.S. 1990. Heterogeneity of chandelier neurons in monkey neocortex: corticotropin-releasing factor- and parvalbumin-immunoreactive populations. *J. Comp. Neurol.* 293:599–615.

Lund, R.D. and Mustari, M.J. 1977. Development of the geniculocortical pathway in rats. *J. Comp. Neurol.* 173:289–306.

Lund, J.S., Boothe, R.G. and Lund, R.D. 1977. Development of neurons in the visual cortex of the monkey (*Macaca nemestrina*). A Golgi study from fetal day 127 to postnatal maturity. *J. Comp. Neurol.* 176:149–88.

Lund, J.S., Harman, A. and Beazley, L. 1994. Common cell types and patterns of laminar distribution in marsupial and eutherian visual cortex identify components essential for neocortical function. *Soc. Neurosci.* 20:311.

Lund, J.S. and Holbach, S. 1991. Postnatal development of thalamic recipient neurons in monkey striate cortex:I. A comparison of spine aquisition and dendritic growth of layer 4C alpha and beta spiny stellate neurons. *J.Comp. Neurol.* 309:115–28.

Lund, J.S. and Lewis, D.A. 1993. Local circuit neurons of developing and mature macaque prefrontal cortex: Golgi and immunocytochemical characteristics. *J. Comp. Neurol.* 328:282–312.

Luskin, M.B., Parnavelas, J.G. and Barfield, J.A. 1993. Neurons, astrocytes, and oligodendrocytes of the rat cerebral cortex originate from separate progenitor cells. An ultrastructural analysis of clonally related cells. *J. Neurosci.* 13:1730–50.

Luskin, M.B., Pearlman, A.L. and Sanes, J.R. 1988. Cell lineage in the cerebral cortex of the mouse studied in vivo and in vitro with a recombinant retrovirus. *Neuron* 1:635–47.

McConnell, S.K. 1991. The generation of neuronal diversity in the central nervous system. *Ann. Rev. Neurosci.* 14:269–300.

McConnell, S.K., Ghosh, A. and Shatz,C.J. 1989. Subplate neurons pioneer the first axon pathway from the cerebral cortex. *Science* 245:978–82.

McConnell, S.K. and Kaznowski, C.E. 1991. Cell cycle

dependence of laminar determination in developing neocortex. *Science* 254:282–5.

Maffei, I. and Galli-Resti, L. 1990. Correlation in the discharges of neighboring rat retinal ganglion cells in prenatal life. *Proc. Natl Acad. Sci. USA* 87:2861–64.

Miller, B., Chou, L. and Finlay, B. 1993. The early development of thalamocortical and corticothalamic projections. *J. Comp. Neurol.* 335:16–41.

Mione, M.C., Danevic, C., Boardman, B., Harris, B. and Parnavelas, J.G. 1994. Lineage analysis reveals neurotransmitter (GABA or glutamate) but not calcium binding protein homogeneity in clonally related cortical neurons. *J. Neurosci.* 14:107–23.

Missler, M., Wolff, A., Merker, H.J. and Wolff, J.R. 1993. Pre- and postnatal development of the primary visual cortex of the common marmoset. II. Formation, remodelling and elimination of synapses as overlapping processes. *J. Comp. Neurol.* 333:53–67.

O'Rourke, N., Dailey, M.E., Smith, S.J. and McConnell, S.K. 1992. Diverse migratory pathways in the developing cerebral cortex. *Science* 258:299–302.

Parnavelas, J.G., Barfield, E.F. and Luskin, M.B. 1991. Separate progenitor cells give rise to pyramidal and non-pyramidal neurons in the rat telencephalon. *Cerebral Cortex* 1: 463–8.

Peters, A. and Jones, E.G. (eds) 1984. In *Cerebral Cortex. Vol.1. Cellular components of the cerebral cortex.* New York and London: Plenum Press.

Price, J. and Thurlow, L. 1988. Cell lineage in the rat cerebral cortex: a study using retroviral-mediated gene transfer. *Development* 104: 473–82.

Rakic, P. 1972. Mode of cell migration to the superficial layers of fetal monkey cortex. *J. Comp. Neurol.* 145:61–84.

Rakic, P. 1974. Neurons in rhesus monkey visual cortex: systematic relationship between time of origin and eventual disposition. *Science* 183:425–7.

Rakic, P. 1979. Genetic and epigenetic determinants of local circuits in the mammalian central nervous system. In *The neurosciences fourth study program*, ed. F.O. Schmitt and F.G.Worden. Cambridge, MA: MIT Press.

Rakic, P. 1988. Specification of cerebral cortical areas. *Science* 241:170–6.

Rakic, P., Bourgeois, J.-P., Zecevik, N. and Goldman-Rakic, P.S. 1986. Concurrent overproduction of synapses in diverse regions of the primate cerebral cortex. *Science* 232:232–5.

Rakic, P. and Williams, R.W. 1986. Thalamic regulation of cortical parcellation: an experimental perturbation of the striate cortex in rhesus monkeys. *Soc. Neurosci. Abstr.* 12:1149.

Rockel, A.J., Hiorns, R.W. and Powell, T.P.S. 1980. The basic uniformity in structure of the neocortex. *Brain* 103:221–44.

Rosenberg, D.R. and Lewis, D.A. Postnatal maturation of the dopaminergic innervation of monkey prefrontal and motor cortices: a tyrosine hydroxylase immunohistochemical analysis. *J. Comp. Neurol.* (In Press).

Schlaggar, B.L., Fox, K. and O'Leary, D.D.M. 1993. Postsynaptic control of plasticity in the developing cortex. *Nature* 364:623–6.

Schlagger, B.L. and O'Leary, D.D.M. 1991. Potential of visual cortex to develop an array of functional units unique to somatosensory cortex. *Science* 252: 1556–60.

Schwartz, M.L. and Goldman-Rakic, P.S. 1991. Prenatal specification of callosal connections in rhesus monkey. *J. Comp. Neurol.* 307:144–62.

Schwartz, M.L., Rakic, P. and Goldman-Rakic, P.S. 1991. Early phenotypic expression of cortical neurons: evidence that a subclass of migrating neurons have callosal axons. *Proc. Nat. Acad. Sci. U.S.A.* 88:1354–58.

Shatz, C.J., Gosh, A., McConnell, S.K., Allendoerfer, K.L., Friauf, E. and Antonini, A. 1990. Pioneer neurons and target selection in cerebral cortical development. *Cold Spring Harbor Symp. Quant. Biol.* 55:469–80.

Shatz, C.J. and Luskin, M.B. 1986. The relationship between the geniculocortical afferents and their cortical target cells during the development of the cat's primary visual cortex. *J. Neurosci.* 6:3655–68.

Shatz, C.J. and Stryker, M.P. 1988. Prenatal tetrodotoxin infusion blocks segregation of retinogeniculate afferents. *Science* 24:87–9.

Sheng, X.M., Marotte, L.R. and Mark, R.F. 1991. Development of the laminar distribution of thalamocortical axons and corticothalamic cell bodies in the visual cortex of the wallaby. *J. Comp. Neurol.* 307:17–38.

Stryker, M.P. and Harris, W.A. 1986. Binocular impulse blockade prevents the formation of ocular dominance columns in cat visual cortex. *J. Neurosci.* 6:2117–33.

Walsh, C. and Cepko, C.L. 1988. Clonally related cortical cells show several migratory patterns. *Science* 241:1342–5.

Walsh, C. and Cepko, C.L. 1992. Widespread dispersion of neural clones across functional regions of the cerebral cortex. *Science* 255:434–40.

Wiesel, T.N. and Hubel, D.H. 1965. Comparison of the effects of unilateral and bilateral eye closure on cortical unit responses in kittens. *J. Neurophysiol.* **28**:1029–40.

Williams, R.W., Ryder, K. and Rakic, P. 1987. Emergence of cytoarchitectonic differences between areas 17 and 18 in the developing rhesus monkey. *Soc. Neurosci. Abstr.* **13**:1044.

Wong, R.O.L., Meister, M. and Shatz, C.J. 1993. Transient period of correlated bursting activity during development of the mammalian retina. *Neuron* **11**:923–38.

Yamamoto, N., Yamada, K., Kurotani, T. and Toyama, K. 1992. Laminar specificity of extrinsic cortical connections studied in coculture preparations. *Neuron* **9**:217–28.

Yurkewicz, L., Valentino, K.L., Floeter, M.K., Fleshman, J.W. and Jones, E.G. 1984. Effects of cytotoxic deletions of somatic sensory cortex in fetal rats. *Somatosens. Res.* **1**:303–27.

2

Development of the primate prefrontal cortex

DAVID A. LEWIS

INTRODUCTION

One of the distinguishing features of the primate brain is the marked expansion of both the absolute and relative size of the prefrontal cortex (PFC). For example, the PFC occupies less than 4% of the total cortical volume in cats, whereas it has been estimated to constitute 11.5% and 30% of the total cortical volume in macaque monkeys and humans, respectively (Fuster 1989). This tremendous increase in the size of the PFC is obviously associated with the presence of substantially enhanced abilities to perform complex cognitive tasks involving active memory, abstract reasoning and judgment. The disruption of many of these types of higher-order functions in psychiatric disorders, such as schizophrenia, has led to a tremendous interest in the functional architecture of the PFC. Although many of the functions of the PFC remain enigmatic, it is clear that in both monkeys and humans the PFC is essential for the integration of information in the temporal domain (Goldman-Rakic 1987b; Fuster 1989). In particular, the dorsolateral PFC appears to govern behavior through the use of transient memory traces that link the temporal discontinuities between recent stimuli and future responses.

This review will focus on the development and refinement of neural circuitry in the primate PFC in order to understand how these changes may underlie the functional maturation of the PFC. The possible relations between these changes in circuitry and the maturation of behaviors thought to be subserved by neural networks that involve PFC circuitry will be considered, but a full review of those data is beyond the scope of this chapter. In addition, this chapter will emphasize the development of the dorsolateral PFC, specifically areas 9 and 46. In adult nonhuman primates, the distinctive cytoarchitectonic fea-

tures of these regions have been described by Walker (1940) and others (Barbas and Pandya 1989; Preuss and Goldman-Rakic 1991), and their intrinsic circuitry and biochemistry as well as their connections with other brain regions have been extensively investigated (see Goldman-Rakic 1987b, 1988; Fuster 1989; Pandya and Yeterian 1990; Barbas 1992; Lewis 1992 for reviews). These regions are thought to bear some homologies to the regions of the human PFC designated with the same numbers by Brodmann (1909). Thus, the development of these areas is of particular interest because they are relatively well-characterized in the adult primate in terms of both function and underlying circuitry. In addition, converging lines of evidence indicate that these regions may be sites of dysfunction and structural pathology in human psychiatric disorders, such as schizophrenia, that may be attributable, at least in some cases, to disturbances in neural development.

MATURATION OF BEHAVIORS SUBSERVED BY PFC CIRCUITRY

In both monkeys and humans, the functional maturation of the dorsolateral PFC appears to be quite protracted, such that adult levels of performance on cognitive tasks mediated by these regions are not achieved until after puberty. One of the cardinal behaviors dependent on the PFC in adults is the performance of delayed-response tasks. These tasks, some versions of which can be performed by both monkey and human subjects, require the subject to retain knowledge of the information provided by an environmental cue in order to perform the appropriate behavioral response after the cue has been removed. For example, in oculomotor delayed-response tasks, subjects are required to hold "on line" or in "working memory" the location of a visual cue in space during a delay period following the removal of the cue (Goldman-Rakic 1987b). The ability to carry out such tasks first appears between 2 and 4 months of age in monkeys (Goldman-Rakic 1987a), and around 1 year of age in humans (Diamond 1985). Performance of these tasks then continues to improve at a slower rate until adult functional competence is achieved around the time of puberty in both monkeys (Goldman 1971; Alexander and Goldman 1978) and humans (Levin *et al.* 1991).

The time course of improved performance with age, as evidenced by the ability to withstand longer delay periods, appears to reflect not only the functional maturation of the PFC, but also the increasing involvement during postnatal development of PFC neural circuitry in the mediation of these behaviors. That is, the emergence of the ability to perform delayed-response tasks during infancy does not appear to depend upon the integrity of the dorsolateral PFC, and may be mediated by circuitry that does not involve these cortical regions. For example, ablation of the dorsolateral PFC in infant monkeys does not produce the same degree of impairment on spatial delayed-response tasks observed in adult animals with such lesions (Alexander and Goldman 1978). In contrast, during the first year of life these behaviors do appear to depend upon the integrity of other brain structures, including the caudate nucleus (Goldman and Rosvold 1972), mediodorsal thalamic nucleus (Goldman 1974; Alexander and Goldman 1978) and orbitofrontal cortex (Goldman 1971; Miller *et al.* 1973).

Studies that have employed reversible cooling of the PFC, which temporarily disrupts neural activity in the affected area, have also demonstrated an age-dependent role of the dorsolateral PFC in certain behaviors (Alexander and Goldman 1978; Alexander 1982). In these studies, cooling of the PFC did not produce impairments in delayed-response performance in monkeys 9–16 months of age. In animals 19–31 months old, cooling produced a modest degree of disruption in task performance compared to pre- and postcooling conditions. In animals 3 years of age, however, cooling of the PFC resulted in a substantial impairment of performance. These findings

suggest that during postnatal development there is an increasing dependence upon the dorsolateral PFC for the mediation of delayed-response behavior, such that the maturation of the PFC augments the function of neural circuits which appear to subserve the same task earlier in life (Alexander and Goldman 1978). Consequently, the improvement in performance on delayed-response tasks with increasing age may reflect both the maturation of the functional architecture of the dorsolateral PFC, and its progressive, integrated participation in the neural circuits that mediate the conduct of these behaviors.

Further evidence for the increasing involvement of PFC circuitry in delayed-response tasks during postnatal development has been derived from electrophysiological studies of this region. In adult animals, specific populations of PFC neurons have been identified whose activity is temporally linked to specific components of the delayed-response task (Fuster *et al.* 1982). In particular, some PFC neurons exhibit elevated firing rates during the delay period of the task, and the loss of this delay-related neuronal activity is associated with errors in the performance of the task (Bauer and Fuster 1976; Funahashi *et al.* 1989). During postnatal development, the percentage of PFC neurons that exhibit delay period activity doubles between 12 and 36 months of age, suggesting that developmental changes in PFC circuitry facilitate the recruitment of these neurons to this functional role (Alexander 1982). In contrast to other brain areas (e.g., mediodorsal thalamic nucleus, caudate nucleus, posterior parietal cortex) that also subserve delayed-response tasks, only the PFC appears to exhibit this type of developmental increase in the number of delay-activated neurons (Alexander 1982).

What changes occur in the neural circuitry of the PFC during postnatal development to support the functional maturation of these and related types of cognitive abilities? What events and time periods during development are necessary for the emergence of functional maturity in the PFC? Although the available data are insufficient to definitively answer these questions, findings from a variety of lines of investigation provide interesting clues. The following sections summarize these data, from prenatal through adolescent periods of development, and suggest important areas for future investigations.

Fig. 2.1 Brightfield
photomicrographs of Nissl-
stained sections through the
lateral prefrontal cortex of
macaque monkey brain ranging
in age from embryonic day 82 to
157. Note the progressive differentiation of the cortical plate
(panel A) into the distinct layers
of the cerebral cortex (panel D).
MZ, marginal zone; CP, cortical
plate; SP, subplate; IZ, intermediate zone; WM, white matter.
Calibration bar = 300 μm.

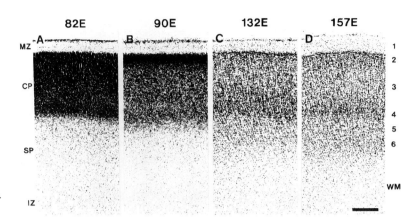

NEUROGENESIS AND NEURONAL MIGRATION IN THE PRIMATE PREFRONTAL CORTEX

Although the time course of emergence of adult abilities mediated by the PFC clearly indicates the importance of postnatal developmental events in the maturation of PFC neural circuitry, these late developmental processes are built on the foundation of neural architecture that arose during earlier periods of development. At the earliest stage of development, the cerebral wall is composed of an outer cell-free marginal zone and an inner ventricular zone, a single layer of pseudostratified epithelium from which all neurons and glia are eventually generated. The first post-mitotic cells migrate from the ventricular zone to form the preplate, a group of loosely-packed cells located below the marginal zone. The continuing processes of neurogenesis and migration subsequently produce a cell-dense zone, the cortical plate (Fig. 2.1A), which splits the preplate cells into two populations: a superficial group in the marginal zone (which later becomes layer 1 of the cerebral cortex) and a deeper zone termed the subplate.

Subplate neurons are not only among the first neurons generated in the cortex, they are also the earliest to mature (Allendoerfer and Shatz 1994). Their axons pioneer descending pathways to the thalamus and other sub-cortical structures (McConnell et al. 1989, 1994), project into the cortical plate (Friauf et al. 1990), and furnish collateral branches within the subplate (Wahle and Meyer

1987; Chun and Shatz 1989a; Friauf, McConnell, and Shatz 1990). Subplate neurons also appear to be the initial synaptic targets for many afferents to the cerebral cortex, including projections from the thalamus (Allendoerfer and Shatz 1994) and the contralateral cerebral cortex (Innocenti 1991). Both thalamic and callosal axons accumulate within the subplate for extended periods of time, especially in primates, before invading the cortical plate (Lund and Mustari 1977; Rakic 1977; Shatz and Luskin 1986). The interactions between subplate neurons and cortical afferents during this "waiting period" (Rakic 1977) appear to be critical for the subsequent formation of proper connections with cortical neurons. For example, following lesions of the subplate, axons from the lateral geniculate nucleus continue to grow past the visual cortex, suggesting that subplate neurons are required for these thalamic axons to recognize their appropriate cortical target (Ghosh et al. 1990). In addition, subplate neurons appear to be essential for the final patterning (the formation of ocular dominance columns) of thalamocortical afferents within layer 4 of the visual cortex (Ghosh and Shatz 1992, 1994). Following the completion of these maturational processes, the majority of subplate neurons die, leaving as a remnant the interstitial neurons of the adult white matter (Kostovic and Rakic 1980; Chun and Shatz 1989b; Woo et al. 1991). Although only limited studies of subplate neurons below the PFC have been conducted, it is likely that subplate neurons play similar roles in early development throughout the cortical mantle.

These characteristics of subplate neurons suggest that abnormalities in these neurons could lead to the alterations in PFC circuitry in schizophrenia or other psychiatric disorders (Akbarian *et al.* 1995; Lewis 1995). For example, due to their early maturation, subplate neurons might be particularly sensitive to pre- or perinatal insults (Allendoerfer and Shatz 1994), the types of events which have been implicated as etiological factors in at least some cases of schizophrenia. Given their importance in the formation of cortical circuitry, even a restricted lesion of the subplate during prenatal development could result in extensive errors in axon targeting and connectivity during later development (Allendoerfer and Shatz 1994). It is also important to note that the number of subplate neurons, the relative size of the subplate to the cortical plate, and the length of time during which subplate neurons persist are all much greater in humans than in the other species in which most studies of the subplate have been conducted (Mrzljak *et al.* 1988; Kostovic and Rakic 1990). Consequently, the role of subplate neurons in the development of the human PFC may be even more complex than is currently understood from animal studies.

After the formation of the subplate, additional waves of neurons continue to be generated and to migrate through the subplate into the cortical plate, which eventually forms layers 2–6 of the adult cerebral cortex (Fig. 2.1). Neurons destined for the deep cortical layers are generated first, followed successively by those that will form the middle and then the superficial cortical layers. This general "inside-out" pattern of cortical development is characteristic of the PFC and all other cortical regions. During the 165 day gestational period of macaque monkeys, neurons that will eventually form the PFC are generated between embryonic days 40 through 90 (E40–90) (Goldman-Rakic *et al.* 1983). By comparison, in the anterior cingulate and motor cortices neurons are born between E40 and 80, and in primary visual cortex neurons are generated until E102 (Berger *et al.* 1992). By E104, all PFC neurons have arrived in their appropriate and final laminar location (Schwartz *et al.* 1991; Rakic and Wikmark, cited in Bourgeois, Goldman-Rakic, and Rakic 1994)

As in other cortical regions, all neurons in the primate PFC are considered to be members of one of two general classes: pyramidal neurons and nonpyramidal, or local circuit, neurons. As a group, pyramidal neurons, which constitute about 70% of cortical neurons (Powell 1981), have several distinguishing features. These include a characteristically-shaped cell body, an apical dendrite that typically ascends towards the pial surface, dendritic spines, and a principal axon which enters the white matter and furnishes excitatory projections to other cortical regions or subcortical areas. In humans, the basic features of PFC pyramidal neurons develop between 17 and 25 weeks of gestation, before the invasion of thalamocortical axons (Mrzljak *et al.* 1988). When apical and basilar dendrites first appear, they lack spines. Between 26 and 34 weeks of gestation, the ingrowth of afferent axons into the PFC coincides with intensive dendritic differentiation and the appearance of dendritic spines on pyramidal neurons in layers 3 and 5 (Mrzljak *et al.* 1988). The progressive increase in total dendritic length of pyramidal neurons during development is the result of both the formation of a greater number of bifurcations and the growth of the terminal segments of each branch (Mrzljak *et al.* 1992).

Consistent with the general "inside-out" pattern of cortical neurogenesis and migration, pyramidal neurons in layer 5 are generated first and achieve the adult size of dendritic arbor earlier than layer 3 pyramids (Mrzljak *et al.* 1992). Although the function of acetylcholinesterase (AChE) in pyramidal neurons is not clear, AChE staining in layer 3 pyramidal neurons begins to appear after the first year of postnatal life. AChE levels then continue to increase, reaching a peak in young adulthood (Kostovic *et al.* 1988), an observation that may be consistent with a late maturation of human PFC.

In contrast to pyramidal neurons, which appear to utilize excitatory amino acids as neurotransmitters, the vast majority of local circuit neurons in the cerebral cortex utilize the inhibitory neurotransmitter GABA. As a group, GABA neurons comprise approximately 25% of all neurons in the primate PFC (Hendry *et al.* 1987), and are comprised of a variety of distinct subtypes (Fairen *et al.* 1984). Based upon differences in axonal features and synaptic targets, at least ten different morphological subclasses of local circuit neurons have been identified in the primate neocortex (Lund 1973; Jones 1975; Fairen *et al.*

1984), and most of these subtypes have been found in both monkey and human PFC (Mrzljak *et al.* 1988, 1992; Lund and Lewis 1993). In addition, GABA neurons are chemically heterogeneous, and separate subpopulations can be identified by the presence of specific neuropeptides or calcium-binding proteins (DeFelipe 1993). For example, the calcium-binding proteins calbindin, calretinin, and parvalbumin are expressed in distinct subgroups of GABA neurons with different laminar distributions in monkey PFC (Condé *et al.* 1994). Together, these morphological and chemical features define subpopulations of GABA neurons that appear to have different roles in PFC circuitry. GABA neurons of the chandelier class, which may also express either the neuropeptide corticotropin-releasing factor (Lewis *et al.* 1989) or the calcium-binding protein parvalbumin (DeFelipe *et al.* 1989; Lewis and Lund 1990), are found primarily in cortical layers 2–5 in monkey PFC (Lewis and Lund 1990; Lund and Lewis 1993). The distinctive axon terminals of these neurons are arrayed as cartridges which form symmetric, inhibitory synapses with the axon initial segment of pyramidal neurons (Szentagothai and Arbib 1974; Jones 1975; Somogyi 1977; Fairen and Valverde 1980; Peters, Proskauer, and Ribak 1982; Hendry *et al.* 1983; DeFelipe *et al.* 1985), the site of action potential generation. Each chandelier cell may contact up to 300 pyramidal neurons within a radius of 150–200 μm from its cell body (Peters 1984). Thus, chandelier cells exert critical inhibitory control over the activity of a localized group of pyramidal neurons, and as a consequence appear to be specialized to regulate the output of a cortical column. In contrast, the axons of wide arbor (basket) neurons, which form symmetric inhibitory synapses with the cell bodies of pyramidal neurons (Jones and Hendry 1984), spread horizontally for considerable distances (up to 1.0 mm) within the PFC (Lund and Lewis 1993). These neurons may be specialized to provide inhibitory constraints on the patterns of intra-areal excitation propagated by horizontally-oriented axon collaterals of PFC pyramidal neurons (Levitt *et al.* 1993; Lund, Yoshioka, and Levitt 1993).

During fetal development in monkeys, GABA immunoreactivity is detectable in neurons as early as E41, very shortly after the onset of cortical neurogenesis (Schwartz and Meinecke 1992). At this early point in development, GABA-positive neurons are distributed throughout the full thickness of the cerebral wall, including the marginal zone, cortical plate, and subplate. In addition, within the subplate, a subset of cells with the bipolar morphology suggestive of migrating neurons are GABA-immunoreactive (Schwartz and Meinecke 1992). This observation suggests that the biochemical phenotype of at least some cortical neurons may appear relatively early in the postmitotic state. By the first postnatal week, both the laminar distribution and density of GABA neurons appear quite similar to the patterns present in mature monkeys (Schwartz and Meinecke 1992).

Among subclasses of GABA neurons, those that express the neuropeptide somatostatin (Kostovic *et al.* 1991) or the calcium-binding proteins calbindin or calretinin (F. Condé and D.A. Lewis, unpublished observations) are also detectable quite early in postnatal development. Expression of the calcium-binding protein parvalbumin (PV), however, is a much later developmental event; i.e. PV immunoreactivity is not detectable in monkey PFC neurons until birth (Condé and Lewis 1993). These findings suggest that different subsets of GABA cells may become functionally mature at different time points in development (Condé and Lewis 1993). Finally, in other chemically-defined subclasses of GABA neurons, such as those that contain the neuropeptides cholecystokinin (CCK) or substance P, peak expression of the neuropeptide seems to occur around birth. The number of neurons expressing detectable levels of these neuropeptides then declines rapidly during the first six postnatal months to levels which remain stable through the remainder of development and into adulthood (Yamashita *et al.* 1990; Oeth and Lewis 1993).

ARRIVAL OF AFFERENT PROJECTIONS TO THE PRIMATE PFC

During the period of cortical neurogenesis and migration, many afferent systems are also making their way to the developing PFC. The first afferents to arrive in the cerebral wall appear to be the monoamines, dopamine, norepinephrine (noradrenaline) and serotonin (Levitt 1982; Marin-Padilla and Marin-Padilla 1982; Berger *et al.* 1992), which suggests that these systems may play an important role in guiding the development of cortical connections. The different groups of brainstem monoaminergic neurons are generated between E27 and E43 in monkeys (Levitt and Rakic 1982), and in humans these cell groups are apparent as early as 6 weeks of gestation (see Berger *et al.* 1992). In humans, monoaminergic axons penetrate the intermediate zone of the developing cortex at 8 gestational weeks, and penetrate the cortical plate at 13 gestational weeks (Zecevic and Verney, 1995). In contrast, axons from the mediodorsal thalamic nucleus do not arrive in the subplate until gestational week 15 in humans (Kostovic and Goldman-Rakic 1983), and the afferent fibers from other cortical regions arrive still later (Goldman-Rakic 1987a).

Monoaminergic axons probably form the first synaptic contacts in the marginal zone and subplate (Kostovic and Rakic 1990). Indeed, in monkey cortex, the earliest synapses formed frequently contain dense core vesicles (Zecevic *et al.* 1989), a feature commonly found in monoaminergic axon terminals in adults. In addition, D_1 and D_2 dopaminergic receptors have been identified in the marginal zone as early as E73 in monkeys (Lidow 1995). By gestational week 24 in humans, numerous presumptive dopamine axons can be identified in the cerebral wall, preferentially distributed in the deep cortical plate and upper subplate. Thus, the cortical plate is already innervated by dopamine axons (Verney *et al.* 1993) when thalamic afferents end their "waiting period" and start penetrating the cortical plate (Kostovic and Goldman-Rakic 1983). Although comparable studies are not available in primates, early developmental lesions of dopamine neurons in rodents have been shown to produce a substantial decrease in the total length of basal dendrites on layer 5 pyramids (Kalsbeek *et al.* 1989), an observation which suggests the critical importance of dopamine axons in cortical development.

Following the arrival of monoaminergic afferents, callosal axons projecting from migrating neurons in the opposite hemisphere begin to arrive in the subplate around E82 in monkeys (Schwartz and Goldman-Rakic 1991), and by E111 large numbers of callosal axons have invaded the cortex. By E133–155, callosal as well as associational projections have clearly-defined columnar arrays of axon terminals (Schwartz and Goldman-Rakic 1984), indicat-

ing that patterns of cortical connectivity may be specified early in maturation. Despite the early appearance of these patterns, callosal axons continue to increase in number during late gestation to reach a peak of 188 million at birth, about 3.5 times the number present in the adult (LaMantia and Rakic 1990). About 70% of callosal axons are eliminated during the first three postnatal months, with the most rapid decline occurring during the first three postnatal weeks. Since the basic patterns of discontinuities in the terminal fields of callosal axons are already evident before birth (Schwartz and Goldman-Rakic 1991), the elimination of callosal axons probably does not play a role in the establishment of those patterns.

SYNAPTOGENESIS IN PRIMATE PFC

Similar to neurogenesis and neuronal migration, synaptogenesis in the PFC and other cortical regions of the primate brain is characterized by an inside-out pattern of development (Bourgeois *et al.* 1994). By E149 in monkeys (approximately 2 weeks prior to term), however, the inside-out gradient of synaptic density is no longer apparent, and the density of synapses is higher in the supragranular layers. This laminar shift in synaptic density eventually results in the mature pattern of distribution of synapses in which up to 70% of PFC synapses are located in the supragranular layers.

Bourgeois and colleagues (1994) have identified five phases of synaptogenesis in the PFC of macaque monkeys. The *precortical phase* extends from E47 through E78, and is characterized by the presence of synapses in the marginal zone and subplate, but not in the cortical plate. During the *early cortical phase* (E78–E104), synapses appear gradually in the cortical plate, but they are present only on dendritic shafts. The *rapid phase* of synaptogenesis lasts from E104 through the second postnatal month. During this period, the number of cortical synapses increases very rapidly, with the peak rate of accumulation taking place around term. The total number of PFC synapses increases to levels that are substantially above adult values. This overshoot in synaptic density occurs to the greatest extent in layers 1–3, is less marked in layers 4 and 5, and is not apparent in layer 6. The *plateau phase*, which lasts from the ages of 2 months to about 3 years, is characterized by a period of high and unchanging synaptic density. Finally, during the *declining phase*, the density of synaptic contacts decreases slowly from 3 years through at least 20 years of age.

Embedded within these periods of change in the overall density of PFC synapses are additional patterns of change that are specific to different types of synapses. For example, the density of synapses on dendritic shafts peaks at the postnatal age of 2 months, and this level appears to be maintained throughout the life span. These synapses account for 25–40% of all synapses, and in terms of total number, they are not overproduced or pruned. In contrast, synapses on the dendritic spines of pyramidal neurons appear to contribute to most or all of the transient over-production of PFC synapses. These synapses decline in density by 50% after the age of 3 years.

Although studied in less detail, synaptogenesis in human PFC appears to undergo a similar pattern of change during postnatal development. For example, as in monkeys, the bulk of synaptogenesis in humans occurs in the second half of gestation and in the early postnatal weeks (Kostovic and Rakic 1990). In addition, in layer 3 of human PFC, synaptic density increases rapidly from birth to reach peak values around 1–2 years of age (Huttenlocher 1979). This elevated density of synapses, which is about 50% above adult levels, is maintained at least until age 7 years, before declining to levels which appear to remain stable from 16 through 72 years of age. Thus, in both monkeys and human PFC, synaptogenesis is characterized by an early period of overproduction, a plateau phase, and then a decline to adult levels.

Interestingly, the overall patterns of synapse produc-tion and regression appear to parallel the timing of meta-bolic changes in human PFC as revealed by positron emission tomography (PET) measures of glucose utiliza-tion (Chugani, Phelps, and Mezziotta 1987). For example, metabolic rates in the PFC begin to increase around 6 months of age, and then continue to rise until peak values are reached around 3 years of age. These levels, approxi-mately 200% above adult values, are maintained through about 8 years of age, and then decline to stable adult levels by the end of the second decade of life. Similarly, regional cerebral blood flow, as measured by single photon emission

computed tomography (SPECT) using [133]XE, increases substantially in the human PFC between 13 and 24 months of age (Chiron *et al.* 1992). In addition, evidence of an overshoot above adult levels was present between 3 and 12 years of age, although this observation was not significant, perhaps due to the small sample size.

Comparison of the monkey and human studies of syn-aptogenesis, however, suggests that the rate and pattern of decrease in synapse density during the declining phase may differ across species. In monkeys, synapse number in the PFC appears to continue to decline throughout ado-lescence and adult life, whereas in humans the declining phase appears to be restricted to adolescence. Given the relatively small sample size of each study, these differences may be more apparent than real. It is possible that these differences reflect differences in the rate of change in syn-aptic number across specific systems in the PFC. Although the overall pattern of postnatal changes in synaptic density has been found to be similar in all regions of primate cortex studied (Rakic *et al.* 1986), regional, laminar and cellular differences in the precise time course of these changes have been observed. For example, in layer 3 of human cerebral cortex, total synaptic density peaks at 6 months of age in primary visual cortex (Huttenlocher and DeCourten 1987), but at 2 years of age in prefrontal regions (Huttenlocher 1979). Laminar differences in the temporal pattern of postnatal synaptic production and elimination have also been described in several regions of monkey neo-cortex. In primary visual cortex, Bourgeois and Rakic (1993) found that the periods of overshoot and regression in the density of synapses in layer 4 were completed prior to 1 year of age. A more protracted pattern of maturation was observed in both the infragranular and supragranular layers of this region. In these layers, the plateau phase of relatively high synaptic density persisted into the third year of life. Laminar differences in postnatal changes in synaptic density have also been observed in monkey PFC. In these cortical regions, the early overshoot and peripu-bertal reduction in synaptic density was most marked in the supragranular layers (Bourgeois *et al.* 1994). Within a cortical layer, there may also be important differences among classes of neurons in the timing of synaptic produc-tion and elimination. For example, in layer 4 of monkey primary visual cortex, changes in the densities of dendritic spines (markers of sites of excitatory synapses) on the alpha and beta types of spiny stellate cells follow markedly different time courses during the first 6 months of life (Lund and Holbach 1991). Thus, it is clearly important for future studies to examine the developmental pattern of change in synaptic inputs to specific populations of PFC neurons.

Similar to synapses, the production of neurotransmitter receptors in the monkey PFC, as measured by quantitative receptor autoradiography, also appears to undergo a distinctive pattern of postnatal development (Lidow, Goldman-Rakic, and Rakic 1991; Lidow and Rakic 1992). For example, the densities of both D_1 and D_2 dopaminergic receptors are relatively low at birth, and then increase to peak values, about twice those present in adult animals, by 2 months of age. These elevated values appear to be maintained until 4 months of age, and to then decline until adult levels are reached at the age of 3 years. D_1 sites are most dense in layers 1 through superficial 3 and in layers 5–6, whereas D_2 sites (which have a much lower overall density) are most numerous in layer 5. These laminar patterns are consistently present throughout development and do not appear to change with the fluctuations in density of receptors. Serotonin 5HT1 and 5HT2 sites undergo a similar increase and decrease in density during development with peak levels observed at 2–4 months in all layers. Similarly, α_1, α_2 and β adrenergic receptors, cholinergic receptors and GABA receptors show the same pattern of increase (with peak levels present between 2 and 4 months of age) and decrease over the same time course. It should be noted that these changes in density of monoaminergic receptors do not correlate well with changes in cortical concentrations of the relevant neurotransmitters (Goldman-Rakic and Brown 1982) or with markers of the afferent axons (Lewis and Harris 1991; Berger *et al.* 1992; Rosenberg and Lewis 1994, 1995), which suggests an independent time course for the development of pre- and postsynaptic markers of these systems (Lidow and Rakic 1992).

LATE POSTNATAL REFINEMENTS IN PREFRONTAL CORTEX CIRCUITRY

Although the studies reviewed above have emphasized the pre- and early postnatal development of the primate PFC,

it is clear from the time course of the functional maturation of this area that significant refinements in the circuitry of the region must also occur during later periods of development. Indeed, the time course of the declining period of synaptic development strongly suggests that the connectivity of the region undergoes substantial changes during adolescence. It is important to determine how specific and inter-related components of PFC circuitry change during postnatal development because of the apparent regional, laminar, and cellular specificity in the timing and course of maturational changes in synaptic density (see preceding section). One system of particular relevance to both the cognitive functions mediated by the PFC, and to the disruption of those functions in disorders such as schizophrenia, comprises of the pyramidal neurons located in layer 3. The axons of these neurons are major contributors to excitatory projections to other cortical regions (see Jones 1984; Barbas 1992 for reviews), and serve as the principal source of horizontally-spreading excitatory connections within a region of PFC (Levitt *et al.* 1993) (see Fig. 2.7a). Thus, these neurons appear to play a critical role not only in the flow of information processing between the PFC and other cortical regions, but also in the recruitment and coordination of activity among spatially-distributed populations of neurons within a PFC region. Consequently, understanding the manner in which the adult pattern of inputs to these neurons is achieved may not only enhance our understanding of the functional maturation of PFC circuitry, but may also provide insight into the possible pathophysiological basis of human neurodevelopmental disorders that impair PFC function.

Dendritic spines are the principal sites of asymmetric, excitatory synaptic inputs to pyramidal neurons (Colonnier 1968; LeVay 1973; Mates and Lund 1983; Saint Marie and Peters 1985), and changes in spine number appear to reflect parallel changes in excitatory inputs to these neurons (Lund and Holbach 1991). In Golgi studies (Anderson *et al.* 1995), the density of dendritic spines on layer 3 pyramidal neurons of monkey PFC undergoes substantial changes during postnatal development (Fig. 2.2). The dendrites of these neurons exhibit a rapid acquisition of spines between birth and 10 weeks of age (Fig. 2.3). They then maintain a high density of spines at a relatively constant value, approximately 50%

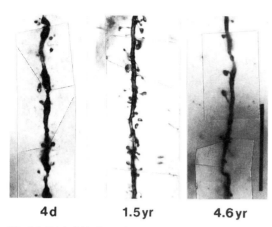

4d   1.5yr   4.6yr

Fig. 2.2 Brightfield photomicrographs of distal apical dendritic segments of layer 3 pyramidal neurons from animals of the indicated ages. Note the increase and decline in spine density over this age range. Calibration bar=20 μm. (Adapted from Anderson *et al*. 1995.)

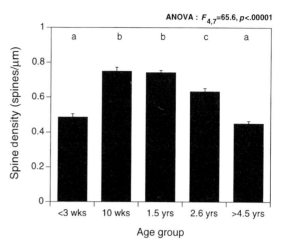

Fig. 2.3 Postnatal changes in relative apical dendritic spine density on layer 3 pyramidal neurons located in monkey PFC. Groups not sharing the same letter are significantly different at $p<0.05$. (Adapted from Anderson *et al*. 1995.)

higher than at birth, over a period of at least 14 months. After 1.5 years of age, this population of neurons undergoes overall spine attrition, again by about 50%, until adult levels are achieved by 4.5 years of age. Spine density then appears to remain stable at these levels at least through 16 years of age. The time course for this acquisition and loss of spines during development is similar on both the apical and basilar dendritic trees of these neurons.

This temporal pattern of change in spine density is both similar to and different from the sequence of developmental changes in synaptic density observed in the supragranular layers of monkey PFC in electron microscopy studies (Bourgeois *et al*. 1994). In these studies of the cortical neuropil, the number of asymmetric synapses on dendritic spines were observed to increase rapidly between birth and 2 months of age, and then to maintain this relatively high level until approximately 3 years of age. The density of axospinous synapses, however, then declined steadily from 3 years of age through adulthood, a pattern of change that differs from the rapid decline in spine density to stable adult levels observed on layer 3 pyramidal neurons in Golgi studies (Anderson *et al*. 1995). The apparent discrepancy in these findings may be a consequence of the different sampling methods employed in

each study. The assessment of the density of axospinous synapses in the supragranular layers included any spines located in these layers, without knowledge of which neuronal populations contributed those spines. Thus, although the total number of asymmetric axospinous synapses in the supragranular layers may decline steadily during the postpubertal period, the number of excitatory inputs to a subpopulation of pyramidal neurons, specifically those with cell bodies located in layer 3, appears to decrease over a shorter period of time during adolescence and then to remain stable through adulthood. Consistent with this interpretation of these data, synaptic density in the infragranular layers of monkey PFC does not appear to follow the same temporal pattern of overproduction and elimination as in the superficial layers (Bourgeois *et al*. 1994). Thus, the timing of axospinous synapse maturation on pyramidal neurons located in these deeper layers, including those synapses on the portions of their dendrites that extend into the supragranular layers, may be dissimilar to that of pyramidal neurons located in the superficial layers. Although additional studies are necessary to confirm this hypothesis, these comparisons suggest that the elimination of PFC axospinous synapses and dendritic spines during the peripubertal age range follows different time courses for specific subpopulations of PFC pyramidal neurons. These differences may provide an anatomical substrate for different rates of maturation of specific functions subserved by PFC circuitry (Alexander and Goldman 1978).

As discussed above, the chandelier class of local circuit GABA neurons provides an important source of inhibitory regulation of pyramidal neuron function in the PFC. The axon terminals of chandelier neurons are arrayed as morphologically-distinct cartridges which form symmetric, inhibitory synapses on the axon initial segment of pyramidal neurons (Szentagothai and Arbib 1974; Jones 1975; Somogyi 1977; Fairen and Valverde 1980; Peters *et al.* 1982; Somogyi *et al.* 1982; Freund *et al.* 1983; Hendry *et al.* 1983; DeFelipe *et al.* 1985; Marin-Padilla 1987). Expression of the calcium-binding protein, parvalbumin (PV), by chandelier neurons in monkey PFC also undergoes substantial changes during postnatal development (Lewis and Lund 1990; Akil and Lewis 1992; Anderson *et al.* 1995). Of particular interest are the PV-immunoreactive axon cartridges of chandelier neurons located in layer 3 (Fig. 2.4), which are likely to provide inhibitory input to layer 3 pyramidal neurons (see Fig. 2.7a). As shown in Fig. 2.5, the density of PV-positive cartridges in monkey PFC increases rapidly during the first 3 months of postnatal development, undergoes a plateau period that lasts until at least until 1.5 years of age, and then declines during the peripubertal age range to stable adult values (Anderson *et al.* 1995). This close temporal match between the postnatal changes in spine density on layer 3 pyramidal neurons, and that of PV-immunoreactive chandelier neuron axon cartridges presumed to surround the axon initial segments of a similar population of pyramidal neurons, indicates the importance of this time frame in the maturation of the circuitry involving layer 3 pyramidal neurons in monkey PFC. Although the change in density of PV-labeled axon cartridges could possibly be due to parallel developmental shifts in the number of chandelier neuron axon terminals, or number of varicosities per cartridge, such changes have not been observed in Golgi studies of chandelier neurons in monkey PFC (Lewis and Lund 1990; Lund and Lewis 1993). For example, Golgi-impregnated chandelier neuron axon cartridges are clearly present in PFC layer 3 in both neonatal and adult monkeys; in contrast, in these same animals PV- immunoreactive cartridges are either not

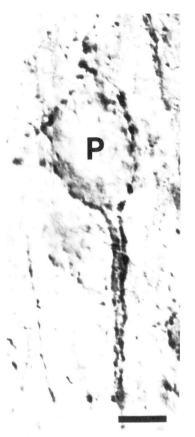

Fig. 2.4 Differential interference contrast photomicrograph of a PV-immunoreactive chandelier neuron axon cartridge in monkey PFC. This cartridge outlines the axon initial segment of an unlabeled pyramidal neuron (P). Calibration bar=10 μm.

detectable or are quite low in density (Lewis and Lund 1990). Thus, it seems likely that the level of PV immunoreactivity per cartridge changes with age.

As levels of PV immunoreactivity appear to be correlated with neuronal activity (Heizmann 1984; Celio 1986; Carr *et al.* 1989), the developmental changes in density of PV-immunoreactive cartridges may reflect the level of activity of the inhibitory synapses furnished by these axon terminals. Thus, during postnatal development at least a subpopulation of chandelier neurons may vary their degree of inhibitory control over specific populations of pyramidal cells. The striking correlation across postnatal development (see Fig. 2.5) between the densities of PV-labeled car-

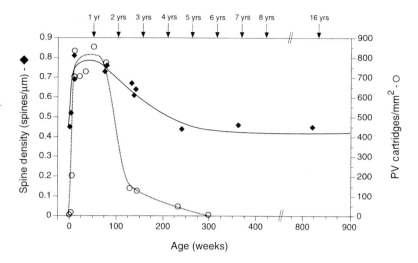

Fig. 2.5. Age-related changes in the mean density of spines on the apical dendrite of layer III pyramidal neurons (diamonds) and of PV-immunoreactive axon cartridges (○) in layer 3 of monkey PFC. Note the synchronous temporal patterns of change in these markers of excitatory and inhibitory inputs to layer III pyramidal neurons. (Adapted from Anderson *et al.* 1995.)

tridges and dendritic spines on layer 3 pyramidal neurons suggests that the strength of inhibitory inputs to these neurons may change to match the strength of the excitatory inputs. Such a coordination between excitatory and inhibitory inputs could be achieved by axon collaterals of layer 3 pyramidal cells contacting chandelier neurons, thus increasing their activity as the excitatory inputs proliferate on the spines of the pyramidal neurons. Based upon studies in other neuronal systems (Changeux and Danchin 1976; Purves and Lichtman 1980), the temporary maintenance of high levels of excitatory inputs to pyramidal neurons may be necessary for appropriate competition among, and ultimately for the proper refinement of, cortical connections. Although the axon collaterals of layer 3 pyramidal neurons in some regions of monkey cortex, have been shown to provide excitatory input to local circuit neurons (Winfield *et al.* 1981), the existence of such a relationship between the pyramidal and chandelier neurons in layer 3 of monkey PFC remains to be established.

These synchronous changes in the density of dendritic spines and a marker of inhibitory inputs to layer 3 pyramidal neurons raises the question of whether these changes are linked to postnatal refinements in other elements of PFC circuitry. For example, the dopaminergic innervation of monkey PFC also undergoes substantial change during postnatal development (Goldman-Rakic and Brown 1982; Lewis and Harris 1991; Lidow *et al.* 1991; Rosenberg and

Lewis 1995). Dopamine afferents to the primate PFC form symmetric contacts with dendritic spines and shafts of pyramidal neurons (Goldman-Rakic *et al.* 1989; Smiley *et al.* 1992), as well as with the dendrites of local circuit neurons (Smiley and Goldman-Rakic 1993) that are GABAergic (Sesack *et al.* 1993). Consequently, the maturational changes in the dopaminergic innervation of PFC layer 3 are of particular interest (see Fig. 2.7a). As summarized in Fig. 2.6, the density of varicosities (possible sites of synaptic specializations or neurotransmitter release) on dopamine axons in layer 3 of monkey PFC increases during the first few postnatal months (Rosenberg and Lewis 1995), parallel to the increase in densities of pyramidal neuron dendritic spines and PV-immunoreactive chandelier neuron axon cartridges. After a plateau period, dopamine varicosities undergo a second marked increase in density, to reach peak values at between 2 and 3 years of age, the typical age of onset of puberty in this species (Plant 1988). The number of dopamine varicosities then rapidly declines to relatively stable adult levels by 5 years of age. This second rise in the density of dopamine varicosities appears to begin prior to the decline in the densities of pyramidal neuron spines and PV-immunoreactive cartridges in layer 3, and to persist until the adult levels of these markers of excitatory and inhibitory inputs are achieved. These patterns suggest that the neuromodulatory effects of dopamine may influence the adoles-

Fig. 2.6. Number (per 5000 μm²) of dopamine axon varicosities in deep layer 3 of monkey PFC area 9. Data are presented as values (mean of triplicate measures) for individual animals (a) and as mean (±SD) values for the same animals clustered into six groups defined by chronological age (b). In (b), groups not sharing the same letter are significantly different at $p < 0.05$. (Adapted from Rosenberg and Lewis 1995.)

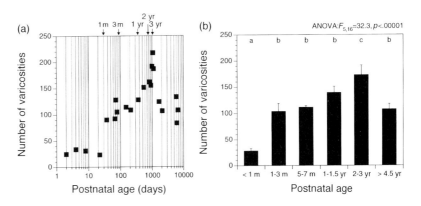

cent refinement of excitatory and inhibitory inputs to layer 3 pyramidal neurons, and that dopamine may have a particularly strong influence on cortical information processing around the time of puberty. These findings are also of particular interest given the converging lines of evidence from lesion, pharmacological, electrophysiological and modeling studies demonstrating the importance of an intact dopamine innervation to the functional integrity of the PFC (Brozoski *et al.* 1979; Sawaguchi *et al.* 1988; Sawaguchi and Goldman-Rakic 1991; Cohen and Servan-Schreiber 1992). It is important to note that these developmental changes in the dopaminergic innervation of monkey PFC appear to be specific to layer 3 (Rosenberg and Lewis 1995).

In contrast to these parallel patterns of developmental changes, the density of cholecystokinin (CCK)-positive neurons in layers 1–superficial 3 is most prominent at birth and falls to a constant adult-like level by 1 year of age (Oeth and Lewis 1993), i.e., as the densities of dendritic spines and PV-immunoreactive cartridges increase, the expression of CCK immunoreactivity declines. These CCK-positive cells belong to two classes of local circuit neurons (Lund and Lewis 1993), narrow arbor neurons connecting layers 2 and 4 and medium arbor neurons with axons confined to layers 2 and superficial 3. Although the synaptic targets of these CCK-containing neurons remain to be identified, they appear to have their major targets in layers 2 and 4, respectively, and to lack a direct influence on neuronal activity in layer 3 (Fig. 2.7a). These data, together with the laminar specificity of postnatal changes

in density of PFC dopamine varicosities, are consistent with the hypothesis of a high degree of specificity in the postnatal refinement of monkey PFC circuitry.

The temporal course of these refinements in different aspects of monkey PFC circuitry is summarized schematically in Figure 2.7b.

CONCLUSIONS

The studies reviewed above indicate that the appearance of the mature functional architecture of the primate PFC depends upon a number of specific developmental events that begin in early prenatal life and extend through the period of adolescence. Prenatally, the formation of the subplate, the genesis and migration of PFC neurons, the ingrowth of various afferent systems, and the formation of synapses all represent processes that, if aberrant, could have profound consequences on the subsequent maturation and functional capacities of PFC circuitry. It must be kept in mind that the plasticity of cortical systems is so great that even resection of the PFC in monkeys 2 months prior to birth does not produce evidence of significant impairments on cognitive tasks during postnatal life (Goldman-Rakic and Galkin 1978). In addition, although progressive and regressive events occur throughout development, multiple converging lines of evidence indicate that the perinatal and peripubertal periods are critical time points for building and refining, respectively, the functional architecture of the primate PFC. Consequently,

Fig. 2.7. (a) Schematic drawing of four components of PFC circuitry. Layer 3 pyramidal neurons (P) furnish projections to other cortical regions, and horizontally-spreading axon collaterals within the same region. Dopamine (DA) axons and parvalbumin (PV)-containing axon cartridges of GABAergic chandelier neurons are thought to provide direct synaptic input to the dendritic shafts and spines and axon initial segment, respectively, of these pyramidal neurons (P). In contrast, CCK-containing GABAergic neurons do not have direct connections with these pyramidal neurons. (b) Age-related changes in these four components of PFC circuitry, plotted as a percentage of the maximal value for each measure. Spines (---) indicate relative dendritic spine density on layer 3 pyramidal neurons. CCK neurons (—) indicate the density of CCK-positive-neurons in layers 2 and superficial 3. DA varicosities (· · ·) indicate the density of varicosities on dopamine axons in deep layer 3. PV cartridges (-·-) indicate the density of chandelier neuron axon cartridges exhibiting parvalbumin immunoreactivity in the deep half of layer 3. Note the marked changes that occur during the perinatal (birth to 2 months of age) and peripubertal (2–4 years of age) periods of development. (b) is adapted from Anderson *et al.* 1995.)

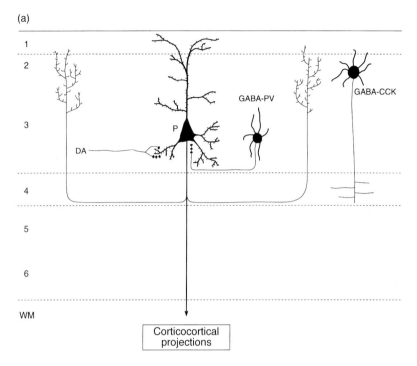

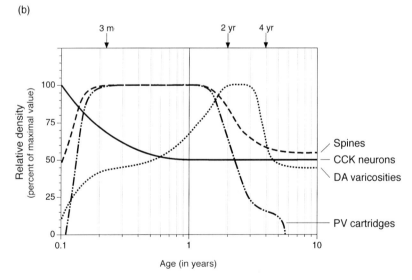

further studies of the development of PFC circuitry during these time periods may provide important insights into how this circuitry may become disrupted in clinical disorders characterized by PFC dysfunction.

ACKNOWLEDGMENTS

Studies described in this chapter that were conducted by the author and colleagues were supported by USPHS grants MH00519, MH43784, and MH45156. The author thanks S. Anderson, J. Classey, F. Condé, J. Lund, K. Oeth and D. Rosenberg for their valuable contributions to those studies, and M. Brady for preparing the figures for this chapter.

REFERENCES

Akbarian, S., Kim, J.J., Potkin, S.G., Hagman, J.O., Tafazzoli, A., Bunney, W.E., Jr, and Jones, E.G. 1995. Gene expression for glutamic acid decarboxylase is reduced without loss of neurons in prefrontal cortex of schizophrenics. *Arch. Gen. Psychiatr.* **52**:258–66.

Akil, M., and Lewis, D.A. 1992. Differential distribution of parvalbumin-immunoreactive pericellular clusters of terminal boutons in developing and adult monkey neocortex. *Exp. Neurol.* **115**:239–49.

Alexander, G.E. 1982. Functional development of frontal association cortex in monkeys: behavioral and electrophysiological studies. *Neurosci. Res. Prog. Bull.* **20**:471–9.

Alexander, G.E., and Goldman, P.S. 1978. Functional development of the dorsolateral prefrontal cortex: an analysis utilizing reversible cryogenic depression. *Brain Res.* **143**:233–49.

Allendoerfer, K.L., and Shatz, C.J. 1994. The subplate, a transient neocortical structure: its role in the development of connections between thalamus and cortex. In *Annual review of neuroscience*, vol. 17, ed. W.M. Cowan, E.M. Shooter, C.F. Stevens and R.F. Thompson, pp.185–218. Palo Alto: Annual Reviews Inc.

Anderson, S.A., Classey, J.D., Condé, F., Lund, J.S., and Lewis, D.A. 1995. Synchronous development of pyramidal neuron

dendritic spines and parvalbumin-immunoreactive chandelier neuron axon terminals in layer III of monkey prefrontal cortex. *Neuroscience* (in press).

Barbas, H. 1992. Architecture and cortical connections of the prefrontal cortex in the Rhesus monkey. *Adv. Neurol.* **57**:91–115.

Barbas, H., and Pandya, D.N. 1989. Architecture and intrinsic connections of the prefrontal cortex in the rhesus monkey. *J. Comp. Neurol.* **286**:353–75.

Bauer, R.H., and Fuster, J.M. 1976. Delayed matching and delayed-response deficit from cooling dorsolateral prefrontal cortex in monkeys. *J. Comp. Physiol. Psychol.* **90**:293–302.

Berger, B., Verney, C., and Goldman-Rakic, P.S. 1992. Prenatal monoaminergic innervation of the cerebral cortex: differences between rodents and primates. In *Neurodevelopment, aging and cognition*, ed. I. Kostovic, S. Knezevic, H. Wisniewski, and G. Spilich, pp. 18–36. Boston: Birkhauser.

Bourgeois, J.P., Goldman-Rakic, P.S., and Rakic, P. 1994. Synaptogenesis in the prefrontal cortex of rhesus monkeys. *Cereb. Cortex* **4**:78–96.

Bourgeois, J.P., and Rakic, P. 1993. Changes of synaptic density in the primary visual cortex of the macaque monkey from fetal to adult stage. *J. Neurosci.* **13**:2801–20.

Brodmann, K. 1909. *Lokalisationslehre der Grosshirnrinde*, p.324. Leipsiz: J.A. Barth.

Brozoski, T.J., Brown, R.M., Rosvold, H.E., and Goldman, P.S. 1979. Cognitive deficit caused by regional depletion of dopamine in prefrontal cortex of rhesus monkeys. *Science* **205**:929–32.

Carr, P.A., Yamamoto, T., Karney, G., Baimbridge, K.G., and Nagy, J.I. 1989. Analysis of parvalbumin and calbindin D28K-immunoreactive neurons in dorsal root ganglia of rat in relation to their cytochrome oxidase and carbonic anhydrase content. *Neuroscience* **33**:363–71.

Celio, M.R. 1986. Parvalbumin in most gamma-aminobutyric acid-containing neurons of the rat cerebral cortex. *Science* **231**:995–8.

Changeux, J.-P., and Danchin, A. 1976. Selective stabilization of developing synapses as a mechanism for the specification of neuronal networks. *Nature* **264**:705–12.

Chiron, C., Raynaud, C., Mazière, B., Zilbovicius, M., Laflamme, L., Masure, M.C., Dulac, O., Bourguignon, M., and Syrota, A. 1992. Changes in regional cerebral blood flow during brain maturation in children and adolescents. *J. Nucl. Med.* **33**:696–703.

Chugani, H.T., Phelps, M.E., and Mezziotta, J.C. 1987. Positron emission tomography study of human brain functional development. *Ann. Neurol.* **22**:487–97.

Chun, J.M., and Shatz, C.J. 1989a. The earliest-generated neurons of the cat cerebral cortex: characterization by MAP2 and neurotransmitter immunohistochemistry during fetal life. *J. Neurosci.* **9**:1648–57.

Chun, J.J.M., and Shatz, C.J. 1989b. Interstitial cells of the adult neocortical white matter are the remnant of the early generated subplate neuron population. *J. Comp. Neurol.* **282**:555–69.

Cohen, J.D., and Servan-Schreiber, D. 1992. Context, cortex, and dopamine: a connectionist approach to behavior and biology in schizophrenia. *Psychol. Rev.* **99**:45–77.

Colonnier, M. 1968. Synaptic patterns on different cell types in the different laminae of the cat visual cortex. An electron microscope study. *Brain Res.* **9**:268–87.

Condé, F., Lund, J.S., Jacobowitz, D.M., Baimbridge, K.G., and Lewis, D.A. 1994. Local circuit neurons immunoreactive for calretinin, calbindin D-28k, or parvalbumin in monkey prefrontal cortex: distribution and morphology. *J. Comp. Neurol.* **341**:95–116.

Condé, F., and Lewis, D.A. 1993. Postnatal development of parvalbumin (PV) immunoreactive local circuit neurons in visual areas of monkey neocortex. *Soc. Neurosci. Abstr.* **19**:675.

DeFelipe, J. 1993. Neocortical neuronal diversity: chemical heterogeneity revealed by colocalization studies of classic neurotransmitters, neuropeptides, calcium-binding proteins, and cell surface molecules. *Cereb. Cortex* **3**: 273–89.

DeFelipe, J., Hendry, S.H.C., and Jones, E.G. 1989. Visualization of chandelier cell axons by parvalbumin immunoreactivity in monkey cerebral cortex. *Proc. Natl. Acad. Sci. USA* **86**:2093–7.

DeFelipe, J., Hendry, S.H.C., Jones, E.G., and Schmechel, D. 1985. Variability in the terminations of GABAergic chandelier cell axons on initial segments of pyramidal cell axons in the monkey sensory-motor cortex. *J. Comp. Neurol.* **231**:364–84.

Diamond, A. 1985. The development of the ability to use recall

to guide action, as indicated by infants' performances on AB. *Child Devel.* **56**:868–83.

Fairen, A., DeFelipe, J., and Regidon, J. 1984. Nonpyramidal neurons, general account. In *Cerebral cortex*, vol. 1, ed. A. Peters and E.G. Jones, pp. 201–45. New York: Plenum Press.

Fairen, A., and Valverde, F. 1980. A specialized type of neuron in the visual cortex of cat: a Golgi and electron microscope study of chandelier cells. *J. Comp. Neurol.* **194**:761–79.

Freund, T.F., Martin, K.A.C., Smith, A.D., and Somogyi, P. 1983. Glutamate decarboxylase-immunoreactive terminals of Golgi-impregnated axoaxonic cells and of presumed basket cells in synaptic contact with pyramidal neurons of the cat's visual cortex. *J. Comp. Neurol.* **221**:263–78.

Friauf, E., McConnell, S.K., and Shatz, C.J. 1990. Functional synaptic circuits in the subplate during fetal and early postnatal development of cat visual cortex. *J. Neurosci.* **10**:2601–13.

Funahashi, S., Bruce, C.J., and Goldman-Rakic, P.S. 1989. Mnemonic coding of visual space in the monkey's dorsolateral prefrontal cortex. *J. Neurophysiol.* **61**:331–49.

Fuster, J.M. 1989. *The prefrontal cortex: anatomy, physiology and neuropsychology of the frontal lobe.* New York: Raven Press.

Fuster, J.M., Bauer, R.H., and Jervey, J.P. 1982. Cellular discharge in the dorsolateral prefrontal cortex of the monkey in cognitive tasks. *Exp. Neurol.* **77**:679–94.

Ghosh, A., Antonini, A., McConnell, S.K., and Shatz, C.J. 1990. Requirement for subplate neurons in the formation of thalamocortical connections. *Nature* **347**:179–81.

Ghosh, A., and Shatz, C.J. 1992. Involvement of subplate neurons in the formation of ocular dominance columns. *Science* **255**:1441–3.

Ghosh, A., and Shatz, C.J. 1994. Segregation of geniculocortical afferents during the critical period: A role for subplate neurons. *J. Neurosci.* **14**:3862–80.

Goldman, P.S. 1971. Functional development of the prefrontal cortex in early life and the problem of neuronal plasticity. *Exp. Neurol.* **32**:366–87.

Goldman, P.S. 1974. An alternative to developmental plasticity: heterology of CNS structures in infants and adults. In *CNS plasticity and recovery of function*, ed. D.G. Stein, J. Rosen, and N. Butters, pp. 149–74. New York: Academic Press.

Goldman, P.S., and Rosvold, H.E. 1972. The effects of selective caudate lesions in infant and juvenile rhesus monkeys. *Brain Res.* **43**:53–66.

Goldman-Rakic, P.S. 1987a. Development of cortical circuitry and cognitive function. *Child Devel.* **58**:601–22.

Goldman-Rakic, P.S. 1987b. Circuitry of primate prefrontal cortex and regulation of behavior by representational memory. In *Handbook of physiology*, vol. 5, ed. F. Plum, and V. Mountcastle, pp. 373–417. Bethesda: American Physiological Society.

Goldman-Rakic, P.S. 1988. Topography of cognition: parallel distributed networks in primate association cortex. *Ann. Rev. Neurosci.* **11**:137–56.

Goldman-Rakic, P.S., and Brown, R.M. 1982. Postnatal development of monoamine content and synthesis in the cerebral cortex of rhesus monkeys. *Dev. Brain Res.* **4**:339–49.

Goldman-Rakic, P.S., and Galkin, T.W. 1978. Prenatal removal of frontal association cortex in the fetal rhesus monkey: anatomical and functional consequences in postnatal life. *Brain Res.* **152**:451–85.

Goldman-Rakic, P.S., Isseroff, A., Schwartz, M.L., and Bugbee, N.M. 1983. The neurobiology of cognitive development. In *Handbook of child psychology: biology and infancy development*, ed. P. Mussen, pp. 281–344. New York: Wiley.

Goldman-Rakic, P.S., Leranth, C., Williams, S.M., Mons, N., and Geffard, M. 1989. Dopamine synaptic complex with pyramidal neurons in primate cerebral cortex. *Proc. Natl. Acad. Sci. USA* **86**:9015–19.

Heizmann, C.W. 1984. Parvalbumin an intracellular calcium-binding protein. Distribution properties and possible roles in mammalian cells. *Experientia* **40**:910–21.

Hendry, S.H.C., Houser, C.R., Jones, E.G., and Vaughn, J.E. 1983. Synaptic organization of immunocytochemically identified GABA neurons in the monkey sensory-motor cortex. *J. Neurocytol.* **12**:639–60.

Hendry, S.H.C., Schwark, E.G., Jones, E.G., and Yan, J. 1987. Numbers and proportions of GABA-immunoreactive neurons in different areas of monkey cerebral cortex. *J. Neurosci.* **7**:1503–19.

Huttenlocher, P.R. 1979. Synaptic density in human frontal cortex – developmental changes and effects of aging. *Brain Res.* **163**:195–205.

Huttenlocher, P.R., and DeCourten, C. 1987. The development of synapses in striate cortex of man. *Hum. Neurobiol.* **6**:1–9.

Innocenti, G.M. 1991. Growth and reshaping of axons in the establishment of visual callosal connections. *Science* **212**:824–7.

Jones, E.G. 1975. Varieties and distribution of nonpyramidal cells in the somatic sensory cortex of the squirrel monkey. *J. Comp. Neurol.* **160**:205–68.

Jones, E.G. 1984. Laminar distribution of cortical efferent cells. In *Cerebral cortex*, vol. 1, ed. A. Peters, and E.G. Jones, pp. 521–53. New York: Plenum Press.

Jones, E.G., and Hendry, S.H.C. 1984. Basket cells. In *Cerebral cortex: cellular components of the cerebral cortex*, vol. 1, ed. E.G. Jones and A. Peters, pp. 309–36. New York: Plenum Press.

Kalsbeek, A., Matthijssen, M.A.H., and Uylings, H.B.M. 1989. Morphometric analysis of prefrontal and cortical development following neonatal lesioning of the dopaminergic mesocortical projection. *Exp. Brain Res.* **78**:279–89.

Kostovic, I., and Goldman-Rakic, P.S. 1983. Transient cholinesterase staining in the mediodorsal nucleus of the thalamus and its connections in the developing human and monkey brain. *J. Comp. Neurol.* **219**:431–47.

Kostovic, I., and Rakic, P. 1980. Cytology and the time of origin of interstitial neurons in the white matter in infant and adult human and monkey telencephalon. *J. Neurocytol.* **9**:219–42.

Kostovic, I., and Rakic, P. 1990. Developmental history of the transient subplate zone in the visual and somatosensory cortex of the macaque monkey and human brain. *J. Comp. Neurol.* **297**:441–70.

Kostovic, I., Skavic, J., and Strinovic, D. 1988. Acetylcholinesterase in the human frontal associative cortex during the period of cognitive development: early laminar shifts and late innervation of pyramidal neurons. *Neurosci. Lett.* **90**:107–12.

Kostovic, I., Stefulj-Fucic, A., Mrzljak, L., Jukic, S., and Delalle, I. 1991. Prenatal and perinatal development of the somatostatin-immunoreactive neurons in the human prefrontal cortex. *Neurosci. Lett.* **124**:153–6.

LaMantia, A.-S., and Rakic, P. 1990. Axon overproduction and elimination in the corpus callosum of the developing rhesus monkey. *J. Neurosci.* **10**: 2156–75.

LeVay, S. 1973. Synaptic patterns in the visual cortex of the cat and monkey. Electron microscopy of Golgi preparations. *J. Comp. Neurol.* **150**:53–86.

Levin, H.S., Culhane, K.A., Hartmann, J., Evankovich, K., and Mattson, A.J. 1991. Developmental changes in performance on tests of purported frontal lobe functioning. *Dev. Neuropsych.* 7:377–95.

Levitt, J.B., Lewis, D.A., Yoshioka, T., and Lund, J.S. 1993. Topography of pyramidal neuron intrinsic connections in macaque monkey prefrontal cortex (areas 9 & 46). *J. Comp. Neurol.* 338:360–76.

Levitt, P. 1982. Central monoamine neuron systems: Their organization in the developing and mature primate brain and the genetic regulation of their terminal fields. In *Gilles de la Tourette Syndrome*, ed. A.J. Friedhoff, and T.N. Chase, pp. 49–59. New York: Raven Press.

Levitt, P., and Rakic, P. 1982. The time of genesis, embryonic origin and differentiation of the brain stem monoamine neurons in the rhesus monkey. *Dev. Brain Res.* 4:35–57.

Lewis, D.A. 1992. The catecholaminergic innervation of primate prefrontal cortex. *J. Neural Transm.* 36:179–200.

Lewis, D.A. 1995. Neural circuitry of the prefrontal cortex in schizophrenia. *Arch. Gen. Psychiatry* 52:269–273.

Lewis, D.A., Foote, S.L., and Cha, C.I. 1989. Corticotropin releasing factor immunoreactivity in monkey neocortex: an immunohistochemical analysis. *J. Comp. Neurol.* 290:599–613.

Lewis, D.A., and Harris, H.W. 1991. Differential laminar distribution of tyrosine hydroxylase-immunoreactive axons in infant and adult monkey prefrontal cortex. *Neurosci. Lett.* 125:151–4.

Lewis, D.A., and Lund, J.S. 1990. Heterogeneity of chandelier neurons in monkey neocortex: Corticotropin-releasing factor and parvalbumin immunoreactive populations. *J. Comp. Neurol.* 293:599–615.

Lidow, M.S. 1995. D_1 and D_2 dopaminergic receptors in the developing cerebral cortex of macaque monkey: a film autoradiographic study. *Neuroscience* 65:439–52.

Lidow, M.S., Goldman-Rakic, P.S., and Rakic, P. 1991. Synchronized overproduction of neurotransmitter receptors in diverse regions of the primate cerebral cortex. *Proc. Natl Acad. Sci. USA* 88:10218–21.

Lidow, M.S., and Rakic, P. 1992. Scheduling of monoaminergic neurotransmitter receptor expression in the primate neocortex during postnatal development. *Cereb. Cortex* 2:401–16.

Lund, J.S. 1973. Organization of neurons in the visual cortex, area 17, of the monkey (*Macaca mulatta*). *J. Comp. Neurol.* 147:455–96.

Lund, J.S., and Holbach, S. 1991. Postnatal development of thalamic recipient neurons in monkey striate cortex: I. A comparison of spine acquisition and dendritic growth of layer 4C alpha and beta spiny stellate neurons. *J. Comp. Neurol.* 309:115–28.

Lund, J.S., and Lewis, D.A. 1993. Local circuit neurons of developing and mature macaque prefrontal cortex: Golgi and immunocytochemical characteristics. *J. Comp. Neurol.* 328:282–312.

Lund, J.S., Yoshioka, T., and Levitt, J.B. 1993. Comparison of intrinsic connectivity in different areas of macaque monkey cerebral cortex. *Cereb. Cortex* 3:148–62.

Lund, R.D., and Mustari, M.J. 1977. Development of the geniculocortical pathway in rats. *J. Comp. Neurol.* 173:289–306.

McConnell, S.K., Ghosh, A., and Shatz, C.J. 1989. Subplate neurons pioneer the first axon pathway from the cerebral cortex. *Science* 245:978–82.

McConnell, S.K., Ghosh, A., and Shatz, C.J. 1994. Subplate pioneers and the formation of descending connections from cerebral cortex. *J. Neurosci.* 14: 1892–907.

Marin-Padilla, M. 1987. The chandelier cell of the human visual cortex: a Golgi study. *J. Comp. Neurol.* 256:61–70.

Marin-Padilla, M., and Marin-Padilla, T.M. 1982. Origin, prenatal development and structural organization of layer I of the human cerebral (motor) cortex. A Golgi study. *Anat. Embryol. (Berl)* 164:161–206.

Mates, S.L., and Lund, J.S. 1983. Spine formation and maturation of type 1 synapses on spiny stellate neurons in primate visual cortex. *J. Comp. Neurol.* 221:91–7.

Miller, E.A., Goldman, P.S., and Rosvold, H.E. 1973. Delayed recovery of function following orbital lesions in infant monkeys. *Science* 182:304–6.

Mrzljak, L., Uylings, H.B.M., Kostovic, I., and Van Eden, C.G. 1988. Prenatal development of neurons in the human prefrontal cortex: I. A qualitative Golgi study. *J. Comp. Neurol.* 271:355–86.

Mrzljak, L., Uylings, H.B.M., Kostovic, I., and VanEden, C.G. 1992. Prenatal development of neurons in the human prefrontal cortex. II. A quantitative Golgi study. *J. Comp. Neurol.* 316:485–96.

Oeth, K.M., and Lewis, D.A. 1993. Postnatal development of

the cholecystokinin innervation of monkey prefrontal cortex. *J. Comp. Neurol.* **336**:400–18.

Pandya, D.N. and Yeterian, E.H. 1990. Prefrontal cortex in relation to other cortical areas in rhesus monkey: architecture and connections. In *Progress in brain research. the prefrontal cortex: its structure, function and pathology*, vol. 85, ed. H.B.M. Uylings, C.G. VanEden, J.P.C. DeBruin, M.A. Corner, and M.G.P. Feenstra, pp. 63–94. Amsterdam: Elsevier.

Peters, A. 1984. Chandelier cells. In *Cerebral Cortex*, vol. 1, ed. E.G. Jones, and A. Peters, pp. 361–80. New York: Plenum Press.

Peters, A., Proskauer, C.C., and Ribak, C.E. 1982. Chandelier neurons in rat visual cortex. *J. Comp. Neurol.* **206**:397–416.

Plant, T.M. 1988. Neuroendocrine basis of puberty in the rhesus monkey (*Macaca mulatta*). In *Frontiers in neuroendocrinology*, vol. 10, ed. L. Martin, and W.F. Ganong, pp. 215–38. New York: Raven Press.

Powell, T.P.S. 1981. Certain aspects of the intrinsic organisation of the cerebral cortex. In *Brain mechanisms and perceptual awareness*, ed. O. Pompeiana, and C.A. Marsan, pp. 1–19. New York: Raven Press.

Preuss, T.M., and Goldman-Rakic, P.S. 1991. Myelo-and cytoarchitecture of the granular frontal cortex and surrounding regions in the strepsirhine primate galago and the anthropoid primate macaca. *J. Comp. Neurol.* **310**:429–74.

Purves, D., and Lichtman, J.W. 1980. Elimination of synapses in the developing nervous system. *Science* **210**:153–7.

Rakic, P. 1977. Prenatal development of the visual system in rhesus monkey. *Phil. Trans. R. Soc. London Ser. B* **278**:245–60.

Rakic, P., Bourgeois, J.-P., Eckenhoff, M.F., Zecevic, N., and Goldman-Rakic, P.S. 1986. Concurrent overproduction of synapses in diverse regions of the primate cerebral cortex. *Science* **232**:232–5.

Rosenberg, D.R., and Lewis, D.A. 1994. Changes in the dopaminergic innervation of monkey prefrontal cortex during late postnatal development: a tyrosine hydroxylase immunohistochemical study. *Biol. Psychiatry* **36**:272–7.

Rosenberg, D.R., and Lewis, D.A. 1995. Postnatal maturation of the dopaminergic innervation of monkey prefrontal and motor cortices: a tyrosine hydroxylase immunohisto-chemical analysis. *J. Comp. Neurol.* **358**:383–400.

Saint Marie, R.L., and Peters, A. 1985. The morphology and synaptic connections of spiny stellate neurons in monkey visual cortex (area 17): a Golgi-electron microscopic study. *J. Comp. Neurol.* **233**:213–35.

Sawaguchi, T., and Goldman-Rakic, P.S. 1991. D1 dopamine receptors in prefrontal cortex: involvement in working memory. *Science* **251**:947–50.

Sawaguchi, T., Matsumura, M., and Kubota, K. 1988. Dopamine enhances the neuronal activity of spatial short-term memory task in the primate prefrontal cortex. *Neurosci. Res.* **5**:465–73.

Schwartz, M.L., and Goldman-Rakic, P.S. 1984. Callosal and intrahemispheric connectivity of the prefrontal association cortex in rhesus monkey: relation between intraparietal and principal sulcal cortex. *J. Comp. Neurol.* **226**:403–20.

Schwartz, M.L., and Goldman-Rakic, P.S. 1991. Prenatal specification of callosal connections in rhesus monkey. *J. Comp. Neurol.* **307**:144–62.

Schwartz, M.L., and Meinecke, D.L. 1992. Early expression of GABA-containing neurons in the prefrontal and visual cortices of rhesus monkeys. *Cereb. Cortex* **12**:16–37.

Schwartz, M.L., Rakic, P., and Goldman-Rakic, P.S. 1991. Early phenotype expression of cortical neurons: evidence that a subclass of migrating neurons have callosal axons. *Proc. Natl Acad. Sci. USA* **88**:1354–8.

Sesack, S.R., Snyder, C.L., and Lewis, D.A. 1993. Synaptic associations between dopamine terminals and GABA interneurons in rat and monkey cortex. *Soc. Neurosci. Abstr.* **19**:927.

Shatz, C.J., and Luskin, M.B. 1986. The relationship between the geniculocortical afferents and their cortical target cells during development of the cat's primary visual cortex. *J. Neurosci.* **6**:3655–68.

Smiley, J.F., and Goldman-Rakic, P.S. 1993. Heterogeneous targets of dopamine synapses in monkey prefrontal cortex demonstrated by serial section electron microscopy: a laminar analysis using the silver-enhanced diaminobenzidine sulfide (SEDS) immunolabeling technique. *Cereb. Cortex* **3**:223–38.

Smiley, J.F., Williams, S.M., Szigeti, K., and Goldman-Rakic, P.S. 1992. Light and electron microscopic characterization of dopamine-immunoreactive axons in human cerebral cortex. *J. Comp. Neurol.* **321**:325–35.

Somogyi, P. 1977. A specific axo-axonal interneuron in the

visual cortex of the rat. *Brain Res.* **136**:345–50.

Somogyi, P., Freund, T.F., and Cowey, A. 1982. The axo-axonic interneuron in the cerebral cortex of the rat, cat and monkey. *Neuroscience* **7**:2577–607.

Szentagothai, J., and Arbib, M. 1974. Conceptual models of neural organization. *Neurosci. Res. Prog. Bull.* **12**:307–510.

Verney, C., Milosevic, A., Alvarez, C., and Berger, B. 1993. Immunocytochemical evidence of well-developed dopaminergic and noradrenergic innervations in the frontal cerebral cortex of human fetuses at midgestation. *J. Comp. Neurol.* **336**:331–44.

Wahle, P., and Meyer, G. 1987. Morphology and quantitative changes of transient NPY-ir neuronal populations during early postnatal development of the cat visual cortex. *J. Comp. Neurol.* **261**:165–92.

Walker, A.E. 1940. A cytoarchitectural study of the prefrontal area of the macaque monkey. *J. Comp. Neurol.* **73**:59–86.

Winfield, D.A., Brooke, R.N.L., Sloper, J.J., and Powell, T.P.S. 1981. A combined Golgi-electron microscopic study of the synapses made by the proximal axon and recurrent collaterals of a pyramidal cell in the somatic sensory cortex of the monkey. *Neuroscience* **6**:1217–30.

Woo, T.U., Beale, J.M., and Finlay, B.L. 1991. Dual fate of subplate neurons in a rodent. *Cereb. Cortex* **1**: 433–43.

Yamashita, A., Shimizu, K., and Hayashi, M. 1990. Ontogeny of substance P-immunoreactive structures in the primate cerebral neocortex. *Dev. Brain Res.* **57**: 197–207.

Zecevic, N., Bourgeois, J.P., and Rakic, P. 1989. Changes in synaptic density in motor cortex of rhesus monkey during fetal and postnatal life. *Dev. Brain Res.* **50**: 11–32.

Zecevic, N., and Verney, C. 1995. Development of the catecholamine neurons in human embryos and fetuses, with special emphasis on the innervation of the cerebral cortex. *J. Comp. Neurol.* **351**:509–35.

3 The genetics of neurodevelopment and schizophrenia

ASTRIDE M. VICENTE
AND JAMES L. KENNEDY

INTRODUCTION

Research into embryonic development over the last decade has put an enormous emphasis on the investigation of the molecular mechanisms by which organisms are formed, from insects to vertebrates. As a result, major insights into the molecular regulation of central nervous system (CNS) development have been achieved. A comprehensive analysis of the hypothesis of a developmental etiology for schizophrenia has to give prime importance to the role of genes in many aspects of CNS formation. The fact that genes have major involvement in the pathogenesis of schizophrenia is well accepted from decades of twin, family and adoption studies (Gottesman 1991; for review see Kendler and Diehl 1993). The inheritance pattern of schizophrenia is not simply Mendelian, however, thus creating an extra degree of challenge. By examining rates of risk to relatives, Risch (1990) has suggested that schizophrenia is an oligogenic disorder, caused by a few, but not many, genes. The rapidly developing technology of molecular genetics permits us to effectively address this level of complexity, providing outstanding opportunities to detect susceptibility genes for schizophrenia. Advances in molecular neurobiology and the genetics of brain development combined with the schizophrenia gene mapping effort are promising tools for the elucidation of the disease mechanisms.

In this chapter, we will review some major genes involved in the development of the CNS, including the early stages of neural induction and pattern formation, neural cell differentiation and migration, and synapse formation and maturation (Table 3.1). We will then discuss the relevance of developmental genes to the etiology of schizophrenia, relating morphological alterations

observed in the brains of schizophrenics to malformations during CNS development that may be attributed to defective expression or function of some of these genes. We will in this manner explore a developmental genetic hypothesis for schizophrenia and describe our approach to the problem.

MOLECULAR BIOLOGY OF CNS PATTERNING

The mature CNS is an extremely complex system with many diverse functions from motor coordination to perception, motivation, and memory. These functions can in part be mapped to specific structures within the CNS, which have characteristic patterns of cell connectivity formed by a wide variety of neural cell types. The regional diversity of neuronal connections is established during development in a complex process that involves the differentiation of neuronal precursors into specific neural cell types, the migration of neurons to their proper positions, the extension of axons and the establishment of synaptic connections with selected target cells. These steps seem to be directed by a well organized plan of morphogenetic patterning present from the very early stages of neural plate formation.

The development of the vertebrate CNS begins with the induction, during gastrulation, of a region of ectoderm that lies along the dorsal midline of the embryo, the neural ectoderm (for a review see Ruiz i Altaba 1994). As a result of neural induction the neural plate is formed. The induction of neural fate in ectodermal cells depends on signals from adjacent mesodermal tissues. Mesodermal cells in an

Table 3.1. *An overview of neurodevelopmental genes and their functions*

Gene function/class:	Gene:	Developmental mechanism:
Neural induction	*Notch*	Neurogenesis
	Delta	
	Noggin	
	Follistatin	
	Hedgehog	
	NeuroD	
Regulation of transcription	*Krox20*	Patterning
	Wnt	
	Hox@	
	Otx	
	Ems	
	Dlx	
	Pax	
Cell adhesion	*N-cadherin*	Cell migration and neurite extension
	L1CAM	
	Integrins	
	Laminin	
	Fibronectin	
	Collagen	
Attraction/repulsion	*Semaphorin*	Axon guidance
	Netrin	
Synaptic proteins	*Synaptotagmin*	Synapse formation and activity
	Synaptobrevin	
	Synaptophysin	
	Synapsin	
	Syntaxin	
	SNAP-25	
Neurotrophins	*NGF*	Neural cell survival
	BDNF	
	NT-3	
	NT-4/5	
	TrkA	
	TrkB	
	TrkC	
Synaptic activity	*NMDA receptors*	Synaptic plasticity
	Fyn	
	CaMKII	
	NO-synthase	

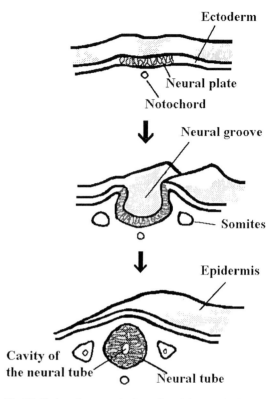

Fig. 3.1 Early embryogenesis: formation of the neural tube.

organizer region, designated the node in mammals, are the initial source of neural-inducing signals that act to de-repress the inherent potential of ectodermal cells to become neural. The cells of the organizer region prolife-rate and migrate to form the axial mesoderm underlying the tissues that will constitute the forebrain, and the noto-chord, which underlies tissue that will give rise to the mid-brain, hindbrain and spinal cord. These mesodermal structures retain their neural-inducing properties throughout neural plate formation. The cells of the devel-oping neural plate also have neural-inducing properties, and have a role in homeogenetic (neural inducing neural) induction of the neural plate. The forming neural plate already displays the regional diversity in cell identity and patterns of cell proliferation and gene expression, along the embryo's mediolateral and anteroposterior axes, that will be present in all stages of development (reviewed in Ruiz i Altaba 1994).

Fig. 3.2 Formation of the brain: the three primary brain vesicles subdivide into five secondary vesicles, from which the adult brain structures are derived.

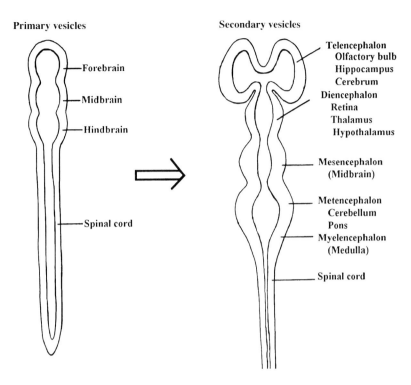

Primary vesicles

Forebrain

Midbrain

Hindbrain

Spinal cord

Secondary vesicles

Telencephalon
Olfactory bulb
Hippocampus
Cerebrum
Diencephalon
Retina
Thalamus
Hypothalamus

Mesencephalon
(Midbrain)

Metencephalon
Cerebellum
Pons
Myelencephalon
(Medulla)

Spinal cord

After formation of the neural plate, this structure folds at the lateral edges to form the neural groove, which then fuses at its dorsal extreme to create the neural tube, in a process called neurulation (Fig. 3.1). The change in shape of the neural plate results from local cell rearrangement from the neural plate but also from the adjacent mesoderm tissue, the somites (which later give rise to axial skeleton, limb musculature and notochord). The cavity of the neural tube gives rise to the ventricular system of the CNS, while the epithelial cells that line the walls of the neural tube (neuroepithelium) generate neurons and glia.

The caudal part of the neural tube gives origin to the spinal cord. The rostral neural tube gives rise to the brain. Initially it forms three brain vesicles: forebrain, midbrain and hindbrain (Fig. 3.2). Forebrain and hindbrain divide subsequently, forming, with the midbrain and spinal cord, the six major regions of the mature CNS: the forebrain gives origin to the telencephalon (including cerebral cortex, basal ganglia, hippocampal formation, and amygdala) and the diencephalon (which lies between the cerebral hemispheres and includes the thalamus, subthalamus,

hypothalamus, and optic cup); the midbrain gives origin to the mesencephalon; the hindbrain gives rise to the metencephalon, which forms the pons and cerebellum and the myelencephalon, which forms the medulla; the caudal part of the neural tube becomes the spinal cord (Fig. 3.2).

The morphogenesis of specific structures within the nervous system is determined by the regional expression of sets of transcription factors, which are DNA-binding proteins that regulate the expression of other genes. Each particular combination of these proteins determines which genes will be expressed in a given cell, and therefore gives an identity to groups of cells that will eventually perform a specific function. This initial process establishes different regulatory states in regions from which different structures will emerge. The initial transcription factors are usually expressed only transiently, but are responsible for the formation of morphological boundaries within which specific types of cells will differentiate and will eventually form the structures of the mature CNS. The regional expression of these molecules in a temporal sequence reflects cascades of gene activation that define pattern formation in the embryo (reviewed in Ruiz i Altaba 1994).

Families of genes encoding transcription factors are expressed in particular morphogenetic and temporal domains in the embryo. Interestingly, these genes and their encoded molecules are often conserved in structure and function among species as different as the fruit fly *Drosophila*, the worm *C. elegans*, the frog *Xenopus*, birds and mammals. The amenability of lower organisms, such as *Drosophila*, to genetic manipulation led to the initial isolation and elucidation of the functions of many of these molecules in neural development, which are now found to be remarkably conserved in higher organisms.

Genes and neural induction

The commitment of undifferentiated cells to a neural fate involves the regulated expression of proneural, neurogenic and neural induction genes in clusters of ectodermal cells, whose action establishes the patterns of neurogenesis in the early CNS-related structures of the embryo.

Proneural genes, such as *mash-1* in mammals, are expressed in subsets of ectodermal cells, where they act as neural fate determination factors, predisposing these cells to become neural. A mechanism of lateral inhibition by neighboring cells regulates whether these prospective neural cells will in fact become neurons. The inhibition mechanism is mediated by signaling involving the interaction of a transmembrane protein encoded by the neurogenic gene *Delta*, expressed by the neural precursors, with a cell membrane receptor on the neighboring cells, encoded by the neurogenic gene *Notch*. These genes, conserved in *Drosophila*, *C. elegans*, *Xenopus* and the chick, regulate commitment to a neural fate, at several stages of neurogenesis (Fortini and Artavanis-Tsakonas 1993; Chitnis *et al.* 1995; Henrique *et al.* 1995).

Several genes encoding molecules with neural-inducing properties have been isolated, and found to be involved in patterning of the early structures of the CNS in different species (reviewed in Kessler and Melton 1994; Ruiz y Altaba 1994). In the amphibian *Xenopus* gastrula stage, the genes *noggin* and *follistatin* encode neural inducers and inhibition of the activin protein by follistatin leads to neural differentiation (Hemmati-Brivanlou and Melton 1992; Massagué 1992; Lamb *et al.* 1993). The family of *hedgehog*

genes, which encode secreted proteins with induction properties, control cell patterning in various embryonic regions, including the node, the notochord, and the neural tube (Ericson *et al.* 1995; Johnson and Tabin 1995). In the vertebrate gastrula, the organizer region is a site of expression of regulatory genes, the *Wnt* genes, which encode a large family of secreted glycoproteins. *Wnt* genes are also expressed in restricted domains in dorsal and ventral midlines of the neural tube where they have a role in the regulation of the proliferation of specific regions in the developing neural tube (Nusse and Varmus 1992). Another transcription factor, encoded by the *neuroD* gene, displays functional characteristics suggestive of a role in the terminal differentiation of neural cells (Lee *et al.* 1995).

The molecular mechanisms of neurogenesis are not fully understood, and many other genes are being characterized that seem to play a role in the determination of cells to a neural fate. These genes define the initial patterning of the neural plate along the embryo's mediolateral and anterioposterior axes that will be present in all stages of development. In later stages of neural tube development some of these genes are still expressed, suggesting that the same molecular mechanisms regulate neurogenesis at different times in development. The homology between these molecules across species indicates that these regulatory and inductive interactions are universal mechanisms for neural cell differentiation.

Morphological segmentation and underlying patterns of gene expression

The early patterning of the neural plate precedes the morphological segmentation observed in the structures that develop later. Repeated and transient bulges along the neural tube, designated neuromeres, are observed. The borders of neuromeres act as actual barriers to cell movement, forming cell lineage restriction boundaries (reviewed in Keynes and Lumsden 1990; Lumsden 1990). These morphological observations, particularly in the hindbrain (rhombomeres) and more recently in the forebrain (prosomeres) have been validated by the observation of a corresponding segmentation pattern of cellular differentiation and gene expression.

In the early stages of hindbrain formation, transient periodic constrictions along its length can be observed,

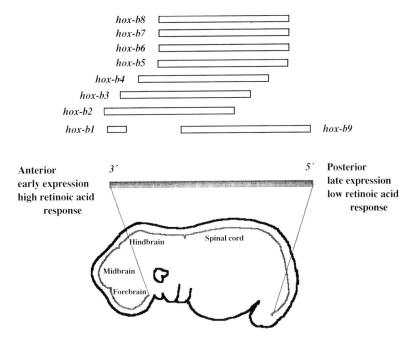

Fig. 3.3 Patterns of expression of *Hox-B* genes in the hindbrain and spinal cord of the mouse embryo. The unshaded bars represent the location of expression of *Hox-B* genes along the embryonic anterior-posterior axis. Genes located towards the 3′ end of the gene cluster are activated at earlier stages of development, have more anterior boundaries of expression in the embryo, and respond to lower doses of retinoic acid.

defining the rhombomeres. During their brief existence, many of the neurons and most of the basic structures of the hindbrain are formed. The cells at the center of each rhombomere display a higher mitotic density and a shorter cell cycle than the cells at the boundaries. This observation, together with a local increase in cell-cell adhesion, suggests that the more tightly cohesive cells at boundaries act as lineage restriction boundaries. Once the rhombomeres are formed, the cells within them will form only the specific structure designated by that region because there is no mixing with the cells of neighboring segments.

An underlying pattern of gene expression confirms the segmentation of the hindbrain, and probably constitutes the molecular basis of rhombomere formation. The zinc-finger gene *Krox20*, which encodes a transcription factor, is expressed as the rhombomeres are being established: its expression is detected in restricted domains in the hindbrain before the morphology characteristic of the rhombomeres is visible (Wilkinson *et al.* 1989). Once the rhombomere boundaries are established, it is observed that *Krox20* accumulates in alternating segments, as is the case with the *pair-rule* regulatory genes responsible, in *Drosophila*, for the striped pattern that defines the initial

segmentation along the anteroposterior axis. These observations suggest that *Krox20* may be analogous to the *pair-rule* genes in insects and may have a function in setting up the repeat pattern of the vertebrate hindbrain.

Homeobox-containing genes (*Hox* genes) encode transcription factors initially isolated from *Drosophila* embryo, where they exhibit segment-restricted patterns of expression. These proteins contain a specific domain, the homeodomain, consisting of a stretch of amino acids arranged in a helix-turn-helix structural motif that binds DNA, regulating the transcription of other genes. In the mouse, these genes are grouped in four gene clusters (*Hox-a,- b,-c,-d*) and, remarkably, their expression is activated in temporal and spatial patterns that match their location along the chromosome cluster: the genes situated towards the 3′ end of the chromosome cluster are expressed in more anterior regions of the embryo and are activated earlier in development (Krumlauf 1994).

During development of the CNS, *Hox* genes are expressed in the neural tube in domains that extend from its caudal end to an anterior limit in the spinal cord or in the hindbrain (Fig. 3.3). These patterns of expression are suggestive of a function in the specification of segment phenotype (reviewed in Krumlauf 1994). Four genes belonging to the *Hox-b* gene cluster are expressed in the hindbrain, and the anterior limits of their expression are coincident with rhombomere boundaries (Wilkinson *et al.* 1989). The positional commitment of the cells within a particular rhombomere seems to be the result of the specific combination of *Hox* genes these cells express. The pattern of expression of these genes suggests that they are involved in the determination of segment phenotype in the hindbrain, but not in its establishment, as they are expressed only after *Krox20* expression patterns have been established and rhombomeres have been formed. The fact that rhombomeres are domains of cell lineage restriction, not allowing cells to cross boundaries, allows for the stable maintenance of segmental domains of gene expression (reviewed in Wilkinson and Krumlauf 1990). It seems likely that the conservation of the clustered organization of the *Hox* genes is linked with the mechanisms necessary to regulate the restricted pattern of gene expression critical for function in anteroposterior patterning (Fig. 3.3).

Other homeobox containing genes expressed in the hindbrain and the midbrain have been isolated in mammals, based upon high sequence homology with *Drosophila* genes. Homologues of the *engrailed (en)* genes, which are involved in embryonic segmentation and nervous system development in *Drosophila*, have been isolated in mice. *en-1* and *en-2* expression is regulated by *wnt*-encoded proteins in a band of cells in the midbrain and anterior hindbrain, defining a specific spatial domain in the developing nervous system. The patterns of expression of these genes suggest roles in segmentation of the neural tube and in the later specification of particular groups of neurons (Joyner, *et al.* 1991).

The temporal patterns of expression of *Krox20, en, wnt* and *Hox-b* genes, as well as other genes that display some spatial/functional analogies to patterning genes in *Drosophila*, suggest that the cascade regulation present in the segmentation of the *Drosophila* embryo may also be important in vertebrates. In the hindbrain segmentation process, the *Hox* genes are expressed after *Krox20, wnt* and the *en* genes, and the KROX20 protein has been shown to bind *Hox-b2* gene promoter regions. This suggests that *Krox20* is required for the establishment and the *Hox* genes for the maintenance of the rhombomeres' correct patterning and growth (reviewed in Krumlauf 1994). *Sonic*

hedgehog, a vertebrate member of the *hedgehog* gene family, has also been shown to activate *Hox* genes in restricted domains, and may be an upstream regulator of these genes (Riddle *et al.* 1993).

Retinoic acid (RA) has also been shown to regulate *Hox* gene family expression, through binding and activating RA receptors. Several *Hox* genes contain sequences in their promoter regions, Retinoic Acid Responsive Elements (RARE), that are bound by activated RA receptors, inducing transcription of the genes. Response of each specific *Hox-b* gene to RA is dose-dependent: genes located downstream (3′ end) on the chromosome, which are expressed in the more anterior portion of the embryo, can be induced by lower doses of RA; the concentration of RA required for induction increases for genes located progressively more towards the 5′ end of the chromosome, which are expressed more posteriorly and at later stages in the embryo (Krumlauf 1994).

Recently a neuromeric model for the morphological organization of the forebrain has been developed, based on temporally and spatially restricted patterns of expression of many developmental genes in the forebrain (Puelles and Rubenstein 1993; Rubenstein *et al.* 1994). Controversy regarding the morphological organization of the neuroepithelium at the forebrain level, and the complexity of the structures it comprises, has hindered the understanding of the developmental patterning of this region. A large number of regulatory genes, many of which are analogous in function or homologous in sequence to embryonic segmentation genes in *Drosophila*, are expressed in the forebrain in regionally restricted patterns. The patterns of expression of these genes have led to the definition of six transverse domains, designated prosomeres, which in turn are subdivided in nonoverlapping regions parallel to the longitudinal axes of the neural tube.

The morphological segmentation of the embryonic forebrain in prosomeres with specific patterns of gene expression allows further investigation of the cellular and molecular mechanisms of forebrain development. Each subdivision coincides with the expression boundaries of several genes, mostly homeobox containing genes such as members of the *Dlx* (Porteus *et al.* 1991; Price *et al.* 1991), *Otx* (Simeone *et al.* 1992a), *Gbx* (Murtha *et al.* 1991), *Nkx* (Price *et al.* 1992) and *Emx* (Simeone *et al.* 1992b) families, which are related to *Drosophila* genes involved in the segmentation of the head.

Segmental expression of members of the paired-box (*Pax*) genes, which constitute another family of transcriptional regulators, is also observed in the developing forebrain (reviewed in Stoykova and Gruss 1994). Several CNS disorders have been found to be caused by mutations in *Pax* genes: Waardenburg's syndrome, characterized by deafness and facial defects, has been attributed to a mutation in *Pax-3* that leads to defective development (Baldwin *et al.* 1992; Tassabehj *et al.* 1992), and *Pax-6* mutations have been reported to cause visual system and other CNS defects (Glaser *et al.* 1994). The expression of these genes is established before any segmentation or axonal outgrowth in the forebrain occurs, which suggests they may play a role in establishing segment identities and axonal pathways at the borders of their expression domains. The temporal and spatial patterns of expression of these *Pax* genes (mainly *Pax-6*) analyzed in conjunction with those of the *Dlx* genes (Porteus *et al.* 1991; Price *et al.* 1991) suggest that the *Pax* genes act earlier than the *Dlx* genes in a presumed cascade of regulatory processes specifying diencephalic regions during development. A good correlation exists between the expression of *Pax* genes in embryo and adult forebrain. This observation suggests that these genes are involved not only in the specification of spatial domains in the developing brain but may also play a role in the differentiation and maintenance of specific neuronal subtypes in the mature CNS.

It is of interest that the main expression areas of several *Pax* genes in the mature brain belong or are related to the subcortical domains of the limbic system. In conjunction with the observed expression of *Pax* genes in the telencephalon, this indicates a role for these genes in the development of the regions of the brain involved in higher cognitive functions. POU domain genes, another family of transcriptional regulators that contain both an homeodomain and a second DNA-binding region, have also been related to the establishment of cortical lamination and neuronal differentiation in hypothalamus and hippocampus (Wegner *et al.* 1993). In contrast with *Hox* genes, whose expression domains have their most anterior limits in the hindbrain-midbrain, *Pax* and *POU* genes appear to be involved in the development of more rostral domains of the CNS, the midbrain and the forebrain. The mechanisms of development of the forebrain are especially relevant for schizophrenia because the structures it comprises are responsible for higher cognitive functions like memory, perception, and motivation.

The cascade of transcription factor activation present in the patterning of the developing CNS does not ultimately explain the mechanisms of morphogenesis, i.e., the mechanics by which cells are directed to differentiate into certain types, migrate to the appropriate locations, and form the correct connections. A major function of the homeodomain regulators may be to control intercellular signaling systems. It is thought that the particular set of homeodomain-encoding genes activated in a region specifies the particular morphology of that domain through regulation of genes encoding molecules with functions in cell-cell interactions. These downstream targets of homeodomain proteins are likely to be genes encoding cell adhesion molecules. Adhesion molecules like cell adhesion molecules (CAMs) and cadherins are expressed in particular spatial and temporal patterns that, in certain cases, correspond to morphogenetic domains during CNS development (Davidson 1993). More importantly it has now been shown that several genes encoding CAMs contain homeodomain-binding sites in their promoter regions. The gene promoters for the adhesion molecules, cytotactin/tenascin, neural cell adhesion molecule (NCAM) and L1CAM contain homeodomain-binding sites, and in vitro studies have shown that cytotactin NCAM and connectin are targets for regulation by *Hox* and *Pax* encoded proteins (Barton *et al.* 1990; Colwell *et al.* 1992; Edelman and Jones 1993; Goomer *et al.* 1994; Holst *et al.* 1994). Cell adhesion molecules are downstream effectors of morphogenesis, regulating cell adhesion, cell migration and interacting with intracellular signaling pathways, and are therefore prime candidates for targets of the hierarchy of gene regulation in embryonic development.

ESTABLISHMENT OF NEURAL CONNECTIVITY: MOLECULAR MECHANISMS

The "wiring" of the CNS is an amazingly complex and delicate process upon which any function of the mature nervous system is dependent. A characteristic feature of neurons is that a single cell forms several connections, mostly through the projection of axons often to distant regions of the brain, where it chooses its target cells in a highly precise and specific way. The formation of the correct pattern of connections by the millions of neurons during development of the CNS occurs in several main steps which involve: the migration of neurons to their appropriate location as part of the primordia of a brain structure; the extension of the axon and migration of its growth cone to the correct target region where a connection is to be made; the recognition of the target cells and establishment of initial synapses; and the refinement of these initial connections through synaptic pruning, generating the highly tuned pattern of neuronal connectivity upon which the functionally mature CNS relies. In recent years, many families of molecules have been implicated in each of these steps, and their precise functions and regulations are being established. We will review some of the molecules fundamental for these processes, with reference to the regulation of the often large families of genes that encode them.

When neuroblasts end the cell cycle and initiate a differentiation process, they leave the ventricular zones where proliferation occurs and migrate to other locations in the nervous system. The migration of neurons leads to the layered pattern of cells present in many structures of the brain, e.g., in the cerebral cortex, hippocampus and cerebellum. A system of radial glial fibres, which retain contacts with both the pial and the lumenal surfaces of the neural tube, provides the primary pathway for migration of neurons. These radial glial fibres guide postmitotic neurons from the ventricular zones to their appropriate layer, in a pattern such that cells initiating migration later will migrate to the most distant locations. Multiple receptor systems involving CAMs have been demonstrated to promote neural migration (reviewed in Hynes and Lander 1992).

The process of axon extension, and underlying mechanisms of growth cone guidance, together with the primary recognition of target cells, generate the initial pattern of neural connections in an activity-independent manner. Once initial neuronal activity is established, activity-dependent mechanisms of refinement and remodeling

of the initial connections take place. The activity-dependent synaptic alterations continue throughout life, driven by input from the external world, and form the basis for higher cognitive processes such as learning and memory.

Activity-independent mechanisms: CAMs and SAMs

The specificity of the initial connections formed before synaptic activity is established is dependent on several molecular mechanisms. A first mechanism relies on the activity of substrate and cell adhesion molecules (SAMs and CAMs) (reviewed in Goodman and Shatz 1993; Goodman 1994). Differential adhesion has been shown to play a major role in growth cone guidance, suggesting that the pattern of expression of cell adhesion molecules on the surface of the growth cones, cells they contact or the extracellular matrix (ECM), may regulate the specification of the axonal pathway. Many adhesion molecules have been characterized and are grouped in several large families according to structural and functional characteristics of the proteins and their encoding genes (reviewed in Hynes and Lander 1992; Hynes 1994; Goodman and Shatz 1993; Letourneau et al. 1994).

Cadherins are calcium-dependent cell-cell adhesion molecules that mediate homophyllic adhesion between cells. They are transmembrane proteins whose activity is mediated by interactions on both sides of the membrane. Domains on the extracellular side are responsible for homophyllic cell recognition, specific to each cadherin. Domains on the intracellular region interact with cytoplasmic proteins designated catenins, which link cadherin molecules to the actin in the cytoskeleton (reviewed in Ranscht and Dours-Zimmermann 1994). Segregation and remodeling of embryonic tissues is associated with the expression of different cadherins. It has been shown in vitro that quantitative differences in cadherin expression create adhesive gradients that specify cell sorting, tissue spreading, and spatial patterning (Steinberg and Takeichi 1994). N-Cadherin has also been shown to promote neurite growth and may be involved in signaling pathways of tyrosine kinases and PKC.

Another major class of cell-cell adhesion molecules are members of the immunoglobulin superfamily, and include NCAM and L1CAM in the CNS. These molecules mediate calcium-independent homophyllic interactions between cells, and are associated with functions such as selective bundling of axons, target selection, segregation of cells into different tissues and induction of neurite outgrowth (reviewed in Rutishauser *et al.* 1988).

NCAM is encoded by a single gene that undergoes alternative splicing to generate several different forms with different spatial and temporal patterns of expression in vertebrates (Gower *et al.* 1988). NCAM's function is also regulated by the molecule's content of polysialic acid (PSA). Neurite outgrowth is induced by NCAM, and this induction is modulated by the content of PSA (Doherty *et al.* 1990), and embryonic and adult forms of NCAM differ significantly in their contents of PSA: NCAM is heavily glycosylated with PSA residues at late embryonic stages, but the concentration of PSA diminishes during development, resulting in higher adhesiveness properties for NCAM. PSA residues in NCAM are present in the adult brain only in selective areas, such as the dentate gyrus and mossy fibers of the hippocampus and the olfactory bulb (reviewed in Linneman and Bock 1989).

NCAM is expressed from the early stages of neural tube development, and its expression is restricted to very specific regions at these early stages, suggesting a role in pattern formation in the neural tube and in maintenance of segmentation boundaries (Bally-Cuif 1993). This hypothesis is further strengthened by the observation that NCAM is regulated by homeotic genes with related patterns of expression (Holst *et al.* 1994; Colwell *et al.* 1992; Perides *et al.* 1994). Later, NCAM is expressed in postmitotic neurons along the neural tube, and is involved in the extension of axonal processes.

The induction and support of neurite outgrowth by CAMs is not solely a result of increased adhesiveness caused by the homophyllic interactions between the receptors. Increasing evidence indicates that CAMs promote cell and axon migration through activation of second messenger pathways and regulation of transcription (Doherty *et al.* 1991; Saffell *et al.* 1992). Alterations in cell adhesion have been shown to induce gene transcription changes for various cell adhesion genes and homeobox-containing transcription factors (Mauro *et al.* 1994).

A third important class of adhesion molecules are the integrins, cell-surface receptors for ECM proteins (for review see Hynes and Lauder 1992; Hynes 1994; DeSimone 1994). The integrins are heterodimeric transmembrane glycoproteins, composed of several α and β subunits which are joined in different combinations with different ligand specificity. Most cells express multiple integrins, which may have the same ligand specificity, or each of which may bind multiple ligands in the ECM. A further level of diversity and complexity is introduced by the existence of alternative splicing in several subunits, generating different cytoplasmic domains with different functional specificities.

Several mechanisms are used by integrins to transmit signals into the intracellular environment (reviewed in Humphries *et al.* 1993). Receptor clustering has been shown to induce changes in the cytoplasmic domain or in the binding and orientation of receptor-associated molecules. Changes in the receptor conformation induced by ligand binding affect the association of intracellular signaling molecules or the cytoskeleton with the integrin's cytoplasmic domain. Integrins can therefore exist in active and inactive states of signal transmission, being stimulated by ligand binding and consequent conformational changes.

Experimental evidence suggests that conformational alterations can be induced by molecules from intra- and extracellular locations, implying that integrins are bidirectionally activated. Intracellularly, integrins associate with cytoskeletal proteins, linking the intracellular moiety with the ECM and providing the basis for intracellular signaling mechanisms mediated by integrins. The observation of differential functions in different subunits, formed by alternative splicing, which diverge in the cytoplasmic domain, further supports a role of intracellular signaling in integrin activity. Ligand binding extracellularly induces conformational alterations that change the activation state of integrins. Activation of integrins alters the cellular patterns of tyrosine phosphorylation, through phosphorylation of the cytoplasmic domains. There is also some evidence that the intracellular signaling events mediated by integrins interact and synergize with those triggered by growth factors (reviewed in Humphries *et al.* 1993; Adams and Watt 1993; Juliano and Haskill 1993; Hynes 1994).

Restricted spatial and temporal distributions of integrins are observed during development. Integrins are found at very early stages in embryos, and may be involved

Fig. 3.4. Structure of CNS
adhesion molecules. Adhesion
molecules are transmembrane
receptors that bind molecules in
the membrane of neighboring
cells or in the extracellular
matrix. Cadherins are homophyllic, calcium-dependent, cell
to cell adhesion molecules.
NCAM mediates cell–cell
adhesion and, as a member of the
immunoglobulin superfamily,
contains several immunoglobulin
domains (Ω). Integrins are
dimeric receptors, composed of α
and β subunits, and bind
extracellular matrix proteins,
mediating cell–matrix adhesion.

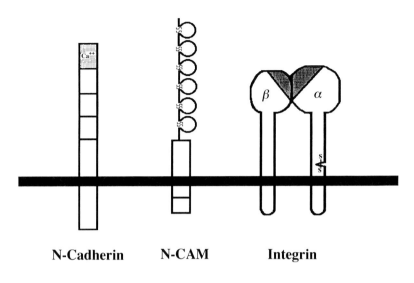

N-Cadherin   **N-CAM**   **Integrin**

■ **Cell membrane**

in implantation, as indicated by gene targeting experiments in mice, in which the α_5 integrin subunit was inactivated. The patterns of expression are possibly regulated by other molecules involved in morphogenesis, as suggested by the observed upregulation of several α integrin subunits by activin and fibroblast growth factor (FGF). Antisense oligonucleotide and antibody experiments in cell culture show inhibition of neural migration or neural cell attachment by antisense oligonucleotides or antibody blockade (Lallier and Bronner-Fraser 1993; reviewed by DeSimone 1994). The multiplicity of integrins isolated thus far suggests that the particular distribution of these ECM receptors on different classes of neurons that confront the same extracellular environment or in the same class of neurons at different stages of development is likely to play a role in determining the patterns of neuronal migration and neurite outgrowth during development (Letourneau et al. 1994 Fig. 3.4).

Embryonic neural tissues contain a dynamic ECM, composed of many types of molecules that have distinct patterns of spatial and temporal expression, including laminin, fibronectin, vitronectin, thrombospondin, collagens, proteoglycans, and tenascin. Expression studies have shown that ECM molecules are very abundant in the CNS at times when differentiation and migration of neurons

occur. This ECM is present transiently and is substantially reduced by the end of embryonic development. The transient ECM is mostly synthesized by embryonic glia. Growth cones migrating in this extracellular environment encounter surfaces expressing diverse molecules, depending on neuronal type, pathway and developmental stage (reviewed in Letourneau et al. 1994).

Chemoattraction and repulsion

Axon guidance mechanisms that do not depend on cell adhesion molecules have been observed, namely repulsion and chemoattraction (reviewed in Goodman and Shatz 1993; Goodman 1994). Repulsion was initially observed in growth cones of different types of neurons whose pathways cross during migration, namely sympathetic and retinal neurons. Upon contact the growth cones retract and collapse, avoiding each other. During migration, growth cones can also be guided by gradients of diffusible molecules, in a phenomenon designated as chemoattraction.

The gene encoding the first growth cone collapse factor, collapsin, has recently been cloned (Lou and Bixby 1993). The sequence of collapsin is highly homologous to a molecule previously identified in insects, Semaphorin I. This molecule redirects growth cones and prevents axons from branching, possibly functioning as an inhibitory signal for branching before the axon reaches its target. Semaphorin I belongs to a family of transmembrane and secreted molecules conserved from insects to humans, the Semaphorins (Kolodkin *et al.* 1993; reviewed in Goodman 1994; Wolpert 1994).

The first chemoattractants for developing axons have also recently been isolated and named netrins (Serafini *et al.* 1994; Kennedy *et al.* 1994). Commissural neurons in the dorsal region of the developing spinal cord are directed towards the floor plate in the ventral side of the spinal cord by a chemoattractive mechanism involving molecules secreted by floor plate cells. This effect can be replicated in vitro by expression of two related genes isolated from chick floor plate, *netrin-1* and *netrin-2*. The two netrins have high gene sequence homology and induce outgrowth from dorsal spinal cord explants as well as attracting growth cones from a distance. Sequence similarity has also been found with a *C. elegans* gene previously isolated, *unc-6*, which had been implicated in axon guidance in the nematode. Analysis of nematode mutants for *unc-6* and data on the vertebrate *netrins* suggest that these molecules may be attractive or repulsive depending on "attractive" or "repulsive" receptors expressed by the growth cones (reviewed by Baier and Bonhoeffer 1994; Goodman 1994).

Synaptic terminal proteins and synaptogenesis

The outgrowth of neurites requires the addition of proteins and other constituents at the growth cone, which is dependent on intracellular trafficking and fusion of intracellular vesicles to the plasma membrane. The formation of the mature nerve terminal also requires the accumulation of large quantities of synaptic vesicles containing neurotransmitters. It has been shown that growth cones are able to secrete neurotransmitters spontaneously before contacting their targets, and that, as soon as neuronal processes come into contact, synapses can be formed. These observations indicate that the components of the synaptic machinery have been synthesized before cellular interactions occur, ensuring that functional synapses form rapidly after cell-cell contact (reviewed in Haydon and Drapeau 1995).

Synaptic terminal proteins are involved in the docking and fusion of synaptic vesicles to the presynaptic plasma membrane and consequent release of neurotransmitters. These proteins are crucial in synaptic activity as well as in mechanisms of nerve terminal formation and synaptic plasticity throughout life (Geddes *et al.* 1990; reviewed in Söllner and Rothman 1994). In the synaptic vesicle membrane, a soluble NSF factor (*N*-ethylmaleimide-sensitive factor) associates with several synaptic vesicle proteins (SNAPs): synaptotagmins, synaptobrevins (VAMPs), synaptophysins, synapsins, and others. These proteins in the synaptic vesicle membrane bind pre-synaptic membrane receptors (SNAREs), such as syntaxins and synaptosomal-associated protein 25 (SNAP-25), leading to membrane fusion and release of neurotransmitters into the synaptic cleft (Fig. 3.5).

The synaptic terminal proteins synaptotagmins, synaptobrevins (VAMPs), synaptophysins, as well as synapsins and SNAP-25, display regulated patterns of expression during embryogenesis that correlate with synaptogenesis (Lou and Bixby 1993). SNAP-25 has been shown to be expressed in axonal growth cones during elongation and synapse formation, and alternative isoforms of this protein may play distinct roles in vesicular fusion processes during axonal outgrowth and in neurotransmitter and peptide release mechanisms (Bark *et al.* 1995). Selective inhibition of SNAP-25 expression with antisense oligonucleotides prevents neurite elongation in vitro and in vivo, affecting the terminal differentiation of specific processes, but not the direction of growth or the general morphology of the neurons (Osen-Sand *et al.* 1993). Synapsin IIb, a member of the synapsin family of synaptic vesicle proteins, has been shown to promote the formation of synapses in neuroblastoma cells (Han *et al.* 1991) and has been implicated in synaptic plasticity (Rosahl *et al.* 1993).

The identification of a large family of synaptic vesicle proteins, with several isoforms, involved in the formation and plasticity of synapses, indicates that these proteins may be responsible in part for the specificity of neural connectivity during development. The fact that the synaptic machinery is present and functional before cell interactions begin may be of importance in the establishing of specific synaptic connections (Haydon and Drapeau 1995). Synaptic terminal proteins are also involved in syn-

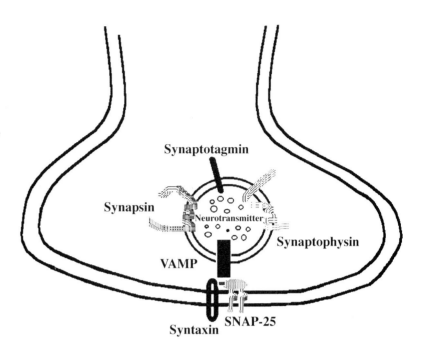

Fig. 3.5. Proteins of the synaptic terminal. The release of neuro-transmitter from synaptic vesicles is dependent on the function of synaptic terminal proteins. Transmembrane proteins in the synaptic vesicle (VAMP, synapsin, synaptophysin, synaptotagmin) interact with proteins in the pre-synaptic membrane (syntaxin, SNAP-25) and mediate the fusion of the vesicle with the membrane and consequent release of neurotransmitter into the synaptic cleft.

aptic plasticity mechanisms. Changes in neurotransmitter release alter the patterns of synaptic connections, and are regulated by release probability which is in turn modulated by the vesicle fusion machinery. Synapsins have been shown to interact with cytoskeleton elements, therefore regulating traffic and fusion of synaptic vesicles. These interactions are dependent on phosphorylation of synapsin, mediated by calcium-calmodulin-dependent protein kinase I (CaMKI), suggesting that protein kinases may also play a role in synaptic plasticity (Sudhof 1995).

Neural cell survival
After neurons reach their targets and connections are established, a substantial proportion undergo cell death. This process matches the number and characteristics of innervating neurons to the requirements of the target tissue and eliminates inappropriately connected neurons. For the most part, molecules secreted by the target cells are responsible for the regulation of cell death. These molecules belong to the neurotrophin family, from which nerve growth factor (NGF) was the earliest molecule to be isolated, and consisting additionally of brain-derived neurotrophic factor (BDNF), and neurotrophins NT-3,

NT-4/5, and NT-6 (reviewed in Meakin and Shooter 1992; Davies 1994). Neurons become dependent on a supply of target-derived neurotrophins for survival when their axons reach their targets in development. The neurotrophin dependence is acquired at a specific time during growth of the innervating neurons as an intrinsic programme for growth and survival that is independent of external signals. Different target-derived neurotrophins act in a developmental sequence to promote the survival and differentiation of specific types of neurons (Buchman and Davies 1993).

Neurotrophin actions are mediated by specific transmembrane receptors with tyrosine kinase activity (trk receptors). Binding of the neurotrophin to its appropriate receptor induces dimerization and autophosphorylation of the receptor and activation of signal transduction pathways, which suggests an important role for these molecules in cellular processes and gene regulation (reviewed in Meakin and Shooter 1992). The neurotrophin receptors were initially identified as tyrosine kinase receptor proto-oncogenes. The trk receptors are partially specific for each neurotrophin: trkA binds NGF, trkB binds BDNF and NT-4, and trkC binds NT-3; a low affinity receptor for NGF, p75, binds all the neurotrophins at a lower affinity.

In the CNS, *trkA* and NGF gene expression are restricted to a few populations of neurons in the basal forebrain and the striatum, but *trkB* and *trkC* and their ligands have broader and more complex patterns of expression (reviewed in Meakin and Shooter 1992; Snider 1994). NT-3 is strongly expressed in the developing hippocampus and neocortex, but its levels decrease with maturation of these regions, and in the adult NT-3 is mostly restricted to the dentate gyrus, and CA1 and CA2 regions (Phillips *et al.* 1990). Expression of *trkC* colocalizes with NT-3 transcripts in the developing CNS, and in limbic and diencephalic structures in the adult (Maisonpierre *et al.* 1990; Lamballe *et al.* 1994). NT-4 is expressed mainly in regions outside of the brain. BDNF is predominantly expressed in the brain, with highest levels in the hippocampus, amygdala and neocortex, the main target regions of the basal forebrain cholinergic system. BDNF has been found to promote survival of basal forebrain cholinergic neurons, dopaminergic neurons from the substantia nigra, hippocampal neurons and sensory neurons derived from neural crest and placode. Levels of BDNF are low in the embryo, but undergo an increase during brain maturation, reaching higher levels than the other neurotrophins in the adult brain (Ip *et al.* 1993; reviewed in Korshing 1993). BDNF has also been found to promote the survival of new neurons generated in the adult forebrain ependymal/subependymal zone, which suggests that it may act as a permissive factor for neuronal recruitment in adulthood (Kirschenbaum and Goldman 1995).

Neurotrophins have been implicated in functions related to axon outgrowth and branching. For example, NGF was the first molecule to be described as having chemoattractive properties in cell culture. Several cellular processes are regulated by neurotrophins, such as the synthesis of transmitter enzymes, peptides and calcium-binding proteins. Neurotrophins also influence the efficacy and activity of developing synapses: BDNF and NT-3 have been shown to cause increases in amplitude and frequencies of synaptic currents in neuromuscular synapses (Lohof *et al.* 1993), and BDNF mRNA is increased after LTP (long-term potentiation, a persistent increase in synaptic connections associated with processes of memory

and learning) in dentate granule cells of rats, which suggests a role in LTP stabilization (Dragunow *et al.* 1993). In cultured embryonic cortical neurons, synaptic activity increases expression of BDNF, and in turn survival of these neurons is dependent on BDNF levels. This suggests that the neurotrophin mediates regulation of survival of postsynaptic neurons by synaptic activity. In the adult hippocampus, BDNF induces enhancement of long-lasting synaptic transmission (Kang and Schuman 1995), and LTP increases levels of BDNF mRNA, which suggests an involvement of this neurotrophin in memory and learning processes.

Recent gene targeting experiments (which inactivate the gene in study) in mice, for several neurotrophins and *trk* receptors, have broadened our knowledge of the in vivo functions of these molecules (reviewed in Snider 1994). Based on the patterns of expression of both the neurotrophins and their receptors in the PNS, the observed phenotypes of these animals were predictable. The effects of the mutation in the CNS of the animals, however, were surprisingly mild considering the wide distribution of the neurotrophins and their receptors in most of the brain. The animals have a short life term due to defects not related to the CNS, so these experiments provide information only on the function of neurotrophins during earlier development, and therefore postnatal functions may be overlooked. For instance, NGF mutant mice die within the first month due to severe PNS defects, and it is therefore possible that the time of responsiveness of NGF-sensitive neurons has not been reached. The CNS of *NT-3* and *trkC* mutant animals displays normal morphology, despite the fact that most regions of the brain express *trkC* and that several neuronal populations in the developing and postnatal brain are NT-3 responsive in vitro (Fariñas *et al.* 1994; Ernfors *et al.* 1994a). Mutation of BDNF leads to subtle phenotypes in the CNS such as reduction of neuronal expression of NPY (member of a family of neuroendocrine hormones) and parvalbumin and calbindin (calcium-binding proteins) in cortex and hippocampus, indicating that this neurotrophin is involved in the regulation of peptides and calcium-binding proteins (Ernfors *et al.* 1994b; Jones *et al.* 1994). Calcium-binding proteins regulate the concentration of calcium induced by neuronal activity and are in turn regulated by levels of electrical activity, possibly through regulation of BDNF, which in cortical neurons is also controlled by neuronal activity (Ghosh *et al.* 1994).

The neurotrophins cross-react with each other's receptors, and therefore a high degree of functional compensation may partially explain the lack of severe defects in neurotrophin knockout animals. This is emphasized by the fact that, in general, receptor mutants display more severe phenotypes than ligand knockouts. Functional cooperation between neurotrophins has also been described in vivo in developing motor neurons (Mitsumoto *et al.* 1994) and several neurotrophins may have parallel functions in the same cellular signaling pathways.

Activity-dependent refinement of connections

Once the first connections are established between migrating axons and their targets, neural activity-dependent refinement and remodeling of the initial connections takes place, leading to the specific and highly tuned patterns of neuronal connectivity found in the mature brain (reviewed in Goodman and Shatz 1993).

Experiments in the developing visual system indicate that the spatial and temporal pattern of neural cell firing leads the process of connection refinement. Synapses undergo strengthening when activity of the presynaptic cell occurs simultaneously with activity in the postsynaptic cell. In these "Hebb synapses" (mechanism proposed by Hebb), if many inputs coincide in activating a cell, they all undergo strengthening. In the adult brain this mechanism is observed in the phenomenon of long-term potentiation (LTP), where coincident activity causes long-lasting changes in transmission. During development, a mechanism similar to LTP may be occurring, in such a way that "cells that fire together wire together."

The exact mechanism by which the postsynaptic cell detects the coincidence in the incoming presynaptic activity, and in turn sends back a signal to all the active presynaptic cells to promote synaptic strengthening, is not known. Evidence suggests that LTP requires activation of the *N*-methyl-D-aspartate (NMDA) receptor, a subclass of glutamate receptors, on postsynaptic neurons following presynaptic release of glutamate (reviewed in Kandel and O'Dell 1992; Goodman and Shatz 1993). The NMDA receptor channel opens only if at the same time it binds

glutamate and the postsynaptic membrane is depolarized. Depolarization of the membrane leads to deblocking of the NMDA channels, which are normally blocked by magnesium ions at the resting membrane potential, and adequate depolarization can only be achieved by simultaneous activity of many pre-synaptic axons.

Activation of the NMDA receptor results in an influx of calcium into the postsynaptic neurons, activating second messenger protein kinases such as *fyn* and CaMKII (calcium-calmodulin-dependent kinase II), which have been shown to be required for LTP (reviewed in Grant and Silva 1994; Pettit *et al.* 1994). The subsequent maintenance of LTP involves an increase in presynaptic transmitter release. A retrograde messenger is thought to mediate the transfer of information from the postsynaptic terminal to the presynaptic terminal for maintenance of LTP. The retrograde messengers are molecules that can be rapidly synthesized by the postsynaptic cell and released into the synaptic cleft. They then diffuse into the presynaptic terminal mediating the activity-dependent enhancement of second messenger pathways in the presynaptic cell. The best studied example of a retrograde messenger is nitric oxide (NO). Inhibitors of NO synthase block induction of LTP and NO increases spontaneous release of transmitter in cultured cells, indicative of a presynaptic effect (reviewed in Kandel and O'Dell 1992).

A similar mechanism may be active for the pruning of inappropriate connections. If a synapse is misplaced, the chances are that it will not be active at the same time as the majority of the properly formed synapses. If postsynaptic activity is not simultaneous with presynaptic activity, synaptic weakening occurs and the asynchronous synapses are eliminated. Such synapses have been studied in adult hippocampus, where they undergo a process named long-term depression (LTD), and the same mechanism is likely to occur during development.

Postsynaptic activity and NMDA receptor activation are required for activity-dependent events during development. NMDA and NO synthase mRNA levels rise sharply in periods of activity-dependent refinement of connections in the visual system of the rat. In addition, studies in vitro indicate that glutamate, acting through NMDA receptors, promotes neuronal survival, neurite extension, and differentiation and stabilization of synapses in development (reviewed in Kandel and O'Dell 1992; Goodman and Shatz 1993).

The synaptic strength alterations occurring in LTP and LTD constitute the basis of memory and learning throughout life (Rose 1991; Grant and Silva 1994; Stevens 1994). It is interesting that the same molecules implicated in these processes are involved in the development of the CNS, in the periods of brain maturation when synaptic plasticity events are occurring at high frequency. There are other important molecular similarities between learning and memory-related synaptic modulation and the establishment of connections during development. For instance, similar cell adhesion molecules and similar intra-cellular signaling mechanisms, regulating gene expression, mediate growth and retraction of connections during synaptic modulation and migration of axons in development. An interesting example is long-term sensitization training in the sea slug *Aplysia*, a model for the study of molecular mechanisms in learning. The process of learning by the organism causes transcription-dependent downregulation of cell adhesion molecules on the surface of sensory neurons (Mayford *et al.* 1992). Antibodies against L1CAM and NCAM have also been shown to reduce LTP in CA1 neurons of rat hippocampal slices, which suggests a role for these adhesion molecules in the development or stabilization of LTP (Lüthl *et al.* 1994).

The study of learning and memory storage processes has provided insight into the molecular basis of higher cognitive functions of the brain. Birds provide interesting model systems for the study of neural plasticity mechanisms in memory and learning. Neurogenesis occurs throughout life in the avian brain and its particular location in regions implicated in song learning and memory has been established in songbirds, that learn new songs every year (reviewed in Doupe 1994a). In food-storing birds an enlargement of the hippocampal area has been shown to occur as a consequence of food-storing and retrieval experience. These behaviours require learning and memorizing, and the enlargement seems to be due to increased survival or recruitment to the hippocampus of newly generated neurons (Clayton and Krebs 1994; reviewed in Doupe 1994b). Adult neurogenesis in mammals has also been described in the dentate gyrus of hippocampus (Bayer *et al.* 1982; Lois and Alvarez-Buylla

1994), where a great deal of plasticity is required for higher cognitive functions throughout life. These observations are again suggestive of common molecular mechanisms used in neural development and in neural plasticity processes later in life, and reinforce the idea of a relation between such molecular mechanisms and the dysfunctions observed in psychiatric disorders such as schizophrenia.

DEVELOPMENTAL MOLECULES AND SCHIZOPHRENIA

The recent developments in noninvasive methods of brain imaging have led to significant advances in the study of the neuropathology of schizophrenia. These imaging studies, as well as neuroanatomical post-mortem analyses are reviewed in more detail elsewhere in this book and are outside the scope of this chapter. We will none the less reference some findings of major relevance for a discussion of genetic approaches to neurodevelopmental factors in schizophrenia.

Accumulating reports on neuropathological alterations in brains of schizophrenics provide a framework for the development of new hypotheses for the etiology of schizophrenia. The most consistently described structural alterations are ventricular enlargement and volumetric abnormalities of temporal lobe structures, hippocampus, amygdala, and entorhinal cortex (reviewed in Bogerts 1990, 1993; Walker 1994). Cytoarchitecture and cell densities have also been reported to be altered in limbic structures: reduced cell numbers or cell size are described in hippocampus, parahippocampal gyrus and entorhinal cortex (reviewed in Bogerts 1993, Arnold *et al.* 1995) as well as disturbed architecture involving cellular disarray in hippocampus and entorhinal and cingulate cortex. Orientation of pyramidal cells in the anterior and middle hippocampal region is altered and disturbances of cell migration from inner to outer layers of the entorhinal cortex have been reported (Conrad *et al.* 1991; Bogerts 1993). The structural disturbances observed in these brain regions are consistent with the symptoms present in schizophrenia: these limbic system structures link the neocortical association areas with the septum-hypothalamus complex, and are therefore key in sensory information processing and sensory gating. Defects in this neural circuit could lead to a dissociation between neocortical cognitive activities and limbic-hypothalamic emotional reactions and to a consequent disturbed emotional experience of external sensory perceptions. Some studies have also described morphometric and anatomical alterations in other brain regions, namely enlargement of the basal ganglia, thalamic abnormalities, reduction of cortical volume and central gray matter (Bogerts 1993; Andreasen *et al.* 1994; reviewed in Walker 1994).

The structural alterations reported in schizophrenia are often subtle and certainly heterogeneous, contributing minimally to the elucidation of the disease if symptoms are to be attributed to defects in single brain regions. Alternatively, it is currently hypothesized that the variety and severity range of symptoms observed in schizophrenia can be explained by defects in several brain regions affecting the same neural circuit that mediates higher cognitive functions. Such neural circuitry would include neocortical association areas, the limbic system and midline and thalamic structures, with possible involvement of the basal ganglia.

The similarity in mechanisms and molecules used both during embryonic development and in postnatal cognitive events may be worth some reflection in relation to one of the many puzzling observations in schizophrenia: the late onset of the disease. Symptoms of acute schizophrenia arise only in early adulthood, making it hard to explain how a defect during prenatal development would lead to noticeable dysfunction only later in life. Nevertheless, accumulating evidence suggests that early premorbid dysfunction in a portion of cases precedes the onset of schizophrenia by many years. Subtle but consistent motor dysfunctions have been reported during childhood in schizophrenic patients, as well as behavior alterations involving attention deficits and possibly learning disabilities (reviewed in Walker 1994; Mirsky *et al.* 1995).

Disturbances of neural circuits including both sensorimotor and frontal and limbic regions are likely to be reflected in motor dysfunctions in earlier years, when metabolic activity is higher in motor-related areas. In adolescence, the peak of brain activity occurs in regions linked to higher cognitive functions, and will be severely impaired by anomalies involving the related neural cir-

cuits, whereas these functions will be mildly affected in earlier years when brain metabolic activity is lower in limbic and frontal areas. A defective molecule could alter the neural circuit early in development but have its most detrimental psychiatric effects later in life, during periods of active neuronal plasticity in the limbic areas, leading to the onset of symptoms.

It is also important to note that regulation of expression of molecules used both during early development and in other processes later in life is likely to play a major role in the correct processing of the molecules' functions. Differential regulation, possibly involving different regulatory molecules or mechanisms, occurs at different stages of life and could be responsible for different phenotypes in different developmental periods. We have referred to the regulation of cell adhesion molecules' expression by homeotic molecules during the early stages of development. In those early stages, the expression of molecules required for the migration of neurons into the appropriate locations will be directed by the specific patterns of expression of the homeotic genes. Cell adhesion molecules such as NCAM, however, are still expressed in the adult and are required for remodeling of synaptic connections. In the adult sea slug *Aplysia*, learning induces a cascade of cell signals that leads to alterations in apCAM (*Aplysia* cell adhesion molecule) expression and synaptic remodeling (Mayford *et al.* 1992). In songbirds, learning and memory of new songs involves synaptic plasticity and also neurogenesis, which is controlled by sexual hormones (Doupe 1994a). In insects, adaptive behaviours are also linked to neurogenesis, which is controlled by hormones (Cayre *et al.* 1994). Adult neurogenesis in mammals has been reported only in limited regions of the brain, namely the olfactory bulb and the dentate gyrus of the hippocampus (Lois and Alvarez-Buylla 1994). Both neurogenesis and synaptic plasticity in the adult require CAMs and one can speculate that their expression in the young adult may be subject to hormonal control. Thus, there are several examples where differential regulation of the same molecules, involved in similar mechanisms of synaptic plasticity, seems to take place in different stages of life.

Morphological post-mortem observations of the brains of schizophrenics have revealed alterations that could be attributable to defective cell migration, namely the disarray of cells found in the hippocampus and the location of cells in inappropriate layers of the entorhinal cortex. CAMs are crucial for cell migration and if defective, could be good candidates for the pathology observed. Kallmann's syndrome, a disorder in which defective migration of olfactory neurons occurs, is caused by deletion of a gene that has homology to NCAM (Franco et al. 1991; Rugarli et al. 1993). A group of X-linked neurologic disorders displaying a range of severity from hydrocephalus to mental retardation with enlargement of the cerebral ventricles involves mutations in the L1CAM gene (Rosenthal et al. 1992; Jouet et al. 1994). Finally, NCAM has recently been implicated in schizophrenia by two different lines of evidence: polymorphic markers on chromosome 11q close to the NCAM location yielded a positive lod score in a large pedigree from Quebec (Merette et al. 1994), although in other families these findings have not been replicated (Vicente et al. 1994); and reduced levels of hippocampal PSA-NCAM (in the normal adult brain PSA-NCAM is only present in the hippocampus) have been reported post-mortem in the brains of schizophrenics (Barbeau et al. 1995). The function of NCAM in mammals has been further analyzed by gene targeting in mice (Tomasiewicz et al. 1993; Cremer et al. 1994). Mice deficient in NCAM are healthy but show a slight reduction in overall brain weight and a strong reduction in olfactory bulb size. It is interesting that a proportion of schizophrenic patients show impairment of the olfactory function (Good et al. 1995). In addition, NCAM deficient mice show significant deficits in spatial learning and impaired exploratory behavior, which suggests that hippocampal activity might be altered. It is of interest that both the morphological and behavior phenotypes are linked to regions where considerable adult plasticity occurs. The findings in these animals are consistent with the expected functions of NCAM and also with a potential role of this molecule in schizophrenia.

Anomalous neuronal connections could result in a variety of psychiatric alterations and cognitive impairments consistent with the heterogeneity of symptoms observed in schizophrenia (Goodman 1989). Some synaptic vesicle proteins have been reported as altered at post-mortem in the brains of schizophrenics. Synapsin levels were reduced in hippocampus of schizophrenics (Browning et al. 1993) and synaptophysin reductions were observed in prefrontal cortex (Glantz and Lewis 1994) and visual association cortices of patients (Sower et al. 1994). Many questions remain to be answered regarding the specific mechanisms of action for each synaptic protein, but their involvement in the regulation of patterns of synaptic connectivity has been firmly established, and suggestive evidence implicates them in schizophrenia. The alterations found in synapsin and synaptophysin, in hippocampus and frontal cortex, can be expected to result in deficiencies in neurotransmitter release with consequent functional impairment of these regions, consistent with the functional neuroanatomy of schizophrenia.

Brain maturation involves remodeling of synaptic connections. During the first 2 years of life, there is a significant increase of synaptic connections in the human frontal cortex. This is followed by a gradual decrease in synaptic density until adolescence, consistent with the synaptic elimination period that characterizes brain maturation (reviewed in Walker 1994; also see Chapter 4 by Stephanis et al.). As we described earlier, the NMDA receptor is crucial in the processes of strengthening and weakening of synapses. Several reports suggest abnormalities in glutamate in the brains of schizophrenic patients, namely in the cingulate cortex, putamen and lateral pallidum, and reduction of glutamate receptors has also been reported (Harrison et al. 1991; reviewed in Walker 1994). NMDA receptor knockout animals die soon after birth of respiratory failure, demonstrating a fundamental neonatal function of the receptor. The brain anatomy of the mutant animals appears normal, which suggests that the NMDA receptor is not vital for CNS formation. The loss of NMDA activity as measured by alterations in calcium flux and membrane currents indicate a main role in synaptic connectivity, fundamental for autonomous neonatal life. The nonviability of the animals makes it impossible to assess the function of the receptor in synaptic plasticity later in life.

Defects in neurotrophins and their receptors could also lead to the impairments observed in schizophrenia. The altered cell numbers reported in several brain areas implicated in schizophrenia are consistent with the role of these molecules in cell survival and death in brain development. BDNF has been shown to promote the survival of dopaminergic neurons from several brain regions, and to increase dopamine turnover in vivo, suggesting an involvement with the dopamine system, which has repeatedly been implicated in schizophrenia. The role of these molecules, mainly BDNF and NT-3, in the regulation of specific types of synaptic transmission that forms the basis of cognitive processes is also very relevant for psychiatric impairments. Data obtained from BDNF gene targeting experiments show no obvious morphological alterations in the CNS, but the information is limited because the animals die early from PNS defects. Some neurological markers are however altered in the young animals, and the high expression of this gene in the normal adult brain indicates that stronger effects in the CNS would be apparent later in life. Motor alterations in the BDNF knockout mice occur early, indicating involvement of the neurotrophin in motor dysfunctions earlier in the developmental process, as seems to occur in children before the onset of symptoms of schizophrenia. The lack of morphological alterations in the animals' CNS observed in gene targeting experiments for any of the neurotrophins could also be due to functional cooperation among these molecules, which is suggested by the overlap in binding affinities to the trk receptors. This functional cooperation has also been observed in specific cellular pathways in vivo: in the *wobbler* mouse, a model of motor neuron disease, both CNTF (ciliary neurotrophic factor) and BDNF are required to completely rescue the defective phenotype, whereas separately each is only able to slow progression of the disease (Mitsumoto *et al.* 1994). Both molecules promote the survival of motor neurons, but through distinct pathways. The functional cooperativity of the neurotrophins with each other and with other molecules, as exemplified in motor neuron disease, argues in favour of the hypothesized oligogenic character of schizophrenia. Supporting the involvement of neurotrophins in schizophrenia are reports of a positive association between the NT3 gene and schizophrenia in a Japanese population (Nanko *et al.* 1994).

Molecules involved in the earlier stages of development are not likely to directly cause the dysfunctions observed in schizophrenia. They are generally active in stages of development where any disruption will cause very severe defects. Knockout animals for many of these molecules are not viable after birth due to a wide range of malformations that often affect more than one system. Some surprising findings have none the less been reported in knockouts for early regulatory genes; for instance, the targeted mutation of the *engrailed* gene in mice results only in mild defects, localized to the cerebellum (Joyner *et al.* 1991). It is important to note that gene targeting experiments lead to the total shutdown of specific genes, often with very severe consequences. Variations in levels of regulatory molecules as opposed to total inactivation can, however, have far reaching consequences in terms of control of gene expression and still not be lethal. Also it should be noted that early regulators such as the homeotic genes control the expression of groups of molecules, therefore possibly affecting more than one process, which would be consistent with the heterogeneity of alterations observed in schizophrenia.

There is substantial evidence for neurodevelopment defects being at least a partial cause of schizophrenia. It provides an explanation for the epidemiology of the disease, the late onset of symptoms, the heterogeneity in symptoms, and in morphological and physiological observations. The combination of advances in the molecular mechanisms of normal neurodevelopment and of genetic strategies allowing the detection of multigenes as causative factors in the disorder will be crucial in the elucidation of the etiology of schizophrenia.

GENETIC STRATEGIES

Human genetics approaches
For the genetic study of complex illnesses such as schizophrenia, two main strategies have been employed. Genetic linkage strategies that use families or affected pairs of relatives have received the most attention to date. The use of affected pairs in genetic studies of another complex disorder, diabetes, has shown great promise for the identification of several genes involved in this illness (Davies 1994). The other major strategy of genetic analysis is the association study which compares a group of unrelated affected individuals to a group of unrelated healthy controls.

Linkage strategies are particularly useful if there is one or a small number of genes involved and genetic hetero-

Fig. 3.6. Allelic variation of a DNA polymorphism in a small family. The segregation of polymorphic markers with a disease in families is the basis of linkage analysis, and has been especially useful in the location of genes for single gene disorders.

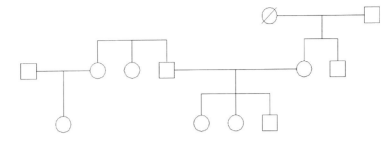

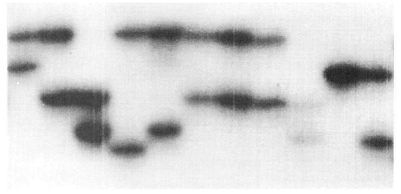

geneity is limited. In a linkage study, a region of a chromosome is identified that is co-inherited with the illness in the family members. The disadvantage of this approach is that the gene causing the disorder in a particular kindred may not have general applicability to the disease in the population. Also, linkage studies require estimation of genetic parameters, such as penetrance, disease gene frequency and mode of inheritance, and are very sensitive to changes in diagnosis. Collections of pairs of affected relatives and small families assesses a wider range of subjects, and avoids most problems in parameter estimation (Weeks and Lange 1988).

Association studies compare groups of unrelated individuals with the disease versus healthy control groups to identify a DNA marker that is in, or close to, the genetic susceptibility locus. Association strategies have the advantage of being free of genetic model specification but are highly susceptible to population stratification effects and sampling error (Kidd 1993). These stratification sampling effects can, however, be largely overcome through the use of the haplotype relative risk (HRR) method (Terwilliger and Ott 1992; Knapp *et al.* 1993). The HRR method uses

the chromosomes from each parent that are not transmitted to the affected child as controls. Thus the HRR strategy overcomes sampling biases that have limited the usefulness of association studies in the past.

The statistical advantages of these designs, when combined with the remarkable advances in the human genetic map and highly informative DNA polymorphisms, creates the overall power of molecular genetics and has already led to the localization of hundreds of disease-causing genes. We have used both linkage (Vicente *et al.* 1993) and HRR (Vicente *et al.* 1994) designs to study neurodevelopment genes in schizophrenia. The combination of these two genetic strategies represents a comprehensive approach for the detection of genes involved in the etiology of schizophrenia (Fig. 3.6).

Animal models

Animal studies are of great importance in the elucidation of the function of specific molecules and as models of disease. Several species are nowadays widely used as systems for the functional analysis of molecules in vivo, which has led to a rapid development of the technology for gene mutation and gene expression, and also to an increasingly more detailed knowledge of the genome of these species.

The simplicity of their nervous system and the possibility of simple mutagenesis and rapid screening makes lower species such as *Drosophila* and *C. elegans* very suitable for the cloning of genes crucial in neurodevelopmental and behavioral mechanisms. The remarkable conservation over evolution of many of the genes implicated in development allowed the isolation and characterization of the mammalian homologues. Reverse genetic approaches such as transgenic methods in mice (Capecchi 1989; Melton 1994) permit the overexpression or the shutdown (knockout) of specific genes in genetically engineered mice. These techniques allow the analysis of the function of the encoded proteins in vivo, contributing in some cases with models for disease mechanisms. Genetic engineering of animals has added to the traditional methods of screening the genome and positional cloning of naturally occurring mice mutations.

The production of knockout animals by gene targeting has some drawbacks. Expression of the gene is completely shutdown, not allowing the analysis of the effect of variable levels of the encoded protein in the organism. Also, gene expression is shutdown from the earliest stages of development and in every cell of the organism. The same molecules appear to be used in different stages of development and in several different tissues, as we have referred to earlier, so the result is that often the animals are not viable due to severe defects in systems not related to the system of interest in the particular study. This is common in the study of the CNS: the same molecules are used in the development of the CNS and peripheral nervous system (PNS), often at different stages, and may have less vital functions in the CNS which will remain unseen due to lethal defects in the PNS. New technologies are being developed that allow the alteration of expression of a gene in particular windows of time and in a tissue-specific way: the Cre-*loxP* transgenics system involves the use of gene promoters to manipulate the turning on of a gene specifically in the tissue and developmental stage of interest (Gu *et al.* 1994); the injection of antisense DNA into specific locations of the brain; and the transfer of genes into the brain mediated by adenovirus vectors (Akli *et al.* 1993; for a review see Takahashi *et al.* 1994). These new techniques

could be especially relevant for an animal model of schizophrenia, considering the late age of onset of the disease.

We have referred, in our discussion of the development of the CNS, to a few examples of gene targeting as important in the elucidation of gene function in vivo, for instance the NCAM and the neurotrophin and trk receptor knockouts. Several mice knockouts are of importance in the elucidation of molecular alterations leading to behavioral anomalies related to higher cognitive functions, and potentially, schizophrenia. Deserving particular attention are animals that show disrupted spatial learning behaviors, such as the NCAM, CaMKII and *fyn* mutants (Cremer *et al.* 1994; Grant and Silva 1994). These mice have subtle anatomical brain defects but are apparently healthy otherwise. Both the CaMKII and *fyn* mutants have disrupted LTP, and the NCAM mutant shows deficits in spatial learning. Another interesting animal model, in which an ibotenic acid lesion is made neonatally in the ventral hippocampal region of rats, shows similar behavior deficits to the CaMKII mutant: both animals display enhanced acoustic startle response, analogous to that seen in schizophrenia patients, and increased exploratory behavior (reviewed by Kotrla, *et al.* in Chapter 13). The neonatal lesion is administered at a developmental period in the rat that corresponds roughly to the third trimester of gestation in humans. The abnormal behavior in the lesioned rats does not arise until puberty, when the circuitry related to the limbic system becomes fully active, a characteristic with an obvious parallel in schizophrenia. It is very interesting that defects in CaMKII, a protein involved in hippocampal plasticity and neural signal transduction, lead to a phenotype similar to that displayed by such an intriguing animal model of schizophrenia.

Animal models of multigenic diseases are for obvious reasons more difficult to create than for single gene disorders, especially if there is no consistent phenotype to single out. Transgenic animals are none the less important to understand the function of candidate genes for the disorder, and analysis of their phenotype may show deficiencies with parallels in the symptomatology observed. The advent of double knockouts, in which two genes are targeted for disruption, can originate morphological and behavior phenotypes that are more consistent with a multigenic disease and lead to a better understanding of the functional cooperation between specific proteins. Improvement in techniques for gene transfer to specific tissues combined with gene targeting may eventually lead to the possibility of downregulating the expression of genes without totally shutting them off, allowing the analysis of the effect of lower levels of the encoded protein as opposed to the effect of total lack of the protein. Forward genetic techniques, the screening of the genome for naturally occurring or chemically-induced mutations, also provide interesting approaches to the study of behavioral disorders. Mutant mice can be screened for quantitative trait loci (QTL) for particular behaviors in the animal that have important parallels in the disease symptoms (Lander and Botstein 1989). This technique can be used to track down several genes contributing to genetic variance in a quantitative trait, and is also currently used for genetic screening of human disease. The QTL method in mice is of further advantage because the mouse genome is thoroughly mapped.

SUMMARY

Evidence from neuroanatomy, brain imaging, molecular biology, and behavior points to an important role for neurodevelopmental factors in the pathogenesis of schizophrenia. We have reviewed the major mechanisms of neurodevelopment to provide a context for our discussion of the action of neurodevelopment genes that we judge to be of significant potential interest in the etiology of the disease. Powerful techniques now exist for the discovery of polymorphisms at these loci, and thus variation in these genes can be correlated with schizophrenic versus non-schizophrenic phenotypes in family-linkage, affected relative pair or case-control association strategies. Thus, by combining knowledge and strategies from clinical, neurobiological and genetic efforts, the etiology of schizophrenia may be elucidated and hopefully progress will be made towards a cure for this disease.

ACKNOWLEDGMENTS

We thank Drs Tsukasa-Saaki and David Nimask for critical reading of the manuscript and helpful comments.

REFERENCES

Adams, J. and Watt, F. 1993. Regulation of development and differentiation by the extracellular matrix. *Development* 117:1183–98.

Akli, S., Caillaud, C., Vigne, E., Stratford-Perricaudet, L., Poenaru, L., Perricaudet, M., Kahn, A., and Peschanski, M. 1993. Transfer of a foreign gene into the brain using adenovirus vectors. *Nature Genetics* 3:224–228.

Andreasen, N., Arndt, S., Swayze II, V., Cizaldo, T., Flaum, M., O'Leary, D., Ehrhardt, J., and Yuh, W. 1994. Thalamic abnormalities in schizophrenia visualized through magnetic resonance image averaging. *Science* 266: 294–8.

Arnold, S.E., Franz, B.R., Gur, R.E., Gur, R.C., Moberg, P.J., Shapiro, R.M., and Trojanowski, J. Q. 1995. Smaller neuron size in schizophrenia in hippocampal subfields that mediate cortical-hippocampal interactions. *Am.J. Psychiatry* 152:738–48.

Baier, H. and Bonhoeffer, F. 1994. Attractive axon guidance molecules. *Science* 265:1541–2.

Baldwin, C., Hoth, C., Amos, J., da-Silva, E., and Milunsky, A. 1992. An exonic mutation in the *HuP2* paired domain gene causes Waardenburg's syndrome. *Nature* 355:637–8.

Bally-Cuif, L., Goridis, C., and Santoni, M.J. 1993. The mouse N-CAM gene displays a biphasic expression pattern during neural tube development. *Development* 117:543–52.

Barbeau, D., Liang, J.J., Quirion, R., Robataille, Y., and Srivastava, L.K. 1995. Decreased expression of the embryonic form of the neural cell adhesion molecule in schizophrenic brains. *Proc. Natl Acad. Sci. USA* 92:2785–9.

Bark, I.C., Hahn, K.M., Ryabinin, A.E., and Wilson, M.C. 1995. Differential expression of SNAP 25 protein isoforms during divergent vesicle fusion events of neural development. *Proc. Natl Acad. Sci. USA* 92:1510–14.

Barton, C.H., Mann, D.A., and Walsh, F.S. 1990. Characterization of the human-N-CAM promoter. *Biochem J* 268:161–8.

Bayer, S.A., Yackel, J.W., and Puri, P.S. 1982. Neurons in the rat dentate gyrus granular layer substantially increase during juvenile and adult life. *Science* 216:890–2.

Bogerts, B. 1990. The neuropathology of schizophrenia. In *Search for the cause of schizophrenia*, ed. H. Häfner and W. Gattaz. Berlin, Heidelberg Springer.

Bogerts, B. 1993. Recent advances in the neuropathology of schizophrenia. *Schizoph.Bull.* **19**:431–45.

Browning, M.D., Dudek, E.M., Rapier, J.L., Leonard, S., and Freedman, R. 1993. Significant reductions in synapsin but not synaptophysin-specific activity in the brains of some schizophrenics. *Biol.Psychiatry* **34**:529–35.

Buchman, V.L. and Davies, A.M. 1993. Different neurotrophics are expressed and act in a developmental sequence to promote the survival of embryonic sensory neurons. *Development* **118**:989–1001.

Capecchi, M. 1989. Altering the genome by homologous recombination. *Science* **244**:1288–92.

Cayre, M., Strambi, C., and Strambi, A. 1994. Neurogenesis in an adult insect brain and its hormonal control. *Nature* **368**:57–9.

Chitnis, A., Henrique, D., Ish-Horowicz, D., Kintner, C., and Lewis, J. 1995. Primary neurogenesis in *Xenopus* embryos regulated by a homologue of the *Drosophila* neurogenic gene *Delta*. *Nature* **375**:761–6.

Clayton, N. and Krebs, J. 1994. Hippocampal growth and attrition in birds affected by experience. *PNAS* **91**:7410–14.

Colwell, G., Li, B., Forrest, D., and Brackenbury, R. 1992. Conserved regulatory elements in the promoter region of the N-CAM gene. *Genomics* **14**:875–82.

Conrad, A.J., Abebe, T., Austin, R., Forsythe, S., and Scheibel, A.B. 1991. Hippocampal pyramidal cell disarray in schizophrenia as a bilateral phenomenon. *Arch. Gen. Psychiatry* **48**:413–17.

Cremer, H., Lange, R., Christoph, A., Plomann, M., Vopper, G., Roes, J., Brown, R., Baldwin, S., Kraemer, P., Scheff, S., Barthels, D., Rajewsky, K., and Wille, W. 1994. Inactivation of the N-CAM gene in mice results in size reduction of the olfactory bulb and deficits in spatial learning. *Nature* **367**: 455–9.

Davidson, E. 1993. Molecular biology of embryonic development: how far have we come in the last ten years? *BioEssays* **16**:603–15.

Davies, A. 1994. Intrinsic programmes of growth and survival in developing vertebrae neurons. *TINS* **17**:195–9.

DeSimone, D. 1994. Adhesion and matrix in vertebrate development. *Cur. Opin. Cell Biol.* **6**:747–51.

Doherty, P., Cohen, J., and Walsh, F. 1990. Neurite outgrowth in response to transfected N-CAM changes during development and is modulated by polysialic acid. *Neuron* **5**:209–19.

Doherty, P., Ashton, S.V., Moore, S.E., and Walsh, F.S. 1991. Morphoregulatory activities of N-CAM and N-cadherin can be accounted for by G protein-dependent activation of L- and N-type neuronal calcium channels. *Cell* **67**:21–33.

Doupe, A. 1994a. Songbirds and adult neurogenesis: a new role for hormones. *PNAS* **91**:7836–8.

Doupe, A. 1994b. Seeds of instruction: hippocampus and memory in food-storing birds. *PNAS* **91**: 7381–4.

Dragunow, M., Abraham, W., Beilharz, E., Lawlor, P., Gluckman, P., and Mason, B. 1993. Brain derived neurotrophic factor expression after long-term potentiation. *Neurosci. Lett.* **160**:232–6.

Edelman, G. and Jones, F. 1993. Outside and downstream of the homeobox. *J. Biol. Chem.* **268**:20683–6.

Ericson, J., Murh, J., Placzek, M., Lints, T., Jessel, T., and Edlund, T. 1995. Sonic hedgehog induces the differentiation of ventral forebrain neurons: a common signal for ventral patterning within the neural tube. *Cell* **81**:747–56.

Ernfors, P., Lee, K-F., and Jaenisch, R. 1994a. Mice lacking brain-derived neurotrophic factor develop with sensory deficits. *Nature* **368**:147–50.

Ernfors, P., Lee, K.-F., Kucera, J., and Jaenisch, R. 1994b. Lack of neurotrophin-3 leads to deficiencies in the peripheral nervous system and loss of limb proprioceptive afferents. *Cell* **77**:503–12.

Fariñas, I., Jones, K., Backus, C., Wang, X.-Y., and Reichardt, L. 1994. Severe sensory and sympathetic deficits in mice lacking neurotrophin-3. *Nature* **369**:658–61.

Fortini, M. and Artavanis-Tsakonas T. 1993. *Notch*: neurogenesis is only part of the picture. *Cell* **75**:1245–7.

Franco, B., Guioli, S., Pragliola, A., Incerti, B., Bardoni, B., Tonlorenzi, R., Carrozzo, R., Maestrini, E., Pieretti, M., Taillon-Mille,. P., Brown, C., Willard, H., Lawrence, C., Persico, M., Camerino, G., and Ballabio, A. 1991. A gene deleted in Kallmann's syndrome shares homology with neural cell adhesion and axonal path-finding molecules. *Nature* **353**:529–36.

Geddes, J., Wilson, M., Miller, F., and Cotman, C. 1990. Molecular markers of reactive plasticity. In *Excitory amino acids and neural plasticity*, ed. Y. Ben-Ari. New York: Plenum Press.

Ghosh, A., Carnahan, J., and Greenberg, M. 1994. Requirement for BDNF in activity-dependent survival of cortical neurons. *Science* **263**:1618–23.

Glantz, L.A. and Lewis, D.A. 1994. Synaptophysin and not rab3A is specifically reduced in the prefrontal cortex of schizophrenic subjects. *Soc. Neurosc. Abstr.* **20**:261.14.

Glaser, T., Jepeal, L., Edwards, J.G., Young, S.R., Favor, J., and Maas, R.L. 1994. Pax6 gene dosage effect in a family with congenital cataracts, aniridia, anophthalmia and central nervous system defects. *Nat. Genet.* **7**:463–71.

Good, K.P., Kopala, L.C., Martzke, J.S., and Honer, W.G. 1995. Converging lateralized olfactory and neuropsychological deficits in male patients with schizophrenia. *Schizophr. Res.* **15**:119.

Goodman, C. 1994. The likeness of being: phylogenetically conserved molecular mechanisms of growth cone guidance. *Cell* **78**:353–6.

Goodman, C. and Shatz, C. 1993. Developmental mechanisms that generate precise patterns of neural connectivity. *Cell, 72/Neuron* **10** (Suppl.): 77–98.

Goodman, R. 1989. Neuronal misconnections and psychiatric disorder: is there a link? *Br. J. Psychiatry* **154**:292–9.

Gottesman, I. 1991. The role of psychosocial and environmental stressors. In *Schizophrenia genesis: the origins of madness*, ed. R.C. Atkinson, G. Lindzey and R.F. Thompson, pp. 150–65. New York: WH Freeman and Company.

Goomer, R.S., Brent, D.H., Wood, I.C., Jones, F.S., and Edelman, G.M. 1994. Regulation *in vitro* of an L-CAM enhancer by homeobox genes *HoxD9* and HNF-1. *PNAS* **91**:7985–9.

Gower, H., Barton, C., Elsom, V., Thompson, J., Moore, S., Dickson, G., and Walsh, F. 1988. Alternative splicing generates a secreted form of N-CAM in muscle and brain. *Cell* **55**:955–64.

Grant, S. and Silva, A. 1994. Targeting learning. *TINS* **17**:71–5.

Gu, H., Marth, J., Orban, P., Mossman, H., and Rajewsky, K. 1994. Deletion of a DNA polymerase ß gene segment in T cells using cell type-specific gene targeting. *Science* **265**:103–6.

Han, H.Q., Bahler, M., Greengard, P., Nichols, R.A., and Rubin, M.R. 1991. Induction of formation of presynaptic terminals in neuroblastoma cells by synapsin IIb. *Nature* **349**:697–700.

Harrison, P.J., McLaughlin, D., and Kerwin, R.W. 1991. Decreased hippocampal expression of a glutamate receptor gene in schizophrenia. *Lancet* **337**:450–2.

Haydon, P. and Drapeau, P. 1995. From contact to connection: early events during synaptogenesis. *TINS* **18**:196–201.

Hemmati-Brivanlou, A. and Melton, D.A. 1992. A truncated activin receptor inhibits mesoderm induction and formation of axial structures in *Xenopus* embryos. *Nature* **359**:609–14.

Henrique, D., Adam, J., Chitnis, A., Ish-Horowicz, D., Lewis, J., and Myat, A. 1995. Expression of a *Delta* homologue in the chick. *Nature* **375**:787–90.

Holst, B., Goomer, R., Wood, I., Edelman, G., and Jones, F. 1994. Binding and activation of the promoter for the neural cell adhesion molecule by Pax-8. *J. Biol. Chem.* **269**:22245–52.

Humphries, M., Mould, A., and Tuckwell, D. 1993. Dynamic aspects of adhesion receptor function – integrins both twist and shout. *BioEssays* **15**:391–7.

Hynes, R. 1994. The impact of molecular biology on models for cell adhesion. *BioEssays* **16**:663–9.

Hynes, R. and Lander, A. 1992. Contact and adhesive specifications in the associations, migrations and targeting of cells and aons. *Cell* **68**:303–22.

Ip, N.Y., Li, Y., Yancopoulos, G.D., and Lindsay, R.M. 1993. Cultured hippocampal neurons show responses to BDNF, NT-3, and NT-4, but not NGF. *J. Neurosc.* **13**:3394–405.

Johnson, R.L. and Tabin, C. 1995. The long and short of *hedgehog* signalling. *Cell* **81**:313–16.

Jones, K., Fariñas, I., Backus, C., and Reichardt, L. 1994. Targeted disruption of the BDNF gene perturbs brain and sensory neuron development but not motor neuron development. *Cell* **76**:989–99.

Jouet, M., Rosenthal, A., Armstrong, G., MacFarlane, J., Stevenson, R., Paterson, J., Metzenberg, A., Ionasescu, V., Temple, K., and Kenwrick, S. 1994. X-linked spastic paraplegia (SPG1), MASA syndrome and X-linked hydrocephalus result from mutations in the L1 gene. *Nat. Genet.* **7**: 402.

Joyner, A., Herrup, K., Auerbach, B., Davis, C., and Rossant, J. 1991. Subtle cerebellar phenotype in mice homozygous for a targeted deletion of the *En-2* homeobox. *Science* **251**:1239–43.

Juliano, R. and Haskill, S. 1993. Signal transduction from the extracellular matrix. *J. Cell Biol.* **120**:577–85.

Kandel, E.R. and O'Dell, T.J. 1992. Are adult learning
mechanisms also used for development? *Science*
258:243–45.

Kang, H., and Schuman, E.M. 1995. Long lasting neurotrophin-
induced enhancement of synaptic transmission in the adult
hippocampus. *Science* 267:1658–62.

Kendler, K.S. and Diehl, S.R. 1993. The genetics of
schizophrenia: a current genetic-epidemiologic perspective.
Schizop. Bull. 19:261–85.

Kennedy, T.E., Serafini, T., de la Torre, J.R., and Tessier-
Lavigne, M. 1994. Netrins are diffusible chemotropic
factors for commissural axons in the embryonic spinal
cord. *Cell* 78:425–35.

Kessler, D.S. and Melton, D.A. 1994. Vertebrate embryonic
induction: mesodermal and neural patterning. *Science*
266:596–604.

Keynes, R. and Lumsden, A. 1990. Segmentation and the origin
of regional diversity in the vertebrate central nervous
system. *Neuron* 4:1–9.

Kidd, K.K. 1993. Association of disease with genetic markers:
deja vu all over again. *Am. J. Med. Genet. (Neuropsych.
Genet.)* 48:71–3.

Kirschenbaum, B. and Goldman, S.A. 1995. Brain-derived
neurotrophic factor promotes the survival of neurons
arising from the adult rat forebrain subependymal zone.
Proc. Natl. Acad. Sci. USA 92:210–14.

Knapp, M., Seuchter, S.A., and Baur, M.P. 1993. The haplotype
relative risk (HRR) method of analysis of association in
nuclear families. *Am. J. Hum. Genet.* 52:1085–93.

Kolodkin, A., Matthes, D., and Goodman, C. 1993. The
semaphorin genes encode a family of transmembrane and
secreted growth cone guidance molecules. *Cell* 75:1389–99.

Korshing, S. 1993. The neurotrophic factor concept: a
reexamination. *J. Neurosc.* 13:2739–48.

Krumlauf, R. 1994. *Hox* genes in vertebrate development. *Cell*
78:191–201.

Lallier, T. and Bronner-Fraser, M. 1993. Inhibition of neural
crest cell attachment by integrin antisense oligonucleotides.
Science 259:692–5.

Lamb, T., Knecht, A., Smith, W., Stachel, S., Economides, A.,
Stahl, N., Yancopolous, G., and Harland, R. 1993. Neural
induction by the secreted polypeptide noggin. *Science*
262:713–18.

Lamballe, F., Smeyne, R., and Barbacid, M. 1994.

Developmental expression of *trk*C, the neurotrophin-3
receptor, in the mammalian nervous system. *J. Neurosci.*
14:14–28.

Lander, E.S. and Botstein, D. 1989. Mapping mendelian factors
underlying quantitative traits using RFLP linkage maps.
Genetics 121:185–99.

Lee, J.E., Hollenberg, S.M., Lipnick, N., Snider, L., Turner,
D.L., and Weintraub, H. 1995. Conversion of *Xenopus*
ectoderm into neurons by NeuroD, a basic helix-loop-helix
protein. *Science* 268:836–44.

Letourneau, P., Condic, M., and Snow, D. 1994. Interactions of
developing neurons with the extracellular matrix. *J.
Neurosci.* 14: 915–27.

Linnemann, D. and Bock, E. 1989. Cell adhesion molecules in
neural development. *Dev. Neurosci.* 11:149–73.

Lohof, A.M., Ip, N.Y., and Poo, M. 1993. Potentiation of
developing neuromuscular synapses by the neurotrophins
NT-3 and BDNF. *Nature* 363:350–53.

Lois, C. and Alvarez-Buylla, A. 1994. Long-distance neuronal
migration in the adult mammalian brain. *Science*
264:1145–8.

Lou, X. and Bixby, J.L. 1993. Coordinate and non-coordinate
regulation of synaptic vesicle protein genes during
embryonic development. *Devel. Biol.* 159:327–37.

Lumsden, A. 1990. The cellular basis of segmentation in the
developing hindbrain. *TINS* 13:329–35.

Luo, Y., Raible, D., and Raper, J.A. 1993. Collapsin: a protein in
brain that induces the collapse and paralysis of neuronal
growth cones. *Cell* 75:217–27.

Lüthl, A., Laurent, J.-P., Figurov, A., Muller, D., and
Schachner, M. 1994. Hippocampal long-term potentiation
and neural cell adhesion molecules L1 and NCAM. *Nature*
372:777–9.

Maisonpierre, P.C., LeBeau, M.M., Espinosa, R., Ip, N.Y.,
Belluscio, L., De La Monte, S.M., Squinto, S., Furth,
M.E., and Yancopoulos, G.D. 1990. Human and rat brain-
derived neurotrophin-3: gene structures, distributions, and
chromosomal localizations. *Genomics* 10:558–68.

Massagué, J. 1992. Receptors for the TGF-ß family. *Cell*
69:1067–70.

Mauro, V., Wood, I., Krushel, L., Crossin, K., and Edelman, G.
1994. Cell adhesion alters gene transcription in chicken
embryo brain cells and mouse embryonal carcinoma cells.
Proc. Natl Acad. Sci. USA 91:2868–72.

Mayford, M., Barzilai, A., Keller, F., Schacher, S., and Kandel, E. 1992. Modulation of an NCAM-related adhesion molecule with long-term synaptic plasticity in aplysia. *Science* **256**:638–44.

Meakin, S. and Shooter, E. 1992. The nerve growth factor family of receptors. *TINS* **15**:323–31.

Melton, D. 1994. Gene targeting in the mouse. *BioEssays* **16**:633–8.

Merette, C., Martinez, M., Rouillard, E., Marcotte, P., Maresca, A., Fournier, J.P., Garneau, Y., Cliche, D., Boutin, P., and Maziade, M. 1994. Update on a linkage trend between schizophrenia (SZ) and the 11q21–22 region in pedigrees of Eastern Quebec. *Am. J. Hum. Genet.* **55**:1137.

Mirsky, A.F., Frenkel, E., Kugelmass, S., and Nathan, M. 1995. Overview and summary: twenty-five-year follow up of high risk children. *Schizophr. Bull.* **21**:227–39.

Mitsumoto, H., Ikeda, K., Klinkosz, B., Cedarbaum, J., Wong, V., and Lindsay, R. 1994. Arrest of motor neuron disease in *wobbler* mice cotreated with CNTF and BDNF. *Science* **265**:1107–10.

Murtha, M.T., Leckman, J.F., and Ruddle, F.H. 1991. Detection of homeobox genes in development and evolution. *Proc. Natl Acad. Sci. USA* **88**:10711–15.

Nanko, S., Hattori, M., Kuwata, S., Sasaki, T., Fukuda, R., Dai, X.Y., Yamaguchi, K., Shibata, Y., and Kazamatsuri, H. 1994. Neurotrophin-3 gene polymorphism associated with schizophrenia. *Acta Psychiatr. Scand.* **89**: 390–2.

Nusse, R. and Varmus, H. 1992. *Wnt* Genes. *Cell* **69**:1073–87.

Osen-Sand, A., Catsicas, M., Staple, J., Jones, K., Ayala, G., Knowles, J., Grenningloh, G., and Catsicas, S. 1993. Inhibition of axonal growth by SNAP-25 antisense oligonucleotides *in vitro* and *in vivo*. *Nature* **364**: 445–8.

Perides, G., Safran, R., Downing, L., and Charness, M. 1994. Regulation of neural cell adhesion molecule and L1 by the transforming growth factor-β superfamily. *J. Biol. Chem.* **269**:765–70.

Pettit, D., Perlman, S., and Malinow, R. 1994. Potentiated transmission and prevention of further LTP by increased CaMKII activity in postsynaptic hippocampal slice neurons. *Science* **266**:1881–5.

Phillips, H.S., Hains, J.M., Laramee, G.R., Rosenthal, A., and Winslow, J.W. 1990. Widespread expression of BDNF but not NT3 by target areas of basal forebrain cholinergic neurons. *Science* **250**:290–4.

Porteus, M., Bulfone, A., Ciaranello, R., and Rubenstein, J. 1991. Isolation and characterization of a novel cDNA clone encoding a homeodomain that is developmentally regulated in the ventral forebrain. *Neuron* **7**:221–9.

Price, M., Lazzaro, D., Pohl, T., Mattei, M., Ruther, U., Olivo, J., Duboule, D., Di Lauro, R. 1992. Regional expression of the homeobox *Nkx-2.2* in the developing mammalian forebrain. *Neuron* **8**:241–55.

Price, M., Lemaistre, M., Pischetola, M., di Lauro, R., and Duboule, D. 1991. A mouse gene related to *Distal-less* shows a restricted expression in the developing forebrain. *Nature* **351**:748–51.

Puelles, L. and Rubenstein, J. 1993. Expression patterns of homeobox and other putative regulatory genes in the embryonic mouse forebrain suggest a neuromeric organization. *TINS* **16**:472–9.

Ranscht, B. and Dours-Zimmermann 1994. T-cadherin, a novel cadherin cell adhesion molecule in the nervous system lacks the conserved cytoplasmic region. *Neuron* **7**:391–402.

Riddle, R., Johnson, R., Laufer, E., and Tabin, C. 1993. *Sonic Hedgehog* mediates the polarizing activity of the ZPA. *Cell* **75**:1401–16.

Risch, N. 1990. Genetic linkage and complex disease, with special reference to psychiatric disorders. *Gen. Epidemiol.* **7**:3–16.

Rosahl, T.W., Hammer, R.E., Herz, J., Malenka, R.C., Missler, M., Selig, D.K., Spillane, D., Sudhof, T.C., and Wolff, J.R. 1993. Essential functions of synapsins 1 and 2 in synaptic vesicle regulation. *Nature* **375**:488–93.

Rose, S. 1991. How chicks make memories: the cellular cascade from *c-fos* to dendritic remodelling. *TINS* **14**:390–7.

Rosenthal, A., Jouet, M., and Kenwrick, S. 1992. Aberrant splicing of neural cell adhesion molecule L1 mRNA in a family with X-linked hydrocephalus. *Nat. Genet.* **2**:107–12.

Rubenstein, J.L.R., Martinez, S., Shimamuram K., and Puelles, L. 1994. The embryonic vertebrate forebrain: the prosomeric model. *Science* **266**:578–80.

Rugarli, E., Lutz, B., Kuratani, S., Wawersik, S., Borsani, G., Ballabio, A., and Eichele, G. 1993. Expression pattern of the Kallmann syndrome gene in the olfactory system suggests a role in neuronal targeting. *Nat. Genet.* **4**:19–26.

Ruiz i Altaba, A. 1994. Pattern formation in the vertebrate neural plate. *TINS* **17**:233–43.

Rutishauser, U., Acheson, A., Hall, A., Mann, D., and Sunshine,

J. 1988. The neural cell adhesion molecule (N-CAM) as a regulator of cell-cell interactions. *Science* 240:53–7.

Saffell, J., Walsh, F., and Doherty, P. 1992. Direct activation of second messenger pathways mimics cell adhesion molecule-dependent neurite outgrowth. *J. Cell Biol.* 118:663–70.

Serafini, T., Kennedy, T.E., Galko, M.J., Mirzayan, C., Jessell, T.M., and Tessier-Lavigne, M. 1994. The netrins define a family of axon outgrowth-promoting proteins homologous to *C. elegans* UNC-6. *Cell* 78:409–24.

Simeone, A., Acampora, D., Gulisano, M., Stornaiuolo, A., and Boncinelli, E. 1992a. Nested expression domains of four homeobox genes in developing rostral brain. *Nature* 358:687–90.

Simeone, A., Gulisano, M., Acampora, D., Stornaiuolo, A., Rambaldi, M., and Boncinelli, E. 1992b. Two vertebrate homeobox genes related to the *Drosophila* empty spiracles gene are expressed in the embryonic cerebral cortex. *EMBO J.* 11:2541–50.

Snider, W. 1994. Functions of the neurotrophins during nervous system development: what the knockouts are teaching us. *Cell* 77:627–38.

Söllner, T. and Rothman, J. 1994. Neurotransmission: harnessing fusion machinery at the synapse. *TINS* 17:344–7.

Sower, A.C., BeLue, R., Bird, E.D., and Perrone-Bizzozero, N.I. 1994. Altered GAP-43 and synaptophysin levels in visual association cortices from schizophrenic brains. *Soc. Neurosc. Abstr.* 20:261.7.

Steinberg, M. and Takeichi 1994. Experimental specification of cell sorting, tissue spreading, and specific spatial patterning by quantitative differences in cadherin expression. *Proc. Natl Acad. Sci. USA* 91:206–9.

Stevens, C. 1994. CREB and memory consolidation. *Neuron* 13:769–70.

Stoykova, A. and Gruss, P. 1994. Roles of *Pax*-genes in developing and adult brain as suggested by expression patterns. *J. Neurosci.* 14:1395–412.

Sudhof, T. 1995. The synaptic vesicle cascade: a cascade of protein-protein interactions. *Nature* 375:645–53.

Takahashi, J.S., Pinto, L.H., and Vitaterna, M.H. 1994. Forward and reverse genetic approaches to behavior in the mouse. *Science* 264:1724–33.

Tassabehji, M., Read, A., Newton, V., Harris, R., Balling, R., Gruss, P., and Strachan, T. 1992. Waardenburg's syndrome patients have mutations in the human homologue of the *Pax-3* paired box gene. *Nature* 355:635–6.

Terwilliger J.D. and Ott, J. 1992. A haplotype-based "Haplotype Relative Risk" approach to detecting allele association. *Hum. Hered.* 42:337–46.

Tomasiewicz, H., Goridis, C., Magnuson, T., Ono, K., Rutishauser, U., Thompson, C., and Yee, D. 1993. Genetic deletion of a neural cell adhesion molecule variant (N-CAM-180) produces distinct defects in the central nervous system. *Neuron* 11:1163–74.

Vicente, A., Honer, W., Bassett, A., Macciardi, F., and Kennedy, J. L. 1993. Antibody-selected candidate gene for schizophrenia: support for the neurodevelopment hypothesis. *Psychiatr. Genet.* 3:166.

Vicente, A., Sasaki, T., King, N., Barr, C., Dixon, L., Bassett, A., Honer, W., Macciardi, and F., Kennedy, J. L. 1994. Schizophrenia and the genetics of neurodevelopment. *Soc. Neurosci. Abstr.* 20:170.

Walker, E. 1994. Developmentally moderated expressions of the neuropathology underlying schizophrenia. *Schizophr. Bull.* 20:453–4.

Weeks, D.E. and Lange, K. 1988. The affected pedigree member method of linkage analysis. *Am. J. Hum. Genet.* 42:315–26.

Wegner, M., Drolet, D.W., and Rosenfeld, M.G. 1993. POU-domain proteins: structure and function of developmental regulators. *Curr. Op. Cell. Biol.* 5: 488–98.

Wilkinson, D., Bhatt, S., Cook, M., Boncinelli, E., and Krumlauf, R. 1989. Segmental expression of Hox-2 homeobox-containing genes in the developing mouse hindbrain. *Nature* 341:405–9.

Wilkinson, D.G. and Krumlauf, R. 1990. Molecular approaches to the segmentation of the hindbrain. *TINS* 13:335–9.

Wolpert, L. 1994. Do we understand development? *Science* 266: 571–2.

4

Glutamate receptors and developmental anomaly in medial temporal lobe in schizophrenia

ROBERT W. KERWIN, PAUL J. HARRISON, AND NICK STEFANIS

INTRODUCTION

There is now strong evidence for neuropathological changes in the medial temporal lobe in schizophrenia. Separate lines of work have uncovered a range of neurochemical abnormalities within medial temporal lobe structures in schizophrenic brains at post-mortem (Kerwin and Murray 1992). The most robust neurochemical abnormalities within this region are seen in the excitatory amino acid neurotransmitter system (Kerwin and Murray 1992). It is also apparent that during embryogenesis the glutamate receptor system plays a key role in controlling development in this region (McDonald and Johnstone 1990), and it would therefore be timely to explore the possibility that these glutamate receptor abnormalities are mechanistically linked to the dysplastic abnormalities seen in the medial temporal lobe of patients with schizophrenia.

THE GLUTAMATE RECEPTOR SYSTEM

The acidic amino acid L-glutamate is the major excitatory amino acid neurotransmitter system throughout the mammalian brain which also possesses a complex and functionally diverse receptor system. Initially, glutamate receptors were classified according to the rank potency of exogenous ligands named after them and three broad types were defined. These were kainic acid-preferring receptors, the kainate receptor; γ-amino-3-hydroxy-5-methyl-isoxazole propionic acid-preferring (AMPA) receptors; and N-methyl-D-aspartic acid-preferring (NMDA) recep-

tors. These are ion channel linked receptors. Later a further family of glutamate receptors was characterized that were metabolically transduced by g proteins, the metabotropic receptor family (for a review see Nakanishi 1992). This classification has undergone some revision with recent molecular cloning studies which suggest that AMPA and kainate genes can be separately defined but are probably assembled together as oligomers. The classification has thus been changed to NMDA and non-NMDA receptors (Seeburg 1993). Broadly speaking, there are seven AMPA genes designated GluR 1–7. GluR 1–4 subunits exhibit traditional AMPA receptor properties; GluR 5–7 exhibit properties similar to low affinity kainate receptors and kainate genes KA1 and KA2 have high affinity kainate properties. The NMDA receptors are assembled from two subunits NR1 and NR2; the NR2 subunit is further divided into NR2 A–D. Many of their receptor subunits also undergo differential splicing and RNA editing to give vast complexity to the system (for a review see Seeburg 1993). Five genetic subunits for the metabotropic receptors have been defined (Schoepp and Conn 1993).

The functions of the ionotropic receptors fall broadly into two categories. Non-NMDA receptors mediate the majority of fast excitatory neurotransmission. They have low permeability to calcium, therefore longer term alterations in cell metabolism, largely mediated by calcium, are unaffected. NMDA receptors flux calcium; therefore these receptors mediate a range of longer term changes, thought to be involved in memory learning and plasticity (McDonald and Johnstone 1990). Metabotropic glutamate receptors linked to second messenger systems probably have a modulatory role on a range of transmitter-mediated activities: they are thought to be particularly important in acting presynaptically to modulate neurotransmitter release.

It has been known since 1957 that glutamate may mediate neurotoxic processes via its own receptors and a role for glutamate in a wide variety of neurological and neurodegenerative processes has been well characterized (Dingledine *et al.* 1990; Meldrum and Garthwaite 1990). Because of the massive diversity of function and ubiquity of the glutamate system it has long been suggested that glutamate may play either a primary or secondary role in the pathophysiology of schizophrenia and glutamate theories for schizophrenia can be dated back to the work of Kim *et al.* (1980). Several separate theories for the role of glutamate systems in schizophrenia have now emerged and there are theories and experimental information concerning all three receptor subclasses for schizophrenia. These are not mutually exclusive and represent the interaction between a functionally diverse system and a complex disease. The theories may indeed be complementary as some abnormalities relate to pathology, others to dopamine glutamate interaction, and others offer hope for pharmacological intervention without postulating an underlying abnormality. The remainder of this review will concentrate on the relationship between medial temporal lobe glutamatergic abnormalities and their trophic function.

DEVELOPMENTALLY DETERMINED ABNORMALITIES

Although the precise magnitude of medial temporal lobe anomaly is in dispute, there is a strong body of evidence which suggests that this is a dysplastic process. Thus, although several early studies failed to show reactive astrocytosis in association with temporal lobe pathology (Falkai and Bogerts 1986; Roberts *et al.* 1986), generalized gliosis remains a feature of many studies (Stevens 1982; 1991).

Cytoarchitectonic and cytoskeletal abnormalities have also been found. The cytoarchitectonic studies show a migrational abnormality of the pre-alpha cells of the

entorhinal cortex which dates the abnormality to the second or third trimester (Jakob and Beckman 1989; Falkai and Bogerts 1986). A cytoskeletal abnormality has been shown in the subicular region of the hippocampus in schizophrenia, where staining for microtubule-associated protein (MAP 2) is severely reduced (Arnold *et al.* 1991). Further replications of these studies have yet to appear. Other migrational anomalies have been found in the temporal lobe with most notably abnormal layering of NADPH staining in neurons (Akbarian *et al.* 1993). Clinical evidence also suggests preschizophrenic putative developmentally triggered abnormalities. These range from perinatal difficulties and prematurity (Lewis and Murray 1987), significantly smaller head circumference (McNeil 1990), to minor physical anomalies (Waddington *et al.* 1990).

GLUTAMATE RECEPTORS AND THE TEMPORAL LOBE IN SCHIZOPHRENIA

Direct evidence of glutamatergic dysfunction in schizophrenia stems from postmortem studies utilizing receptor autoradiography, homogenate binding techniques and in situ hybridization, the most consistent finding so far being the loss of non-NMDA receptors and associated mRNA in hippocampus and entorhinal cortex. Kerwin *et al.* (1988), using enriched homogenates, found a loss of kainate receptor subtypes in hippocampus. In the first systematic localization of glutamate receptors subtypes in human hippocampus, Kerwin *et al.* (1990), demonstrated a significant reduction of kainate binding in CA4 and CA3 regions of the hippocampus and of quisqualate in CA4, while no abnormalities were observed for the NMDA receptor.

Later studies have shown losses of the mRNA encoding AMPA/kainate receptors. With the initial cloning of a rat brain non-NMDA glutamate receptor that encoded a region homologous to both kainate and AMPA receptor genes (glu R1), studies in schizophrenia were extended to look at the encoding mRNAs. Although the human gene sequence was not available it was shown that there was a homologous messenger mRNA in human brain (Harrison *et al.* 1991) and this was subsequently confirmed by partial sequencing of the gene (McLaughlin *et al.* 1993). Using this "pan probe" in an in situ habitization experiment Harrison et al. (1991), reported a 70% reduction of non-NMDA mRNA in the CA3 region of the hippocampus of schizophrenics. Thus, the reduced density of non-NMDA receptors found previously (Kerwin et al. 1990) is accompanied by, and presumably secondary to, reduced gene expression. The loss of glu-R1 mRNA in schizophrenia was gene-specific at least to a point in that other mRNA species were unaltered in the same specimens. This selectivity of gene expression involvement is in line with other data showing that overall gene expression in the schizophrenic brain is unaltered in terms of total or poly-adenylated messenger RNA content (Perrett et al. 1992). Recently, these findings have been replicated in a different series of brains and shown to be independent of pathology in the hippocampus (Eastwood et al. 1995).

Recently the complexity of a glutamate receptor gene family has become increasingly apparent and the mRNA data in schizophrenia (Harrison et al. 1991) must be reinterpreted in this light. There are now at least ten non-NMDA glutamate receptors subunit genes known, many of which undergo differential splicing and RNA editing (Gasic and Heinemann 1991). Non-NMDA receptor subunits are encoded by several genes whose products are preferentially activated by, though not selective for, α-amino-3-hydroxy-5-methyl-4-isoxazole propionate (AMPA) or kainate (KA). AMPA-preferring non-NMDA receptor genes comprise GluR1–4 also known as GluRA-D (Keinanen et al. 1990) whilst GluR5–7, KA 1 and KA2 are the genes encoding putative low and high affinity KA receptors (Hollman and Heinemann 1994). GluR1–4 transcripts have distinct expression patterns and are differentially spliced into "flip" and "flop" isoforms and GluR2 undergoes post-transcriptional RNA editing (Sommer et al. 1990). These features of non-NMDA glutamate receptor genes were determined initially in rodents but they are broadly similar for the human brain. The probe used in our initial study (Harrison et al. 1991) detected a region common to several transcripts (AMPA and KA); given that the interpretation of what the alterations mean for schizophrenia is different if several genes are affected than if only one, we have now repeated and extended our previous study using a new series of brains in which AMPA GluR2 mRNA as well as GluR1 mRNA

have been measured. A regional loss of GluR1 and GluR2 mRNA in dentate gyrus, CA4, CA3 and subiculum was observed in the range 25–70% (Eastwood et al. 1995). Although the underlying mechanism for the reduction of non-NMDA glutamate receptors and their respective genes is not clear, there might be a correlate of the neuro-developmental anomaly thought to underlie the pathogenesis of schizophrenia.

As for NMDA receptors, some studies provide no evidence for overall change in the NMDA receptors judged from autoradiography of the agonist recognition site (Kerwin et al. 1990), whilst other studies found a modest 15–20% elevation in the hippocampus. Post-mortem studies of the glycine regulatory site have revealed consistent elevations in temporal cortex (Waziri et al. 1992; Ishimaru et al. 1994).

To date there are four post-mortem studies of sigma and phencyclidine sites in schizophrenia. Simpson et al. (1992), reported a large reduction in the (3H)-3PPP binding in the amygdala, hippocampus, and frontal cortex of schizophrenics. Reynolds et al. (1991) using a specific sigma ligand (3H) DTG reported a clear deficit of sigma sites in cerebellum of schizophrenics. Weissman et al. (1991), found a reduction of sigma binding sites in the temporal lobe of schizophrenics using (3H) haloperidol but no reduction was observed on the PCP site. On the contrary Shibuya et al. (1992), found no reduction in sigma-binding sites between schizophrenics and controls in all brain areas studied.

Another possible way in which excitatory amino acids could be involved in the developmental pathogenesis of schizophrenia concerns their role in neuronal damage associated with hypoxia. It is now firmly established that excessive endogenous activity at excitatory amino acid receptors mediates some of the adverse consequences of ischemia (Collins 1986) and that psychotomimetic antagonists such as phencyclidine and MK801 can protect against this (Lyeth et al. 1989). It is therefore possible to conceptualize a role for excitatory amino acids in developmental processes adversely affected by pre- or perinatal hypoxia.

Indeed, Cruzio (1991) has suggested that cerebral ischemia secondary to viral infection or birth complications may lead to neuronal loss possibly mediated at glutamate receptors. Cruzio points out that large heritable differences in hippocampal anatomy are found between different inbred strains of mice, particularly with regard to the density of their infra- and intrapyramidal mossy fiber systems. Such different strains of mice show differing susceptibility to anoxia, thus providing a possible model for the interaction of genes and early environmental hazard in schizophrenia. This as yet untested hypothesis raises the possibility that, in view of the known interaction of genetic predisposition and obstetric complications in the offspring of schizophrenics, glutamate receptor blockers administered at the first sign of birth hypoxia might be of prophylactic value.

TESTING SPECIFIC HYPOTHESES

We have considered the combined literature on glutamatergic abnormalities in the medial temporal lobe in schizophrenia, developmental dysplasia in this region and the trophic role of glutamate. It should, therefore, be possible to test hypotheses regarding a causal link between these related phenomena. It is the general case that many classical neurotransmitters play a role of trophic factors during neuronal development. In particular glutamate plays an important role in hippocampal development (for a review see McDonald and Johnstone, 1990). As for the specific role of non-NMDA receptors, these control neurite outgrowth, polarity and orientation of pyramidal cells (Mattson 1988). It is likely that any dysplastic pathology in the first instance will be accompanied by abnormalities in cytoskeletal assembly. Abnormalities in immunocytochemical markers for cytoskeletal elements MAP 1B and MAP 2 have been reported in the hippocampus in schizophrenia (Arnold et al. 1991). Both NMDA and non-NMDA receptors control cytoskeletal assembly via protein kinase phosphorylation-mediated mechanisms (Bigot and Hunt 1991). Therefore, the specific hypothesis is that a primary abnormality in non-NMDA receptors disrupts cytoskeletal assembly resulting in a dysplastic abnormality in the hippocampal and that this leaves a residue of abnormal developmental message for non-NMDA receptors. The first task is to determine if there is an abnormality in the developmental form. It has been possible to show a differential localization of the flip and flop of GluR2 and to demonstrate an increased ratio of flip over flop in the brains of schizophrenics (Monyer et al. 1991; Eastwood et al. 1996). The next step would be to perform neuronal stereology and immunocytochemistry of MAPs and other elements of the cytoskeleton to look for an association. Proving the link will probably require neuronal expression systems containing cytoskeletal elements and a normal and "schizophrenic" pattern of non-NMDA gene products, and determine if there are any abnormalities in cytoskeletal assembly or phosphorylation state. In any event, there is a sufficient body of knowledge in the neurochemistry and neuropathology of schizophrenia to explore the fundamental developmental neurobiology of dysplastic mechanisms and their genetic and trophic origins.

REFERENCES

Akbarian, S., Vinuela, A., Kim, J.J., Potkin, S.G., Bunney, W.E., and Jones, E.G. 1993. Distorted distribution of nucotinamide-adenine dinucleotide phosphate-diaphorase neurons in temporal lobe of schizophrenics in anomalous cortical development. *Arch. Gen. Psychiat.* **50**:178–81.

Arnold, S., Lee, V., Gur, R., and Trojanowski, J.Q. 1991. Abnormal expression of two microtubule associated proteins (MAP2 and MAP5) in specific subfields of the hippocampal formation. *Proc. Natl. Acad. Sci. USA* **88**:10950–4.

Bigot, D. and Hunt, S.P. 1991. The effects of quisqualate and nocodazole on the organization of MAP2 and neurofilaments in spinal cord neurones in vitro. *Neurosci. Lett.* **131**:21–6.

Collins, R.C. 1986. Selective vulnerability of the brain. New insights from the excitatory synapse. *Metab. Brain Dis.* **1**:231–40.

Cruzio, W.E. 1991. The neuropsychology of schizophrenia: a perspective from neurobehavioural genetics. *Behav. Brain Sci.* **14**:23–4.

Dingledine, R., McBain, C.J., and McNamara, J.O. 1990. Excitatory amino acids in epilepsy. *Trends Pharmacol. Sci.* **11**:334–48.

Eastwood, S.L., McDonald, B., Burnet, P.W.J., Beckwith, J.P.,

Kerwin, R.W., and Harrison, P.J. 1995. Decreased
expression of MRNAs encoding non-NMDA glutamate
receptors GluR1 and GluR2 in medial temporal lobe
neurons in schizophrenia. *Mol. Brain. Res.* **29**:211–23.

Eastwood, S.L., Porter, R.H.P., Burnet, P.W.J, *et al.* 1996. Non-
NMDA glutamate receptor expression in schizophrenia.
Schizophr. Res. **18**:174 (abstract).

Falkai, P. and Bogerts, B. 1986. Cell loss in the hippocampus of
schizophrenia. *Eur. Arch. Psychiat. Neurol. Sci.* **236**:154–61.

Harrison, P., McLaughlin, D., and Kerwin, R.W. 1991.
Decreased hippocampal expression of a glutamate receptor
gene in schizophrenia. *Lancet* **337**: 450–2.

Hollman, M. and Heinemann, S. 1994. Cloned glutamate
receptors. *Ann. Neurosci.* **17**:31–108.

Ishimaru, M., Kurumagi, A., and Toru, M. 1994. Increases in
strychnine-insensitive glycine binding sites in cerebral
cortex of chronic schizophrenics : evidence for glutamate
hypothesis. *Biol. Psychiat.* **35**:84–95.

Jakob, H. and Beckmann, H. 1989. Gross and histological
criteria for developmental disorders in brains of
schizophrenics. *J. R. Soc. Med.* **82**:466–9.

Kethaänen, K., Wisden, W., Sommer, B. Wernerp, H.A.,
Verdoorn, T.A., Sakmann, B., and Seeberg, P.H. 1990.
A family of AMPA selective glutamate receptors. *Science*
249:556–60.

Kerwin, R.W. and Murray, R.M. 1992. A developmental
perspective on the pathology and neurochemistry of the
temporal lobe in schizophrenia. *Schizophr. Res.* **7**:1–12.

Kerwin, R.W., Patel, S., and Meldrum, B.S. 1990.
Autoradiographic localisation of the glutamate receptor
system in control and schizophrenic post-mortem
hippocampal formation. *Neuroscience* **39**:25–32.

Kerwin, R.W., Patel, S., Meldrum, B.S., Czudek, C., and
Reynolds, G.P. 1988. Asymmetrical loss of glutamate
receptor subtype in left hippocampus in schizophrenia.
Lancet **8585**:583–4.

Kim, J.S., Kornhuber, H.H., Schmid-Burgk, W., and
Holzmuller, B. 1980. Low cerebrospinal fluid glutamate
in schizophrenia patients and a new hypothesis on
schizophrenia. *Neurosci. Lett.* **20**:379–82.

Lewis, S.W. and Murray, R.M. 1987. Obstetric complications,
neurodevelopmental deviance and risk of schizophrenia.
J. Psychiat. Res. **21**:413–21.

Lyeth, B.G., Jenkins, L.W., Hamm, R.J., Dizon, E., Phillips,
L.L., Clifton, G.L., Young, H.F., and Hayes, R.L. 1989.
Pretreatment with MK801 reduces behavioural deficits
following traumatic brain injury. *Soc. Neurosci.* **15**:113
(abstract).

McDonald, J.W. and Johnstone, M.W. 1990. Physiological and
pathophysiological roles of excitatory amino acids during
central nervous system development. *Brain Res. Rev.*
15:41–70.

McLaughlin, D.P., Cheetham, M.F., and Kerwin, R.W. 1993.
Expression of alternatively spliced glutamate receptors in
human hippocampus. *Env. J. Pharmacol. Mol. Pharmacol.*
244:89–92.

McNeil, T.F. 1990. Head circumference at birth in
schizophrenic patients. Paper presented at the *WPA
Regional Symposium,* in August: in Oslo.

Mattson, M.P. 1988. Neurotransmitters in the regulation of
neuronal cytoarchitecture. *Brain Res. Rev.* **13**:179–212.

Meldrum, B. and Garthwaite, J. 1990. Excitatory amino acid
neurotoxicity and neurodegenerative disease. *Trends
Pharmacol. Sci.* **11**:379–87.

Monyer, H., Seeburg, P., and Wisden, W. 1991. Glutamate
operated channels: developmentally early and mature
forms arise by alternative splicing. *Neuron* **6**:799–810.

Nakanishi, S. 1992. Molecular diversity of the glutamate
receptors. *Clin. Neuropharmacol.* **15**:4A-5A.

Perrett, C.W., Whatley, S.A., Ferrier, I.N., and Marchbanks,
R.M. 1992. Changes in relative levels of specific brain
mRNA species associated with schizophrenia and
depression. *Mol. Brain Res.* **12**:163–71.

Reynolds, G.B., Brown, J.E., and Middlemiss, D.N. 1991. 3H
ditolylguequidine binding to human brain sigma sites is
diminished after haloperidol treatment. *Eur. Pharmacol.*
194:235–6.

Roberts, G.W., Colter, N., Lofthouse, R., Bogerts, B., Zech, N.,
and Crow, T.J. 1986. Gliosis in schizophrenia. *Biol.
Psychiat.* **21**:1043–50.

Roberts, G.W. 1990. Schizophrenia: a neuropathological
perspective. *Br. J. Psychiat.* **158**:8–17.

Schoepp, D.P. and Conn, P.J. 1993. Metabotropic glutamate
receptors in brain function and pathology. *Trends
Pharmacol. Sci.* **14**:13–20.

Seeburg, P.H. 1993. The molecular biology of glutamate
receptor channels. *Trends Neurosci.* **16**:359–65.

Shibuya, H., Movi, H., and Toru, M. 1992. Sigma receptors

in schizophrenic cerebral cortics. *Neurochem. Res.* **17**:983.

Simpson, M.D.C., Slater, P., Royston, M.C., and Deakin, J.F.W. 1992. Alterations in phencyclidine and sigma sites in schizophrenic brains effects the disease process and neuroleptic medication. *Schizophr. Res.* **6**:41–8.

Sommer, B., Kethaänen, K., Verdoorn, T.A., Wisden, W., Burnashev, N., Herb, A., Kohler, M., Takagi, T., Sakmann, B., and Seeburg, P.H. 1990. Flip and flop: a cell specific functional switch in glutamate-operated channels of the CNS. *Science* **249**:1580–85.

Stevens, J.R. 1982. Neuropathology of schizophrenia. *Arch. Gen. Psychiat.* **39**:1131–9.

Stevens, J.R. 1991. Schizophrenia static or progressive pathophysiology. *Schizophr. Res.* **4**:184–6.

Waddington, J.L., O'Callaghan, E., and Larkin, C. 1990. Physical anomalies and neurodevelopmental abnormality in schizophrenia: new clinical correlates. *Schizophr. Res.* **3**:90.

Waziri, R., Baruah, S., and Sherman, A.D. 1992. Abnormal serine-glycine metabolism in the brains of schizophrenics. *Schiz. Res.* **8**:233–43.

Weissman, A.D., Casanova, M.F., Kleinman, J.E., London, E.D., and De Souza, E.B. 1991. Selective loss of cerebral cortical sigma but not PCP binding sites in schizophrenia. *Biol. Psychiat.* **29**:41.

5

Magnetic resonance imaging studies of developing brain

TERRY L. JERNIGAN
AND ELIZABETH R. SOWELL

INTRODUCTION

In recent years, evidence has accumulated that implicates neurodevelopmental factors in the pathogenesis of several major psychiatric disorders, particularly those within the schizophrenia spectrum. Contributing to this evidence are findings in adult patients of neuroanatomical anomalies suggestive of altered brain development. Attempts to model the processes by which such anomalies arise depend of necessity on our understanding of normal brain maturation. High resolution magnetic resonance imaging (MRI), by virtue of its lack of medical contraindications, is an appropriate method for monitoring brain maturation in young subjects. In this chapter, the results of MRI studies of normally developing children will be summarized. As the reader will discover, the work carried out to date concentrates heavily on the earliest postnatal developmental stages, when brain growth is most pronounced. Also, the majority of the studies attempt to detect and describe changes in the signal characteristics of the different tissues while only a few studies have examined morphological changes. As new developments in imaging methods continue to improve anatomical precision and reduce imaging time, and as sensitive morphometric techniques become more widely used, it is likely that much more detail about the nature and course of human brain maturation will emerge. A particularly exciting development, functional magnetic resonance imaging (fMRI), promises to greatly expand the uses of MRI in neurodevelopmental research.

The considerable advantages of MRI for use in developmental populations are balanced to some extent by a few logistical difficulties. Most imaging protocols used for research purposes require several minutes for image acquisition during which time the subject must remain motionless if the images are to be of high quality. Many young children are unable to exercise the needed restraint to complete such examinations without sedation, and some investigators have been reluctant to use sedation in groups of normally developing children. For this reason, much of the information available about very young children comes from studies of children undergoing clinical evaluation. Although attempts are made to exclude subjects in whom the experimental measures might be influenced by covert disease processes, the findings may nevertheless be subtly affected. The problems associated with subject movement during imaging are likely to abate to some extent with newer, very fast, imaging protocols. Even with conventional protocols, however, investigators usually find that, with special coaching, most children over 6 years of age can participate successfully without sedation.

STUDIES OF CHANGING TISSUE CHARACTERISTICS

One of the major strengths of MRI derives from the excellent signal contrast it provides between gray and white matter in the brain. This contrast, which is due to the myelination of white matter, evolves postnatally, and is therefore easily observable with MRI. As the process of myelination occurs the water content of the brain decreases. Myelination gliosis results in increases in lipid and protein content in the myelinating tissue. These changes are reflected in signal changes on MRI. Barkovich *et al.* (1988) and Girard *et al.* (1991) have discussed the relationship between MRI signal changes and the mechanisms governing myelination.

Barkovich *et al.* (1988) examined the changes on T1–weighted (T1W) and T2–weighted (T2W) MR images in 82 infants ranging from 4 days to 2 years of age. The contrast between signal intensity in the white and gray matter was rated subjectively within 14 different brain regions. At birth, very little contrast was observed; however, by 3–6 months of age contrast was observable in central frontal lobe regions with T1W images. On the other hand, this region did not reliably show gray/white contrast on T2W images until 11–16 months of age. These authors noted that the signal changes that accompany myelination progress systematically from the brainstem into cerebellum and cerebrum. They speculated that the earlier changes on T1W images may reflect beginning development of the myelin sheath, whereas the changes on T2W images may be more strongly related to myelination per se. Martin *et al.* (1988) also attempted to stage the progress of myelination subjectively in four regions: the internal capsule, and within frontal, temporal, and occipital lobes. Fifty infants and young children were studied with both T1W and T2W images. The authors also noted that T1W images were more useful for monitoring the earliest stages of myelination, and described a pattern in which myelination generally proceeded rostrally. Based on T1W and T2W images from 36 infants ranging from 3 weeks to 2 years of age, Hayakawa *et al.* (1990) described three stages of brain maturation during this period. It was noted that on T1W images of infants less than 4 weeks of age the signal intensity of white matter was actually detectably lower than that of gray matter throughout much of the brain. Some limited areas of high signal, however, were detectable in brainstem, cerebellum, internal capsule, and centrum semiovale. Between 1 and 6 months of age, however, the white matter and gray matter were generally isointense, although some additional high signal areas could be observed in the corpus callosum, optic radiations, and perirolandic gyri. In the final stage, usually after 7 months of age, high signal areas extended into the rest of the cerebral hemispheres. Like other authors, Hayakawa *et al.* found the T2W images relatively uninformative in the infants. They noted that gray and white matter did not

show adult-like signal contrast on T2W images until around 18 months of age.

Finally, Dietrich *et al.* (1988) focused on the changes in the centrum semiovale region on T2W images in 34 normal infants. They reported that the signal intensity of white matter was generally higher than that of gray matter until 8 months of age, was isointense with gray matter from 8 to 12 months, and was clearly lower after 12 months.

Two studies focused not on the progression of myelination over the first few years, but on the variability observed on MRI in the immediate perinatal period. McArdle *et al.* (1987) examined 51 infants ranging in age from 29 to 42 weeks after conception, using T1W images. Lower white matter than gray matter intensity was observed in the youngest infants, with the images of the older infants showing little signal contrast. Quantitative measures of the signal of white matter were collected and expressed as ratios with the signal of vitreous fluid in the orbital region. Analysis of age-related changes in these measures confirmed that the loss of contrast observed in the older infants was reflective of increasing signal intensity in white matter. These authors also attempted to describe qualitatively the prominent changes in cortical gyration that occur during this age range. Girard *et al.* (1991) also studied newborns, aged 40–62 weeks postnatal, and described similar changes on T1W and T2W images. These authors attempted to relate specific observed changes in MRI signals to biochemical alterations that attend processes of brain maturation.

A few studies have examined the changes in tissue characteristics over a wider age range. Hayakawa *et al.* collected T2W MR images in 90 subjects ranging from 6 months to 60 years of age. They selected a single 10 mm section through the centrum semiovale in each subject and traced first the outline of the entire cerebral hemisphere and then the visual border between low signal (presumably white matter) and high signal (presumably cortical) regions within the hemisphere. The area of the low signal region was then expressed as a proportion of the hemisphere area. The proportion ranged from about 23% in 6 to 12 month-old subjects to around 55% at age 60 years. The increase was most dramatic between 6 and 36 months of age, but gradual continuing increases were apparent throughout childhood. These data are consistent with earlier post-mortem studies of myelination, notably Yakovlev and Lecours (1967), which suggests continuing myelination into the third decade of life.

Signal values within different brain regions were measured from T2W images of 66 normal subjects ranging from 4 to 50 years of age (Autti *et al.* 1994) . These values were standardized to the values from water and cerebrospinal fluid samples. The results showed that signal values throughout the brain decreased rapidly during the first decade and continued to decline until around 18 years of age. The decreases were generally parallel for white matter and deep gray matter regions; however, the globus pallidus and thalamus values decreased more rapidly than those in other regions. The authors pointed out that these changes associated with late brain maturation, because they occur in both white and gray matter, were generally not apparent on visual inspection of the images.

Holland *et al.* (1986), examined 59 subjects including newborns, children, and adolescents up to 16 years of age. They reported qualitative changes in infants consistent with those described above. These authors also computed estimates of T1 and T2 relaxation times from several regions within the brain. Mean estimated T1 of white matter declined dramatically during the first year of life from 1615 ms at birth to 580 ms at 1 year of age. Only a slow decline, to 487ms, occurred in the older group. Gray matter T1 changed similarly from 1590 ms at birth (lower than white matter) to 890 ms at 1 year (higher than white matter). At age 14 years, T1 of gray matter was reduced only slightly further to 805 ms.

At birth, T2 estimates were very similar in gray and white matter (88 and 91 ms, respectively) and gray and white matter values declined similarly over the first 6 months (to 67 and 64 ms, respectively). By 1 year of age, however, white matter values had declined to 57 ms while gray matter values remained at 68 ms. By age 14 years, both white and gray matter values showed some further decline (to 49 and 59 ms, respectively).

Hassink *et al.* (1992) also computed estimates of T2 within several white matter regions throughout the cerebral hemispheres. They compared small groups of subjects who were either 8, 10, or 24–25 years of age. Significant decreases were observed in the oldest group for all regions except the splenium of the corpus callosum. Only the internal capsule showed a significant decrease from 8 to 10 years of age.

In summary, numerous qualitative studies, and a few quantitative investigations, all suggest that the earliest stages of myelination are best visualized on T1W images. Contrast consistent with myelination of white matter appears first in caudal and posterior regions and generally proceeds rostrally and anteriorly. After 18 months of age, continuing changes are observable on T2W images. Quantitative studies suggest definite decreases in brain relaxation times that are sometimes not visually discernible in the images. These decreases continue at least into the postpubertal period.

STUDIES OF MORPHOLOGICAL CHANGES

The studies reviewed above focused on changing MR signal characteristics of white and gray matter during brain maturation; however, changes also occur in the sizes and shapes of specific brain structures. In this section, systematic attempts to describe these changes as they are manifest in MR images will be discussed. The earliest studies described the changes in qualitative terms; however, recent studies have included morphometric techniques that permit quantitative analysis of the results.

Among the most dramatic morphological changes observable on MRI in the earliest stages of development is cortical gyration. Martin *et al.* (1988) described four stages of cortical gyration from lissencephaly through the fully mature pattern. Stage 1 was defined by a smooth brain surface; stage 2 by the appearance of the primary gyri separated by shallow fluid-filled sulci; stage 3 by the presence of deeply infolded sulci containing no CSF; and stage 4 by deep, fluid-filled sulci separating primary and secondary gyri. Generally, gyration was rated as stage 2 in full-term newborns. The authors reported that stage 4 was reached by 25% of the infants by 87 weeks after conception, and by 75% of the infants by 143 weeks. Barkovich and Truwit (1990) published an *Atlas of Neonatal Brain Development* that describes and illustrates with representative images the gross morphological changes associated with brain maturation, beginning at 31 weeks gestation. Some of the developmental changes illustrated are: myelination, corpus callosum development, cortical gyration, bone marrow signal changes, and normal iron deposition. When relevant, both T1W and T2W images are provided for contrast.

The corpus callosum has been the subject of a number of morphological studies because it is well visualized in the midsagittal plane. Barkovich and Kjos (1988) studied developmental changes in the callosum during the first year of life. They described the morphology of the callosum as "uniformly thin" in the first month. They observed that first the genu and then the splenium undergo rapid growth spurts during the next five months, resulting in their characteristic "bulbous" appearance. Signal contrast associated with myelination was noted in T1W images, first in the splenium around 4 months of age, and then in the genu at about 6 months, so that the callosum was described as essentially adult-like on midsagittal images at about 8 months of age. Though these results are essentially the same as those observed by others, it should be noted that all of the infants underwent MRI examination for clinical reasons, and nearly half because of seizures. Thus some caution regarding the generalizability of detailed observations is warranted.

Rauch and Jenkins (1994) conducted a study of corpus callosum size in subjects over a much larger age range. Development of the callosum was assessed by computing a callosal index. The area of the callosum on a midsagittal section was divided by the area of the cerebrum on the same section. Continuing age-related increases in this index were observed over the first two decades. Interestingly, no gender differences in the index were observed.

Raininko et al. (1994) also examined changes on MRI from infancy to old age, focusing on brainstem structures. A number of linear measurements were made of mesencephalon, pons, and medulla oblongata in 174 subjects ranging in age from 4 months to 86 years. Eighty-six of these subjects were under 21 years of age. Examination of the differences between the age groups revealed that linear measurements of the dimensions of the mesencephalon did not appear to increase beyond 6 years of age, though the peduncular region may continue to grow slightly into

adolescence. The dimensions of the medulla oblongata were also similar to adults by the time the children were 6–8 years of age; however, both sagittal and coronal dimensions of the pons appeared to increase until age 20 years.

Volumetric studies of extended processes of brain maturation

In general, the development of the mammalian nervous system is known to involve both progressive and regressive events (Purves and Lichtman 1980). Neuronal proliferation occurs mostly prenatally and is followed by a dramatic, mostly postnatal, glial proliferation that gives rise to the brain growth spurt. Many more neurons are generated than survive, and the maturation of the surviving neurons involves the elimination of many processes and synapses. Although it has been well demonstrated, both in postmortem and brain imaging studies, that the human brain has an adult-like size and appearance by age 5 years or so, there is also evidence for important changes continuing into adulthood. As noted above, Yakovlev and Lecours (1967) demonstrated continuing myelination of subcortical white matter, particularly in what they referred to as "supralimbic" regions, into the third decade of life, using post-mortem material. Huttenlocher (1979) and Huttenlocher and de Courten (1987) examined synaptic density in cortical regions of autopsied brains and found evidence for significant decreases in late childhood and adolescence. Additional evidence comes from work in non-human primates (Zecevic and Rakic 1991) which has demonstrated marked reductions in cortical synaptic density during the peripubertal period of development. MRI has made it possible to look for correlates of these later maturational changes in normally developing older children and adolescents.

Excellent tissue contrast in MR images has encouraged the development of methods for doing automated or semi-automated tissue segmentation of MRI brain datasets. Such segmentation permits quantitative analysis of estimated volumes of the different tissue compartments in the brain, and also greatly facilitates the neuromorphological analysis of more specific brain regions and structures. In a series of studies (Jernigan and Tallal 1990; Jernigan et al. 1991; E.R. Sowell and T.L. Jernigan, in press) such methods have been applied to the investigation of late-childhood and adolescent brain maturation.

The methods employed in these studies involved the use of a dual-echo spin echo imaging protocol that renders two registered images for each brain section, one of which is T2–weighted and the other proton density weighted. Combining the information in these images, and using additional information about signal values in manually selected tissue samples, each pixel determined to be within the brain was classified as most like gray matter, white matter, or cerebrospinal fluid (CSF). Consistently identifiable anatomical landmarks and structural boundaries were then designated by trained image-analysts who were unaware of any subject characteristics. In this way, cerebral regions and structural boundaries were defined either manually or, when boundaries could not be visually identified on a reliable basis, using a combination of manual and stereotactic procedures.

In 1990, Jernigan and Tallal reported that a group of young subjects aged 8–10 years had a significantly higher proportion of gray to white matter in the cerebral hemispheres than did a group of young adults. A later study (Jernigan et al. 1991) examined the brains of these subjects in greater detail, and included a larger group of 39 subjects ranging in age from 8 to 35 years.

This study showed that the volume of the total cerebral cranial vault increased only very slightly across this age range, although there was evidence that dorsal, particularly dorsal frontal, regions might grow more during this period than other regions. More interestingly, there were highly significant age-related decreases in the volume of the cortex in these dorsal regions, with concomitant increases in CSF in the overlying sulci. In contrast, no significant volume decreases were observed in the ventral cortical regions.

The gray matter volume decreases observed were not confined to cortical areas. A number of subcortical gray matter structures, including the caudate and lenticular nuclei and the thalamus, showed volume decreases similar to those observed in dorsal cortical regions; and there were significant volume increases in the adjacent ventricular CSF. Unexpectedly, one of the subcortical gray matter regions measured, a region including hypothalamus, septal nuclei, and other very anterior structures in the dien-

cephalon, actually showed a significant volume increase across the age range. Jernigan et al. (1991) speculated that the regional cortical volume decreases they observed might be related to the reductions in synaptic density that had been reported by others (Huttenlocher 1979; Huttenlocher and de Courten 1987; Zecevic and Rakic 1991), and thus might reflect the later stages of functional maturation of these cortical regions. They also raised the possibility that the unexpected volume increase in the anterior diencephalic region might be related to trophic effects of gonadal steroid hormones in the peripubertal period. The density of receptors for these hormones has been reported to be very high within several of the structures in this region (e.g., hypothalamus and septal nuclei) (Stumph and Sar 1978; Rainbow et al. 1982).

Sowell and Jernigan (in press) recently conducted a study to extend the findings reviewed above. Many of the same subjects were examined, and the sample was extended to include 57 male and female subjects, again ranging from 8 to 35 years of age. The study was designed to examine in more detail the ventral cortical regions in which no age-related volume decreases had been observed in the earlier study. As this region contained both neocortical and limbic structures, and because the earlier study had suggested that related limbic structures in the hypothalamus might show changes distinct from that of other gray matter structures, attempts were made to separate the limbic from nonlimbic cortical regions. To this end, the structures on the mesial surface of the temporal lobe were circumscribed and volumed separately from the remaining ventral cortical regions of the frontal and temporal lobes. The results showed that, contrary to our earlier findings, both ventral cortical regions showed age related changes. The mesial temporal lobe structures, however, increased significantly in volume, while the remaining cortical structures decreased significantly.

To summarize the results of these studies, significant decreases in estimated volumes of neocortical, basal ganglia, and nonlimbic diencephalic structures were observed, as were significant increases in the volume of the adjacent CSF spaces. In combination, these observations suggest that regressive changes continue through late childhood and adolescence, perhaps in association with completion of the myelination process and reductions in synaptic density. On the other hand, there is evidence for continued growth as well during this period, in limbic regions of the temporal lobe and diencephalon. These volume increases may be related to hormonal factors. Trophic effects of gonadal steroid hormones on neural tissue have been demonstrated (Jones 1988).

Events such as those reflected in the MRI changes just described may have widespread functional implications, and may play an important role in the pathogenesis of major psychiatric disorders. In particular, an understanding of such processes of late brain maturation may help to explain the onset of symptoms in many psychiatric patients during adolescence and early adulthood. A part of the pathophysiology of schizophrenia, for example, may be a disturbance of the final regressive events that stabilize patterns of connectivity in late-maturing neural systems. The fact that both volume increases and volume decreases were observed in different regions suggests that these morphological effects arise dynamically as a result of multiple processes, and it is not yet clear whether these processes are related, or relatively independent, and whether they have different specific functional correlates. Further studies of normally developing individuals, with MRI and other evolving techniques, may address some of these questions.

Since these studies by Jernigan and associates, other investigators have also examined children and adolescents with neuromorphometric techniques. In a study of normal youngsters and subjects with attention deficit hyperactivity disorder, the caudate nucleus was carefully volumed by Castellanos et al. (1994). In 48 normal boys ranging in age from 5.5 to 17.8 years, significant age-related volume reductions were observed in the caudate nucleus, consistent with the results of Jernigan et al. These authors also reported that the normal caudate nucleus shows a slight, but significant, volume asymmetry, with the right caudate being somewhat larger.

An impressive study was recently reported by Pfefferbaum et al. (1994). They examined 88 subjects ranging in age from 3 months to 30 years who underwent MRI for clinical evaluations (as well as a cohort of adult subjects who were normal volunteers). In all of the clinical cases included the MRI films had been read as normal, and there was no clinical evidence for the presence of a neuro-

logical disorder. Most referrals were for headaches or dizziness. A semi-automated image-segmentation method was used to process the MRI data. This method yielded estimates of cranial size, cortical gray matter volume, white matter volume in the cortical region, and sulcal and ventricular CSF volume. The data were analyzed with a series of nonlinear regression methods. Results suggested brain growth until 10 years of age. The cortical gray matter volume increased significantly until about 4 years of age and then declined thereafter. The white matter volume increased steadily until about age 20 years. CSF volumes showed no significant monotonic changes in the young subjects. There was some evidence that the sulcal volumes first decreased and then increased in the range from birth to 30 years of age. Although the overall brain size of male subjects was significantly larger than that of female subjects there were no further sex differences or interactions between age and sex. These results, like those of the earlier studies, show that morphometric techniques can be used to monitor ongoing progressive and regressive processes during neurodevelopment.

A NEW METHOD: FUNCTIONAL MAGNETIC RESONANCE IMAGING

A particularly exciting possibility for future studies of developing children and adolescents involves the use of MRI for functional brain imaging (fMRI). It was recently demonstrated that the MR signal used to construct images of the brain's structure is also influenced by local functional properties of the tissue (for a review see Cohen and Bookheimer 1994). Specifically, the signal is slightly altered by the degree of oxygenation of the blood, because deoxyhemoglobin is paramagnetic and therefore slightly reduces the MR signal. When mental activity requires increased neuronal function there is an increase in blood flow to the areas of the brain involved in that activity. Although there is probably also an increase in oxygen use by the neurons in these areas, this increase is not commensurate with the increase in blood flow. In consequence, the blood in the areas involved becomes more oxygenated (has a lower concentration of deoxyhemoglobin), and this results in a local increase in the MR signal. Using specialized MRI techniques, this signal change can be measured and mapped throughout the brain. Thus there is the potential to use fMRI to determine the different patterns of brain activity that characterize different mental activities, by comparing the results obtained in people while they are doing different mental tasks.

Techniques for applying fMRI are evolving rapidly and the method is under very heavy use for mapping sensory, perceptual, and cognitive functions, mostly in young adult volunteers. It is very likely that the regional patterns of brain activation for specific mental activities change during development. If such changes can be determined, the results are likely to shed considerable light on the evolution of normal brain functions. A number of specific behavioral deficits are known to be prevalent in specific psychiatric disorders. It is an exciting prospect that fMRI may someday be used to elucidate the ways in which brain organization for these functions differs in patients. Furthermore, it may be possible to determine whether a shift from normal to abnormal organization occurs during the development of a psychiatric disorder by tracking developmental changes in young subjects at-risk to develop these disorders.

In summary, MRI has contributed to our understanding of normal brain maturation and has made it possible to detect deviant brain development during life. Although some detailed, quantitative studies have been conducted, many questions remain about the specific nature and location of structural changes in the brain during development, and especially about their functional significance. It is feasible to address many of these questions using MRI in normal children. Future studies should use longitudinal designs, very high resolution structural imaging protocols, and should, whenever possible, combine anatomical studies with the use of well-validated behavioral activation paradigms and fMRI.

ACKNOWLEDGMENT

Investigations conducted in our laboratory were supported by funds from the Medical Research Service of the department of Veterans Affairs to Dr Terry Jernigan, and grant P01 DC01289 from the National Institutes of Health for the Center for Developmental Cognitive Neuroscience.

REFERENCES

Autti, T., Raininko, R., Vanhanen, S.L., Kallio, M., and Santavuori, P. 1994. MRI of the normal brain from early childhood to middle age. II. Age dependence of signal intensity changes on T2–weighted images. *Neuroradiology* 36:649–51.

Barkovich, A.J. and Kjos, B.O. 1988. Normal postnatal development of the corpus callosum as demonstrated by MR imaging. *Am. J. Neuroradiol.* 9:487–91.

Barkovich, A.J., Kjos, B.O., Jackson, D.E., and Norman, D. 1988. Normal maturation of the neonatal and infant brain: MR imaging at 1.5 T. *Neuroradiology* 166:173–180.

Barkovich, A.J. and Truwit, C.L. 1990. *Practical MRI Atlas of Neonatal Brain Development*. New York: Raven Press.

Castellanos, F.X., Giedd, J.N., Eckburg, P., Marsh, W.L., Vaituzis, A.C., Kaysen, D., Hamburger, S.D., and Rapoport, J.L. 1994. Quantitative morphology of the caudate nucleus in attention deficit hyperactivity disorder. *Am. J. Psychiatry* 151:1791–6.

Cohen, M.S. and Bookheimer, S.Y. 1994. Localization of brain function using magnetic resonance imaging. *Trends Neurosci.* 17:268–77.

Dietrich, R.B., Bradley, W.G., Zaragoza, E.J., Otto, R.J., Taira, R.K., Wilson, G.H., and Kangarloo, H. 1988. MR evaluation of early myelination patterns in normal and developmentally delayed infants. *Am. J. Roentgenol.* 150:889–96.

Girard, N., Raybaude C., and du Lac, P. 1991. MRI study of brain myelination. *J. Neuroradiol.* 18:291–307.

Hassink, R.I., Hiltbrunner, B., Muller, S., and Lutschg, J. 1992. Assessment of brain maturation by T2–weighted MRI. *Neuropediatrics* 23:72–4.

Hayakawa, K., Konishi, Y., Kuriyama, M., Konishi, K., and Matsuda, T. 1990. Normal brain maturation in MRI. *Eur. J. Radiol.* 12: 208–15.

Holland, B.A., Haas, D.K., Norman, D., Brant-Zawadzki, M., and Newton, T.H. 1986. MRI of normal brain maturation. *Am. J. Neuroradiol.* 7:201–8.

Huttenlocher, P.R. 1979. Synaptic density in human frontal

cortex:developmental changes and effects of aging. *Brain Res.* **163**:195–205.

Huttenlocher, P.R., and de Courten, C. 1987. The development of synapses in striate cortex of man. *Hum. Neurobiol.* **6**:1–9.

Jernigan, T.L. and Tallal, P. 1990. Late childhood changes in brain morphology observable with MRI. *Devel. Med. Child Neurol.* **32**: 379–85.

Jernigan, T.L., Trauner, D.A., Hesselink, J.R., and Tallal, P.A. 1991. Maturation of the human cerebrum observed in vivo during adolescence. *Brain* **114**: 2037–49.

Jones, K.J. 1988. Steroid hormones and neurotrophism: relationship to nerve injury. *Metab. Brain Dis.* **3**:1–18.

McArdle, C.B., Richardson, C.J., Nicholas, D.A., Mirfakhraee, M., Hayden, C.K., and Amparo, E.G. 1987. Developmental features of the neonatal brain:MR imaging, Part I. Gray-white matter differentiation and myelination. *Radiology* **162**:223–9.

Martin, E., Kikinis, R., Zuerrer, M., Boesch, C., Briner, J., Kewitz, G., and Kaelin, P. 1988. Developmental stages of human brain: an MR study. *J. Comput. Assist. Tomogr.* **12**:917–22.

Pfefferbaum, A., Mathalon, D.H., Sullivan, E.V., Rawles, J.M., Zipursky, R.B., and Lim, K.O. 1994. A quantitative magnetic resonance imaging study of changes in brain morphology from infancy to late adulthood. *Arch. Neurol.* **51**:874–87.

Purves, D. and Lichtman, J.W. 1980. Elimination of synapses in the developing nervous system. *Science* **210**:153–7.

Rainbow, T.C., Parsons, B., MacLusky, N.J., and McEwen, B.S. 1982. Estradiol receptor levels in rat hypothalamic and limbic nuclei. *J. Neurosci.* **2**:1439–45.

Raininko, R., Autti, T., Vanhanen, S.L., Ylikoski, A., Erkinjuntti, T., and Santavuori, P. 1994. The normal brain stem from infancy to old age: a morphometric MRI study. *Neuroradiology* **36**:364–8.

Rauch, R.A. and Jenkins, .J.R. 1994. Analysis of cross-sectional area measurements of the corpus callosum adjusted for brain size in male and female subjects from childhood to adulthood. *Behav. Brain Res.* **64**:65–78.

Sowell, E.R. and Jernigan, T.L. Further MRI evidence of late brain maturation: limbic volume increases and changing asymmetries during childhood and adolescence. *Developmental Neuropsychology* (in press).

Stumph, W.E. and Sar, M. 1978. Anatomical distribution of estrogen, androgen, progestin, corticosteroid and thyroid hormone target sites in the brain of mammals: phylogeny and ontogeny. *Am. Zoo.* **18**:435–45.

Yakovlev, P.I. and Lecours, A.R. 1967. The myelogenetic cycles of regional maturation of the brain. In *Regional development of the brain in early life*, ed. A. Minkowski, pp. 3–70. Oxford: Blackwell Scientific.

Zecevic, N. and Rakic, P. 1991. Synaptogenesis in monkey somatosensory cortex. *Cerebral Cortex* **1**:510–23.

6

^{31}P magnetic resonance spectroscopy studies of developing brain

JAY W. PETTEGREW, RICHARD J. MCCLURE,
MATCHERI S. KESHAVAN, NANCY J. MINSHEW,
KANAGASABAI PANCHALINGAM,
AND WILLIAM E. KLUNK

INTRODUCTION

^{31}P magnetic resonance spectroscopy (MRS) provides a powerful noninvasive technique to study neurodevelopmental processes. Many of these neurodevelopmental events involve either the formation of membranes, such as the proliferation of dendritic spines in synaptic development, or the degradation of membranes, such as synaptic pruning. ^{31}P MRS is well suited to monitor both types of processes by measuring metabolite levels implicated in membrane synthesis and degradation. Also, high-energy phosphate metabolite levels are obtained that reflect the energy metabolism associated with these processes. In this chapter we describe the biochemical changes in neuronal development in the brain that we can monitor by ^{31}P MRS and its relevance to in vivo ^{31}P MRS studies of neuropsychiatric disorders.

NORMAL BRAIN DEVELOPMENT

Human brain

A basic understanding of neuronal development in the human brain is essential to interpret the biochemical changes monitored by ^{31}P MRS. The four major stages that characterize neuronal development of the human brain are: (1) neuronal proliferation; (2) migration of neurons to specific sites throughout the CNS; (3) organization of the neuronal circuitry; and (4) myelination of the neuronal circuitry (Volpe 1995).

The external form of the brain is established during the first 6 weeks of gestation. This is followed by neuronal proliferation that peaks during the second to fourth month of gestation. Glial proliferation begins later, occurring from approximately 5 months of gestation to 1 year (or more) of age (Volpe 1995). All neurons and glia originate from the ventricular and subventricular zones of cellular membranes throughout the CNS.

The second stage of neuronal development is characterized by the migration of millions of nerve cells from the ventricular and subventricular zones to loci within the CNS where they remain for life. The time for this stage overlaps the neuronal proliferation stage, peaking in the third to fifth month of gestation. Two major events are involved: (1) radial migration in the cerebral cortex to form the cerebral cortex and deep nuclear structures; and (2) radial migration in the cerebellum to form Purkinje cells, the dentate, and other roof nuclei, and tangential migration in the cerebellum to form the internal granule cell layer of the cerebellar cortex. The migration of neurons in the cerebral cortex is completed by 20–24 weeks of gestation (Volpe 1995).

The third stage of neuronal development, organization of the neural circuitry, is most active from the sixth month of gestation to several years postnatal. However, the timing of this organizational activity varies with the region of the brain under consideration. Of particular relevance to research in adult neuropsychiatric disorders is the fact that the organization of neural circuitry in the prefrontal cortex can extend well into adolescence, overlapping with the timing of the onset of major psychiatric disorders such as schizophrenia. The major events associated with neural organization include: (1) proper alignment, orientation, and layering of cortical neurons; (2) dendritic and axonal differentiation; (3) synaptic development; (4) synaptic pruning (cell death and/or selective elimination of neuronal processes); and (5) glial proliferation and differentiation (Volpe 1995). ^{31}P MRS is well suited to monitor both the process of synaptic development involving the proliferation of dendritic spines and neuronal cell death by measuring levels of metabolites implicated in membrane synthesis and degradation, respectively. Perinatal insults and intrauterine disturbances can potentially result in disordered neuronal organization (Volpe 1995). Based on the increased incidence of schizophrenia among offspring who have had intrauterine or perinatal insults, it has been argued that schizophrenia may involve neurodevelopmental events (Murray and Lewis 1987; Weinberger 1987).

Myelination is the fourth stage of neuronal development and involves the formation of a sheath of myelin membranes around axons. This process begins in the second trimester of pregnancy and continues well into adult life. Myelination proceeds at different rates, dependent upon the brain region, but myelination of many regions of the brain is complete after 2–3 years. Intrauterine and perinatal insults also can lead to potential disturbances in this stage (Volpe 1995).

Rat brain

Membrane phospholipid metabolism and high-energy phosphate metabolism are significantly involved in these neurodevelopmental events and measurement of the respective metabolites by ^{31}P MRS reveals insights about these events. Ex vivo ^{31}P MRS studies of rat brain development form the basis for in vivo studies of human brain development. A brief description of the development of rat brain is provided for comparison with the human stages of development.

Brain maturation and development of the rat can be arbitrarily divided into four periods (McIlwain and Bachelard 1985). Period 1 is characterized by cellular division and extends up to birth in the rat. The rat brain at birth has approximately 15% of its adult weight and has no recordable electrical activity. In Period 2 (from birth to 10 days of age) there is growth in the size of individual cells, rapid outgrowth of axons, and the rapid development of dendritic connections. During this period there is a rapid increase in brain lipid content that peaks at approximately 10 days. Period 3 (10–20 days of age in the rat) is characterized by rapidly increasing synaptic densities and nerve terminals, and the development of electroencephalographic activity. This period is accompanied by increases in cell volume and the associated K^+ space and decreases in the extracellular Na^+ and Cl^- spaces. The rates of glucose uptake, glycolysis, and oxidative phosphorylation all steadily increase from birth to reach their adult levels during Period 2. Naturally occurring cell death has been demonstrated to occur during the period of synaptogenesis that corresponds to Periods 2 and 3 in the rat (Pittman and Oppenheim 1979; Cowan *et al.* 1984; Clarke 1985; Oppenheim 1985). 5'-Adenosine triphosphate (ATP) activity, including activity requiring additional Na^+ and K^+, increases during Periods 2 and 3. Period 4 in the rat extends from 20 days and is associated with active myelination but little further brain growth. During this period, creatine phosphokinase activity reaches maximal levels. Senescence in rats is thought to develop after 12 months of age and certainly by 24 months of age.

^{31}P MAGNETIC RESONANCE SPECTROSCOPY

A basic knowledge of MRS methods is useful to understand the power and limitations of this technique in the study of brain development and schizophrenia. In this chapter, we focus primarily on ^{31}P MRS as this is a major focus of our ongoing research.

Information available from ^{31}P MRS studies

Resonance peaks in the MRS spectra are defined and identified by chemical shift. Chemical shifts are the difference between the resonance position of a nucleus and the resonance position in the same spectrum of an arbitrarily chosen reference nucleus. Chemical shifts are one of the primary spectral characteristics used for identification of the origin of MRS resonances. A typical reference for ^{31}P MRS is 85% orthophosphoric acid. Chemical shifts are

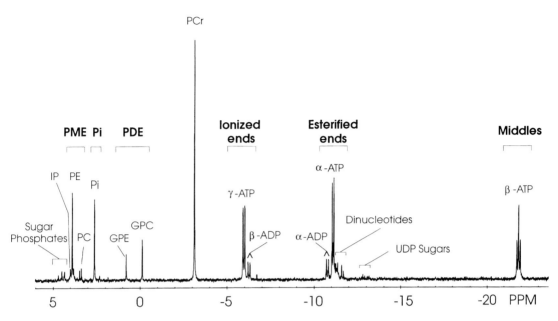

PCr

PME Pi PDE

Ionized
ends

Esterified
ends

Middles

IP PE
Pi

α-ATP

β-ATP

γ-ATP

Sugar
Phosphates

PC

GPC

GPE

β-ADP α-ADP

Dinucleotides

UDP Sugars

5 0 -5 -10 -15 -20 PPM

Fig. 6.1. ^{31}P MRS in vitro spectrum of perchloric acid extract of freeze- clamped rat brain tissue at a magnetic field strength of 11.7 Tesla, pH 9.6. Ionized ends=γATP and βADP, the esterified ends=αATP and αADP, and middles=βATP. *Abbreviations*: ADP, 5′-adenosine diphosphate; ATP, 5′-adenosine triphosphate; GPC, glycerophosphocholine; GPE, glycerophosphoethanolamine; IP, phosphoinositol; PC, phosphocholine; PCr, phosphocreatine; PDE, phosphodiesters; PE, phosphoethanolamine; Pi, inorganic orthophosphate; PME, phosphomonoesters; and UDP, uridine diphosphate. Reprinted from McClure *et al.*, 1995, ^{31}P magnetic resonance in schizophrenic study of brain metabolism spectroscopy. In H. Hafner and W.F. Gattaz (eds) *Search for the causes of schizophrenia*, vol. 3, pp. 227–51. Berlin: Springer (with permission).

usually reported in parts per million (ppm or δ) which are independent of field strength since they are obtained by dividing the resonating frequency by the applied frequency and multiplying by 10^6.

Resonances that are readily identified in the ex vivo ^{31}P MRS spectrum (Fig. 6.1) of a perchloric acid (PCA) extract of freeze-clamped rat brain include: (1) phosphomonoesters (PME), α-glycerol phosphate (α-GP, 4.35δ), inositol phosphate (IP, 4.05δ), phosphoethanolamine (PE, 3.94δ), and phosphocholine (PC, 3.43δ); (2) inorganic orthophosphate (Pi, 2.66δ); (3) the phosphodiesters (PDE), glycerol 3-phosphoethanolamine (GPE, 0.66δ) and glycerol 3-phosphocholine (GPC, −0.13δ); (4) PCr (−3.12δ); (5) the nucleotide triphosphates, predominantly ATP, γ−5.80δ, α−10.92δ, β−21.7δ; (6) the nucleotide diphosphates, predominantly

5′-adenosine diphosphate (ADP); β−6.11δ, α−10.61δ; (7) dinucleotides such as nicotinamide adenine dinucleotide (NAD) (−11.37δ); and (8) a complex resonance band centered around −12.89δ composed of nucleoside diphospho- derivatives such as uridine diphosphosugars and cytidine diphospho- derivatives such as cytidine diphosphocholine and cytidine diphosphoethanolamine. To obtain reliable measures of the unstable high-energy phosphate metabolites (e.g., PCr, ATP, ADP) the PCA extraction is carried out on rat brain tissue freeze-clamped with liquid nitrogen at the time of harvesting (Fig. 6.1).

Resonances which are quantifiable by in vivo ^{31}P MRS include PME, Pi, PCr, and ionized ends (predominantly terminal phosphates of ADP and ATP), esterified ends (predominantly ADP and ATP), and middle phosphates (mainly ATP) of the nucleoside phosphates. Resolution of

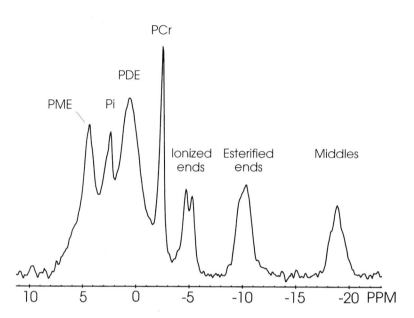

Fig. 6.2. ³¹P MRS in vivo spectrum of human brain (dorsal prefrontal cortex) at a magnetic field strength of 1.5 Tesla. Ionized ends, γATP and βADP; esterified ends, αATP and αADP; middles, βATP; PCr, phosphocreatine; PDE, phosphodiesters; Pi, inorganic orthophosphate; and PME, phosphomonoesters. Reprinted from McClure *et al.*, 1995, ³¹P magnetic resonance study of brain metabolism. In H. Hafner and W.F. Gattaz. *Search for the causes of schizophrenia*, ed. Berlin: Springer (with permission).

the in vivo ³¹P MRS spectra of brain (Fig. 6.2) is diminished compared to ex vivo MRS spectra of extracts. This loss of resolution of spectral peaks is due in part to the lower magnetic field strength (1.5 Tesla) of in vivo studies compared with ex vivo studies (11.7 Tesla), since higher field strength gives greater dispersion of the chemical shift. The production of high field magnets sufficiently large enough to accommodate humans limits the field strength feasible for in vivo MRS. Radio frequency power absorption by the subject's head, which increases with field strength, also limits the highest practical magnetic field strength for in vivo MRS to approximately 4 Tesla. In vivo MRS spectral peaks are broadened relative to the narrow in vitro spectra peaks of molecules in solution by T_2 spin relaxation effects that reflect the environment of the molecules in living tissue. Field inhomogeneity within the sample is another important contributor to line broadening. Chemical exchange also can contribute to line broadening. Complexation with and dissociation from a cation provide two different local magnetic field environments for an excited nucleus in that molecule. If the rate of chemical exchange (the time spent in each local magnetic field) is comparable to the time of rotation about the applied magnetic field axis, the resultant resonances are unresolvable and result in one broad resonance line. The identification

of the origin of in vivo resonance signals requires detailed knowledge of in vitro spectra of brain extracts under conditions as close as possible to in vivo conditions.

High-energy phosphate resonances
The brain is exquisitely dependent on a continuous supply of high-energy phosphates. The in vivo resonances related to high-energy phosphate metabolism, Pi, PCr, and the nucleoside phosphate resonances are derived from small, rapidly tumbling molecules. The linewidth of the nucleoside phosphate resonances can be increased by increasing intracellular levels of free Ca^{2+} or Mg^{2+} which form complexes with nucleoside phosphates producing chemical exchange line broadening (Pettegrew *et al.* 1988). The intracellular pH is determined by the chemical shift difference between the PCr and Pi resonances (Petroff *et al.* 1985). High-energy phosphate metabolism can be assessed by observing the PCr and ATP resonances as well as a final product of energy utilization, Pi.

Phospholipid resonances
PME and PDE resonances are related to phospholipid membrane metabolism. The PME resonance represents both small, rapidly tumbling molecules that give narrow linewidths and large, slowly moving macromolecules that

give broad linewidths. The small molecules include PE, PC, IP, and small amounts of phosphoserine, sugar phosphates, and monophosphates such as α-glycerophosphate. The macromolecules are relatively mobile proteins containing phosphorylated serine and threonine residues. The macromolecular component appears to be minor because at least two-thirds of the total in vivo PME concentration (3 μmol/g, Bottomley *et al.* 1992), is accounted for by small, water-soluble metabolites. PE contributes about 1 μmol/g (Klunk *et al.* 1994).

The PDE resonance also has both small and large molecular components. The small molecules are mainly glycerophosphocholine (GPC) and glycerophosphoethanolamine (GPE), which give relatively narrow linewidths. The large molecules are choline, ethanolamine, and serine phospholipids in small, mobile structures such as synaptic vesicles and certain bilayer phospholipids such as those in the endoplasmic reticulum (Kilby *et al.* 1991; Murphy *et al.* 1992; Pettegrew *et al.* 1994) which give broad resonance components. Phospholipids in myelin, external cell membranes, and large organelle membranes are too immobile to be observed with in vivo ^{31}P MRS (Kilby *et al.* 1991). In practice, the broadest components are typically not observed due to the choice of spectral acquisition parameters or are removed by processing the spectral baseline. Thus, as typically applied, in vivo ^{31}P MRS measures GPE, GPC, and mobile/vesicular phospholipids in the PDE peak. The latter appear to predominate as the concentration of GPE plus GPC approaches 3 μmol/g brain in water-soluble extracts and the total in vivo PDE peak has been estimated to be on the order of 15 μmol/g (Bottomley *et al.* 1992).

PME and PDE levels determined by ^{31}P MRS provide a measure of membrane phospholipid metabolism. The PME are building blocks of phospholipids and the relative concentrations of these metabolites are a measure of the active synthesis of membranes (Vance 1991). Sources of PME are: (1) phosphorylation of their respective bases by kinases; (2) phospholipase C cleavage of their respective phospholipids; or (3) phosphodiesterase cleavage of their respective PDE such as GPC and GPE. The PME are broken down by phospholipase D to release Pi and the constituent base. The water soluble PDE, such as GPE and GPC, are the major products of membrane phospho-lipid degradation (Vance 1991). The small molecular components of PDE are products of phospholipase $A_1 + A_2$ activity toward their phospholipids and are converted to their respective PME by PDE phosphodiesterase activity. In spite of their high abundance in the brain, the physiological function of water-soluble PDE remains unknown.

Quantitation of in vivo MRS spectra

As in vivo MRS resonance peaks are broad, of variable linewidth, and poorly resolved, peak areas are usually obtained from curve-fitting software programs such as NMR1 of New Methods Research, Inc., or the GE SAGE/IDL software. Figure 6.3 gives an example of curve-fitting an in vivo ^{31}P spectrum.

We report in vivo MRS data in relative units of mol % by using tissue metabolites as their own internal reference (Pettegrew *et al.* 1991; Klunk *et al.* 1994). The best method of quantification would be based on comparison of sample signal to a reliable internal standard; however, no reliable internal standard exists for in vivo MRS. In order to express in vivo data in absolute units of μmole/g, several studies have used external standards, either attached in some fashion to the head and measured simultaneously (Bottomley *et al.* 1988, 1992) or in "phantoms" which are analyzed separately (Gruetter *et al.* 1992). Other studies obtain estimates of absolute concentration by assuming a known, unchanging concentration of one "reference" metabolite such as creatine (Frahm *et al.* 1989; Sappey-Marinier *et al.* 1992). This quantitation method measures a molar ratio despite the expression of data in absolute units. The external standard procedure introduces errors based on partial volume effects which are not present in the mole % values.

Signal acquisition

In our initial schizophrenia study, ^{31}P MRS data were acquired using a pulse sequence which minimizes the loss of spectral information due to delayed acquisition (Pettegrew *et al.* 1991). Localization of the brain area of interest was achieved by using a radio frequency field gradient produced by a surface coil as described by Bendall (1986). This localization technique is effective for studying 15–20 ml volumes of brain areas that are close to the surface of the skull, but it is not suitable for studying brain areas more distant from the surface coil. There are technical limitations to all of the localization methods presently employed. More detailed information concerning these in vivo MRS localization methods can be found in the literature (Aue 1986; Lim *et al.* 1994).

Our in vivo ^{31}P MRS spectra are obtained using a General Electric Signa System with the spectroscopy research accessory (Aue 1986). The field strength is 1.5 Tesla, yielding a phosphorus frequency of 25.895 MHz. Details of the ^{31}P MRS in vivo parameters are given in Pettegrew *et al.* (1991). Our in vivo results compare quite favorably with previously published ex vivo results (Glonek *et al.* 1982; Cohen *et al.* 1984; Pettegrew *et al.* 1987, 1990) verifying the validity of the in vivo method used in the present study. The ^{31}P MRS inter-rater intraclass coefficients ($N=10$) are: PME, 0.97; Pi, 0.97; PDE, 0.99; PCr, 0.98; ionized ends, 0.87; esterified ends, 0.94; and middles, 0.74.

INVESTIGATION OF BRAIN DEVELOPMENT USING ^{31}P MRS

Ex vivo ^{31}P MRS study of rat brain development

Ex vivo MRS spectra of rat brain provide a foundation for interpreting in vivo results of ^{31}P MRS studies. Ex vivo ^{31}P MRS studies of PCA freeze-clamped brain tissue extracts of animals within the previously defined age periods provide basic information that can be used to help interpret the results from in vivo studies of human brain. The age and anatomical events of these periods of development are shown in Table 6.1.

Striking changes are seen in brain levels of the α-GP, PE, PC, GPE, GPC, PCr and Pi (Pettegrew *et al.* 1990) during development (Fig. 6.4). The PME (PE and PC) are high in the immature brain at birth and rapidly decrease from the newborn period to 3 months of age ($p=0.0001$). The levels of α-GP and PC then remain relatively constant

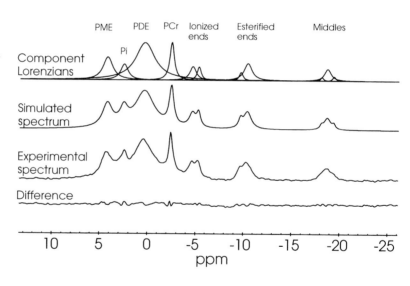

Fig. 6.3. Quantification of the ^{31}P MRS in vivo spectrum of brain. The experimental spectrum is shown after baseline correction in the trace labeled experimental spectrum. Component Lorenzians (top trace) are then fit to the individual peaks. Addition of the Lorentzians produces the trace labeled simulated spectrum. The goodness of fit to the experimental data is controlled by ensuring that the difference (bottom trace) between the experimental and simulated spectra is negligible. Reprinted from *Neurobiology of Aging*, **15**, Alterations of cerebral metabolism in probable Alzheimer's disease: a preliminary study, Pettegrew *et al.*, pp. 117–32, Copyright 1994, with kind permission from Elsevier Science Inc., The Boulevard, Langford Lane, Kidlington OX5 1GB, UK.

Table 6.1. *Magnetic resonance spectroscopy correlates with rat brain development*

			^{31}P MRS findings[1]	
Period	Age	Anatomical event	Phospholipid metabolism	High-energy phosphate metabolism
II	Birth to 10 days	Neuronal organization •Rapid increase in brain lipid content •Synaptogenesis •Programmed cell death starts	PME levels high PDE levels low PME/PDE>150	•PCr levels low •Pi levels high •PCr/Pi ratio low
III	10–20 days	Neuronal organization •Synaptogenesis •EEG activity appears •Programmed cell death continues	PME levels decreasing PDE levels increasing	•Rapid increase in PCr and PCr/Pi ratio •Rapid decrease in Pi level, which correlates with development of glycolytic and oxidative pathways •Increase in Na$^+$–K$^+$ ATPase and EEG activity
IV	20 days–12 months	Myelination	PME/PDE≈1–2	•Slight increase in PCr and Pi levels •PCr/Pi: no change
V	>12 months	Aging and senescence	PME/PDE<1	•Slight increase in Pi and PCr •Slight increase in PCr/Pi suggests decrease in PCr utilization

Notes:

[1] There were no changes in adenosine triphosphate with age.

Abbreviations: PCr: phosphocreatine; PME: phosphomonoester; PDE: phosphodiester; Pi: inorganic orthophosphate; ATPase: adenosine triphosphatase; EEG: electroencephalographic.

(Reprinted from McClure *et al.* 1994, Magnetic spectroscopy applications for the neurosciences, *Neuroprotocols, 5,* pp. 80–90, with permission from Academic Press, Inc.)

until 12 months of age, but the levels of PE increase slightly $(0.01<p<0.05)$. From 12 to 24 months, the levels of PC decrease $(0.0001<p<0.001)$ (Fig. 6.4b). In contrast, the PDE (GPE and GPC) are very low or undetectable in the newborn period and then rapidly rise up to 3 months of age $(p=0.0001)$ after which the levels rise at a slower rate up to 24 months of age (Fig. 6.4a). The PME/PDE ratio, an estimate of membrane phospholipid anabolic/catabolic activity (Pettegrew *et al.* 1987) is high in the newborn period, rapidly decreases up to 3 months of age $(p=0.0001)$ and then remains relatively constant up to 12 months of age. After 12 months of age the PME/PDE

ratio decreases slightly $(0.01<p<0.05)$ which suggests that membrane phospholipid breakdown is proceeding slightly faster than membrane phospholipid synthesis.

These ^{31}P MRS results suggest very high phospholipid anabolic activity without appreciable catabolic activity from 12 h to 10 days of age in rat brain. This metabolic profile coincides with an increase in the size of neuronal cells, the rapid outgrowth of axons and the rapid development of dendritic connections reported to occur in Period 2. After 10 days of age, there is a rather rapid increase in PDE which are catabolic breakdown products of membrane phospholipids. The PME levels start to decrease at

Fig. 6.4. Effect of animal age
on the brain levels (mol%;
mean ± SEM) of the
phosphodiesters (a) and the
phosphomonoesters (b).
Reproduced with permission
from the *Journal of Neuropathology and Experimental
Neurology*, 1990, **49**, 237–49.

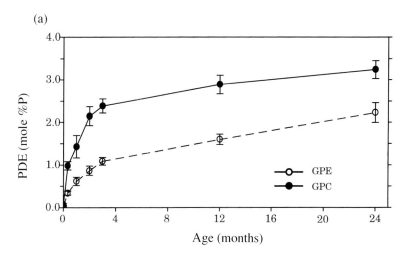

(a)

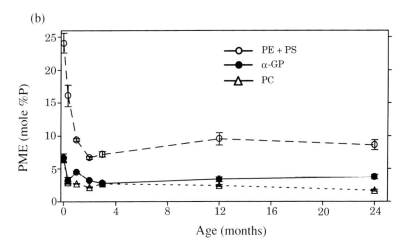

(b)

10 days of age, but the PME/PDE ratio remains high (>10). The increasing PDE levels observed from 10 to 30 days of age could represent the metabolic correlates of naturally occurring cell death and the remodeling of neuritic connections. Cell death has been demonstrated to occur naturally during neural development and, in particular, occurs at about the time of rapid synaptogenesis which is from birth to 20 days of age in the rat (Pittman and Oppenheim 1979; Cowan *et al.* 1984; Clarke 1985; Oppenheim 1985). From 1 to 3 months of age the PME continue to decrease and the PDE continue to increase, although not as rapidly as before. The PME/PDE ratio

falls from 10 to 2 indicating that the rate of phospholipid synthesis is decreasing. The changes in PME and PDE occurring from 1 to 3 months of age could reflect active myelination which is known to occur during this time in the rat. After 3 months of age, the turnover rate for phospholipids (PME/PDE) remains relatively constant until 12 months of age. From 12 to 24 months of age, the PME/PDE ratio decreases further ($0.01 < p < 0.05$) which suggests that membrane catabolism is proceeding slightly faster than anabolism.

Levels of PCr, a very labile brain high-energy phosphate, are quite low in the newborn period and appear to decrease even further up to 5 days of age. After 5 days of age, the PCr levels rapidly increase up to 1 month of age, with less rapid increases between 1 and 3 months of age (12 h versus 3 months, $p=0.0001$). After 3 months of age, the PCr levels undergo less dramatic but steady increases up to 24 months of age. In contrast, the levels of Pi are relatively high in the newborn, decrease up to 5 days of age followed by increases up to 10 days of age. After 10 days of age, the Pi levels drop rapidly until 3 months of age ($0.01 < p < 0.05$). From 3 months of age until 12 months of age, the Pi levels appear to increase slightly with more rapid increases from 12 to 24 months of age.

The PCr/Pi ratio is quite low in the newborn period until 5 days of age after which time the PCr/Pi ratio rapidly increases up to 3 months of age ($p=0.0001$). After 3 months of age, the PCr/Pi ratio remains relatively constant up to 24 months of age. The rapid increase in the PCr/Pi ratio up to 1 month of age correlates with the development of the glycolytic and oxidative pathways, increasing $Na^+–K^+$ ATPase activity, and the onset of electroencephalographic activity. The PCr/Pi ratio appears to increase slightly after 12 months of age, which suggests decreased utilization of PCr. The brain levels of ATP do not undergo similar changes; there are no significant differences in brain ATP content comparing animals of 12 h versus 3 months, 3 months versus 12 months, or 12 months versus 24 months of age.

In vivo ^{31}P MRS study of human brain development

An understanding of the changes in high-energy phosphate and membrane phospholipid metabolism associated with normal human brain development is necessary in order to properly interpret the ^{31}P MRS findings in disease states such as schizophrenia that have been suggested to be a consequence of a disruption or distortion of one or more aspects of this process. In vivo ^{31}P MRS of the dorsal prefrontal cortex (15–20 cm^3 volume) was performed on 100 normal subjects aged 10–45 years who were recruited as controls for the autism, Down's syndrome, and schizophrenia studies in our laboratory (Pettegrew *et al.*, unpublished observations). All control subjects had normal medical, neurological, and psychiatric examinations, a negative current and past history of

evidence of developmental, neurologic, or psychiatric disorders, and had a negative family history for neuropsychiatric disorders. During late childhood and early adolescence, there was an exponential decrease in the levels of PME and the oxidative metabolic rate (V/V_{max} calculated from the ratio of Pi/PCr) and an exponential increase in the levels of PCr in the prefrontal cortex of these 100 normal controls. The changes in brain levels of PME and PCr between 10 and 20 years of age probably reflect synaptic pruning of the prefrontal cortex. This is the time period of normal synaptic pruning of the prefrontal cortex.

An in vivo ^{31}P MRS study of humans by Buchli *et al.* (1994) was conducted on 16 term neonates, 17 infants, and 28 healthy adults. This study utilized a volume-selective pulse sequence (ISIS) to localize 125, 216, and 343 cm^3 volumes of interest in the brain of neonates, infants, and adults, respectively. This volume contained approximately 45% parietal lobes, 15% frontal lobes, 10% occipital lobes, and 20% basal ganglia lobes in all three groups. The study found high PME levels and low PDE levels in the neonates compared with adults. Also, the concentrations of ATP, Pi, PCr and PDE increased significantly by factors of 1.8, 1.9, 2.4, and 3.5, respectively from birth to adulthood. Also, the pH decreased significantly from 7.11 to 7.02 during brain development. These changes are consistent with the ex vivo ^{31}P MRS rat brain development studies (Pettegrew *et al.* 1990). In addition, Buchli *et al.* (1994) reported a linewidth broadening and a change in chemical shift of the PME resonance from neonates to adults which may indicate a change in the chemical composition of PME with age.

The ^{31}P MRS animal and human studies of brain development have provided the basis for evaluating possible abnormalities in brain development in disease states such as autism and schizophrenia, as discussed below.

IN VIVO ^{31}P MRS STUDIES IN SCHIZOPHRENIA AND AUTISM

In vivo ^{31}P MRS studies in schizophrenia

Evidence that schizophrenia is associated with membrane phospholipid alterations in peripheral cells (for reviews see

Fig. 6.5. Phospholipid metabolite levels in mol %P of schizophrenic subjects compared with controls. Relative mol %P obtained from in vivo ^{31}P MRS spectra of human brain (dorsal prefrontal cortex). Ionized ends=γATP and βADP, the esterified ends=αATP and βADP, and middles=βATP. *Abbreviations*: PCr, phosphocreatine; PDE, phosphodiesters; Pi, inorganic orthophosphate; and PME, phosphomonoesters. Reprinted from McClure *et al.*, 1995, ^{31}P magnetic resonance study of brain metabolism. In *Search for the causes of schizophrenia*, ed. H. Hafner and W.F. Gattaz Berlin:Springer.

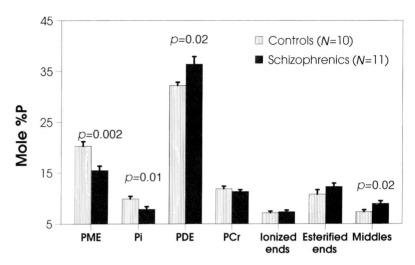

Rotrosen and Wolkin 1987; Horrobin *et al.* 1989, 1994), stimulated our studies of brain membrane phospholipid metabolism using ^{31}P MRS. Reduced activity of the prefrontal cortex ("hypofrontality") is seen in schizophrenia as evidenced by decreased glucose utilization and regional blood flow in positron emission tomography (PET) and single photon emission tomography studies (for a review see Andreasen *et al.* 1992). Our overall hypotheses were that: (1) schizophrenia would be associated with neurochemical abnormalities in membrane phospholipid metabolism, as evidenced by a reduction in membrane building blocks (PME) and an increase in membrane products (PDE); and (2) schizophrenia would be associated with abnormal utilization of high-energy phosphates such as ATP and PCr in the prefrontal cortex in view of the observation of hypofrontality in schizophrenia. To examine these hypotheses, we studied brain high-energy phosphate and membrane phospholipid metabolism in the dorsal prefrontal cortex of neuroleptic-naive, first-episode schizophrenic patients (Pettegrew *et al.* 1991). In this study, neuroleptic-naive patients were chosen to minimize the confounding lasting effects of neuroleptics on membrane phospholipids; patients at an early stage of the illness were chosen to exclude the possible effects on find-

ings of length of illness and hospitalization and to differentiate between cause and consequence. Eleven schizophrenic patients, and ten matched healthy controls were studied. There were no significant group differences between patients and controls for age, sex, race, education or parental education. Analysis of the ^{31}P MRS spectra of the dorsal prefrontal cortex of the schizophrenic patients (Pettegrew *et al.* 1991) demonstrated decreased levels of PME ($p=0.002$) and Pi ($p=0.01$) compared with control subjects (Fig. 6.5). The schizophrenic group showed increased levels of PDE ($p=0.02$) and ATP ($p=0.02$). There were no group differences in the levels of PCr, ADP or intracellular pH.

Alterations in phospholipid metabolites similar to those observed in schizophrenia (decreased PME, increased PDE) were seen in a "healthy" control subject who was studied 2 years before her first psychotic episode. This suggests that the phospholipid alterations seen in schizophrenia may represent "trait" markers (Keshavan *et al.* 1991). The ^{31}P MRS findings appear to persist with neuroleptic treatment (J.W. Pettegrew, unpublished observations). Longitudinal studies of subjects at risk for schizophrenia (e.g., first-degree relatives of schizophrenic probands) and of schizophrenic subjects in episode as well as untreated remission are needed to clarify state-trait issues.

Other in vivo ^{31}P MRS studies of schizophrenic patients (O'Callaghan *et al.* 1991; Williamson *et al.* 1991; Fukuzako *et al.* 1992; Stanley *et al.* 1994, 1995; Deicken *et al.* 1995; Kato *et al.* 1995) have appeared in the literature since our original study (Pettegrew *et al.* 1991). The recent study by Stanley *et al.* (1995) examined a 2–3 cm slice of the prefrontal cortex by ^{31}P MRS using a fast rotating gradient spectroscopy pulse sequence to localize a 15–20 cm^3 region. Stanley *et al.* (1995) compared 11 drug-naive, eight newly diagnosed medicated, and ten chronic medicated schizophrenic patients with matched controls and found significantly lower PME levels in all of the schizophrenia groups and significantly higher PDE levels in the drug-naive group compared with controls. With the exception of one study (O'Callaghan *et al.* 1991), which examined the temporal lobe, the phospholipid findings of our initial study have been replicated in part in three independent studies (Deicken *et al.* 1995; Kato *et al.* 1995; Stanley *et al.* 1995). The results with respect to alterations in high-energy phosphate metabolism in schizophrenia, have been inconsistent across studies. The most recent study of Stanley *et al.* (1995) found no significant differences in the high-energy phosphate metabolite levels in schizophrenic patients versus controls. The differences across these studies may lie in the MRS methodology or may relate to variability in the clinical status of the schizophrenic patients, e.g., medicated or unmedicated, acute or chronic.

Altered membrane metabolism in schizophrenia

What are the possible causes of these biochemical alterations? Possible causes for decreased observable levels of PME in schizophrenia brain are: (1) decreased kinase activity; (2) decreased phospholipase C activity; (3) decreased PDE phosphodiesterase activity; (4) increased phospholipase D activity; (5) increased chemical exchange with divalent cations leading to decreased MRS observability; or (6) increased NMR molecular correlation times of the PMEs with resulting decreased MRS observability. Possible causes for increased PDE in schizophrenic brain include decreased PDE phosphodiesterase activity and increased phospholipase $A_1 + A_2$ activity. Gattaz *et al.*

(1987, 1990) has reported increased activity of phospholipase A_2 in plasma from schizophrenic patients. Other possible causes of the increased observable PDE are decreased correlation times (a MRS parameter related to molecular motion) leading to increased MRS observability, or decreased chemical exchange with divalent cations resulting in increased MRS observability. Decreased PDE phosphodiesterase activity could account for both the decreased PME and increased PDE levels observed in the schizophrenic patients studied.

Decreased PME and increased PDE levels could suggest decreased synthesis and increased breakdown of membrane phospholipids in schizophrenia. Demisch *et al.* (1987) have reported a significantly decreased incorporation of ^{14}C-labeled arachidonic acid in PtdC, PtdE and PtdI in patients with schizoaffective and schizophreniform disorders which could suggest decreased membrane phospholipid synthesis. Decreased levels of membrane PtdC have been observed in erythrocytes in some schizophrenics (Stevens 1972; Henn 1980; Hitzemann *et al.* 1984) and decreased PtdE has been reported as well (Keshavan *et al.* 1993). It is possible, therefore, that the PME and PDE alterations could represent metabolic alterations which antedate the onset of anatomical changes.

Exaggerated synaptic pruning in schizophrenia

At a cellular level, we propose the abnormality in membrane metabolism described above is manifested as an exaggeration of normal synaptic pruning that occurs during early adolescence in nonhuman primates (Rakic *et al.* 1986; Bourgeois and Rakic 1993; Bourgeois *et al.* 1994; Rakic *et al.* 1994) and humans (Huttenlocher 1979; Huttenlocher *et al.* 1982). The synaptic loss associated with normal pruning is predominantly of presumptive excitatory asymmetric junctions on dendritic spines (Smiley and Goldman-Rakic 1993), which probably utilize amino acids such as glutamate as the neurotransmitter (Storm-Mathisen and Otterson 1990). We hypothesize a decrease in synaptic contacts and dendritic arborizations around cortical neurons in schizophrenia in brain regions such as the prefrontal cortex, superior temporal gyrus, and inferior parietal lobule (Fig. 6.6). The increased levels of PCr and ATP seen in the brains of some schizophrenic subjects and the progressive elevations of these

Fig. 6.6. Hypothesized effect of synaptic pruning on neurochemical and neurohistological indices.

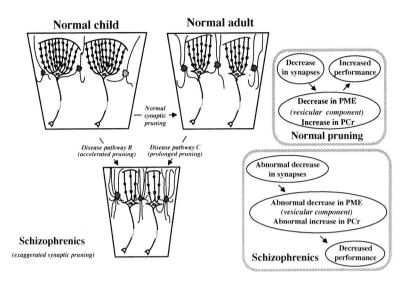

high-energy phosphates with worsening clinical and neuropsychological functioning also are consistent with our hypothesis of exaggerated pruning of synapses in schizophrenia. We suggest that exaggerated pruning might result in an increased percentage of nonsynaptic components (glial cell bodies and processes; neuronal cell bodies and processes without synapses) and a decrease in the highest energy-consuming component, i.e., the synapse, in a given brain region. Our observation of elevation of high-energy phosphates supports this view. Studies have demonstrated a higher metabolic rate of O_2 consumption for neurons ($122 \times 10^{-6} \mu l$ O_2/cell/h) compared with neuroglia ($2.5 \times 10^{-6} \mu l$ O_2/cell/h) (Hess 1961), for grey matter (5.8 ml O_2 per 100 g brain per min) compared with white matter (1.8 ml O_2 per 100 g brain per min) ($p < 0.05$) (Frey 1994), and for children age 6 years (5.2 ml O_2 per 100 g brain/min) compared to adults age 21 years (3.5 ml O_2/100 g brain/min) (Kennedy and Sokoloff 1957; Sokoloff 1966; Chugani et al. 1987). In addition, research on anesthetic agents shows that synaptic activity in a normal awake "steady-state" is enough to drive high-energy phosphate levels below that which would occur in inactive neurons. Anesthesia has been shown to increase PCr and ATP in parallel to the decrease in neuronal activity (Hein et al. 1975; McCandless and Wiggins 1981). In addition, Sokoloff (1991, 1993) has shown that the synapse

is the site of highest energy consumption during increased activity and that most of this consumption is in the recovery period rather than during the activity itself. This is consistent with the studies of Jansson et al. (1979) who showed that PCr and ATP levels are lower in isolated cerebral nerve endings than in whole brain. Unlike nerve tissue in general, synaptosomes preferentially utilize endogenous PCr and ATP stores. Jansson et al. (1979) conclude that synaptic transmission primarily depends on local stores of high-energy phosphates rather than on the availability of glucose per se. Finally, the notion that elevated PCr is a reflection of exaggerated synaptic pruning is supported by our own preliminary data on normal neurodevelopmental changes which show an exponential decrease in PME levels and oxidative metabolic rate (V/V_{max}) and an exponential increase in PCr levels during the period of normal synaptic pruning which occurs during late childhood and early adolescence (Pettegrew et al., unpublished observations). Our findings are in keeping with the findings of Buchli et al. (1994) who report that human brain levels of PME decrease from the neonatal to adult period. It is therefore likely that ^{31}P MRS findings in schizophrenia reflect processes similar to what happens during normative postnatal development, but exaggerated relative to controls.

An exaggeration or altered timing of normal programmed synaptic pruning may occur during adolescence in schizophrenia (Pettegrew *et al.* 1991; Keshavan *et al.* 1994) as initially suggested by Feinberg (1982a). An exaggeration of regressive synaptic events involving apical and basal dendrites could produce brain structural changes similar to those observed in schizophrenia in which the predominant reduction is in grey but not white matter (Pakkenberg 1987; Zipursky *et al.* 1992; Harvey *et al.* 1993; Schlaepfer 1994). An exaggeration of normal neuronal cell death, however, should produce decreased numbers of neurons and their projection axons and, there-fore, reduce the volume of both gray and white matter. Recent neuropathological work by Selemon *et al.* (1995) showing neuropil reductions in the dorsolateral prefrontal cortex of schizophrenic patients is in support of the possibility of exaggerated synaptic pruning in this dis-order.

Several clinical observations point to neurodevelop-mental abnormalities in schizophrenia: onset in adoles-cence in most and earlier age of onset among males; pronounced premorbid neurodevelopmental abnormal-ities such as asociality and "soft" neurological signs; impaired cognitive and neuromotor functioning; minor physical anomalies; presence of structural abnormalities at the onset of illness which may predate the illness; and absence of a relationship between illness duration and brain abnormalities (for reviews see Weinberger 1987; Waddington 1993). The timing of the neurodevelopmental abnormality, however, remains controversial. In "early" neurodevelopmental models, a fixed lesion from early life interacts with normal neurodevelopmental events occur-ring much later (Murray and Lewis 1987; Weinberger 1987). The "late" neurodevelopmental model originally proposed by Feinberg (1982b) and subsequently by others (Hoffman and McGlashan 1993), posits that schizo-phrenia may result from a deviation in normal brain maturational processes that occur during early adoles-cence, involving large-scale synaptic elimination or pruning in brain regions critical for cognitive develop-ment. The abnormality in schizophrenia could be due to an exaggeration of the normal synaptic pruning process, perhaps involving basal and apical dendrites of cortical neurons (Pettegrew *et al.* 1991). Alternatively, abnormal neurodevelopment in schizophrenia may result from faulty myelination processes in critical brain regions (Benes *et al.* 1994).

Schizophrenia and prefrontal glutamatergic pathways
The descending prefrontal glutamatergic pathway is a major input to both the striatum and the limbic cortex. Exaggerated synaptic pruning of the dendrites of the pre-frontal-limbic glutamatergic neurons could produce a reduced neuropil volume resulting in what might appear as an enhanced clustering of cells as observed for pre-α-cells in the parahippocampal gyrus (Falkai *et al.* 1988). Excessive synaptic pruning of prefrontal-striatal gluta-matergic neurons ending on striatal dopaminergic termi-nals could decrease the tonic release of dopamine from the dopaminergic terminals resulting in secondary upregula-tion of the postsynaptic dopaminergic receptors. Post-mortem (Seeman *et al.* 1984; Jaskiw and Kleinman 1988; Kornhuber *et al.* 1989) and in vivo imaging studies exam-ining this issue (Wong *et al.* 1986; Farde *et al.* 1987) have been conflicting, however, and further research is needed. The phasic release of dopamine is thought to be responsive to stress; if upregulation of postsynaptic dopaminergic receptors occurs as discussed above, stress could result in exaggerated mesolimbic activity resulting in positive symptoms. Neuroleptics which block postsynaptic D_2 receptors could modulate the mesolimbic activity back toward normal. This formulation has been suggested by Grace (1991).

In vivo ^{31}P MRS studies in autism
Autism is an early onset developmental disorder that results in the failure of social, verbal and nonverbal lan-guage, and reasoning abilities to develop normally during infancy and early childhood. Neuropathological findings have suggested that the disruption of development begins no later than 30 weeks of gestation (Bauman and Kemper 1985). Neuropathologic findings also have characterized autism as a disorder of neuronal organization (Bauman and Kemper 1985, 1994). Several aspects of neuronal organiza-tion have been implicated by research findings, specifically the elaboration of dendritic and axonal ramifications, the establishment of synaptic connections, and the selective elimination of neuronal processes (Minshew *et al.* in press).

In addition to being a developmental disorder of

neuronal organization, autism in high functioning individuals has many clinical similarities to schizophrenia related to the overlap in negative symptoms. The clinical similarity is sufficient for a misdiagnosis of schizophrenia to be common in such cases and to result in the inclusion in DSM-IV of Pervasive Developmental Disorder in the differential diagnosis of schizophrenia, schizophreniform disorder, schizotypal personality disorder, and schizoid personality disorder (American Psychiatric Association 1994). In a comparison study of high functioning autistic and schizophrenic subjects, autistic individuals were demonstrated to exhibit many of the negative symptoms associated with schizophrenia but lacked the positive symptoms (Rumsey *et al.* 1986). At comparable levels of general intellectual ability, negative symptoms are even more pronounced in autistic individuals than they are in schizophrenia. This overlap in clinical symptomatology, along with similarities in neurobiological findings, suggests that these two disorders may involve the same neural systems but at different points in brain maturation and by different mechanisms. Current hypotheses about localization are now very similar in these two disorders. A comparison of the ^{31}P MRS characteristics of these two disorders could therefore be particularly interesting.

Studies of cerebral cortex and its metabolic status are highly relevant to recent research findings in autism and to current neurologic models for autism which all propose dysfunction of cerebral association cortex as the final common pathway for the behavioral expression of this syndrome. Evidence for the central involvement of cerebral cortex, particularly frontal and parietal cortices, in the pathophysiology of autism is now extensive. Neurophysiological studies in the past 10 years have consistently identified abnormalities in late evoked response potentials including the P300 potential and the frontally distributed Nc, while documenting the absence of abnormalities in early and middle latency potentials related to the posterior fossa and lower brain regions (Novick *et al.* 1979, 1980; Courchesne *et al.* 1984, 1985, 1987 Rumsey *et al.* 1984, 1989). Oculomotor studies have similarly documented abnormalities in the cortical control of eye movements by frontal and parietal neural systems and the integrity of more basic eye movements and oculomotor reflexes related to the function of lower brain regions (Ornitz *et al.*

1985; Minshew *et al.* 1990, 1995). Neuropsychological studies of high functioning autistic individuals have provided evidence of the generalized involvement of higher order cognitive abilities, including numerous findings referable to frontal cortical systems (Rumsey and Hamburger 1988; Ozonoff *et al.* 1991; Minshew *et al.* 1992a, 1992b).

Evidence of alterations in the production and remodeling of brain membranes in autism has come from numerous sources and has included the truncation in dendritic tree development apparent in limbic structures, increase in brain weight at autopsy (Bauman and Kemper 1994), the overgrowth of cortical gray and white matter apparent in MRI measurements of supratentorial structures (Piven *et al.* 1992, 1995), and increase in head circumference observed clinically (Bailey *et al.* 1993). In addition, a PET study examining functional connections between brain regions has reported a decrease in the intra- and interhemispheric connections of frontal and parietal cortex with other cortical and subcortical regions (Horwitz *et al.* 1987; Horwitz and Rumsey 1994), providing evidence of a decrease in the neural connections of cortex with other brain regions and a potential functional correlate for the decrease in dendritic tree development in the limbic structures. Recent neurochemical studies have reported evidence of increased CSF levels of glial acidic protein and gangliosides in autistic and autistic-like children, providing additional evidence of alterations in synaptosomal membrane metabolism (Ahlsen *et al.* 1993).

With regard to energy metabolism, there is no clinical evidence to suggest that autism is associated with a primary failure in bioenergetics; however, the evidence suggests that neurophysiological abnormalities may result in secondary changes in bioenergetics. In a series of studies of normal individuals, PET and evoked potential mapping studies have provided evidence of increasing brain activation with decreasing IQ, new task learning, and incorrect answers, suggesting that more neural circuits are recruited in these situations (Gevins *et al.* 1983, 1987, 1989; Haier *et al.* 1992; Squire *et al.* 1992). These findings are reminiscent of some early evoked potential studies in autism which suggested reliance on less efficient alternative neural pathways for the processing of information (Novick *et al.* 1979, 1980).

The first ^{31}P MRS study in autism was undertaken to investigate the in vivo brain chemistry of the cerebral cortex and its potential relationship to the pathophysiology of autism (Minshew *et al.* 1993). In this ^{31}P MRS study of autism, high-energy phosphate and membrane phospholipid metabolism were investigated in the dorsal prefrontal cortex under resting conditions in 11 nonsedated nonmentally retarded autistic adolescents and young adults who met research diagnostic criteria for Autistic Disorder and 11 matched normal controls (Minshew *et al.* 1989). Emphasis was placed on the study of non-mentally retarded autistic individuals, the accuracy of the diagnosis of autism using research diagnostic instruments, and outside verification of diagnosis, and individual matching of autistic and control subjects on variables most likely to have an impact on CNS structure and function, e.g., age, Full Scale and Verbal IQ, gender, and socioeconomic status. Neuropsychologic and language parameters reflecting the overall severity of autism and of the cognitive and language deficits in high functioning autistic individuals (Rumsey and Hamburger 1988; Minshew *et al.* 1992a; Venter *et al.* 1992) were chosen a priori for correlational analyses with the MRS metabolite levels to determine if there were any relationships between measures of brain chemistry and the clinical disorder.

Intergroup metabolite differences
The significant metabolic alterations observed in the dorsal prefrontal cortex of the autistic subjects relative to the controls were: (1) decreased levels of PCr; and (2) decreased levels of esterified ends or αATP. The levels of PME, Pi, PDE, ionized ends (αATP and βADP), middles (βATP) and intracellular pH were not significantly different between autistic and control subjects.

A decrease in PCr levels, in the absence of changes in intracellular pH, suggests increased utilization of PCr to maintain ATP levels, e.g., a hypermetabolic state. This finding is consistent with the increase in glucose utilization reported with PET in a group of 18 high functioning young adult autistic subjects (Rumsey *et al.* 1985). The biological import of this finding is somewhat of an enigma, but neurophysiological studies suggest that alterations in bioenergetics may be the consequence of neurophysiologic alterations. As previously mentioned, Novick and cowork-

ers (1979, 1980) have suggested that the P300 abnormalities in autism may be the consequence of reliance on less efficient, alternative pathways for information processing. In neurophysiologic studies of normal individuals, Gevins and coworkers have observed that incorrect responses during cognitive-evoked potential paradigms result in greater activation of frontal cortex and related pathways than correct answers (Gevins *et al.* 1983, 1987, 1989). Similarly, PET studies in normal individuals have suggested that brain function is more efficient, e.g., fewer neural circuits are activated, as IQ score increases, once a new task has been learned, and when a correct answer is given (Haier *et al.* 1992; Squire *et al.* 1992). Additional MRS, PET, and functional MRI studies using cortical activation techniques are needed to further investigate brain connectivity and function in autism.

The decrease in esterified ends observed in the autistic group could be of multiple origins. Contributors to this resonance include the α-phosphate of ATP and ADP, dinucleotides such as nicotinamide adenine dinucleotide, cytidine diphosphocholine, cytidine diphosphoethanolamine and uridine diphosphosugars. Hence, a decrease in this resonance could reflect diminished levels of one or more of these constituents. In addition to ATP and the dinucleotides, the contributors to this resonance are found predominantly in the pathways of membrane biosynthesis and lipid and protein glycosylation. The absence of alterations in the β-ATP levels, the only peak whose sole contribution is from ATP, suggests that the decrease in esterified ends in autism may be related to alterations in these membrane- and glycosylation-related biosynthetic activities. The significance of this finding for the pathophysiology of autism is unclear. Alterations in protein glycosylation, however, could theoretically be related to the alterations reported in immune status in autism (Warren *et al.* 1986, 1990a, 1990b), as highly glycosylated proteins are involved in normal immune function (Gennis 1989).

Intragroup clinical-metabolic correlations
When the ^{31}P MRS metabolite levels were correlated with IQ scores (Wechsler 1974, 1981) and selected scores from tests of reasoning ability (Wisconsin Card Sorting Test; Grant and Berg 1948; Making Inferences subtest from the

Fig. **6.7.** Correlations in normal group were nonsignificant. All correlations derived by linear regression analysis. Reprinted from Minshew, N.J. 1994. In vivo brain chemistry of autism ^{31}P magnetic resonance spectroscopy studies. In *The Neurobiology of Autism*, ed. M.L. Bauman and T.L. Kemper, pp. 86–101. Reprinted by permission of the Johns Hopkins University Press, Baltimore.

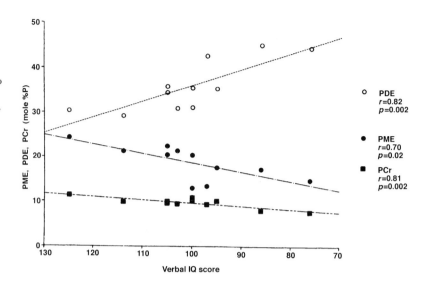

Test of Language Competence; Wiig and Secord 1989), secondary memory (delayed recall scores from the California Verbal Learning Test; Delis *et al.* 1987), and semantic language comprehension (Test of Language Competence; Wiig and Secord 1989; Token Test; Benton and Hamsher 1978), a number of significant clinical-metabolic correlations were observed in the autistic group but were not present in the control group. The correlations were generally quite robust and demonstrated a consistent pattern across the different clinical parameters. As clinical performance declined, the levels of the most labile high-energy phosphate compound (PCr) and of the membrane building blocks (PME) decreased, and the levels of the membrane breakdown products (PDE) increased (Fig. 6.7). These findings are consistent with a hypermetabolic energy state and undersynthesis and enhanced degradation of brain membranes. The clinical-metabolic correlations with PCr provide additional support for the biologic significance of an altered energy state, possibly secondary to the neurophysiological abnormalities in autism. The phospholipid correlations are particularly intriguing, in view of the histoanatomical observations of a truncation in the development of the dendritic tree in autism (Bauman and Kemper 1985; Raymond *et al.* 1989) and the increased CSF levels of glial acidic protein and gangliosides (Ahlsen *et al.* 1993). The metabolic evidence of

undersynthesis and enhanced degradation of brain phospholipids may provide a possible molecular/metabolic basis for the observed histoanatomical findings, as the presence of this metabolic pattern during fetal brain development could be expected to result in undersynthesis of brain membranes in affected neural systems. In addition, this metabolic pattern also includes the potential for membrane degradation, and thus may provide a potential molecular/metabolic mechanism for the clinical regression that occurs at presentation in nearly one-third of autistic children and the deterioration that occurs in a small subgroup in adolescence.

The clinical-metabolic correlations observed in the autistic subjects were not present in the control subjects. This suggests that the correlations in the autistic subjects are not merely an exaggerated form of normal biological variability, but may represent a true qualitative alteration in brain metabolism.

In summary, this preliminary study reports alterations in high-energy phosphate and membrane phospholipid metabolism in the brain in autism, which correlate with the clinical deficits and severity of this disorder. As with the functional correlation findings with PET in autism (Horwitz and Rumsey 1994), the clinical-metabolic correlations are scientifically and statistically the most significant, and provide the greatest insights into the pathophysiology of autism. This would suggest that future MRS studies should incorporate such correlations as a central element of their design.

CONCLUSION

A major attribute of in vivo MRS is its ability to measure levels of metabolites in the living human brain; however, this field is at an early, developing stage. Many technological hurdles remain to be overcome, including improvements in sensitivity, localization techniques, volume minimization, signal baseline correction, and quantitation. The ability of ^{31}P MRS to monitor high-energy phosphates as well as membrane phospholipid metabolites provide a useful tool to study neurodevelopment and provide new insights into the pathophysiology of possible neurodevelopmental diseases such as schizophrenia and autism. As MRS is safe and noninvasive, repeated measurements can be carried out in the same individual over a period of time making longitudinal studies possible. ^{31}P MRS has the potential to provide new information on the possible evolution of regional biochemical changes in schizophrenia and other psychiatric disorders.

ACKNOWLEDGMENTS

This work was supported by NIMH grants MH46614 (J.W.P., R.J.M., and M.K.), 45203 and 45156, and 46614; NINDS grant NS-3355 (N.J.M.) and an NIA grant AG08974 (J.W.P., R.J.M., N.J.M., K.P., and W.E.K.).

REFERENCES

Ahlsen, G., Rosengren, L., Belfrage, M., Palm, A., Haglid, K., Hamberger, A., and Gillberg, C. 1993. Glial fibrillary acidic protein in the cerebrospinal fluid of children with autism and other neuropsychiatric disorders. *Biol. Psychiatry* 33:734–43.

American Psychiatric Association. 1994. *Diagnostic and Statistical Manual-IV*. Washington, DC: American Psychiatric Association.

Andreasen, N.C., Rezzi, K., Alliger, R., Swayze, II, Falum, M., Kirchner, P., Cohen, G., and O'Leary, D.S. 1992. Hypofrontality in neuroleptic-naive patients and in patients with chronic schizophrenia. *Arch. Gen. Psychiatry* 49:943–58.

Aue, W.P. 1986. Localization methods for in vivo nuclear magnetic resonance spectroscopy. *Magn. Reson. Med.* 1:21–72.

Bailey, A., Luthert, P., Bolton, P., LeCouteur, A., and Rutter, M. 1993. Austism and megalencephaly. *Lancet* 341:1225–6.

Bauman, M.L. and Kemper, T.L. 1985. Histoanatomic observations of the brain in early infantile autism. *Neurology* 35:866–74.

Bauman, M.L. and Kemper, T.L. 1994. Neuroanatomic observations of the brain in autism. In *The Neurobiology of Autism*, ed. M. Bauman and T.L. Kemper, pp. 119–45. Baltimore: Johns Hopkins University Press.

Bendall, M.R. 1986. Surface coil techniques for in vivo NMR. *Bull. Magn. Reson.* 8: 17–44.

Benes, F.M., Turtle, M., Khan, Y., and Farol, P. 1994. Myelination of a key relay zone in the hippocampal formation occurs in the human brain during childhood, adolescence and adulthood. *Arch. Gen. Psychiatry* 51: 477–84.

Benton, A.L. and Hamsher, K.D. 1978. *Multilingual Aphasia Examination*. Iowa City: University of Iowa.

Bottomley, P.A., Charles, H.C., Roemer, P.B., Flamig, D., Engeseth, H., Edelstein, W.A., and Mueller, O.M. 1988. Human in vivo phosphate metabolite imaging with ^{31}P NMR. *Magn. Reson. Med.* 7:319–36.

Bottomley, P.A., Cousins, J.P., Pendrey, D.L., Wagle, W.A., Hardy, C.J., Eames, F.A., McCaffrey, R.J., and Thompson, D.A. 1992. Alzheimer dementia: quantification of energy metabolism and mobile phosphoesters with P-31 NMR spectroscopy. *Radiology* 183:695–9.

Bourgeois, J.-P., Goldman-Rakic, P.S., and Rakic, P. 1994. Synaptogenesis in the prefrontal cortex of Rhesus monkeys. *Cerebral Cortex* 4:78–96.

Bourgeois, J.-P. and Rakic, P. 1993. Changes of synaptic density in the primary visual cortex of the Macaque monkey from fetal to adult stage. *J. Neurosci.* 13:2801–20.

Buchli, R., Martin, E., Boesiger, P., and Rumpel, H. 1994. Developmental changes of phosphorus metabolite concentrations in the human brain: a ^{31}P magnetic

resonance spectroscopy study in vivo. *Pediatr. Res.* 35:
431–5.

Chugani, H.R., Phelps, M.E., and Mazziotta, J.C. 1987.
Positron emission tomography study of human brain
functional development. *Ann. Neurol.* 322:487–97.

Clarke, P.G. 1985. Neuronal death in the development of the
vertebrate nervous system. *Trends Neurosci.* 8:345–9.

Cohen, M.M., Pettegrew, J.W., Kopp, S.J., Minshew, N., and
Glonek, T. 1984. P-31 nuclear magnetic resonance analysis
of brain: normoxic and anoxic brain slices. *Neurochem. Res.*
9:785–801.

Courchesne, E., Courchesne, R.Y., Hicks, G., and Lincoln, A.J.
1985. Functioning of the brain stem auditory pathway in
non-retarded autistic individuals. *Electroencephalogr. Clin.
Neurophysiol.* 61:491–501.

Courchesne, E., Elmasian, R.O., and Yeung-Courchesne, R.
1987. Electrophysiologic correlates of cognitive processing:
P3b and Nc, basic, clinical and developmental research. In
Textbook of clinical neurophysiology, ed. A.M. Halliday,
S.R. Butler and R. Paul, pp. 645–76. Sussex, England:
John Wiley and Sons.

Courchesne, E., Kilman, B.A., Galambos, R., and Lincoln, A.J.
1984. Autism: Processing of novel auditory information
assessed by event-related brain potentials.
Electroencephalogr. Clin. Neurophysiol. 59:238–48.

Cowan, W.M., Fawcett, J.W., O'Leary, D.D., and Stanfield, B.B.
1984. Regressive events in neurogenesis. *Science*
225:1258–65.

Deicken, R.F., Merrin, E.L., Floyd, T.C., and Weiner, M.W.
1995. Correlation between left frontal phospholipids and
Wisconsin Card Sort Test performance in schizophrenia.
Schizophr. Res. 14:177–81.

Delis, D.C., Kramer, J.H., Kaplan, E. and Ober, B.A. 1987.
California Verbal Learning Test. New York: Psychological
Corporation.

Demisch, L., Gerbaldo, H., Heinz, K., and Kirsten, R. 1987.
Transmembranal signaling in schizophrenic and affective
disorders: studies on arachidonic acid and phospholipids.
Schizophr. Res. 22:275–82.

Falkai, P., Bogerts, B., and Rozumek, M. 1988. Cell loss and
volume reduction in the entorhinal cortex of
schizophrenics. *Eur. Arch. Psychiatry Neurol. Sci.*
24:515–21.

Farde, L., Wiesel, F.A., Hall, H., Halldin, C., Stone-Elander, S.,
and Sedvall, G. 1987. No D2 receptor increase in
PET study of schizophrenia. *Arch. Gen. Psychiatry*
44:671–2 (letter).

Feinberg, I. 1982a. Schizophrenia: caused by a fault in
programmed synaptic elimination during adolescence?
J. Psychiatr. Res. 17 (Suppl. 4):319–34.

Feinberg, I. 1982b. Schizophrenia and late maturational brain
changes in man. *Psychopharmacol. Bull.* 18:29–31.

Frahm, J., Bruhn, H., Gyngell, M.L., Merboldt, K.D., Hanicke,
W., and Sauter, R. 1989. Localized proton NMR
spectroscopy in different regions of the human brain in
vivo. Relaxation times and concentrations of cerebral
metabolites. *Magn. Reson. Med.* 11:47–63.

Frey, K.A. 1994. Positron emission tomography. In *Basic
neurochemistry: molecular, cellular and medical aspects*, 5th
edn. ed. G.J. Siegel, B.W. Agranoff, R.W. Albers and P.B.
Molinoff, pp. 935–55. New York: Raven Press.

Fukuzako, H., Takeuchi, K., Fujimoto, T., Hokazono, Y.,
Hirakawa, K., VeYama, K., Matsumoto, K., and Fukuzako,
T. 1992. ^{31}P magnetic resonance spectroscopy of
schizophrenic patients with neuroleptic resistant positive
and negative symptoms. *Biol. Psychiatry* 31 (Suppl.): 204A-
205A (abstract).

Gattaz, W.F., Hubner, C.V., Nevalainen, T.J., Thuren, T., and
Kinnunen, P.K. 1990. Increased phospholipase A_2 activity
in schizophrenia; a replication study. *Biol. Psychiatry*
28:495 501.

Gattaz, W.F., Kolisch, M., Thuren, T., Virtanen, J.A., and
Kinnunen, P.K. 1987. Increased plasma phospholipase-A_2
activity in schizophrenic patients: reduction after
neuroleptic therapy. *Biol. Psychiatry* 22:421–6.

Gennis, R.B. 1989. *Biomembranes: molecular structure and
function.* New York: Springer.

Gevins, A.S., Cutillo, B.A., Bressler, S.L., Morgan, N.H.,
White, R.M., Illes, J., and Greer, D.S. 1989. Event-related
covariances during a bimanual visuomotor task. II.
Preparation and feedback. *Electroencephalogr. Clin.
Neurophysiol.* 74:147–60.

Gevins, A.S., Morgan, N.H., Bressler, S.L., Cutillo, B.A.,
White, R.M., Illes, J., Greer, D.S., Doyle, J.C., and Zeitlin,
G.M. 1987. Human neuroelectric patterns predict
performance accuracy. *Science.* 235:580–5.

Gevins, A.S., Schaffer, R.E., Doyle, J.C., Cutillo, B.A.,
Tannehill, R.S., and Bressler, S.L. 1983. Shadows of

thought: shifting lateralization of human brain electrical patterns during brief visuomotor task. *Science* **220**:97–9.

Glonek, T., Kopp, S.J., Kot, E., Pettegrew, J.W., Harrison, W.H., and Cohen, M.M. 1982. P-31 nuclear magnetic resonance analysis of brain: the perchloric acid extract spectrum. *J. Neurochem.* **39**:1210–19.

Grace, A.A. 1991. Phasic versus tonic dopamine release and the modulation of dopamine system responsivity: a hypothesis for the etiology of schizophrenia. *Neuroscience.* **41**:1–24.

Grant, D.A. and Berg, E.A. 1948. *Wisconsin Card Sorting Test.* Odessa, FL: Psychological Assessment Resources.

Grillon, C., Courchesne, E., and Akshoomoff, N. 1989. Brainstem and middle latency auditory evoked potentials in autism and developmental language disorder. *J. Aut. Dev. Disord.* **19**:255–69.

Gruetter, R., Rothman, D.L., Novotny, E.J., and Shulman, R.G. 1992. Localized ^{13}C NMR spectroscopy of myo–inositol in the human brain in vivo. *Magn. Reson. Med.* **25**:204–10.

Haier, R.J., Siegel, B.V.J., MacLachlan, A., Soderling, E., Lottenberg, S., and Buchsbaum, M.S. 1992. Regional glucose metabolic changes after learning a complex visuospatial/motor task: a positron emission tomographic study. *Brain Res.* **570**:134–43.

Harvey, I., Ron, M.A., Du Boulay, G., Wicks, D., Lewis, S.W., and Murray, R.M. 1993. Reduction of cortical volume in schizophrenia on magnetic resonance imaging. *Psychol. Med.* **23**:591–604.

Hein, H., Krieglstein, J., and Stock, R. 1975. The effects of increased glucose supply and thiopental anesthesia on energy metabolism of the isolated perfused rat brain. *Naunyn Schmiedebergs Arch. Pharmacol.* **289**: 399–407.

Henn, F. 1980. Biological concepts of schizophrenia. In *Perspectives in schizophrenia research*, ed. C. Baxter and T. Melnachuk, pp. 209–23. New York: Raven Press.

Hess, H. 1961. The rates of respiration of neurons and neuroglia in human cerebrum. In *Regional neurochemistry*, ed. S.S. Kety and J. Elkes, pp. 200–2. Oxford: Pergamon Press.

Hitzemann, R., Hirschowitz, D., and Garver, D. 1984. Membrane abnormalities in the psychoses and affective disorders. *J. Psychiatr. Res.* **18**:319–26.

Hoffman, R.E. and McGlashan, T.H. 1993. Parallel distributed processing and the emergence of schizophrenic symptoms. *Schizophr. Bull.* **19**:119–40.

Horrobin, D.F., Glen, A.I.M., and Vaddadi, K. 1994. The membrane hypothesis of schizophrenia. *Schizophr. Res.* **13**: 195–207.

Horrobin, D.F., Manku, M.S., and Morse-Fisher, N. 1989. Essential fatty acids in plasma phospholipids in schizophrenia. *Biol. Psychiatry* **25**:562–8.

Horwitz, B., Grady, C.L., Schlageter, N.L., Duara, R., and Rapoport, S.I. 1987. Intercorrelations of regional cerebral glucose metabolic rates in Alzheimer's disease. *Brain Res.* **407**:294–306.

Horwitz, B. and Rumsey, J.M. 1994. Positron emission tomography: implications for cerebral dysfunction in autism. In *The neurobiology of autism*, ed. M. Bauman and T.L. Kemper, pp. 102–18. Baltimore: Johns Hopkins University Press.

Huttenlocher, P.R. 1979. Synaptic density in human frontal cortex. Developmental changes and effects of aging. *Brain Res.* **163**:195–205.

Huttenlocher, P.R., deCourten, C., Garey, L.J., and Van Der Loos, H. 1982. Synaptogenesis in human visual cortex: evidence for synapse elimination during normal development. *Neurosci. Lett.* **33**:247–52.

Jansson, S.E., Harkonen, M.H., and Helve, H. 1979. Metabolic properties of nerve endings isolated from rat brain. *Acta Physiol. Scand.* **107**:205–12.

Jaskiw, G. and Kleinman, J. 1988. Postmortem neurochemistry studies in schizophrenia. In *Schizophrenia: a scientific focus*, ed. S.C. Schulz and H.K. Tamminga, pp. 264–73. New York: Oxford University Press.

Kato, T., Shioiri, T., Murashita, J., Hamakawa, H., Inubushi, T., and Takahashi, S. 1995. Lateralized abnormality of high-energy phosphate and bilateral reduction of phosphomonoester measured by phosphorus-31 magnetic resonance spectroscopy of the frontal lobes in schizophrenia. *Psychiatry Res.* **61**:151–60.

Kennedy, C. and Sokoloff, L. 1957. An adaptation of the nitrous oxide method to the study of the cerebral circulation in children; normal values for cerebral blood flow and cerebral metabolic rate in childhood. *J. Clin. Invest.* **36**: 1130–7.

Keshavan, M.S., Anderson, S., and Pettegrew, J.W. 1994. Is schizophrenia due to excessive synaptic pruning in the prefrontal cortex? *J. Psychiatr. Res.* **28**: 239–65.

Keshavan, M.S., Mallinger, A.G., Pettegrew, J.W., and Dippold, C. 1993. Erythrocyte membrane phospholipids in psychotic patients. *Psychiatry Res.* **49**:89–95.

Keshavan, M.S., Pettegrew, J.W., Panchalingam, K., Kaplan, D., and Bozik, E. 1991. Phosphorus 31 magnetic resonance spectroscopy detects altered brain metabolism before onset of schizophrenia. *Arch. Gen. Psychiatry.* **48**:1112–3.

Kilby, P.M., Bolas, N.M., and Radda, G.K. 1991. 31P-NMR study of brain phospholipid structures in vivo. *Biochim. Biophys. Acta* **1085**:257–64.

Klunk, W.E., Xu, C.J., Panchalingam, K., McClure, R.J., and Pettegrew, J.W. 1994. Analysis of magnetic resonance spectra by mole percent: Comparison to absolute units. *Neurobiol. Aging* **15**:133–40.

Kornhuber, J., Riederer, P., Reynolds, G.P., Beckmann, H., Jellinger, K., and Gabriel, E. 1989. 3H-spiperone binding sites in post-mortem brains from schizophrenia patients: relationship to neuroleptic drug treatment, abnormal movements, and positive symptoms. *J. Neural Transm.* **75**:1–10.

Lim, K.O., Pauly, J., Webb, P., Hurd, R., and Macovski, A. 1994. Short TE phosphorus spectroscopy using a spin-echo pulse. *Magn. Reson. Med.* **32**: 98–103.

McCandless, D.W. and Wiggins, R.C. 1981. Cerebral energy metabolism during the onset and recovery from halothane anesthesia. *Neurochem. Res.* **6**: 1319–26.

McIlwain, H. and Bachelard, H.S. 1985. *Biochemistry and the central nervous system.* 5th edn. Edinburgh: Churchill Livingstone.

McClure, R., Keshavan, M.S., Minshew, N.J., Pancha Iingam, K., and Pettegrew, J.W. [31]P Magnetic resonance spectroscopy study of brain metabolism in schizophrenia. In *Search for the Causes of Schizophrenia*, 3, ed. H. Hafner and W.F. Gattaz, pp. 225–51. Berlin Heidelberg: Springer-Verlag.

Minshew, N.J., Furman, J.M., Goldstein, G., and Payton, J.B. 1990. The cerebellum in autism: a central role or epiphenomenon? *Neurology* **40** (Suppl. 1):173 (abstract).

Minshew, N.J., Goldstein, G., Dombrowski, S.M., Panchalingam, K., and Pettegrew, J.W. 1993. A preliminary ^{31}P MRS study of autism: evidence for under synthesis and increased degradation of brain membranes. *Biol. Psychiatry* **33**:762–73.

Minshew, N.J., Goldstein, G., Munez, L.R., and Payton, J.B. 1992a. Neuropsychological functioning in non-mentally retarded autistic individuals. *J. Clin. Exp. Neuropsychol.* **14**:740–61.

Minshew, N.J., Panchalingam, K., Dombrowski, S.M., and Pettegrew, J.W. 1992b. Developmentally regulated changes in brain membrane metabolism. *Biol. Psychiatry* **31**:62A [abstract].

Minshew, N.J., Pettegrew, J.W., Payton, J.B., and Panchalingam, K. 1989. Metabolic alterations in the dorsal prefrontal cortex of autistic patients with normal IQ. *Ann. Neurol.* **26**:438 [abstract].

Minshew, N.J., Sweeney, J.A., and Bauman, M.L. (in press). Neurologic aspects of autism. In *Handbook of autism and pervasive developmental disorders*, 2nd edn., ed. D.J. Cohen and F.R. Volkmar. New York: John Wiley and Sons.

Minshew, N.J., Sweeney, J.A., and Furman, J.M. 1995. Evidence for a primary neocortical systems abnormality in autism. *Soc. Neurosci. Abstr.* **21**:735 [abstract].

Murphy, E.J., Bates, T.E., Williams, S.R., Watson, T., Brindle, K.M., Rajagopalan, B., and Radda, G.K. 1992. Endoplasmic reticulum: the major contributor to the PDE peak in hepatic ^{31}P-NMR spectra at low magnetic field strengths. *Biochim. Biophys. Acta* **1111**:51–8.

Murray, R.M. and Lewis, S.W. 1987. Is schizophrenia a neurodevelopmental disorder? *Br. Med. J.* **295**:681–2.

Novick, B., Kurtzberg, D., and Vaughn, H.G.J. 1979. An electrophysiologic indication of defective information storage in childhood autism. *Psychiatry Res.* **1**:101–8.

Novick, B., Kurtzberg, D., and Vaughn, H.G.J. 1980. An electrophysiologic indication of auditory processing defects in autism. *Psychiatry Res.* **3**: 107–14.

O'Callaghan, E.O., Redmond, O., Ennis, R., Stack, J., Kinsella, A., Ennis, J.T., Conall, L., and Waddington, J.L. 1991. Initial investigation of the left temporoparietal region in schizophrenia by ^{31}P magnetic resonance spectroscopy. *Biol. Psychiatry* **29**:1149–52.

Oppenheim, R.W. 1985. Naturally occurring cell death during neural development. *Trends Neurosci.* **8**:487–93.

Ornitz, E.M., Atwell, C.W., Kaplan, A.R., and Westlake, J.R. 1985. Brainstem dysfunction in autism: results of vestibular stimulation. *Arch. Gen. Psychiatry* **42**:1018–25.

Ozonoff, S., Pennington, B.F., and Rogers, S.J. 1991. Executive function deficits in high-functioning autistic individuals: relationship to theory of mind. *J. Child Psychol. Psychiatry.* **32**:1081–105.

Pakkenberg, B. 1987. Post-mortem study of chronic schizophrenic brains. *Br. J. Psychiatry* **151**:744–52.

Petroff, O.A.C., Prichard, J.W., Behar, K.L., Alger, J.R., den Hollander, J.A., and Shulman, R.G. 1985. Cerebral intracellular pH by ^{31}P nuclear magnetic resonance spectroscopy. *Neurology* **35**:781–88.

Pettegrew, J.W., Keshavan, M.S., Panchalingam, K., Strychor, S., Kaplan, D.B., Tretta, M.G., and Allen, M. 1991. Alterations in brain high-energy phosphate and phospholipid metabolism in first episode, drug-naive schizophrenia. A pilot study of the dorsal prefrontal cortex by in vivo ^{31}P NMR spectroscopy. *Arch. Gen. Psychiatry* **48**:563–8.

Pettegrew, J.W., Kopp, S.J., Minshew, N.J., Glonek, T., Feliksik, J.M., Tow, J.P., and Cohen, M.M. 1987. ^{31}P nuclear magnetic resonance studies of phosphoglyceride metabolism in developing and degenerating brain: preliminary observations. *J. Neuropathol. Exp. Neurol.* **46**:419–30.

Pettegrew, J.W., Panchalingam, K., Klunk, W.E., McClure, R.J., and Muenz, L.R. 1994. Alterations of cerebral metabolism in probable Alzheimer's disease; a preliminary study. *Neurobiol. Aging* **15**:117–32.

Pettegrew, J.W., Panchalingam, K., Withers, G., McKeag, D., and Strychor, S. 1990. Changes in brain energy and phospholipid metabolism during development and aging in the Fischer 344 rat. *J. Neuropathol. Exp. Neurol.* **49**:237–49.

Pettegrew, J.W., Withers, G., Panchalingam, K., and Post, J.F. 1987. ^{31}P nuclear magnetic resonance (NMR) spectroscopy of brain in aging and Alzheimer's disease. *J. Neural Transm. Suppl.* **24**:261–8.

Pettegrew, J.W., Withers, G., Panchalingam, K., and Post, J.F.M. 1988. Considerations for brain pH assessment by ^{31}P NMR. *Magn. Reson. Imaging* **6**:135–42.

Pittman, R. and Oppenheim, R.W. 1979. Cell death of motoneurons in the chick embryo spinal cord. IV. Evidence that a functional neuromuscular interaction is involved in the regulation of naturally occurring cell death and the stabilization of synapses. *J. Comp. Neurol.* **187**:425–46.

Piven, J., Arndt, S., Bailey, J., Havercamp, S., Andreasen, N.C., and Palmer, P. 1995. An MRI study of brain size in autism. *Am. J. Psychiatry* **152**: 1145–9.

Piven, J., Nehme, E., Simon, J., Barta, P., Pearlson, G., and Folstein, S. 1992. Magnetic resonance imaging in autism: measurement of the cerebellum, pons and fourth ventricle.

Biol. Psychiatry **31**:491–504.

Rakic, P., Bourgeois, J.P., Eckenhoff, M.F., Zecevic, N., and Goldman-Rakic, P.S. 1986. Concurrent overproduction of synapses in diverse regions of the primate cerebral cortex. *Science* **232**:232–5.

Rakic, P., Bourgeois, J.P., and Goldman-Rakic, P.S. 1994. Synaptic development of the cerebral cortex: implications for learning, memory, and mental illness. In *The self-organizing brain: from growth cones to functional networks*, ed. J. van Pelt, M.A. Corner, H.B.M. Uylings and F.H. Lopes da Silva, pp. 227–43. Amsterdam: Elsevier Science.

Raymond, G., Bauman, M., and Kemper, T. 1989. The hippocampus in autism: Golgi analysis. *Ann. Neurol.* **26**:483–4 (abstract).

Rotrosen, J. and Wolkin, A. 1987. Phospholipid and prostaglandin hypothesis in schizophrenia. In *Psychopharmacology: the third generation of progress*, ed. H.Y. Meltzer, pp. 759–64. New York: Raven Press.

Rumsey, J.M., Andreasen, N.C., and Rapoport, J.L. 1986. Thought, language, communication, and affective flattening in autistic adults. *Arch. Gen. Psychiatry* **43**:771–7.

Rumsey, J.M., Duara, R., Grady, C., Rapoport, J.L., Margolin, R.A., Rapoport, S.I., and Cutler, N.R. 1985. Brain metabolism in autism. Resting cerebral glucose utilization rates as measured with positron emission tomography. *Arch. Gen. Psychiatry* **42**:448–55.

Rumsey, J.M., Grimes, A.M., Pikus, A.M., Duara, R., and Ismond, D.R. 1984. Auditory brainstem responses in pervasive developmental disorders. *Biol. Psychiatry* **19**:1403–18.

Rumsey, J.M. and Hamburger, S.D. 1988. Neuropsychological findings in high-functioning men with infantile autism, residual state. *J. Clin. Exp. Neuropsychol.* **10**.201–21.

Sappey-Marinier, D., Calabrese, G., Hetherington, H.P., Fisher, S.N., Deicken, R., Van Dyke, C., Fein, G., and Weiner, M.W. 1992. Proton magnetic resonance spectroscopy of human brain: applications to normal white matter, chronic infarction, and MRI white matter signal hyperintensities. *Magn. Reson. Med.* **26**:313–27.

Schlaepfer, T.E. 1994. Decreased regional cortical gray matter volume in schizophrenia. *Am. J. Psychiatry* **151**:842–8.

Seeman, P., Ulpian, C., Bergeron, C., Riederer, P., Jellinger, K., Gabriel, E., Reynolds, G.P., and Tourtellotte, W.W. 1984. Bimodal distribution of dopamine receptor densities in brains of schizophrenics. *Science* 225: 728–31.

Selemon, L.D., Rajkowska, G., and Goldman-Rakic, P.S. 1995. Abnormally high neuronal density in the schizophrenic cortex. A morphometric analysis of prefrontal area 9 and occipital area 17. *Arch. Gen. Psychiatry* 52:805–18.

Smiley, J.F. and Goldman-Rakic, P.S. 1993. Heterogeneous targets of dopamine synapses in monkey prefrontal cortex demonstrated by serial section electron microscopy: a laminar analysis using the silver enhanced diaminobenzidine-sulfide (SEDS) immunolabeling technique. *Cerebral Cortex* 3:223–38.

Sokoloff, L. 1966. Cerebral circulatory and metabolic changes associated with aging. *Res. Publ. Assoc. Res. Nerv. Ment. Dis.* 41:237–54.

Sokoloff, L. 1991. Measurement of local cerebral glucose utilization and its relation to local functional activity in the brain. *Adv. Exp. Med. Biol.* 291: 21–42.

Sokoloff, L. 1993. Function-related changes in energy metabolism in the nervous system: localization and mechanisms. *Keio J. Med.* 42:95–103.

Squire, L.R., Ojemann, J.G., Miezin, F.M., Petersen, S.E., Videen, T.O., and Raichle, M.E. 1992. Activation of the hippocampus in normal humans: a functional anatomical study of memory. *Proc. Natl Acad. Sci. USA.* 89: 1837–41.

Stanley, J.A., Williamson, P.C., Drost, D.J., Carr, T.J., Rylett, R.J., Morrison-Stewart, S., and Thompson, R.T. 1994. Membrane phospholipid metabolism and schizophrenia: an in vivo ^{31}P-MR spectroscopy study. *Schizophr. Res.* 13:209–15.

Stanley, J.A., Williamson, P.C., Drost, D.J., Carr, T.J., Rylett, J., Malla, A., and Thompson, R.T. 1995. An in vivo study of the prefrontal cortex of schizophrenic patients at different stages of illness via phosphorus magnetic resonance spectroscopy. *Arch. Gen. Psychiatry* 52:399–406.

Stevens, J.D. 1972. The distribution of phospholipid fractions in the red cell membrane of schizophrenics. *Schizophr. Bull.* 6:60–1.

Storm-Mathisen, J. and Otterson, O.P. 1990. Immunocytochemistry of glutamate at the synaptic level. *J. Histochem. Cytochem.* 38:1733–43.

Vance, D.E. 1991. Phospholipid metabolism and cell signalling in eucaryotes. In *Biochemistry of lipids, lipoproteins and membranes*, vol. *20*, ed. D.E. Vance and J. Vance, pp. 205–40. New York: Elsevier.

Venter, A., Lord, C., and Schopler, E. 1992. A follow-up study of high functioning autistic children. *J. Child Psychol. Psychiatry* 33:489–507.

Volpe, J.J. 1995. Neuronal proliferation, migration, organization, and myelination. In *Neurology of the newborn*, 3rd edn., pp. 43–92. Philadelphia: W.B. Saunders.

Waddington, J.L. 1993. Schizophrenia: Developmental neuroscience and pathobiology. *Lancet* 341: 531–6.

Warren, R.P., Cole, P., Odell, J.D., Pingree, C.B., Warren, W.L., White, E., Yonk, J., and Singh, V.K. 1990a. Detection of maternal antibodies in infantile autism. *J. Am. Acad. Child Adolesc. Psychiatry* 29:873–7.

Warren, R.P., Margaretten, N.C., Pace, N.C., and Foster, A. 1986. Immune abnormalities in patients with autism. *J. Aut. Dev. Disord.* 16:189–97.

Warren, R.P., Yonk, L.J., Burger, R.A., Cole, P., Odell, J.D., Warren, W.L., White, E., and Singh, V.K. 1990b. Deficiency of suppressor-inducer (CD4+CD45RA+) T cells in autism. *Immunol. Invest.* 19:245–51.

Wechsler, D. 1974. *Wechsler Intelligence Scale for Children – Revised Manual*. New York: Psychological Corporation.

Wechsler, D. 1981. *Wechsler Adult Intelligence Scale – Revised Manual*. New York: Psychological Corporation.

Weinberger, D.R. 1987. Implications of normal brain development for the pathogenesis of schizophrenia. *Arch. Gen. Psychiatry* 44:464–9.

Wiig, E.H. and Secord, W. 1989. *Test of Language Competetence – Expanded Edition*. New York: Psychological Corporation.

Williamson, P., Drost, D., Stanley, J., Carr, T., Morrison, S., and Merskey, H. 1991. Localized phosphorus-31 magnetic resonance spectroscopy in chronic schizophrenic patients and normal controls. *Arch. Gen. Psychiatry* 48:578 (letter).

Wong, D.F., Wagner, H.N., Tune, L.E., Dannals, R.F., Pearlson, G.D., Links, J.M., Tamminga, C.A., Broussolle, E.P., Ravert, H.T., Wilson, A.A., Toung, J.K.T., Malat, J., Williams, J.A., Lorcan, A., O'Tuama, O., Snyder, S.H., Kuhar, M.J., and Gjedde, A. 1986. Positron emission tomography reveals elevated D$_2$ dopamine receptors in drug-naive schizophrenics. *Science* 234:1558–63.

Zipursky, R.B., Lim, K.O., Sullivan, E.V., Brown, B.W., and Pfefferbaum, A. 1992. Widespread cerebral gray matter volume deficits in schizophrenia. *Arch. Gen. Psychiatry* 49:195–205.

7 Position emission tomography studies of developing brain

HARRY T. CHUGANI AND DIANE C. CHUGANI

INTRODUCTION

Recent studies have shown that even after the brain has reached its adult size and weight, maturational changes continue to occur at least until age 16–18 years. The average brain weight for a fullterm male at birth is about 370 g. By 1 year, brain weight has more than doubled and by 3 years, average brain weight has tripled to 1080 g. By 6–14 years, the average brain weight is 1350 g. This developmental profile is quite different from that which describes the energy requirement of the central nervous system at various stages of development. In this chapter, we review data pertaining to the functional maturation of the brain as indicated by energy demand of its various components. These data are related to synaptogenesis and brain plasticity, and finally, to the study of psychopathology.

ENERGY REQUIREMENTS OF THE DEVELOPING BRAIN

It has been known for some time that the immature brain consumes more oxygen and glucose than a brain that is fully developed (Himwich and Fazekas 1941; Tyler and van Harreveld 1942). For example, the utilization of both oxygen and glucose in excised rat cerebral cortex, striatum, cerebellum, and brainstem were shown to be higher during the period between the fourth and seventh postnatal weeks compared with adult values (Tyler and van Harreveld 1942). This phenomenon was found also to be present in humans by Kennedy and Sokoloff (1957), who demonstrated that the average global cerebral blood flow (an indirect measure of energy demand in the brain) in nine normal children (aged 3–11 years) was approximately 1.8 times that of normal young adults. Moreover, average global cerebral oxygen utilization was approximately 1.3 times higher in children than in adults.

Such studies proliferated with the development of in vivo autoradiography using radiolabeled tracer substances which allowed local cerebral blood flow (LCBF), and more directly, the actual rates of local cerebral glucose utilization (LCMRglc) to be estimated for individual brain regions with high spatial resolution in laboratory animals (Freygang and Sokoloff 1958; Sokoloff et al. 1977; Sakurada et al. 1978). These studies demonstrated that, in most species, phylogenetically older structures (e.g., brainstem, cerebellum, thalamus) already demonstrate considerable activity compared with telencephalic structures in the neonatal period. As the animal matures and various phylogenetically newer regions in the brain become functionally active, the animal develops a more complex behavioral repertoire (Kennedy et al. 1972; Gregoire et al. 1981; Duffy et al. 1982; Abrams et al. 1984; Nehlig et al. 1988; Chugani et al. 1991). For example, Kennedy et al. (1982) compared the patterns of glucose metabolism between newborn and adult monkeys, and found a relationship between an increase of glucose metabolism in a particular brain structure and the emergence of behavior related to that structure. These autoradiography methods also led to further studies of the phenomenon whereby the energy demand of the immature brain exceeds that of the fully developed brain. Kennedy et al. (1972) found that, as in humans, dogs also undergo a developmental period during which LCBF in most structures exceeds adult blood flow rates. In the cat, there were two periods during development when LCMRglc for a number of brain regions exceeded adult values (Chugani et al. 1991).

Fig. 7.1. Positron emission tomography images of glucose utilization in the newborn brain showing: (a) sensorimotor cortex (short arrow) and cingulate cortex (long arrow); (b) thalamus (thick arrow) and basal ganglia (thin arrow); the latter is only occasionally seen in neonates; (c) brainstem (thick arrow) and mesial temporal region (thin arrow); (d) cerebellar vermis (thick arrow) and mesial temporal (hippocampal) region (thin arrow). Most of the frontal, parietal, temporal and occipital cortex, as well as the cerebellar cortex, show relatively low rates of glucose utilization during this period.

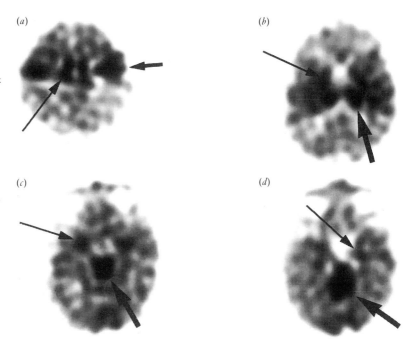

POSITRON EMISSION TOMOGRAPHY: PRINCIPLES

Although CBF and oxygen utilization could be determined in the human brain, the methods used were best suited for measurements involving the whole brain or large regions of the brain. In addition, substrate utilization in small children could not be accurately measured. With the development of positron emission tomography (PET), it became possible to measure not only LCBF and LCMRglc noninvasively, but a variety of other biochemical and physiological parameters in the brain, including oxygen utilization, protein synthesis, and even neurotransmitter uptake, binding and release (Mazziotta and Gilman 1992). This technology, developed at Washington University in St Louis by Ter-Pogossian *et al.* (1975) and Phelps *et al.* (1975), uses arrays of detectors sensitive to the unique features of positron-electron annihilation which results in paired photons being released in opposite directions. Mathematical models which describe the in vivo behavior of selected chemical tracers labeled with positron-emitting isotopes are applied in order to allow quantitative assessments of the brain function being studied.

BRAIN GLUCOSE METABOLISM IN HUMAN INFANTS

With PET, it is possible to measure substrate utilization in the brains of even small infants. Using this methodology, we demonstrated that the pattern of glucose utilization in the human infant evolves during the first year of life from a simple neonatal pattern to one that resembles an adult pattern.

In the newborn brain, several basic areas such as the primary sensory and motor cortex, thalamus, brainstem and cerebellar vermis appear to be already metabolically active (Chugani and Phelps 1986; Chugani *et al.* 1987; Chugani 1994). Improved spatial resolution of newer PET scanners have suggested that the cingulate cortex and the hippocampal region should be added to this list of areas; sometimes the basal ganglia also show considerable glucose metabolism in newborns, but this is not a consistent finding (Fig. 7.1) (H.T. Chugani, unpublished observations). The relatively simple pattern of behavior seen in newborns is perhaps related to the functional inactivity of most brain regions at this time. For example, reaching movements are relatively poor and imprecise, and are referred to as 'prereaching' (von Hofsten 1982) due to inadequate visuomotor integration. In addition, intrinsic brainstem reflex behaviors are prominent in newborns. These reflexes include the Moro, root and grasp responses (Andre-Thomas and Saint-Anne Dargassies 1960) which later become suppressed.

At 2–3 months, PET scans show increases of glucose metabolism in parietal, temporal and primary visual cortex, basal ganglia, and cerebellar hemispheres (Fig. 7.2), but not the frontal cortex. These changes in glucose metabolism coincide with improved skills involving visuospatial and visuosensorimotor integration (Bronson 1974), the disappearance or reorganization of brainstem reflex neonatal behaviors (Andre-Thomas and Saint-Anne Dargassies 1960; Parmelee and Sigman 1983), and evidence of increasing cortical contribution to the electroencephalogram (Kellaway 1979).

As the infant continues to mature beyond 6 months, vast areas in the frontal cortex begin to show increases of glucose utilization. Initially, between 6 and 8 months, lateral and inferior portions of frontal cortex become active (Fig. 7.3), and lastly, the dorsal and medial frontal regions show increased glucose utilization between 8 and 12 months (Fig. 7.4). Frontal lobe maturation in glucose utilization coincides with the appearance of more cognitively-related behaviors and abilities, such as the phenomenon of stranger anxiety (Kagan 1972), and improved performance on the delayed response task (Fuster 1984; Goldman-Rakic 1984). Increased glucose requirement in frontal cortex also coincides with the expansion of dendritic fields (Schade and van Groenigen 1961) and the increased capillary density (Diemer 1968) observed in frontal cortex during the same period of development. By approximately 1 year of age, the infant's pattern of glucose utilization resembles that of the adult, but further changes are yet to come (see next section).

To summarize at this point, it appears that in the first year of life, the ontogeny of glucose metabolism follows a phylogenetic order, with functional maturation of older anatomical structures preceding that of newer areas (Chugani and Phelps 1986; Chugani *et al.* 1987; Chugani 1994). Furthermore, there is at least a general relationship between the maturational sequence of regional glucose metabolism and the behavioral maturation of the infant; this anatomical-behavioral relationship is the basis for the

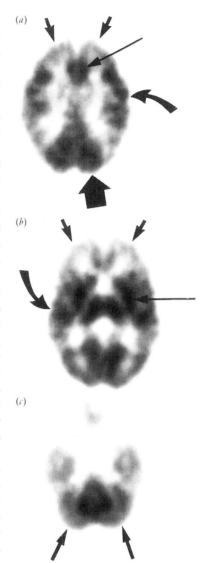

Fig. 7.2. Positron emission tomography images of glucose utilization in a 3–month-old infant showing: (a) increase of glucose metabolism in parietal cortex (curved arrow) and occipital cortex (thick arrow); note the persistently high metabolism in cingulate cortex (long arrow) and the low metabolism in frontal cortex (short arrows); (b) increase of glucose metabolism in temporal cortex (curved arrow) and basal ganglia (long arrow); note the low metabolism in frontal cortex (short arrows); (c) increase of glucose metabolism in cerebellar hemispheres (short arrows).

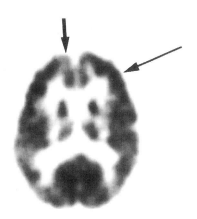

Fig. 7.3. Selected positron emission tomography image of glucose utilization in an 8–month-old infant. The *lateral* frontal cortex (long arrow) shows a maturational rise in glucose metabolism before the *mesial* portion of the frontal cortex (short arrow).

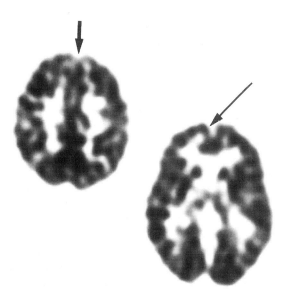

Fig. 7.4. Selected positron emission tomography images of glucose utilization in a 10–month-old infant. The *inferior* mesial frontal cortex (long arrow) shows a maturational rise in glucose metabolism before the *superior or dorsal* mesial portion of the frontal cortex (short arrow).

development of complex neuroanatomical networks that mediate human behavior.

GLUCOSE METABOLIC RATES

Although the brain of a 1-year-old shows a similar distribution pattern of glucose utilization as that of an adult, the *rate* at which glucose is being used by various brain regions undergoes maturational changes that continue until early adulthood (16–18 years). The most dramatic changes occur in the cerebral cortex (Fig. 7.5) where LCMRglc rises from the low neonatal values (about 30% lower than adult rates) to reach adult values by the second year. Thereafter, cortical LCMRglc *surpasses* adult rates and by about 4 years, a plateau is reached which extends until about 9–10 years; during this plateau period, LCMRglc in the child's cerebral cortex is over two-fold that in the adult. At about 9–10 years, LCMRglc begins to decline and gradually reaches adult values by 16–18 years (Chugani *et al.* 1987; Chugani 1994). Again, the hierarchical ordering of structures in terms of the degree to which maturational increases in LCMRglc exceed adult values is based on phylogeny. Thus, phylogenetically older structures (e.g., brainstem) do not show a significant increase of LCMRglc over adult values and are relatively metabolically mature even at birth. Intermediate increases in LCMRglc over adult values occur in a number of subcortical structures such as the basal ganglia and thalamus, and finally, neocortical regions show the greatest magnitude of change in LCMRglc during development as compared to adult values (Fig. 7.5).

REGRESSIVE PHENOMENA DURING DEVELOPMENT

It is clear, from the data presented above, that brain development in humans is both dynamic and protracted. Brain glucose metabolism is one of many processes characterized by an initial overshoot and a subsequent regression during development (Changeux and Danchin 1976; Jacobson 1978; Cowan *et al.* 1984). Overgrowth and elimination phases have also been described in neurons and their processes and synaptic contacts. The prolifera-

Fig. **7.5**. Absolute values of local cerebral metabolic rates for glucose (LCMRglc) for cortical brain regions plotted as a function of age in normal infants and children, and corresponding adult values. In the infants and children, points represent individual values of LCMRglc; in adults, points are mean values from seven subjects, in which the size of the symbols equals the standard error of the mean.

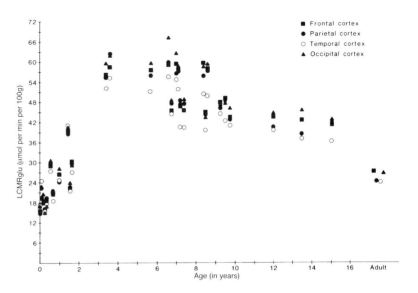

tion and overproduction of neurons in humans occur pre-natally, whereas programmed cell death (apoptosis) begins prenatally and continues until about the second postnatal year (Rabinowicz 1979). Surviving neurons undergo a similar phenomenon postnatally characterized by over-production of their arborization and synaptic contacts, fol-lowed by an elimination or 'pruning' phase (Huttenlocher, 1979; Huttenlocher *et al.* 1982; Huttenlocher and de Courten, 1987). Synaptic elimination in humans probably continues well into adolescence; for example, synaptic density in frontal cortex of children up to 11 years of age have been shown to exceed that in adults (Huttenlocher 1979). It is believed that regressive phenomena, including synaptic elimination, do not occur randomly but are based, in many systems, on neuronal activity during a critical period (Rauschecker and Marler 1987). Thus, neuronal activity leads to stabilization and less vulnerability to elimination. Recent studies have suggested that in the visual cortex of kittens, this activity-dependent stabiliza-tion may involve activation of the *N*-methyl-*D*-aspartate (NMDA) subclass of glutamate receptors (Rauschecker and Hahn 1987; Bear *et al.* 1990), resulting perhaps in the expression of specific neuronal proteins.

GLUCOSE METABOLISM, SYNAPTOGENESIS AND PLASTICITY

It is interesting that the developmental curve for syn-aptogenesis in humans (Huttenlocher 1979; Huttenlocher *et al.* 1982; Huttenlocher and de Courten 1987) runs almost parallel to the curve which describes LCMRglc for cerebral cortex shown in Fig. 7.5 (Chugani *et al.* 1987; Chugani 1994). As the major portion of glucose in the brain, under normal conditions, is used to maintain resting membrane potentials (Mata *et al.* 1980; Kadekaro *et al.* 1985; Nudo and Masterton 1986), there should be a direct relationship between the degree of "connectivity" and the energy demand of the brain in the resting state.

We have, therefore, hypothesized that the ascending portion of the glucose metabolism curve shown on Fig. 7.5 represents a period of synaptic overproduction in the cere-bral cortex. The "plateau" period during which LCMRglc exceeds adult values corresponds to the period of increased energy requirement by cortex due to the pres-ence of synaptic exuberance which must be maintained. Finally, the gradual decline of LCMRglc marks the time of synaptic elimination or the "pruning" process which is also a time when the brain begins to lose its developmental plasticity (Chugani et al. 1989; Chugani 1994).

A number of studies have been performed in our laboratory to test the validity of these hypotheses. For example, we have determined the relationship between LCMRglc, synaptogenesis and plasticity in the kitten visual cortex (Chugani et al. 1991). Using quantitative ^{14}C-2-deoxyglucose autoradiography, we found low values of LCMRglc in the newborn kitten. After 15 days of age, many brain regions (particularly telencephalic structures) underwent sharp increases of LCMRglc to reach, or exceed, adult rates by 60 days. At 90 and 120 days, a slight decline of LCMRglc was observed, but this was followed by a second, larger peak occurring at about 180 days. Only after 180 days did LCMRglc decrease to reach final adult values. Thus, the kitten goes through two developmental phases during which LCMRglc in many telencephalic structures exceed adult values. The second peak (around 180 days) appears not to coincide with any known major neuroanatomical changes in the brain, but rather, occurs at a time when cats undergo sexual maturation (Kling 1965). Therefore, the high energy requirement in the brain may be related to hormonal factors (reviewed in Pfaff 1982); studies in the cat relating LCMRglc to puberty and hormones are lacking.

On the other hand, there are abundant data relating synaptogenesis to developmental plasticity in the cat. As the best studied in this regard is probably area 17 in the kitten visual system, we focused on this area. There are few synapses in this region in newborn kittens (Voeller et al. 1963; Winfield 1981); correspondingly, LCMRglc values in area 17 are low (Chugani et al. 1991). During the second and third weeks postnatally, there is a well-documented rapid increase of synaptic density which reaches a peak at about 70 days (Winfield 1981, 1983); this phase of synaptogenesis coincides with the period when LCMRglc values rise dramatically in area 17. Moreover, the same period is characterized as a "critical period" in the visual system of kittens. During this time, there is considerable plasticity manifested when the visual system is injured or experimentally manipulated (Morest 1969; Hubel and Wiesel 1970; Spinelli et al. 1972; Pettegrew 1974; Timney 1983). This "critical period" of development in kitten visual cortex extends from 4 weeks to about 3 months of life, during

which LCMRglc values are high in this brain region. Following this period, there is diminishing plasticity associated with regression of exuberant synapses and connections (Barlow 1975; Hirsch and Leventhal 1978; Sherman and Spear 1982), and a corresponding decline of LCMRglc presumably due to diminished energy requirement.

In order to further test the hypothesis that resting LCMRglc are an indication of synaptic density, we have studied this relationship in nonhuman primates. Morphometric studies of synaptogenesis in monkeys are both expensive and cumbersome, but have been performed in the rhesus monkey. In this species, there is a period between 2 and 6 months postnatally when the cerebral cortex contains more synapses than the adult rhesus (Rakic et al. 1986). The timing of synaptic decline appears to be the same for all cortical regions studied indicating that this may be a genetically programmed phenomenon. Studies performed in our laboratory by Jacobs et al. (1995) have found that LCMRglc of cerebral cortex in infant rhesus is at about 60% of adult levels until after 2 months postnatally when LCMRglc rises steeply to about 155% of adult values by 6 months; after this, there is a gradual decline of LCMRglc in cerebral cortex to reach adult values following a time course similar to that of synaptic pruning in rhesus. Thus, as in the cat, maturational changes of resting LCMRglc in the developing rhesus appear to parallel periods of synaptic overproduction and subsequent regression.

Based on the data reviewed above, we believe that the resting LCMRglc for cerebral cortex in children (Fig. 7.5) is an indirect measure of the degree of "connectivity" in the developing central nervous system. Furthermore, these data provide the basis for exploring how LCMRglc and synaptogenesis might relate to developmental brain plasticity in children. As is well known, children can sustain damage to large areas of the brain and yet show remarkably little functional deficit compared with adults who have sustained comparable lesions (for a review see Finger and Wolf 1988). A central hypothesis in our laboratory is that the period between 8 and 10 years, when LCMRglc in cerebral cortex begins to decline (Fig. 7.5) also marks the time when developmental brain plasticity begins to diminish in children. The implications of such a relationship are obvious, as this would have an impact on medical decision-making (e.g., in surgery for uncontrolled epilepsy), early exposure of infants and children to an enriched environment, educational curricula, and in the context of this book, theories of psychopathology.

There is a large amount of evidence to suggest that, indeed, brain plasticity in children begins to decrease at about 8–10 years, thus supporting our hypothesis. Much of this evidence is in the language and visual system domains, and this will be reviewed briefly.

Children who have been deprived of exposure to language since birth, as for example those raised in the wilderness (so-called "feral" children), can still acquire reasonably normal language skills but only if intense speech and language therapy is introduced prior to the age of 10 years (Curtiss 1981). Following damage to the language-dominant hemisphere, there is better recovery of language skills if the injury occurs prior to about 8–10 years than if the injury occurs later (Basser 1962; Curtiss 1977). In fact, based on an extensive review of this subject, Lenneberg (1967) postulated that there must be a "critical period for language acquisition" ending at about the age of 10 years, after which there is a more limited (but not absent) potential to acquire language skills.

Analyses in the visual system domain have also suggested a similar timing of diminished plasticity in children. A number of studies have evaluated the upper age limit beyond which stimulus deprivation of one eye in young children, caused by monocular occlusion such as a cataract or certain kinds of strabismus, will induce an irreversible reduction of visual acuity known as amblyopia (Marg 1982). Two large clinical surveys have found that amblyopia can be prevented from occurring if the monocular occlusion is corrected prior to about 8–10 years of age, but not after (Awaya 1978; Vaegan and Taylor 1979). In addition, the compromise in visual depth perception induced by unilateral enucleation (e.g., for orbital tumors) can be minimized if enucleation is performed prior to about 8 years of age (Schwartz et al. 1987).

IMPLICATIONS FOR RESEARCH ON PSYCHOPATHOLOGY

The LCMRglc developmental curve depicted in Fig. 7.5 consists of several segments, the neurobiological signifi-

cance of which has been reviewed in this chapter. The timing of these segments coincides with the age when important clinical events occur in a number of psychopathologies, and allow for the generation of several hypotheses.

Feinberg et al. (1990) have noted that the maturational curves for LCMRglc, synaptogenesis, and delta wave amplitude during sleep in children are similar, and can be best described with a gamma distribution model. The proposal is made that because the early symptoms of schizophrenia occur at early adolescence when the maturational curves begin their down slope, errors in synaptic pruning localized to certain areas of the brain (e.g., frontal cortex) may play an important role in this disorder. A detailed analysis of this hypothesis is presented by Feinberg in Chapter 17, and will not be further discussed here.

Analysis of the signs and symptoms of another psychopathology, namely infantile autism, indicates that the "autistic regression" which most typically occurs between 18 and 24 months of age coincides with the time when LCMRglc in children is at its highest rate of increase (Fig. 7.5). Up until this point, mild delays in motor milestones and deficits in attachment behaviors may be observed. During the second year, however, deficits become more severe and regression in skills occurs. The time course of this blooming of autistic behaviors in children coincides with the period of high glucose demand and profuse synaptogenesis. Furthermore, during the period of rapid synaptic proliferation, a number of events occur in the ontogeny of serotonin neurotransmission. For example, animal studies have demonstrated the expression of a transient dense serotonergic projection to cerebral cortical primary sensory areas during the period of synaptogenesis in rat cortex (D'Amato et al. 1987). In addition, a transient expression of $5HT_{1B}$ serotonin receptors localized presynaptically on thalamocortical afferents in rats has been demonstrated during the same time period (Bennett-Clarke et al. 1993; Leslie et al. 1992). Electrophysiological studies have demonstrated that serotonin strongly inhibits excitatory thalamocortical transmission in rat somatosensory cortex at this time (Rhoades et al. 1994).

Evidence for an abnormality in serotonin metabolism in some autistic persons has been well documented. Hyperserotonemia, originally described by Schain and

Freedman (1961), and altered free plasma tryptophan levels (Hoshino *et al.* 1992) measured in autistic subjects are evidence of metabolic abnormalities of this neurotransmitter. Although attempts to document central abnormalities in serotonin metabolism have not demonstrated a convincing alteration in autistic subjects, more sensitive methods, such as PET studies with the tryptophan analog ^{11}C-α-methyl-tryptophan may be useful in this regard. Further, abnormalities may be particularly prominent during this developmental window. We propose that the severe behavioral manifestations during the second year of life in autistic children may be attributed, in part, to abnormal connections formed in the cortex due to faulty serotonergic modulation of excitatory thalamocortical neurons during this critical period. The role of a transient dense serotonergic innervation on synapse formation in human cortex may provide insight and potential *early* interventions in this devastating developmental disorder. Pharmacological modulation of central serotonergic tone following this period may ameliorate some abnormal behaviors, but we suggest that once this critical period is past, correction of the established synaptic patterns responsible for these aberrant behaviors through pharmacological or dietary manipulations are not likely to be effective. In fact, clinical trials with the serotonin-depleting drug fenfluramine report only limited behavioral improvement (for a review see Campbell 1988).

In this chapter, we have demonstrated that studies correlating neuroanatomy with metabolism in the developing brain can contribute significantly to our concepts of human behavior and brain function. As the technology of PET becomes more refined, particularly with respect to the development of more specific tracers designed to measure various biochemical processes in the maturing brain, we can expect important breakthroughs in the neurobiology of psychiatric disorders.

REFERENCES

Abrams, R.M., Ito, M., Frisinger, J.E., Patlak, C.S., Pettigre, K.D., and Kennedy, C. 1984. Local cerebral glucose utilization in fetal and neonatal sheep. *Am. J. Physiol.* **246**:R608–R618.

Andre-Thomas, C.Y. and Saint-Anne Dargassies, S. 1960. The neurological examination of the infant. London: *Medical Advisory Committee of the National Spastics Society.*

Awaya, S. 1978. Stimulus vision deprivation amblyopia in humans. In *Strabismus*, ed. R.D. Reinecke, pp.31–44. New York: Grune and Stratton.

Barlow, H.B. 1975. Visual experience and cortical development. *Nature* **258**:199–203.

Basser, L.S. 1962. Hemiplegia of early onset and the faculty of speech with special reference to the effects of hemispherectomy. *Brain* **85**:427–60.

Bear, M.F., Kleinschmidt, A., Gu, Q.A., and Singer, W. 1990. Disruption of experience-dependent synaptic modifications in striate cortex by infusion of an NMDA receptor antagonist. *J. Neurosci.* **10**:909–25.

Bennett-Clarke, C.A., Leslie, M.J., Chiaia, N.L., and Roades, R.W., 1993. Serotonin 1B receptors in the developing somatosensory and visual cortices are located on thalamocortical axons. *Proc. Natl Acad. Sci. USA* **90**:153–7.

Bronson, G. 1974. The postnatal growth of visual capacity. *Child Devel.* **45**:873–90.

Campbell, M. 1988. Fenfluramine treatment of autism. *J Child Psych.* **29**:1–10.

Changeux, J. P. and Danchin, A. 1976. Selective stabilization of developing synapses as a mechanism for the specification of neuronal networks. *Nature* **264**:705–12.

Chugani, H.T. 1994. Development of regional brain glucose metabolism in relation to behavior and plasticity. In *Human behavior and the developing brain*, ed. G. Dawson and K.W. Fischer, pp. 153–75. New York: Guilford Publications, Inc.

Chugani, H.T., Hovda, D.A., Villablanca, J.R., Phelps, M.E., and Xu, W.F. 1991. Metabolic maturation of the brain: a study of local cerebral glucose utilization in the developing cat. *J. Cerebr. Blood Flow Metab.* **11**:35–47.

Chugani, H.T., Mazziotta, J.C., and Phelps, M.E. 1989. Sturge-Weber syndrome: a study of cerebral glucose utilization with positron emission tomography. *J. Pediatr.* **114**:244–53.

Chugani, H.T. and Phelps, M.E. 1986. Maturational changes in cerebral function in infants determined by 18FDG positron emission tomography. *Science* **231**:840–3.

Chugani, H.T., Phelps, M.E., and Mazziotta, J.C. 1987. Positron emission tomography study of human brain functional development. *Ann. Neurol.* **22**:487–97.

Chugani, H.T., Phelps, M.E., and Mazziotta, J.C. 1989.

Metabolic assessment of functional maturation and neuronal plasticity in the human brain. In *Neurobiology of early infant behavior*, ed. G. Dawson and K. W. Fischer pp. 153–75. Wenner-Gren International Symposium Series, vol. 55 (pp. 323–30). New York: Stockton Press.

Cowan, W.M., Fawcett, J.W., O'Leary, D.D.M., and Stanfield, B.B. 1984. Regressive events in neurogenesis. *Science* 225:1258–65.

Curtiss, S. 1977. *Genie: a psycho linguistic study of a modern-day "wild child"*. New York: Academic Press.

Curtiss, S. 1981. Feral children. In *Mental retardation and developmental disabilities XII* , ed. J. Wortis, pp. 129–61. New York: Brunner/Mazel.

D'Amato, R.J., Blue, M.E., Largent, B.L., Lynch, D.R., Ledbetter, D.J., Molliver, M.E., and Snyder, S.H. 1987. Ontogeny of the serotonergic projection to rat neocortex: transient expression of a dense innervation to primary sensory areas. *Proc. Natl Acad. Sci. USA* 84:4322–6.

Diemer, K. 1968. Capillarisation and oxygen supply of the brain. In *Oxygen transport in blood and tissue*, ed. D. W. Lubbers, U.C. Luft, G. Thews, and E. Witzleb, pp. 118–23. Stuttgart: Thieme Inc.

Duffy, T.E., Cavazzuti, M., Cruz, N.F., and Sokoloff, L. 1982. Local cerebral glucose metabolism in newborn dogs: effects of hypoxia and halothane anesthesia. *Ann. Neurol.* 11:233–46.

Feinberg, I., Thode, H.C., Chugani, H.T., and March, J.D. 1990. Gamma distribution model describes maturational curves for delta wave amplitude, cortical metabolic rate and synaptic density. *J. Theor. Biol.* 142:149–61.

Finger, S. and Wolf, C. 1988. The "Kennard effect" before Kennard: the early history of age and brain lesions. *Arch. Neurol.* 45:1136–42.

Freygang, W.H. and Sokoloff, L. 1958. Quantitative measurement of regional circulation in the central nervous system by the use of radioactive inert gas. *Adv. Biol. Med. and Phys.* 6:263–79.

Fuster, J.M. 1984. Behavioral electrophysiology of the prefrontal cortex. *Trends Neurosci.* 7:408–14.

Goldman-Rakic, P.S. 1984. The frontal lobes: uncharted provinces of the brain. *Trends Neurosci.* 7:425–9.

Gregoire, N., Pontier, R., and Salamon, G. 1981. Local cerebral glucose utilization in the newborn brain. *Eur. Neurol.* 20:162–8.

Himwich, H.E. and Fazekas, J.F. 1941. Comparative studies of the metabolism of the brain in infant and adult dogs. *Am. J. Physiol.* 132:454–9.

Hirsch, H.V.B. and Leventhal, A.G. 1978. Functional modification of the developing visual system. In *Handbook of sensory physiology, vol.IX: Development of sensory systems*, ed. M. Jaconson, pp. 279–335. Berlin-Heidelberg: Springer.

Hoshino, Y., Kaneko, M., and Kumashiro, H. 1992. Blood serotonin and free tryptophan concentration in autistic children. In *Neurobiology of infantile autism*, ed. H. Naruse and E.M. Ornitz, pp. 289–92. Amsterdam: Elsevier Science Publishers.

Hubel, D.H. and Wiesel, T.N. 1970. The period of susceptibility to the physiological effects of unilateral eye closure in kittens. *J. Physiol.* 206:419–36.

Huttenlocher, P.R. 1979. Synaptic density in human frontal cortex-developmental changes and effects of aging. *Brain Res.* 163:195–205.

Huttenlocher, P.R. and de Courten, C. 1987. The development of striate cortex in man. *Hum. Neurobiol.* 6:1–9.

Huttenlocher, P.R., de Courten, C., Gary, L.J., and van der Loos, H. 1982. Synaptogenesis in human visual cortex: evidence for synapse elimination during normal development. *Neurosci. Lett.* 33:247–52.

Jacobs, B., Chugani, H.T., Allada, V., Chen, S., Phelps, M.E., Pollack, D.B., and Raleigh, M.J. 1995. Developmental changes in brain metabolism in sedated rhesus macaques and vervet monkeys revealed by positron emission tomography. *Cerebral Cortex* 3:222–33.

Jacobson, M. 1978. *Developmental neurobiology*, 2nd edn., pp. 302–7. New York: Plenum Press.

Kadekaro, M., Crane, A.M., and Sokoloff, L. 1985. Differential effects of electrical stimulation of sciatic nerve on metabolic activity in spinal cord and dorsal root ganglion in the rat. *Proc. Nat. Acad. Sci. USA* 82:6010–13.

Kagan, J. 1972. Do infants think? *Sci. Am.* 226:74–82.

Kellaway, P. 1979. An orderly approach to visual analysis: parameters of the normal EEG in adults and children. In *Current practice of clinical electroencephalography*, ed. D.W. Klass and D.D. Daly, pp. 69–147. New York: Raven Press.

Kennedy, C., Grave, G.D., Jehle, J.W., and Sokoloff, L. 1972. Changes in blood flow in the component structures of the

dog brain during postnatal maturation. *J. Neurochem.*
19:2423–33.

Kennedy, C., Sakurada, O., Shinohara, M., and Miyaoka, M.
1982. Local cerebral glucose utilization in the newborn
macaque monkey. *Ann. Neurol.* 12:333–40.

Kennedy, C. and Sokoloff, L. 1957. An adaptation of the nitrous
oxide method to the study of the cerebral circulation in
children; normal values for cerebral blood flow and
cerebral metabolic rate in childhood. *J. Clin.Invest.*
36:1130–37.

Kling, A. 1965. Behavioural and somatic development following
lesions of the amygdala in the cat. *J. Psychiat. Res.*
3:263–73.

Lenneberg, E. 1967. *Biological foundations of language*, pp.
125–87. New York: John Wiley.

Leslie, M.J., Bennett-Clarke, C.A., and Rhoades, R.W. 1992.
Serotonergic 1B receptors form a transient vibrissa-related
pattern in primary somatosensory cortex of the developing
rat. *Dev. Brain Res.* **69**:143–48.

Marg, E. 1982. Prentice Memorial Lecture: is the animal model
for stimulus deprivation amblyopia in children valid or
useful? *Am. J. Optometry Physiol. Optics* **59**:451–64.

Mata, M., Fink, D.J., Gainer, H., Smith, C.B., Davidsen, L.,
Savaki, H., Schwartz, W.J., and Sokoloff, L. 1980. Activity-
dependent energy metabolism in rat posterior pituitary
primarily reflects sodium pump activity. *J. Neurochemistry*
34:213–15.

Mazziotta, J.C. and Gilman, S. 1992. *Clinical brain imaging:
principles and applications.* Contemporary Neurology Series.
Philadelphia: F.A. Davis Co.

Morest, D.K. 1969. The growth of dendrites in the mammalian
brain. *Z. Anat. Entwicklungsgeschichte* **128**:290–317.

Nehlig, A., Pereira De Vasconcelos, A., and Boyet, S. 1988.
Quantitative autoradiographic measurement of local
cerebral glucose utilization in freely moving rats during
postnatal development. *J. Neurosci.* 8:321–33.

Nudo, R.J. and Masterton, R.B. 1986. Stimulation-induced
{14C}2–deoxyglucose labeling of synaptic activity in the
central auditory system. *J. Comp. Neurol.* 245:553–65.

Parmelee, A.H. and Sigman, M.D. 1983. Perinatal brain
development and behavior. In *Biology and infancy, vol. II,*
ed. M. Haith and J. Campos, pp. 95–155. New York: John
Wiley.

Pettigrew, J.D. 1974. The effect of visual experience on the
development of stimulus specificity by kitten cortical
neurones. *J. Physiol.* 237:49–74.

Pfaff, D.W. 1982. Neurobiological mechanisms of sexual
motivation. In *The physiological mechanisms of motivation,*
ed. D.W. Pfaff, pp. 287–317. New York: Springer.

Phelps, M.E., Hoffman, E.J., Mullani, N.A., and Ter-Pogossian,
M.M. 1975. Application of annihilation coincidence
detection to transaxial reconstruction tomography. *J. Nucl.
Med.* **16**:210–24.

Rabinowicz, T. 1979. The differentiated maturation of the
human cerebral cortex. In *Human growth, vol. 3.
Neurobiology and nutrition,* ed. F. Falkner and J. M. Tanner,
pp. 97–123. New York: Plenum Press.

Rakic, P., Bourgeois, J.P., Eckenhoff, M.F., Zecevic, N., and
Goldman-Rakic, P.S. 1986. Concurrent overproduction of
synapses in diverse regions of the primate cerebral cortex.
Science 232:232–5.

Rauschecker, J.P. and Hahn, S. 1987. Ketamine-xylazine
anaesthesia blocks consolidation of ocular dominance
changes in kitten visual cortex. *Nature* 326:183–5.

Rauschecker, J.P. and Marler, P. 1987. What signals are
responsible for synaptic changes in visual cortical
plasticity? In *Imprinting and cortical plasticity,* ed. J.
Rauschecker and P. Marler, pp. 193–220. New York: John
Wiley.

Rhoades, R.W., Bennett-Clarke, C.A., Shi, M.-Y., and Mooney,
R.D. 1994. Effect of 5–HT on thalamocortical synaptic
transmission in the developing rat. *J. Neurophysiol.*
72:2438–50.

Sakurada, O., Kennedy, C., Jehle, J., Brown, J.D., Carbin, G.L.,
and Sokoloff, L. 1978. Measurement of local cerebral blood
flow with iodo[^{14}C] antipyrine. *Am. J. Physiol.*
234:H59–H66.

Schade, J.P. and van Groenigen, W.B. 1961. Structural
organization of the human cerebral cortex. *Acta Anat.*
47:74–111.

Schain R.J., and Freedman D.X. 1961. Studies on 5–hydroxy
indole metabolism in autistic and other mentally retarded
children. *J. Pediatr.* 58:315–20.

Schwartz, T.L., Linberg, J.V., Tillman, W., and Odom, J.V.
1987. Monocular depth and vernier acuities: a comparison
of binocular and uniocular subjects. *Invest. Ophthalmol.
Visual Sci.* **28**(Suppl.):304.

Sherman, S.M. and Spear, P. D. 1982. Organization of visual

pathways in normal and visually deprived cats. *Physiol. Rev.* **62**:738–855.

Sokoloff, L., Reivich, M., Kennedy, C., Desrosie, M.H., Patlak, C.S., Pettigre, K.D., Sakurada, O., and Shinohara, M. 1977. The [^{14}C] deoxyglucose method for the measurement of local cerebral glucose utilization: theory, procedure, and normal values in the conscious and anesthetized albino rat. *J. Neurochem.* **28**:897–916.

Spinelli, D.N., Hirsch, H.V.B., Phelps, R.W., and Metzler, J. 1972. Visual experience as a determinant of the response characteristics of cortical receptive fields in cats. *Exp. Brain Res.* **15**:289–304.

Ter-Pogossian, M.M., Phelps, M.E., Hoffman, E.J., and Mullani, N.A. 1975. A positron emission transaxial tomograph for nuclear imaging (PETT). *Radiology* **114**:89–98.

Timney, B. 1983. The effects of early and late monocular deprivation on binocular depth perception in cats. *Devel. Brain Res.* **7**: 235–43.

Tyler, D.B., and van Harreveld, A. 1942. The respiration of the developing brain. *Am. J. Physiol.* **136**:600–3.

Vaegan, and Taylor, D. 1979. Critical period for deprivation amblyopia in children. *Trans. Ophthalmol. Soc. UK* **99**:432–9.

Voeller, L., Pappas, G.D., and Purpura, D.P. 1963. Electron microscope study of development of cat superficial neocortex. *Exp. Neurol.* **7**: 107–30.

Von Hofsten, C. 1982. Eye-hand coordination in the newborn. *Devel. Psychol.* **18**:450–61.

Winfield, D.A. 1981. The postnatal development of synapses in the visual cortex of the cat and the effects of eyelid suture. *Brain Res.* **206**:166–71.

Winfield, D.A. 1983. The postnatal development of synapses in different laminae of the visual cortex in the normal kitten and in kittens with eyelid suture. *Devel. Brain Res.* **9**:155–69.

8

Long-term effects of different early rearing experiences on social, emotional, and physiological development in nonhuman primates

STEPHEN J. SUOMI

INTRODUCTION

The basic idea that certain early experiences can have important consequences for adult functioning has been a central feature of many developmental theories throughout the history of psychiatry, psychology, and ethology alike. From his earliest writings on psychoanalysis, Freud argued that events transpiring during an individual's first 3 years had life-long influences on that individual's personality and intrapsychic dynamics. In the 1930s Konrad Lorenz appropriated the embryological concept of critical periods to account for permanent social preferences established via imprinting mechanisms by precocial birds shortly after hatching. Behaviorally oriented psychologists generated social learning theories in the 1950s which postulated that the most important aspects of personality development initially were derived from a newborn's early experiences with feeding. John Bowlby, borrowing concepts from both psychoanalytic and ethological frameworks, formulated a theory of social attachment in the 1960s and 1970s which had as its most basic premise the notion that all of an individual's social relationships throughout life were influenced in fundamental ways by the initial attachment relationship with one's mother. Developmental neuroscience approaches of the 1980s and 1990s have focused on issues relating to differential nervous system plasticity during different phases of development, especially long-term neurobiological changes associated with events experienced during early critical or sensitive periods. At the heart of all of these

approaches has been the basic belief that "the child is the father of the man," that early experiences can and do shape adult functioning.

Not surprisingly, for many years researchers and clinicians alike have searched for causal links between the experiences of human infants and children and adult behavioral and emotional characteristics. Direct, unambiguous links, however, have not been easy to establish empirically (Lewis, in press). While clinical reports suggesting powerful, clear-cut relationships between specific early experiences and later proclivities abound, the retrospective nature of most of these reports precludes the establishment of scientifically acceptable causality. There also is a dearth of relevant prospective data, largely a consequence of the formidable ethical and practical obstacles that daunt researchers' attempts to design and carry out appropriately controlled human longitudinal studies that follow individuals from infancy to adulthood. As a result, theoretical speculations regarding specific long-term consequences of certain early experiences have generally outstripped the actual human data.

By contrast, over the past half-century there have been a wealth of studies prospectively investigating the consequences of different early physical and social environments on behavioral and physiological development in many species of animals. Most of these studies have been carried out with rodents, birds, and invertebrates, and from the body of this work have come many compelling and convincing accounts of how specific early experiences come to affect adult behavior, sensory capabilities and perceptual preferences, neuroendocrine and psychophysiological activities, and, increasingly in recent years, neurochemical and neuroanatomical functioning. Of course, the relevance of these extensive and often exciting findings for considerations of relationships between human early experiences and adult characteristics is largely dependent on the degree to which the animal phenomena in question generalize to the human case. The most compelling generalizations between animals and humans typically occur when the animal data come from our closest evolutionary relatives – nonhuman simian primates.

Monkeys and apes share most of our genes (e.g., the genetic overlap between humans and rhesus monkeys is approximately 94% while between chimpanzees and humans the overlap is 98–99%; Lovejoy 1981; Sibley *et al.* 1990), and so many aspects of their morphology and physiology are homologous with ours. The basic patterns and sequences of brain development are also highly conserved across the primate order, especially among Old World monkeys, apes, and humans. Moreover, the rich behavioral and emotional repertoires and cognitive capabilities of monkeys and apes provide opportunities for modeling aspects of human socioemotional development that are simply not feasible with rodents or other nonprimate animals (Suomi in press, a). These behavioral and emotional patterns provide a face validity for primate models that cannot be matched in any other species.

This chapter reviews recent findings regarding long-term effects of different early rearing experiences on adult social, emotional, and physiological functioning in nonhuman primates. Much of the relevant research comes from studies with rhesus monkeys (*Macaca mulatta*) in both laboratory and field settings, and these will provide the main focus of the review. The chapter will begin with a description of species-normative patterns of social and emotional development from infancy to adulthood in rhesus monkeys living in the wild. Next, two clearly aberrant patterns of development that spontaneously appear in wild populations of rhesus monkeys will be examined. These two abnormal developmental trajectories are of special interest because in many ways they appear to mimic distinctive features of human internalizing and externalizing disorders, respectively. Recent laboratory studies have demonstrated that specific types of early rearing

experiences greatly increase the risk that each of these aberrant developmental patterns will emerge, at least for some individuals. These patterns include behavioral as well as physiological abnormalities, and each will be described in detail. The chapter will close with a discussion of the relevance of these findings from studies with nonhuman primates for understanding developmental issues in human psychopathology.

SPECIES-NORMATIVE PATTERNS OF SOCIAL AND EMOTIONAL DEVELOPMENT IN RHESUS MONKEYS

Rhesus monkeys are perhaps the most extensively studied species of nonhuman primates in the world, a fact that should not seem surprising given that they not only are among the most populous and widespread species of nonhuman primates living in natural habitats today, but also are able to adapt to a wide variety of captive environments with relative ease. In the wild, rhesus monkeys live in large, distinctive social groups (termed "troops") that range in size from several dozen to several hundred individuals. Each troop is organized around several multigenerational matrilines, a consequence of the species-normative pattern in which all females remain in the troop in which they were born for their entire lives, whereas virtually all males emigrate from their natal troop around puberty, eventually joining other nearby troops (Lindburg 1971). Each rhesus monkey troop is also characterized by multiple dominance hierarchies, both between and within matrilines, as well as among the adolescent and adult males that have immigrated into the troop (Sade 1967). This pattern of social organization is relatively common among Old World monkey species, especially within the genus *Macaca* (Lindburg 1991).

Rhesus monkey infants are born with strong behavioral propensities, clear-cut perceptual biases, and a host of physical and social features that make them highly attractive to conspecifics, ensuring that they become a major focus of attention within their respective extended families. At the same time, each infant's behavioral predispositions and preferences serve to channel virtually all of its energy and effort toward maintaining physical contact with its mother, providing the initial basis for the establishment of a strong attachment relationship with her. As a result, rhesus monkey infants spend virtually all of their first days and weeks of life in the immediate presence of their mothers, who provide them with nourishment, physical and psychological warmth, and protection (Harlow *et al.* 1963).

In their second month of life rhesus monkey infants begin to leave their mothers for brief exploratory forays. By this time each infant has already established a strong social attachment bond with its mother, and it uses her as a "secure base" from which to organize the exploration of its immediate environment. In the course of such exploration the infant encounters other members of its troop, and in the succeeding weeks and months it spends increasing amounts of time away from its mother engaging in extensive interactions with others, especially peers. From 6 months of age onward play with peers becomes the predominant social activity for young rhesus monkeys. These play interactions become increasingly complex and involve specific sequences and patterns of behavior that appear to simulate virtually all adult social activities, including reproductive behavior and dominance/aggressive interactions (Suomi and Harlow 1975).

Puberty in rhesus monkeys begins on average near the end of the third year of life (for females) and the start of the fourth year (for males), and it is clearly associated with major life transitions for both sexes. Although females remain in their natal troop throughout this period and thereafter, their interactions with peers decline dramatically, and they redirect much of their social activities toward other members of their own matriline, including the infants that they subsequently bear (Berman 1982). Pubertal males, by contrast, leave their natal troop and typically join all-male gangs for varying periods before they attempt to enter a new troop (Berard 1989). It should be noted that adolescence and early adulthood is clearly the most dangerous period of life for a male rhesus monkey – in the wild, the mortality rate for males from the time they leave their natal troop until they are successfully integrated into a new troop approaches 50% (Dittus 1979). It is also clear that individual males employ different "strategies" in their efforts to join a new troop, and that each strategy entails a different set of potential risks and benefits (Suomi *et al.* 1992).

The above-described sequences of behavioral ontogeny and pattern of social troop organization have been consistently documented not only in rhesus monkey troops living in the wild but also in groups maintained in captivity and can therefore be considered normative for the species. Relatively few (i.e., less than 2%) rhesus monkeys in the wild live beyond 20 years of age. In contrast, rhesus monkeys maintained in captive environments (where there is typically plenty of food, no predators, and comparatively few parasites) routinely live until their late 20s or early 30s, during which time they exhibit clear-cut signs of aging. For example, captive females typically undergo menopause in their mid-to-late twenties (Walker 1995), whereas the vast majority of rhesus monkey females in the wild perish well before the first signs of menopause, a situation parallel to that of most human females prior to the last few centuries.

NON-NORMATIVE PATTERNS OF DEVELOPMENT AMONG FREE-RANGING RHESUS MONKEYS

Although the vast majority of rhesus monkeys living in the wild follow the general sequence of development outlined above, there are substantial differences among individual monkeys in the precise timing and relative ease through which they make major developmental transitions, as well as how they manage the day-to-day challenges and stresses that are an inevitable consequence of life in complex social groups. Recent research has identified two subgroups of individuals born and raised in natural settings who exhibit aberrant developmental trajectories that often result in increased long-term risk of morbidity and even mortality.

High reactivity

Members of one subgroup, comprising approximately 20% of most populations of rhesus monkeys studied to date, consistently exhibit unusual behavioral disruption and enhanced physiological arousal in the face of a wide range of stimuli that most of the other monkeys in their social group often find interesting and readily explore (with minimal physiological arousal). These *high-reactive* (or "uptight") individuals typically respond instead with behavioral expressions of fear and anxiety and with significant (and often prolonged) activation of the hypothalamic-pituitary-adrenal (HPA) axis, sympathetic nervous system arousal, and increased noradrenergic turnover (Suomi 1986).

High-reactive rhesus monkeys can usually be identified within their first month of life, and in the absence of dramatic environmental change their tendency toward extreme behavioral and physiological responsiveness to relatively mild environmental perturbations appears remarkably stable from infancy to adulthood. High-reactive infants typically begin leaving their mothers for brief exploratory forays later chronologically and tend to explore less overall than other infants in their birth cohort. Similarly, high-reactive youngsters tend to be shy and withdrawn in their initial encounters with agemates. Laboratory studies of high-reactive juveniles placed in novel playrooms with unfamiliar peers have demonstrated that they also exhibit higher and more stable heart rates and more elevated levels of plasma corticotropin (ACTH) and cortisol than those of their less reactive interaction partners (Suomi 1991a). In the absence of obvious environmental challenge, however, high-reactive infants and juveniles usually are indistinguishable, both behaviorally and physiologically, from others in their birth cohort.

On the other hand, behavioral and physiological differences between high-reactive and other infants and juveniles often become exaggerated when environmental perturbations are extreme and/or prolonged. For example, virtually all rhesus monkey youngsters annually experience repeated functional maternal separations when their mothers leave the troop for several hours or even days to consort with selected males during the 2–3 month breeding season each year. The vast majority of these juveniles initially react with behavioral agitation and obvious physiological arousal, much as Bowlby (1960,1973) described for human infants and young children experiencing involuntary maternal separation. Most of these monkeys soon begin to adapt to their mothers' repeated departures and typically expand their interactions with others in their social group while their mothers are away in consort (Berman et al. 1994). In contrast, high-reactive juveniles often lapse into a behavioral depression characterized by increasing lethargy and social withdrawal, obvious eating and sleeping difficulties, and a striking fetal-like huddling posture sometimes maintained for hours on end (Suomi 1991b). Such reactions are reminiscent of Bowlby's description of the "despair" phase of prototypical human response to maternal separation (Bowlby 1960, 1973).

Laboratory studies of rhesus monkey responses to social separation have both replicated and extended these findings from the field. Relative to their like-reared peers, high-reactive infants and juveniles are not only more likely to exhibit depressive-like behavioral responses to separation but also tend to show greater and longer HPA activation, more dramatic sympathetic arousal, more rapid central norepinephrine (noradrenaline) turnover, and greater selective immunosuppression (Suomi 1991a). They also typically fail to suppress cortisol output following dexamethasone challenge during separation (but not during reunion), unlike their less reactive peers (Kalin et al. 1983), and they appear to be differentially responsive to both tricyclic and serotonin selective reuptake inhibitor (SSRI) medications, especially during periods of social separation (Suomi 1991b).

These differential patterns of behavioral and physiological response to separation remain quite stable throughout development. Rhesus monkeys who exhibited depressive reactions to separations as infants are at high risk to display extreme reactions to subsequent separations throughout their juvenile, adolescent, and even adult years, relative to those whose early separation reactions were mild (Suomi 1995). An increasing body of evidence has demonstrated significant heritability for such differences in behavioral and physiological reactivity, although the specific patterns of heritability differ somewhat among the various behavioral and physiological measures examined to date (Higley et al. 1993).

Recent field studies have shown that high-reactive rhesus monkey adolescent males usually emigrate from their natal troop at significantly older ages than the rest of their birth cohort. When they do finally leave their home troop, high-reactive young males typically employ much more conservative strategies for entering a new troop than do less reactive male peers (Suomi et al. 1992). High-reactive young females appear to be at greater risk for inadequate maternal care of their first-born offspring than are other primiparous mothers (Suomi and Ripp 1983).

Although reliable information regarding relative morbidity and mortality rates among high-reactive rhesus monkeys of different age-sex classes in field settings does not currently exist (the relevant data are only now being collected), some recent findings from captive rhesus monkeys living in multiacre outdoor enclosures are intriguing. During periods of relatively low environmental stress, high-reactive monkeys of all ages and both sexes tended to have significantly *lower* rates of accidents and injuries than low-reactive members of their troop. During periods of high environmental stress, however, the accident and injury rates among high-reactive individuals skyrocketed, while such rates remained surprisingly stable, and consequently lower, for the low-reactive group members (Boyce *et al.* in press). These findings suggest that high reactivity in rhesus monkeys can serve as a protective factor in benign environments but can become a significant risk factor under conditions of high and/or prolonged environmental stress. These and other data collected under field-like conditions clearly demonstrate that high reactivity in rhesus monkeys need not inevitably lead to negative outcomes. On the contrary, under some circumstances high reactivity can be associated with highly advantageous and occasionally optimal life-long consequences (Suomi, in press b).

High impulsivity

A second subgroup of rhesus monkeys that typically exhibit aberrant developmental trajectories in wild populations can be generally characterized as unusually impulsive in their behavioral activities, especially those that result in aggressive interchanges. These individuals, rarely comprising more than 5–10% of the populations and more "obvious" among males than females, also tend to have chronically low central serotonin metabolism, as indexed by cerebrospinal fluid (CSF) levels of 5–hydroxy-indoleacetic acid (5–HIAA), the primary central serotonin metabolite in primates.

Both the behavioral and physiological features that characterize these "impulsive" or "jumpy" monkeys appear relatively early in development and are notably stable from then on (Higley *et al.* 1994). Impulsive individuals, especially males, distinguish themselves from

same-sex peers in early play interactions: they seem to lack the ability to moderate their behavioral responses, and consequently their rough-and-tumble play interactions often escalate into tissue-damaging aggressive exchanges, disproportionately at their own expense. Impulsive juvenile males also display a propensity for making dangerous leaps from treetop to treetop, occasionally with disastrous outcomes. CSF samples obtained from free-ranging populations of rhesus monkeys reveal that these impulsive individuals also have disproportionately low concentrations of 5–HIAA that typically remain low as these monkeys start to mature (Mehlman *et al.* 1994).

It appears that relatively few of these young impulsive males actually get the opportunity to mature fully. Instead, most are expelled from their natal troop well before puberty, a result more likely a consequence of social incompetence than any general aggressive tendencies per se (Mehlman *et al.* 1995). These monkeys are usually too inexperienced and socially inept to be able to readily join other social groups, and most eventually become solitary and typically perish within a year (Higley *et al.* in press). The likelihood that they can make significant contributions to any troop's gene pool does not seem great.

On the other hand, females who exhibit excessive impulsive-aggressive behavior also characteristically have chronically low CSF 5–HIAA concentrations. Unlike males, they are unlikely to be expelled from their natal troop (or even matriline) at any time during their lives, although laboratory studies suggest that they typically remain at the bottom of their respective dominance hierarchies. These females also clearly produce and rear infants, although laboratory studies again suggest that they often are inept and incompetent mothers (Higley *et al.* 1996a).

In sum, rhesus monkeys who behave impulsively (and have low central serotonin turnover) early in life tend to exhibit aberrant developmental trajectories that often result in premature death for males and chronically low social dominance for females. There is increasing and compelling evidence that these behavioral and physiological features are highly heritable; certainly they are developmentally stable.

Thus, both high reactivity and high impulsiveness – and their specific physiological concomitants – are typically associated with developmental trajectories for rhesus monkeys that differ substantially from species-normative patterns. Their long-term outcomes, however, are not always negative and can, in some circumstances, even be optimal. An increasing body of data from studies with other nonhuman primate species clearly indicates that these two basically aberrant developmental trajectories are not limited to rhesus monkeys, but rather have turned up in virtually all primate species that have been investigated to date. Other investigators have reported seemingly analogous phenomena in an impressive variety of nonprimate and even nonmammalian species (Kagan *et al.* 1994).

EFFECTS OF DIFFERENTIAL EARLY SOCIAL EXPERIENCE ON DEVELOPMENTAL TRAJECTORIES

It has long been known that early social experiences can have dramatic long-term behavioral and emotional consequences for rhesus monkeys and other nonhuman primate species. Research by Harlow and his Wisconsin colleagues, among others, in the 1960s clearly demonstrated that extreme social deprivation throughout infancy almost always results in extreme (and often permanent) behavioral abnormalities and severe social and emotional deficits, especially evident in aggressive, reproductive, and parenting activities (e.g., Harlow *et al.* 1965). Few of these early social isolation studies included any measures of physiological functioning, although long-term follow-up and post-mortem investigations did find significant differences from socially reared control subjects in various aspects of brain physiology and neuroanatomy, even down to the level of ultrastructural differences within certain cell types (Suomi 1982).

While the evidence that prolonged early social isolation inevitably has severe long-term consequences for rhesus monkeys is overwhelming, the relevance of these findings for cases involving early social deprivation of human infants and young children seems unclear, given that (fortunately) virtually no human infants experience the degree of social deprivation for comparable developmental periods as the early rhesus monkey studies entailed. Perhaps as a consequence, more recent studies of early social deprivation have utilized rearing environments that provide a much greater degree of social stimulation during "deprivation" periods, e.g., access to foster mothers and/or peers, than did the early isolation experiments. Monkeys reared in such environments develop few, if any, of the bizarre, idiosyncratic stereotypic patterns of behavior so characteristic of isolated repertoires; instead, most aspects of their social and emotional development generally mimic species-normative patterns. Nevertheless, even relatively "mild" forms of early social deprivation can have significant short- and long-term behavioral and physiological consequences (Suomi 1991c).

Effects of early peer rearing

Numerous studies have examined the effects of rearing infant monkeys away from their mothers but in the company of other infants like themselves. A frequently used rearing paradigm for these studies involves separating infants from their mothers at birth, hand-rearing them in a nursery for the first month, and then introducing them to same-age peers, with whom they live continuously (usually in mixed-sex groups of four to six infants) until 6 months of age, after which they are moved into larger peer groups that also contain mother-reared age mates and sometimes older adults. Both peer-reared and mother-reared youngsters continue to live in these mixed social groups at least until puberty.

Rhesus monkey infants reared according to this protocol readily develop strong attachment bonds to each other, much as mother-reared infants develop an attachment to their biological mother. Peers are not nearly as effective as a typical monkey mother, however, in providing a "secure base" for exploration or in reducing fear in the face of novelty or stress, and the attachment relationships these peer-reared monkeys develop with each other are likely to be "anxious" in nature. As a consequence, while peer-reared monkeys show normal physical and motor development and relatively normal complex social behavioral repertoires, they seem reluctant to explore novel objects, they tend to be shy in initial encounters with unfamiliar peers, and they typically drop to the bottom of their respective dominance hierarchies when grouped with mother-reared monkeys of their age (Suomi 1995).

Differences between peer-reared and mother-reared

rhesus monkeys become considerably more dramatic under conditions of greater environmental stress. For example, peer-reared monkeys consistently exhibit more severe behavioral and physiological reactions to social separation than do their mother-reared cohorts (Higley and Suomi 1989). Such differences in separation reactions persist from infancy to adolescence, if not beyond. Interestingly, the general nature of the separation reactions of peer-reared monkeys – excessive self-directed and stereotypic behavior, high and prolonged adrenocortical activation, increased central noradrenergic turnover, and selectively decreased immune system responsiveness – seems to mirror that of "naturally" high-reactive mother-reared subjects. Peer-reared monkeys characteristically exhibit "high-reactive-like" biobehavioral responses to other environmental stressors as well. Thus, early peer rearing appears to have the effect of making monkeys more high-reactive than they might have been if reared "naturally", i.e., by their biological mother (Suomi 1995).

Early peer rearing appears to have another long-term developmental consequence for rhesus monkeys as well – it tends to make them more impulsive, especially if they are males. Like the previously described impulsive monkeys growing up in the wild, peer-reared monkeys initially exhibit impulsive tendencies in the context of juvenile play, and as they approach puberty the frequency and severity of their aggressive episodes greatly exceeds that of mother-reared group members of similar age. Both peer-reared males and females tend to be toward the bottom of their respective dominance hierarchies in mixed social groups, and peer-reared juveniles and adolescents of both sexes are more likely to be removed from such mixed groups for both social and veterinary reasons than are the mother-reared group members. These behavioral differences in dominance and impulsive aggression between peer-reared and mother-reared juveniles and adolescents remain robust when the monkeys are subsequently moved into newly formed social groups composed initially of strangers, and they appear to be quite stable developmentally (Higley et al. 1996b).

It is of considerable interest that peer-reared monkeys also consistently show lower CSF concentrations of 5–HIAA than their mother-reared age mates. These group differences in 5–HIAA levels appear relatively early (i.e.,

well before 6 months of age), they persist through the transition to mixed group housing at 6 months, and they remain remarkably stable at least until adolescence despite significant developmental drops in 5–HIAA levels for mother- and peer-reared monkeys alike (Higley et al. 1992). Thus, peer-reared monkeys as a group resemble the impulsive subgroup of wild-living (and mother-reared) monkeys not only behaviorally but also in terms of serotonergic functioning throughout development.

In summary, early peer-rearing not only seems to make rhesus monkey youngsters more highly reactive but also more impulsive, and the resulting developmental trajectories not only resemble those of naturally occurring subgroups of rhesus monkeys in the wild but also continue in that vein long after the differential peer-rearing procedures have been completed. What processes or mechanisms might be responsible for such diverse and long-term developmental consequences of early peer rearing?

One set of aberrant processes associated with early peer rearing derives not from what such rearing provides but from what it does not, i.e., the stimulation normally coming from the infant's biological mother. Mothers obviously provide many different levels and types of stimulation to their infants over the first 6 months of life, and different investigators have emphasized different aspects of these maternal contributions. For example, Hofer (1995) has stressed the regulatory contributions a mother provides, including early entrainment of circadian and other biological rhythms emerging in the infant's rapidly developing nervous system. Kraemer has emphasized the different sets of expectations an infant develops when it grows up with its mother instead of with same-age peers (Kraemer 1992).

Other investigators have focused on differences in the types of attachment relationships infants form with their mothers compared with those involving peers. For them, the secret to the peer-reared monkeys' increased reactivity to environmental challenge can be traced to the insecure attachment an infant develops with a like-reared peer, relative to that shared with a mother. Peer-reared monkeys become insecurely attached because they cannot serve each other as either secure bases or reliable fear-reducing, soothing sources of stimulation nearly as effectively as can a mother. This, according to attachment-oriented researchers, is the real basis of peer-reared monkeys' high reactivity (Suomi 1995).

Multiple explanations for the enhanced impulsiveness and reduced serotonin turnover shown by peer-reared monkeys also abound: they include many of the same factors postulated above for reactivity. In addition, some researchers have proposed that some of the peer-reared monkeys' seeming impulsiveness and social ineptness might be a consequence of the restricted and somewhat crude patterns of play they develop with their peer partners (Higley and Suomi 1996). Put simply, peer-reared monkeys are not usually very good play partners, and hence peer-reared monkeys are, to some degree, play-deprived even though they live with continuous access to potential playmates. One long-term consequence of play deprivation might entail restricted opportunities to develop and practice impulse control, a normal feature of complicated rough-and-tumble play patterns in mother-reared juvenile monkeys (Suomi 1979).

These various explanations for both the immediate and the long-term consequences of early peer rearing are neither mutually exclusive nor necessarily exhaustive. Indeed, it seems unlikely that any single factor, process, or mechanism could account for all the diverse behavioral and physiological effects attributed to early peer rearing. Instead, it appears more likely that multiple factors are at work – individually, interactively, or both.

Effects of early environmental perturbations

The laboratory rearing conditions for rhesus monkeys described above clearly do not match the social and sensory richness of species-normative natural habitats; rather, they involve some degree of chronic deprivation during presumably important, if not crucial, periods of development. It is perhaps not surprising that such early deprivation is associated with long-term risk for behavioral, emotional, and physiological dysfunction, especially in the face of subsequent environmental challenge. What is instead noteworthy is that such dysfunctional patterns closely resemble patterns seen in subgroups within rhesus monkey troops living in the wild.

While most monkeys living in the wild do not experience chronic maternal deprivation from birth (if they do, they seldom survive infancy), they inevitably experience

relatively brief periods of physical, physiological, and emotional stress, often unpredictable and occasionally intense, even life-threatening. To what extent do such episodic experiences have long-term consequences? To date, relevant data from the field are generally too sparse to be definitive, although active current efforts are already yielding interesting preliminary tendencies. On the other hand, some recent laboratory studies clearly indicate that seemingly "minor" environmental perturbations can have striking long-term behavioral and physiological consequences, especially when such perturbations affect the mother–infant relationship.

For example, Rosenblum and his colleagues (1994) have studied the effects of systematically manipulating ease of access to food for mothers and their infants and have found significant effects that persist at least until puberty. The basic experimental paradigm has involved a procedure in which groups of female bonnet macaques (members of the same genus as rhesus macaques) and their infants must forage for their daily diet; the time and effort required for sufficient foraging to sustain the diet can be altered experimentally. Perhaps the most striking findings to date have come from comparisons between groups of mothers and infants provided with essentially an ad lib supply of food (low foraging demand (LFD)) and those whose food availability switched biweekly from ad lib (LFD) to a condition of relatively high foraging demand (requiring several hours of foraging each day to maintain normal dietary intake). These latter groups experienced such biweekly shifts for a total of 14 weeks, beginning when the infants were on average 11 weeks old (variable foraging demand (VFD)). After the 14-week experimental period, both LFD and VFD groups were maintained on identical ad lib feeding schedules (Andrews and Rosenblum 1991).

Andrews and Rosenblum found minimal behavioral differences between the LFD and VFD mothers and their infants, respectively, during periods of differential foraging. When VFD and LFD dyads, however, were subsequently challenged by brief introductions to a novel playroom, VFD infants left their mothers to explore less frequently and engaged in less social play than LFD infants, reflecting "less secure" attachments to their mothers (Andrews and Rosenblum 1991). Brief (20½ h) separations, however, did not distinquish the two groups of infants behaviorally, although individual differences in the nature and intensity of reaction tended to be highly stable across repeated separations (Andrews and Rosenblum 1993).

Surprising long-term consequences of the 14–week period of VFD treatment during infancy emerged when VFD and LFD monkeys were challenged pharmacologically by a noradrenergic probe (yohimbine) and a serotonergic probe (mCPP), respectively, when they were 3 years old. VFD monkeys were generally hyperresponsive to the noradrenergic yohimbine, increasing patterns characteristic of "behavioral inhibition" (Kagan et al. 1984); in contrast, they were generally hyporesponsive to the serotonergic probe (Rosenblum et al. 1994). Moreover, at 4 years of age VFD monkeys exhibited persistently elevated CSF levels of corticotropin-releasing factor (CRF) relative to those of LFD monkeys (Coplan et al. 1996).

These findings thus demonstrate that seemingly minor environmental perturbations, e.g., 14 weeks of varied food availability, can have significant, indeed dramatic, behavioral and physiological consequences that sometimes become apparent only later in life. Presumably, these effects resulted from the differential treatment of infants by VFD and LFD mothers during the 14-week period, rather than differential foraging by the infants themselves. It is therefore of considerable interest that the effects of VFD on these infants, in the words of Andrews and Rosenblum (1991:686) "a consequence of less secure attachment" conceptually, seem quite similar (in pattern if not in degree) to the behavioral and physiological consequences of peer-rearing in rhesus monkeys. Both cases involve insecure early attachments and both are associated with subsequent behavioral and physiological manifestations of increased reactivity and, to some extent, impulsivity.

A different form of environmental "perturbation" was utilized by Mineka et al. (1986) to study the effects of differential early experience among peer-reared rhesus monkeys. Their focus was on controllability, i.e., the degree to which young monkeys had "control" of access to highly desirable features of their environment. Some youngsters could obtain food treats and fruit drinks by pulling chains or pressing panels in their group cage, whereas others served as "yoked controls," i.e., they received exactly the same food and liquid treats, at the very

same time, as the monkeys with "control". These two conditions – "mastery" and yoked control – were maintained over the monkeys' first 11 months of life.

This ostensibly subtle difference in environmental controllability was associated with significant differences in behavior between 7 and 10 months of age, with the mastery group demonstrating less fearful behavior in response to novel objects and more exploratory behavior in a standard playroom than did members of the yoked control group. In contrast, there were minimal differences between mastery and control monkeys when they were in their respective home cages (Mineka et al. 1986).

When these monkeys were 3 years old, they were subjected to a pharmacological challenge, using the benzodiazepine receptor inverse agonist β-carboline-3-carboxylic acid ethyl ester (B-CCE), an experimental anxiogenic compound (Insel et al. 1988). Prior to drug treatment, monkeys with previous mastery experience were slightly more playful, less passive, and had lower plasma cortisol levels than their previously yoked counterparts. Treatment with B-CCE significantly increased activity and responsiveness to human observers, and decreased self-directed behavior, in the mastery monkeys, whereas B-CCE treatment decreased exploration and increased anxious-like behavior in the previously yoked control monkeys. Thus, early experience with an absence of control of access to highly preferred food and drink was associated with both short-term deficits in response to novel physical environments and increased long-term susceptability to the effects of an anxiogenic compound.

SOME GENERAL PRINCIPLES AND IMPLICATIONS FOR CONSIDERATION OF HUMAN PSYCHOPATHOLOGY

The research findings reviewed in the previous sections clearly indicate that certain early experiences can result in dramatic long-term alterations of developmental trajectories for macaque monkeys. Although the precise nature and timing of the relevant early experiences differed somewhat from study to study, as did the long-term consequences, it is nevertheless possible to glean some general principles from this body of data.

First, even though the early experience manipulations carried out in these laboratory studies were predominantly behavioral in nature, the long-term consequences included physiological as well as behavioral features in these monkeys. Specifically, early experience with peer-rearing, variable foraging schedules, or lack of control of access to desirable treats resulted in long-term alteration of hypothalamic-pituitary-adrenal activity in all cases and changes in both noradrenergic and serotonergic functioning in most. Such alterations occurred in spite of the fact that significant heritability could be demonstrated for most, if not all, of the affected physiological systems (Higley *et al.* 1993). Thus, biological systems, even highly heritable ones, seem essentially as vulnerable to the effects of adverse early experiences as are behavioral repertoires or social relationships. The general principle that the brain itself can be changed by certain early experiences is strongly supported by the extant nonhuman primate data.

A second general principle involves the environmental circumstances under which long-term effects of early experiences were most likely to be expressed. Simply put, the most dramatic displays of early experience effects seemed to occur in the context of stress or challenge. In the absence of challenge, both behavioral and physiological consequences of specific early experiences remained largely masked. Thus, the actual nature and magnitude of early experience effects may be as dependant on contemporaneous eliciting conditions as on the original experiences themselves. Both appear to be necessary to produce the above-described long-term behavioral and physiological effects. An obvious implication of this general principle is that benign physical and social environments can serve as powerful protective factors for individuals whose early experiences were far from optimal.

A third general principle pertains to the specific nature of the alterations in developmental trajectories resulting from the various types of early experiences described above. By and large, these altered developmental trajectories seemed strikingly similar in many fundamental respects to the aberrant developmental trajectories seen in certain subgroups of rhesus monkeys living in wild populations. Thus, both early peer-rearing and experience with variable foraging demands (and, to a lesser extent, lack of control of access to desirable foodstuffs) seem to

make monkeys more behaviorally and physiologically reactive and, for at least some individuals, more impulsive as well. These findings raise the possibility that the most common forms of aberrant behavioral and physiological development seen in wild monkeys have multiple potential etiological pathways for seemingly similar adverse outcomes. Whether these particular outcomes are largely limited to those individuals who carry a heritable risk or can be induced in essentially any individual who experiences adverse early enviornments is currently a focus of intense investigation. At the very least, such findings suggest that the aberrant developmental trajectories seen in wild populations may also reflect deviant early experiences over and above any heritable predispositions.

What are the implications of these three general principles for consideration of human psychopathology? One must keep in mind that these principles have been derived from studies of rhesus and other macaque monkeys, who are clearly not furry little humans with tails but rather members of other, albeit quite closely related, species of primates. One should therefore be cautious in making any cross-species generalizations to specific cases of human psychopathology.

On the other hand, the degree to which behavioral and physiological manifestations of high reactivity and extreme impulsiveness in monkeys resemble characteristic features of human internalizing and externalizing disorders, respectively, is truly striking, with parallels extending even to the general incidence rates within each species. The nonhuman primate data make it clear that early experiences can play crucial roles in the development of such disorders in monkeys who lack the linguistic and mental imagery capabilities central to all human cultures (Suomi; in press, a). It is hard to believe that humans would not be at least as potentially sensitive to the long-term behavioral and physiological effects of adverse early experiences as their evolutionary cousins appear to be.

REFERENCES

Andrews, M. W. and Rosenblum, L. A. 1991. Security of attachment in infants raised in variable- or low-demand environments. *Child Dev.* **62**:686–93.

Andrews, M. W. and Rosenblum, L. A. 1993. Assessment of attachment in differentially reared infant monkeys (*Macaca radiata*): response of separation and a novel environment. *J. Comp. Psychol.* **107**:84–90.

Berard, J. 1989. Male life histories. *Puerto Rico Health Sci. J.* **8**:47–58.

Berman, C. M. 1982. The ontogeny of social relationships with group comparisons among free-ranging infant rhesus monkeys: I. Social networks and differentiation. *Animal Behav.* **30**:149–62.

Berman, C.M., Rasmussen, K.L.R., and Suomi, S.J. 1994. Responses of free-ranging rhesus monkeys to a natural form of social separation: I. Parallels with mother-infant separation in captivity. *Child Develop.* **65**:1028–41.

Bowlby, J. 1960. Grief and mourning in infancy and early childhood. *Psychoanal. Study Child* **15**:9–52.

Bowlby, J. 1973. *Separation: anger and anxiety*. New York: Basic Books.

Boyce, W.T., O'Neill-Wagner, P.L., Price, C.S., Haines, M.C., and Suomi, S.J. (in press). Stress reactivity and violent injuries in free-ranging rhesus monkeys. *Health Psychol.*

Coplan, J.D., Andrews, M.W., Rosenblum, L.A., Owens, M.J., Friedman, S., Gorman, J.M., and Nemeroff, C.B. 1996. Persistent elevations of cerebrospinal fluid concentrations of corticotropin-releasing factor in adult nonhuman primates exposed to early-life stressors: implications for the pathophysiology of mood and anxiety disorders. *Proc. Natl Acad. Sci. USA* **93**:1619–23.

Dittus, W.P.J. 1979. The evolution of behaviors regulating density and age specific rates in a primate population. *Behaviour* **69**:265–302.

Harlow, H.F., Dodsworth, R.O., and Harlow, M.K. 1965. Total social isolation in monkeys. *Proc. Natl Acad. Sci. USA* **54**:90–6.

Harlow, H.F., Harlow, M.K., and Hansen, E.W. 1963. The maternal affectional system of rhesus monkeys. In: *Maternal behavior in mammals*, ed. H. L. Rheingold, pp. 254–81. New York: John Wiley.

Higley, J.D., King, S. T., Hasert, M.F., Champoux, M., Suomi, S.J., and Linnoila, M. 1996a. Stability of interindividual differences in serotonin function and its relationship to severe aggression and competent social behavior in rhesus monkey females. *Neuropsychopharmacol.* **14**:67–76.

Higley, J.D., Linnoila, M., and Suomi, S.J. 1994. Ethological contributions. In *Handbook of aggressive behavior in psychiatric patients*, ed. R.T. Ammerman, pp. 17–32. New York: Raven Press.

Higley, J.D. Mehlman, P.T., Taub, D.M., Higley, S., Fernald, B., Vickers, J., Lindell, S.G., Suomi, S.J., and Linnoila, M. (in press). Excessive mortality in young free-ranging nonhuman primates with low CSF 5–HIAA concentrations. *Arch. Gen. Psychiat.*

Higley, J.D., and Suomi, S.J. 1989. Temperamental reactivity in nonhuman primates. In *Handbook of temperament in children*, ed. G.A. Kohnstam, J.E. Bates, and M.K. Rothbard, pp. 153–67. New York: John Wiley.

Higley, J.D. and Suomi, S.J. 1996. Reactivity and social competence affect individual differences in reaction to severe stress in children: investigations using nonhuman primates. In *Intense stress and mental disturbance in children*, ed. C.R. Pfeffer, pp. 3–58. Washington, DC: American Psychiatric Press.

Higley, J.D., Suomi, S.J., and Linnoila, M. 1992. A longitudinal assessment of CSF monoamine metabolite and plasma cortisol concentrations in young rhesus monkeys. *Biolog. Psychiat.* **32**:127–45.

Higley, J.D., Suomi, S.J., and Linnoila, M. (1996b). A nonhuman primate model of Type II alcoholism? (Part 2): diminished social competence and excessive aggression correlates with low CSF 5–HIAA concentrations. *Alcoholism: Clin. Exp. Res.* **20**:643–50.

Higley, J.D., Thompson, W.T., Champoux, M., Goldman, D., Hasert, M.F., Kraemer, G.W., Scanlan, J.M., Suomi, S. J., and Linnoila, M. 1993. Paternal and maternal genetic and environmental contributions to CSF monoamine metabolites in rhesus monkeys (*Macaca mulatta*). *Arch. Gen. Psychiat.* **50**:615–23.

Hofer, M.A. 1995. Hidden regulators: implications to a new understanding of attachment, separation, and loss. In *Attachment theory: social, developmental, and clinical perspectives*, ed. S. Goldberg, R. Muir, and J. Kerr, pp. 203–32. Hillsdale, NJ: Analytic Press.

Insel, T.R., Scanlan, J.M., Champoux, M., and Suomi, S.J. 1988. Rearing paradigm in a nonhuman primate affects response to B–CCE challenge. *Psychopharmacol.* **96**:81–6.

Kagan, J., Snideman, N., Arcus, D., and Reznick, J.S. 1994. *Galen's prophecy: temperament in human nature*. New York: Basic Books.

Kalin, N.H., Shelton, S.E., McKinney, W.T., Kraemer, G.W., Scanlan, J.M., and Suomi, S.J. 1983. Stress alters dexamethasone suppression test in rhesus monkeys. *Psychopharmacol. Bull.* **19**:542–5.

Kraemer, G.W. 1992. A psychobiological theory of attachment. *Behav. Brain Sci.*, **15**:493–541.

Lewis, M. (in press). Maternal soothing and infant stress. In *Soothing and stress*, ed. M. Lewis and D.S. Ramsay. Hillsdale, NJ: Lawrence Erlbaum Associates.

Lindburg, D.G. 1971. The rhesus monkey in North India: An ecological and behavioral study. In: *Primate behavior: developments in field and laboratory research*, Vol. 2, ed. L.A. Rosenblum, pp. 1–106. New York: Academic Press.

Lindburg, D.G. 1991. Ecological requirements of macaques. *Lab. Animal Sci.* **41**:315–22.

Lovejoy, C.O. 1981. The origins of man. *Science* **211**:341–50.

Mehlman, P.T., Higley, J.D., Faucher, T., Lilly, A.A., Taub, D.M., Vickers, J., Suomi, S.J., and Linnoila, M. 1994. Low cerebrospinal fluid 5–hydroxyindoleaceatic acid concentrations are correlated with severe aggression and reduced impulse control in free-ranging nonhuman primates (*Macaca mulatta*). *Am. J. Psychiat.* **151**:1485–91.

Mehlman, P.T., Higley, J.D., Faucher, I., Lilly, A.A., Taub, D.M., Vickers, J., Suomi, S.J., and Linnoila, M. 1995. CSF 5–HIAA cocentrations are correlated with sociality and the timing of emigration in free-ranging primates. *Am. J. Psychiat.* **152**:901–13.

Mineka, S., Gunnar, M., and Champoux. M. 1986. Control and early socioemotional development: infant rhesus monkeys reared in controllable versus uncontrollable environments. *Child Dev.* **57**:1241–56.

Rosenblum, L.A., Coplan, J.D., Friedman, S., Bassoff, T., Gorman, J.M., and Andrews, M.W. 1994. Adverse early experiences affect noradrenergic and serotonergic functioning in adult primates. *Biol. Psychiatr.* **35**:221–7.

Sade, D.S. 1967. Determinants of social dominance in a group of free-ranging rhesus monkeys. In *Social Communication among primates*, ed. S. Altmann, pp. 99–114. Chicago: University of Chicago Press.

Sibley, C.O., Comstock, J.A., and Alquist, J.E. 1990. DNA hybridization evidence of hominoid phylogeny: a reanalysis of the data. *J. Mol. Evol.* **30**:202–36.

Suomi, S.J. 1979. Peers, play, and primary prevention in primates. In: *Primary prevention of psychopathology*, vol. 3: *Social competence in children*, ed. M.W. Kent and J.E. Rolf, pp. 127–49. Hanover, NH: Universities Press of New England.

Suomi, S.J. 1982. Abnormal behavior and primate models of psychopathology. In *Primate behavior*, ed. J.L. Fobes and J.E. King, pp. 171–215. New York: Academic Press.

Suomi, S.J. 1986. Anxiety-like disorders in young primates. In *Anxiety of childhood*, ed. R. Gittelman, pp. 1–23. New York: Guildford Press.

Suomi, S.J. 1991a. Up-tight and laid-back monkeys: individual differences in the response to social challenges. In *Plasticity of development*, ed. S. Brauth, W. Hall, and R. Dooling, pp. 27–56. Cambridge: MIT Press.

Suomi, S.J. 1991b. Primate separation models of affective disorders. In *Neurobiology of learning, emotion, and affect*, ed. J. Madden, pp. 195–214. New York: Raven Press.

Suomi, S.J. 1991c. Early stress and adult emotional reactivity. In *The childhood environmental and adult disease* (CIBA Foundation Symposium 156), ed. G.R. Bock and J. Whelan, pp. 171–88. Chichester: John Wiley.

Suomi, S.J. 1995. Influence of Bowlby's Attachment Theory on research on nonhuman primate biobehavioral development. In *Attachment Theory: Social, Developmental, and Clinical Perspectives*, ed. S. Goldberg, R. Muir, and J. Kerr, pp. 185–201. Hillsdale, NJ: Analytic Press.

Suomi, S.J. 1996. Nonverbal communication in nonhuman primates: Implications for the emergence of culture. In *Where nature meets culture: nonverbal communication in social interaction*, ed. P. Molnar and U. Segerstrale. Hillsdale, NJ: Erlbaum Associates.

Suomi, S.J. (in press, b). Biological, maternal, and life style interactions with the psychosocial environment: primate models. In *Environmental and nonenvironmental determinants of the east-west life expectancy gap in Europe*, ed. C. Hertzman, S. Kelly, and M. Bobak. Amsterdam: Kluwer Publishers.

Suomi, S.J., and Harlow, H.F. 1975. The role and reason of peer friendships. In *Friendship and peer relations*, ed. M. Lewis and L.A. Rosenblum, pp. 310–34. New York: Basic Books.

Suomi, S.J., Rasmussen, K.L.R., and Higley, J.D. 1992. Primate models of behavioral and physiological change in adolescence. In *Textbook of adolescent medicine*, ed. E.R. McAnarney, R.E. Kreiipe, D.P. Orr, and G.D. Comerci, pp. 135–9. Philadelphia: J.B. Saunders.

Suomi, S.J., and Ripp, C. 1983. A history of motherless mother monkey mothering at the University of Wisconsin Primate Laboratory. In *Child abuse: the nonhuman primate data*, ed. M. Reite and N. Caine, pp. 49–77. New York: Alan R. Liss.

Walker, M.L. 1995. Menopause in female rhesus monkeys. *Am. J. Primatol.* **35**:59–71.

Development and psychopathology

9

From birth to onset: a developmental perspective of schizophrenia in two national birth cohorts

PETER JONES AND D. JOHN DONE

Childhood developmental milestones and IQ scores were ascertained prospectively in the 1946 and 1958 British birth cohort studies. Subjects have been followed to date and those with adult onset schizophrenia, identified. Motor and cognitive development during childhood were shown to differentiate children destined to develop schizophrenia; developmental milestones were late and psychomotor dysfunction continued throughout childhood. Children destined to develop schizophrenia had lower IQ but there was no evidence that a subgroup of cases with poor scores accounted for these effects. Models of developmental pathways to schizophrenia, the distribution of risk within the general population, and the specificity of these effects are discussed.

INTRODUCTION

In contrast to the relatively new idea that some chronic physical diseases of adult life may have their origins in childhood (Barker 1994), it has long been acknowledged that adult psychological illness may arise more commonly in individuals with certain personality traits and that these may have been continuous with childhood characteristics (Rutter 1984). The development of explanatory models that include remote events has added a new level of complexity to our understanding of several diseases, together with new opportunities to uncover their causes. Regarding mental illnesses, mechanisms proposed include straightforward continuity of symptoms, as seen between childhood conduct disorder and adult antisocial personality disorder (Robins 1966; Rutter and Giller 1983),

continuity both of intrinsic (e.g., personality) and of extrinsic risk factors from childhood through to adult life, and the persistence of personality characteristics which lead to behaviours placing individuals at risk of mental illness (Rutter 1984; Rodgers 1990a 1990b).

Among the psychoses, schizophrenia has been seen to stem from childhood psychological abnormalities such as social awkwardness and withdrawal (Watt 1978) as, in the guise of dementia praecox, it was first described (Kraepelin 1896). The specificity of these abnormalities is not clear. On the one hand, recent evidence suggests that affective psychosis, too, may have some links to development in childhood (van Os et al. in press) and adolescence (Sands and Harrow 1995). On the other hand, any specific pattern of social and cognitive dysfunction may lead to various outcomes in adult life, not only schizophrenia and affective psychosis. The developmental abnormalities, however, are quite distinct from the hallucinations, delusions, and thought disorder which characterize the adult psychosis, although there is some evidence of continuity of negative symptoms (Foerster et al. 1989). Thus, it is not immediately clear as to which of the models described above might best describe the mechanisms underlying this awkward discontinuity of symptoms. Compounding the difficulty in providing a convincing model to fit the data that are available, we are still far from a useful description of the childhood characteristics which predict psychosis. This is distinct from affective disorders where childhood symptomatology is not unlike the adult disorder and shows continuities with it (van Os et al. 1996).

Currently, the more biological explanations tend to favor a modified version of the continuity of symptom model: early and late psychological abnormalities being manifestations of the same underlying brain lesion, the normal development of surrounding brain areas and their corresponding functions having a pathoplastic effect on those manifestations (Weinberger 1987). This is the fundamental version of the neurodevelopmental hypothesis of schizophrenia (Murray and Lewis 1987). A description of the psychological development of psychosis, however, will need to explain the transition from nonpsychotic dysfunction in childhood to psychotic dysfunction in adulthood. It may be that future work will uncover underlying characteristics of the phenotype which are present throughout life.

Given these difficulties, is the evidence that early events are important particularly strong? It comes from diverse sources. Histopathological studies of adults with schizophrenia indicate that developmental processes may have gone awry in some areas, particularly in the formation of hippocampal structures (Jakob and Beckman 1986; Roberts 1990) and the frontal cortex (Akbarian et al. 1993a, 1993b). Some findings have proved difficult to replicate, although there is, presumably, some microscopic basis to the macroscopic structural differences that have been demonstrated in neuroimaging studies of schizophrenia (Jones et al. 1994a). Pregnancy and delivery complications have been found to be more common in the histories of adults with schizophrenia than controls in many (Lewis et al. 1989; O' Callaghan et al. 1990; Buka et al. 1993) but not all studies (Done et al. 1991) and, if there is a true association, its nature and the direction of causality is a matter of debate (Goodman 1988; Sacker et al. 1995). Similarly, there is evidence of an association in populations between schizophrenia and prenatal exposure to influenza (Mednick et al. 1988; Sham et al. 1992; but see also Crow 1992; Crow and Done 1992; Selten and Slaets 1994; Erlenmeyer-Kimling et al. 1994; Susser et al. 1994), maternal malnutrition (Susser and Lin 1992) and, possibly, with urban rather than rural upbringing (Lewis et al. 1989).

It is assumed that these associations indicate causal agency, or are markers of damage to the immature brain which, at maturity, may lead to psychosis. During infancy and childhood the damage is manifest only in moderately dysfunctional ability in a variety of domains because the mechanisms and structures necessary for producing the specific phenomena of psychosis have simply not yet developed. A useful parallel to this is the development of cognitive ability; in infancy a performance level is undifferentiated across cognitive and motor tasks but in adulthood ability varies across different types of cognitive task (Plomin 1987). The moderate dysfunction that has been reported includes the personality traits noted above, the minor differences in neurological development which have been demonstrated (Fish 1977; Erlenmeyer-Kimling et al. 1980; Walker and Lewine 1990; Fish et al. 1992) and also the decrements in mean intelligence scores which have been noted both in historical cohort studies of children who later develop schizophrenia and in groups of adults with the condition (Aylward et al. 1984).

Given all these strands of evidence pointing to very early developmental events as being involved in schizophrenia, possibly involving the early determination of brain structure (Jones and Murray 1991), why study intervening psychological and neurological events any further? Why not concentrate on possible causal factors at early stages in development and the processes which are involved with the precipitation of psychosis in later life? We believe there are several reasons. Accurate and precise description of prepsychotic traits is a prerequisite to the identification of high-risk individuals, facilitating early diagnosis and prompt treatment. The latter has been shown consistently to affect prognosis (Johnstone et al. 1986; Wyatt 1991; Loebel et al. 1992) and is an important and realistic aim. Prevention in high-risk individuals may, perhaps, be possible. In the meantime, any reduction in the risk of developing schizophrenia will not only be clinically valuable, but will also hasten our understanding of etiology and best practice in prevention. Such goals will rely on the accurate characterization of traits which precede psychosis.

A model where all overt abnormalities in childhood are manifestations of a single underlying process continuous with psychosis is parsimonious, but not necessarily correct. In the normal population there is no relationship between WAIS scores and MMPI profiles (Lacks and Keefe 1970; Bloom and Eaton 1975; Gaines and Morris

1978), which suggests that personality and general intelligence, or g, may be generated by largely independent neural systems. Thus, dysfunctional personality and low intelligence could act independently as risk factors for schizophrenia, presence of one and absence of the other will determine whether an individual crosses a threshold of risk where the disorder becomes inevitable. It is only with a detailed and unbiased description of the period prior to psychosis that these possibilities can be tested and extended to examine the notion of "robust" personality and high intelligence as *protective* factors.

Unfortunately, demonstrating such associations between early events and a disorder with onset most commonly in the third or fourth decade of life is not easy: it is accepted that a proportion of individuals are different or odd prior to psychosis but the details and the true proportion are difficult to define. Retrospective study designs are prone to recall biases and spurious associations, and the less obvious departures from normality will not be remembered. Often, the best that can be achieved is a classification of complex early characteristics as either present or absent, normal or abnormal; the subsequent consideration of the nature of the risk conferred is similarly dichotomized (Gittleman-Klein and Klein 1969; Watt and Lubensky 1976; Cannon-Spoor *et al.* 1982; Done *et al.* 1994). Few studies in this area have had population controls. Most rely on the demonstration of differences in group means, leading to further emphasis on "abnormality" versus "normality", as well as to a lack of comparability between studies.

In general, evidence of childhood developmental deviance, defined as either present or absent, in around a third to a half of adults with schizophrenia (Rutter 1984) has given rise to the notion that these individuals may have a distinct subtype of the disorder. If the early characteristics were defined in fine detail in population-based samples, then evidence of a familiar dose–response relationship may be revealed, just as is the case with many risk factors for chronic disease. We aim to shed light on the question as to whether early developmental events are involved in the minority or majority of schizophrenia. In the latter, etiology may still be diverse, but may act through homogeneous developmental mechanisms.

Longitudinal studies of general population samples are one of the best ways of investigating the questions outlined above, although these, too, have their problems; large samples are required to yield adequate numbers of cases and the childhood information, while unbiased, is often not ideally suited to the purpose. In the UK there have been three such studies with suitable childhood data in which the participants have lived through any or all of the period of risk for psychosis; the three birth cohort studies of 1946, 1958 and 1970. In this chapter we review some of the evidence that has arisen from the first two of these samples: the Medical Research Council (MRC) National Survey of Health and Development, and the National Child Development Study.

The MRC National Survey of Health and Development has its origins in a survey of all births in England, Scotland and Wales during the week 3–9 March 1946 carried out to investigate the determinants of the falling birth rate before the Second World War, and to assess the needs and demands of parents and the maternity services in the planned National Health Service to be introduced 2 years later. Multiple and illegitimate births were excluded as, at that time, they would have been even more difficult to trace than the legitimate singletons. Following the original survey of 13 687 births, the group was stratified by socioeconomic class and disproportionately sampled. All the children of nonmanual workers and agricultural workers and a random, one in four sample of the remaining manual occupational groups (which predominated in the population) were included in the follow-up sample, a cohort of 5362 children. This group has been followed regularly and a large amount of data collected over the ensuing decades. Regular contact is maintained through a birthday card and the cohort was last interviewed in 1989. Another interview and comprehensive health check are planned for the late 1990s. The cohort has been described elsewhere extensively, most recently by Wadsworth (1991). Data on childhood analyzed in this study come from the 11 contacts with the survey members prior to age 16 years during which data were collected by health visitors, school nurses and doctors, teachers, mothers and the children themselves.

The National Child Development Study has its origins

in the British Perinatal Mortality Survey of 1958 which included some 98% of all births in England, Scotland and Wales registered during the week 3–9 March 1958, the same birth week as the National Survey of Health and Development (NSHD). Four subsequent attempts (ages 7, 9, 16 and 23 years) to trace members of the cohort to monitor physical, educational, and social development became known as the National Child Development Study (NCDS 1–4) . The numbers of subjects followed up at each stage were 15 398, 15 303, 14 761, and 12 537.

First, we review previous work (Done *et al.* 1991, 1994; Jones *et al.* 1994b) which has investigated the occurrence of abnormal motor, speech and other cognitive development in children in these cohorts who, as adults, went on to develop psychosis. Data from each sample were considered separately, one being an independent test of the results from the other. Second, we have gone on to attempt to combine data in areas where data in the samples were comparable and results in each were similar. Our aim was to test the specific hypothesis that abnormality in development of psychomotor skills and cognitive functioning in children destined to develop schizophrenia as adults is best described not as excessively "abnormal", as would be predicted by the contemporary neurodevelopmental hypothesis, but as a continuous risk (*or protective*) factor for the illness. The data available allowed emphasis on the distribution of risks within the population, rather than concentrating on cases alone. Finally, we have considered the specificity of our findings among the psychoses and mental illness in general, and have speculated on possible mechanisms for the effects we have demonstrated.

METHODS OF CASE FINDING IN THE TWO BIRTH COHORTS

National Survey of Health and Development (NSHD)

Survey members at risk of being identified in adult life as having schizophrenia comprised all those alive and living in the UK at age 16 years ($n=4746$, 52.2% were men). There were 81 survey members for whom there was evidence, up to age 43 years and 8 months, of a diagnosis of schizophrenia, use of regular neuroleptic medication,

undefined severe mental illness or a psychiatric admission for unknown cause. The majority of hospital admissions were identified from both the Mental Health Enquiry, a national register, now defunct, and from reports from the survey members. Of these 81 survey members, 30 (20 male) met DSM-IIIR criteria for schizophrenia or schizoaffective disorder when all available clinical material was scrutinized (for details, see Jones *et al.* 1995). Age at onset (range 17–43 years) was defined as the age at which cases first contacted medical services for psychosis or, when this was not available, the age at which the NSHD became aware of the psychiatric disorder. Mean age at onset for schizophrenia was 24.3 years (95% CI 21.5 to 27.0), with men presenting, on average, 2.5 years earlier (95% CI -3.3 to 8.2). As yet, operational classifications of psychotic conditions in this survey are available only for schizophrenia, although later we refer to work by van Os *et al.* (in press) in which a group of survey members with chronic, severe affective symptoms has been defined.

Control subjects were defined as the entire risk set, excluding those identified as cases of schizophrenia, although a 6.8% random sample ($n=300$) was used for the preparation of some graphs.

National Child Development Study (NCDS)

Survey members who had been discharged from psychiatric hospital for any reason between 1974 and 1986 were identified from the Mental Health Enquiry (see earlier). Case notes were retrieved from hospitals and Present State Examination (PSE diagnosis CATEGO) (Wing *et al.* 1974) diagnoses were derived through use of the syndrome checklist (Done *et al.* 1991).

The control group was a randomly selected 10% sample of NCDS subjects never admitted to hospital for psychiatric treatment, who had been traced at least once in any NCDS sweep. The numbers of subjects in each group, have been reported elsewhere. We focus here only on cases with data collected on at least two of the three sweeps at 7, 11 and 16 years, and with a PSE/CATEGO diagnosis of "narrow schizophrenia" ($n=29$), affective psychosis ($n=29$), which included manic and psychotic depression, and a group of unusual patients admitted to hospital with a diagnosis of neurosis ($n=71$), as they had predominantly anxious and/or depressive symptoms at each age.

Table 9.1. *Age at reaching developmental milestones*

Milestone	Modal value*	Control mean* (SD)	Case-control difference* (95% CI)
Sitting	6	6.5 (1.5)	0.1 later (0.5 earlier – 0.8 later)
Standing	12	11.4 (2.2)	0.2 later (0.6 earlier – 1.0 later)
Walking	12	13.5 (2.4)	1.2 later (0.1 later – 2.3 later)
Teething	6	6.8 (2.2)	0.2 earlier (1.0 earlier – 0.6 later)
Talking	18	14.3 (4.2)	1.2 later (0.4 earlier – 2.8 later)

Note: * Months.

Source: Jones *et al.* 1994b.

COMPARISONS OF CHILDHOOD VARIABLES

Early milestones and motor function in childhood and adolescence

National Survey of Health and Development

A health visitor interview was conducted at age 24–26 months, during which mothers were asked to recall the age at which sitting/standing/walking alone, beginning to talk and cutting of first tooth were reached (Jones *et al.* 1994b). The mean ages at which speech and gross motor milestones were reached were consistently later for children who later developed schizophrenia than for controls (Table 9.1), particularly for walking (cases 1.2 months later, 95% CI difference 0.1 to 2.3 months later, $p=0.005$).

At age 2 years, there was an excess of preschizophrenic cases over controls who had not yet reached all their milestones, compared with those where all milestones were seen by the health visitors to have been attained (two of 25 cases versus 64 of 3854 controls; OR=4.8, $\chi^2=5.4$, $p=0.02$); speech was the milestone not attained in both these cases. School doctors were more likely to note non-structural speech defects in the preschizophrenic children than in their peers and, throughout childhood, health professionals were more likely to note any speech problem in the preschizophrenic group (OR=2.8; 95% CI 0.9 to 7.8). It is notable from Table 9.1 that the preschizophrenic children appeared to show a small delay on all milestones, indicating that they may be delayed in terms of some latent developmental factor.

Van Os *et al.* (in press) have identified 75 adults in the NSHD who suffered severe depressive symptoms at age 36 years when survey members were given the PSE (Wing *et al.* 1974), and who continued to complain of such symptoms at age 43 years when the next interview took place. Scrutiny of what clinical records were available indicated that the majority of these individuals had marked clinical depression. Classification according to operational criteria is awaited but members of this group appear to have suffered a chronic severe depressive disorder. Attainment of motor milestones had been later in women with this condition (OR=1.5 per month; 1.1 to 2.2) but not in men. Similarly, women had been noted to have more speech defects between the ages of 6 and 15 years (OR=3.6; 1.8, 7.5).

National Child Development Study

In order to analyze motor dysfunction, the principal component analysis (PCA) was also used to elicit factors from the numerous standardized ratings of motor signs (e.g., balancing on one leg) and neurological soft signs (e.g., tics, twitches, epileptic attacks) which had been noted by school doctors when the survey members were age 7 years, and then again at 11 years.

At age 7 years, six factors could be identified in the complete sample which were, in order of importance: coordination/clumsiness, epilepsy, laterality, incontinence and skull deformity, tics, stammer. Those who developed narrow schizophrenia were significantly more abnormal than the controls on the coordination/clumsiness ($p=0.001$), and on the incontinence ($p<0.10$) factors.

Preaffective psychosis was also associated with more abnormality on the coordination/clumsiness factor ($p=0.008$) whereas the preneurotics produced factor scores well within the normal range on all factors.

At age 11 years, some seven valid factors were identified in the complete sample. In order of importance, these were: balance, hand preference/relative hand skill, coordination, convulsions, central nervous system (CNS) impairment, tics and twitches, and a category of miscellaneous deficits (articulation and incontinence problems). At this age, those who later developed narrowly-defined schizophrenia (Done *et al.* 1991) were significantly more abnormal on hand preference/relative hand skill ($p=0.09$) due to reduced laterality of hand skill, coordination ($p<0.001$), CNS impairment ($p<0.001$) and on the miscellaneous deficits factor (predominantly incontinence; $p=0.002$). Preaffective psychosis was associated with significant abnormality in ratings of coordination ($p=0.04$), CNS impairment ($p=0.06$), and tics and twitches ($p=0.01$). At 11 years, preneurotics scored significantly poor on one factor; coordination ($p=0.01$).

Findings from the two cohorts compared
The data available from the two cohorts did not allow direct replication from one to the other; however, the data are complementary. Those from the 1946 cohort indicated that motor and speech development during the first 2 years of life were slightly delayed prior to schizophrenia. Throughout childhood, school doctors noted abnormalities in speech not due to structural problems. Data from the 1958 cohort confirm that these differences were not merely reflections of developmental timing; at ages 7 and 11 years, speech and other aspects of CNS function were rated as being qualitatively abnormal prior to schizophrenia.

That subjects with chronic severe depression in the NSHD and preaffective psychotics in the NCDS also demonstrated motor and other CNS abnormality, which suggests that there is little specificity of this effect to schizophrenia amongst the psychoses, but there was little convincing evidence that these abnormalities were apparent in children in the NCDS who would later develop neurosis. Most of these measures are unlikely to be caused by social disadvantage, and formal statistical adjustment

indicated they were independent of socioeconomic class. We feel, therefore, that the most parsimonious explanation is that the early developmental delays and the later, more qualitative abnormalities, are manifestations of a single mechanism underlying the development of psychosis which results from a difference in CNS development.

EDUCATIONAL ACHIEVEMENT: COGNITIVE TEST SCORES AND IQ

National Survey of Health and Development
Results of cognitive tests were available for ages 8, 11 and 15 years (Jones *et al.* 1995). Briefly, four tests were given at age 8 years: a nonverbal picture recognition test, a reading comprehension test (sentence completion), a word recognition test, and a vocabulary test. At age 11 years, four tests yielded verbal and non-verbal IQ, arithmetic, reading and vocabulary scores. At age 15 years, tests gave similar scales to those at 11 years: verbal and nonverbal IQ, reading comprehension, and mathematics.

Mean, unadjusted scores in the individual educational tests at ages 8, 11 and 13 years have been reported elsewhere (Jones *et al.* 1994b); cases scored consistently lower than the controls in all tests, at all three ages across all subscores. The pattern of differences between the means, together with the confidence limits, suggested that deficits in the scores of the cases were most marked for verbal, nonverbal and mathematical skills, and least for reading and vocabulary, although all scores were highly correlated. In the present investigation, these scores were analyzed as a single variable at each age.

At each age, principal components analysis of normalized scores resulted in a single factor, the first principal component (PC 1), analogous to a general intelligence (g) score. This IQ factor explained some 75% of the variance in scores at each age and comprised similar (72–91%) contributions from each subtest. Mean values of this factor, expressed as standard deviations from the mean (z-scores), were lower in the cases than controls at age 8 years (difference=0.3 SD lower, 95% CI −0.1 to 0.7), age 11 years (difference=0.2, 95% CI −0.1 to 0.5) and at 15 years when the gap was greater (difference=0.48, 95% CI 0.1 to 0.9). The age 15 years score was entered into an ANCOVA,

Table 9.2. *Association between IQ score* at age 8, 11 and 15 years and later schizophrenia in the NSHD*

Age (years)		IQ tertile based on population distribution (one-third of controls in each tertile)			Summary or for linear trend in association (95% CI)
		Lowest ability	Middle ability	High ability	
8	Number of cases	11	7	6	
	Adjusted OR**	1	0.6	0.5	0.7 (0.4–1.2) $p=0.2$
11	Number of cases	14	6	6	
	Adjusted OR**	1	0.5	0.4	0.6 (0.4 – 0.99) $p=0.04$
15	Number of cases	13	8	4	
	Adjusted OR**	1	0.6	0.3	0.5 (0.3 – 0.9) $p=0.01$

Notes:

 *First principal component derived from all scores at any age.

**Adjusted for confounding by sex and social class. One-third of controls in each tertile. Lowest ability as baseline odds.

together with sex, socioeconomic status and previous IQ score at age 11 years. The main effect of case versus control was significant ($F=5.7$, $p=0.02$) in the model, as was an interaction term between case and sex ($F=7.1$, $p=0.01$). Unexpectedly, this interaction was due to girl "pre-cases" at 15 years having particularly low IQ scores after adjustment. Being counter to many previous studies (Aylward *et al.* 1984) and counter to our hypothesis in entering the interaction term, this effect is difficult to interpret without replication.

The distribution of the principal component loadings were divided by their tertiles into thirds, based upon the control data (Table 9.2), as described above. The raw data form the body of the table with the bottom line being a summary odds ratio adjusted for sex and social class, obtained from logistic regression. This represents the increased odds of developing schizophrenia if a score is in the middle tertile versus the highest group, or the lowest versus the middle. Similar results were obtained using quartiles but occasional empty cells made analysis problematic. There was no evidence that a nonlinear trend (e.g., quadratic) gave a better fit to the data, nor in this analysis was there statistical evidence of an interaction with sex; the gradients of risks were very similar for girls and boys.

Thus, the impression from the initial investigation of differences in mean values was confirmed but there was also a clear pattern in the adjusted odds ratios. Cases were consistently over-represented in the lowest third of the test scores, even at age 8 years, after which the effect appeared to become more marked. A stepwise logistic regression was used to analyze these repeated measures further, taking into account sex, social class, and the effect of previous score. Inclusion of the g factor score at age 15 years into a model containing sex and social class resulted in a significant improvement in the fit of the model (reduction in deviance; likelihood ratio statistic (LRS)=7.7, $p=0.005$). Addition of the g factor score at age 11 years resulted in a slight and nonsignificant decrease in deviance (LRS=1.3; $p=0.5$) and change in the odds ratio associated with the 15 year score (OR=0.59, $p=0.03$). Similarly, addition of the g factor score at age 8 years resulted in a tiny improvement in the fit of the model (LRS=0.6; $p=0.7$) associated with a change in the odds ratio associated with the 15 year score which remained statistically significant (OR=0.64; $p=9.04$). Adjustment for teachers' ratings of anxiety in social situations, a measure shown to be high in those who would develop schizophrenia, indicated that this rating and lower IQ were independent of each other as risk factors for the disorder, both being independent of a child's social class (Jones *et al.* 1994b).

The most parsimonious conclusion from the statistical model outlined above is that the majority, or even all, of the children destined to become cases of schizophrenia, clever or dull, showed a slight decrement in observed IQ, thereby shifting the entire distribution and resulting in a lower group mean. The division of the distribution into thirds, rather than more divisions, was relatively crude and it was possible that the observed effect may have been due to a minority of the cases with very deviant scores. Inspection of the frequency distributions of IQ scores for cases and controls at each of the three ages indicated that this was not the case. This case is discussed below.

If low IQ were a risk factor for schizophrenia, was it related to age at onset? In the NSHD there was no evidence of an association between these two variables within the case group, either alone ($r=-14$, $p=0.5$) or when corrected for sex and social class in a multiple regression equation ($\beta=-0.11$, $p=0.65$), which suggests that low IQ in childhood is found for later onsets as well as earlier onsets confirming some recent findings (Heaton *et al.* 1994).

In conclusion, general ability in the NSHD was adequately summarized by the first principal component at each age and this score was lower in cases than controls. The deficit between cases and controls became statistically significant at 15 and remained so when account was taken of regression to the mean in ANCOVA or a logistic regression model. Cases tended to score below the controls at all three ages: the lower the IQ score, the greater the risk (odds) of becoming a case, regardless of sex or social class or age of onset. There was no evidence of a subgroup of cases with very low scores or that cases arose solely from a subgroup of the population with low IQ. These data are compatible with the notion that the majority of cases had, to some degree, a decrement existing in their childhood IQ.

Results to date regarding chronic, severe depression (van Os *et al.* 1996) largely replicate those for schizophrenia; however, the magnitude of the effects was somewhat smaller, particularly in boys.

National Child Development Study

The general ability tests used in the NCDS were similar to those used in the NSHD and, conveniently, were administered at two intervening ages. Thus, reading comprehension and math were assessed at 7, 11 and 16 years. An IQ test providing scores for verbal and performance IQ was administered at the age of 11 years. Other psychometric tests used at 11 years included copying designs and the

"draw-a-man" test. A variety of qualitative assessments made by the teacher at ages 7 and 11 years were also available, and gave some idea about the proportion of the pre-onset cases who were regarded by teachers as below average or poor in their school performance.

At the ages of 7 and 11 years children who later developed schizophrenia performed more poorly than the population controls on a wide range of tasks which included verbal and performance IQ ($p<0.01$ for both types of IQ), reading ($p<0.01$), mathematics ($p<0.01$), general knowledge about the world ($p<0.01$), oral ability ($p<0.01$) and quality of speech ($p<0.001$). Different types of assessment, namely psychometric tests and qualitative assessments by the teachers, produced similar results. Not only was there a consistent deficit across many of the varied tests, but this deficit was found consistently at three different ages (7, 11 and 16 years): a linear trend comparison of the preschizophrenics and control subjects for the reading comprehension and the mathematics data showed no change in group differences between 7 and 16 years for either reading comprehension ($F=1.05$, $p=0.3$) or mathematics ($F<1$). The deficit was approximately 0.7 and 0.6 of a standard deviate (z-score) for male and female preschizophrenics, respectively.

These effects are in line with those reported by Aylward *et al.* (1984) and are consistent with, although rather larger than, the effect sizes in the NSHD. In both studies, the cognitive deficit appeared to be broadly based, (not only reading and mathematics). Assessment of pragmatic or crystallized aspects of intelligence, which may include knowledge of the world, reading comprehension, verbal IQ, were as deficient as mechanical (or fluid aspects of intelligence), e.g., performance IQ. This would suggest a nonspecific cognitive deficit, present at the earliest age of assessment (7 years of age). In the NCDS, there was no evidence that the deficit varied over time whereas, in the NSHD, there was some evidence that test performance deteriorated. Thus, the NCDS tests suggest that preschizophrenic children do not show any cognitive decline, and also that the rate of acquisition of knowledge between the ages of 7 and 16 years compares with that of the normal controls. Indeed, there was a significantly greater stability of this cognitive deficit compared with the normal controls across the age period covered. Using covariance analysis, social disadvantage, lack of family interest and obstetric complications (see Done *et al.* 1991) did not account for the observed IQ deficit.

In the NCDS we investigated the specificity of childhood cognitive dysfunction to schizophrenia, as two other groups of adult psychopathology had been classified.

Children who were later to develop an affective psychosis showed only a minor cognitive deficit. Preaffective psychotic cases scored below the control means on all tasks including verbal and performance IQ ($p=0.18$ and $p<0.05$ respectively) with group difference on the full scale score worthy of note ($p=0.06$), reading comprehension ($p<0.13$), mathematics ($p<0.14$), but only the teachers report of below average/poor at number work ($p=0.05$) distinguished the two groups on the various ratings made by the teacher. A linear trend comparison the preaffective psychotics and control subjects for the reading comprehension data, however, showed a significant decline between 11 and 16 ($F=6.55, p=0.01$) with a similar , but nonsignificant trend for the mathematics data . The deficit on reading and mathematics was approximately 0.2–0.3 of a standard deviate (z-score).

Children who in adult life developed anxiety and/or depressive disorders also manifested marked deficits on all of the psychometric tests, namely verbal ($p<0.001$) and performance IQ ($p<0.001$) , reading ($p=0.01$), and math ($p<0.01$). When an analysis of covariance was carried out on the reading and math measures, with social disadvantage measures as covariates, the deficit of these preneurotics compared with controls was reduced markedly. Social disadvantage did account for the IQ differences in a covariance analysis. Hence some cognitive deficits appeared to result from social disadvantage. With linear trend analysis, performance of the females, but not males, deteriorated over time on reading comprehension ($F=5$, $p=0.03$) but not mathematics ($F=1.24$, $p=0.24$). Teachers ratings also indicated that academic dysfunction was broadly based.

IQ: findings of the two cohorts compared

These results from both cohorts suggest that cognitive dysfunction in terms of general ability scores is nonspecific in all three prepatient groups. There may be some differences in effects from the two cohorts, however. In the preschizophrenic children in the NCDS the abnormal personality previously reported in this sample (Done *et al.* 1994) accounted for about half of the cognitive deficit, which suggests a partial relationship between abnormal personality and cognitive deficit in this group, whereas for the preneurotic subjects abnormal personality was independent from the cognitive deficit. This is somewhat different from the results from the NSHD where social anxiety and IQ were independent of each other at age 15 years as predictors of IQ for preschizophrenic cases. Whereas the measurement of IQ was very similar in the two studies, abnormality of personality was measured differently in the two cohorts. In the NSHD the measure used is reported social anxiety based on the Pintner Scales (Pidgeon 1964, 1968). In the NCDS, the Bristol Social Adjustment Guide (Done *et al.* 1994), a psychometric assessment of social maladjustment, gave a rather different measure.

Thus, the discrepancy in the relationship between IQ and behavior in the children who would develop psychiatric disorder is difficult to interpret with any certainty. In both studies, disruptive, naughty behaviours were strongly related to school performance in the general population. This trait was not found to be related to the occurrence of schizophrenia in the NSHD and the IQ effects were, in fact, adjusted for rather different behavioral characteristics in the two samples. Additional differences between the samples, such as diagnostic classification and age at onset, are discussed later.

Preschizophrenic children in both cohorts were performing below average across a variety of tasks. On measures of IQ the deficit was in the order of five IQ points at age 8 years in the NSHD and ten IQ points in the NCDS at age 11 years. Unlike earlier reports, both studies find this deficit in the girls as well as the boys. Social disadvantage in childhood did not account for this deficit in either cohort. The cognitive deficit was broadly based in both cohorts covering verbal and nonverbal reasoning tasks, mathematics and reading comprehension. On the basis of these results it is unlikely that a specific cognitive deficit be found in preschizophrenic children from early psychometric assessment.

There are some discrepancies in results from the two cohorts. In the NSHD some cognitive decline (but not

Fig. 9.1. IQ distributions
through childhood: controls and
cases. Groups: 1 NSHD controls
at age 8 years (*n*=300) 2 NSHD
cases at age 8 years 3 NSHD
controls at age 11 years 4 NSHD
cases at age 11 years 5 NCDS
cases at age 11 years (data from
the 1958 cohort) 6 NSHD
controls at age 15 years 7 NSHD
cases at age 15 years.

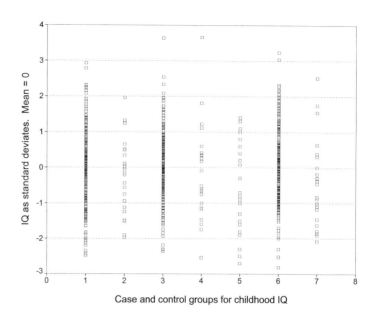

statistically significant) was apparent between 8 and 15 years in the preschizophrenic children, whereas no such decline in this group was found in the NCDS. It is unlikely that different methods of diagnosis (DSM-III-R and PSE/CATEGO) could account for this finding. Neither disruptive behavior, nor social anxiety accounted for the cognitive deficit in the NSHD, although social maladjustment did account for a substantial proportion, but not all, of the cognitive deficit in the NCDS. Thus, it appears that the cognitive dysfunction may well be independent of any personality dysfunction, but that dysfunctional personality and low IQ could act additively.

The distinction between early and late onset cases could only be undertaken in the NSHD where survey members had been followed over a longer period. The results from this cohort indicate that the cognitive deficit was not confined to the early onset cases; statistical power was low but there was no hint of an effect.

Is there a subgroup of cognitive impaired individuals who develop schizophrenia or is there a population shift ?

Availability of over 50 standardized IQ scores on 11-year-old children who will develop schizophrenia as adults,

together with population controls, represents a valuable opportunity, but one where various assumptions must be made, given that they arise from two different cohorts. We must presume that they are similar samples taken at two time points from the same hypothetical population of children at risk of schizophrenia, all liable to the same disorder.

Frequency distributions of IQ scores were plotted so as to examine overlap between cases and controls, in order to investigate the existence of a subgroup of particularly abnormal cases of schizophrenia – analogous to a developmental subtype of the disorder. Given the comparability of the IQ tests administered in the two samples and the similarity of the deficits demonstrated in both sets of children who developed schizophrenia, IQ data at age 11 years were examined together for both cohorts. Both sets of IQ scores had been "normalized" to give a population mean of 100 and standard deviation of 15. Frequency distributions of these IQ scores were simply examined by eye for evidence of bimodality between cases and controls and within the case group alone.

Figure 9.1 shows the distributions of IQ scores for controls and cases side by side at each age. Frequency distributions were examined using a single, 6.8% random sample of controls (*n*=300) from the NSHD so as to facilitate the

Fig. 9.2. IQ at 11 years. NSHD and NCDS cases combined. Control samples (*n*=300) from NSHD. Children (55 cases) who developed schizophrenia as adults (see text).

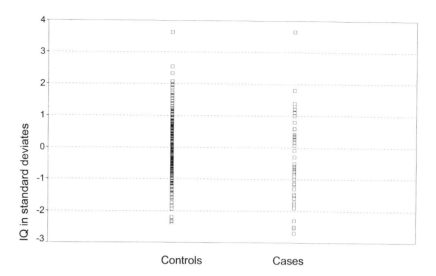

preparation of graphs. This sampling was performed once only using the SPSS-PC procedure "sample". Groups 4 and 5 are the 11-year-old scores for the children destined to develop schizophrenia in the NSHD and the NCDS, respectively, all other scores coming from the NSHD.

It was clear that there was no subgroup of cases with particularly low IQ. Scores for the majority of cases were within two standard deviations of the mean value for the controls, although scores above the mean were less common than scores below it. The impression was that cases became more frequent within the distribution at progressively lower scores, another way of expressing the predictions of the logistic regression model presented earlier.

From both cohorts, there were 55 children with an IQ score at age 11 years out of a total of 59 who later developed schizophrenia; four scores were missing from the NSHD. At this age, the scores of children who would develop schizophrenia from the NCDS were somewhat lower (mean 0.6 SD below the population mean) than those of similar children from the NSHD (mean 0.2 SD below the mean); however, the variances were very similar ($F=0.4$, $p=0.9$) and the difference between the means was not statistically significant (difference 0.4 SD; 95% CI -0.2 to 1.1; $p=0.2$) for the two case groups.

Given that our previous hypothesis was that the two sets of cases were independent samples of the same hypo-

thetical population of children at risk for schizophrenia, we went on to combine these two samples of "cases", assuming the difference in scores of the two groups to be largely due to sampling error. There may be some confounding effect from the disproportionate sampling method employed by the NSHD, whereby only a random one in four sample of children of manual workers was included in the follow-up sample, together with all other children. This effect would have been likely to be small.

Despite these caveats, inspection of the frequency distributions of IQ for the samples combined (Fig. 9.2) is of interest. Inspection of the tails of the distribution of the cases' scores reveals no evidence of a subgroup, and the overall impression is of a general shift of the distribution, albeit with the visual distraction of the single case with IQ approaching 4 standard deviations above the population mean. Unfortunately, there was insufficient statistical power to attempt a formal, confirmatory admixture analysis, although we think these data speak for themselves. Cases were rarer from the population above the mean value than they were from that below it.

The parsimonious explanation is that the lower the IQ at age 11 years, the greater the risk of schizophrenia; the shift of 0.4 standard deviation (95% CI 0.05 to 0.75) shown by the combined case population may have been due to an effect on *each* individual. Whether this may be a deleterious effect lowering IQ or some manifestation of a *protective effect* associated with higher IQ is considered below.

DISCUSSION

We have assumed that the NSHD and the NCDS are two independent samples of the same theoretical population of children who are at risk of the same disorder: adult onset schizophrenia in those born 12 years apart is the same disorder or range of disorders. Thus, results are not only comparable but conclusions from one cohort may be inferred for the other. This approach has dangers and we acknowledge, for instance, that the definition of schizophrenia was somewhat different in the two samples. We think it was a useful heuristic exercise, however, particularly as our initial comparisons were in some sense a test of these assumptions, and showed similar results for the two samples.

Low statistical power is a methodological problem in studies of this kind but is counterbalanced by several strengths. Moreover, the comparison of results from the two cohorts has made it possible to identify areas of independent replication. The longitudinal nature of the data collection and the use of standardized cross-sectional information, such as the educational tests, avoided problems with biased recall. It is of interest to note that the mean age of teething, as recalled by NSHD mothers when the children were age 24 months, was slightly earlier for the case group, indicating that the other (later) milestone findings, which accord with current hypotheses, were unlikely to be the result of recall bias (Jones *et al.* 1994b). Furthermore, comparisons in the NCDS of subjective ratings, by teachers, and objective ratings derived from psychometric tests, for both reading and mathematics correlated highly (+0.7 and +0.8) confirming the reliability of recall by the teachers.

Selection of cases proceeded blind to information collected before age 16 years in both cohorts, and several independent sources of information were employed to identify the cases. In particular, use of the Mental Health Enquiry meant that survey members who had dropped out of both cohorts could still be included as cases. Affected subjects are incident cases so that results were not

biased by the effects of chronicity or survival which are the bane of cross-sectional samples. Attrition is low in both cohorts, only one permanent refusal of follow-up before age 16 years in the NSHD, and in the NCDS some 75% of cases with score at 7 years also provided scores at 11 and 16 years, so the risk set was representative of the generations born in the UK during the period 1946–58. Similar proportions of cases and controls had missing exposure data and cases with and without missing data had onset at similar ages.

We avoided dividing the cases according to clinical characteristics owing to their small number and our reliance on case histories which often had inadequate detail to permit, positive/negative symptom scores to be rated. If differences in developmental associations do exist between possible subtypes of the adult clinical syndrome, our estimates of associations will have represented underestimates of the true effect in which ever subgroup is primarily involved. Our observation of the distribution of IQ scores and the age of reaching milestones, do not indicate a subgroup performing well below average with the remainder coming at random from the normal population. Thus, we consider that there is a systematic shift of the distribution for the schizophrenia population as a whole.

The risk of schizophrenia was within expected limits in both cohorts. Case identification was designed to ensure high specificity rather than sensitivity; with such a small number of cases, false positive cases would have been a serious problem. Nevertheless, the estimated risk of 0.63% and 0.38% for schizophrenia by ages 43 and 27 years in the two cohorts compares very favorably with the predicted risk of 0.6% and 0.36% by ages 40 and 27 years (Jones *et al.* 1995).

No statistically significant predictors of schizophrenia emerged from the measures of social class in either study, although the trend in both cohorts was for higher social status at birth, something which has also been found in recent investigations involving the 1966 North Finland birth cohort (Isohanni *et al.* in press). Furthermore, covariance analyses using socioeconomic status, social disadvantage and life event measures failed to make any impression on the cognitive deficit in the preschizophrenics in either cohort. The more modest cognitive deficit in the pre-affective psychotics in the NCDS could not be accounted for by social disadvantage; however some cognitive deficits found in the preneurotics of the same age, namely on reading comprehension and mathematics, appear to be accounted for by social factors. These findings do not rule out an effect for social disadvantage in the precipitation of schizophrenia in adulthood, where the evidence suggests that socioeconomic disadvantage may be a factor, although the direction of causality is difficult to establish for a disorder which, as we have shown, has multiple manifestations prior to psychosis (Jones et al. 1993).

Within the early motor milestones, later walking was the only statistically significant predictor of the cases, although there was a pattern for the cases to have reached all motor milestones later than the controls. The delay in motor development identified in the NSHD appeared also to result in persistent coordination and miscellaneous motor problems evident throughout childhood and adolescence in the NCDS. Delays in motor development and other perturbations of motor development have been noted in schizophrenia in studies using a variety of designs (Robins 1966; Walker and Lewine 1990; Ambelas 1992; Fish et al. 1992) and, given that our control groups included children with gross motor disabilities, these motor findings are likely to be genuine effects.

In the NCDS, the only school-based assessments which distinguished the preschizophrenic children from the other patient groups were the qualitative assessment of "speech difficulties ", at both 7 and 11 years, together with an objective test of word mispronunciation at 7 years. Whereas the pre-affective psychotic and preneurotic children fell within the normal range, 32% of mothers for the age 7 years group and 41% of teachers for the age 11 years group reported "speech difficulties" which were not due to stammer or stutter. In the NSHD, school doctors noted similarly nonspecific speech defects more commonly in children who would get schizophrenia. Given that the base rates in the control population were low (in NCDS 8% and 11%, respectively) these group differences were highly significant and the results suggest that a qualitative distinction might exist between the manner in which speech is produced by preschizophrenics as early as 7 years compared with the other groups of children.

As discussed above, the evidence for abnormal speech development prior to schizophrenia is, therefore, strong and complementary from both studies. The study by van Os et al. (1996) of chronic, severe depressives in the NSHD did find evidence of speech irregularities in childhood but only in girls, and any delays present were of lesser magnitude than in schizophrenia. The interaction with sex was an unexpected finding and difficult to interpret, although in accord with notions of severe affective disorders being more akin to schizophrenia in women than in men (Murray 1994). On all other cognitive tests the distinction between preschizophrenics, pre-affective psychotics and preneurotics appears to be simply one of magnitude, preschizophrenics consistently performing worse on all tests than the other two groups, whose performance was also below average.

One can only speculate on the pathogenesis of these neurodevelopmental findings. The deficits in motor development may reflect some abnormal process of neural development, perhaps involving myelination of motor tracts. Normal myelination of hippocampal pathways extends into adolescence and this, or some perturbation, has been suggested as a mechanism for the delayed appearance of positive schizophrenic phenomena (Benes 1989) in adulthood. It is possible that delayed motor milestones were a manifestation of similar mechanisms. Such explanations are beyond epidemiology.

The finding of poor educational performance predicting later schizophrenia reinforces evidence from several types of epidemiological studies indicating a premorbid deficit in intelligence (Aylward et al. 1984; Jones et al. 1994c). The findings from both cohorts suggest that deficits are found in female as well as male preschizophrenics, something which has not been reported before. It was not the case that specific deficits are found, instead there appears to be a small but reliable reduction in general intelligence reported by previous workers (Crawford et al. 1992). The magnitude of the deficit suggested by our combined analysis was within the range 0.05 to 0.75 of a standard deviate (i.e. one to 11 IQ points) which is small and does not even merit the consideration of preschizophrenic individuals being labeled as having "low intelligence". Given the longitudinal nature of the data, with the same subjects involved at each age, and the population base of the study, these findings are strong evidence in favor of prepsychotic intelligence deficits in schizophrenia.

The data reported here, however, indicate that a general intelligence, "g", deficit is also linked to the development of affective psychosis and neurotic disorders. Could "g" act as a protective factor by reducing the risk of onset of psychosis in general and possibly other psychopathologies, too? Done et al. (1996) have noted that low IQ has been reported as a risk factor, or high IQ as a protecting factor for antisocial behavior, personality disorder and for post-traumatic stress disorder (PTSD). We have no data which would allow us to assess the contribution of genetic influences on the deficits that we have found, influences which may be distinct for some of these psychological disorders. Complementary to this idea of protection are preliminary results from a 20-year follow-up of children in a psychiatric clinic who later developed schizophrenia (Munro et al. 1996). In this high-risk sample, IQ at first presentation was the single most important factor in predicting outcome in terms of GAF and GAS scores when considered together with other characteristics at baseline including social class and features of the presenting complaint; the higher the IQ the better the outcome. Moreover, repeat IQ at follow-up revealed no sign of a significant change (Russell et al. 1996), evidence against an ongoing illness process.

Developmental risk for schizophrenia – evidence for a subgroup?

Analysis of categorical ratings of abnormality versus normality has tended to focus attention on the notion of a subgroup of cases who showed prepsychotic deviance, with the assumption that other cases are normal, for example low versus normal IQ, or late versus normal milestones. This approach ignores the wide range of scores found in the general population and the fact that categorical ratings are often artificial, applying arbitrary or poorly defined cut-off points. Examining frequency distributions for evidence of subgroups of cases was simple, though none the less interesting and informative. There are sophisticated statistical techniques, such as admixture analysis (Harvey et al. 1990) for examining whether a frequency distribution is better described by two or more separate distributions but such techniques have low statistical

power and were inappropriate for our data sets. Larger case series based upon hospital admissions would not be ideal, even if premorbid data were available, owing to the dangers of referral bias with particularly abnormal or deviant individuals preferentially included. The simple plots showed clearly that case scores overlapped closely with control scores and that subgroups within the cases were unlikely to account for differences in the mean scores between cases and controls; a different explanatory model was required.

We applied our statistical approach to this question only in the NSHD because of the caveats involved in combining the samples (see earlier). Again, the approach exploited the population basis of this investigation and allowed conclusions to be drawn concerning the population at risk of schizophrenia by defining which parts of that total population were responsible for the largest proportion of disorder. Linear trends in the associations between subsequent schizophrenia and educational test scores gave further indication (though not independent of merely looking at the distributions) that the notion of a distinct, developmentally deviant subgroup who later suffer from schizophrenia may not portray the true situation. In terms of IQ, the risk of schizophrenia appeared to be distributed through the population, such that, for any child, the lower the score in the educational tests the more likely they were to develop schizophrenia as adults; the risk of schizophrenia within the general population was not confined to a particular group. As schizophrenia is relatively rare, larger numbers in a cohort study (i.e., a larger population at risk) or, more efficiently, a population-based "nested" case control study, would be required to examine the exact nature and distribution of this risk. Nevertheless, the simplest conclusion is that it is linear.

If there is a "developmental majority" in schizophrenia, rather than a minority subtype with developmental roots, the risk may be analogous to, for instance, blood pressure and the risk of stroke. If blood pressure were measured only with an instrument registering only two levels, "high" or "normal", stroke may be found to be associated with a subgroup of individuals with hypertension. This strategy ignores the fact that many, indeed the majority of cases will have, so called, normal values and, more importantly, that the risk of stroke associated with blood pressure is linear over a wide range of values; the higher the blood pressure, the greater the risk of having a stroke.

This in no way indicates that the linear associations demonstrated in the present study are causal, nor does it exclude etiological heterogeneity. They do allow consideration of how genetic and environmental etiological factors may operate in terms of a liability-threshold model. One possibility is that there is no specific early causal factor for schizophrenia, but that the normal genetic and environmental determinants of behavior, cognition and neurodevelopment also determine the risk of schizophrenia. Familiality of schizophrenia could be the result of the complex mix of effects involved in these processes also tending to cluster in families, although evidence from adoption studies, risk to progeny in discordant monozygotic twins and retrospective accounts of life events indicate genetic rather than cultural transmission.

The alternative is that specific causal factors are involved. Their effect(s), which may occur early in life, probably effecting neural development, are betrayed in the associations demonstrated. Thus, a subject who would have had a high IQ in the absence of the particular gene or environmental factor scores a little lower when affected by this factor. Poor information processing could interact with other dysfunctional psychological systems concerned with motor ability, motivation, affect, etc., leading to less competence in social situations. Nevertheless, this subject may still function well within the normal range and would escape detection by a test designed to detect abnormality. Another subject who would have been at the lower end of the normal range of cognitive functioning in the absence of the factor, would be pushed into the realms of, so called, pathological functioning when affected by the factor. This subject would be detected by the test described above. All cases would be prone to this process and, as a group, their functioning would slip towards the lower end of normal.

Under such a model, a higher proportion of subjects with schizophrenia than previously thought may have suffered attenuated development, although the majority of these will remain undetected by tests designed to detect gross abnormality. The alternative, with IQ as a protective factor, may involve "resilience" to independent events, be they neurobiological factors predisposing to psychosis, psychosocial factors associated with precipitation, or both.

This model also offers an explanation of the overlap between cases and controls which is evident in virtually all studies of schizophrenia, be they of neuropathology, IQ, or of prepsychotic social functioning. It explains why, in studies of monozygotic twins, the affected twins may show little abnormality as a group but when compared with their co-twin in a paired analysis, predicted differences become apparent (Suddath *et al.* 1990). A similar explanation has recently been suggested for the overlapping distributions of sizes of cerebral structures in schizophrenia and controls (Jones *et al.* 1994a). Here again, it is suggested that a much larger proportion of schizophrenia than previously imagined may be associated with disease-related changes, or merely differences, in cerebral structure.

As we have argued before (Jones *et al.* 1994b), for normally distributed risk factors such as IQ, the models predict that the majority of affected individuals arise from the majority of the population who are around the average value, very high risk individuals are very rare. This has implications not only for understanding the mechanism by which risk factors might operate but also for early intervention and perhaps even prevention (Rose 1992).

In conclusion, this investigation replicates a body of literature by demonstrating that children destined to develop schizophrenia in adult life can be differentiated from their peers across a variety of characteristics beginning with early milestones of motor and speech development. Initial events, either genetic or environmental, occur early and commence their influence on psychological functioning at an early age. The epidemiological base of the study indicated that the incidence of schizophrenia was not confined to a subgroup of the population in terms of childhood educational performance but appeared to arise increasingly frequently as ability declined in these domains. These effects may not be specific to schizophrenia with respect to severe affective disorder. Such tentative conclusions require replication but, if true, provide a further, longitudinal dimension to the schizophrenia/psychosis phenotype yet to be explained in terms of basic neurobiology. Continuing investigations in this and other longitudinal investigations, particularly if results can be pooled, will facilitate further exploration of the longitudinal phenotype of schizophrenia before the emergence of psychosis.

ACKNOWLEDGMENTS

We thank Professor M.E.J. Wadsworth for facilitating
work regarding severe mental illness in the NSHD, to
many other colleagues for helping us to develop the ideas
that we have presented, and to both the UK Medical
Research Foundation and the Stanley Foundation for
funding.

REFERENCES

Akbarian, S., Bunney, W.E., Potkin, S.G., Wigal, S.B., Hagman,
    J.O., Sandman, C.A., and Jones, E. G. 1993a. Altered
    distribution of nicotinamide-adenine dinucleotide
    phosphate-diaphorase cells in frontal lobe of
    schizophrenics implies disruption of cortical development.
    Arch. Gen. Psychiatry 50:169–77.

Akbarian, S., Viñuela, A., Kim, J.J., Potkin, S.G., Bunney, W.E.,
    and Jones, E.G. 1993b. Disrupted distribution of
    nicotinamide-adenine dinucleotide phosphate-diaphorase
    neurons in temporal lobe of schizophrenics implies
    abnormal cortical development. *Arch. Gen. Psychiatry*
    50:178–89.

Ambelas, A. 1992. Preschizophrenics: adding to the evidence,
    sharpening the focus. *Br. J. Psychiatry* 160:401–4.

American Psychiatric Association: *Diagnostic and statistical
    manual of mental disorders* 1987. Third edition – revised.
    Washington, DC: American Psychiatric Association.

Aylward, E., Walker, E., and Bettes, B. 1984. Intelligence in
    schizophrenia: meta-analysis of the research. *Schizophr.
    Bull.* 10:430–59.

Barker, D.J.P. 1994. Mothers, babies and disease in later life.
    London: British Medical Journal Publishing Group.

Benes, F.M. 1989. Myelination of cortico-hippocampal relays
    during late adolescence. *Schizophr. Bull.* 10:430–59.

Bloom, R.B. and Eaton, A.D. 1975. Intellectual functioning and
    psychopathology: A canonical analysis of the WAIS and
    MMPI relationships. *J. Clin. Psychol.* 31:697–8.

Buka, S.L., Tsuang, M.T. and Lipsitt, L.P. 1993.
    Pregnancy/delivery complications and psychiatric
    diagnosis. A prospective study. *Arch. Gen. Psychiatry*
    50:151–6.

Cannon-Spoor, H.E., Potkin, S.G., and Wyatt, R.J. 1982.

Measurement of premorbid adjustment in chronic
    schizophrenia. *Schizophr. Bull.* 8:470–84.

Crawford, J.R., Besson, J.A.O., Bremner, M., Ebmeier, K.P.,
    Cochrane, R.H.B., and Kirkwood, K. 1992. Estimation of
    premorbid intelligence in schizophrenia. *Br. J. Psychiatry*
    161:69–74.

Crow, T.J. 1992. Maternal viral infection hypothesis. *Br.
    J. Psychiatry* 161:570–1.

Crow, T.J. and Done, D.J. 1992. Prenatal exposure to influenza
    does not cause schizophrenia. *Br. J. Psychiatry* 161:390–3.

Done, D.J., Crow, T.J., Johnson, E.C., and Sacker, A. 1994.
    Childhood antecedents of schizophrenia and affective
    illness: social adjustment at ages 7 and 11. *Br. Med.
    J.* 309:699–703.

Done, J., Johnstone, E.C., Frith C.D., Golding J., Shepard P.M.,
    and Crow T.J. 1991. Complications of pregnancy and
    delivery in relation to psychosis in adult life: data from
    the British Perinatal Mortality Survey. *Br. Med.
    J.* 302:1576–80.

Erlenmeyer-Kimling, L., Cornblatt, B., Friedman, D. *et al.*
    1980. Neurological, electrophysiological and attentional
    deviations in children at risk of schizophrenia. In
    Schizophrenia as a brain disease, ed. F.A. Henn and H.
    Nasrallah, pp. 61–98. New York: Oxford Univeersity Press.

Erlenmeyer-Kimling, L., Folnegovic, Z., Hrabak-Zerjavic, V.,
    Borcic, B., Folnegovic-Smalc, V., and Susser, E. 1994.
    Schizophrenia and prenatal exposure to the 1957 A2
    influenza epidemic. *Am. J. Psychiatry*, 151: 1496–8.

Fish, B. 1977. Neurobiological antecedents of schizophrenia in
    children. *Arch. Gen. Psychiatry* 34:1297–313.

Fish, B., Marcus, J., Hans, S.L., Auerbach, J.G., and Perdue, S.
    1992. Infants at risk for schizophrenia: sequelae of a genetic
    neurointegrative defect. *Arch. Gen. Psychiatry* 49:221–35.

Foerster, A., Lewis, S.W., Owen, M.J., and Murray, R.M. 1989.
    Pre-morbid adjustment and personality in psychosis.
    Effects of sex and diagnosis. *Br. J. Psychiatry* 158:171–6.

Gaines, T. and Morris, R. 1978. Relationships between MMPI
    increases of psychopathology and WAIS sub-test scores
    and intelligence quotients. *Perceptual and Motor Skills*
    47:399–402.

Gittleman-Klein, R. and Klein, D.F. 1969. Premorbid social
    adjustment and prognosis in schizophrenia. *J. Psychiat.
    Res.* 7:35–53.

Goodman, R. 1988. Are complications of pregnancy and birth

causes of schizophrenia? *Dev. Med. Child Neurol.* **30**:391–406.

Harvey, I., McGuffin, P., Williams, M., and Toone, B.K. 1990. The ventricle-brain ratio (VBR) in functional psychoses: an admixture analysis. *Psychiat. Res.: Neuroimaging* **35**:61–9.

Heaton, R., Paulsen, J.S., McAdams, L.A., Kuck, J., Zisook, S., Braff, D., Harris, M.J., and Jeste, D.V. 1994. Neuropsychological deficits in schizophrenia: relationship to age, chronicity and dementia. *Arch. Gen. Psychiatry* **51**:469–75.

Isohanni, M., Moring, J., Rasanen, P., Hakko, H., Partanen, U., Koiranen, M. and Jones, P.B. 1997. The validity of diagnoses of first-onset schizophrenia in the Finnish Hospital Discharge Register: a comparison of clinical and scientific views in a national birth cohort. *Social Psychiatry Psychiatr. Epidemiol.* **31** (in press).

Jakob, H. and Beckmann, H. 1986. Prenatal developmental disturbances in the limbic allocortex in schizophrenics. *J. Neural Trans.* **63**:303–26.

Johnstone, E.C., Crow, T.J., Johnson, A.L. and MacMillan, J.F. 1986. The Northwick Park study of first episode schizophrenia. 1. Presentation of the illness and problems relating to admission. *Br. J. Psychiatry* **148**:115–20.

Jones, P.B., Bebbington, P., Foerster, A., Lewis, S.W., Murray, R.M., Russell, A., Sham, P.C., Toone, B.K. and Wilkins, S. 1993. Premorbid social underachievement in schizophrenia. Results from the Camberwell Collaborative Psychosis Study. *Br. J. Psychiatry* **162**:65–71.

Jones, P.B., Guth, C.W., Lewis, S.W., and Murray, R.M. 1994c Low intelligence and poor educational achievement precede early onset schizophrenic psychosis. In *The Neuropsychology of Schizophrenia*, ed. S. David and J. Cutting. Hove: Lawrence Erlbaum.

Jones, P.B., Harvey, I., Lewis, S.W., Toone, B.K., van Os, J., Williams, M., and Murray, R.M. 1994a. Cerebral ventricle dimensions as risk factors for schizophrenia and affective psychosis. An epidemiological approach to analysis. *Psychol. Med.* **24**:995–1011.

Jones, P.B. and Murray, R.M. 1991. The genetics of schizophrenia is the genetics of neurodevelopment. *Br. J. Psychiatry* **158**:615–23.

Jones, P.B., Murray, R.M., and Rodgers, B. 1995. Childhood risk factors for schizophrenia in a general population birth cohort at age 43 years. In *Neural development in schizophrenia: theory and practice*, ed. S. A. Mednick, pp. 151–76. New York: Plenum Press.

Jones, P.B., Rodgers, B., Murray, R.M., and Marmot, M.G. 1994b. Child developmental risk factors for adult schizophrenia in the British 1946 birth cohort. *Lancet* **344**:1398–402.

Kraepelin, E. 1896. Dementia Praecox, pp. 426–41 of the 5th edition of *Psychiatrie Barth: Leipzig*. Translated (1987) by J. Cutting and M. Shepherd. In *The Clinical Roots of the Schizophrenia Concept*. Cambridge: Cambridge University Press.

Lacks, P. B. and Keefe, K. 1970. Relationship among education, the MMPI and WAIS measures of psychopathology. *J. Clin. Psychol.* **26**:468–70.

Lewis, S.W., Owen, M.J. and Murray, R.M. 1989. Obstetric complications and schizophrenia: methodology and mechanisms. In *Schizophrenia – a scientific focus*, ed. S.C. Schulz and C.A. Tamminga, pp. 56–68. New York: Oxford University Press.

Loebel, A.D., Lieberman, J.A., Alvir, J.M.J., Meyerhoff, D.I., Geisler, S.H., and Szymanski, S.R. 1992. Duration of psychosis and outcome in first-episode schizophrenia. *Am. J Psychiatry* **149**:1183–8.

Mednick, S.A., Machon, R.A., Huttenen, M.O., and Bonnett, D. 1988. Adult schizophrenia following prenatal exposure to an influenza epidemic. *Arch. Gen. Psychiatry* **45**:188–92.

Murray, R.M. 1994. Neurodevelopmental schizophrenia: The rediscovery of dementia praecox. *Br. J. Psychiatry* **165**(Suppl. 25): 6–12.

Murray, R.M. and Lewis, S.W. 1987. Is schizophrenia a neurodevelopmental disorder? *Br. Med. J.* **295**:681–2.

O'Callaghan, E., Larkin, C., and Waddington, J.L. 1990. Obstetric complications in schizophrenia and the validity of maternal recall. *Psychol. Med.* **20**:89–94.

Pidgeon, D.A. 1964. Tests used in the 1954 and 1957 surveys. In *The home and the school*, ed. J.W.B. Douglas, pp. 129–32. London: MacGibbon and Kee.

Pidgeon, D.A. 1968. Appendix: details of the fifteen year tests. In *All our futures*, ed. J.W.B. Douglas, J.M. Ross, and H.R. Simpson, pp. 194–7. London: Peter Davies.

Plomin, R. 1987. Developmental behavioral genetics and infancy. In *Handbook of infant development*, ed. J. D. Osofsky. New York: John Wiley.

Roberts, G.W. 1990. Schizophrenia: a neuropathological perspective. *Br. J. Psychiatry* **157**:1–10.

Robins, L.N. 1966. *Deviant Children Grown Up. A Sociological and Psychiatric Study of Sociopathic Personality*. Baltimore: Williams and Wilkins.

Rodgers, B. 1990b. Behavior and personality in childhood as predictors of adult psychiatric disorder. *J. Child Psychol. Psychiatry* **31**:393–414.

Rodgers, B. 1990a. Adult affective disorder and early environment. *Br. J. Psychiatry* **157**:539–50.

Rose, G. 1992. *The Strategy of Preventive Medicine*. Oxford: Oxford University Press.

Rutter, M. 1984. Psychopathology and development: 1. childhood antecedents of adult psychiatric disorder. *Austr. N.Z. J. Psychiatry* **18**:225–34.

Rutter, M.L. and Giller, H. 1983. *Juvenile delinquency: trends and perspectives*. Penguin: Harmondsworth.

Sacker, A., Done, D.J., Crow, T.J., and Golding, J. 1995. Antecedents of schizophrenia and affective illness. Obstetric complications. *Br. J. Psychiatry* **166**:734–41.

Sands, J.R. and Harrow, X. 1995. Vulnerability to psychosis in unipolar major depression: is premorbid functioning involved? *Am. J. Psychiatry* **152**:1009–15.

Selten. J.-P.C.J. and Slaets, J.P.J. 1994. Second trimester exposure to 1957 A$_2$ influenza epidemic is not a risk factor for schizophrenia. *Schizophr. Res.* **11**: 95.

Sham, P.C., O'Callaghan, E., Takei, N., Murray, G.K., Hare, E.H., and Murray, R.M. 1992. Increased risk of schizophrenia following prenatal exposure to influenza. *Br. J. Psychiatry* **160**:461–6.

Suddath, R.L., Christison, G.W., Torrey, E.F., Casanova, M.F., and Weinberger, D.R. 1990. Anatomical abnormalities in the brains of monozygotic twins discordant for schizophrenia. *New Engl. J. Medicine* **322**:789–94.

Susser, E. and Lin, S.P. 1992. Schizophrenia after exposure to the Dutch Hunger Winter of 1944–1945. *Arch. Gen. Psychiatry* **49**:983–8.

Susser, E., Lin, S.P., Brown, A.S., Lumey, L.H., and Erlenmeyer Kimling, L. 1994. No relation between risk of schizophrenia and prenatal exposure to influenza in Holland. *Am. J. Psychiatry* **151**:922–4.

Van Os, J.J., Jones, P.D, Lewis, G., Wadsworth, M., and Murray, R. M. 1996. Evidence for similar developmental precursors of chronic affective illness and schizophrenia in a general population birth cohort. *Arch. Gen. Psychiatry* (in press).

Wadsworth, M.E.J. 1991. *The Imprint of Time. Childhood History and Adult Life*. Oxford: Clarendon Press.

Walker E. and Lewine, R.J. 1990. Prediction of adult-onset schizophrenia from childhood home movies of the patients. *Am. J. Psychiatry* **147**:1052–6.

Watt, N. and Lubensky, A. 1976. Childhood roots of schizophrenia. *J. Consult. Clin. Psychology* **44**:363–75.

Watt, N.F. 1978. Patterns of childhood social development in adult schizophrenics. *Arch. Gen. Psychiatry* **35**:160–5.

Weinberger, D.R. 1987. Implications of normal brain development for the pathogenesis of schizophrenia. *Arch. Gen. Psychiatry* **44**:660–9.

Wing, J.K., Cooper, J.E., and Sartorius, N. 1974. *The Measurement and Classification of Psychiatric Symptoms*. London: Cambridge University Press.

Wyatt, R.J. 1991. Neuroleptics and the natural course of schizophrenia. *Schizophr. Bull.* **17**:325–51.

10 Developmental aspects of schizophrenia

MICHAEL F. POGUE-GEILE

INTRODUCTION

As indicated by this volume, consideration of the developmental aspects of schizophrenia has become an increasingly important area for theorizing and research (Randall 1980; Feinberg 1982–83; Murray and Lewis 1987; Weinberger 1987; Pogue-Geile 1991; Walker 1991; Waddington and Buckley, 1996). Although long a subject of research interest (Mednick and McNeil 1968; Garmezy and Streitman 1974), this reinvigorated attention is important both because it is clear that schizophrenia develops in ways that need to be explained and because consideration of its developmental aspects may also provide clues to its etiology and pathophysiology.

The aim of this chapter is therefore to examine conceptualizations of development in general, consider carefully the developmental aspects of schizophrenia, briefly describe current models of the development of schizophrenia, and review research on both the description and causation of age of onset of schizophrenia (see also Pogue-Geile 1991,1996).

GENERAL CONCEPTIONS OF DEVELOPMENT: IS SCHIZOPHRENIA A DEVELOPMENTAL DISORDER, AND IF SO, WHY?

In seeking to define the term "developmental" we will first rule out some uses from our intended meaning. First, the term developmental is often used casually to refer to something having to do with childhood. This usage is generally not employed in the scientific literature because development can obviously occur after childhood. Development is also often used to refer to an *individual* and the changes and consistencies he or she exhibits over time. In contrast, here we are concerned not with an individual but rather with a *characteristic* (i.e., schizophrenia). It may also help to distinguish between "development" and "developmental" here. Virtually all characteristics "develop", in the sense that there is some sequence of preceding states. For example, even the common cold develops over *time*, in that preceding the classic signs and symptoms there is some more or less variable sequence of events beginning with infection. Understanding these antecedents is important, but stating that a cold "develops" is a truism. In contrast, we will restrict our use here of the term "developmental" to those characteristics that are associated with *age*.

We will base the following discussion and definitions on general concepts of developmental phenomena that are frequently used in developmental psychology. A central idea here is that of a characteristic's "developmental function", which is usually defined as a graph of the quantity of the characteristic, such as total vocabulary, across age (Wohlwill 1973; McCall 1981,1993). To the extent that a developmental function is not flat or uniform across age, some developmental aspect to the characteristic is implicated. One can distinguish two general ways in which a developmental function could deviate from a flat, uniform distribution. First, a plot could be *linear*, but with some nonzero slope across age. Here, change is occurring across age, but the rate of change is constant and not associated with age (i.e., the acceleration is always zero). For example, suppose that special summer courses emphasizing vocabulary building increase one's vocabulary by some constant number of words each year with no forgetting across years. Further, suppose that an individual takes these courses every year across some age span. The developmental function for total vocabulary for the individual in this example would be a linear one with a positive slope. In such a linear example, the causes of the constant rate of increase in vocabulary over time would need to be explained, but there would be no need to consider anything special about one age period versus another.

In contrast, the developmental function could be *nonlinear*, in which case the rate of change across age (or acceleration) may vary with age. Modifying this example, if an individual only took a special vocabulary building course once (such as the summer before college entrance examinations), then the developmental function for vocabulary would show a change in slope (i.e., some positive acceleration) at that age for the individual. In this case, one would need to invoke something special about this particular age versus other age periods in order to explain this acceleration.

Although both linear and nonlinear functions may be considered developmental, in some sense, the nonlinear case might be considered more truly "developmental" because some age periods differ from others in their rate of change. This will be our preference here and we will narrowly define for our purposes as "developmental", those developmental functions that show some nonlinear relationship with age.

Developmental functions may be plotted for both individuals and means of groups, but the two should be distinguished because the developmental function for an individual in some sense does not distinguish between changes across "time" and changes with "age". Continuing with our example, some nonlinear change in slope would be observed in total vocabulary at a particular age for an individual if an intensive summer course in vocabulary building were taken. In a group, if the probability of taking the course were equal for all ages, then the *mean* developmental function for the group would be linear, suggesting no special association between *age* and vocabulary increase. For an individual we cannot know whether changes over time are associated with "age" in general. Therefore, in the current context, the concept of "age" has meaning largely in reference to a group, such that a characteristic may be said to be associated with age to the extent that its quantity differs *on average* across age in some groups. Age in itself cannot cause changes in a

characteristic, but rather it may best be considered as a potentially useful summary variable that serves to indicate the extent to which causal factors are associated in some group with "time from birth". In a similar fashion, differences in incidence rates across geographic areas may be studied to provide clues to spatial variation in causal factors, but geographic location is not considered as causal itself. In addition, attributions to age effects must be distinguished in some manner from the historical time at which the group members reach a particular age (i.e., birth cohort effects). When we say that beginning to walk is a developmental phenomenon because the cumulative distribution of first independent steps has a peak acceleration at about *age* 1 year old, the emphasis is on the age of the individuals. An implicit presumption is that this is largely the case regardless of whether the children are 1 year old in 1990 or 1995. If the peak of first steps were at 1 year old for a particular birth cohort, but differed markedly for others, then we would probably be less willing to attribute a special importance to age-associated causes and instead might be more interested in causal factors associated with historical time. In any case, such birth cohort effects on developmental phenomena are clearly possible and important and need to be investigated and distinguished from age effects (e.g., Schaie 1983). Therefore, our definition here of a developmental phenomenon will be reserved to those characteristics that show a nonlinear mean developmental function across age in some group that is relatively consistent across birth cohorts.

How should schizophrenia be considered within this developmental function framework? First, some measurement of schizophrenia needs to be defined and because we are interested in the beginning of schizophrenia rather than some other aspect we will choose a measure of its clinical *onset*. This is often taken as when an individual meets relevant criteria for a diagnosis of schizophrenia, although there are other possibilities. In quantitative terms, this schizophrenia variable could be scored dichotomously with individuals not diagnosed with schizophrenia at a particular age scored as "0" and those who meet criteria scored as "1". There would usually be the added and important constraint that change could only be unidirectional, from normal to schizophrenia, but not vice versa, and therefore once an individual is diagnosed they would receive "1"s for all succeeding ages. A plot of this mean developmental function for "schizophrenia score" by age in a group is the same as a cumulative age incidence distribution for schizophrenia because the mean of a dichotomous variable (0 or 1) is the proportion of the group scoring 1.

Although there may be other ways to define "developmental", at least according to the present definition it seems clear that the onset of schizophrenia is a developmental phenomenon. The primary reason is that the onset of the syndrome of signs and symptoms by which schizophrenia is currently defined has a cumulative age incidence distribution, or developmental function, that is nonlinear with a peak change in slope or acceleration usually taken to occur during young adulthood (see below). Schizophrenia's cumulative age distribution therefore suggests that the risk for onset of schizophrenia varies with an individual's age, which may be taken as evidence that the onset of schizophrenia is a developmental phenomenon according to the definition above. Given the plausibility of the existence of brain abnormalities (albeit currently largely unspecified) in schizophrenia, it further seems reasonable to conceive of the onset of schizophrenia as some sort of *neuro*-developmental phenomenon. From this analysis it should be clear that the onset of schizophrenia is a developmental phenomenon and that currently our primary evidence for a role of developmental processes in schizophrenia comes from the nature of the age incidence distribution in schizophrenia and its peak during the young adulthood. In the following sections we will particularly focus our attention on the age distribution of schizophrenia onset.

CAUSATION AND DEVELOPMENTAL PHENOMENA

Before discussing the developmental function of schizophrenia specifically, we will first consider some more general aspects of the causes of developmental functions, as the existence of age-related change in itself implies nothing about the causes of such developmental phenomena.

The causes of any individual difference and/or change over time may be broadly divided into either genetic or environmental sources. In considering causes of differences among *individuals* in some characteristic, it is traditionally presumed that they may be ascribed to genetic differences, environmental differences, and/or some combination (additive or nonadditive, i.e., gene x gene, gene x environment, and environment x environment interactions) of the two (e.g., Falconer 1981). Similarly, changes over *time* within an individual may be ascribed to genetic changes, environmental changes, or some combination of the two. Although the causes for changes over time within an individual are often attributed to environmental changes, it is also clear that changes in gene *expression* may occur over time. While an individual's DNA does not change over time (except for new somatic mutations), the pieces of the DNA that are expressed as proteins may change over time, just as gene expression varies across the different tissues within an individual. The causes of changes in gene expression over time may be either due to the consequences of previous changes in gene expression or to changes in environmental exposures. The acknowledgment and investigation of this dynamic aspect of genetic influence is the cornerstone of developmental genetics and developmental behavior genetics (e.g., Plomin 1986; Hahn *et al.* 1990).

Next, we will distinguish several different aspects of mean developmental functions. This is important as the causes of each may differ. First, it is important in considering developmental functions to bear in mind that the causes of mean changes across time may or may not contribute to individual differences at any particular age (and *vice versa*). This is an issue that is well appreciated in the developmental psychology and developmental behavior genetic literatures (McCall 1981; Plomin 1986). To illustrate this point, let us return to a variation of the example of the increase in vocabulary following an intensive vocabulary course, only now all individuals in a group took the course at the same age. In this example, a mean increase in vocabulary across the relevant age period could be ascribed to environmental exposure to the class. At that particular age, however, *individual differences* in total vocabulary must be due to factors other than exposure to the class, such as individual differences in previous education and genotype, because in this example all individuals in the group were exposed to the course at the same age. A similar example could be imagined in which changes in gene expression over time may cause within person changes in a characteristic, but individual differences at any particular age may be due to other causes. For example, a mean increase in height during puberty may be caused by the new expression of select "height growth" genes, whereas individual differences in height at any particular age would also be caused by individual differences in other "height" genes, as well as environmental experiences, such as diet. In considering causes for changes over time in developmental functions, it must also be noted that the existence of time "lags" between environmental exposure/gene expression and changes in measured phenotype may occur. For example, even in the simple case of measles there is usually a delay of several days, or "incubation period" between infection and the occurrence of symptoms (Armenian and Khoury 1981; Armenian and Lilienfeld 1983). Thus, the cause for the increase in some characteristic during a particular time period may not necessarily be found during that time period, but rather at some earlier point.

A related concept is that of a threshold. Here, although environmental exposures and gene expression relevant to a particular characteristic may occur over some time period, they may only produce an observable change in the phenotype when their summation (as opposed to a particular combination) exceeds some *threshold*. This is a special example of a nonlinear effect resulting from the addition of multiple effects. A familiar example of this phenomenon is the failure of a light bulb after a certain number of hours of use. What counts here is not a particular time that the light is switched on, but the total *number* of hours that it has been on.

A nonlinear mean developmental function implies that changes over time for individuals as discussed above *covary* with age in a group for some reason(s). Two general ways in which mean nonlinear developmental functions arise may be distinguished. First, it may be that changes in acceleration with age are created by a *covariation* between age and exposure to some environmental causal factor(s). Such an *age–environment covariation* could arise for various reasons. Similarly, an *age–gene expression covariation* could exist in which the expression of certain genes covaries with age. To continue with our vocabulary

example, if exposure to the vocabulary enhancing course is associated with age in a group such that many individuals take the course at the same age (e.g., the summer prior to taking college entrance examinations) then there will be an acceleration in the mean developmental function at this age. The causes for this *covariation* between age and course exposure may be different from the causes of the increase in vocabulary itself. Thus, although the course itself improves vocabulary, the covariation between course exposure and age is caused by other factors, such as a personal and/or parental desire to perform well on college entrance examinations that peaks at a particular age. Similarly, to the extent that some "height growth" genes are expressed at a similar age across individuals, then an acceleration in height will be observed in the group. Again, although expression of the height growth genes may cause the increase in height, the covariation between age and this expression may be due to other factors, such as the expression of "puberty" genes, which activate expression of the height genes.

It is also important here to distinguish between two aspects of this covariation between causes of changes and age. A mean nonlinear developmental function usually exhibits both a *peak* acceleration as well as some *variation* in acceleration. For the vocabulary example, as was mentioned above a possible cause of the peak acceleration might be the desire to perform well on college entrance examinations that peaks at a particular age due to general societal age-graded expectations. In contrast, the causes of variation in acceleration across age might be due to other factors that influence individual differences in the age at which such courses are taken. That is, because in this example the developmental function for vocabulary presumably shows some variation in acceleration (i.e., not all individuals take the course at the same age), then there may be other factors that influence these individual differences in age of vocabulary increase (e.g., why some individuals take the course at earlier or later ages, such as individual differences in social class, etc.). Similarly, in the height example, the causes for the peak height growth gene expression at a particular age may be different from the causes of individual differences in age for such gene expression (such as individual differences in "puberty" genes, diet, and/or sexual experience).

To summarize, phenotypic changes over time may be due to either changes in environmental exposure or gene expression. The causes of changes over time within individuals may (or may not) be different from the causes of individual differences at any particular age. It is also important to distinguish between the causes of changes themselves and the causes of any covariation between them and age. Furthermore, for characteristics that covary with age in a group (i.e., exhibit a mean nonlinear developmental function) the causes of the peak acceleration may (or may not) be different from the causes of variation across age in acceleration. It is hoped that this discussion of some of the general aspects of developmental functions and their causation will provide a context for considering the specific case of clinical onset schizophrenia, which exhibits such a nonlinear developmental function.

MODELS OF SCHIZOPHRENIA DEVELOPMENT

Next we will discuss how most current models attempt to explain this developmental aspect of schizophrenia, namely its nonlinear mean developmental function for onset with a peak acceleration in young adulthood (see also Pogue-Geile 1991, 1996). However, most recent "developmental" models of schizophrenia have primarily emphasized hypotheses concerning the *development of the pathophysiology* of schizophrenia, rather than the *developmental* aspects of schizophrenia (i.e., age of onset). That is, these models have primarily focused on attempting to describe the sequence of states (both physical and psychological) that precede the clinical onset of schizophrenia, much as one might try to describe the sequence of changes that precede the onset of the symptoms of a cold. These crucial questions of when and how pathogenesis begins are obviously important in their own right and these models have had important heuristic value in stimulating research, but they differ in several ways from questions about why schizophrenia onset is a developmental phenomenon that shows a peak acceleration in its developmental function in young adulthood. Interestingly, the most popular of these recent models hypothesizes that the development of the brain and psychological pathologies that are specific to

schizophrenia first occur "early" and are abnormalities in in utero brain development (Murray and Lewis 1987; Weinberger 1987; Pogue-Geile 1991). The etiology of individual differences in these early abnormalities has been hypothesized to be genetic (i.e., expressed in utero) and/or environmental (e.g., in utero viral infection or other obstetrical insults), with more emphasis recently being paid to environmental hypotheses. The in utero developmental period has been emphasized primarily because of the dramatic brain changes that occur at that time. Such hypotheses require some additional mechanism to explain the long "delay" between these early abnormalities and the much later onset of schizophrenia symptoms.

It is in the secondary context of attempting to explain this hypothesized delay that these early development models have addressed questions of the developmental aspects of schizophrenia and its age of peak clinical onset in young adulthood. The problem for the early development models of the "delay" in manifestation of clinical symptoms has been dealt with in one of two general ways.

One approach, perhaps best exemplified by Meehl (1962, 1989) (although not considered explicitly), is that pathogenic experiences necessary (but not sufficient) for schizophrenia occur during childhood and adolescence in some individuals who have early brain abnormalities due to an early expressed gene until a critical combination or number is reached, usually no earlier than young adulthood, when schizophrenia symptoms then become manifest. In this model some individuals with early brain abnormalities due to a mutant gene are not exposed to the relevant noxious experiences and thus never develop clinical schizophrenia, although they manifest a *forme fruste*, termed schizotypy. Why the occurrence or accumulation of these contributory experiences peaks during young adulthood is not considered explicitly. In such models, environmental experiences across ages serve *both* to affect eventual risk for schizophrenia among those who have the early genetically caused brain abnormalities, as well as to delay the onset of schizophrenia until young adulthood because for whatever reason it takes that long to be exposed to the experiences necessary to produce the clinical syndrome.

In contrast, some more recent early development models (e.g., Randall 1980; Murray and Lewis 1987;

Weinberger 1987) have hypothesized a role for normal developmental brain changes during young adulthood in accounting for the "delay" in onset of schizophrenia symptoms. In these models, individual differences in brain abnormalities that are sufficient to produce schizophrenia eventually are present in utero but only produce schizophrenia symptoms following normal developmental brain changes that typically occur during young adulthood that "release" them. The causes of these normal brain developmental changes during young adulthood are usually not considered explicitly. Here, presumably normal later experiences and/or genetic expression serve only to time the onset of symptoms, but not to alter risk across individuals.

Although they have received considerably less attention by researchers to date than these early development theories, other models hypothesize that brain abnormalities specific to schizophrenia appear *late*, usually during young adulthood and relatively close in time to the onset of clinical symptoms. They do not postulate separate processes for the onset of pathogenesis and the onset of symptoms, and these "late development" models are more directly concerned with the developmental aspect of schizophrenia: its peak age of onset in young adulthood.

A late development model that has been perhaps most clearly proposed is that by Feinberg (1982–83), who hypothesized that schizophrenia may arise from abnormalities in brain changes that normally take place during young adulthood. Gottesman and Shields (1972) were also some of the early proponents of a developmental model in which liability for schizophrenia changed across age as a function of environmental and gene influences. In Feinberg's model, either abnormalities in which normal brain changes fail to terminate (e.g., synaptic pruning) or do not begin appropriately (e.g., myelinization) are suggested as possibilities (e.g., Keshavan *et al.* 1994). Rather than hypothesizing that normal developmental processes during young adulthood release early brain abnormalities, such late development models hypothesize abnormalities only in these young adulthood brain changes – a considerably simpler theoretical proposition. Such late hypotheses are not only parsimonious, but are also plausible as it is clear that a range of brain changes do occur during late adolescence and young adulthood. The causes of these young adult brain abnormalities are not usually considered

explicitly. Elsewhere we have suggested that to the extent that such normal brain changes during young adulthood are due to changes in gene expression, then the hypothesized brain abnormalities in schizophrenia may also be due to abnormalities in gene expression (Pogue-Geile 1991). Since it is clear that different genes may be expressed at different times during development (Plomin 1986), it seems plausible that abnormalities in genes that normally begin or end expression in the brain during young adulthood may play a role in schizophrenia. Such genes that control normal brain changes during adulthood are just beginning to be identified (Hahn *et al.* 1990).

In summary, both early and late development models of schizophrenia emphasize the development of schizophrenia pathophysiology but have obvious differences in terms of the age when brain abnormalities specific to schizophrenia are hypothesized to occur. Both, however, appeal to developmental changes during young adulthood to account for the developmental aspects of schizophrenia, namely its peak age of clinical onset in young adulthood, although the recent early development models posit separate processes for early pathogenesis and late clinical onset and the late development models hypothesize only a single process for both. Interestingly, neither early nor late development models usually address explicitly the causes of schizophrenia's developmental aspect. In any case, both these recent models of schizophrenia development further attest to the importance of understanding the nature and causes of the developmental function of schizophrenia onset.

THE DEVELOPMENTAL FUNCTION OF SCHIZOPHRENIA ONSET

Next we will consider in more detail the nature of schizophrenia's developmental function. Specifically, we seek estimates of the peak and shape of schizophrenia's age incidence distribution; however, estimation of such age incidence distributions for relatively rare disorders with widely varying ages of onset presents a range of practical and methodological difficulties. These methodological points will be discussed in order to describe the potential biases that our current estimates may exhibit. Our intention here is not to provide a comprehensive review of all such studies, but rather only to obtain a single "best estimate" of schizophrenia's age-incidence distribution for purposes of discussion. Therefore, data from only one of the most methodologically rigorous studies of incident (new) cases will be selected for detailed consideration. Studies of representative prevalent (established) cases will not be reviewed because they are potentially biased by post-onset mortality, censoring, and retrospective recall. Studies without total or representative samples of cases are also not considered because the age of onset distribution may be artefactual and adjustments for the population age distribution cannot be made.

Before considering the methodological issues and findings, a few general points will be addressed. First, is the important issue of how to define clinical "onset". Although there are a variety of approaches, clinical onset is most commonly defined as when an individual exhibits enough symptoms and signs to meet diagnostic criteria, which may be termed "diagnostic onset". The age-incidence distribution for diagnostic onset may therefore vary depending on the specific diagnostic criteria employed. Onset is also sometimes defined as the first occurrence of *any* psychopathological symptom (i.e., depression or anxiety) or as the first occurrence of any *psychotic* symptom (i.e., delusions or hallucinations). We prefer the latter for the current purposes because it is so difficult to know whether early nonspecific symptoms, such as anxiety or depression, reflect the onset of schizophrenia or are unrelated to schizophrenia. Second, developmental functions for schizophrenia will be presented separately for males and females because it has been an almost uniform observation that the age of onset distributions for schizophrenia differ by sex (Angermeyer and Kühn 1988; Lewine 1988). This is an important observation whose meaning however is still far from clear.

Birth cohort incidence studies

The "ideal" method for estimating a cumulative age incidence distribution (i.e., a developmental function for a dichotomous characteristic) would be a prospective longitudinal study from birth to death of a large birth cohort that is representative of the population of some geographic region. Annual (although the more frequent the better) repeated personal assessments would identify the onset of new (incident) cases in a reliable and consistent manner across the duration of the study without regard to contact with clinical services. Competing sources of morbidity and mortality would be assessed and adjusted for. Attrition to the initial sample would be absent or minimal. A cumulative distribution of onset during each succeeding year could then be plotted and covariates investigated. It would also be ideal to replicate this study across several different birth cohorts to assess and control for cohort effects. Although an ideal, obviously such a study of the age of onset distribution for a relatively rare diagnosis, such as schizophrenia, with a late and widely varying age of onset presents considerable challenges.

To the best of our knowledge, no such prospective studies that are large enough to provide stable age of onset data on schizophrenia have been reported to date, (see Jones and Done in Chapter 9), although there exist two birth cohort studies of the age incidence of schizophrenia using retrospective methods. Both Fremming (1951) in Denmark and Helgason (1964) in Iceland performed studies in which a birth cohort was defined retrospectively (date of birth approximately 70 years before the time of the study) and treatment contacts, mortality and emigration in the interim were assessed using records and proband and informant recall. Although having many strengths, both these studies were too small to yield stable sex specific age of onset distributions: Fremming only identified 34 and Helgason only 36 schizophrenic patients.

Cross-sectional treated incidence studies

A more practical and common design identifies treated incident cases from clinic records. The typical study of this sort attempts to identify all new cases treated for schizophrenia in some defined geographic area during a single period, such as 1 year, and orders them into age bands based on their age at first treatment. Census figures are then used to provide the total population in the geographic area in that year who are in a particular age band. The probability of onset (incidence) during each age band can then be calculated by dividing the number of incident cases by the relevant number of individuals in the general population in the age band.

These designs have the advantage of attempting to

identify a *complete* sample of treated cases from a defined area, which is absolutely essential, as otherwise any differences across ages may merely reflect the artefacts of a particular clinic admitting policy. Studies are compromised to the extent that they do not include all treating agencies in a catchment area. For example, if pediatric or geriatric clinics are not included in a study, then the incidence for younger or older cases may be underestimated. Likewise, studies that include outpatient clinics and general practitioners are to be preferred to the extent that first treatments occur in these settings and not only in inpatient units.

Use of incident cases is an advantage in that they are not biased if the diagnosis is associated with increased mortality after treatment (which schizophrenia is). That is, patients who die some time after treatment will still be counted in an incidence study, but would be missed in a prevalence study; however, estimates from treated incident cases (as well as all other methods) will still be biased if the condition is associated with increased mortality (or out migration) before treatment.

A potential complication in such studies is the identification of "new" cases. Without careful checking across sites it is possible that individuals will be counted multiple times as they are treated for schizophrenia at different clinics at different times, which would inflate the age-incidence. Existence of a "case-register" is an advantage here in that such registers organize treatment contacts for a geographic area by individual rather than by admission, and thus eliminate duplicate counts for readmissions.

Another issue relevant to the definition of new cases is whether only *first* admissions are surveyed for diagnoses of schizophrenia or whether *all* admissions (first and readmissions) are surveyed to identify admissions with a first diagnosis of schizophrenia. In the former design, schizophrenic patients whose first admission yielded a nonschizophrenic diagnosis will not be counted, whereas in the latter, and preferred, strategy such individuals will be ascertained. The percentage of schizophrenic patients with previous hospital admissions for nonschizophrenic diagnoses has been estimated using case-registers to be approximately 27% in Denmark and 14% in Mannheim, Germany (Häfner *et al.* 1989). The age-incidence distribution will be distorted to the extent that these cases are

missed and vary systematically by age. Unfortunately, usually only studies using case-registers are able to employ this latter approach because of the effort involved in screening all admissions and checking their previous diagnoses.

Relying on only treated cases is a disadvantage to the extent that not all cases are treated and therefore, this method is best in areas that can demonstrate as complete a rate of treatment as possible. This would be a particular problem if the rate of treatment varied with age.

If only clinic data are available, then the result is the age-incidence distribution for *treatment* of schizophrenia. This will differ from the age-incidence distribution of diagnostic onset to the extent that there is some delay between diagnostic onset and treatment contact. If this delay is a constant across all ages, then the shape of the distribution will be unaffected, but it will be shifted to older ages by the amount of delay. If the delay between diagnostic onset and treatment varies by age, then the shape of the age-incidence distribution will be distorted in unknown ways.

Furthermore, the use of only clinic data on treated cases assumes that the clinic diagnoses are consistent across different clinics and that there are no tendencies among clinics or clinicians to avoid the diagnosis at particular ages. For example, underestimation will occur if clinicians are reluctant to assign diagnoses of schizophrenia to young or old patients for some reason. This is especially a problem if the diagnostic system used clinically has an age cutoff for diagnosing schizophrenia. For example, some diagnostic systems, such as the Diagnostic and Statistical Manual, third edition (DSM-III; American Psychiatric Association 1980), prohibit diagnosing schizophrenia after the age of 45 years, in which case, the incidence of schizophrenia after age 45 years is by definition zero.

In an effort to avoid some of these problems, several studies using this general design ascertain potential cases from treatment facilities but then assign diagnoses based on personal interview. Such studies provide important advantages in terms of the consistency of diagnosis and elimination of "false positives", but they suffer from the same problems concerning untreated cases as studies that rely only on clinic diagnoses. Studies that employ personal interviews of treated cases have an additional advantage in that they can also attempt to retrospectively date the age of diagnostic onset based on some operational definition, which may precede the age at treatment. Although not ideal due to potential recall biases, this information is an improvement over the biases produced when there may be a considerable and/or variable delay between clinical and treatment onset.

The use of census figures is important because it adjusts for the age structure of the population, which is rarely flat due to changes in the size of birth cohorts across time and increased mortality with age. For example, even within one birth cohort there are always fewer older than younger persons because of increased mortality with age. Similarly, the sizes of birth cohorts usually vary over time, with the "baby boom" after the Second World War as one example. Therefore, even if the risk of schizophrenia is invariant, there should be more *total* cases of schizophrenia at younger than older ages and in larger than smaller birth cohorts because of the different number of persons at risk. If these variations in the number of individuals at risk are not adjusted for, they could be mistaken for changes in risk with age.

Such adjustments for population age structure are based upon the assumption that the population based on census figures is in fact the population from which the incident cases are derived. This is so only if migration (in or out of the geographic area) is not related to later treatment for schizophrenia. This is probably not a problem for studies of large geographic areas, although smaller scale studies might be biased due to tendencies of symptomatic individuals to migrate to seek or avoid particular treatment sites.

The best studies of this general design measure incidence over some relatively brief time period, such as 1 or 2 years; however, it is common to extend the study over longer periods to increase the number of incident cases observed and thus increase statistical precision. A potential disadvantage with this practice is that it becomes more difficult to define a census population for the denominator, particularly if there may be an undetected net in or out migration during the period of the study. For example, if an area experienced a net loss of population during a study period that was undetected, then the resulting risk figures would be underestimates. If the population loss varied with age, then it would confound estimates of age effects.

Another potential bias from using census figures is that cases that were incident at previous ages are typically not removed from the census figures at succeeding ages. Although this is not a major problem for studies of schizophrenia because of its relative rarity, in general only individuals who have not previously been cases should be included as at risk for becoming a new case.

A more basic potential disadvantage of such cross-sectional studies is that they confound age and cohort effects because individuals who differ in age at any single time point also differ in their birth cohort. That is, differences in risk between two age bands may be due either to differences in the ages of the sample (e.g., 20 versus 30 years old) and/or to differences due to their birth cohort (e.g., born in 1975 or 1965). If historical, secular events relevant for schizophrenia (such as viral epidemics) or other potential risk factors (e.g., ethnic composition due to migration) vary across birth cohorts, then they may confound cross-sectional estimates of age effects. Birth cohort effects appear to be present for other psychopathologies (e.g., depression) and have also been hypothesized to be present for schizophrenia (e.g., due to viral epidemics). To the extent that such birth cohort effects are present, they confound cross-sectional estimation of age effects.

With these methodological comments in mind let us turn to one of the largest and most rigorous of such studies of schizophrenia's age incidence, although there are other excellent incidence studies of schizophrenia also available (e.g., Jablensky *et al.* 1992). In their "ABC" (Age, Beginning, Course) study, Häfner and colleagues (Häfner *et al.* 1993) attempted to identify all first treated cases of schizophrenia from a catchment area of 1.5 million persons in the Mannheim/Heidelberg region of Germany during 1987–89. Care was taken to ensure that all ten mental hospitals (including day hospitals and child and adolescent units) providing treatment to the area were surveyed, although outpatient clinics and general practitioners were not included. Cases were identified from among first admissions with a broad diagnostic screen based on the International Classification of Disease, ninth edition (ICD-9) categories of schizophrenia or schizophrenia-like diagnoses with a broad age range of 12–59 years old. Inclusion of readmissions was minimized by careful

Fig. 10.1. Cumulative age incidence distribution of hospital admissions for broad definition of schizophrenia (ICD-9) in Mannheim, Germany (Reprinted from *Schizophrenia Research* 8, Hambrecht, Maurer, and Häfner, Evidence for a gender bias in epidemological studies of schizophrenia, pp. 223–31, 1992, with kind permission of Elsevier Science – NL, Sara Burgerhartstraat 25, 1055 KV Amsterdam, The Netherlands.)

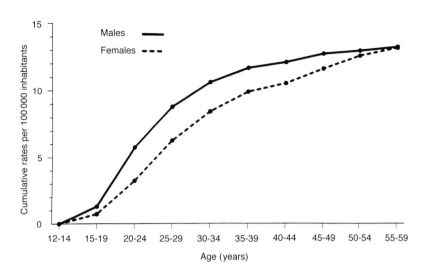

cross-checking. Only first hospital admissions were screened and therefore schizophrenic patients with previous nonschizophrenic hospital diagnoses were not included, although individuals with previous outpatient or general practitioner nonschizophrenic diagnoses would be counted. Other studies had estimated that hospitalization for schizophrenia in this area approached 100% and that few cases from this catchment area were hospitalized in neighboring areas. All such first admissions ($n = 392$) were then approached and 276 (71%) patients were able to be interviewed using both a structured interview to date the onset of the disorder (Häfner *et al.* 1992) as well as the Present State Examination (PSE), which was used to produce reliable diagnoses of schizophrenia using either the CATEGO algorithm (Wing *et al.* 1974) or DSM-III. Adjustments to the incidence for those patients not interviewed were made. Annual incidence rates were calculated based on the sex and age specific census data.

Figure 10.1 presents the cumulative annual age-incidence distributions (or developmental functions) for hospital diagnoses of broad definition ICD-9 schizophrenia from this study separately for males and females (Hambrecht *et al.* 1992). Onset here was defined as first hospital admission. First, it should be noted that the cumulative incidence of schizophrenia is equal for males and females (cumulative annual incidence = 13.21 and 13.14 per 100000, respectively). Although some recent

studies have suggested that total risk for schizophrenia may be higher in males than females, most studies observe no sex difference (Hambrecht *et al.* 1994). As can be seen in this figure, and is almost uniformly observed (Angermeyer and Kühn 1988), however, the *shape* of the age incidence distributions differs between males and females. At earlier ages, males show a steeper slope than females, whereas at later ages females show the steeper slope.

Figure 10.2 presents these same sex-specific age-incidence data noncumulatively (Hambrecht *et al.*, 1992). As can be seen, for males the peak annual incidence of hospital admission occurs in the age-band of 20–24 years, whereas for females the peak annual incidence is in the age band for 25–29 years, with a second small peak at 45–49 years old. For both males and females the greatest increase across ages (highest acceleration) in hospital admissions occurs between the age ranges of 15–19 and 20–24, with males having a greater increase than females (+26.5 and +15.7 per 100000, respectively), suggesting that the *beginning* of increased risk for schizophrenia hospitalization occurs at a similar age for both males and females and is some time during the late teens and early twenties.

Figure 10.3 presents data from this same study on the onset of psychotic symptoms (as opposed to hospital admission) from those broad definition schizophrenic patients who were interviewed (Häfner *et al.* 1991).

Fig. 10.2. Noncumulative age incidence distribution of hospital admission for broad definition of schizophrenia (ICD-9) in Mannheim, Germany (Reprinted from *Schizophrenia Research* 8, Hambrecht, Maurer, and Häfner, Evidence for a gender bias in epidemological studies of schizophrenia, pp. 223–31, 1992, with kind permission of Elsevier Science – NL, Sara Burgerhartstraat 25, 1055 KV Amsterdam, The Netherlands.)

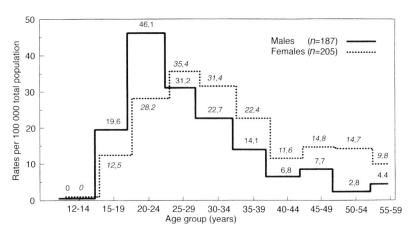

Fig. 10.3. Age distribution of first recalled psychotic symptom among hospital admissions with broad definition of schizophrenia (ICD-9) with personal interviews in Mannhein, Germany. Males, *n*=125; females, *n*=139. (Reprinted from *Nervenarzt* **62**, Häfner, Maurer, Löffler, and Riecher-Rössler, Schizophrenie und lebensalter, pp. 536–48, 1991, with kind permission of Elsevier Science – NL, Sara Burgerhartstraat 25, 1055 KV Amsterdam, The Netherlands.)

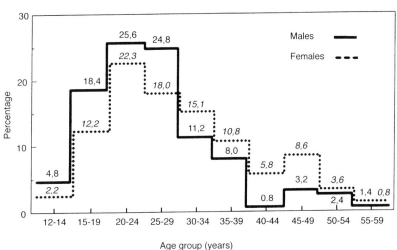

Although retrospective, these data should provide a better estimate of the distribution of actual clinical onset given the potential delay between onset of schizophrenia symptoms and hospital admission. Here it can be seen that the peak age of onset of psychotic symptoms is in the 20–24 years old age range for both males and females, with females again showing a second smaller peak in the 45–49 years age range. The greatest increase across age ranges in onset of psychosis occurs between age ranges 12–14 and 15–19 years old for both males and females (+13.6% and +10% of patients respectively), which suggests again that the beginning of increased risk for the onset of psychosis

occurs at about the same age for males and females and that it begins some time during the late teen years.

Presuming that these may be among our current best estimates of the age of onset distribution of schizophrenia, at least in Western Europe, what conclusions should we draw from them? First, it appears that an increase in risk of schizophrenia onset *begins* during the late teen years and rapidly reaches its peak in the twenties for both males and females, although males have a higher risk during this early period. Second, risk diminishes rapidly from its peak in the twenties through the thirties for both males and females. Risk is almost completely expended by the forties for males, whereas it extends through the fifties for females. These sex differences are usually hypothesized to be due to a delay in onset for some females caused by an initial protective effect of estrogen that diminishes as females experience menopause and estrogen levels decline (e.g., Seeman and Lang 1990).

Although arguably one of the best such studies, these conclusions should be tempered by some methodological aspects of the study. First, these distributions may be distorted in unknown ways to the extent that cases were missed because they were never hospitalized (although this was probably rare) or because they were not first hospitalized with a diagnosis of schizophrenia (which may be more problematic). Second, all these distributions employed a broad definition of schizophrenia based on hospital diagnoses of ICD-9 schizophrenia, paranoid states, paranoid reaction, or borderline schizophrenia. It will be important to see whether analyses, which are in preparation, employing narrower more operationalized definitions based on CATEGO or DSM-III diagnoses replicate these initial observations. Finally, it must be recalled that these figures are based on cross-sectional data, i.e., differences between "age" bands reflect both age differences and birth cohort differences, which are confounded. To the extent that later birth cohorts may be at decreased risk for schizophrenia (which although controversial has been suggested by some, e.g., Der *et al.* 1990), then it may be that these cross-sectional distributions are excessively broadened into the older age ranges.

CAUSES OF THE DEVELOPMENTAL FUNCTION OF SCHIZOPHRENIA ONSET

What causes the age of clinical onset for schizophrenia to show its peak acceleration during the late teens and early twenties? This is a basic question regarding the causes of the peak of a developmental function. Unfortunately, it is quite difficult to investigate directly the causes of a measure of central tendency in a group. One approach is to describe the age distribution of hypothesized causal factors and attempt to match their age at peak incidence to the age at peak acceleration of the observed developmental function. The causes of the age distribution peak for the

putative causal factors would then need to be understood. This strategy is a valuable one for hypothesis generation and has been emphasized by Feinberg (1982–1983; see later). Another approach is to investigate the causes of the *variation* in age of schizophrenia onset and assume that the causes of the variability also explain the peak acceleration, although as discussed earlier, this may not necessarily be the case. With this caveat in mind let us consider such studies of variation in age of onset.

Studies of causes of the *variation* in age of onset in schizophrenia have generally taken one of two different approaches. First, like many individual differences its causes have been studied using family and twin studies of age of onset among affected cases in an attempt to determine the relative importance of genetic, shared environmental, and nonshared environmental influences. As has been reviewed by Kendler *et al.* (1987), it seems clear that age of onset is correlated between affected first degree relatives (i.e., parent–offspring and siblings). When adjustments for censoring effects are made these correlations are in the 0.40 range across studies (Kendler and MacLean 1990; MacLean *et al.* 1990), which suggests substantial familiality. The origins of this familiality would appear to be largely genetic, as concordant monozygotic (MZ) twins show higher correlations in age of onset (correlations uncorrected for censoring range across studies from 0.57 to 0.86; Kendler *et al.* 1987) than concordant dizygotic (DZ) twins and siblings. In addition to this genetic influence there also appears to be a role for environmental influences that are not shared between twins because the correlation in age of onset between affected MZ twins is less than 1.0.

Furthermore, it appears that these genetic influences on variation in age of onset may be largely *independent* of age of onset associated variation among probands in liability to schizophrenia itself. Two kinds of evidence suggest this interpretation. First, the correlation in age of onset is lower in concordant DZ twins compared with concordant MZ twins (Neale *et al.* 1989). If differences in age of onset were related to qualitative transmissible etiological differences among schizophrenic patients, then correlations between affected pairs should be approximately the same regardless of whether they are MZ, DZ pairs, or any other class of relative. For example, if there were two kinds of schizophrenia, early and late onset forms, and each were caused by a different major genetic locus, then correlations in age of onset between affected relatives should be the same in DZ twins as MZ twins because affected first (and even second) degree relatives would have a very high probability of sharing the same disease allele. As this does not seem to be the case, it appears that *variation* in age of onset, although perhaps largely genetically influenced, may be influenced by genes that do not cause schizophrenia itself. The general failure of age of onset to correlate with risk for schizophrenia among relatives, which is discussed later, is also consistent with this interpretation.

A second approach to studying the causes of variation in age of onset of schizophrenia has been to correlate age of onset with factors hypothesized to contribute to the cause of schizophrenia. Most frequently such studies have investigated either risk for schizophrenia among relatives (as a potential indicator of variation in genetic liability among probands) or measures of obstetrical abnormalities (as potential indexes of variation in perinatal insult). Interestingly, variables that might be hypothesized to cause variation in age of onset, but not schizophrenia itself, have rarely been studied. Due to space constraints, the aim in the following is not a comprehensive review of these literatures, but rather a brief overview of the primary issues and findings.

There is a long tradition of studies that have correlated age at onset among schizophrenic probands and some aspect of familial risk for schizophrenia. The general rationale here is that if proband age of onset is correlated with *degree* of transmissible liability then it should be associated with the risk for schizophrenia among relatives. For example, in a multiple threshold framework if early onset schizophrenia is a quantitatively more transmissible etiological form (e.g., five genes are required) than the late onset form (e.g., only two genes required), then relatives of early onset schizophrenia should be at increased risk compared with relatives of late onset forms.

Many such studies suffer from a range of methodological difficulties. For example, many have simply classified schizophrenic probands as either being positive or negative for family history of schizophrenia depending on whether none or one (or more) relatives are affected. This is not the most statistically powerful method because

important information is lost concerning variation in risk (number of relatives and their age structure) within family history positive and negative groups (Eaves *et al.* 1986). Other common difficulties with these studies include lack of personal diagnostic interviews with relatives, unrepresentative proband samples, truncated age of onset among probands, uncontrolled effects of censoring among relatives, and difficulty in controlling for correlations in age of onset among affected relatives. A review of the best of such studies, however, finds little if any evidence for a correlation between age of onset and familial risk for schizophrenia (Kendler *et al.* 1987; Neale *et al.* 1989; Kendler and MacLean 1990) which suggests again that variation in age of onset is not importantly associated with variation in transmissible causes of schizophrenia itself.

Studies have also investigated potential "environmental" causes of variation in age of onset of schizophrenia, with an almost exclusive emphasis on perinatal abnormalities, although it is generally recognized that perinatal abnormalities need not reflect only environmental exposures. In these studies, age of onset among patients is correlated with degree of obstetrical complications, either based on maternal recall or contemporaneous hospital records. Although not unanimous, several studies have reported significant negative associations between obstetrical complications and age of onset among patients (e.g., Pollack and Greenberg 1966; Owens *et al.* 1988; O'Callaghan *et al.* 1990, 1992; see also Reddy *et al.* 1990). Overall these data suggest that perinatal abnormalities may reflect causal factors that can shorten the time until onset of schizophrenia. It may be that perinatal abnormalities also increase liability to schizophrenia itself (McNeil 1988). One interpretation of these findings in the context of the apparent substantial genetic influence on variation in age of onset reviewed above is that perhaps perinatal abnormalities primarily reflect the action of nonshared environmental influences (recall that the correlation in age of onset between MZ twins is less than 1.0). It is possible that such perinatal abnormalities may also reflect genetic influences on age of onset.

To summarize from what little is known concerning the causes of *variation* in age of onset in schizophrenia, it appears that genetic influences are important, but that they may be largely uncorrelated with genetic influences that cause schizophrenia itself. The effects of these age of onset relevant genetic influences in the absence of the schizophrenia phenotype are unknown. Environmental influences (largely of the nonshared variety) also appear to be present, although probably of less importance than genetic influences. Perinatal abnormalities may be associated with early age of onset and may largely reflect nonshared environmental effects. It may be that these putative causes of variation in age of onset might also explain the peak acceleration across age in schizophrenia onset although this is not necessarily the case.

SUMMARY, SPECULATION, AND FUTURE DIRECTIONS

In summary, we have argued that the clearest evidence that schizophrenia should be considered as a "developmental" disorder is that its age of clinical onset shows a nonlinear distribution, or developmental function. Furthermore, both early and late development models of schizophrenia emphasize the importance of the age distribution of clinical onset, although this is of primary concern for late development models and is secondary for early development models. These points all highlight the importance of understanding further schizophrenia's developmental function. Discussion of general qualities of developmental functions indicated the potentially important distinction between the causes of individual differences and changes over time and the causes of their age distribution. Critical discussion of methods and description of some of our best data concerning the age distribution of clinical onset identified the peak acceleration of schizophrenia's developmental function during the late teens and early twenties. Review of studies of the causes of variation in age of onset suggested that this variation may be primarily genetically influenced (along with some nonshared environmental influences), but that these genetic influences appear to be largely independent of the genetic causes of schizophrenia itself. It is possible that perinatal abnormalities may reflect some of these nonshared environmental influences on age of clinical onset.

Based on these and other points, a clearly speculative and hopefully heuristic developmental model of schizo-

phrenia suggests itself. First, we assume that individual differences in liability to schizophrenia are caused by genetic and nonshared environmental differences (Gottesman and Shields 1982). It seems likely that multiple genetic loci are involved, either in a multifactorial threshold or oligogenic fashion (McGue and Gottesman 1989).

What effect might these mutant alleles have? Careful study of brain and psychological abnormalities among schizophrenic patients early in the course of their disorder and their relatives are obviously important strategies to answer this question. To date however, this approach has generally been largely atheoretical and little constrained by the phenomenology of schizophrenia or other considerations. Brute-force brain and mind "scans" (similar to total genome scans) may nevertheless eventually be successful but it seems that an additional approach, initially proposed by Feinberg (1982–1983), that acknowledges the important information provided by schizophrenia's developmental function should also be helpful and might constrain the search. Feinberg has emphasized the potential usefulness in hypothesis generation of identifying other "candidate" endophenotypes (Gottesman and Shields 1972) by comparing the normal developmental functions of other characteristics with the developmental function of schizophrenia onset. To the extent that other phenotypes show similar developmental functions as that for schizophrenia onset, then they may also play a role in schizophrenia, either as "releasers" of other early developed liability or, if abnormal, as endophenotypes for schizophrenia itself.

Although there are a number of brain and psychological phenomena that show a developmental function with changes in acceleration during the late teens and early twenties, Feinberg and others (e.g., Keshavan et al. 1994) have emphasized synaptic density (number of synapses per unit volume) as potentially relevant for schizophrenia. As initially described by Huttenlocher (1979, 1994), synaptic density appears to show a rapid rise following birth until a peak at about 2 years old followed by a decline until a plateau is reached during the late teens. The age at which this apparent plateau is reached is interestingly close to the greatest acceleration in onset of schizophrenia. Synaptic density may be considered as the result of two opposing processes: synapse generation and synapse elimination or pruning. Presumably (although not necessarily) both these processes show anatomical variation, but for our purposes here we will not address the issue of *where* the abnormalities critical for schizophrenia are localized. Following Feinberg's reasoning (Feinberg *et al.* 1990) we propose that a neuron is initially in a "synaptic generation" state in which synapses are able to be generated based on local microenvironment variation in such substances as nerve growth factors and target neuron signals. We propose that the synaptic generation state is largely the result of the expression of "synaptic generation" genes. The expression of the synaptic generation genes is suppressed when some maximum number of synapses are formed, with the negative feedback signal perhaps involving some sort of contact inhibition. It is proposed that the suppression of the synaptic generation genes promotes the expression of "synaptic pruning" genes, which place the neuron in a "synaptic pruning" state, which allows a neuron to eliminate synapses based on local environmental conditions, such as use below some threshold. We further propose that the expression of the synaptic pruning genes is terminated by feedback that is based on the number of synapses below some threshold of use. When there are zero synapses below the use threshold, then the synaptic pruning genes would be suppressed. Following the synaptic pruning state, the neuron is in a steady state in which the number of synapses cannot be changed.

There may be genetic polymorphisms relevant to schizophrenia in at least two aspects of this hypothesized system. First, there may be individual differences in "synapse pruning threshold" genes that determine the minimum *threshold* of use, below which a synapse is "pruned" if the neuron is in a synaptic pruning state. We propose that alleles at such genetic loci that produce an inappropriately high synapse use threshold would lead to excessive pruning and often the clinical symptoms of schizophrenia. Furthermore, we hypothesize that there are polymorphisms in the synaptic pruning genes that produce variation in the *rate* of pruning. This variation would *not* contribute to liability to schizophrenia. In the general population without genetic liability to schizophrenia (i.e., no alleles that increase the threshold needed for a synapse to be spared from pruning) these poly-

morphisms influencing rate of pruning would produce individual differences in the age at which pruning terminates. Similarly, among schizophrenia patients, these polymorphisms would produce individual differences in age of clinical onset. Given the sex difference in age of onset distributions, it is further proposed that the expression of these synaptic pruning rate genes is in some fashion modulated by genes on the sex chromosomes that produce a slower rate of pruning among females. In addition to genetic variation influencing these two stages of the system, nonshared environmental variation would affect both these parameters.

Although obviously speculative and abstract, this kind of hypothetical model is consistent with several observations. Most recent anatomical evidence suggests that it is much more likely that schizophrenic patients exhibit a relative reduction than an excess of some sort in brain tissue. The answers to the questions of what is reduced and where are more controversial. In the context of this controversy, a hypothesis of reduced synaptic density due to excessive pruning is nevertheless quite plausible and is consistent with much of the available data (e.g., Selemon *et al.* 1995). The apparent multiple genetic influence on liability to schizophrenia is also acknowledged in the model by the hypothesized polymorphisms in genes influencing the synaptic use threshold required to avoid pruning. The presumed genetic influence on age of schizophrenia onset that is independent of schizophrenia liability is reflected in the hypothesized genetic variation that influences the rate of synaptic pruning. This feature importantly allows for liability-independent variation in age of onset of schizophrenia that does not imply abnormalities in synaptic density among individuals without genetic liability to schizophrenia. It does, however, imply that in the nonrisk population there would be variation in the age at which synaptic pruning would terminate and that this would roughly follow the distribution of the age of onset of schizophrenia. What sort of psychological effects this might predict is unclear at this point. The peak age of onset of schizophrenia is also attended to in this model because of its emphasis on abnormalities in the *termination* of synaptic pruning, which apparently normally occurs during the late teens and early twenties when synaptic density reaches a plateau. Schizophrenic abnormalities in excessive pruning would most often become manifest during this time period, and as such, this model would be classed as a late development model. Obviously this hypothetical model is speculative, abstract, and undoubtedly incorrect in many if not all ways. It is offered in the hope that it will have some heuristic value in leading to attempts to specify it more precisely and thus to falsify it.

As should be clear from this chapter, it will be claimed that questions relevant to late development models of schizophrenia are important and understudied. The period of young adulthood is important regardless of whether processes during this time serve to "release" early abnormalities or whether abnormalities in these late processes themselves are critical for schizophrenia. From the above analysis, I would echo Feinberg's (1982–1983) call for the study of normal developmental processes during this period. Although it is not certain that phenotypes with developmental functions that show interesting parallels to schizophrenia's clinical age of onset will be relevant to schizophrenia, it is definitely the case that the age of onset distribution of schizophrenia, both its peak and its variation, are important facts about schizophrenia that beg for explanation, and studies of normal development during young adulthood seem to be one of the primary approaches to these questions.

The apparent genetic influence on age of onset and the certain genetic influence on schizophrenia liability itself also points to several lines of enquiry. First, it is important to understand the nature of genetic influences on normal developmental changes during the young adult period as a way to understand better the variation in schizophrenia's age of onset. Second, genetic studies of schizophrenia liability could be more informed by such late development hypotheses. Thus, genes that change expression in brain during young adulthood might be important candidates in genetic association studies.

Finally, a late developmental analysis should affect when we look for environmental influences. It is clear that there are important nonshared environmental influences on both the liability to schizophrenia as well as on variation in age of onset. Although not fashionable recently, it may be that the study of environmental experiences during young adulthood will prove useful. There is evidence that psychological experiences may influence the course of

schizophrenia (e.g., Ventura et al. 1989), and it should not be surprising that similar experiences may also contribute to causing the first episode. Experiences that become more prevalent during young adulthood should be likely candidates to further our environmental understanding of the epigenesis of this enigmatic syndrome.

ACKNOWLEDGMENTS

Preparation of this manuscript was supported in part by grants MH 43666, HL40962, and MH 45156. Thanks are also due my colleague, Robert McCall, PhD, for discussions on these issues as well as Dr Heinz Häfner for his kind and thorough correspondence regarding the details of the ABC study.

REFERENCES

American Psychiatric Association. 1980. *Diagnostic and Statistical Manual of Mental Disorders*, 3rd ed. Washington, DC: American Psychiatric Press.

Angermeyer, M.C. and Kühn, L. 1988. Gender differences in age of onset of schizophrenia. *Eur. Arch. Psychiatry Neurol. Sci.* **237**:351–64.

Armenian, H.K. and Khoury, M.J. 1981. Age at onset of genetic diseases. *Am. J. Epidemiol.* **113**:596–605.

Armenian, H.K. and Lilienfeld, A.M. 1983. Incubation period of disease. *Epidemiol. Rev.* **5**:1–15.

Der G., Gupta, S., and Murray, R.M. 1990. Is schizophrenia disappearing? *Lancet* **335**:513–6.

Eaves, L.J., Kendler, K.S., and Schulz, S.C. 1986. The familial sporadic classification: Its power for the resolution of genetic and environmental etiologic factors. *J. Psychiat. Res.* **20**:115–30.

Falconer, D.S. 1981. *Introduction to quantitative genetics*, 2nd ed. New York: Longman.

Feinberg, I. 1982–1983. Schizophrenia: caused by a fault in programmed synaptic elimination during adolescence? *J. Psychiatric Res.* **17**:319–39.

Feinberg, I., Thode, H.C., Chugani, H.T., and March, J.D. 1990. Gamma distribution model describes maturational curves for delta wave amplitude, cortical metabolic rate, and synaptic density. *J. Theoret. Biol.* **142**:149–61.

Fremming, K.H. 1951. *The expectation of mental infirmity in a sample of the Danish population.* London: Cassell.

Garmezy, N. and Streitman, S. 1974. Children at risk: the search for the antecedents of schizophrenia. Part I. Conceptual models and research methods. *Schizophr. Bull.* **8**:19–90.

Gottesman, I.I. and Shields, J. 1972. *Schizophrenia and genetics : a twin study vantage point.* New York: Academic Press.

Gottesman, I.I. and Shields, J. 1982. *Schizophrenia: the epigenetic puzzle.* New York: Cambridge University Press.

Hahn, M.E., Hewitt, J.K., Henderson, N.D., & Benno, R.H. 1990. *Developmental behavior genetics: neural, biometrical, and evolutionary approaches.* New York: Oxford University Press.

Häfner, H., Maurer, K., Löffler, W., and Riecher-Rössler, A. 1991. Schizophrenie und lebensalter. *Nervenarzt* **62**:536–48.

Häfner, H., Maurer, K., Löffler, W., and Riecher-Rössler, A. 1993. The influence of age and sex on the onset and early course of schizophrenia. *Br. J. Psychiatry* **162**:80–6.

Häfner, H., Riecher, A., Maurer, K., Löffler, W., Munk-Jørgensen, P., and Strömgren, E. 1989. How does gender influence age at first hospitalization for schizophrenia? A transnational case register study. *Psychol. Med.* **19**:903–18.

Häfner, H., Riecher-Rössler, A., Hambrecht, M., Maurer, K., Meissner, S., Schmidtke, A., Fätkenheuer, B., Löffler, W., and van der Heiden, W. 1992. IRAOS: an instrument for the assessment of onset and early course of schizophrenia. *Schizophr. Res.* **6**:209–23.

Hambrecht, M., Maurer, K., and Häfner, H. 1992. Evidence for a gender bias in epidemiological studies of schizophrenia. *Schizophr. Res.* **8**:223–31.

Hambrecht, M., Riecher-Rössler, A., Fätkenheuer, B., Louzã, M.R., and Häfner, H. 1994. Higher morbidity risk for schizophrenia in males: fact or fiction? *Compreh. Psychiatry* **35**:39–49.

Helgason, T. 1964. Epidemiology of mental disorders in Iceland. *Acta Pychiatr. Scand. (Suppl).* **173**.

Huttenlocher, P.R. 1979. Synaptic density in human frontal cortex: developmental changes and the effects of aging. *Brain Res.* **163**: 195–205.

Huttenlocher, P.R. 1994. Synaptogenesis in human cerebral cortex. In *Human behavior and the developing brain*, ed. G. Dawson and K.W. Fischer, pp. 137–51. New York: Guilford Press.

Jablensky, A., Sartorious, N., Ernberg, G., Anker, M., Korten, A., Cooper, J.E., Day, R., & Bertelsen, A. 1992. Schizophrenia: manifestations, incidence, and course in different cultures. A World Health Organization Ten-Country Study. *Psychol. Med., Monograph Suppl.* **20**.

Keshavan, M.S., Anderson, S., & Pettegrew, J.W. 1994. Is schizophrenia due to excessive pruning of the prefrontal cortex? The Feinberg hypothesis revisited. *J. Psychiatric Res.* **28**:239–65.

Kendler, K.S. and MacLean, C.J. 1990. Estimating familial effects on age at onset and liability to schizophrenia: I. Results of a large sample family study. *Genet. Epidemiol.* **7**:409–17.

Kendler, K.S., Tsuang, M.T., and Hays, P. 1987. Age at onset in schizophrenia: a familial perspective. *Arch. Gen. Psychiatry* **44**:881–90.

Lewine, R.R.J. 1988. Gender and schizophrenia. In *Handbook of schizophrenia, vol. 3, Nosology, epidemiology and genetics of schizophrenia.* Ed. M.T. Tsuang & J.C. Simpson, pp. 379–97. New York: Elsevier.

McCall, R.B. 1981. Nature-nurture and the two realms of development: a proposed integration with respect to mental development. *Child Dev.* **52**:1–12.

McCall, R.B. 1993. Developmental functions for general mental performance. In *Current topics in human intelligence*, vol. 3, ed. D.K. Detterman, pp. 3–29. Norwood, NJ: Ablex.

McGue, M. and Gottesman, I.I. 1989. Genetic linkage in schizophrenia: Perspectives from genetic epidemiology. *Schizophr. Bull.* **15**:453–64.

MacLean, C.J., Neale, M.C., Meyer, J.M., and Kendler, K.S. 1990. Estimating familial effects on age at onset and liability to schizophrenia: II. Adjustment for censored data. *Genet. Epidemiol.* **7**:419–26.

McNeil, T.F. 1988. Obstetric factors and perinatal injuries. In *Handbook of schizophrenia, vol. 3, Nosology, epidemiology, and genetics*, ed. M.T. Tsuang and J.C. Simpson, pp. 319–44. New York: Elsevier.

Mednick, S.A. and McNeil, T.F. 1968. Current methodology in research on the etiology of schizophrenia: serious difficulties which suggest the use of the high-risk-group method. *Psychol. Bull.* **70**:681–93.

Meehl, P.E. 1962. Schizotaxia, schizotypia, and schizophrenia. *Am. Psychol.* 17:827–38.

Meehl, P.E. 1989. Schizotaxia revisited. *Arch. Gen. Psychiatry* **46**: 935–44.

Murray, R.M. and Lewis, S.W. 1987. Is schizophrenia a neurodevelopmental disorder? *Br. Med. J.* **295**:681–2.

Neale, M.C., Eaves, L.J., Hewitt, J.K., MacLean, C.J., Meyer, J.M., and Kendler, K.S. 1989. Analyzing the relationship between age at onset and risk to relatives. *Am. J. Hum. Genet.* **45**:226–9.

O'Callaghan, E., Gibson, T., Colohan, H.A., Buckley, P., Walshe, D.G., Larkin, C., and Waddington, J.L. 1992. Risk of schizophrenia in adults born after obstetric complications and their association with early onset of illness: a controlled study. *Br. Med. J.* **305**:1256–9.

O'Callaghan, E., Larkin, C., Kinsella, A., and Waddington, J.L. 1990. Obstetric complications, the putative familial-sporadic distinction, and tardive dyskinesia in schizophrenia. *Br. J. Psychiatry* **157**:578–84.

Owen, M.J., Lewis, S.W., and Murray, R.M. 1988. Obstetric complications and schizophrenia: a computed tomographic study. *Psychol. Med.* **18**:331–9.

Plomin, R. 1986. *Development, genetics, and psychology*. Hillsdale, NJ: Lawrence Erlbaum.

Pogue-Geile, M.F. 1991. The development of liability to schizophrenia: early and late developmental models. In *Schizophrenia: a life-course developmental perspective*, ed. E. F. Walker, pp. 277–298. New York: Academic Press.

Pogue-Geile, M.F. 1996. Developmental processes and schizophrenia. In *The neurodevelopmental basis of schizophrenia*, ed. J.L. Waddington and P.F. Buckley. Austin, TX: R.G. Landes.

Pollack, M. and Greenberg, I.M. 1966. Perinatal complications in hospitalized schizophrenic and nonschizophrenic patients. *J. Hillside Hosp.* **15**:191.

Randall, P.L. 1980. A neuroanatomical theory on the etiology of schizophrenia. *Medical Hypotheses* **6**:645–58.

Reddy, R., Mukherjee, S., Schnur, D.B., Chin, J., and DeGreef, G. 1990. History of obstetric complications, family history, and CT scan findings in schizophrenic patients. *Schizophr. Res.* **3**:311–14.

Schaie, K.W. 1983. *Longitudinal studies of adult psychological development*. New York: Guilford.

Seeman, M.V. and Lang, M. 1990. The role of estrogens in schizophrenia gender differences. *Schizophr. Bull.* **16**:185–94.

Selemon, L.D., Rajkowska, G., and Goldman-Rakic, P.S. 1995. Abnormally high neuronal density in the schizophrenic cortex. *Arch. Gen.Psychiatry* **52**:805–18.

Ventura, J., Nuechterlein, K.H., Lukoff, D., & Hardesty, J.P. 1989. A prospective study of stressful life events and schizophrenic relapse. *J. Abn. Psychol.* **98**:407–11.

Waddington, J.L. and Buckley, P.F. 1996. *The neurodevelopmental basis of schizophrenia*. Austin, TX: R.G. Landes.

Walker, E.F. 1991. *Schizophrenia: a life-course developmental perspective*. New York: Academic Press.

Weinberger, D.R. 1987. Implications of normal brain development for the pathogenesis of schizophrenia. *Arch. Gen. Psychiatry* **44**:660–4.

Wing, J.K., Cooper, J.E., and Sartorious, N. 1974. *The measurement and classification of psychiatric symptoms*. New York: Cambridge University Press.

Wohlwill, J.F. 1973. *The study of behavioral development*. New York: Academic Press.

11 Sex differences in schizophrenia

GRETCHEN L. HAAS AND DAVID J. CASTLE

INTRODUCTION

Sexual dimorphism in psychopathology is perhaps best illustrated by sex differences in the phenomenology and course of schizophrenia. Clinical observations of sex differences in the timing and course of schizophrenia were documented by Kraepelin (1919/1987) nearly a century ago. Such observations received little clinical recognition until they became the focus of formal empirical research in the 1980s. A growing body of empirical data generated during the past decade now provides confirmatory support for early post-hoc epidemiologic and clinical research findings which indicated an earlier age at onset, poorer premorbid psychosocial adjustment, and greater risk for relapse among males.

The recent interest in sex differences in schizophrenia stems, in no small part, from efforts to identify factors which contribute to the clinical heterogeneity of this disorder. A "second wave" of research on sex differences in schizophrenia is now directed at understanding the etiology and pathophysiology of sex-related heterogeneity. In this chapter, we will review the current state of knowledge of sex differences in the epidemiology, phenomenology and clinical course of schizophrenia. Evidence of sex differences in normal human development will be presented, followed by a discussion of implications for the pathophysiology of schizophrenia. Finally, we will discuss the relevance of sex differences to an emerging neurodevelopmental model of schizophrenia, evidence for and against this model, and competing etiologic models of the disorder.

EPIDEMIOLOGY

Published incidence rates for schizophrenia vary significantly for males and females, depending on the relative restrictiveness of the definition of the disorder. Research data show a substantial range of male:female incidence ratios, from well below 1.0:1.0 to well above 3.0:1.0 (Hambrecht *et al.* 1994). Lewine and colleagues (Lewine *et al.* 1984) reported that when using the more inclusive diagnostic schema such as the International Classification of Diseases, 9th Revision (ICD-9; World Health Organization 1977) or the New Haven Schizophrenia Index (NHSI; Astrachan *et al.* 1972), nearly equivalent numbers of males and females were identified as having schizophrenia, whereas the application of more stringent diagnostic systems tended to exclude proportionately more females, yielding higher male/female ratios, e.g., a 2.8:1.0 ratio for Research Diagnostic Criteria (RDC; Spitzer *et al.* 1975), a 7.0:1.0 ratio for St. Louis "Feighner" criteria (Feighner *et al.* 1972) and a 1.4:1.0 ratio for Schneider's First Rank Symptoms (Schneider 1959). Using Feighner criteria, Castle *et al.* (1993) observed a sex ratio of 2.47:1.0, whereas using the more broad ICD-9 criteria, they obtained a sex ratio of 1.1:1.0. In a population-based clinical incidence study, Iacono and Beiser (1992) reported data that reflect consistently high male:female ratios: for Feighner and RDC, ratios are 2.7:1.0 for each; for the ICD-9 and DSM III diagnoses, they are 3.0:1.0 for each; and for the 12-point Flexible System (Carpenter *et al.* 1973, 1980) a ratio of 3.17:1.0 was obtained. The relatively small size of the total sample ($N=100$), and the female sample ($n=25$), in particular, suggest that comparisons of sex ratios across the diagnostic categories are likely to be unreliable due to sensitivity to error with small sample sizes.

An excess of males relative to females among samples of patients assigned diagnoses of schizophrenia is a phenomenon commonly attributed to the greater risk for affective disturbance (i.e., mood syndromes and affective symptoms) among women, in contrast to men, in the general population (Tsuang *et al.* 1976). Hence, it has been widely assumed that females, more often than males, are excluded from schizophrenia based solely on the presence of affective symptomatology. This is a reasonable explanation; however, several other factors potentially contribute to the observed sex imbalance in some studies. First, diagnostic criteria which include upper age limits (e.g., age 40 years for Feighner Criteria and age 45 years for RDC and DSM-III-R (*Diagnostic and Statistical Manual*, 3rd Edition, American Psychiatric Association, 1980) criteria) exclude proportionately more females than males (Hambrecht *et al.* 1992a; Castle *et al.* 1993). Castle and colleagues found that among patients with schizophrenia onset over age 45 years, the sex ratio reverses (0.5:1.0), regardless of the diagnostic criteria applied (Castle *et al.* 1993). Case register samples that include the full age range yield sex ratios that more closely approximate 1:1, e.g., 1.13:1.0 and 1.16:1.0 for the ICD and RDC, respectively, in one study (Castle *et al.* 1993), 10:10 for broadly-defined ICD in another (Hambrecht *et al.* 1992a), and 1.0:1.0 and 0.9:1.0 for the DSM-III (restrictive versus broad) diagnoses, respectively (Hambrecht *et al.* 1994).

A greater tendency for females to manifest late (age >45 years) onset schizophrenia has now been documented in several investigations (Castle and Howard 1992; Castle *et al.* 1993; Häfner *et al.* 1993). It is not clear, however, whether the preponderance of females among later-onset cases compensates (for their relative under-representation at early ages) sufficiently to yield overall equivalent lifetime incidence rates for males and females. Although there has been a burgeoning interest in late-onset schizophrenia, only a few studies (see Castle and Howard 1992; Castle *et al.* 1993) have adequately addressed the very late onset (>60 years) group. Thus, more exacting study of incidence rates for males and females will require more demographically inclusive sampling methods.

Premorbid adjustment levels may also influence the diagnostic classification status. Using more restrictive definitions of schizophrenia which include criteria pertaining to premorbid adjustment, e.g., the single marital status inclusion criterion (from the St Louis "Feighner" Criteria), females are less likely (than males) to be assigned the diagnosis of schizophrenia. In a case-record study

which sampled all first-contact patients with nonaffective functional psychoses from a defined geographic area and including all cases age 16 years and older, Castle *et al.* (1993) found an excess of males with poor premorbid adjustment in the early-onset (age <25 years) narrowly-defined DSM-III-R schizophrenia group. The authors concluded that males are particularly vulnerable to a form of schizophrenia characterized by poor premorbid functioning, absence of affective symptoms, and evolution of a chronic course. Based on these sex-related characteristics, they also concluded that males are more likely to be represented among schizophrenia samples selected using more restrictive criteria (e.g., RDC, Feighner, and DSM-III-R schizophrenia).

What appears to be a greater prominence of deficit symptoms among males (Pogue-Geile and Harrow 1984; Lewine 1985; Goldstein and Link 1988; Goldstein *et al.* 1990; Haas *et al.* 1991) might also contribute to the higher proportion of males among the narrowly defined, core-deficit schizophrenia syndrome cases described by Kraepelin, and a higher prevalence of schizophrenia using definitions which include negative symptoms, e.g., the DSM-III-R (American Psychiatric Association 1987) and the DSM-IV (American Psychiatric Association 1994).

Finally, the well-documented finding that females tend to have fewer relapses, fewer rehospitalizations and better clinical outcome than males would suggest that among any consecutive-admission series of *inpatients*, the population of females with schizophrenia will tend to be underrepresented. Clinical contact-based samples tend to reflect a higher prevalence of females than found among inpatient-based samples. For example, sex analyses of the multinational WHO studies yield an overall male:female ratio of 1.10:1.00 (Hambrecht *et al.* 1992b) for the Determinants of Outcome Study ($N=1292$) and 1.19:1.00 for the Assessment and Reduction of Psychiatric Disability Study ($N=510$) (Hambrecht *et al.* 1992a). Rates generated from community (population-based) samples tend to yield even higher proportions of females relative to males. The few such studies that have been conducted using contemporary diagnostic criteria yield some of the lowest male:female incidence ratios, e.g. 0.63:1.00 for a community sample from Iceland (Helgason 1964), 0.87 for a case-register sample from northeastern Italy (deSalvia *et al.*

1993), 0.82 from the NIMH Epidemiologic Catchment Area Study (Keith *et al.* 1991) and 0.55 for a two-stage re-evaluation study (von Korff 1985) of the Eastern Baltimore Mental Health Survey, one of the ECA survey sites. Thus, community samples suggest that, using broadly-defined schizophrenia criteria, the proportion of males with schizophrenia may actually be exceeded by the proportion of females with the disorder. Although the complexities of comparing community-based point prevalence data with clinical register incidence data are many (for a review see Jablensky 1986), results of the community-based epidemiologic studies at least raise the important question of whether clinical samples (and hospital-based samples, in particular) tend to underestimate the incidence of schizophrenia among females.

Cross-cultural studies reveal higher male:female incidence ratios for sites in the developing, compared with the industrial, cultures. Interestingly, the authors of the sex-specific reports on the multicenter WHO Study on Determinants of Outcome of Severe Mental Disorders (Hambrecht *et al.* 1992a) suggest that variance in sex ratios across various research sites can be attributed to service-related selection effects; they report that in the WHO multicenter studies, increasing scarcity of treatment facilities led to women receiving less adequate treatment in the developing countries. Females tended to be increasingly underrepresented, leading to greater male:female sex ratios for the less developed countries. Link and Dohrenwend (1980) have reported the reverse pattern among psychiatrically disordered individuals in the USA, i.e., a tendency for males to be underrepresented among treated samples.

Efforts to address the question of sex differences in relative risk for schizophrenia continue, therefore, to be rather complicated. Population-based data from community samples would seem ideal; however, community sampling approaches tend to yield relatively small sample sizes because of the low base rate of schizophrenia in the general population. Thus, the sex ratio estimates from this type of database tend to be sensitive to relatively minor numeric sampling error. For this reason, there is a need for studies which aim to ascertain all clinical contact cases in a geographically restricted area. The sex ratios obtained by Iacono and Beiser (1992) in such a study, using DSM-III-R criteria, are relatively high in comparison with most USA

and European samples. Thus, there is a need for replication of this type of study before more exact estimates of the sex differences in relative risk for schizophrenia can be established.

In conclusion, although there continues to be debate about the magnitude of male:female incidence ratios in schizophrenia, in general, males tend to predominate in clinical samples of schizophrenia patients. At least three factors have a significant impact on the sex ratio composition of any sample: (1) the age range sampled; (2) the relative restrictiveness of the diagnostic criteria used; and (3) the source of the sample, i.e., inpatient versus outpatient versus community-sampled cases.

CLINICAL FEATURES AND COURSE OF ILLNESS

Sex differences in age at onset of illness

The most consistently observed sex difference in schizophrenia is the tendency for males to manifest the illness at an earlier age (Lewine 1980, 1981; Loranger 1984; Angermeyer and Kuhn 1988; Häfner *et al.* 1991c; Haas and Sweeney 1992). Transcultural studies and transhistorical studies have yielded remarkably consistent findings of a 3 to 5-year differential in age at onset, with an earlier onset for males. On review of these findings, it appears that the modal age at onset for males is in the range of 19–24 years, whereas for females, the modal age tends to fall in the late 20s (25–30 years). Consistent with the finding of an earlier age at onset of illness for males, age at first hospitalization also tends to be earlier than for females (Watt and Szulecka 1979; Lewine 1980; Leventhal *et al* 1984; Loranger 1984; Häfner *et al.* 1989; Folnegovic, 1990; Häfner *et al.* 1991).

Lewine (1985) has questioned whether reported differences in age at onset are artefactual, reflecting a lower societal tolerance for psychopathology in males and thus a greater readiness to hospitalize males at the onset of psychiatric symptoms. In his review of the early literature, he cites evidence that the magnitude of sex differences in age at onset of psychotic symptoms is equivalent to the magnitude of sex differences in the age at first hospitalization. From this, he concludes that the differential in timing of the first episode cannot be attributed to differential delay from onset to first admission. Also running counter to the social/family tolerance explanation of sex differences in age at onset data are more recent epidemiological data from Häfner *et al.* (1989) and Bromet *et al.* (1992) which suggest that there are no sex differences in latency from onset of first psychotic symptoms to first treatment contact or hospitalization. These findings argue that the sex differential in age at onset does not reflect a socially-mediated delay in female admissions to hospital but rather a primary sex difference in the timing of onset of the disorder.

At least two studies directly address the question of whether familial tolerance for symptoms differs with the sex of the proband (Gibbons *et al.* 1984; Goldstein and Kreisman 1988). In a large, catchment-based sample ($N = 364$) of individuals with a diagnosis of schizophrenia, Gibbons *et al.* (1984) noted that more females (63%) than males (41%) were living with relatives and more females (40%) than males (13%) were currently married. Rated "distress" levels of family members did not differ with the sex or marital status of the proband. As noted by Seeman and Hauser (1984), however, one cannot rule out the possibility that family members who experienced extreme "distress" in living with their schizophrenic relative may have elected to live apart, thus introducing a downward bias in distress ratings for those residing with the proband at the time of study contact. Goldstein and Kreisman (1988) assessed family attitudes toward symptomatology as predictors of rehospitalization. Their sample included both first episode (54.5%) and multiple episode mixed psychotic (80% DSM-III schizophrenia) patients and evaluated family attitudes as predictors of postadmission rehospitalization. Results indicated that overall, familial tolerance for symptomatology was equivalent for male and female offspring, although parental readiness to rehospitalize offspring depended on the sex of the offspring *and* the sex of the parent. Whereas at milder levels of symptom severity, no sex differences were found, for individuals with severe psychotic symptoms, mothers and fathers/significant others tended to be more rejecting of responsibility for the care of (and ready to hospitalize) the same-sex offspring, the highest level of rejection (and readiness to rehospitalize) was found among fathers with sons who had

schizophrenia (Häfner *et al.* 1991). Whether this pattern of differential familial response to severe psychotic symptoms clearly extends to the period of prodromal and first-episode symptom cannot be determined from this study. Thus, although social factors appear to play a role in readiness to rehospitalize a family member, whether family and community tolerance for *prodromal and onset features of illness* vary with the sex of the patient and thereby contribute to variance in the dating of onset and/or recognition of frank psychotic symptoms has yet to be determined. Although the possibility exists that age at onset differences reflect differential sensitivity to symptoms or differential bias in recall of timing of symptom onset, the evidence regarding tolerance for symptomatology and the timing of symptom onset argues against the differential tolerance hypothesis.

An alternative explanation for an earlier onset and more severe illness among males presumes that objective levels of sex role-related stress may be greater for males during late adolescence and early adulthood, when pressures for independence, dominance and competitive behavior increase, with entry into a primary "breadwinner" role. What have been traditional sex role-related differences in the expectations for males and females cannot be ruled out as an explanation for findings of sex differences in premorbid functioning. The impact of such social role factors would be expected to be equivalent for all psychoses; the existing data do not support this expectation. Sex differences in age at onset of psychotic symptoms appear to be specific to schizophrenia. For example, in a review of published studies of age at onset of schizophrenia, Angermeyer and Kühn (1988) found sex differences in age at onset and age at first hospitalization among individuals with schizophrenia, but not among those with affective psychoses. Consistent with this observation, women were observed to develop affective psychoses at the same age as men in a sample from New Zealand (Joyce 1984). When sex differences in age at onset of affective psychoses have been found, females reportedly developed affective psychoses at an earlier age than males (Weissman and Klerman 1977).

A second argument against the sex role explanation of age at onset differences is that in an era of changing sex roles, one would expect to observe a narrowing of the age at onset gap with females developing schizophrenia at an earlier age. The fact that recent studies of first episode schizophrenia continue to show the expected sex difference in age at onset suggests that sex-related role pressures are unlikely to be a causal determinant of differences in age at onset. None the less, systematic investigation of the impact of social factors on the timing of onset of schizophrenia is lacking.

In addition to social factors, biological parameters have been implicated as contributors to variance in age at onset of illness. For example, variance in age at onset may be genetically controlled (Kendler *et al.* 1987), or alternatively, may reflect different etiologies of schizophrenia, with familial forms manifesting illness at an earlier age. A rather diverse range of studies reveal age at onset-related variance in premorbid adjustment (Haas *et al.* 1992), clinical psychopathology (Haas *et al.* 1995a) and structural abnormalities of cortical volumes (Haas *et al.* 1995b). Whether these findings reflect primary sex-related variance or age at onset-related variance in clinical manifestations of illness is an important question because it may shed light on different pathophysiologies and/or etiologies of the disorder.

Sex differences in premorbid functioning

In addition to a later age at onset, females tend to have better psychosocial adjustment prior to illness onset (Farina *et al.* 1962; Schooler 1963; Childers and Harding 1990; Dworkin 1990; Foerster *et al.* 1991a). Retrospective studies have reported higher scores for females on measures of premorbid social and sexual adjustment, including the Premorbid Adjustment Scale (PAS; Childers and Harding 1990), the Phillips Prognostic Rating Scale (Phillips 1953; Zigler and Phillips 1962; Bruce and Kim 1992), the Zigler-Phillips Social Competence Scale (Zigler and Phillips 1960) and the Premorbid Social Adjustment Scale (Foerster *et al.* 1991a), an instrument derived from the Cannon-Spoor Premorbid Adjustment Scale (Cannon-Spoor *et al.* 1982).

Consistent with findings of superior premorbid psychosocial adjustment, females are more likely than males to be married or involved in a conjugal heterosexual relationship prior to the onset of illness (Eaton 1975; Walker *et al.* 1985; Seeman 1986; Riecher-Rossler *et al.*

1969; Rosen *et al.* 1969), and to have higher levels of premorbid social functioning and occupational achievement (Deister and Merneros 1992; Westermeyer and Harrow 1986); they are less likely to have premorbid asocial behavior or behavior disorders (Salokangas 1983). In a study of premorbid adjustment in schizophrenia and affective disorders, males with schizophrenia showed the most deviant patterns of premorbid adjustment with more prominent schizotypal traits, including asociality and social avoidance (Foerster *et al.* 1991a).

Studies of premorbid intellectual deficits have demonstrated more severe IQ deficits among schizophrenic males than among schizophrenic females, when compared with their well siblings (Offord 1974). Similarly, a review of the data on sex differences in premorbid intellect showed consistent findings of more prevalent premorbid IQ deficits among males (Aylward *et al.* 1984). On review of these findings, Aylward *et al.* (1984) suggest that the more severe premorbid intellectual and psychosocial deficits among males raise the possibility that a subtype of schizophrenia characterized by premorbid developmental deficits or premorbid functional decline may be more common among males than females.

Premorbid psychosocial dysfunction might also predispose to an earlier onset of illness among males. Such an explanation presumes that premorbid incompetence is not necessarily an intrinsic characteristic of schizophrenia but that it may represent an independent deficit which contributes to a reduced capacity to cope with stress and thereby increases vulnerability to onset of psychosis. According to this model, genetically vulnerable individuals with superior premorbid social and academic/occupational skills would be better able to cope with interpersonal stress, and hence, better protected against the onset of psychosis.

Sex differences in the phenomenology and course of illness

The question of whether sex differences in schizophrenia reflect variant forms of the disease has generated interest in determining whether males and females manifest phenomenologically different forms or phenotypes of the disorder. It has been suggested that an "amotivational" pattern may be more characteristic of males (Lewine

1985), consistent with the hypothesis that the "deficit syndrome" or classical *dementia praecox* may be more typical of males than females. There is some evidence that females present more severe psychotic symptoms than males (Goldstein and Link 1988); however, most studies that have found sex differences in the primary symptomatology of schizophrenia have shown differences that are essentially restricted to deficit features, with males presenting more severe negative symptoms (Pogue-Geile and Harrow 1984; Lewine 1985; Goldstein and Link 1988; Goldstein *et al.* 1990; Haas *et al.* 1991).

Although some reviews discuss sex differences in psychotic symptomatology, primary data-based reports of sex differences in psychotic symptoms are few, showing females with an elevation of a single psychotic symptom dimension, e.g., paranoid delusions (Forrest and Hay 1972; Goldstein and Link 1988; Hambrecht *et al.* 1992b) or sexual delusions, in a sample of early onset cases (Galdos *et al.* 1993). A majority of studies report no significant differences in active psychotic symptoms (Bardenstein and McGlashan 1990; Haas *et al.* 1990; Salokangas and Stengård 1990; Häfner *et al.* 1991 Shtasel *et al.* 1992; Chaves *et al.* 1993; Perry *et al.* 1995).

While a higher prevalence of affective disorders among females in the general population would suggest that females with schizophrenia may be at greater risk for affective symptoms, the data bearing on this question is surprisingly limited and inconsistent in this regard, with one study reporting evidence of more severe depressive mood and obsessive symptoms among females (Lewine *et al.* 1984; Lewine and Meltzer 1984; Kelsoe *et al.* 1988; Nasrallah and Wilcox 1989) and others reporting no significant differences in affective symptomatology (Haas *et al.* 1990; Chaves *et al.* 1993).

Sex differences in the temporal course of symptomatology, in response to treatment, were examined in the NIMH Treatment Strategies in Schizophrenia (TSS) Study of a controlled double-blind trial of antipsychotic treatment (Schooler *et al.* in press). In a subsidiary set of analyses, sex differences in symptomatology were examined across three treatment delivery conditions (low-dose, standard-dose and targeted-dose depot fluphenazine), and two phases of study (open-label stabilization phase and double-blind controlled maintenance treatment). At all assessment points, males evidenced more severe negative symptoms; sex differences in psychopathology were otherwise restricted to more severe anxiety in females during the maintenance phase of treatment (Haas, Frances, and the TSS Collaborative Study Group 1992). As suggested above, such differences in negative symptom constellations appear to be the most consistently observed sex differences in the phenomenology of schizophrenia, and may account, in part, for the tendency for male to female ratios to exceed 1.0:1.0.

Antipsychotic treatment response

Several studies have reported sex differences in response to neuroleptic treatments. Goldberg *et al.* (1966) reported greater drug-placebo differences among female, as contrasted with male, schizophrenia inpatients treated in a random assignment clinical trial of chlorpromazine, fluphenazine, thioridazine, and placebo. The authors surmised that these sex differences might reflect sex-related differences in the etiology of the disorder (with more males presenting a stress-reactive form of disorder that responds adequately well to environmental support and placebo medication, and more females, a genetically based disorder that requires active treatment with medication). Females showed superior symptom remission in response to controlled doses of neuroleptics (Ghadirian *et al.* 1982) and on standard- and low-dosage neuroleptic regimens (Hogarty *et al.* 1974). Females have been reported to have higher blood plasma levels of neuroleptic at controlled doses of drug (Simpson *et al.* 1990), lower oral clearance rates (Ereshevsky *et al.* 1991), greater prolactin response to dopaminergic blockade (Meltzer and Fang 1976; Nathan *et al.* 1983) and, at younger ages, females show evidence of a superior clinical response (compared with males) at lower doses in both naturalistic dosage titration studies (Chouinard *et al.* 1986; Seeman 1988) and retrospective case-review studies (Seeman 1983; D'Mello and McNeil 1990). Some evidence indicates that this sex effect may diminish with age and reverse after the menopause (Seeman 1983).

The TSS Study (Schooler *et al.* in press) presented an opportunity to examine sex differences in the temporal course of response to a controlled double-blind trial of three dosing strategies of neuroleptic treatment delivery: standard-dose, low-dose and targeted-dose delivery of intramuscular neuroleptic. In all conditions, females (compared with males) showed a significantly longer duration of adequate response to the controlled dosage of medication, i.e., without need for adjunct dosing (Woerner, Borenstein, and the TSS Collaborative Study Group 1992). Females also showed superior levels of social adjustment during the first month following discharge into the community. This sex difference in social adjustment was attenuated during the maintenance phase of treatment (Haas, Frances, and the TSS Collaborative Study Group 1992).

Preliminary evidence of sex differences in the therapeutic effects of antipsychotics suggest that there is a need for systematic empirical study of the sex-specific action of neuroleptics in men and women. Sex differences in the pharmacokinetics (bioavailability of drug after administration) are suggested by evidence of differences in secretion of gastric acid, gastrointestinal transit time, and gonadal hormones appear to influence absorption rates by altering transit time (for a review see Yonkers *et al.* 1992). Similarly, such sex-related factors as the percentage of adipose tissue and changes in weight across the menstrual cycle are known to influence the volume of distribution of a drug, and thus, may influence serum concentrations of the drug. Finally, hormones may influence the pharmacodynamic as well as pharmacokinetic properties of drugs; ovarian hormones may improve the effects of antipsychotics by directly acting to block dopamine receptors.

The relatively broad and diverse range of findings regarding sex differences in neuroleptic response indicate a need for controlled pharmacological studies specifically designed to examine sex differences in antipsychotic drug response. Speculation regarding the existing clinical data would suggest that there are at least three potential sources of sex-related variance in neuroleptic response that call for further study: (1) sex differences in pharmacodynamics (e.g., estrogen may enhance the therapeutic effects of antidopaminergic drugs and variance in endogenous estrogen levels may alter therapeutic response over different phases of the menstrual cycle); (2) sex differences in pharmacokinetics (e.g., the percentage of adipose tissue can influence the volume of distribution and the cumulative storage of medication, such that females may have lower serum concentrations on initiation of treatment, but greater cumulative storage of medication in adipose tissue); and

(3) possible sex differences (not adequately studied) in the metabolism of drugs. Research into the role of sex differences in antipsychotic drug response is of particular importance. A better understanding of the specific properties of drug action on females, over the menstrual cycle, are important for titration of medication; they also have relevance for side-effect prevention strategies for men and women. Confirmation of superior response to pharmacotherapeutic intervention among females (in contrast to the competing hypothesis of superior medication compliance) could explain much of the sex-related variance in long-term clinical outcome.

Psychosocial treatment response
There have been few formal studies which examined sex differences in response to psychosocial treatments for schizophrenia. A clinical trial of an inpatient family intervention (IFI) added to a multimodal hospital treatment for schizophrenia yielded evidence of sex differences in treatment response, with females alone showing better and more sustained (6- and 18–month follow-up) improvement with the addition of IFI (Spencer *et al.* 1988; Haas *et al.* 1990). Moreover, families of females assigned to the IFI treatment showed more positive changes in attitudes towards their family member with schizophrenia (than families of females assigned to the comparison treatment) at the follow-up evaluation. The reason why female patients and their families showed superior outcome with IFI in the absence of similar results for males is not clear; however, research on family attitudes toward patients suggests that families of males tend to be more critical and rejecting toward the patient than families of females (Hogarty *et al.* 1979). Subsequent findings of these investigators (Hogarty 1985; Hogarty *et al.* 1991), suggest that families of females with schizophrenia may be characteristically less critical of their patient/family members, and thus, more positively disposed toward a family intervention than are families of male patients with schizophrenia. Alternatively, females may be better able to tolerate the stress of interpersonal therapeutic interventions.

Long-term outcome
On balance, recent long-term, naturalistic follow-up studies tend to show evidence of superior outcomes for

women with schizophrenia (Seeman 1986; Goldstein 1988; Angermeyer *et al.* 1989, 1990). In a study of 175 patients, evaluated approximately 8 years following first hospital admission, Salokangas (1983) found that men were more often hospitalized and had longer hospital stays; adjustment to work and social role demands also tended to be superior for women. Similarly, in a study of 90 schizophrenic patients followed for 10 years, females experienced fewer rehospitalizations and had shorter hospital stays (than did males) as well as better social and occupational (work) adjustment (Goldstein 1988). On examination of the diagnostic characteristics of the subjects, the authors noted that these findings could not be attributed to variation in application of diagnostic criteria.

Interestingly, in reviews of the long-term outcome data, Watt *et al.* (1983) and Salokangas (1983) noted that superior outcomes for females are characteristic of the more recent studies; Watt *et al.* (1983) noted that studies carried out during the neuroleptic drug treatment era, revealed a higher proportion of females (than males) remaining out of the hospital. Similarly, Salokangas noted that a pattern of superior social functioning outcomes for females is characteristic of relatively recent outcome studies: in studies of patients hospitalized in the first half of the century (Lindelius 1970; Bleuler 1972; Ciompi and Müller 1976; Ciompi 1980), "social prognosis" i.e., social functioning outcomes did not vary with sex; only in more recent follow-up studies (Affleck *et al.* 1976; Lo and Lo 1977; Bland and Orn 1978; Nyman 1978), that one finds that levels of social functioning outcomes prove to be superior among females. Salokangas attributes the lack of sex differences in earlier studies to a restriction of variance in prognosis associated with relatively homogeneous diagnostic (narrowly-defined schizophrenia) groups. Another explanation may be that the relatively recent pattern of superior social functioning and less frequent rehospitalization is a function of superior neuroleptic treatment outcomes (be they due to superior compliance or treatment response). Support for this hypothesis comes from Salokangas' (1983) examination of treatment data which indicated that females were more reliable in attending outpatient clinic appointments during the 8-year follow-up period. The investigator concluded that females are more willing to seek help and thus have a shorter delay in seeking treatment when symptoms return. Salokangas reasoned that risk for relapse may be elevated among males due to their reluctance to seek help until a time when the symptoms have exacerbated to the point that inpatient admission is indicated.

Summary of findings on course, treatment response and outcome

In summary, there is evidence of significant sex-related variance in schizophrenia, spanning multiple dimensions of the disorder: age at onset, premorbid functioning, clinical symptomatology, treatment response and long-term outcome. To evaluate the potential relevance of these sex differences to the etiology of schizophrenia, and in particular, as they may relate to a neurodevelopmental model of schizophrenia, an overview of sex differences in normal neurodevelopment follows.

SEX DIFFERENCES IN NORMAL NEURO-DEVELOPMENT

There is a great deal of evidence attesting to the fact that the brains of adult men and women differ in important ways from each other. Perhaps the most consistently reported differences are in performance on certain neuropsychological tests. In reviewing such studies, Kimura (1992) suggested that men, on average, perform better than women in tests requiring imaginal rotation or other manipulation of an object; on tests of mathematic reasoning; on navigating through a route; and on target-directed motor skills. In contrast, women tend to be better at tests of perceptual speed; arithmetic calculation; recalling landmarks from a route; and at certain precision manual tasks. They also tend to exhibit greater verbal fluency (McGee 1982).

In a related area, much work has been done on sex differences in cerebral laterality. A simplified summary of the differences in "thinking" between the two hemispheres is that the left excels in intellectual, rational, verbal and analytical thinking, whereas the right excels in overall perception, in emotional, nonverbal, and intuitive thinking (Ames 1991). It has been suggested that men are more "logical", and women more "intuitive" thinkers, although of course, it is simplistic to explain such effects purely in terms of laterality. Thus, as Ames (1991) put it, "the two hemispheres function together in both sexes, but appear to differ in the manner in which they do so".

In a detailed and careful review of the literature on sex differences in cerebral laterality, McGlone (1980) noted that one of the few conclusions which could be drawn was that males tend to exhibit more lateralization of cerebral function than do females. The quest for anatomical correlates of this difference in cerebral laterality has been fraught with difficulty, not least of which includes the confounding effects of handedness. Numerous studies have concentrated on sex differences in the corpus callosum, which forms the "bridge" between the hemispheres. Witelson (1989), in a careful post-mortem study controlling for handedness, found the area of the isthmus of the corpus callosum to be larger in women, and interpreted this as evidence "compatible with the neuropsychological hypothesis of greater bihemispheral representation of functions in females for only posterior cortical regions . . .".

There is also evidence that certain other brain structures are sexually dimorphic. Swaab and Fliers (1985) reported that the preoptic nucleus of the hypothalamus is consistently larger in males than females; the nucleus appear to play a role in the expression of male sexual behavior. And in voles at least, the hippocampus (a structure which has come to excite contemporary interest in schizophrenia research) is consistently larger in males, while in rats, the hippocampal-dentate complex shows sex-differential laterality effects (Diamond 1989).

Importantly, many of these differences are evident very early in life, perhaps as early as the age of 3 years for some of the neuropsychological tests. Looked at another way, it appears that it is early (prenatal and early neonatal) influences which define the later sexual dimorphism in the brain and consequent differences in behavior. Thus, the roots of these differences appear to lie in the early development of the brain. To understand these differences, we must look at the hormonal influences on brain development, specifically the sex hormones. It should be noted that the role of genes, particularly those in the pseudo-autosomal region of the sex chromosomes, in the determination of cerebral laterality is not directly addressed here; the interested reader is referred to Crow (1988) for a full exposition of the possible relevance to schizophrenia.

Testosterone secretion in the human male fetus begins as early as weeks 12 through 18, once the testicular Leydig cells develop. It is the influence of testosterone which appears to be responsible for most of the sex differences in the brain; certainly it is this hormone which has been best studied in this regard. Once testosterone enters the brain, it is changed to dihydrotestosterone or more often, to estradiol; thus, at least some of the effects of testosterone on the brain are, paradoxically, mediated through estrogen receptors (Seeman 1989).

One of the most powerful organizational effects of the testosterone surge in males is on the hypothalamus, the area in the brain which determines much of male and female reproductive behavior. As reported earlier, it has been shown that the preoptic area of the hypothalamus is larger in males than females.

The precise manner in which testosterone exerts its effects on neuronal organization is unclear. It has however been shown that hypothalamic neurons from newborn rats, when exposed to androgenizing steroids, show increased outgrowth of new axons and dendrites. This suggests that the sex steroids affect neuronal circuitry by controlling the growth rate of axons and dendrites of select steroid-sensitive cells (Ames 1991).

The lifelong effects of early exposure of the brain to sex hormones, and the far lesser role played by later exposure to such hormones, suggests a certain "critical period" during which the brain is receptive to their organizational influences. Furthermore, as Kimura (1992) has pointed out, these early hormonal effects "are not limited to sexual or reproductive behaviours; they appear to extend to all known behaviours in which males and females differ". This view is supported by both animal work involving castration of neonatal males, which results in a reversal of sex-typed behaviors as adults, and by "natural experiments" in humans, such as studies of girls with congenital adrenal hyperplasia, who were exposed to an excess of androgens at a prenatal and early neonatal stage, and who as adults tend to behave and problem-solve in a "male" way.

Organizational effects aside, testosterone also appears

to slow the development of the male brain, expressly the left (dominant) hemisphere. Thus, Taylor (1969) hypothesized that the female brain develops more rapidly, in terms of myelinization, establishment of neuronal connections, and lateralization of function, but that development reaches a plateau earlier; male brains develop more slowly, and continue to do so for longer. This sex difference in rates of cerebral maturation implies that the male brain is vulnerable to environmental factors which might adversely affect neurodevelopment for longer than is the female brain.

Clinical and animal studies support the view that the male brain is particularly vulnerable to the effects of early adverse influences. For example, in the literature on low birth weight fetuses, male infants have been shown to be more vulnerable to peri-intraventricular hemorrhage (Amato et al. 1987), while Brothwood et al. (1986) found in a 1 and 2-year follow-up of very low birth weight infants that males showed significantly more impairment of development than females in all areas save locomotor. Boys also seem more likely to suffer longer-term consequences of early brain abnormality; for example, Lunsing et al. (1992) followed up a group of children shown to have minor neurological dysfunction at birth, and found that at the age of 12 years, children exhibiting minor neurological dysfunction were most likely to be male and to have been neurologically abnormal at birth or to have been born preterm and/or to have experienced early environmental adversity in combination with asphyxia. In experiments on rats, Grimm and Frieder (1985) have shown that prenatal insult to the developing brain impairs later performance on complex learning tasks in males but not females, while postnatal insult affects the two sexes equally.

IMPLICATIONS FOR THE PATHOPHYSIOLOGY OF SCHIZOPHRENIA

Sex differences in cortical structure and function
Neuropsychological, neuropathological and neuroimaging studies provide evidence of left hemisphere cortical abnormalities in schizophrenia. Investigators (Boklage 1977; Flor-Henry 1987; Crow et al. 1989) have speculated

that an illness-related arrest of cortical development may selectively affect the later-maturing (Chi et al. 1977) prefrontal and temporal regions of the left (rather than the right) hemisphere, and more dramatically in the later-to-mature male cortex (Taylor 1969). According to this model, abnormalities of the dorsolateral prefrontal cortex (DLPFC) and medial temporal region, would be more common (or severe) among males, and lateralized to the left side. In normal individuals, there is a greater right/left structural asymmetry in males (Wada et al. 1975), increasing with age (Diamond 1989), and evidence of greater hemispheric lateralization of spatial and verbal abilities among males (McGee 1982) as well as a tendency for superior visuospatial versus verbal functioning among males (Kimura and Harshman 1984). Among normal females a reverse pattern of structural asymmetry is observed (i.e., greater left than right) along with a tendency for better verbal functioning among females contrasted with males (Kimura and Harshman 1984). Evidence of superior functional recovery from posterior left temporal lobe brain injury in normal females compared with males (McGlone 1978, Kimura 1992) has been interpreted as consistent with greater equipotentiality of hemispheric involvement in verbal functioning among females. In aggregate, these observations have led neuropsychologists to suggest that functional recovery (or compensation of deficits) associated with injury to the left temporal region are generally better in females (Filskov and Catanese 1986). Thus, in schizophrenia, cognitive deficits presumed to be associated with left temporal lobe dysfunction might be better compensated (or recovered) in the female brain.

Abnormalities of frontal and temporolimbic cortical regions in schizophrenia
Restricted by the technical limitations of computerized tomography (CT), early attempts to uncover a biological basis for schizophrenia in brain morphology focused largely on measurement of the cerebral ventricles (Johnstone et al. 1976; Johnstone 1987) to provide evidence of cortical atrophy (Weinberger et al. 1979). Evidence of gross structural abnormalities of frontal cortex (such as reduced cortical area (Andreasen 1986)) has been scant, and attempts to replicate have generally

failed (Kelsoe *et al.* 1988). For example, Flaum *et al.* (1990) reviewed neuroimaging studies of individuals with schizo-phrenia, which reported sex effects; most had small sample sizes and lacked statistical power, but of the six studies which found a sex effect, males had larger ventricle/brain rations (VBR) than females in five. In three of their own four studies, Flaum *et al.* (1990) found males had signifi-cantly larger ventricles than controls, but that there was no such effect for females. Andreasen *et al.* (1993) have shown that in male, but not female, schizophrenic patients, the normal positive correlation between IQ and the volume of various brain structures (e.g., temporal lobe) is lost, imply-ing greater abnormality in male than female schizophrenic patients. Not all neuroimaging studies of schizophrenic patients have found such sex differences (Nasrallah *et al.* 1990; Gur *et al.* 1991). In fact, in a recent study reported by Flaum *et al.* (1995), no evidence of sex differences in structural volumetric magnetic resonance imaging (MRI) indices of regions of interest was found in schizophrenia (i.e., no sex by diagnosis interaction effects beyond larger total brain volumes among both schizophrenic and control males). As Flaum *et al.* conclude, however, the contrast between their findings and evidence from previous studies showing greater structural brain abnormalities among males with schizophrenia suggest that no firm conclusions can yet be drawn about sex-related variation in structural abnormalities of the brain in schizophrenia.

Abnormalities of the laminar organization of frontal cortex (Benes *et al.* 1986; Akbarian *et al.* 1993) provide pre-liminary evidence of developmental abnormalities of this brain region. Other evidence of frontal cortical abnormal-ities derives from three independent bodies of empirical data: (1) functional imaging of frontal cortex (Ingvar and Franzen 1974; Weinberger *et al.* 1986; Berman *et al.* 1988) recently showing reduced glucose metabolism in pre-frontal cortical regions (Ingvar and Franzen 1974; Buchsbaum *et al.* 1990); (2) oculomotor studies of pre-frontal cortical function (Goldman-Rakiç 1987; Park and Holzman 1992; Sweeney *et al.* 1996); and (3) evidence of neuropsychological deficits on putative tests of prefrontal function (Weinberger *et al.* 1986; Keilp *et al.* 1988). Morphometric studies using MRI confirm ventricular enlargement in schizophrenia (Kelsoe *et al.* 1988) and, more importantly, provide evidence of structural

abnormalities of temporolimbic cortical regions (Suddath *et al.* 1989; Bogerts *et al.* 1990). Several post-mortem studies indicate cytoarchitectonic abnormalities of the medial temporal lobe, the superior temporal sulcus, and associated limbic structures in patients with schizophrenia (Scheibel and Kovelman 1981; Kovelman and Scheibel 1984; Bogerts *et al.* 1985; Brown *et al.* 1986; Jakob and Beckmann 1986; Conrad and Scheibel 1987).

Evidence of neurodevelopmental deficits prominent among schizophrenic males

By several reports, temporal lobe abnormalities (Bogerts *et al.* 1985; Falkai *et al.* 1992; Woodruff *et al.* 1993) including enlargement of the temporal horns of the lateral ventricles (Brown *et al.* 1986), hippocampal and parahippocampal dysplasias (Bogerts *et al.* 1985; Falkai *et al.* 1992) and structural abnormalities of the planum temporalus (Brown *et al.* 1986; Falkai *et al.* 1992; Lieberman *et al.* 1992a) tend to be more prominent among males. Interestingly, consis-tent with temporal lobe abnormalities in schizophrenia, corpus callosum dimensions may be smaller in schizo-phrenia, specifically in the posterior region, the fibers pre-sumed to support communication between the right and left temporal lobes. Some investigators have found corpus callosum dimensions to be more reduced among males (Raine *et al.* 1990; Woodruff *et al.* 1993). The potentially confounding influence of handedness and/or differences in the methods for subdivision of the callosal regions are likely to account for the conflicting findings on sex differ-ences in corpus callosum areas. Thus, it is premature to draw any conclusions regarding a possible sexual dimor-phism of the corpus callosum in schizophrenia.

RELEVANCE OF SEX DIFFERENCES TO OTHER ETIOLOGICAL FACTORS IN SCHIZOPHRENIA

Genetic liability to schizophrenia

Evidence for a genetic liability to schizophrenia is based on familial studies showing heritability to be approximately 30–50% (Gottesman and Shields 1976). Studies of mono-zygotic twins are, overall equivocal regarding sex differ-ences in concordance rates (Abe 1983; Kringlen 1987;

Rosenthal 1962) although evidence of an increased concor-dance among same-sex compared with opposite-sex sib-lings has been forwarded in support of the hypothesis that a pseudo autosomal dominant gene on the short arm of the sex chromosome (Crow 1990, 1992) may occur in schizo-phrenia. With few exceptions (Rosenthal 1962; Kringlen 1987), empirical work prior to the 1990s (e.g., Rosenthal and Bigelow 1972; Gottesman and Shields 1976) has sup-ported the notion that there are no sex differences among probands in terms of familial risk for schizophrenia. More recent reports which suggest that there is a greater preva-lence of familial cases of schizophrenia among female pro-bands (Bellodi et al. 1986; Goldstein et al. 1990, 1992; Pulver et al. 1990) have inspired speculation that a familial form of schizophrenia may be more common among females (Goldstein et al. 1990; Murray et al. 1992). Several of these studies fail to adjust for number of years of each family member's exposure to risk per family member per proband. Goldstein et al. (1992) did include an age-related period of risk adjustments; however, the use of hospital chart availability as a criterion for case selection may have introduced bias. Alternatively, what appears to be a higher prevalence of family history of schizophrenia among females may be due to a higher prevalence of a nongenetic neurodevelopmental form of schizophrenia among males. Given evidence that non-genetic factors likely account for less than 10% of the variance in schizophrenia (Crow et al. 1989; McGuffin 1992) such atypical cases may account for the excess of males observed in recent studies, even when using broad-band definitions and age-adjusted commu-nity-based epidemiological samples (Lewine 1985; Waddington et al. 1990). So-called "non-genetic" cases would be expected to show a low frequency of schizo-phrenia among first-degree relatives. Evidence supporting the hypothesis of a higher prevalence of a nonfamilial form among males, might also explain why some studies have reported a relatively higher rate of familial schizophrenia among female compared with male probands.

Social environmental factors and stress vulnerability among males

The impact of stress on the course of schizophrenia is rec-ognized by clinicians and researchers alike. As discussed above, one explanation for an earlier onset and more severe

illness among males presumes that sex role-related stress may be greater for males during late adolescence and early adulthood when pressures for independence, dominance and competitive behavior come into play, triggering onset in a biologically vulnerable individual (Farina et al. 1963; Forrest and Hay 1971; Seeman 1985). Stressful life events appear influential in precipitating onset (Michaux et al. 1967; Bleuler 1972; Kirkegaard-Sorensen and Mednick 1975) and relapse (Brown and Birley 1968; Kirkegaard-Sorensen and Mednick 1975; Leff and Vaughn 1980; Nuechterlein et al. 1992) in schizophrenia. Preliminary data from a study of first-hospitalization schizophrenic patients, using the Life Events and Difficulties Scale (LEDS) developed by Brown and Harris (1978), suggests that in a majority of cases the onset of an illness episode is temporally linked to a severely stressful life event during the preceding 6 months; the latency from stressful life event to onset appears to be shorter for males, suggesting that the timing of onset among males may be more closely linked in time to acute stressors. Males in general appear to be more physiologically stress-reactive (Polefrone and Manuck 1987) . Thus, social environmental stressors may modify the timing of the first psychotic episode and contribute to the earlier onset in males.

Obstetric and perinatal factors

A neurodevelopmental model imputing a form of central nervous system (CNS) trauma accommodates evidence of an association between schizophrenia and trauma during the second trimester of pregnancy (Mednick and Cannon 1991). This model posits that during a critical period of early brain development (e.g., the second trimester of pregnancy) such varied putative etiologic agents as obstet-ric complications (McNeil and Kaij 1978), winter birth (Häfner et al. 1987), and maternal exposure to viral influenza cause insult to the developing brain, and thus contribute to nonspecific risk factors for schizophrenia in a subgroup of predominantly male cases.

Several researchers have found a higher prevalence of obstetric complications among males than females (Wilcox and Nasrallah 1987; Owen et al. 1988; Foerster et al. 1991b). This high prevalence does not necessarily suggest that birth complications represent a specific and sufficient causal factor in schizophrenia in males. Pregnancy and birth complications may increase risk for schizophrenia only in individuals with a genetic predisposition (Fish *et al.* 1992; Marcus *et al.* 1993), perhaps more commonly among boys (Marcus *et al.* 1993). Also consistent with a model of genetically-controlled neurodevelopmental abnormality is evidence that temporal lobe dysplasias in schizophrenia do not resemble the gross abnormalities associated with perinatal brain insult (Falkai *et al.* 1990). Structural brain abnormalities in adult schizophrenics appear to be associated with male sex, cognitive deficits and obstetric complications (Pearlson *et al.* 1989; Rosenthal and Bigelow 1972).

Estrogen protection hypothesis

Age at schizophrenia onset may be delayed, and the severity of symptoms diminished, among females, due to the protective effects of estrogen (Seeman 1985; Häfner *et al.* 1991a; Riecher-Rössler and Häfner 1993). Evidence that estrogen levels may influence the vulnerability to relapse in females comes from clinical studies which show a strong temporal correlation between relapse and low levels of endogenous estrogen (as during menstruation or the immediate premenstrual phase (Janowsky *et al.* 1969), postpartum (Kendell *et al.* 1987), and after the menopause (Seeman 1983). Thus, estrogen may confer some neuroleptic-like (antipsychotic) protection against psychotic symptoms in females. Moreover, the predominantly female phenomenon of onset after age 45 years coincides with the age of decline in estrogen levels. Animal studies show that chronic treatment with exogenous estrogen serves effectively to reduce dopamine (DA) transmission (DiPaolo and Falardeau 1985; Häfner *et al.* 1991a; Gattaz *et al.* 1994).

Gattaz *et al.* (1994) found that women who entered the hospital during the low-estrogen phase of their cycle (and thus were moving towards higher-estrogen levels during active treatment) required lower neuroleptic doses than women who entered the hospital during the high-estrogen phases of their cycle. In general, a superior therapeutic response to antipsychotic treatment and lower clinical dosing of females compared with males, particularly at earlier ages, is consistent with the estrogen protection hypothesis. Haas *et al.* (1992) analyzed data from the NIMH Collaborative Study of Treatment Strategies in Schizophrenia (Haas, Frances and the Collaborative Study

Group 1992) and found superior survival rates among females compared with males at standard controlled levels of injectable neuroleptic wherein variance in medication compliance is limited. On the whole, women treated with a long-term regimen of a conventional neuroleptic tend to have better outcomes and to require lower doses of neuroleptics than males (Hogarty 1974; Goldstein *et al.* 1978; Seeman 1986). Taken together, these findings suggest that estrogen may play a key role in modulating the timing of symptom onset and the severity of its presentation, as well as enhancing neuroleptic treatment response in females with schizophrenia.

CONCLUSIONS: IMPLICATIONS FOR A NEURODEVELOPMENTAL MODEL OF SCHIZOPHRENIA

Several independent lines of investigation have identified sex differences in the psychopathology, neurobiology and psychosocial deficits of schizophrenia. The findings have been generally consistent in revealing a more severe form of illness among males associated with more severe premorbid deficits. Sex differences in age at onset of psychotic symptoms and course of illness have important implications for understanding the etiology and pathophysiology of schizophrenia. Whether sex differences in the severity and course of schizophrenia derive from essential differences in the pathophysiology of the illness, whether they are secondary to differences in the timing of onset or the effects of other sex-related factors on the subsequent course of illness remains to be determined. Evidence of developmental deficits and premorbid dysfunction is consistent with contemporary neurodevelopmental models of schizophrenia.

The details of the neurodevelopmental model of schizophrenia have been comprehensively outlined elsewhere in this volume. It is useful here to remind ourselves of the characteristics of neurodevelopmental disorders in general, and to assess how well schizophrenia fits into the broader scheme of neurodevelopmental disorders. Goodman (1991) has suggested the main characteristics of neurodevelopmental disorders to be: (1) males predominate; (2) such disorders are over-represented amongst individuals with brain abnormalities; (3) there is an association with pre- and perinatal complications; and (4) there are increased rates of non-right handedness.

It seems reasonable to assert that there is little evidence to justify the view that all the conditions commonly subsumed under the label "schizophrenia" have a neurodevelopmental origin; however, a compelling case can be made that certain characteristics of one/some of these disparate conditions can be interpreted in a neurodevelopmental framework. In particular, it has been proposed elsewhere (Castle and Murray 1991; Murray et al. 1992) that it is severe early-onset schizophrenia that shows most of the features of neurodevelopmental illness. To follow Goodman's (1991) points, as detailed above:

(1) There is undoubtedly an excess of males among individuals with early-onset schizophrenia, particularly when the illness is stringently defined (Castle et al. 1993; and as reviewed earlier).

(2) Despite methodological difficulties in neuroimaging studies of schizophrenia (described earlier), and the fact that they have not generally been set up to examine sex differences, it seems reasonable to conclude that structural brain abnormalities are more commonly a feature of male than female cases of schizophrenia.

(3) In etiological terms, males with schizophrenia, expressly those with an early onset of illness, appear more likely than females to have a history of those obstetric complications implicated in the etiology of the condition (Lewis et al. 1989; Castle and Murray 1991; O'Callaghan et al. 1992; and as reviewed earlier).

(4) The left temporal lobe seems to be of particular importance in the pathogenesis of schizophrenia (Crow et al. 1989; Suddath et al. 1990) but direct studies of cerebral laterality in schizophrenia have met with mixed success. Some evidence suggests that "pathological" left-sided hand and eye preference may be associated with a severe form of schizophrenia to which males are particularly prone. For example, studies have shown an association between left handedness/crossed dominance and early onset of illness (Piran et al.

1982), inferior social competence (Merrin 1984), and increased VBR and poor performance on neuropsychological tests (Witelson 1989).

Other characteristics of early onset male-predominant schizophrenia are also compatible with a neurodevelopmental illness: a tendency to worse premorbid functioning (Zigler and Levine 1973; Klorman et al. 1977; Zigler et al. 1977; Lewine 1981; Childers and Harding 1990; Foerster et al. 1991a; Castle et al. 1993), lower premorbid IQ and poorer school performance (Offord 1974) amongst males who subsequently develop schizophrenia (for a review see Aylward et al. (1984), more negative symptoms (for a review see Bardenstein and McGlashan 1990), and generally worse outcome among males compared with females (Seeman 1986; Goldstein 1988; Angermeyer et al. 1989, 1990) with schizophrenia.

Thus, a more severe premorbid course of schizophrenia is suggestive of a neurodevelopmental form of schizophrenia that may be more common among males. Competing hypotheses would suggest that more severe deficits in males derive from a greater cumulative morbidity associated with an earlier age of onset or age-related complications of onset rather than from sex differences in the pathophysiological substrates of the disorder.

Further investigation of sex differences in schizophrenia is needed to address key questions regarding the nature of sex differences in the disorder. What accounts for the striking sex difference in the timing of onset of the disorder? Do sex differences in structural abnormalities reflect variant pathophysiological substrates of the disorder? Do gonadal hormones play a role in modulating the neurodevelopmental trajectories of individuals with a biological genetic vulnerability to schizophrenia in males and females? What are the sex effects on clinical diagnosis? What are the implications of sex differences in symptomatology and functioning for the planning of treatments effective for males and females?

It is currently unclear whether increased risk for progressive clinical decline is attributable to early age of onset or something more specific about males. It is also unclear whether reduced morbidity in females derives primarily from delayed onset or sex-related protective factors. The answers to these questions may be important in efforts to develop interventions to modify the course of schizo-phrenia. Such efforts may require the development of different interventions for men and women. A knowledge of sex-related risk and protective factors may also eventually help to: (1) identify forms of schizophrenia with unique etiology and pathophysiology; (2) enhance understanding of risk and protective factors which modulate the severity and course of schizophrenia; (3) identify sex-specific protective factors which might delay onset and minimize severity of illness in females; and (4) develop more effective diagnostic and treatment strategies for schizophrenic patients.

ACKNOWLEDGMENT

This work was supported in part by US Public Health Service Grants R01–MH48492 (G.L.H.), and R29–MH43613 (G.L.H.) from the National Institute of Mental Health.

REFERENCES

Abe, K. 1983. The morbidity rate and environmental influence in monozygotic cotwins of schizophrenics. *Br. J. Psychiatry* **115**:519–31.

Affleck, J.W., Burns, J., and Forrest, A.D. 1976. Long-term follow-up of schizophrenic patients in Edinburgh. *Acta Psychiatr. Scand.* **53**:227–37.

Akbarian, S., Bunney, W.E., Potkin, S.G., Wigal, S.B., Hagman, J.O., Sandman, C.A., and Jones, E.G. 1993. Altered distribution of nicotinamide-adenine dinucleotide phosphate-diaphorase cells in frontal lobe of schizophrenics implies disturbances of cortical development. *Arch. Gen. Psychiatry* **50**:169–87.

Amato, M., Howald, H., and von Muralt, G. 1987. Fetal sex and distribution of peri-intraventricular hemorrhage in preterm infants. *Eur. Neurol.* **27**:20–3.

American Psychiatric Association. 1980. *DSM-III: Diagnostic and Statistical Manual of Mental Disorders*, 3rd edn. Washington, DC: The Association.

American Psychiatric Association. 1987. *DSM-III-R: Diagnostic and Statistical Manual of Mental Disorders*, 3rd edn. Washington, DC: The Association.

American Psychiatric Association. 1994. *DSM-IV: Diagnostic and Statistical Manual of Mental Disorders*, 4th edn. Washington, DC: The Association.

Ames, F.R. 1991. Sex and the brain. *S. Afr. Med. J.* **80**:150–2.

Andreasen, N. 1986. Structural abnormalities in the frontal system in schizophrenia: a magnetic resonance imaging study. *Arch. Gen. Psychiatry* **43**:136–44.

Andreasen, N.C., Flaum, M.A., Swayze, V.W., Harris, G., Cizadlo, T., and Gupta, S. 1993. Gender differences in the brain in schizophrenia. *Paper presented at the Annual Meeting of the American Psychiatric Association,* San Francisco, CA.

Angermeyer, M.C., Goldstein, J.M., and Kühn, L. 1989. Gender differences in schizophrenia: rehospitalization and community survival. *Psychol. Med.* **19**:365–82.

Angermeyer, M.C. and Kühn, L. 1988. Gender differences in age at onset of schizophrenia. An overview. *Eur. Arch. Psychiatry Neurol. Sci.* **237**:351–64.

Angermeyer, M.C., Kühn, L., and Goldstein, J.M. 1990. Gender and the course of schizophrenia: differences in treated outcomes. *Schizophr. Bull.* **16**: 293–307.

Astrachan, B.M., Harrow, M., Adler, D., Brauer, L., Schwartz, A., Schwartz, C., and Tucker, G. 1972. A checklist for the diagnosis of schizophrenia. *Br. J. Psychiatry* **121**:529–39.

Aylward, E., Walker, E., and Bettes, B. 1984. Intelligence in schizophrenia: meta-analysis of the research. *Schizophr. Bull.* **10**:430–59.

Bardenstein, K.K. and McGlashan, T.H. 1990. Gender differences in affective, schizoaffective, and schizophrenic disorders: a review. *Schizophr. Res.* **3**:159–72.

Bellodi, L., Bussoleni, C., Scorza-Smeraldi, R., and Grassi, G. 1986. Family study of schizophrenia: exploratory analysis for relevant factors. *Schizophr. Bull.* **12**:120–8.

Benes, F.M., Davidson, J., and Bird, E.D. 1986. Quantitative cytoarchitectural studies of the cerebral cortex of schizophrenics. *Arch. Gen. Psychiatry* **43**: 31–5.

Berman, K.F., Illowsy, B.P., and Weinberger, D.R. 1988. Physiological dysfunction of dorsolateral prefrontal cortex in schizophrenia: IV. Further evidence for regional and behavioral specificity. *Arch. Gen. Psychiatry* **45**: 616–22.

Bland, R.C. and Orn, H. 1978. 14-year outcome in early schizophrenia. *Acta Psychiatr. Scand.* **58**:327–38.

Bleuler, M. 1972. *The schizophrenic disorders: long-term patient and family studies.* New Haven: Yale University Press.

Bogerts, B., Ashtari, M., Degreef, G., and Alvir, J.M. 1990. Reduced temporal limbic structure volumes on magnetic resonance images in first episode schizophrenia. *Psychiatr. Res. Neuroimaging* **35**:1–13.

Bogerts, B., Meertz, E., and Schonfeldt-Bausch, R. 1985. Basal ganglia and limbic system pathology in schizophrenia: a morphometric study of brain volume and shrinkage. *Arch. Gen. Psychiatry* **42**:784–91.

Boklage, C.E. 1977. Schizophrenia, brain asymmetry development, and twinning: cellular relationship with etiological and possibly prognostic implications. *Biol. Psychiatry* **12**:19–35.

Bromet, E.J., Schwartz, J.E., Fennig, S., and Geller, L. 1992. The epidemiology of psychosis: The Suffolk County Mental Health Project. *Schizophr. Bull.* **18**: 243–55.

Brothwood, M., Wolke, D., Gamsu, H., Benson, J., and Cooper, D. 1986. Prognosis of the very low birth weight baby in relation to gender. *Arch. Dis. Child.* **61**:559–64.

Brown, G.W. and Birley, J.L.T. 1968. Crises and life changes and the onset of schizophrenia. *J. Health Soc. Behav.* **9**:203–14.

Brown, R., Colter, N., Corsellis, J.A., Crow, T.J., Frith, C.D., Jagoe, R., Johnstone, E.C., and Marsh, L. 1986. Post-mortem evidence of structural brain changes in schizophrenia: differences in brain weight, temporal horn area, and parahippocampal gyrus compared with affective disorder. *Arch. Gen. Psychiatry* **43**:36–42.

Brown, G.W. and Harris, T.O. 1978. *The Bedford College Life Events and Difficulty Schedule*, London: Bedford College.

Bruce, M.L. and Kim, K.M. 1992. Differences in the effects of divorce on major depression in men and women. *Am. J. Psychiatry* **149**:914–17.

Buchsbaum, M.S., Nuechterlein, K.H., Haier, R.J., and Wu, J. 1990. Glucose metabolic rate in normals and schizophrenics during the Continuous Performance Test assessed by positron emission tomography. *Br. J. Psychiatry* **156**:216–27.

Cannon-Spoor, H., Potkin, S.G., and Wyatt, R.J. 1982. Measurement of premorbid adjustment in chronic schizophrenia. *Schizophr. Bull.* **8**:470–84.

Carpenter, W.T. Jr., Bartko, J.J., and Strauss, J.S. 1980. A postscript on the 12–point flexible system for the diagnosis of schizophrenia: a report from the international pilot study of schizophrenia. *Psychiatr. Res.* **3**:357–64

Carpenter, W.T., Jr., Strauss, J.S., and Bartko, J.J. 1973. Flexible

system for diagnosis of schizophrenia: report from the WHO international pilot study of schizophrenia. *Science* **182**:1275–8.

Castle, D.J. and Howard, R. 1992. What do we know about the aetiology of late-onset schizophrenia? *Eur. Psychiatry* **7**:99–108.

Castle, D.J. and Murray, R. 1991. The neurodevelopmental basis of sex differences in schizophrenia. *Psychol. Med.* **21**:565–75.

Castle, D.J., Wessely, S., and Murray, R.M. 1993. Sex and schizophrenia: effects of diagnostic stringency, and associations with and premorbid variables. *Br. J. Psychiatry* **162**:658–64.

Chaves, A.C., Seeman, M.V., Mari, J.J., and Maluf, A. 1993. Schizophrenia: impact of positive symptoms on gender social role. *Schizophr. Res.* **11**:41–5.

Chi, J., Dooling, E., and Gilles, F. 1977. Gyral development of the human brain. *Ann. Neurol.* **1**:86–93.

Childers, S.E. and Harding, C.M. 1990. Gender, premorbid social functioning, and long-term outcome in DSM-III schizophrenia. *Schizophr. Bull.* **16**: 309–18.

Choinard, G., Annable, L., and Steinberg, S. 1986. A controlled clinical trial of fluspirilene, a long-acting injectable neuroleptic, in schizophrenic patients with acute exacerbation. *J. Clin. Psychopharmacol.* **6**:21–6.

Ciompi, L. 1980. The natural history of schizophrenia in the long term. *Br. J. Psychiatry* **136**:413–20.

Ciompi, L. and Müller, C. 1976. Lifestyle and age of schizophrenics. A catamnestic long-term study into old age. *Monographien aus dem Gesamtgebiete der Psychiatrie* **12**:1–242.

Conrad, A.J. and Scheibel, A.B. 1987. Schizophrenia and the hippocampus: the embryological hypothesis extended. *Schizophr Bull.* **13**:577–87.

Crow, T. 1992. Sex differences, sexual selection and sex linkage in psychoses. *Paper presented at the Annual Meeting of The Royal College of Psychiatrists*, Dublin, Ireland.

Crow, T.J. 1988. Sex chromosomes and psychosis: the case for a pseudo autosomal locus. *Br. J. Psychiatry* **153**:675–83.

Crow, T.J. 1990. Nature of the genetic contribution to psychotic illness: a continuum viewpoint. *Acta Psychiatr. Scand.* **81**:401–08.

Crow, T.J., Ball, J., Bloom, S.R., and Brown, R. 1989. Schizophrenia as an anomaly of development of cerebral asymmetry: a post-mortem study and a proposal concerning the genetic basis of the disease. *Arch. Gen. Psychiatry* **46**:1145–50.

Crow, T.J., Colter, N., Frith, C.D., and Johnstone, E.C. 1989. Developmental arrest of cerebral asymmetries in early onset schizophrenia. First International Symposium: Imaging the brain in psychiatry and related fields (1988, Wurzburg, Federal Republic of Germany). *Psychiatry Res.* **29**: 247–53.

DeSalvia, D., Barbato, A., Salvo, P., and Zadro, F. 1993. Prevalence and incidence of schizophrenic disorders in Portogruaro. An Italian case register study. *J. Nervous Mental. Dis.* **181**:275–82.

D'Mello, D.A. and McNeil, J.A. 1990. Sex differences in bipolar affective disorder: neuroleptic dosage variance. World Psychiatric Association Regional Symposium (1988, Washington, DC). *Compr. Psychiatry* **31**: 80–3.

Deister, A. and Marneros, A. 1992. Sex differences in functional psychoses: comparison between schizophrenic, schizoaffective and affective disorders. *Fortschr. Neurologie Psychiatr.* **60**:407–19.

Diamond, M. 1989. Sex and the cerebral cortex. *Biol. Psychiatry* **25**:823–25.

DiPaolo, T. and Falardeau, P. 1985. Modulation of brain and pituitary dopamine receptors by estrogens and prolactin. *Prog. Neuropsychopharmacol. Biol. Psychiatr.* **9**:473–80.

Dworkin, R.H. 1990. Patterns of sex differences in negative symptoms and social functioning consistent with separate dimensions of schizophrenic psychopathology. *Am. J. Psychiatry* **147**:347–9.

Eaton, W.W. 1975. Marital status and schizophrenia. *Acta Psychiatr. Scand.* **52**: 320–9.

Ereshefsky, L., Saklad, S.R., Watanabe, M.D., Davis, C.M., and Jann, M.W. 1991. Thiothixene pharmacokinetic interactions: a study of haptic enzyme inducers, clearance inhibitors, and demographic variables. *J. Clin. Psychopharmacol.* **11**:296–301.

Falkai, P., Bogerts, B., Greve, B., and Pfeiffer, U. 1992. Loss of sylvian fissure asymmetry in schizophrenia: a quantitative post mortem study. *Schizophr. Res.* **7**:23–32.

Falkai, P., Bogerts, B., and Rozumek, M. 1988. Limbic pathology in schizophrenia: the entorhinal region—a morphometric study. *Biol. Psychiatry* **24**:515–21.

Farina, A., Garmezy, N., and Barry, H. 1963. Relationship of marital status to incidence and prognosis of schizophrenia. *J. Consult. Clin. Psychol.* **67**: 624–30.

Farina, A., Garmezy, N., Zalusky, M., and Becker, J. 1962. Premorbid behavior and prognosis in female schizophrenic patients. *J. Consult. Clin. Psychol.* **26**: 56–60.

Feighner, J., Robins, E., Guze, S., Woodruff, R., Winokur, G., and Munoz, R. 1972. Diagnostic criteria for use in psychiatric research. *Arch. Gen. Psychiatry* **26**:57–63.

Filskov, S.B. and Catanese, R.A. 1986. Effects of sex and handedness on neuropsychological testing. In *Handbook of clinical neuropsychology*, 2nd edn., ed. S.B. Filskov and T.J. Boll, pp. 198–212. New York: John Wiley.

Fish, B., Marcus, J., Hans, S.L., and Auerbach, J.G. 1992. Infants at risk for schizophrenia: sequelae of a genetic neurointegrative defect. A review and replication analysis of pandysmaturation in the Jerusalem Infant Development Study. *Arch. Gen. Psychiatry* **49**:221–35.

Flaum, M., Arndt, S., and Andreasen, N.C. 1990. The role of gender in studies of ventricle enlargement in schizophrenia: a predominantly male effect. *Am. J. Psychiatry* **147**:1327–32.

Flaum, M., Swayze, V.W., O'Leary, D.S., Yuh, W.T., Ehrherdt, J.C., Arndt, S.V., and Andreasen, N.C. 1995. Effects of diagnosis, laterality and gender on brain morphology in schizophrenia. *Am. J. Psychiatry* **152**: 704–14.

Flor-Henry, P. 1987. Cerebral dynamics, laterality and psychopathology. In *Cerebral Dynamics, Laterality and Psychopathology*, ed. R. Takahashi.

Foerster, A., Lewis, S., Owen, M. and Murray, R. 1991a. Premorbid adjustment and personality in psychosis. Effects of sex and diagnosis. *Br. J. Psychiatry* **158**:171–6.

Foerster, A., Lewis, S.W., Owen, M.J., and Murray, R.M. 1991b. Low birth weight and a family history of schizophrenia predict poor premorbid functioning in psychosis. *Schizophr. Res.* **5**:13–20.

Folnegović, Z., Folnegović-Smalc, V., and Kulčar, Z. 1990. Characteristics of male and female schizophrenics at first admission. Special Issue: Cross-cultural psychiatry. *Br. J. Psychiatry* **156**:365–68.

Forrest, A.D. and Hay, A.J. 1971. Sex differences and the schizophrenic experience. *Acta Psychiatr. Scand.* **47**: 137–47.

Forrest, A.D. and Hay, A.J. 1972. The influence of sex on schizophrenia. *Acta Psychiatr. Scand.* **6**:53–8.

Galdos, P.M., van Os, J.J., and Murray, R.M. 1993. Puberty and the onset of psychosis (see comments). *Schizophr. Res.* **10**:7–14.

Gattaz, W.F., Vogel, P., Riecher-Rössler, A., and Soddu, G. 1994. Influence of the menstrual cycle phase on the therapeutic response in schizophrenia. *Biol. Psychiatry* **36**:137–39.

Ghadirian, A.M., Chouinard, G., and Annable, L. 1982. Sexual dysfunction and plasma prolactin levels in neuroleptic-treated schizophrenic outpatients. *J. Nerv. Mental Dis.* **170**:463–7.

Gibbons, J.S., Horn, S.H., Powell, J.M., and Gibbons, J.L. 1984. Schizophrenic patients and their families. A survey in a psychiatric service based on a DGH unit. *Br. J. Psychiatry* **144**:70–7.

Goldberg, S.C., Schooler, N.R., Davidson, E.M., and Kayce, M.M. 1966. Sex and race differences in response to drug treatment among schizophrenics. *Psychopharm. Bull.* **9**:3–47.

Goldman-Rakič, P.S. 1987. Circuitry of primate prefrontal cortex and regulation of behavior by representational memory. In *Handbook of Physiology: The Nervous System. Vol. 5*, ed. F. Plum, pp. 373–417. Bethesda, MD: American Physiological Society.

Goldstein, J., Faraone, S., Chen, W., and Tsuang, M. 1992. Gender and the familial risk for schizophrenia: disentangling confounding factors. *Schizophr. Res.* **7**:135–40.

Goldstein, J.M. 1988. Gender differences in the course of schizophrenia. *Am. J. Psychiatry* **145**:684–9.

Goldstein, J.M., Faraone, S.V., Chen, W.J., and Tolomiczencko, G.S. 1990. Sex differences in the familial transmission of schizophrenia. *Br. J. Psychiatry* **156**:819–26.

Goldstein, J.M. and Kreisman, D. 1988. Gender, family environment and schizophrenia. *Psychol. Med.* **18**:861–72.

Goldstein, J.M. and Link, B.G. 1988. Gender and the expression of schizophrenia. *J. Psychiatr. Res.* **22**:141–55.

Goldstein, M.J., Rodnick, E.H., Evans, J.R., May, P.R.A., and Steinberg, M.R. 1978. Drug and family therapy in the aftercare of acute schizophrenics. *Arch. Gen. Psychiatry* **35**:1169–77.

Goodman, R. 1991. Developmental disorders and structural brain development. In *Biological risk factors for psychosocial disorders*, ed. M. Rutter and P. Casaer, pp. 20–49. Cambridge, England: Cambridge University Press.

Gottesman, I.I. and Shields, J. 1976. A critical review of recent adoption, twin and family studies of schizophrenia: behavioral genetics perspectives. *Schizophr. Bull.* **2**:360–401.

Grimm, V.E. and Frieder, B. 1985. Differential vulnerability of male and female rats to the timing of various perinatal insults. *Int. J. Neurosci.* **27**:155–64.

Gur, R.E., Mozley, P.D., Resnick, S.M., and Shtasel, D. 1991. Magnetic resonance imaging in schizophrenia: I. Volumetric analysis of brain and cerebrospinal fluid. *Arch. Gen. Psychiatry* **48**:407–12.

Haas, G.L., Escobar, M., Sweeney, J.A., and Keshavan, M.S. 1995a. Sex differences in age at onset in schizophrenia: evidence for a subgroup of females with delayed illness onset. *Schizophr. Res.* **15**:1–2.

Haas, G.L., Frances, A.J. and the TSS Collaborative Study Group. 1992. Gender differences in changes in psychopathology: response to maintenance medication and family treatment. *Poster presented at the 31st Annual Meeting of the American College of Neuropsychopharmacology*, San Juan, Puerto Rico.

Haas, G.L., Glick, I.D., Clarkin, J.F., and Spencer, J.H. 1990. Gender and schizophrenia outcome: a clinical trial of an inpatient family intervention. *Schizophr. Bull.* **16**:277–92.

Haas, G.L., Keshavan, M.S., Schooler, N.R., Bagwell, W.W., and Pettegrew, J.W. 1995b. Temporal cortical volume correlates with illness duration in first episode schizophrenia. *Poster presented at the 34th Annual Meeting of the American College of Neuropsychopharmacology*, San Juan, Puerto Rico.

Haas, G.L. and Sweeney, J. 1992. Premorbid and onset features of first-episode schizophrenia. *Schizophr. Bull.* **18**:373–86.

Haas, G.L., Sweeney, J.A., Hien, D.A., Goldman, D., and Deck, M. 1991. Gender differences in schizophrenia. *Paper presented at the Third International Congress on Schizophrenia Research*, Tucson, Arizona.

Häfner, H., Behrens, S., de Vry, J., and Gattaz, W.F. 1991a. An animal model for the effects of estradiol on dopamine-mediated behavior: implications for sex differences in schizophrenia. *Psychiatry Res.* **38**:125–34.

Häfner, H., Haas, S., Pfeifer-Kurda, M., and Eichhorn, S. 1987. Abnormal seasonality of schizophrenic births: a specific finding? *Eur. Arch. Psychiatry Neurol. Sci.* **236**:333–42.

Häfner, H., Maurer, K., Löffler, W., and Riecher-Rössler, A.

1991b. Schizophrenie und Lebensalter. Schizophrenia and the life cycle. *Nervenarzt* **62**:536–48 (abstract).

Häfner, H., Maurer, K., Löffler, W., and Riecher-Rössler, A. 1993. The influence of age and sex on the onset and early course of schizophrenia. *Br. J. Psychiatry.* **162**:80–6.

Häfner, H., Riecher-Rossler, A., Fätkenheuer, B., and Hambrecht, M. 1991c. Sex differences in schizophrenia. *Psychiatria Fennica (Suppl).* **22**:123–156.

Häfner, H., Riecher, A., Maurer, K., and Löffler, W. 1989. How does gender influence age at first hospitalization for schizophrenia? A transnational case register study. *Psychol Med.* **19**:903–18.

Hambrecht, M., Maurer, K., and Häfner, H. 1992a. Evidence for a gender bias in epidemiological studies of schizophrenia. *Schizophr. Res.* 8: 223–31.

Hambrecht, M., Maurer, K., Häfner, H., and Sartorius, N. 1992b. Transnational stability of gender differences in schizophrenia? An analysis based on the WHO study on determinants of outcome of severe mental disorders. *Eur. Arch. Psychiatr. Clin. Neurosci.* **242**:6–12

Hambrecht, M., Riecher-Rössler, A., Fätkenheuer, B., Louzã, M.R., and Häfner, H. 1994. Higher morbidity risk for schizophrenia in males: fact or fiction? *Compr. Psychiatry* **35**:39–49.

Helgason, T. 1964. Epidemiology of mental disorders in Iceland. *Acta Psychiatr. Scand.* **40**:67–95.

Hogarty, G.E. 1974. Drug and sociotherapy in the aftercare of schizophrenic patients: III. Adjustment of nonrelapsed patients. *Arch. Gen. Psychiatry* 31: 609–18.

Hogarty, G.E. 1985. Expressed emotion and the schizophrenic relapse. In *Controversies in schizophrenia*, ed. M. Alpert, pp. 354–63. New York: Guilford Press.

Hogarty, G.E., Anderson, C.M., Reiss, D.J., and Kornblith, S.J. 1991. Family psychoeducation, social skills training, and maintenance chemotherapy in the aftercare treatment of schizophrenia: II. Two-year effects of a controlled study on relapse and adjustment. *Arch. Gen. Psychiatry* **48**: 340–7.

Hogarty, G.E., Goldberg, S., and Schooler, N.S. 1974. Drug and sociotherapy in the aftercare of schizophrenic patients: II. Two-year relapse rates. *Arch. Gen. Psychiatry* **31**:603–08.

Hogarty, G.E., Schooler, N.R., Ulrich, R., Mussare, F., Ferro, P., and Herron, E. 1979. Fluphenazine and social therapy in the aftercare of schizophrenic patients. *Arch. Gen. Psychiatry* **36**:1283–94.

Iacono, W. and Beiser, M. 1992. Where are the women in first-episode studies of schizophrenia? *Schizophr. Bull.* 18:471–80.

Ingvar, D. and Franzen, G. 1974. Abnormalities of cerebral blood flow distribution in patients with chronic schizophrenia. *Acta Psychiatr. Scand.* **50**:425–62.

Jablensky, A. 1986 Epidemiology of schizophrenia: a European perspective. *Schizophr. Bull.* **12**:52–73.

Jakob, H. and Beckmann, H. 1986. Prenatal developmental disturbances in the limbic allocortex in schizophrenics. *J. Neural Transm.* **65**: 303–26.

Janowsky, D., Gorney, R., Castelnuovo-Tedesco, P., and Stone, C. 1969. Premenstrual-menstrual increases in psychiatric admission rates. *Am. J. Obstet. and Gynecol.* **103**:189–91.

Johnstone, E.C. 1987. In vivo and post-mortem evidence of structural changes. In *Biological perspectives in schizophrenia. Dahlem Workshop Report LS 40*, ed. H. Helmchen and F.A. Henn, pp. 187–200. Cambridge: John Wiley and Sons.

Johnstone, E.C., Crow, T.J., Frith, C.D., Husband, J., and Kreel, L. 1976. Cerebral ventricular size and cognitive impairment in chronic schizophrenia. *Lancet* 2:924–26.

Joyce, P.R. 1984. Age of onset in bipolar affective disorder and misdiagnosis as schizophrenia. *Psychol. Med.* 14:145–9.

Keilp, J.G., Sweeney, J.A., Jacobsen, P., Solomon, C., St. Louis, L., Deck, M., Frances, A., and Mann, J.J. 1988. Cognitive impairment in schizophrenia: specific relations to ventricular size and negative symptomatology. *Biol. Psychiatry* **24**:47–55.

Keith, S.J., Regier, D.A., and Rae, D.S. 1991. Schizophrenic disorders. In *Psychiatric disorders in America: the Epidemiologic Catchment Area Study.* ed. L.N. Robins and D.A. Regier DA, pp. 33–52. New York: Free Press.

Kelsoe, J.R., Cadet, J.L., Pickar, D., and Weinberger, D.R. 1988. Quantitative neuroanatomy in schizophrenia: a controlled magnetic resonance imaging study. *Arch. Gen. Psychiatry* **45**:533–41.

Kendell, R.E., Chalmers, J.C., and Platz, C.L. 1987. Epidemiology of puerperal psychoses. *Br. J. Psychiatry* **150**:662–73.

Kendler, K.S., Tsuang, M.T., and Hays, P. 1987. Age at onset in schizophrenia: a familial perspective. *Arch. Gen. Psychiatry.* **44**: 881–90.

Kimura, D. 1992. Sex differences in the brain. *Scientific American* September: 118–25.

Kimura, D. and Harshman, R. 1984. Sex differences in brain organization for verbal and non-verbal functions. *Prog. Brain Res.* **61**:423–41.

Kirkegaard-Sorensen, L. and Mednick, S.A. 1975. Registered criminality in families with children at high risk for schizophrenia. *J. Abnorm. Psychol.* **84**:197–204.

Klorman, R., Strauss, J.S., and Kokes, R.F. 1977. Premorbid adjustment in schizophrenia: III. The relationship of demographic and diagnostic factors to measures of premorbid adjustment in schizophrenia. *Schizophr. Bull.* **3**: 214–25.

Kovelman, J.A. and Scheibel, A.B. 1984. A neurohistological correlate of schizophrenia. *Biol. Psychiatry* **19**:1601–21.

Kraepelin, E. 1919/1987 *Dementia praecox and paraphrenia.* Huntington, New York: Robert E. Krieger Publishing Co., Inc..

Kringlen, E. 1987. Contributions of genetic studies on schizophrenia. In *Search for the causes of schizophrenia*, ed. H. Hafner, W.F. Gattaz and W. Janzarik, pp. 123–43. Heidelberg: Springer.

Leff, J. and Vaughn, C. 1980. The interaction of life events and relatives' expressed emotion in schizophrenia and depressive neurosis. *Br. J. Psychiatry* **136**:146–53.

Leventhal, D.B., Schuck, J.R., and Rothstein, H. 1984. Gender differences in schizophrenia. *J. Nervous Mental Dis.* **172**:464–7.

Lewine, R. 1985. Schizophrenia: an amotivational syndrome in men. *Can. J. Psychiatry* **30**:316–18.

Lewine, R.J. and Meltzer, H.Y. 1984. Negative symptoms and platelet monoamine oxidase activity in male schizophrenic patients. *Psychiatr. Res.* **12**:99–109.

Lewine, R.R. 1980. Sex differences in age of symptom onset and first hospitalization in schizophrenia. *Am. J. Orthopsychiatry* **50**:316–22.

Lewine, R.R. 1981. Sex differences in schizophrenia: timing or subtypes? *Psychol. Bull.* **90**:432–44.

Lewine, R.R., Burbach, D., and Meltzer, H.Y. 1984. Effect of diagnostic criteria on the ratio of male to female schizophrenic patients. *Am. J. Psychiatry* **141**:84–7.

Lewis, S.W., Owen, M.J., and Murray, R.M. 1989. Obstetric complications and schizophrenia: methodology and mechanisms. In *Schizophrenia: Scientific Progress*, ed. C. Schulz and C.A. Tamminga, pp. 56–68. New York, NY,

US: Oxford University Press.

Lieberman, J., Alvir, J., Woerner, M., Degreef, G., Bilder, R.M., Ashtari, M., Bogerts, B., Mayerhoff, Geisler, H., Loebel, A., Levy, D.L., Hinrichsen, G., Szymanski, S., Koreen, A., Borenstein, M., and Kane, J.M. 1992a. Prospective study of psychobiology in first-episode schizophrenia at Hillside Hospital. *Schizophr. Bull.* **18**: 351–71.

Lieberman, J., Borenstein, M. and the TSS Study Group. 1992b. Clinical response of first episode schizophrenic patients to maintenance medication and family treatment. *Poster presented at the 31st Annual Meeting of the American College of Neuropsychopharmacology*, San Juan, Puerto Rico.

Lindelius, R. 1970. A study of schizophrenia. *Acta Psychiatr. Scand.* **21**:6–126.

Link, B. and Dohrenwend, B. 1980. Formulation of hypotheses about the ratio of untreated to treated cases in the true prevalence studies of functional psychiatric disorders in adults in the United States. In *Mental Illness in the United States*, ed. B.P. Dohrenwend, B.S. Dohrenwend, M.S. Gould, B. Link, et al, pp. 133–49. New York: Praeger.

Lo, W.H., Lo, T. 1977 A ten-year follow-up study of Chinese schizophrenics in Hong Kong. *Br. J. Psychiatry* **131**:63 6.

Loranger, A.W. 1984. Sex differences in age at onset of schizophrenia. *Arch. Gen. Psychiatry* **41**:157–61.

Lunsing, R.J., Hadders-Algra, M., Huisjes, H.J., and Touwen, B.C. 1992. Minor neurological dysfunction from birth to 12 years. II: Puberty is related to decreased dysfunction. *Dev. Med. Child Neurol.* **34**: 404–9.

Marcus, J., Hans, S.L., Auerbach, J.G., and Auerbach, A.G. 1993. Children at risk for schizophrenia: the Jerusalem Infant Development Study. II. Neurobehavioral deficits at school age. *Arch. Gen. Psychiatry* **50**:797–809.

McGee, M.G. 1982. Spatial abilities: the influence of genetic factors. In *Spatial orientation: developments and physiological bases*, ed. M. Potegal, pp. 199–222. New York: Academic Press.

McGlone, J. 1978. Sex differences in functional brain asymmetry. *Cortex* **14**: 122–8.

McGlone, J. 1980. Sex differences in human brain asymmetry: a critical survey. *Behav. Brain Sci.* **3**:215–63.

McGuffin, P. 1992. The strength of the genetic evidence – is there room for an environmental influence in etiology of schizophrenia? *Paper presented at the Annual Meeting of The Royal College of Psychiatrists*, Dublin, Ireland.

McNeil, T.F. and Kaij, L. 1978. Obstetric factors in the

development of schizophrenia: complications in the births of preschizophrenics and in reproduction by schizophrenic parents. In *The nature of schizophrenia: new approaches to research and treatment*, ed. L.C. Wynne, R.L. Cromwell and S. Matthysse, pp. 401–29. New York: John Wiley.

Mednick, S.A.and Cannon, T.D. 1991. Fetal development, birth and the syndromes of adult schizophrenia. In *Fetal neural Development and Adult Schizophrenia*, ed. S.A. Mednick, T.D. Cannon, C.E. Barr and M. Lyon, New York, NY: Cambridge University Press.

Meltzer, H.Y. and Fang,V.S. 1976. The effect of neuroleptics on serum prolactin in schizophrenic patients. *Arch. Gen. Psychiatry* 33:270–86.

Merrin, E.L. 1984. Motor and sighting dominance in chronic schizophrenics. Relationship to social competence, age at first admission, and clinical course. *Br. J. Psychiatry* 145: 401–6.

Michaux, W., Gansereit, K., McCabe, O., and Kurland, A. 1967. The psychopathology and measurement of environmental stress. *Commun. Ment. Health J.* 3: 358–72.

Murray, R.M., O'Callaghan, E., Castle, D.J., and Lewis, S.W. 1992. A neurodevelopmental approach to the classification of schizophrenia. *Schizophr.Bull.* 18:319–32.

Nasrallah, H.A., Schwarzkopf, S.B., Olson, S.C., and Coffman, J.A. 1990. Gender differences in schizophrenia on MRI brain scans. *Schizophr. Bull.* 16: 205–10.

Nasrallah, H.A. and Wilcox, J.A. 1989. Gender differences in the etiology and symptoms of schizophrenia: genetic versus brain injury factors. *Annal. Clin. Psychiatry* 1:51–3.

Nathan, R., Sachar, E., Ostrow, L., Asnis, G.M., Halbreich, U., Halpern, F., Renzi, N.L., and Slotnick, V. 1983. A preliminary study of sex-related differences in prolactin responses to dopamine blockade and insulin hypoglycemia and in penfluridol plasma levels in schizophrenic patients. *Psychopharmacology* 80:46–9.

Nuechterlein, K., Dawson, K., Gitlin, M., and Ventura, J. 1992. Developmental processes in schizophrenic disorders: longitudinal studies of vulnerability and stress. *Schizophr. Bull.* 18:387–425.

Nyman, A.K. 1978. Non-regressive schizophrenia. Clinical course and outcome. *Acta Psychiatr. Scand., (Suppl.)* 272:1–143.

O'Callaghan, E., Gibson, T., Colohan, H.A., Buckley, P., Walshe, D.G., and Larkin, C. 1992. Risk of schizophrenia in adults born after obstetric complications and their association with early onset of illness: a controlled study. *Br. Med. J.* 305:1256–59.

Offord, D.R. 1974. School performance of adult schizophrenics, their siblings and age mates. *Br. J. Psychiatry* 125:12–19.

Owen, M.J., Lewis, S.W., and Murray, R.M. 1988. Obstetric complications and schizophrenia: a computed tomographic study. *Psychol. Med.* 18:331–9.

Park, S. and Holzman, P.S., 1992. Schizophrenics show spatial working memory deficits, *Arch. Gen. Psychiatry.* 49:975–82.

Pearlson, G.D., Kim, W.S., Kubos, K.L., and Moberg, P.J. 1989. Ventricle–brain ratio, computed tomographic density, and brain area in 50 schizophrenics. *Arch. Gen. Psychiatry* 46:690–7.

Perry, W., Moore, D., and Braff, D. 1995. Gender differences on thought disturbance measures among schizophrenic patients. *Am. J. Psychiatry* 152:1298–301.

Phillips, L. 1953. Case history data and prognosis in schizophrenia. *J. Nerv. Ment. Dis.* 117:515–25.

Piran, N., Bigler, E.D., and Cohen, D. 1982. Motoric laterality and eye dominance suggest unique pattern of cerebral organization in schizophrenia. *Arch. Gen. Psychiatry* 39:1006–10.

Pogue-Geile, M.F. and Harrow, M. 1984. Negative and positive symptoms in schizophrenia and depression: a follow up. *Schizophr. Bull.* 10:371–87.

Polefrone, J.M. and Manuck, S.B. 1987. Gender differences in cardiovascular and neuroendocrine response to stressors. In *Gender and Stress*, ed. C.B. Rosalind, L. Biener and G. K. Baruch, pp. 13–38. New York: Free Press.

Pulver, A.E., Brown, C.H., Wolyniec, P., and McGrath, J. 1990. Schizophrenia: age at onset, gender and familial risk. *Acta Psychiatr. Scand.* 82:344–51.

Raine, A., Harrison, G.N., Reynolds, G.P., and Sheard, C. 1990 Structural and functional characteristics of the corpus callosum in schizophrenics, psychiatric controls, and normal controls: a magnetic resonance imaging and neuropsychological evaluation. Fifth Biennial Winter Workshop on Schizophrenia (1990, Badgastein, Austria). *Arch. Gen. Psychiatry* 47: 1060–4.

Riecher-Rössler, A., Fätkenheuer, B., Löffler, W., Maurer, K., and Häfner, H. 1992. Is age of onset in schizophrenia influenced by marital status? Some remarks on the difficulties and pitfalls in the systematic testing of a "simple" question. *Soc. Psychiatry Psychiatr. Epidemiol.* 27:122–8.

Riecher-Rössler, A. and Häfner, H. 1993. Schizophrenia and oestrogens: is there an association? *Eur. Arch. Psychiatry Clin. Neurosci.* **242**:323–8.

Roberts, G.W. 1990. Schizophrenia: the cellular biology of a functional psychosis. *Trends Neurosci.* **13**: 207–11.

Rosen, B., Klein, D.F., and Gittleman-Klein, R. 1969. Sex differences in the relationship between premorbid asociality and posthospital outcome. *J. Nerv. Ment. Dis.* **149**:415–20.

Rosenthal, D. 1962. Familial concordance by sex with respect to schizophrenia. *Psychol. Bull.* **59**:401–21.

Rosenthal, R. and Bigelow, L. 1972. Quantitative brain measurements in chronic schizophrenia. *Br. J. Psychiatry* **121**:259–64.

Salokangas, R.K. 1983. Prognostic implications of the sex of schizophrenic patients. *Br. J. Psychiatry* **142**:145–51.

Salokangas, R.K. and Stengård, E. 1990. Gender and short-term outcome in schizophrenia. *Schizophr. Res.* **3**:333–45.

Scheibel, A.B. and Kovelman, J.A. 1981. Disorientation of the hippocampal pyramidal cell and its processes in the schizophrenic patient. *Biol. Psychiatry* **16**:101–2.

Schneider, K. 1959. *Klinische psychopathologie*, 5th edn. New York: Grune and Stratton.

Schooler, C. 1963. Affiliation among schizophrenics: preferred characteristics of the other. *J. Nerv. Ment. Dis.* **137**:438–46.

Schooler, N., Keith, S., Severe, J., Mathews, S., Bellack, A., Glick, I., Gargreaves, W., Kane, J., Ninan, P., Frances, A., Jacobs. M., Lieberman, A., Mancc, R., Simpson, G., and Woerner, M. Relapse and rehospitalization during maintenance treatment of schizophrenia: the effects of dose reduction and family treatment. *Arch. Gen. Psychiatry* (in press).

Seeman, M. and Hauser, P. 1984. Schizophrenia: the influence of gender on family environment. *Int. J. Family Psychiatry* **5**: 227–32.

Seeman, M.V. 1983. Interaction of sex, age, and neuroleptic dose. *Compr. Psychiatry* **24**:125–8.

Seeman, M.V. 1985. Sex and schizophrenia. *Can. J. Psychiatry* **30**:313–5.

Seeman, M.V. 1986. Current outcome in schizophrenia: women vs men. *Acta Psychiatr. Scand.* **73**:609–17.

Seeman, M.V. 1989. Prenatal gonadal hormones and schizophrenia in men and women. *Psychiatr. J. Univ. Ottawa* **14**:473–5.

Seeman, P. 1988. Tardive dyskinesia, dopamine receptors, and neuroleptic damage to cell membranes. *J. Clin. Psychopharmacol. (Suppl.)* **8**:3S–9S.

Shtasel, D., Gur, R.E., Gallacher, F., Heimberg, C., Cannon, T., and Gur, R.C. 1992. Phenomenology and functioning in first-episode schizophrenia. *Schizophr. Bull.* **18**:449–69.

Simpson, G.M., Yadalam, K.G., Levinson, D.F., Stephanos, M.J., Sing Lo, E.E., and Cooper, T.B. 1990. Single dose pharmacokinetics of fluphenazine after fluphenazine decanoate administration *J. Clin. Psychopharmacol.* **10**:417–21.

Spencer, J.H., Glick, I.D., Haas, G.L., and Clarkin, J.F. 1988. A randomized clinical trial of inpatient family intervention: III. Effects at 6–month and 18–month follow-ups. *Am. J. Psychiatry* **145**:1115–21.

Spitzer, R.L., Endicott, J., and Robins, E. 1975. *Research diagnostic criteria*, New York: Biometrics Research Division, New York State Psychiatric Institute.

Sweeney, J.A., Mintun, M.A., Kwee, S., Wiseman, M.B., Brown, D.L., Rosenberg, D.R., and Carl, J.R. 1996. Positron emission tomography study of voluntary saccadic eye movements and spatial working memory. *J. Neurophysiol.* **75**:454 68.

Suddath, R.L., Casanova, M.F., Goldberg, T.E., and Daniel, D.G. 1989. Temporal lobe pathology in schizophrenia: a quantitative magnetic resonance imaging study. 141st Annual Meeting of the American Psychiatric Association (1988, Montreal, Canada). *Am. J. Psychiatry* **146**:464–72.

Suddath, R.L., Christison, G.W., Torrey, E.F., and Casanova, M.F. 1990. Anatomical abnormalities in the brains of monozygotic twins discordant for schizophrenia. *New Engl. J. Med.* **322**:789–94.

Swaab, D.F. and Fliers, E. 1985. A sexually dimorphic nucleus in the human brain. *Science* **228**:1112–15.

Taylor, D.C. 1969. Differential rates of cerebral maturation between sexes and between hemispheres. Evidence from epilepsy. *Lancet* **2**:140–2.

Tsuang, M.T., Dempsey, G., and Rauscher, F. 1976. A study of "atypical schizophrenia": comparison with schizophrenia and affective disorder by sex, age of admission, precipitant, outcome, and family history. *Arch. Gen. Psychiatry* **33**:1157–60.

Von Korff, M. 1985. Prevalence of treated and untreated DSM-III schizophrenia: results of a two–stage community survey. *J. Nerv. Mental Dis.* **173**:577–81.

Wada, J.A., Clarke, R., and Hamm, A. 1975. Cerebral
    hemispheric asymmetry in humans. Cortical speech zones
    in 100 adults and 100 infant brains. *Arch. Neurol.*
    32:239–46.

Waddington, J.L., O'Callaghan, E., and Larkin, C. 1990.
    Physical anomalies and neurodevelopmental abnormality in
    schizophrenia: new clinical correlates. *Schizophr. Res.* 3:90.

Walker, E., Bettes, B.A., Kain, E., and Harvey, P. 1985.
    Relationship of gender and marital status with
    symptomatology in psychotic patients. *J. Abnorm. Psychol.*
    94:42–50.

Watt, D., Katz, K., and Shepherd, M. 1983. The natural history
    of schizophrenia: a 5–year prospective follow–up of a
    representative sample of schizophrenics by means of a
    standardized clinical and social assessment. *Psychol. Med.*
    13:663–70.

Watt, D.C. and Szulecka, T.K. 1979. The effect of sex, marriage
    and age at first admission on the hospitalization of
    schizophrenics during 2 years following discharge. *Psychol.
    Med.* 9:529–39.

Weinberger, D.R., Berman, K.F., and Zec, R.F. 1986.
    Physiologic dysfunction of dorsolateral prefrontal cortex in
    schizophrenia: I. Regional cerebral blood flow evidence.
    Arch. Gen. Psychiatry 43:114–24.

Weinberger, D.R., Torrey, E.F., Neophytides, A.N., and Wyatt,
    R.J. 1979. Lateral ventricular enlargement in chronic
    schizophrenia. *Arch. Gen. Psychiatry* 36: 735–9.

Weissman, M.M. and Klerman, G.L. 1977. Sex differences and
    the epidemiology of depression. *Arch. Gen. Psychiatry*
    34:98–111.

Westermeyer, J.F. and Harrow, M. 1986. Predicting outcome in
    schizophrenics and nonschizophrenics of both sexes: the
    Zigler-Phillips Social Competence Scale. *J. Abnorm.
    Psychol.* 95:406–9.

Wilcox, J.A. and Nasrallah, H.A. 1987. Perinatal insult as a risk
    factor in paranoid and nonparanoid schizophrenia.
    Psychopathology 20:285–7.

Witelson, S.F. 1989. Hand and sex differences in the isthmus
    and genu of the human corpus callosum. A post-mortem
    morphological study. *Brain* 112:799–835.

Woerner, M.G., Borenstein, M., and the TSS Study Group.
    1992. Gender effects on outcome of maintenance
    medication and family treatment. *Poster presented at the
    American College of Neuropsychopharmacology Annual
    Meeting*, San Juan, Puerto Rico.

Woodruff, P.W., Pearlson, G.D., Geer, M.J., Barta, P.E., and
    Chilcoat, H.D. 1993. A computerized magnetic resonance
    imaging study of corpus callosum morphology in
    schizophrenia. *Psychol. Med.* 23:45–56.

World Health Organization. 1977. *Manual of the International
    Statistical Classification of Diseases, Injuries, and Causes of
    Death*, 9th revision, Geneva: WHO.

Yonkers, K.A., Kando, J.C., Cole, J.O., and Blumenthal, S. 1992.
    Gender differences in pharmacokinetics and
    pharmacodynamics of psychotropic medication (see
    comments). *Am. J. Psychiatry* 149:587–95 Review.

Zigler, E. and Levine, J. 1973. Premorbid adjustment and
    paranoid-nonparanoid status in schizophrenia: a further
    investigation. *J. Abnorm. Psychol.* 82: 189–99.

Zigler, E., Levine, J., and Zigler, B. 1977. Premorbid social
    competence and paranoid-nonparanoid status in female
    schizophrenic patients. *J. Nerv. Mental Dis.* 164:333–9.

Zigler, E. and Phillips, L. 1960. Social effectiveness and
    symptomatic behaviors. *J. Abnorm. Soc. Psychol.* 61:231–8.

Zigler, E. and Phillips, L. 1962. Social competence and the
    process-reactive distinction in psychopathology. *J. Abnorm.
    Psychol.* 65:215–22.

12 Psychopathology and brain dysfunction: structural imaging studies

SHÔN LEWIS

INTRODUCTION

Noninvasive structural imaging techniques began to have an impact on schizophrenia research in the early 1980s. Computed tomography (CT) allowed the limited quantitative analysis of brain structure during life in large samples of schizophrenic subjects and controls. Using CT, the main measurable region within the brain was the area or volume occupied by the lateral cerebral ventricles. CT became the focus of most of the research in the first years of the 1980s because of its measurability. Early studies were more or less unanimous in showing statistical enlargement of lateral ventricles in schizophrenic patients compared with matched controls. Paradoxically, the size of this effect became less and less as the studies became more and more sophisticated in terms of the representative nature of the patient and control samples. Initially, the enlargements of cerebral fluid spaces was taken to represent a process of cerebral atrophy. It was the change of interpretation of these findings in the mid-1980s that was one of the founding observations which fueled the emergence of the neurodevelopmental hypothesis of schizophrenia.

Historical aspects

The interpretation of the first wave of CT studies in the early 1980s was that the fluid spaces were enlarged in the manner of so-called secondary hydrocephalus: an increased volume of cerebrospinal fluid as a result of wasting of brain tissue. Clinicians were familiar with this picture as being typical of global neurodegenerative conditions such as Alzheimer's disease, alcoholism, and other progressive dementias. The notion, in the mid-1980s, that the natural history of these findings was perhaps neurodevelopmental rather than degenerative has been criticized as going beyond the limits of the data (Lewis 1990): later CT studies were to show the effect size of lateral ventricular enlargement to be considerably less than initially claimed. None the less the value of this reinterpretation was essentially heuristic. Formulating schizophrenia as a neurodevelopmental disorder has been one of the most productive scientific milestones, generating a host of testable hypotheses.

It is sobering to reflect that a similar reformulation about dementia praecox happened in the first decade of the 20th century, but has been largely forgotten. Before plausible hypotheses about the cause of schizophrenia became lost in psychobiology and psychoanalysis, there were a few years when opinion leaders on both sides of the Atlantic came similarly to reinterpret neuropathological findings in schizophrenia. This included Kraepelin, whose initial model was that it was a neurodegenerative disorder. In the second half of his career, Kraepelin reformulated his thinking, proposing that many cases of dementia praecox might be the result of prenatal developmental abnormalities such as cerebral infection during pregnancy. What had been seen as atrophic lesions in the brain were revised as being "early hypoplasias" (for a review see Lewis 1989). Writers such as Rosanoff and Southard clearly saw the pathological findings in their case series as being of embryological rather than adult acquired origin and "a congenital or early acquired basis for the development of dementia praecox" was proposed. The possible importance of "intrauterine disease" was mooted and, in a striking anticipation of current thinking, MacKenzie (1912) considered that dementia praecox patients were "the victims of a brain deformity which does not manifest itself till late in life"; Turner (1912) put forward the hypothesis that developmentally acquired structural brain deficits remained quiescent until the stresses of adult life acted upon them to produce psychotic symptoms.

These formulations seem swiftly to have been lost in the paradigm shift that resulted from psychoanalytic theory particularly in the USA between the wars. It was not until the deployment of noninvasive brain imaging in the late 1970s coincided with, and to some extent generated, the renaissance in biological psychiatry, that neuroscientific approaches to schizophrenia were sufficiently mature again to see the re-emergence of the neurodevelopmental hypothesis.

THE COMPUTED TOMOGRAPHY LITERATURE: SUBCORTICAL CHANGES

By the early 1990s there were over 50 controlled studies in the world literature which examined some aspect of brain structure in schizophrenic patients using CT. A critical review needs to consider only those studies in which controls were prospectively ascertained healthy volunteers, scanned concurrently with the patient group. The 21 studies meeting these criteria have been reviewed (Lewis 1990). In comparison with less well-controlled studies, a relatively high proportion of these studies failed to show significant CT abnormalities in schizophrenic patients. Of these 21 studies nine could not demonstrate lateral ventricular enlargement in the patient group and a further three showed this at only marginal degrees of statistical significance.

Besides lateral ventricular size, studies increasingly looked for a difference in other cerebral fluid spaces, in particular enlargement of the third ventricle and cerebral cortical sulci. Several studies reported an enlarged third ventricle or enlarged cortical sulci in the absence of significant lateral ventricular changes. Other claims, such as enlarged cerebellar sulci, widened Sylvian and interhemispheric fissures, and asymmetry of occipital pole size, have not been well replicated.

The disparity even between well-controlled studies again points to the likelihood of methodological confounding factors. Although the studies reviewed had as their minimum requirement a control group of prospectively scanned healthy volunteers, the decision about which variables should be matched between patients and controls is still at issue. Certainly, age and sex should be matched. In addition, there is evidence that other demographic factors can influence measures of brain structure: social class (Pearlson *et al.* 1985), height, ethnicity (Nimgaonkar *et al.* 1988) and educational level (DeMeyer *et al.* 1988), for example. Another issue left in need of further clarification by CT was the specificity of reported abnormalities to schizophrenia. Most of the changes in schizophrenia have also been reported in other severe "functional" psychiatric disorders, including affective disorders, obsessive-compulsive disorder and anorexia nervosa.

Focal neurodevelopmental lesions

As well as the minor degrees of enlargement of ventricles and sulci found in the majority of studies there are a handful of reports in the literature of gross focal brain lesions in schizophrenia: aqueduct stenosis (Reveley and Reveley 1983), arachnoid and septal cysts (Kuhnley *et al.* 1981; Lewis and Mezey 1985), and agenesis of the corpus callosum (Lewis *et al.* 1988).

Four studies enable an estimate to be made of the prevalence of such focal lesions on brain imaging in schizophrenia. Owens *et al.* (1980), in their series of 136 schizophrenic patients, found "unsuspected intracranial pathology" as a focal finding on CT in 12 cases (9%), excluding lesions due to leukotomy. Five of these 12 were aged over 65 years. Lewis (1987) examined a series of 228 Maudsley Hospital patients who met Research Diagnostic Criteria (RDC) for schizophrenia and who had been consecutively scanned for clinical reasons. Patients with a history of epilepsy or intracranial surgery, or who were aged over 65 years at the time of scan, were excluded. The original scan reports were examined and the films of those not unequivocally normal were reappraised by a neuroradiologist blind to the original report. In 41 patients the scan showed a definite intracranial abnormality. This was in the nature of enlarged fluid spaces in 28 cases, but in 13 patients (6%) there was a discrete focal lesion. These 13 lesions varied widely in location and probable pathology, although left temporal and right parietal regions were most commonly implicated. The third study (S.W. Lewis and M.A. Reveley, unpublished results) was an attempt to examine a geographically defined sample of schizophrenic patients, ascertained as part of a large, multidisciplinary survey (Brugha *et al.* 1988). All catchment area residents who, on a particular census day, were aged 18–65 years and were in regular contact with any psychiatric day service were approached. Of 120 eligible people, 83 consented to CT and psychiatric interview. Fifty of these met RDC for schizophrenia or schizoaffective disorder. In four of these 50 patients clinically unsuspected focal lesions were found: low density in the right caudate head; a left occipitotemporal porencephalic cyst; low-density regions in the right parietal lobe; agenesis of the corpus callosum (described further by Lewis *et al.* 1988). None of 50 matched healthy volunteers showed focal pathology on CT. Using MRI, O'Callaghan *et al.* (1992) found definite focal neurodevelopmental lesions in four of 47 prospectively scanned cases of schizophrenia: one had partial agenesis of the corpus callosum.

Given the differences in the nature of the patient samples, these three studies are in rough agreement about the prevalence of unexpected focal (usually neurodevelopmental) abnormalities on CT: between 6 and 9%.

Cerebral cortical volume deficits in schizophrenia

The widespread use of X-ray CT as a research tool in schizophrenia set the scene for the establishment of the neurodevelopmental hypothesis. None the less, the limitations of X-ray CT were considerable in that it showed little in the way of anatomical detail within brain substance. This meant that testing hypotheses to do with abnormalities in specific brain compartments was not possible. The field has had to wait for the emergence of magnetic resonance imaging (MRI) to enable this. MR images derive from proton density rather than electron density and effectively reflect differences in water content between different tissues. This enables the white matter to be differentiated from gray matter within the brain and coupled with multiplanar resegmentation and high resolution, this has led to the testing of more interesting

hypotheses in schizophrenia than was ever possible with CT.

In the late 1980s the first wave of MRI studies essentially aimed at replicating the findings already established with CT: that there were increases in the volume of cerebrospinal fluid (CSF) spaces in schizophrenic subjects compared with controls. The new interest in post-mortem studies (see Chapter 13 by Kotrla *et al.*) had by the end of the 1980s focused attention on histopathological changes in the medial temporal lobe. A second wave of MRI studies pursued this notion and reported measurable reduction in gray matter volume in medial temporal lobe structures including hippocampus – amygdala and parahippocampal gyrus. These changes are probably bilateral although some earlier studies found evidence that changes were largely confined to the left side (Bogerts *et al.* 1993).

Most recently, a third wave of studies has extended the area of interest from the gray matter of the medial temporal lobe to cortical gray matter in general. The first studies to look at this systematically were Zipursky *et al.* (1992) and Harvey *et al.* (1993). Both these groups used carefully ascertained subjects with controls matched on a variety of measures, with covariance for age and head size. Both reported a generalized reduction in cortical gray matter volume over the brain of between 4 and 18% in schizophrenia compared with control subjects. A series of similar studies has now been reported at least in abstract form and these are tabulated in the Table 12.1. Zipursky's group replicated their findings, which were originally in male subjects, in female subjects (Lauriello *et al.* 1995). In both studies, there was a percentage reduction in cortical grey matter volume of about 7%, equivalent to about 1.2 standard deviations of the normal control mean. This was significant at the $p < 0.01$ level in each study. The volume reduction was confined to cerebral cortical gray matter and not white matter and this has been replicated subsequently in other studies (Table 12.1). Harvey *et al.* (1993) matched healthy community controls for age, sex, ethnicity and family socioeconomic status and showed a significant reduction in cortical gray matter volume. In a subsequent study by this group reduction was found to be specific to patients with schizophrenia when compared with patients with bipolar disorder, who did not show such a deficit (Harvey *et al.* 1994). Results from three first episode

Table 12.1. *Is there decreased cerebral cortical volume in schizophrenia? MRI studies*

	No. of subjects Patients: controls	Analysis controlled for	Cortical volumes Patient versus controls: Mean (SD): ml	%Reduction in cortical gray, with significance
Zipursky *et al.* (1992) (1992)	22:20	Age, height, sex (all male) handedness, ethnicity	z-scores quoted 1.15 of 1 SD	$P<0.01$
Harvey *et al.* (1993)	48:34:26 BP	Age, sex, ethnicity, family SES, height, intracranial volume	Men 264 versus 275 Women 235 versus 225	Women 4.4% Men 4.0% $P=0.03$
Schlaepfer *et al.* (1994)	46:60:27 BP	Age, sex, family SES	688(97) versus 722 (73) versus 700(90) BP	4.7%: NS
Bilder *et al.* (1994)	53:45 (first episode)	Age, height	Men 999(114) versus 1038(7) Women 894(85) versus 919(90)	Men: 3.8%NS Women: 2.8%
Pieri *et al.* (1995)	17:15 (first episode)	Age, sex, cranial size, ethnicity, family SES	704(87) versus 746 (122)	5.6% $P<0.01$
Lim *et al.* (1995)	29:53 (first episode)	Volume intracranial	z-scores quoted	0.63 of 1 SD $P<0.05$
Lauriello *et al.* (1995)	19:20	Age, sex (all female)	z-scores quoted	1.2 of 1SD $P<0.01$

Notes:
NS: not significant; SES: socioeconomic status

studies have been reported. Preliminary results from the studies of Pieri *et al.* (1995) and Lim *et al.* (1995) both showed significant cerebral cortical gray matter volume reductions in schizophrenic patients. The study of Bilder *et al.* (1994) showed a 4% reduction in mean cortical gray matter volume compared with healthy controls, but this did not achieve statistical significance. Although this study examined a well-characterized sample of first episode patients, there was a marked imbalance in important confounding variables such as ethnicity between patient and control groups in this study, now known to be a potent confounding variable (Harvey *et al.* 1993); also volumetric measures were covaried simply by height rather than intracranial size. Schlaepfer *et al.* (1994) found a 5% reduction in cortical gray matter volume in schizophrenic subjects. Although this did not achieve statistical significance, interestingly, those regions of cortex thought to comprise heteromodal association cortex, if measured separately, were significantly reduced compared with controls.

Collectively, these recent findings are compelling and suggest there is a 5–8% global reduction in cortical gray matter volume in schizophrenia. Several of the studies (Table 12.1) have looked for and failed to find a correlation between length of illness and degree of volumetric reduction, which suggests again that this change is developmental rather than degenerative in pathology. Certainly, neurodegenerative disorders such as chronic alcoholism and Alzheimer's disease lead to a parallel reduction in volume of cortical gray and subcortical white matter. The latter is not seen in schizophrenia.

These findings allow us to assemble a more refined hypothesis about the pathogenesis of schizophrenia. Schizophrenia is likely to be a mainly genetic neurodevelopmental disorder of cerebral cortex, perhaps particularly the association cortex. This hypothesis records well with other recent findings documenting premorbid cognitive and behavioural deficits in preschizophrenic children. For instance, Jones et al. (1994) found evidence for delays in motor and cognitive milestones at many developmental points suggesting that, in the long view, schizophrenia does seem to involve developmental disturbances attributable to widespread regions of the cerebral cortex. If there is a neurodevelopmental abnormality of cortical genesis in schizophrenia, what is known about processes leading to cortical dysgenesis in general?

The causes of cortical dysgenesis

With the exception of the recent reports of enlargements in striatal structures, which seem to be a consequence of chronic neuroleptic administration (Chakos et al. 1994), the structural brain changes reported in schizophrenia do not appear to be progressive. As noted, the most recent findings of global or at least widespread volumetric reductions in cerebral cortical gray matter are of interest because, in contrast to degenerative brain disorders such as is seen in Alzheimer's disease or chronic alcoholism, there is no concomitant loss of white matter volume (Zipursky et al. 1992). Furthermore, unlike enlarged lateral ventricles which have been reported in a wide variety of psychiatric and neurological disorders, reduced

cortical volume seems to be specific to schizophrenia (Harvey et al. 1994). The pathological process responsible is in the nature of a cortical dysgenesis rather than a cortical atrophy. Is this the process central to the pathogenesis of schizophrenia?

The stages of normal brain development are detailed elsewhere in this volume. The embryology of cortical development begins with the mitotic proliferation of precursor cells in the germinal plate. The postmitotic neuroblasts migrate outwards along radial glial tracts, sticking on as a result of specific cell adhesion molecules. This mainly occurs between the seventh and 16th weeks of gestation. The first cohort of cells to migrate will form the deepest layer of the mature cortex. A quarter to a half of these early neuroblasts will later undergo programed cell death (Sarnat 1991). Techniques of tagging cell clones with retroviral vectors have shown that clones of cells show widespread dispersion into the cortical plate, at least to begin with, and there is a subsequent process of transverse migration within the cortical plate (Walsh and Cepko 1993). Ninety per cent are destined for the neocortex, the remainder going to form hippocampus, dentate gyrus and piriform cortex, whose pattern of development is somewhat different. Slightly later migratory movements involve clustering of cells with similar morphologies. Within this model, genetic mutations might affect neuroblasts either at the early progenitor stage, as with periventricular gray matter heterotopias, or the slightly later clustered stage, as in tuberous sclerosis. In neuronal clones in in vitro culture, all cells go on either to express γ-aminobutyric acid (GABA) or glutamate, in proportions similar to those found in vivo: about 1:4. The presence of glutamate in the cell culture will reduce the numbers of cells expressing it. Further stages of neuronal development include growth of axons, production of electrical excitability and neurotransmitters, and myelination, the last of which can continue into adolescence. Sulcal and gyral development starts in the 16th gestational week and carries for months after birth, possibly a faster rate of growth in the more superficial layers of the cortex causing a steady mechanical buckling of the surface.

Cerebral cortical dysgenesis is the term encompassing a variety of disorders of cortical development and organization. In theory, it can result from the failure of processes of migration either in its initiation, or in stopping inappropriately short of its true destination, in overshooting its true destination, or in the processes of apoptosis or further maturation. Failures at particular stages have been equated with particular morphological disorders (Rakic 1988). Traditional terminology in cortical dysgenesis names a range of overlapping conditions (Harding 1992). Pachygyria and microgyria are malformations of gyri. Lissencephaly is agyria with a reduction in the number of cortical layers and results from early disruptions in the generation of cortical neuroblasts. Schizencephaly comprises developmental clefts in the cortex and can arise from focal ischemia in the second trimester. Ectopic neuroblast migration can result in gray matter heterotopias, or focal cortical dysplasias where there is local disruption of cortical layering and the gray-white boundary. Developmental disruptions at the histological rather than gross level with misplaced neurons, for instance in the subcortical white matter, are often called microdysgenesis and have been reported in mental retardation and generalized epilepsy (Meencke 1994). Cortical dysgenesis is sometimes associated with neurodevelopmental tumors such as gangliogliomas. Cortical dysgenesis shows etiological heterogeneity with a variety of autosomal disorders such as Type 1 lissencephaly (chromosome 17p) or tuberous sclerosis (chromosome 9p) and X-linked disorders such as subependymal (periventricular) gray matter heterotopia, mostly seen in women, and Aicardi syndrome, the latter incorporating callosal agenesis. Environmental risk factors include intrauterine infections, poisons such as ethanol and mercury, local ischemia and ionizing radiation.

Schizophrenia as a neurodevelopmental syndrome: comparison with cerebral palsy

In an earlier review of the possible role of congenital risk factors in the etiology of schizophrenia (Lewis 1989) cerebral palsy was suggested as being a prototype neurodevelopmental disorder which might bear comparison in some respects to schizophrenia, and epidemiological comparisons have been made by McGrath and Murray (1995). Further recent research into the epidemiology, etiology, natural history and brain imaging aspects of cerebral palsy invites a revisit.

Both disorders, schizophrenia and cerebral palsy, are defined in terms of clusters of symptoms rather than any unifying pathology underlying them (Table 12.2). The current consensus definition is that cerebral palsy is an "umbrella term covering a group of nonprogressive, but often changing motor impairment syndromes secondary to lesions or anomalies of the brain arising in the early

Table 12.2. *Schizophrenia and cerebral palsy: an epidemiological comparison*

	Cerebral palsy	Schizophrenia
Nosological Status	Syndrome	Syndrome
Clinically apparent only after	Age 2 years	Age 16 years
Prevalence	2 per 1000	5 per 1000
Structural brain imaging	Gross anomalies in 15% periventricular atrophy; diffuse rather than focal changes; left hemisphere more usual	Gross anomalies in 5%: periventricular atrophy; diffuse rather than focal changes; left hemisphere more usual?
Risk factors:		
Family history	Yes	Yes
Maternal reproductive history (thyroid disorder)	Yes	Unknown
Major and minor physical anomalies	Yes	Yes
Low birth weight	Yes	Possibly (Rifkin *et al.* 1994)
Twin birth	Yes	Yes (Klaning *et al.* 1994)
Low social class	Yes	Yes
Weak association with BCs	Yes	Yes
Primary prevention	Unlikely: less than 3% of the top 5% high-risk pregnancies lead to cerebral palsy	Unlikely
Incidence trends	Increasing	Unknown

Note: BC: birth complications.

stages of its development" (Kuban and Leviton 1994). This statement is strikingly close to the notions concerning the nature of schizophrenia which emerged in the late 1980s (Murray and Lewis 1987; Weinberger 1987). The underlying notion here is that there is a nonprogressive underlying lesion whose cognitive and behavioral manifestations change over time as a result of essentially normal developmental changes occurring in the brain. Within this definition the main difference between the neurodevelopmental context of cerebral palsy and schizophrenia is that the critical gray areas involved mature much earlier in cerebral palsy (basal ganglia and associated pathways) than presumed critical sites in schizophrenia, such as the dorsolateral prefrontal cortex. Both are recognized to have a latent period which involves the disappearance of some symptoms and signs and the reappearance of others. In cerebral palsy, early relatively nonspecific signs such as hypotonia in the first months often evolve after the first months of life into extrapyramidal abnormalities and spasticity. As Kuban and Leviton note "the presumption is that myelination of axons and maturation of neurons in the basal ganglia are required before spasticity, dystonia and athetosis can be manifested". Recent work looking at large epidemiological cohorts over long periods of time has suggested that a similar picture is indeed true in schizophrenia (Jones et al. 1994). Early nonspecific cognitive motor and behavioral anomalies come and go long before the characteristic cluster of paranoid-hallucinatory symptoms emerge in early adult life.

The epidemiology of schizophrenia and cerebral palsy are compared in the Table 12.2. The classical risk factor mooted for cerebral palsy in the past was to do more or less specifically with perinatal hazards and what was once called birth asphyxia. Epidemiological case-control studies have shown this essentially to be a fallacy and it might rather be that the birth complications are themselves secondary to an already established trajectory of abnormal development in utero. In addition genetic factors in cerebral palsy are more important than was formerly realized. In terms of the risk factors established for cerebral palsy there are some similarities and many differences with schizophrenia. One of the most potent risk factors for cerebral palsy remains very low birth weight and although there is some evidence that low birth weight

might be a weak risk factor for schizophrenia (Rifkin et al. 1994); this work needs replication. Low social class is an independent risk factor for both disorders as are minor physical anomalies and twin gestation. That schizophrenia is more common in twins was predicted several years ago (Lewis et al. 1987) and has recently been demonstrated satisfactorily in a national dataset (Löffler et al. 1994).

The brain imaging findings also are more similar between the two conditions than might be supposed. Gross anomalies are surprisingly infrequent in cerebral palsy. As noted above, such anomalies occur in 5–10% of unselected samples of people with schizophrenia (Lewis 1990). Diffuse rather than focal change seems to be usual on structural brain imaging studies in cerebral palsy and this is also the emerging case for schizophrenia where recent careful studies as noted earlier have shown reductions in cortical cerebral volume. It is likely that genetic factors are more important in schizophrenia than they are in cerebral palsy, although the two play a part in both conditions. The long-running debate about preferential involvement of the left compared with the right temporal lobe in schizophrenia on brain imaging also has a curious echo in the literature on cerebral palsy. Right-sided hemiplegia occurs twice as often as left-sided hemiplegia in cerebral palsy.

It is a mistake, however, to get too consumed by the comparison between cerebral palsy, defined as a motor disorder, and schizophrenia, defined as a cognitive behavioral disorder. None the less, in some senses cerebral palsy, whose etiology is better understood, can act as a prototype neurodevelopmental disorder in generating testable hypotheses about schizophrenia. As ever, the power of epidemiology in unravelling both disorders cannot be underestimated. The most pervasive problem with brain imaging studies in schizophrenia is the lack of adherence to basic epidemiological principles. Despite the high technology, brain imaging in schizophrenia is really epidemiology after all.

REFERENCES

Bilder, R.M., Wu, H.W., Bogerts, B., Degreef, G., Ashtari, M., Alvir, J.M.J., Snyder, P.J., and Lieberman, J.A. 1994.

Absence of regional hemispheric volume asymmetries in first episode schizophrenia. *Am. J. Psychiatry* **151**:1437–47.

Bogerts, B., Lieberman, J., Ashtari, M., Degreef, G., Gilder, R., Lerner, G., Johns, C., and Masiar, S. 1993. Hippocampus-amygdala volumes and psychopathology in chronic schizophrenia. *Biol. Psychiatry* **33**:236–46.

Brugha, T. S., Wing, J.K., Brewin, L.R., Mcartthy, B., Mangen, S., Lesage, A., and Mumford, J. 1988. The problems of people in long-term psychiatric care. An introduction to the Camberwell High Contact Survey. *Psychol. Med.* **18**:443–56.

Chakos, M.H., Leiberman, J.A., Bilder, R.M., Borenstein, M., Lerner, G., Bogerts, B., Wu, H., Kinon, B., and Ashtari, M. 1994. Caudate volume increases in first episode schizophrenia after treatment. *Am. J. Psychiatry* **151**:1430–6.

DeMyer, M.K., Gilmor, R.L., Hendrie, H.C. Augustyn, G.T., and Jackson, R.K. 1988. Magnetic resonance brain images in schizophrenic and normal subjects: influence of diagnosis and education. *Schizophr. Bull.* **14**:21–38.

Harding, B.N. 1992. Malformations of the nervous system. In *Greenfield's Neuropathology*, ed. J.H. Adams and L.W. Duche, pp. 521–638. London: Edward Arnold.

Harvey, I., Persaud, R., Ron, M.A., Baker, G., and Murray, R.M. 1994. Volumetric MRI measurements in bipolars compared with schizophrenics and healthy controls. *Psychol.Med.* **24**:689–99.

Harvey, I., Ron, M.A., Du Boulay, G., Wicks, S.W., Lewis, S.W., and Murray, R.M. 1993. Reduction of cortical volume in schizophrenia on magnetic resonance imaging. *Psychol. Med.* **23**: 591–604.

Jones, Rodgers, B., Murray, R., and Marnot, M. 1994. Child development risk factors for adult schizophrenia in the British birth cohort. *Lancet* **344**: 1398–402.

Kläning, U., Mortensen, P.B., and Kyvik, K.O. (1996) Increased occurrence of schizophrenia and other psychiatric illnesses amongst twins. *Br. J. Psychiatry* **168**:668–92.

Kuban, K.C. and Levitan, A. 1994. Cerebral palsy. *New Engl. J. Medicine* **16**:1760.

Kuhnley, E.J., White, D.H., and Granoff, A.L. 1981. Psychiatric presentation of an arachnoid cyst. *J. Clin. Psychiatry* **42**:167–8.

Lauriello, J., Hoff, A., Weinecke, S., DeMent, S., Faustman, W.O., Sullivan, E.V., Lim, K.O., and Pfefferbaum, A. 1995.

Cortical gray matter volume deficits in women with schizophrenia. *Schizophr. Res.* **15**:95–6.

Lewis, S.W. 1987. Schizophrenia with and without intracranial abnormalities on CT scan. Unpublished MPhil thesis, University of London.

Lewis, S. W. 1989. Congenital risk factors for schizophrenia. *Psychol. Med.* **19**:5–13.

Lewis, S.W. 1990. Computed tomography in schizophrenia 15 years on. *Br. J. Psychiatry* **9**:16–24.

Lewis, S.W. and Mezey, G.C. 1985. Clinical correlates of septum pellucidum cavities: an unusual association with psychosis. *Psychol. Med.* **15**:43–54.

Lewis, S.W., Reveley, M.A., David, A.S., and Ron, M.A. 1988. Agenesis of the corpus callosum and schizophrenia. *Psychol. Med.* **18**:341–7.

Lewis, S.W., Reveley, A.M., Reveley, M.A., Chitkara, B., and Murray, R.M. 1987. The familial-sporadic distinction as a strategy in schizophrenia research. *Br. J. Psychiatry* **151**:306–13.

Lim, K.O., Tew, W., Koshner, M., Chow, K., Matsumoto, B., and DeLisi, L.E. 1995. Cortical gray matter volume deficit is present in first episode schizophrenia. *Schizophr. Res.* **15**:90.

Löffler, W., Häfner, H., Fatkenheuer, B., Maurer, K., Riecher-Rossler, A., Lutzhoft, J., Shadhede, S., Munk-Jørgensen, P., and Stromgren, E. 1994. Validation of Danish Case Register Diagnosis for Schizophrenia. *Acta Psychiatr. Scand.*. **90**:1996–203.

Mackenzie, I. 1912. The physical basis of mental disease. *J. Mental Sci.* **58**:405–77.

McGrath, J. and Murray, R. M. 1995. Risk factors for schizophrenia from conception to birth. In *Greenfield's neuropathology, 5th* edn. D.R. Weinberger and S R Hirsch. Oxford:Blackwell.

Meencke, H. J. 1994. Minimal developmental disturbances in epilepsy and MRI. In *Magnetic resonance scanning and epilepsy*, ed. S. D. Shorvon, D. R. Fish, G. Bydder and H. Stefan. New York:Plenum Press.

Murray, R. M. and Lewis, S. W. 1987. Is schizophrenia a neurodevelopmental disorder? *Br. Med. J.* **295**:681–2.

Nimgaonkar, V. L., Wessley, S., and Murray, R. M. 1988. Prevalence of familiality, obstetric complications and structural brain damage in schizophrenic patients. *Br. J. Psychiatry* **153**:191–7.

O'Callaghan, E., Buckley, P., Redmond, O., Stack, J., Ennis, J.T., Larkin, C., and Waddington, J.L. 1992. Abnormalities of cerebral structure on MRI:interpretation in relation to the neurodevelopmental hypothesis. *J. R. S. Med.* **86**:224.

Owens, D.G.C., Johnstone, E.C., Bydder, G.M., and Kreel, L. 1980. Unsuspected organic disease in chronic schizophrenia demonstrated by computed tomography. *J. Neurol., Neurosurg. Psychiatry* **43**:1065–9.

Pearlson, G. D., Garbacz, D. J., Moberg, P. J., Ahn, H.S., and DePaulo, J. R. 1985. Symptomatic, familial, perinatal and social correlates of computerised axial tomography (CAT) changes in schizophrenics and bipolars. *J. Nerv. Ment. Dis.* **173**:42–50.

Pieri, J., Gupta, B.K., Bagwell, W., Haas, G.L., Sweeney, J.A., Schooler, N.R., Sanders, R.D., Pettegrew, J.W., and Keshavan, M.S. 1995. MRI abnormalities in first episode schizophrenia: association in neurological impairment. *Schizophr. Res.* **15**:87–8.

Rakic, P. 1988. Defects of neuronal migration and the pathogenesis of cortical malformations. In *Progress in brain research*, vol. 73, ed. G. J. Boer, M. G. P. Feenstra and F. Van Haaren, pp. 15–37. Amsterdam:Elsevier.

Reveley, A. M. and Reveley, M. A. 1983. Aqueduct stenosis and schizophrenia. *J. Neurol., Neurosurg. Psychiatry* **46**:18–22.

Rifkin, L., Lewis, S.W., Jones, P.B., Toone, B.K., and Murray, R.M. 1994. Low birthweight and poor premorbid function predict cognitive impairment in schizophrenia. *Br. J. Psychiatry* **165**:357–62.

Sarnat, B.H. 1991. Cerebral dysplasias as expressions of altered maturational processes. *Can. J. Neurol. Sci.* **18**:196–204.

Schlaepfer, T. E., Harris, G. J., Tien, A. Y., Peng, I. W., Lee, S., Fedeman, E. B., Chase, G. A., Barta, P. E., and Pearlson, G. D. 1994. Decreased regional cortical gray matter volume in schizophrenia. *Am. J. Psychiatry* **151**:842–8.

Turner, J. 1912. The classification of insanity. *J. Ment. Sci.* **58**: 1–25.

Walsh, C. and Cepko, C.L. 1993. Clonal dispersion in proliferative layers of developing cerebral cortex. *Nature* **362**:632–5.

Weinberger, R.D. 1987. Implications of normal brain development for the pathogenesis of schizophrenia. *Arch. Gen. Psychiatry* **44**:660–9.

Zipursky, R.B., Lim, K.O., Sullivan, E.V., Brown, B.W., and Pfefferbaum, A. 1992. Widespread gray matter volume deficits in schizophrenia. *Arch. Gen. Psychiatry* **49**:195–205.

13

Neuropathology, neurodevelopment and schizophrenia

KATHRYN J. KOTRLA, AMY K. SATER,
AND DANIEL R. WEINBERGER

INTRODUCTION

The neurodevelopmental hypothesis of schizophrenia suggests that subtle anomalous brain development occurs in utero which reveals itself symptomatically, years later, as the heterogeneous symptoms of schizophrenia (Weinberger 1987). The evidence in support of this hypothesis is circumstantial, in part because normal human brain development is not amenable to direct investigation. Neuroimaging studies, however, consistently find abnormalities in the structure or function of multiple brain regions in schizophrenia, most notably in the temporal and frontal lobes. Neuropathological investigations of these areas, though incomplete, indicate a pattern of subtle aberrations of cortical organization, which could arise only during development. The field of developmental neurobiology is actively exploring neuronal determination, migration, and synapse formation resulting in normal cortical development. Such studies also illuminate the consequences of abnormalities at different developmental stages. This chapter will first examine findings from neuroimaging and neuropathological investigations in schizophrenia to determine how tenable the indirect support for the "neurodevelopmental hypothesis" appears. Next, advances from developmental neurobiology likely relevant to the findings in schizophrenia will be highlighted. Lastly, the chapter will offer speculation on how a neurodevelopmental event could result in an illness of adolescent or early adult onset, how the "dopamine hypothesis" can be reconciled with the "neurodevelopmental hypothesis", and areas of research likely to provide new insights into the etiology of schizophrenia.

NEUROIMAGING AND NEUROPATHOLOGICAL FINDINGS IN SCHIZOPHRENIA

During the first half of this century, schizophrenia earned the distinction as the "graveyard of neuropathologists" due to a frustrating and inconsistent search for brain abnormalities associated with the illness. The lack of gross abnormalities was partly responsible for theories suggesting a "schizophrenogenic" mother or a "double-bind" family caused schizophrenia. Soon after, with the advent of computerized tomography (CT), Johnstone et al. (1976) reported that schizophrenic patients had enlarged ventricles compared with normal controls, linking schizophrenia with brain abnormalities. This finding has been consistently replicated in subsequent CT studies (for a review see Shelton and Weinberger 1986), and with magnetic resonance imaging (MRI) (for a review see Kotrla and Weinberger 1995).

The spatial resolution of MRI allows investigators to determine where brain abnormalities are found. Reductions of the order of 10–15% have been reported in the overall size of the temporal lobe (Dauphinais et al. 1990), in temporal lobe gray matter (Suddath et al. 1990), and in specific mesial (Bogerts et al. 1990; Suddath et al. 1990; Shenton et al. 1992) and lateral (Shenton et al. 1992) temporal lobe structures in schizophrenic patients. Recent MRI studies suggest subtle volumetric reductions in widespread cortical areas, including the frontal and parietal secondary association areas (Zipursky et al. 1992; Schlaepfer et al. 1994; Andreasen et al. 1994). Data from diverse research groups converge on the finding of subtle brain abnormalities, yet speak not at all as to when they first occur or how they progress, questions important in understanding the etiology of the abnormalities.

In studies exploring these questions, it appears that schizophrenic patients show enlarged ventricles at the onset of their illness (Weinberger *et al.* 1982; Degreef *et al.* 1992), and that the ventriculomegaly (Vita *et al.* 1988) and reduced volumes of temporal lobe structures (Marsh *et al.* 1994) do not worsen with time. These findings strongly suggest that schizophrenia is not due to a progressive, degenerative illness like Alzheimer's disease or Huntington's disease; however, while not contrary to the neurodevelopmental hypothesis, they provide no evidence that the lesion is neurodevelopmental in origin.

Post-mortem morphometric studies of brains from schizophrenic patients are convincingly consistent with in vivo imaging studies. Schizophrenia is associated with enlarged ventricles (Brown *et al.* 1986) and apparently focal decreases in the size of mesial temporal lobe structures and other brain areas. Specifically, thinner parahippocampal cortices (Brown *et al.* 1986), reduced hippocampal volumes (Bogerts *et al.* 1985; Falkai and Bogerts 1986; Jeste and Lohr 1989), and smaller thalami (Pakkenberg 1990) have been reported in schizophrenic brains. Likewise, reduced neuronal counts have been reported in schizophrenic patients in selected cortical and periventricular regions (Bogerts *et al.* 1985; Jeste and Lohr 1989). It should be noted that there have also been negative reports (Heckers *et al.* 1990) regarding hippocampal volume, and mixed reports regarding the volume of the nucleus accumbens (Bogerts *et al.* 1985) in schizophrenia, and the reasons for the inconsistencies are unclear.

One crucial, relatively consistent observation is the lack of gliosis in schizophrenia. With the exception of one study that probably included cases of secondary encephalopathies (Stevens 1982), recent studies in neocortex (Benes *et al.* 1986; Bruton *et al.* 1990; Benes *et al.* 1991), hippocampus (Roberts *et al.* 1986), or parahippocampal cortex (Falkai *et al.* 1988), have not found evidence of either acute or chronic gliosis. Since proliferation of glial cells is seen in most degenerative brain conditions and encephalopathies that arise after birth, this negative result is more consistent with events that predate the responsivity of glial cells to injury, which is before the third trimester of gestation (Weinberger 1995).

Perhaps more convincing, and of considerable interest in understanding the developmental neurobiology of schizophrenia, are a series of studies exploring cortical cytoarchitecture in schizophrenia. In potentially landmark work, Jakob and Beckmann (1986) studied 64 brains of schizophrenics compared with ten controls. In 20 of the schizophrenic brains, the rostral entorhinal region in the parahippocampal gyrus showed poor development of layers II and III, with heterotopic groups of nerve cells belonging to layer II displaced in layer III. Twenty-two brains showed equivocal changes in the lamination pattern in these regions; 22 brains lacked these cytoarchitectural abnormalities. Interestingly, patients with more disorganized and florid symptoms (hebephrenic) with an earlier onset of illness were likely to have the changes in cytoarchitecture. These authors suggest "an abnormal ontogenetic development of a small part of the entorhinal region in the fourth to fifth month of gestation," specifically an abnormality of migration of these neurons, resulting in the formation of heterotopic islands of neurons, and the abnormal cytoarchitecture.

Had this finding been confined to a single study, its importance would be limited; however, independent investigators have confirmed the abnormalities in the entorhinal cortex (Arnold *et al.* 1991). Others (Benes *et al.* 1991) have found reduced numbers of small neurons and abnormalities of neuronal aggregates (Benes and Bird 1987) in the anterior cingulate. Likewise, in schizophrenics, layer II in the prefrontal cortex shows reduced numbers of small neurons and higher densities of pyramidal neurons in layer V (Benes *et al.* 1991).

More recently, Akbarian *et al.* (1993a) used a neuron-specific stain for nicotinamide-adenine dinucleotide phosphate-diaphorase (NADPH-d) and compared five brains from schizophrenics with five matched controls. NADPH-d is an interesting marker in that it stains neurons positive for nitric oxide synthase; such neurons are relatively resistant to neonatal hypoxia or ischemia, neurodegenerative disorders, and neurotoxic factors. NADPH-d staining cells are seen in cortex and in subcortical white matter where they are likely to be the remnants of "subplate" neurons, essential in the formation of normal thalamocortical connections (Ghosh *et al.* 1990). In the prefrontal cortex of the schizophrenic cases, these neurons were shown to be decreased in the cortex and its immediately subjacent white matter, but present in abnormally high numbers in the deeper regions of prefrontal white matter. Similar results in seven schizophrenic-control matches were found in the lateral temporal lobe (Akbarian *et al.* 1993b). The authors suggest that anomalous brain development in schizophrenia involves abnormalities of neuronal migration or programed cell death.

The number of studies exploring the extent, type, and location of cytoarchitectural abnormalities in schizophrenia is limited. Nevertheless, each one implicates a failure of neurons assuming the correct laminar location, a process that occurs during the second trimester of intrauterine brain development (Rakic 1988a). One crucial link not addressed by post-mortem studies is the functional impact of cortical abnormalities. Fortunately, functional neuroimaging with single photon emission computed tomography (SPECT) and positron emission tomography (PET), can at least image these brain regions as they function in vivo. For example, there are known neuroanatomical connections between the prefrontal cortex, parietal association areas, and mesial temporal lobe "limbic" areas (Weinberger 1993), some of the areas abnormal on neuropathological examination.

This neuronal network is involved in performing memory tasks in nonhuman primates (Goldman-Rakic *et al.* 1990), and is activated in humans during the performance of the Wisconsin Card Sorting Test (WCST), an abstract problem-solving test requiring attention and working memory (Berman *et al* in press). In a recent study, monozygotic twins discordant for schizophrenia underwent PET blood flow scans while performing the WCST. In all but one pair, the ill twin had relatively decreased prefrontal rCBF; the mesial temporal lobe limbic region in the ill twin was invariably hyperactive (Weinberger *et al.* 1993). Likewise, in PET studies of schizophrenic patients at rest, patients show different rCBF deficits correlated along three symptom dimensions: disorganization, delusions and hallucinations, and negative symptoms (Liddle *et al.* 1992). Importantly, those areas with blood flow abnormalities included the prefrontal and medial temporal cortex (Liddle *et al.* 1992). In vivo studies do not speak as to when or how the functional abnormality arose. Finding functional consequences in cerebral areas defined as abnormal

in neuropathological investigations, however, is essential to correlate neurodevelopmental abnormalities with the clinical symptoms of schizophrenia.

Taken as a whole, data from different research modalities support the notion of subtle, likely widespread abnormalities in cortical organization. Structural neuroimaging suggests these can be appreciated at the onset of illness, and do not progress appreciably with time. Neuropathology provides the strongest evidence available for a neurodevelopmental event. The lack of gliosis is suggestive of an in utero event. The subtle cytoarchitectural abnormalities, with heterotypic placement of neurons, virtually identifies the timing of the insult to during development. And functional neuroimaging is able to provide a speculative link between regions of purported abnormality and functional consequences with associated neuropsychological and clinical deficits. Neuropathologists have suggested that the subtle abnormalities they find in schizophrenia are due to aberrations in neuronal migration or in cell death. Developmental neurobiology is actively exploring the processes by which neurons are determined, assume their proper location and connections, and survive during periods of cell death. What follows is a discussion of these processes.

ASPECTS OF CORTICAL DEVELOPMENT

The wonder of development is that the complexity of the human brain arises from a flat sheet of embryological ectoderm. Cerebral cortex throughout the brain has well characterized architectonic regions; neocortex has six layers with layer I being the most superficial, extending into the deepest layer VI. Each layer has characteristic interconnections, with the superficial layers connecting with other cortical areas, and the deeper layers connecting to subcortical structures. To have neurons choosing the correct fate, attaining the correct laminar position, finding the correct target, and expressing the correct neurotransmitters requires subtle interplay between genetic and epigenetic factors. The final breathtakingly complex set of connections in human cortex depends on a series of much simpler decisions as neurons become progressively more restricted in the choices they make.

The initial decision to form a brain depends on the embryonic mesoderm inducing the overlying ectoderm to become nervous system (McConnell 1991). This neural plate invaginates to form the neural tube (Marin-Padilla 1988) as cells are progressively determined to form forebrain, midbrain, and hindbrain even before the first neurons have been generated (Nowakowski 1991a).

Within the neural tube, future neurons are generated from a rapidly dividing pseudostratified epithelium, in a ventricular zone on the lumenal surface of the cerebral vesicle. All cortical neurons in nonhuman primates are born by mid-gestation; in humans cortical neurons are born from around day 40 until day 125 of gestation (Rakic 1988a). During or shortly after the DNA synthesis phase of the neuron's final mitotic division, before migration from the ventricular zone, the neuron's fate is decided, i.e., the decision of laminar identity (to which cortical layer belongs) is made, likely depending on microenvironmental signals (McConnell and Kaznowski 1991). If newly-born neurons destined for deep cortical layers are transplanted into cortex making superficial layers, the transplanted neurons migrate to the deep layers. If cells are transplanted earlier (closer to the DNA synthesis phase), some cells populate the deep layers; others are influenced by the environment to alter their identity to the superficial layers (McConnell and Kaznowski 1991).

Further fate restrictions likely linked to the environment also occur around the time of neurogenesis. Remarkably, the decision to be limbic cortex as distinct from other cortical areas is made very early. The expression of limbic-associated membrane protein (LAMP) is limited to meso- and allocortical regions including the prefrontal, cingulate, perirhinal, and hippocampal cortices (Barbe and Levitt 1991). This suggests that very early after neurogenesis, the cells destined to form these cortical areas are molecularly marked, and can be recognized as distinct by cell surface markers. Furthermore, this membrane glycoprotein appears to be a critical component in the formation of circuits involving neurons in these areas, and in the ability for limbic thalamus to locate this cortex as target (Barbe and Levitt 1992). The LAMP label persists as a cell surface marker into adulthood (Barbe and Levitt 1991).

Other localizing information seems to be provided around neurogenesis. It appears likely that positional information in the neuroepithelium is imparted to preplate cells around the time they are generated, and that this information is deployed in the subplate to control the targeting of ingrowing thalamocortical axons, at least in the neocortex (Ghosh et al. 1990; Ghosh and Shatz 1992; O'Leary et al. 1994). So even as neurons are generated, their laminar fate is decided, some cortical area restrictions have occurred, and information is imparted which allows for further restriction of fate as development progresses. Abnormalities in the assignment of laminar identity or cortical area markers could result in disordered cortical layers or in the formation of incorrect afferent connections, respectively.

Once neurons are born in the ventricular or subventricular zone, they migrate, bypassing earlier-born neurons, to assume their final laminar position (Rakic 1988a). This results in the inside-out development of cortex where relatively older neurons settle into the inner lamina nearer to the ventricular surface, and younger neurons migrate further out to the outside, superficial surface of developing brain. The first postmitotic neurons leave the neuroepithelium and accumulate beneath the pial surface to form the preplate. Later generated cortical plate neurons populate layers II–VI of the adult cortex (Luskin and Shatz 1985).

To reach their laminar location, neurons migrate along radial glial fibers that stretch from the ventricular to superficial surface (Rakic 1972), a journey that may take place over tens of millimeters (Nowakowski 1991a). These cortical plate neurons aggregate within the preplate, splitting it into a superficial, marginal zone (future layer I) and a deep subplate zone (Luskin and Shatz 1985). This requires neurons to traverse a rapidly expanding zone containing afferents from the thalamus (which are cuing on and likely synapsing with subplate neurons (Friauf et al. 1990; Ghosh et al. 1990), and other cortical areas.

Migration, moreover, is far from automatic. There is the suggestion of transient synapses, and expression of neurotransmitters and neuromodulators, which suggests a chemical interaction between the migrating neurons and the embryonic environment (Rakic 1988a) that can influence the rate of neuronal migration (Komuro and Rakic 1993). Also, contact interaction between migrating neurons and the surfaces of neighboring cells plays a crucial role in selecting migratory pathways, and in choosing to stop migration (Rakic 1990). Abnormalities affecting neuronal migration might result in disturbances in the normal lamination of the cerebral cortex (Marin-Padilla 1988). Remarkably, the vast majority of neurons find the correct position. It is estimated that a certain, small percentage of neurons migrate to an abnormal location; all but a handful of these neurons degenerate during the later phase of naturally occurring cell death (Rakic 1988a).

Once a neuron reaches its proper location, in the correct cortical layer, the neuron must detach from the radial glial fiber to continue differentiation. As seen in cortical transplantation studies, though, stopping migration is likely to be an active process. There is evidence to suggest that neurons with a laminar identity share specific adhesion to each other (McConnell 1991), likely due to cell surface markers.

Likewise, the signals for differentiation into final neuronal and neurotransmitter type could arise from multiple sources: previously generated neurons, glia, the extracellular matrix, various trophic factors, growth factors, and local neurotransmitters (McConnell 1991). One critical factor in neuronal differentiation appears to be cortical afferents (Patterson and Nawa 1993). The differentiation of neurons in layers VI, V, and IV coincides with the ingrowth of thalamocortical fibers, which have been waiting in the subplate (Ghosh and Shatz 1992), that of layer III with the arrival of interhemispheric fibers, and that of layer II with the arrival of corticocortical fibers (Marin-Padilla 1988). The formation of specific neural connections is likely due to a cell-cell recognition system between cortical or subcortical neurons and their final targets (Yamamoto et al. 1992). The choice of neurotransmitter is likewise determined by afferent and efferent connections, local influences like glia, and circulating hormonal levels (Patterson and Nawa 1993).

Once cortical areas are created and have assumed their connections, there is a period of naturally occurring cell death in widespread areas. The extent of cell death is controlled by influences from the synaptic targets of the cells, the afferent input to the neurons, and local glial-derived and extracellular matrix molecules (Oppenheim 1991). If the amount of target (for example, neurons in a particular cortical area) or afferent input is diminished, more cell death results; likewise, if target or afferents are increased, the number of surviving neurons increases. Notably, even in adults, neurons continue to be dependent upon their efferent and afferent connections both for their survival and the maintenance of normal morphology and biosynthetic events (Oppenheim 1991).

The above discussion illustrates the dynamic nature of cortical development. While neurons are undergoing progressive genetic and molecular restrictions in cell type, location, morphology, connections, and neurochemistry, they are doing so in response to a myriad of environmental influences including local extracellular matrix molecules, local neuronal and non-neural cell interactions, and the amount and quality of afferent and efferent connections. Abnormalities in this developmental cascade could arise at virtually any step of the process. And since later developmental decisions are dependent on earlier ones, any major misstep may result in widespread consequences.

IMPLICATIONS FOR SCHIZOPHRENIA

How can basic developmental neurobiology be reconciled with the neuropathological studies, neuroimaging results and clinical observations in schizophrenia? Findings to be explained from the neuropathology include the heterotopic location of layer 2 neurons into layer 3 (Jakob and Beckman 1986; Arnold et al. 1991), the abnormal position of NADPH-d neurons (Akbarian et al. 1993a, 1993b), and the finding of reduced cell numbers in limbic, cingulate, and prefrontal cortex (Bogerts et al. 1985; Benes and Bird 1987; Jeste and Lohr 1989; Benes et al. 1991). Finding neurons in heterotopic locations can be explained by genetic or environmental abnormalities, which could affect any step in the complicated process of laminar identity and migration.

The functional consequences of heterotopy is unclear, however. Ionizing radiation, for example, causes corticospinal neurons to migrate abnormally, forming ectopic clusters in subcortical white matter and supragranular layers. Importantly, these cells still project to appropriate targets despite their abnormal location (Jensen and Killackey 1984). The same holds in the reeler mutant mouse, where despite an inverted lamination pattern in the cerebral cortex, relatively normal projection patterns remain subcortically (Caviness and Rakic 1978; Caviness and Pearlman 1984). Of crucial importance, though, is the nature of the insult. With radiation, it is possible that cells have received their correct molecular identity, and express the cell surface molecules required to attract the proper afferents as well as to find the suitable target. In contrast, if the defect causing the heterotopy was of recognizing the correct lamina, then the same defect could result in faulty connections with afferent fibers, and in efferent projections. If the cytoarchitectural abnormalities in schizophrenia have clinical meaning, they must reflect a defect not only in migration, but in the ability to attract the correct afferents or make normal efferent connections.

Post-mortem studies in schizophrenia cannot determine if abnormal cell location translates into abnormal connections. The existence of heterotopic neurons argues that these cells have made afferent and efferent connections, or they would likely have been eliminated via cell death (Oppenheim 1991). This is particularly striking in finding NADPH-d staining neurons in the deep white matter area in schizophrenia (Akbarian *et al.* 1993a, 1993b); these neurons are thought to be remnants of the subplate, which is normally virtually eliminated during a wave of cell death (Friauf *et al.* 1990). This argues that despite their abnormal location, some factor or connection maintains these neurons.

If *abnormal* afferent and efferent connections account for the survival of heterotopic neurons, and there is no evidence to support or refute this in schizophrenia, the disruption of normal connectivity is likely to have profound consequences. For example, if somatosensory input is routed to visual cortex, V1 neurons retain a projection to the spinal cord, acting like normal somatosensory cortex (O'Leary 1992). If normal thalamic input is withheld from primary visual cortex (via early enucleation), a novel cytoarchitectonic area results (Rakic *et al.* 1991). If one area of cortex is abnormal, then there will be ramifications of this in the organization and function of cortical and subcortical areas from which it gets its afferents, and to which it sends its efferents. Moreover, as cortical areas depend on their afferent and efferent connections to survive cell death and maintain cell numbers, it is possible that the reports of

reduced cell numbers in schizophrenia are due not to primary lesions in these areas but to the effects of disordered cortex elsewhere. This is consistent with the subtle volume reductions found in cortical areas in schizophrenia using neuroimaging methods.

It is clear from the above mentioned studies that while disordered cortical organization could be widespread in schizophrenia, it need not be. Because the nervous system uses molecular markers to label cells as they become progressively determined to form certain cortical areas, lamina, and cell types, a migratory defect could effect only a discrete population of neurons with its unique molecular identity. In fact, clinically it could be argued that the defect in schizophrenia must be circumscribed for childhood development to proceed in a grossly normal fashion. It would be more likely for widespread defects in migration to present earlier with observable neurological and cognitive disorders (Rakic 1988b). For example, there are a series of mutant mice strains characterized by abnormalities of neural migration in the hippocampus. One, the hippocampal lamination defect mutation (Hld) is an autosomal dominant mutation characterized by an inversion of the laminar organization of the pyramidal cell layer of area CA3c, caused by disrupted migration of only the late-generated cells in this area (Nowakowski 1991b). This mutant underscores that heterotypic neuronal lamination can be limited to certain cell types in specific cortical areas, due to their identifying molecular markers (Jakob and Beckmann 1986).

Moreover, basic developmental neurobiology informs that in rat brain the cortical areas destined to become prefrontal, cingulate, perirhinal, and hippocampal areas have a specific molecular marker (LAMP) as postmitotic neurons begin migrating (Barbe and Levitt 1991), and that this molecule may be critical in the formation of circuits between these cortical areas (Barbe and Levitt 1992). Thus it seems reasonable to speculate that in human brain frontal-temporal networks have similar markers, and that such molecules may prove crucial in the neurodevelopmental abnormalities that result in schizophrenia, where these networks function abnormally. Fortunately, with the explosion of molecular techniques, it may prove possible to test such a speculation. For example, in *Drosophila*, a gene has been identified which encodes a protein likely to be involved in the development of specific neural circuits; the homologue has been identified in humans (Kolodkin *et al.* 1993). Likewise, the human gene responsible for the Kallmann syndrome, characterized by anosmia and hypogonadism, has been cloned; this adhesive protein is likely needed for the selection and/or synaptogenesis between olfactory neurons and mitral cells in the olfactory bulb (Rugarli and Ballabio 1993), and is expressed in only selected cerebral areas during development (Legouis *et al.* 1993). It may then become possible to molecularly map the neuroanatomical cerebral networks postulated to be abnormal in schizophrenia and determine if abnormalities are limited to one labeled region.

Animal experimentation illuminates the behavioral consequences that discrete lesions and their interconnections can produce. Rats are a good model because the first postnatal week in the rat cortex corresponds, neurodevelopmentally, to the second trimester of gestation in primates (Weinberger and Lipska, 1995). When lesions are induced in the ventral hippocampus of neonatal rats with ibotenic acid, the rats show no initial effects on a host of tested behaviors. With the onset of puberty, behavioral abnormalities emerge which appear to be more like those produced by analogous adult lesions of limbic and prefrontal cortices (Lipska and Weinberger 1993). Apparently, a discrete lesion has marked functional consequences in interconnected cortical areas.

The rat model is also striking in revealing the behavioral abnormalities at adolescence. The mechanisms by which the behavioral abnormalities emerge in the rat at puberty are unknown, but are not simply the result of hormonal changes (Lipska and Weinberger 1994). Behaviors emerging at adolescence though, are not surprising. In human neuropsychological studies, task performance changes through adolescence, and are thought to be due to the normal maturation of the frontal lobes (Grattan and Eslinger 1991). Likewise, in studies of perinatal dorsolateral prefrontal cortical ablations, deficits appear after adolescence. Specifically, while performing a working memory task, monkeys showed impairment only after puberty (Goldman 1971). Notably, this same temporal pattern was not evident in orbitofrontal cortex, where deficits were manifested early in life (Goldman 1971).

It seems likely that developmental mechanisms are

continuing to account for the emergence of frontal lobe-dependent cognitive processes with adolescence, but it is unknown what molecular and cellular changes are driving the functional maturation. Schizophrenia has been consistently linked with abnormalities of neural circuits between the frontal and limbic temporal lobes, both with functional neuroimaging (Weinberger *et al.* 1992), neuropsychological (Gold *et al.* 1994), and neuropathological studies (Jakob and Beckmann 1986; Arnold *et al.* 1991; Akbarian *et al.* 1993a, 1993b). If these circuits undergo a normal developmental process during the first two decades of life, then as they are due to become functionally mature, abnormalities within the network may manifest themselves symptomatically as schizophrenia. Importantly, if adolescence triggers a developmental sequence, then abnormalities in one area could have widespread consequences, analogous to embryonic events, which could account for the irreversible breakdown in functioning seen in some schizophrenic patients.

This type of speculation represents a dramatic shift away from considering schizophrenia only in terms of dopaminergic function. As schizophrenia responds to dopamine antagonists, abnormalities in dopaminergic function are somehow involved in psychotic symptoms. The decision of neurotransmitter production, and the regulation of that production, however, are again developmental processes subject to a myriad of target-derived, afferent and efferent influences (Patterson and Nawa 1993). If the cytoarchitectural abnormalities uncovered in neuropathological investigations have any clinical meaning, then disordered brain connectivity is likely to lead to multiple instances of abnormal neurotransmitter balance. All schizophrenics do not respond to dopamine antagonists with a remission of their psychotic symptoms. Even with diminution of positive symptoms, many of the pervasive cognitive deficits appear to remain (Goldberg *et al.* 1991), which argues that dopamine alone is insufficient to explain the illness.

It seems more fruitful to expend energy in the active exploration of the "neurodevelopmental hypothesis" of schizophrenia as it relates to the development of intracortical networks. One set of networks that has been implicated in schizophrenia is frontal–temporal. Developmental neurobiology has demonstrated that the formation of complex networks depends on a much simpler restriction in cell choice and fate, guided by an intricate interplay between the genome and the environment. The molecules leading to and resulting from these decisions are being discovered at a dazzling rate, and can be followed from the level of the genome to their expression at the cell surface. The networks thought to be dysfunctional in schizophrenia may soon have molecular markers from the exploration of normal development. Advances in neuroimaging, such as functional MRI, may allow investigators to image an individual subject multiple times, to determine if all networks function abnormally (Kotrla *et al.* 1994) and how cerebral dysfunction in response to tasks is correlated with symptoms. Such studies should further inform the search for specific neuronal network abnormalities. Perhaps it is time to think in terms of the specific molecular triggers and cell surface markers controlling laminar identity and connection formation, and begin exploring if these molecules are implicated in schizophrenia. As such, with advances in technology from clinical and basic neurosciences, the "neurodevelopmental hypothesis" may be refined into a testable state.

CONCLUSIONS

The neurodevelopmental hypothesis of schizophrenia is attractive in that it acknowledges the dynamic nature of normal brain development, and recognizes the plasticity that persists in the mature brain. To date, however, it remains largely untested. Structural neuroimaging studies in schizophrenia reveal subtle cortical volume reductions in multiple cerebral areas, most consistently temporal lobe structures. The limited number of neuropathological investigations of these and interconnected frontal lobe and cingulate cortex are important for the absence of gliosis, and the findings of disordered cytoarchitectural organization, with neurons in heterotopic locations. If these results are replicated, this virtually identifies the timing of the aberration as during development. Unfortunately, this speaks not at all to the functional consequences of cortical abnormalities. Functional neuroimaging in schizophrenia has shown abnormalities in a frontal-temporal lobe

network (Weinberger *et al.* 1992, 1993) during the performance of a task, and deficits in these areas during rest (Liddle *et al.* 1992). Although the mechanism of these deficits remains unknown, these studies provide a crucial correlation between neuropathological abnormalities and functional consequences.

During normal development, the decisions about cortical area, laminar location, and possibly afferent recognition, are made around the time of neurogenesis (McConnell 1991) and depend upon a complex interplay between the genome and the environment; these decisions are expressed via cell surface markers that molecularly label neurons. Neurons in heterotopic locations are usually eliminated via cell death (Oppenheim 1991), or retain their capacity for correct connections (Caviness and Rakic 1978; Caviness and Pearlman 1984; Jensen and Killackey 1984). For the heterotopy in schizophrenia to have clinical meaning, then arguably the deficit likely extends beyond neuronal laminar location to the ability to form correct afferent and efferent connections. Abnormal connectivity of one cortical area could have widespread ramifications throughout interconnected cortical and subcortical regions (Rakic *et al.* 1991; O'Leary *et al.* 1994); speculatively, this could account for reports of reduced cell numbers and subtle cortical and subcortical volume reductions in neuropathological and neuroimaging (respectively) studies in schizophrenia. If schizophrenia is due to a neurodevelopmental event, the molecules involved in labeling cortical circuits may provide candidates for exploration.

If the etiology of schizophrenia lies in utero, why is its expression delayed? The cerebral areas most implicated by neuropathology and neuroimaging are part of a fronto–temporal network implicated in complex cognitive processes like memory and attention (Mesulam 1990). This network appears to have undergone a normal maturational process to reach functional maturity around adolescence (Goldman 1971; Grattan and Eslinger 1991). Importantly, at least one molecule has been identified in rat brain which marks and is necessary for connections between hippocampus, perirhinal, cingulate, and prefrontal cortices (Barbe and Levitt 1992). It is possible that as this network becomes essential for normal brain functioning, with abnormalities in the network being revealed symptomatically as schizophrenia.

With the advances in molecular developmental neuro-biology, the neurodevelopmental hypothesis of schizo-phrenia can be focused around specific neural networks and the molecules necessary for their normal develop-ment. This type of conceptualization shifts away from considering a single neurotransmitter system as causal to an end result of diffuse cortical abnormalities. As technol-ogy advances the neurodevelopmental hypothesis may become testable.

REFERENCES

Andreasen, N.C., Flashman, L., Flaum, M., Arndt, S., Swayze II, V., O'Leary, D.S.K., Ehrhardt, J.C., and Yuh, W.T.C. 1994. Regional brain abnormalities in schizophrenia measured with magnetic resonance imaging. *JAMA.* 272:1763–9.

Akbarian, S., Bunney, W.E., Potkin, S.G., Wigal, S.B., Hagman, J.O., Sandman, C.A., and Jones, E.G. 1993a. Altered distribution of nicotinamide-adenine dinucleotide phosphate–diaphorase cells in frontal lobe of schizophrenics implies disturbances of cortical development. *Arch. Gen. Psychiatry* 50: 169–77.

Akbarian, S., Vinuela, A., Kim, J.J., Potkin, S.G., Bunney, W.E., and Jones, E.G. 1993b. Distorted distribution of nicotinamide-adenine dinucleotide phosphate-diaphorase neurons in temporal lobe of schizophrenics implies anomalous cortical development. *Arch. Gen. Psychiatry* 50:178–87.

Arnold, S.E., Hyman, B.T., van Hoesen, G.W., and Damasio, A.R. 1991. Some cytoarchitectural abnormalities of the entorhinal cortex in schizophrenia. *Arch. Gen. Psychiatry* 48:625–32.

Barbe, M.F. and Levitt, P. 1991. The early commitment of fetal neurons to the limbic cortex. *J. Neurosci.* 11:519–33.

Barbe, M.F. and Levitt, P. 1992. Attraction of specific thalamic input by cerebral grafts depends on the molecular identity of the implant. *Proc. Natl Acad. Sci. USA* 89:3706–10.

Benes, F.M. and Bird, E.D. 1987. An analysis of the arrangement of neurons in the cingulate cortex of schizophrenic patients. *Arch. Gen. Psychiatry* 44: 608–16.

Benes, F.M., Davidson, J., and Bird, E.D. 1986. Quantitative cytoarchitectural studies of the cerebral cortex of schizophrenics. *Arch. Gen. Psychiatry* 43: 31–5.

Benes, F.M., McSparren, J., Bird, E.D., SanGiovanni, J.P., and Vincent, S.L. 1991. Deficits in small interneurons in prefrontal and cingulate cortices of schizophrenic and schizoaffective patients. *Arch. Gen. Psychiatry* 48:996–1001.

Berman, K.F., Randolph, C., Gold, J., Goldberg, T.E., Coppola, R., Ostrem, J.L., Carson, R.E., Herscovitch, P., and Weinberger, D.R. Activation of a cortical network during performance of the Wisconsin Card Sorting Test: a positron emission tomography study. *Neuropsychologia* (in press).

Bogerts, B., Ashtari, M., Degreef, G., Alvir, J.M.J., Bilder, R.M., and Lieberman, J.A. 1990. Reduced temporal limbic structure volumes on magnetic resonance images in first episode schizophrenia. *Psychiatry Res. Neuroimaging* 35:1–13.

Bogerts, B., Meertz, E., and Schonfeldt-Bausch, R. 1985. Basal ganglia and limbic system pathology in schizophrenia. *Arch. Gen. Psychiatry* 42:784–91.

Brown, R., Colter, N., Corsellis, N., Crow, T.J., Frith, C.D., Jagoe, R., Johnstone, E.C., and Marsh, L. 1986. Post-mortem evidence of structural brain changes in schizophrenia. *Arch. Gen. Psychiatry* 43:36–42.

Bruton, C.J., Crow, T.J., Frith, C.D., Johnstone, E.C., Owens, D.G.C., and Roberts, G.W. 1990. Schizophrenia and the brain: a prospective cliniconeuropathological study. *Psychol. Med.* 20:285–304.

Caviness, V.S. Jr. and Pearlman, A.L. 1984. Mutation-induced disorders of mammalian forebrain development. In *Organizing principals of neural development*, ed. S.C. Sharma, pp. 277–305. New York: Plenum Press

Caviness, V.S. Jr. and Rakic, P. 1978. Mechanisms of cortical development: a view from mutations in mice. *Annu. Rev. Neurosci.* 1:297–326.

Dauphinais, R.D., DeLisi, L.E., Crow, T.J., Alexandropoulos, K., Colter, N., Tuma, I., and Gershon, E.S. 1990. Reduction in temporal lobe size in siblings with schizophrenia: a magnetic resonance imaging study. *Psychiatry Res. Neuroimaging* 35:137–47.

Degreef, G., Ashtari,M., Bogerts, B., Bilder, R.M., Jody, D.N., Alvir, J.M.J., and Lieberman, J.A. 1992. Volumes of ventricular system subdivisions measured from magnetic resonance images in first-episode schizophrenic patients. *Arch. Gen. Psychiatry* **49**:531–7.

Falkai, P. and Bogerts, B. 1986. Cell loss in the hippocampus of schizophrenics. *Eur. Arch. Psychiatry Neurol. Sci.* **236**:154–61.

Falkai, P.z, Bogerts, B., and Rozumek, M. 1988. Limbic pathology in schizophrenia: the entorhinal region – a morphometric study. *Biol. Psychiatry* **24**:515–21.

Friauf, E., McConnell, S.K., and Shatz, C.J. 1990. Functional synaptic circuits in the subplate during fetal and early postnatal development of cat visual cortex. *J. Neurosci.* **10**:2601–13.

Ghosh, A., Antonini, A., McConnell, S.K., and Shatz, C.J. 1990. Requirements for subplate neurons in the formation of thalamocortical connections. *Nature* **347**:179–81.

Ghosh, A. and Shatz, C.J. 1992. Pathfinding and target selection by developing geniculocortical axons. *J. Neurosci.* **12**:39–55.

Gold, J.M., Herman, B.P., Randolph, C., Wyler, A.R., Goldberg, T.E., and Weinberger, D.R. 1994. Schizophrenia and temporal lobe epilepsy: a neuropsychological analysis. *Arch. Gen. Psychiatry* **51**:265–72.

Goldberg, T.E., Gold, J.M., and Braff, D.L. 1991. Neuropsychological functioning and time-linked information processing in schizophrenia. In *American psychiatric press: review of psychiatry*, vol. 10, ed. A. Tasman and S.M. Goldfinger, pp. 60–78. Washington, DC: APPA Press.

Goldman, P.S. 1971. Functional development of the prefrontal cortex in early life and the problem of neuronal plasticity. *Exp. Neurol.* **32**:366–87.

Goldman-Rakic, P.S., Funahashi, S., and Bruce, C.J. 1990. Neocortical memory circuits. *Cold Spring Harbor Symp. Quantit. Biol.* **55**:1025–38.

Grattan, L.M. and Eslinger, P.J. 1991. Frontal lobe damage in children and adults: a comparative review. *Dev. Neuropsychol.* **7**:283–326.

Heckers, S., Heinsen, H., Heinsen, Y.C., and Beckmann, H. 1990. Limbic structures and lateral ventricle in schizophrenia. *Arch. Gen. Psychiatry* **47**:1016–22.

Jakob, H. and Beckmann, H. 1986. Prenatal developmental disturbances in the limbic allocortex in schizophrenics. *J. Neural. Transmission* **65**:303–26.

Jensen, K.F., and Killackey, H.P. 1984. Subcortical projections

from ectopic neocortical neurons. *Proc. Natl Acad. Sci. USA* **81**:964–8.

Jeste, D.V. and Lohr, J.B. 1989. Hippocampal pathologic findings in schizophrenia. *Arch. Gen. Psychiatry* **46**:1019–24.

Johnstone, E.C., Crow, T.J., Frith, C.D., Husband, J., and Kreel, L. 1976. Cerebral ventricular size and cognitive impairment in chronic schizophrenia. *Lancet* **2**:924–6.

Kolodkin, A.L., Matthes, D.J., and Goodman, C.S. 1993. The *semaphorin* genes encode a family of transmembrane and secreted growth cone guidance molecules. *Cell* **75**:1389–99.

Komuro, H. and Rakic, P. 1993. Modulation of neuronal migration by NMDA receptors. *Science* **260**:95–7.

Kotrla, K.J., Mattay, V.S., Duyn, J.H., van Gelderen, P., Jones, D.W., Barrios, F.A., Sexton, R.H., Moonen, C.T.W., Frank, J.A., and Weinberger, D.R. 1994. Three dimensional functional MRI in schizophrenics and normal volunteers performing the Wisconsin Card Sorting Test. *Biol. Psychiatry* **35**:623.

Kotrla, K.J. and Weinberger, D.R. 1995. Brain imaging in schizophrenia. *Ann. Rev. Med.* **46**:113–21.

Legouis, R., Aycr-Le Lievre, C., Leibovici, M., Lapointe, F., and Petit, C. 1993. Expression of the *KAL* gene in multiple neuronal sites during chicken development. *Proc. Natl Acad. Sci. USA* **90**:2461–5.

Liddle, P.F., Friston, K.J., Frith, C.D., Hirsch, S.R., Jones, T., and Frackowiak, R.S.J. 1992. Patterns of cerebral blood flow in schizophrenia. *Br. J. Psychiatry* **160**:179–86.

Lipska, B.K. and Weinberger, D.R. 1993. Neonatal excitotoxic hippocampal damage as an animal model of schizophrenia. *ACNP Abstracts* 32nd Annual Meeting, p. 54.

Lipska, B.K. and Weinberger, D.R. 1994. Gonadectomy does not prevent novelty or drug-induced motor hyper-responsiveness in rats with neonatal hippocampal damage. *Dev. Brain Res.* **78**:253–8.

Luskin, M.B. and Shatz, C.J. 1985. Studies of the earliest generated cells of the cat's visual cortex: cogeneration of subplate and marginal zones. *J. Neurosci.* **5**:1062–75.

McConnell, S.K. 1991. The generation of neuronal diversity in the central nervous system. *Annu. Rev. Neurosci.* **14**:269–300.

McConnell, S.K. and Kaznowski, C.E. 1991. Cell cycle dependence of laminar determination in developing neocortex. *Science* **254**:282–5.

Marin-Padilla, M. 1988. Early ontogenesis of the human cerebral cortex. In *Cerebral Cortex*, vol. 7, ed. A. Peters and E.G. Jones, pp. 1–34. New York: Plenum Press.

Marsh, L., Suddath, R.L., Higgins, N., and Weinberger, D.R. 1994. Medial temporal lobe structures in schizophrenia: relationship of size to duration of illness. *Schizophr. Res.* 11:225–38.

Mesulam, M.M. 1990. Large-scale neurocognitive networks and distributed processing for attention, language, and memory. *Ann. Neurol.* 28:597–613.

Nowakowski, R.S. 1991a. Some basic concepts of the development of the central nervous system. In *Fetal neural development and adult schizophrenia*, ed. S.A. Mednick, T.D. Cannon, C.E. Barr and M. Lyon, pp.17–39. Cambridge: Cambridge University Press.

Nowakowski, R.S. 1991b. Genetic disturbances of neuronal migration: some examples from the limbic system of mutant mice. In *Fetal neural development and adult schizophrenia*, ed. S.A. Mednick, T.D. Cannon, C.E. Barr and M. Lyon, pp. 69–96. Cambridge: Cambridge University Press.

O'Leary, D.D.M. 1992. Development of connectional diversity and specificity in the mammalian brain by the pruning of collateral projections. *Curr. Op. Neurosci.* 2:70–7.

O'Leary, D.D.M., Schlaggar, B.L., and Tuttle, R. 1994. Specification of neocortical areas and thalamocortical connections. *Annu. Rev. Neurosci.* 17:419–39.

Oppenheim, R.W. 1991. Cell death during development of the nervous system. *Annu. Rev. Neurosci.* 14:453–501.

Pakkenberg, B. 1990. Pronounced reduction of total neuron number in mediodorsal thalamic nucleus and nucleus accumbens in schizophrenics. *Arch. Gen. Psychiatry* 47:1023–8.

Patterson, P.H. and Nawa, H. 1993. Neuronal differentiation factors/cytokines and synaptic plasticity. *Cell* 10:123–37.

Rakic, P. 1972. Mode of cell migration to the superficial layers of fetal monkey neocortex. *J. Comp. Neur.* 145:61–84.

Rakic, P. 1988a. Specification of cerebral cortical areas. *Science* 241:170–6.

Rakic, P. 1988b. Defects of neuronal migration and the pathogenesis of cortical malformations. In *Progress in brain research*, vol. 73, ed. G.J. Boer, M.G.P. Feenstra, M. Mirmiran, D.F. Swaab, and F. Van Haaren, pp. 15–37.

Amsterdam: Elsevier Science Publishers.

Rakic, P. 1990. Principles of neural cell migration. *Experientia* 46:882–91.

Rakic, P., Suner, I., and Williams, R.W. 1991. A novel cytoarchitectonic area induced experimentally within the primate visual cortex. *Proc. Natl Acad. Sci. USA* 88:2083–7.

Roberts, G.W., Colter, N., Lofthouse, R., Bogerts, B., Zech, M., and Crow, T.J. 1986. Gliosis in schizophrenia: a survey. *Biol. Psychiatry* 21:1043–50.

Rugarli, E.I. and Ballabio, A. 1993. Kallmann syndrome: from genetics to neurobiology. *JAMA* 270:2713–16.

Schlaepfer, T.E., Harris, G.J., Tien, A.Y., Peng, L.W., Lee, S., Federman, E.B., Chase, G.A., Barta, P.E., and Pearlson, G.D. 1994. Decreased regional cortical gray matter volume in schizophrenia. *Am. J. Psychiatry* 151:842–8.

Shelton, R.C. and Weinberger, D.R. 1986. Computerized tomography in schizophrenia: a review and synthesis. In *Handbook of schizophrenia, vol. 1: the neurology of schizophrenia*, ed. H.A. Nasrallah and D.R. Weinberger, pp. 207–50. Amsterdam: Elsevier.

Shenton, M.E., Kikinis, R., Jolesz, F.A., Pollak, S.D., LeMay, M., Wible, C.G., Hokama, H., Martin, J., Metcalf, D., Coleman, M., and McCarley R.W. 1992. Abnormalities of the left temporal lobe and thought disorder in schizophrenia. *New Engl. J. Med.* 327:604–12.

Stevens, J.R. 1982. Neuropathology of schizophrenia. *Arch. Gen. Psychiatry* 39:1131–9.

Suddath, R.L., Christison, G.W., Torrey, E.F., Casanova, M.F., and Weinberger, D.R. 1990. Anatomical abnormalities in the brains of monozygotic twins discordant for schizophrenia. *New Engl. J. Med.* 322:789–94.

Vita, A., Sacchetti, E., Valvassori, G., and Cazzullo, C.L. 1988. Brain morphology in schizophrenia: a 2– to 5–year CT scan follow-up study. *Acta Psychiatr. Scand.* 78:618–21.

Weinberger, D.R. 1987. Implications of normal brain development for the pathogenesis of schizophrenia. *Arch. Gen. Psychiatry* 44:660–9.

Weinberger, D.R. 1993. A connectionist approach to the prefrontal cortex. *J. Neuropsychiatry Clin. Neurosci.* 5:241–53.

Weinberger, D.R. 1995. Schizophrenia as a neurodevelopmental disorder: a review of the concept. In *Schizophrenia*, ed. S.R. Hirsch and D.R. Weinberger. London: Blackwood.

Weinberger, D.R., Berman, K.F., Ostrem, J.L., Abi-Dargham, A., and Torrey, E.F. 1993. Disorganization of prefrontal–hippocampal connectivity in schizophrenia: a PET study of discordant MZ twins. *Soc. Neurosci. Abst.* **19**:7.

Weinberger, D.R., Berman, K.F., Suddath, R., and Torrey, E.F. 1992. Evidence of dysfunction of a prefrontal–limbic network in schizophrenia: a magnetic resonance imaging and regional cerebral blood flow study of discordant monozygotic twins. *Am. J. Psychiatry* **149**:890–7.

Weinberger, D.R., DeLisi, L.E., Perman, G.P., Targum, S., and Wyatt, R.J. 1982. Computed tomography in schizophreniform disorder and other acute psychiatric disorders. *Arch. Gen. Psychiatry* **39**:778–83.

Weinberger, D.R. and Lipska, B.K. 1995. Cortical maldevelopment, antipsychotic drugs, and schizophrenia: a neuroanatomical reductionism. *Schizophr. Res.* **16**:87–110.

Yamamoto, N., Yamada, K., Kurotani, T., and Toyama, K. 1992. Laminar specificity of extrinsic cortical connections studied in coculture preparations. *Neuron* **9**:217–28.

Zipursky, R.B., Lim, K.O., Sullivan, E.V., Brown, B.W., and Pfefferbaum, A. 1992. Widespread cerebral gray matter volume deficits in schizophrenia. *Arch. Gen. Psychiatry* **49**:195–205.

14 Neurodevelopmental models of affective disorders

HENRY A. NASRALLAH

INTRODUCTION

Affective disorders, particularly bipolar disorder, show many features which, considered collectively, are suggestive of a neurodevelopmental model of etiology (Nasrallah 1991). Although there has been a wide acceptance of neurodevelopmental pathology in schizophrenia (Weinberger 1986; Lewis and Murray 1987; Nasrallah 1990) the literature is almost devoid of references to affective disorders in neurodevelopmental terms. Yet there are numerous clinical and neurobiological similarities and overlap between schizophrenia and severe affective disorders such as bipolar disorder (Crow 1990; Squires and Saederup 1991; Nasrallah 1994). Many of the neurodevelopmental "stigmata" in schizophrenia (Nasrallah 1993) have been described in bipolar disorder as well (Nasrallah 1991) despite the relative dearth of studies that attempted to address this issue.

In this chapter, the various clinical and neurobiological features reported in bipolar disorder consistent with a neurodevelopmental model will be presented. Most of those features had been initially found in schizophrenia samples and subsequently described in bipolar disorder as well. Where appropriate, suggestions for further research to help consolidate or repudiate the neurodevelopmental model of affective disorders will be offered.

DEVELOPMENTAL SIMILARITIES BETWEEN SCHIZOPHRENIA AND BIPOLAR DISORDER

Schizophrenia is widely regarded as a neurodevelopmental disorder. This concept is primarily based on several types of biological data that point to various types of adverse events or brain lesions that most likely occurred during fetal life or perinatally (Murray et al. 1988; Nasrallah 1991). There also is systematic evidence that there are behavioral antecedents to the initial psychotic episode, usually in late adolescence or early twenties. For example, there are longitudinal studies of infants at risk for schizophrenia describing abnormal neurological functioning and erratic psychomotor developmental patterns (Fish 1987). Furthermore, recent evidence points to abnormal behavior, affect and motor coordination during the latency years of children who ultimately developed schizophrenia (Walker and Lewine, 1990).

Bipolar affective disorder is similar to schizophrenia with regards to the above findings. Excess winter births has been reported in both schizophrenia and bipolar disorder (Hare 1975; Boyd et al. 1987; Kendell and Kemp 1989). Obstetric complications are also observed in both disorders (Dalen 1965; Lewis and Murray 1987). In fact, the excess in schizophrenic offspring in women exposed to the influenza A virus during the second trimester (Mednick et al. 1988; O'Callaghan et al. 1991; Kunugi et al. 1992) has been attributed to an affective diathesis interacting with a neurodevelopmental adverse event (Takei et al. 1993). Mednick's group also recently reported an excess bipolar disorder in offspring of women exposed to the influenza A virus during the second trimester (Machon et al. 1995). A shared genetic linkage between schizophrenia and affective disorders has been proposed based on a family history of psychopathology (Baron and Gruen 1991). Further like schizophrenia, bipolar disorder often manifests during childhood (Kraepelin 1921; Fristad et al. 1992) although it is frequently misdiagnosed as hyperactivity disorder. The peak onset of bipolar disorder is similar to schizophrenia, occurring in adolescence and early twenties (Goodwin and Jamison 1990).

In summary, there are several lines of evidence which suggest that schizophrenia and bipolar affective disorder demonstrate developmental similarities prenatally, during childhood and at onset. They share many clinical signs, symptoms and treatments. Even the course and prognosis of bipolar disorder can be as poor as that of schizophrenia in a subset of the patients, which suggests developmental similarities across the life span.

IN VIVO NEUROBIOLOGICAL MARKERS OF NEURODEVELOPMENTAL IMPAIRMENT IN SCHIZOPHRENIA AND BIPOLAR DISORDER

Over the past decade, many brain imaging studies have documented in vivo neuroanatomical abnormalities in various brain regions in bipolar disorder (Nasrallah et al. 1989; Guze and Gitlin 1994; Nasrallah 1994). All of the same abnormalities had been described in schizophrenia (Shelton and Weinberger 1986) and have become an important part of the total evidence for a neurodevelopmental hypothesis of schizophrenia (Nasrallah 1991; Weinberger and Lipska 1995). The neurodevelopmental pathogenesis of bipolar disorder is conceptualized on the basis of the presence of the same cortical and subcortical maldevelopments observed in schizophrenia, which include:

1. Cerebral ventricular enlargement, which was the first structural brain imaging finding reported in bipolar patients, which suggests that this finding is not specific to schizophrenia (Nasrallah et al. 1982a). The clinical significance of ventriculomegaly in bipolar disorder is possibly related to a poorer outcome (Nasrallah et al. 1984) similar to schizophrenia.

2. Lack of progression in cerebral ventricular enlargement is a strong indication of a "static" (non-atrophic) developmental etiology. This was first reported in schizophrenia (Nasrallah et al. 1986) and subsequently in bipolar disorder

(Woods et al. 1990). On the other hand, evidence of progression in some schizophrenics (Schwarzkopf et al. 1990) and bipolars (Vita et al. 1988) has also been reported which suggests that there may be some nondevelopmental (neurodegenerative?) factors in both disorders.

3. Cortical sulcal and fissure widening, a dysplastic cortical maldevelopment that initially was thought to be atrophy (Nasrallah et al. 1982b) has been reported in 25% of bipolars and 40% of schizophrenics.

4. Cerebellar "atrophy" has been reported in both disorders (Nasrallah et al. 1981). Although some studies suggest a neurodevelopmental etiology for hypoplasia of some vermal lobules in schizophrenia (Nasrallah et al. 1991), no such data are available for bipolar patients.

5. Reduced cerebral volume on magnetic resonance imaging (MRI) scans has been reported in schizophrenia (Andreasen et al. 1986; Nasrallah et al. 1990). This decrease in brain volume has been widely accepted as a neurodevelopmental hypoplasia because it is accompanied by a decrease in cranial volume or circumference. The author has reported a similar cerebral hypoplasia in bipolar patients (Nasrallah et al. 1991a).

6. Hypoplastic limbic structures, such as the hippocampus and parahippocampal gyrus have been shown to be reduced on MRI brain scans (Bogerts et al. 1990; Suddath et al. 1990). One study has reported a similar pattern in bipolar disorders (Olson et al. 1990), but more controlled quantitative studies are needed to confirm this finding in bipolar patients.

7. Superior temporal gyrus volume reduction, especially on the left, has been reported in schizophrenic patients with auditory hallucinations (Barta et al. 1990). Only one study has examined the volume of the superior temporal gyrus in bipolar disorder, reporting an increase in the right temporal gyrus in hallucinating compared with nonhallucinating bipolar patients (Nasrallah et al. 1993a). It is possible to speculate that structural pathology of the superior temporal

gyrus may be associated with auditory hallucinations in both schizophrenia and bipolar disorder.

8. Caudate nucleus volume has been reported to be increased in schizophrenia (Brier *et al.* 1992; Nasrallah *et al.* 1993b) and decreased in depression (Krishnan *et al.* 1992). It has been shown that antipsychotic drugs treatment increases the volume of the caudate nucleus in schizophrenia (Chakos *et al.* 1993). Thus, although caudate volume was reported not to be increased in bipolar disorder (Nasrallah *et al.* 1993c) further studies in neuroleptic-treated and untreated bipolar groups should be conducted.

9. Congenital brain anomalies are increased in both schizophrenia as well as in bipolar disorder on MRI brain scans, especially in males (Jurjus *et al.* 1993). This finding suggests that neuro-developmental factors may be involved in both disorders.

POST-MORTEM NEUROPATHOLOGIC SIGNATURES OF NEURO-DEVELOPMENTAL IMPAIRMENT IN SCHIZOPHRENIA AND BIPOLAR DISORDER

In tandem with the avalanche of in vivo brain imaging studies, there has been a resurgence of post-mortem studies that have added to the accumulating evidence for neurodevelopmental impairment in schizophrenia. Gross morphological changes have been reported in the brains of schizophrenic patients, such as reduced total brain volume (Pakkenberg 1987) and decreased volume and distorted morphology of limbic structures (Falkai *et al.* 1988; Arnold *et al.* 1991). There are very few similar studies in bipolar or other affective patients, with only one study (Altshuler *et al.* 1990) that looked at the brains of suicide victims and found some similarities to schizophrenia with regards to smaller parahippocampal gyrus and shape distortions of the hippocampal cortex. Although suicide tends to occur with the highest frequency in bipolar and unipolar patients, there is a need for diagnosis-specific

post-mortem studies to establish neurodevelopmental antecedents in affective disorders.

Histopathological studies in schizophrenia have also rapidly accumulated over the past decade, showing a strong degree of consistency implicating neurodevelopmental errors in various frontal and limbic structures (Nasrallah 1993; Bogerts and Falkai 1995). The collective weight of those studies is significant in demonstrating that schizophrenia is associated with impairment of basic central nervous system developmental processes (Nowakowski 1987) of neuronal proliferation, migration, and differentiation. The findings of decreased neuronal size, abnormal location of neurons, missing neurons, and disoriented neurons represent a histoarchitectural signature of maldevelopment on a serious scale. Furthermore, as most of those neuropathological studies in schizophrenia report little if any gliosis, the timing of the "lesions" is placed squarely during fetal life.

In order to demonstrate that affective illnesses are also neurodevelopmental, the above type of post-mortem body of evidence is essential. Unfortunately, there is but one such post-mortem histological study that reports neuronal histopathology on a scale similar to schizophrenia in the entorhinal (limbic) cortex of four bipolar patients (Beckmann and Jakob 1991). It is vital that further post-mortem investigations be conducted in rigorously diagnosed bipolar and unipolar affective disorders to shed further light on the possible neurodevelopmental origins of those disorders.

FUNCTIONAL IMAGING SIMILARITIES IN SCHIZOPHRENIA AND AFFECTIVE DISORDERS

After more than a decade of positron emission tomography (PET) research, the main pathological findings in both schizophrenia and affective disorders are quite similar, implicating a dysfunction in frontal lobe blood flow and metabolism (Baxter *et al.* 1989; Pearlson 1991; Dolan *et al.* 1993). As frontal lobe pathology is generally believed to be of neurodevelopmental origin (Andreasen *et al.* 1986), both schizophrenia and affective disorder may overlap in that regard. In addition, a more recently applied functional imaging technique, magnetic resonance spectroscopy (MRS) also reveals almost identical neurochemical abnormalities of frontal lobe phosphorus metabolism in both schizophrenia (Pettegrew *et al.* 1995) and bipolar disorder (Deicken *et al.* 1995). Those high energy phosphate abnormalities point to a neurodevelopmental abnormality in frontal lobe function in both disorders.

CONCLUSIONS

It is reasonable to conclude from the above overview of various types of evidence that bipolar disorder and schizophrenia appear to share several neurodevelopmental features. It is difficult to generalize to all affective disorders due to the lack of some key studies, such as post-mortem histoarchitecture in affective disorders. Neurodevelopment is a vast time/space process and it is likely that both schizophrenia and bipolar disorder are associated with various disruptions along the complex process of neurodevelopment. The exact "when", "where" and "why" of the neurodevelopmental lesion(s) are extremely difficult to define with accuracy especially via studies that are far removed from the critical phases and intricate processes of brain macro- and microdevelopment. There are vast permutations of possible neurodevelopmental impairments not only in time and space but also with regards to genetic/environmental factors and their interactions. At this point, the state of knowledge with regards to the genetic origins and biological environmental factors in major psychiatric diagnostic categories such as schizophrenia and affective disorder are essentially primitive at best. Thus, even if we conclude that the evidence so far suggests impaired neurodevelopment in bipolar disorder or schizophrenia, a great deal of knowledge needs to be generated through methodologically-sound studies designed specifically for this purpose.

It has been estimated that over a third of the human genome is expressed primarily in the brain (Sutcliffe *et al.* 1984). Brain development is probably intricately orchestrated by hundreds if not thousands of genes. Thus, there are theoretically infinite types of possible neurodevelopmental aberrations especially when random adverse environmental events are taken into account. Thus, it is

reasonable to conclude that neurodevelopmental pathology in schizophrenia, bipolar disorder (or any psychiatric disorder) is a heterogeneous continuum. In comparing studies of neurodevelopmental abnormalities in schizophrenia and mania, it should be kept in mind that the probability of dissimilarity is far higher than the probability of similarity in the cause(s) and outcome(s) of a neurodevelopmental lesion(s).

Finally, an important question begs an answer in psychiatric research: If a disorder is genetically transmitted, what are the influences of the abnormal gene(s) on basic brain development and is that gene expressed during the sculpting of the brain's structural and neurochemical anatomy? It may turn out that all heritable psychiatric disorders and not just schizophrenia or bipolar disorder are "neurodevelopmental" in their evolution.

ACKNOWLEDGMENT

I thank Beth Deley for assistance with manuscript preparation.

REFERENCES

Altshuler, L.L., Casanova, M.F., Goldberg, T.E., and Kleinman, J.E. 1990. The hippocampus and parahippocampus in schizophrenic, suicide, and control brains. *Arch. Gen. Psychiatry* 47:1029–34.

Andreasen, N.C., Nasrallah, H.A., Dunn, V., Ehrhardt, J.C., Grove, W.M., Olson, S.C., Coffman, J.A., and Crossett, J.H. 1986. Structural abnormalities in the frontal system in schizophrenia: a magnetic resonance imaging study. *Arch. Gen. Psychiatry* 43:136–144.

Arnold, S.E., Hyman, B.T., van Hoesen GW., and Damasio, A.R. 1991. Some cytoarchitectural abnormalities of the entorhinal cortex in schizophrenia. *Arch. Gen. Psychiatry* 48:625–32.

Baron, M. and Gruen, R.S. 1991. Schizophrenia and affective disorder: are they genetically linked? *Br. J. Psychiatry* 159:267–70.

Barta, P.B., Pearlson, G.D., Powers, R.E., Richards, S.S., and Tune, L.E. 1990. Auditory hallucinations and smaller superior temporal gyral volume in schizophrenia. *Am. J. Psychiatry* **147**:1457–62.

Baxter, L.R., Schwartz, J.M., Phelps, M.E., Mazziotto, J.D., Guze, B.H., Selin, C.E., Gerner, R.H., and Sumida, R.M. 1989. Reduction of prefrontal cortex glucose metabolism common to three types of depression. *Arch. Gen.Psychiatry* **46**:243–50.

Beckmann, H. and Jakob, H. 1991. Prenatal disturbances of nerve cell migration in the entorhinal region: a common vulnerability factor in functional psychoses? *J. Neural. Transm.* **84**:155–64.

Bogerts, B., Ashtari, M., Degreef, G., Alvir, J.M.J., Bilder, R.M., and Liberman, J.A. 1990. Reduced temporal limbic structure volumes on magnetic resonance images in first episode schizophrenia. *Psychiatry Res. Neuroimaging.* **35**:1–13.

Bogerts, B. and Falkai, P. 1995. Post-mortem brain abnormalities in schizophrenia. In *Contemporary issues in the treatment of schizophrenia*, ed. C.L. Shriqui and H.A. Nasrallah, pp. 43–60, Washington, DC: American Psychiatric Press.

Boyd, J.H., Pulver, A.E., and Stewart, W. 1987. Season of Birth: Schizophrenia and bipolar disorder. *Schizophr. Bull.* **12**:173–85.

Brier, A., Buchanan, R.W., Elkashy, A., Munson, R.C., Kirkpatrick B., and Gellad, F. 1992. Brain morphology and schizophrenia. A magnetic resonance imaging study of limbic, prefrontal cortex and caudate structures. *Arch. Gen. Psychiatry* **49**:921–6.

Chakos, M.H., Lieberman, J.A., Bilder, R.M., Lerner, G., Bogerts, B., and Ashtari, M. 1993. Prospective MRI study of caudate pathomorphology in first episode schizophrenia. *Schizophr. Res.* **9**:196.

Crow, T.J. 1990. The continuum of psychosis and its genetic origins. *Br. J. Psychiatry* **156**:788–97.

Dalen, R. 1965. Family history, the electroencephalogram and perinatal factors in manic conditions. *Acta Psychiatr. Scand.* **41**:527–63.

Deicken, R.F., Fein, G., and Weiner, M.W. 1995. Abnormal frontal lobe phosphorous metabolism in bipolar disorder. *Am. J. Psychiatry* **152**:915–18.

Dolan, R.J., Bench, C.J., Liddle, P.F., Friston, K.J., Frith, C.D., Grasby, P.M., and Frackowiak, R.S.J. 1993. Dorsolateral prefrontal cortex dysfunction in the major psychoses:

symptom or disease specificity? *J. Neurol. Neurosurg. Psychiatry* **56**:1290–4.

Falkai, P., Bogerts, B., and Rozumek, M. 1988. Cell loss and volume reduction in the entorhinal cortex of schizophrenics. *Biol. Psychiatry* **24**:515–21.

Fish, B., 1987. Infant predictors of the longitudinal course of schizophrenic development. *Schizophr. Bull.* 13:395–410.

Fristad, M.A., Weller, E.B., and Weller, R.A. 1992. Bipolar disorder in children and adolescents. *Child Adolescent Psychiat. Clin. N. Am.* 1:13–29.

Goodwin, F.K. and Jamison, K.R. 1990. *Manic-depressive illness.* New York: Oxford University Press.

Guze, B.H. and Gitlin, M. 1994. The neuropathologic basis of major affective disorders: neuroanatomic insights. *J. Neuropsychiat. Clin. Neurosci.* **6**: 114–21.

Hare, E.H., 1975. Manic-depressive psychosis and season of birth. *Acta Psychiatr. Scand.* **52**:69–79.

Jurjus, G.J., Nasrallah, H.A., Brogan, M., and Olson, S.C. 1993. Developmental brain anomalies in schizophrenia and bipolar disorder: a controlled MRI study. *J. Neuropsychiatry Clin. Neurosci.* **5**:375–8.

Kendell, R.E.and Kemp, I.W. 1989. Comparison of winter and summer-born schizophrenia and winter-and-summer-born affectives. In *Schizophrenia: scientific progress*, ed. S.C. Schulz, C.A. Tamminga, pp. 28–35, New York: Oxford University Press.

Kraepelin, E. 1921. *Manic-depressive insanity and paranoia*, Edinburgh: E & S Livingstone.

Krishnan, K.R.R., McDonald, W.M., Escalona, P.R., Doraiswamy, P.M., Na., D., Hussain, M.M., Figiel, G.S., Boyko, O.B., Ellinwood, E.H., and Nemeroff, C.B. 1992. Magnetic resonance imaging of the caudate nuclei in depression. *Arch. Gen. Psychiatry* **49**:553–7.

Kunugi, H., Nanko, S., and Takei, N. 1992. Influenza and schizophrenia in Japan. *Br. J. Psychiatry* **161**:274–5.

Lewis, S.W. and Murray, R.M. 1987. Obstetric complications, neurodevelopmental deviance and risk of schizophrenia. *J. Psychiatr. Res.* **21**:413–21.

Machon, R.A., Mednick, S.A., and Huttunen, M.O. 1995. Fetal viral infection and adult schizophrenia: empirical findings and interpretation. In *Neural development and schizophrenia: theory and research* , ed. S.A. Mednick and J.M. Hollister, p. 199. New York: Plenum Press.

Mednick, S.A., Machon, R.A., Huttunen, M.O., and Bonnett,

D. 1988. Adult schizophrenia following prenatal exposure to an influenza epidemic. *Arch. Gen. Psychiatry* **45**:189–92.

Murray, R.M., Reveley, A.M., and Lewis, S.W. 1988. Family history, obstetric complications and cerebral abnormality in schizophrenia. In *The handbook of schizophrenia, vol. 3: Nosology, epidemiology and genetics of schizophrenia*, ed. M.T. Tsuang and J.C. Simpson, pp. 563–77. Amsterdam: Elsevier Science Publishers.

Nasrallah, H.A. 1990. Brain structure and function in schizophrenia: evidence for fetal neurodevelopmental impairment. *Curr. Opin. Psychiatry* **3**:75–8.

Nasrallah, H.A. 1991. Neurodevelopmental aspects of bipolar affective disorder. *Biol. Psychiatry* **29**:1–2.

Nasrallah, H.A. 1993. Neurodevelopmental pathogenesis of schizophrenia. *Psychiatr. Clin. N. Am.* **16**:269–80.

Nasrallah, H.A. 1994. The continuum of psychoses between schizophrenia and bipolar disorder: the neuroanatomic evidence. *Neurol. Psychiatr. Brain Res.* **2**:206–9.

Nasrallah, H.A., Chu, O., Olson, S.C., and Martin, R. 1993a. Superior temporal gyrus volume in schizophrenia and bipolar disorder. *Biol. Psychiatry* **33**:122.

Nasrallah, H.A., Chu, O., Olson, S.C., Martin, R., and Lynn, M. 1993b. Caudate volume in bipolar disorder: a controlled MRI study. *Biol. Psychiatry* **33**:66.

Nasrallah, H.A., Chu, O., Olson, S.C., and Martin, R. 1993c. Increased caudate volume in schizophrenia: a controlled MRI study. *Schizophr. Res.* **9**:204.

Nasrallah, H.A., Coffman, J.A., and Olson, S.C. 1989. Structural brain-imaging findings in affective disorders: an overview. *J. Neuropsychiat. Clin, Neurosci.* **1**:21–6.

Nasrallah, H.A., Coffman, J.A., Schwarzkopf, S.B., and Olson, S.C. 1990. Reduced cerebral volume in schizophrenia. *Schizophr. Res.* **3**:17.

Nasrallah, H.A., Jacoby, C.G., and McCalley-Whitters, M. 1981. Cerebellar atrophy in schizophrenia and mania. *Lancet* **1**:1102.

Nasrallah, H.A., McCalley-Whitters, M., and Jacoby, C.G. 1982a. Cerebral ventricular enlargement in young manic males: a controlled CT study. *J. Affect.Disorder* **4**:15–19.

Nasrallah, H.A., McCalley-Whitters, M., and Jacoby, C.G. 1982b. Cortical atrophy in schizophrenia and mania: a comparative CT study. *J. Clin. Psychiatry* **43**:439–41.

Nasrallah, H.A., McCalley-Whitters, M., and Pfohl, B. 1984.

Clinical significance of large cerebral ventricles in manic males. *Psychiatry Res.* **13**:151–6.

Nasrallah, H.A., Olson, S.C., McCalley-Whitters, M., and Jacoby, C.G. 1986. Cerebral ventricular enlargement in schizophrenia: a preliminary follow-up study. *Arch. Gen. Psychiatry* **43**:157–9.

Nasrallah, H.A., Olson, S.C., and Schwarzkopf, S.B. 1991a. Cerebral volume is reduced in bipolar disorder: a controlled MRI study. *Biol. Psychiatry* **29**: 172.

Nasrallah, H.A., Schwarzkopf, S.B., Coffman, J.A., and Olson, S.C. 1991. Perinatal brain injury and cerebellar vermal lobules I–X in schizophrenia. *Biol. Psychiatry* **29**:567–74.

Nowakowski, R.S. 1987. Basic concepts of CNS development. *Child Dev.* **58**:568–95.

O'Callaghan, E., Sham, P., Takei, N., Glover, G., and Murray, R.M. 1991. Schizophrenia after prenatal exposure to 1957 A$_2$ influenza epidemic. *Lancet* **337**:1248–50.

Olson, S.C., Bogerts, B., Coffman, J.A., Schwarzkopf, S.B., and Nasrallah, H.A. 1990. Medial-temporal and ventricular abnormalities by MRI. Comparing major psychoses. *Biol. Psychiatry* **27**:59.

Pakkenberg, B. 1987. Post mortem study of chronic schizophrenic brains. *Br. J. Psychiatry* **151**:744–52.

Pearlson, G.P. 1991. PET scans in schizophrenia: what have we learned? *Ann. Clin. Psychiatry* **3**:97–101.

Pettegrew, J.W., Keshavan, M.S., Minshew, N.J., and McClure, R.J. 1995. 31P-MRS of metabolic alterations in schizophrenia and neurodevelopment. In *NMR spectroscopy in psychiatric brain disorders.* ed. H.A. Nasrallah and J.W. Pettegrew, pp. 45–78, Washington DC: American Psychiatric Press.

Schwartzkopf, S.B., Olson, S.C., Coffman, J.A., and Nasrallah, H.A. 1990. Third and lateral ventricular volumes in schizophrenia: support for progressive enlargement of both structures. *Psychopharmacol. Bull.* **26**:385–91.

Shelton, R.C. and Weinberger, D.R. 1986. X-ray computerized tomography studies in schizophrenia: a review and synthesis, In *The handbook of schizophrenia, volume 1. The neurology of schizophrenia*, ed. H.A. Nasrallah and D.R. Weinberger, pp. 207–50, Amsterdam: Elsevier Science Publishers.

Squires, R.F. and Saederup, E. 1991. A review of evidence for GABAergic predominance/glutamatergic deficit as a common etiological factor in both schizophrenia and affective psychoses: more support for a continuum hypothesis of "functional" psychosis. *Neurochem. Res.* **16**:1099–111.

Suddath, R.L., Christison, G.W.,Torrey, E.F., and Weingerger, D.R. 1990. Cerebral anatomical abnormalities in monozygotic twins discordant for schizophrenia. *New Engl. J. Med.* **322**:789–94.

Sutcliffe, J.G., Milner, R.J., Gottesfeld, J.M, and Reynolds, W. 1984. Control of neuronal gene expression. *Science* **225**:1308–15.

Takei, N., O'Callaghan, E., Sham, P.C., Glover, G., and Murray, R.M., 1993. Does prenatal influenza divert susceptible females from later affective psychosis to schizophrenia? *Acta Psychiatr. Scand.* **88**:328–36.

Vita, A., Sacchetti, E., Valvassori, G., and Cazzullo, C.Z. 1988. Brain morphology in schizophrenia: a 2 to 5 year CT scan follow up study. *Acta Psychiatr. Scand.* **78**:618–21.

Walker, E. and Lewine, R., 1990. Prediction of adult-onset schizophrenia from childhood home movies of the patients. *Am. J. Psychiatry* **147**:1052–56.

Weinberger, D.R. 1986. The pathogenesis of schizophrenia: a neurodevelopmental theory. In *The neurology of schizophrenia*, ed. H.A. Nasrallah and D.R. Weinberger, pp. 397–406. Amsterdam: Elsevier Science Publishers.

Weinberger, D.R. and Lipska, B. 1995. Cortical maldevelopment, antipsychotic drugs and schizophrenia: a search for common ground. *Schizophr. Res.* **16**:87–110.

Woods, B.T., Yurgelum-Todd, D., Benes, F.M., Frankenburg, F.R., Pope, H.G., and McSparsen, J., 1990. Progressive ventricular enlargement in schizophrenia: comparison to bipolar affective disorder and correlation with clinical course. *Biol. Psychiatry* **27**:341–52.

15

Heterogeneity within obsessive-compulsive disorder: evidence for primary and neurodevelopmental subtypes

TOMAS BLANES AND PHILIP MCGUIRE

INTRODUCTION

Obsessive-compulsive disorder (OCD) is not subcategorized in the Diagnostic and Statistical Manual (DSM)-IV, and although International Classification of Diseases (ICD)-10 maintains the traditional clinical subtypes of patients with predominantly obsessions, predominantly compulsions, or mixed obsessions and compulsions, most patients have both obsessions and compulsions, and multivariate analysis of large data sets fails to identify the ICD subtypes (Rasmussen and Tsuang 1986). The basis of OCD has, until recently, been obscure, but in the last decade, a diversity of research involving detailed clinical evaluation, epidemiology, pharmacology, neuroendocrinology, and functional neuroimaging has advanced our understanding of its pathophysiology. This newly acquired data also provides a means of distinguishing categories of patient within OCD with respect to more than just their clinical features. In this chapter, we will suggest that much of it points to the existence of two subtypes, which can be termed "neurodevelopmental" and "primary".

EPIDEMIOLOGY

Sex differences

In contrast to the anxiety and affective disorders, to which it is usually thought to be related, OCD is evenly distributed between the sexes. While it is often episodic, with stress-related exacerbations followed by partial remis-

sions, there is a group of patients whose illness follows a chronic deteriorating course. These patients are more likely to be men, with an early age of illness onset, and comparatively severe symptoms (Rasmussen and Tsuang 1986). This is consistent with the predominance of males among childhood onset OCD (King and Tonge 1991), and the lower age of first admission and poorer outcome in males who develop OCD as adults (Thomsen, in press). Children with OCD are also more likely to show neurological signs than adults, with 80% exhibiting tics, and a third displaying choreiform movements (Denckla 1989).

These data suggest the existence of a subgroup of patients, characterized by male sex, early onset, severe symptoms, neurological signs, and a chronic course. This putative form of OCD thus bears some resemblance to neurodevelopmental disorders such as autism, dyslexia, and attention deficit disorder.

Other conditions with obsessive-compulsive features

In recent years obsessive-compulsive phenomena have been associated with an increasing variety of clinical conditions other than OCD. These can be divided into two groups with respect to the phenomenology of the obsessive-compulsive features. The first is characterized by obsessive thoughts or preoccupations, and includes anorexia nervosa (Kasvikis et al. 1986; Fahy et al. 1993), body dysmorphic disorder (Phillips et al. 1993), depersonalization (Torch 1978), hypochondriasis (Fallon et al. 1993), anxiety (Rasmussen and Eisen 1988), and mood disorders (Goodwin *et al.* 1969). The second group is typified by stereotyped ritualistic or driven behaviours, and includes tic disorders (Denckla 1989), Tourette's syndrome (Robertson *et al.* 1988), trichotillomania (Jenike 1989), Sydenham's chorea (Swedo *et al.* 1989) and pervasive developmental disorders such as autism (Maurer and Damasio 1982).

The first group of conditions are commoner in women, have a relatively late age of onset, and a high comorbidity with mood and anxiety disorders. They are also associated with neuroendocrinological evidence of serotonergic dysfunction and clinical responsiveness to serotonergic antidepressants (Hollander *et al.* 1989, 1990a; Kaye *et al.* 1991a, 1991b; Fallon *et al.* 1993). Conversely, the second group predominantly affect males, have an earlier age of onset, are more associated with neurological features, and have been linked with basal ganglia dysfunction. Moreover, follow-up data in childhood OCD suggest that girls are more likely to subsequently develop disorders in the first category, whereas boys with OCD are more likely to suffer from pervasive developmental disorders (Thomsen, in press).

PHARMACOLOGY AND NEUROENDOCRINOLOGY

Antidepressants whose principal action is at serotonergic synapses, such as clomipramine, fluoxetine and fluvoxamine, have an ameliorating effect on obsessional symptoms (Thoren *et al.* 1980a; Perse *et al.* 1987; Goodman *et al.* 1989; Jenike *et al.* 1989). This is not merely secondary to their effect on mood (Insel *et al.* 1983; Mavissakalian *et al.* 1985), and these drugs are more effective than non-serotonergic antidepressants (Insel *et al.* 1983; Goodman *et al.* 1990; Piccinelli *et al.* 1995). While the extent to which their impact on obsessive-compulsive phenomena depends on the inhibition of transmitter reuptake, or effects on receptor densities is unclear (Peroutka and Snyder 1981), their clinical efficacy suggests that OCD involves an abnormality of serotonergic transmission. This is consistent with data from neuroendocrine studies, which indicate that patients with OCD show reduced hypothalamic sensitivity to serotonergic probes, such as D-fenfluramine (Bastani *et al.* 1990; Hollander *et al.* 1992; Lucey *et al.* 1992).

By no means do all patients with OCD benefit from treatment with serotonergic antidepressants, however, and some studies have failed to identify neuroendocrinological evidence of serotonergic dysfunction in OCD (Charney *et al.* 1988; Lesch *et al.* 1991). Moreover, among patients with OCD, a clinical response appears to be more likely in those with neuroendocrinological evidence of serotonergic dysfunction (Thoren *et al.* 1980b), and the magnitude of the response has been correlated with a reduction in serotonin markers (Winslow and Insel 1990). Until recently it was thought that a patient's clinical features could not be used to predict response to treatment, but recent data suggest that patients with harm avoidance and a history of coexisting anxiety disorders are more likely to benefit from pharmacological (and behavioral) treatment. Conversely, a preoccupation with an inner sense of imperfection or symmetry, repetition, and feeling that actions are never completed to a satisfactory level, anticipates a poor response, as well as being associated with symptoms attributable to basal ganglia dysfunction (Rasmussen and Tsuang 1986; Rasmussen and Eisen 1988). Of those who fail to respond to serotonergic antidepressants, up to 50% have a concurrent diagnosis of chronic tics or schizotypal personality disorder, and most with these features respond to augmentation with antipsychotic medication (McDougle *et al.* 1990, 1994). Nonresponders to treatment may also be more likely than responders to have an early age of onset, and to display functional neuroimaging abnormalities and neuropsychological deficits, but less likely to resist their obsessional symptoms (Hollander *et al.* 1990b, 1992).

These observations suggest that while impaired serotonergic function is common in OCD, it may not be a feature in a subgroup of patients with a relatively early age of illness onset, certain types of obsessional phenomena and signs of "organic" dysfunction.

BRAIN DYSFUNCTION IN OCD

Soft neurological signs and neuropsychology
Careful observation of the mental state in a number of neurological conditions indicates that obsessions and

compulsions may be evident in patients with posten-cephalitic Parkinsonism (Jellife 1932), Huntington's disease (Cummings and Cunningham 1992), Sydenham's chorea (Swedo *et al.* 1989), Gilles de la Tourette's syndrome (Pauls *et al.* 1986), and lesions of the neostriatum (Weilburg *et al.* 1989), globus pallidus (Laplane *et al.* 1989), and frontal lobes (Eslinger and Damasio 1985). A common feature of these conditions is that all are thought to involve pathological changes in the basal ganglia and/or the inferior prefrontal cortex. Just as certain conditions with a probable "organic" basis can be associated with obsessional features, a detailed clinical examination in OCD reveals a variety of "soft" neurological signs, such as involuntary movements, mirror movements and disturbed fine motor coordination (Conde Lopez *et al.* 1990; Khanna 1991). Soft signs are not universal, however, and are commoner in patients who are male, have severe symptoms, a poor response to treatment with serotonergic antidepressants, and visuospatial deficits on neuropsychological testing (Hollander *et al.* 1990b, 1992; Hymas *et al.* 1991). Conversely, neuropsychological deficits attributable to frontal lobe dysfunction (Behar *et al.* 1984) appear to be negatively correlated with the number of soft signs in OCD, but positively associated with evidence of serotonergic dysfunction (Hollander *et al.* 1990b; Towey *et al.* 1993).

Neuroimaging

The application of functional neuroimaging techniques such as positron emission tomography (PET) and single photon emission computed tomography (SPET) to the study of OCD has produced striking results, with several studies reporting increased neural activity in the inferior prefrontal ("orbitofrontal"), anterior cingulate cortex, and/or the neostriatum, relative to controls (Baxter *et al.* 1988; Nordahl *et al.* 1989; Swedo *et al.* 1989; Machlin *et al.* 1991; Sawle *et al.* 1991; McGuire *et al.* 1994; Perani *et al.* 1995). Moreover, when symptomatic patients are successfully treated, metabolic abnormalities in these regions appear to resolve (Benkelfat *et al.* 1990; Hoehn-Saric *et al.* 1991a; Baxter *et al.* 1992; Swedo *et al.* 1992; Perani *et al.* 1995). Close inspection of the literature, however, reveals that most studies found abnormalities before treatment in one of these three regions, rather than in all three together.

Similarly, the site where neural activity changed in association with treatment varies between studies, with some reporting reductions in the striatum (Baxter *et al.* 1992), but others finding decreases in medial (Hoehn-Saric *et al.* 1991a) or inferior prefrontal cortex (Benkelfat *et al.* 1990; Swedo *et al.* 1992). Furthermore, some studies have described reduced activity in frontal and striatal regions in symptomatic patients (Martinot *et al.* 1990; Lucey *et al.* 1995), and increases in activity after successful treatment. Nevertheless, the main findings from functional neuroimaging studies are relatively consistent, in contrast to those from structural neuroimaging studies of OCD, which have described reduced (Luxemberg *et al.* 1988), normal (Garber *et al.* 1989; Kellner *et al.* 1991) and significantly increased (Scarone *et al.* 1992) caudate volume. These differences between studies may be attributed to confounding effects of mood, anxiety and medication, and the use of different scanning methods (McGuire 1995), but they might also reflect the examination of a population of patients which is heterogeneous.

Whether neuroimaging abnormalities are characteristic of a particular subgroup of patients with OCD remains to be investigated. Given that frontal deficits on neuropsychological testing may be associated with serotonergic dysfunction (Hollander *et al.* 1990b; Towey *et al.* 1993), frontal abnormalities might be particularly evident in patients who respond to treatment with serotonergic drugs. This would be consistent with the observation that a frontal lobe syndrome, with disinhibition or apathy, can develop following administration of serotonergic antidepressants to sensitive patients (Hoehn-Saric *et al.* 1991b). Conversely, patients with severe symptoms, visuospatial deficits, soft neurological signs, and who are unresponsive to serotonergic pharmacotherapy, may be less likely to show frontal changes, but might display abnormalities elsewhere. For example, ventricular enlargement (Behar *et al.* 1984) and small caudate volume (Luxemberg *et al.* 1988) have been reported in patients with early-onset OCD.

CONCLUSIONS

Recent data from a diversity of sources suggests that OCD is not a homogeneous condition, and indicates the exis-

Table 15.1. *Putative subtypes of obssessive-compulsive disorders*

Subtype	Primary	Neurodevelopmental
Sex	F>M	M>F
Age of onset	Late	Early
Course	Episodic	Chronic
Symptoms	Mild	Severe
Neuropsychological impairment	Frontal	Visuospatial
Soft signs	+	+++
Associated conditions	Mood, anxiety, and eating disorders	Neurodevelopmental
Response to serotonergic pharmacotherapy	+++	+

tence of two subtypes (Table 15.1). The features which distinguish them do not seem to be exclusively associated with one or other category, and the subtypes may be seen as representing the extremes of a continuum. "Neurodevelopmental" OCD appears to be more common in males, begins at an earlier age, and has a more chronic course, with more severe symptoms. It is associated with soft neurological signs, visuospatial deficits, and other neurodevelopmental disorders, and a poor response to treatment with serotonergic antidepressants. "Primary" OCD is more common in females, has a later age of onset, a more episodic course, and less severe symptoms. It is associated with frontal (as opposed to visuospatial) neuropsychological deficits, mood, anxiety and eating disorders, and a good response to serotonergic pharmacotherapy (Table 12.1).

This form of subcategorization is remarkably similar to that recently proposed for schizophrenia. Murray and his colleagues (Murray 1994; see Bullmore *et al.* in Chapter 18) also describe a "neurodevelopmental" subtype, which is commoner in males, has an early onset, severe symptoms, and a chronic, unremitting course. It is also relatively unresponsive to pharmacological treatment, and more likely to be associated with structural abnormalities as detected with neuroimaging techniques, a history of obstetric complications and soft neurological signs. On the other hand, schizophrenia in females tends to have a relatively late onset, an episodic course, with less severe symptoms, which are more responsive to treatment. It may also be more common in patients with a family history of affective disorders. These similarities suggest that the etiologies of the corresponding subtypes of the two conditions may also be alike. The causes of schizophrenia remain uncertain, although there is indirect evidence that one factor may be an environmental insult to the fetus during pregnancy (O'Callaghan *et al.* 1991). As the concept of subtypes of OCD is even more recent, there has been little research directed at examining the validity of this form of classification. Such work would help to assess its usefulness, and might, as it has with schizophrenia, provide clues as to the condition's etiology. At a more practical level, it may ultimately prove important for the clinician to take into account the sex, age of onset, distinctive symptoms, course, psychiatric comorbidity, neurological signs and cognitive impairment when evaluating a patient with OCD.

REFERENCES

Bastani, B., Nash, J.F., and Meltzer, H.Y. 1990. Prolactin and cortisol responses to MK-212, a 5–HT agonist in OCD. *Arch. Gen. Psychiatry* **47**:833–9.

Baxter, L.R., Schwartz, J.M., Bergman, K.S., Szuba, M.P., Guze, B.H., Mazziotta, J.C., Alazraki, A., Huah-Kwang, F., Munford, P., and Phelps, M.E. 1992. Caudate glucose metabolic rate changes with both drug and behavior therapy for obsessive-compulsive disorder. *Arch. Gen. Psychiatry* **49**:681–9.

Baxter, L., Schwartz, J., Mazziotta, J., Phelps, M.E., Pahl, J.J., Guze, B.H., and Fairbanks, L. 1988. Cerebral glucose metabolic rates in nondepressed patients with obsessive-compulsive disorder. *Am. J. Psychiatry* **145**:1560–3.

Behar, D., Rapoport, J.L., Berg, C.J., Denckla, M.B., Mann, L., Cox, C., Fedio, P., Zahn, T., and Wolfman, M.G. 1984. Computerized tomography and neuropsychological test measures in adolescents with obsessive compulsive disorder. *Am. J. Psychiatry* **141**:363–9.

Benkelfat, C., Nordahl, T.E., Semple, W.E., King, C., Murphey, D.L., and Cohen, R.M. 1990. Local cerebral glucose metabolic activity in obsessive-compulsive disorder: patients treated with clomipramine. *Arch. Gen. Psychiatry* **47**:840–8.

Conde Lopez, V., de la Gandara Martin, J.J., Blanco Lozano, M.L.,Cerezo Rodriguez, P., Martinez Roig, M., and De Dios Francos, A. 1990. Minor neurological signs in obsessive compulsive disorders. *Actas Luso Esp. Neurol. Psiquiatr. Cienc. Afines* 18:143–64.

Charney, D., Goodman, W., Price, L., Woods, S.W., Rasmussen, S.A., and Heninger, G.R. 1988. Serotonin function in obsessive-compulsive disorder. A comparison of the effects of tryptophan and *m*-chlorophenylpiperazine in patients and healthy subjects. *Arch. Gen. Psychiatry* **45**:177–85.

Cummings, J.L. and Cunningham, K. 1992. Obsessive-compulsive disorder in Huntington's disease. *Biol. Psychiatry* **31**:263–70.

Denckla, M. 1989. Neurologic examination. In *Obsessive-compulsive disorder in childhood and adolescents*, ed. J.L. Rapoport, pp. 107–15. Washington, DC:American Psychiatric Association.

Eslinger, P.J., and Damasio, A.R. 1985. Severe disturbance of higher cognition after bilateral frontal lobe ablation: patient EVR. *Neurology* 35, 1731–41.

Fahy, T.A., Osacar, A., and Marks, I. 1993. History of eating disorder in female patients with obsessive-compulsive disorder. *Int. J. Eating Disorders* 14:439–43.

Fallon, B.A., Licbowitz, M.R., Salman, E., Schneier, F.R., Jusino, C., Hollander, E., and Klein, D.F. 1993. Fluoxetine for hypochondriacal patients without major depression. *J. Clin. Psychopharmacol.* 13:438–41.

Garber, H.J., Ananth, J.V., Chiu, L.C., Griswold, V.J., and Oldendorf, W.H. A. 1989. Nuclear magnetic resonance study of obsessive-compulsive disorder. *Am. J. Psychiatry* 146:1001–5.

Goodman, W.K., Price, L.P., Delgado, P.L., Palumbo, J., Krystal, J.H., Nagy, L.M., Rasmussen, S.A., Heninger, G.R., and Charney, D.S. 1990. Specificity of serotonin reuptake inhibitors in the treatment of obsessive-compulsive disorder. *Arch. Gen. Psychiatry* **47**: 577–85.

Goodman, W.K., Price, L.H., Rassmussen, S.A., Delgado, P.L., Heninger, G.R., and Charney, D.S. 1989. Efficacy of fluvoxamine in obsessive compulsive disorder: a double blind comparison with placebo. *Arch. Gen. Psychiatry* **46**:36–44.

Goodwin, D.W., Guze, S.B., and Robins, E. 1969. Follow up studies in obsessional neurosis. *Arch. Gen. Psychiatry* **20**:182–87.

Hoehn-Saric, R., Harris, G.J., Pearlson, G.D., Cox, C.S., Machlin, S.R., and Camargo, E.E. 1991b. A fluoxetine induced frontal lobe syndrome in an obsessive-compulsive patient. *J. Clin. Psychiatry* 52:131–3.

Hoehn-Saric, R., Pearlson, G., Harris, G.J., Machlin, S.R., and Camargo, E.E. 1991a. Effects of fluoxetine on regional cerebral blood flow in obsessive-compulsive patients. *Am. J. Psychiatry* **148**:1243–5.

Hollander, E., DeCaria, C.M., Nitesai, A., Gully, R., Suckow, R.F., Cooper, T.B., Gorman, J.M., Klein, D.F., and Liebowitz, M.R. 1992. Serotonergic function in obsessive-compulsive disorder: behavioral and neuroendocrine responses to oral *m*-chlorophenylpiperazine and fenfluramine in patients and normal volunteers. *Arch. Gen. Psychiatry* **49**:21–8.

Hollander, E., Liebowitz, M.R., DeCaria, C., Fairbanks, J., Fallon, B., and Klein, D.F. 1990a. Treatment of depersonalization with serotonin reuptake blockers. *J. Clin. Psychopharm.* **10**.200–3.

Hollander, E., Liebowitz, M.R., Winchel, R., Klumker, A., and Klein, D.F. 1989. Treatment of body dysmorphic disorder with serotonin reuptake blockers. *Am. J. Psychiatry* **146**:768–70.

Hollander, E., Schiffman, E., Cohen, B., Rivera-Stein, M., Rosen, W., Gorman, J.M., Fyer, A., Papp, L., and Liebowitz, M.R. 1990b. Signs of central nervous system dysfunction in obsessive-compulsive disorder. *Arch. Gen. Psychiatry* **47**:27–32.

Hymas, N., Lees, A., Bolton, D., Epps, K., and Head, D. 1991. The neurology of obsessional slowness. *Brain* 114:2203–33.

Insel, T.R., Murphy, D.L., Cohen, R.M., Alterman, I., Kilts, C., and Linnoila, M. 1983. A double-blind trial of clomipramine and clorgyline. *Arch. Gen. Psychiatry* **40**: 605–12.

Jellife, S.E. 1932. Psychopathology of forced movements and the oculogyric crisis of lethargic encephalitis. *Nervous and Mental Diseases Monograph* No. 55. New York and Washington.

Jenike, M.A. 1989. Obsessive-compulsive and related disorders: a hidden epidemic. *New Engl. J. Med.* 321:539–41.

Jenike, M.A., Bulltoph, L., Bear, L., Ricciardi, J., and Holland,

A. 1989. An open trial of fluoxetine in obsessive-compulsive disorder. *Am. J. Psychiatry* **146**:909–11.

Kasvikis, Y.G.,Tsakiris, F., Marks, I.M., Basoglu, M., and Noshirvani, H.F. 1986. Past history of anorexia nervosa in women with obsessive compulsive disorder. *Int. J. Eating Disorders* **5**:1069–75.

Kaye, W.H., Gwirtsman, H.E., George, D.T., and Ebert, M.H. 1991a. Altered serotonin activity in anorexia nervosa after long-term weight restoration: does elevated CSF 5–HIAA correlate with rigid and obsessive behavior? *Arch. Gen. Psychiatry* **48**:556–62.

Kaye, W.H., Weltzin, T.E., Hsu, L.K.G., and Bulik, C.M. 1991b. An open trial of fluoxetine in patient with anorexia nervosa. *J. Clin. Psych.* **52**: 464–71.

Kellner, C., Jolley, R., Holgate, R., Austin, L., Lydiard, R.B., Laraia, M., and Ballenger, J.C. 1991. Brain MRI in obsessive-compulsive disorder. *Psychiatry Res.* **6**:45–9.

Khanna, S. 1991. Soft neurological signs in obsessive compulsive disorder. *Biol. Psychiatry* **29**:442S.

King, N.G. and Tonge, B.J. 1991. Childhood obsessive compulsive disorder. *J. Paediatr. Child. Health* **27**:139–40.

Laplane, D., Levasseur, M., Pillon, B., Dubois, Baulac, M., Mazoyer, B., Dinh, S.T., Sette, G., Danze, F., and Baron, J.C. 1989. Obsessive-compulsive and other behavioral changes with bilateral basal ganglia lesions. *Brain* **112**:699–725.

Lesch, K., Hoh, A., Disselkamp-Tietze, J., Weismann, M., Osterheider, M., and Schulte, H.M. 1991. 5–Hydroxytryptamine 1a receptor reponsivity in obsessive-compulsive disorder. *Arch. Gen. Psychiatry* **48**:540–7.

Lucey, J.V., Costa, D.C., Blanes, T., Busatto, G.F., Pilowsky, L.S., Takei, N., Marks, J.M., Ell, P.J., and Kerwin, R.W. 1995. Regional cerebral blood flow in obsessive-compulsive disordered patients at rest. *Br. J. Psychiatry* **167**:629–34.

Lucey, J.V., O'Keane, V., Butcher, G., Clare, A.W., and Dinan, T.G. 1992. Cortisol and prolactin responses to *d*-fenfluramine in nondepressed patients with obsessive-compulsive disorder: a comparison with depressed and healthy controls. *Br. J. Psychiatry* **161**:517–21.

Luxemberg, J.S., Swedo, S.E., Flament, M.F., Freidland R.P., Rapoport, J., and Rapoport, S.I. 1988. Neuroanatomical abnormalities in obsessive compulsive disorder detected with quantitative X-ray computed tomography. *Am. J. Psychiatry* **145**:1089–93.

McDougle, C.J., Goodman, W.K., Leckman, J., Lee, N.C., Heninger, G.R., and Price, L.H. 1994. Haloperidol addition in fluvoxamine-refractory obsessive compulsive disorder: a double blind placebo control study in patients with and without tics. *Arch. Gen. Psychiatry.* **51**:302–81.

McDougle, C.J., Goodman, W.K., and Price, L. 1990. Neuroleptic addition in fluvoxamine-refractory obsessive compulsive disorder. *Am. J. Psychiatry* **147**:652–7.

McGuire, P.K. 1995. The brain in obsessive compulsive disorder. *J. Neurol. Neurosurg. Psych.* **59**:457–9.

McGuire, P.K., Bench, C., Marks, I., Frith, C.D., Dolan, J.R., and Frackowiak, R.S.J. 1994. Functional anatomy of obsessive-compulsive phenomena. *Br. J. Psychiatry* **164**: 459–68.

Machlin, S.R., Harris G.J., Pearlson, G.D., Hoehn-Saric, R., Jeffery, P., and Camargo, E.E. 1991. Elevated medial-frontal cerebral blood flow in obsessive-compulsive patients: a SPECT study. *Am. Psychiatry* **148**:1240–2.

Martinot, J.L., Allilaire, J.F., Mazoyer, B.M., Hantouche, E., Huret, J.D., Legaut-Demare, F., Deslauriers, A.G., Hardy, P., Pappata, S., Baron, J.C., and Syrota, A. 1990. Obsessive-compulsive disorder: a clinical, neuropsychological and positron emission tomography study. *Acta Psychiatr. Scand.* **82**:233–42.

Maurer, R.G.and Damasio, A.R. 1982. Childhood autism from the point of view of behavioral neurology. *J. Autism Dev. Disorders* **12**:195–205.

Mavissakalian, M., Turner, S.M., Michelson, L., and Jacob, R. 1985. Tricyclic antidepressants in obsessive-compulsive disorder. Anti-obsessional or antidepressant agents? II. *Am. J. Psychiatry* **42**: 572–6.

Murray, R.M. 1994. Neurodevelopmental schizophrenia: the rediscovery of dementia praecox. *Br. J Psych.* (Suppl.) **25**:6–12.

Nordahl, T.E., Benkelfat, C., Semple, W., Gross, M., King, A.C., and Cohen, R.M. 1989. Cerebral glucose metabolic rates in obsessive compulsive disorder. *Neuropsychopharmacology* **2**:23–8.

O'Callaghan, E., Sham, P., Takei, N., Glover, G., and Murray, R.M. 1991. Schizophrenia after prenatal exposure to 1957 A$_2$ influenza epidemic. *Lancet* **337**:1248–50.

Pauls, D.L., Towbin, K., Leckman, J.F., Zahner, G.E.P., and Cohen, D.J. 1986. Gilles de la Tourette syndrome and

obsessive compulsive disorder: evidence supporting
a genetic relationship. *Arch. Gen. Psychiatry*
43: 1180–2.

Perani, D., Colombo, C., Bressi, S., Bonfanti, A., Grassi, F.,
Scarone, S., Bellodi, L., Smeraldi, E., and Fazio, F. 1995.
[18F]FDG PET study in obsessive-compulsive disorder.
A clinical/methodological correlation study after
treatment. *Br. J. Psychiatry* **166**:244–50.

Peroutka, S.J. and Snyder, S.H. 1981. Long-term antidepressant
treatment decreases 3H-spiroperidol-labeled serotonin
receptor binding. *Science* **210**:88–90.

Perse, T.L., Greist, J.H., Jeffereson, J.W., Rosenfeld, R., and
Dar, R. 1987. Fluvoxamine treatment of obsessive-
compulsive disorder. *Am. Psychiatry* **144**:1543–8.

Phillips, K.A., McElroy, S.L., Keck, P.E., Pope, H.G., and
Hudson, J.I. 1993. Body dysmorphic disorder: 30 cases of
imagined ugliness. *Am. J. Psychiatry* **150**:302–8.

Piccinelli, M., Pini, S., Bellatuono, C., Wilkinson, G., and
Wilkinson, G. 1995. Efficacy of drug treatment in
obsessive-compulsive disorder. A meta-analytic review.
Br. J. Psychiatry **166**:424–44.

Rasmussen, S.A. and Eisen, J.L. 1988. Clinical and
epidemiological findings of significance in OCD.
Psychopharmacol. Bull. **24**:466–70.

Rasmussen, S.A. and Tsuang, M.T. 1986. DSM-III obsessive
compulsive disorder: clinical characteristics and family
history. *Am. J. Psychiatry* **143**:317–22.

Robertson, M.M., Trimble, M.R., and Lees, A.J. 1988. The
psychopathology of Gillete de la Tourette syndrome.
A phenomenological analysis. *Br. J. Psych.* **152**:383–90.

Sawle, G., Hymas, N., Lees, A., and Frackosiak, R.S.J. 1991.
Obsessional slowness: functional studies with positron
emission tomography. *Brain* **114**:2191–202.

Scarone, S., Colombo, C., Livian, S., Abbrazzese, M., Ronchi,
P., Marco, L., Giuseppe, S., and Smeraldi, E. 1992.
Increased right caudate size in obsessive-compulsive

disorder: detection with magnetic resonance imaging.
Psychiatry Res. Neuroimaging **45**:115–21.

Swedo, S.E., Pietrini, P., Leonard, H.L., Schapiro, M.B.,
Rettew, D.C., Goldberger, E.L., Rapoport, S.I., Rapoport,
J.L., and Grady, C.L. 1992. Cerebral glucose metabolism in
childhood-onset obsessive-compulsive disorder. *Arch. Gen.
Psychiatry* **49**:690–4.

Swedo, S.E., Rapoportf, J.L., Cheslow, D.L., Leonard, H.L.,
Ayoub, E.M., Hosier, D.M., and Wald, E.R. 1989. High
prevalence of obsessive-compulsive symptoms in patients
with Sydenham's Chorea. *Am. J. Psychiatry* **146**:246–9.

Thomsen, P.H. Obsessive compulsive disorder in children and
adolescents. A 6- to 22-year follow up study. Clinical
description. *Eur. Child. Adolesc. Psychiatry* (In Press).

Thoren, P., Asberg, M., Bertilsson, L., Wellstrom, B., Sjoqvist,
F., and Traskman, L. 1980b. Clomipramine treatment of
obsessive compulsive disorder II. Biochemical aspects.
Arch. Gen. Psychiatry **37**:1289–94.

Thoren, P., Asberg, M., Cronholm, B., Jornestedt, L., and
Traskman, L. 1980a. Clomipramine treatment of obsessive
compulsive disorder. I. A control trial. *Arch. Gen.
Psychiatry* **37**:1281–5.

Torch, E.M. 1978. Review of the relationship between
obsessions and depersonalization. *Acta Psychiatr. Scand.*
58:191–8.

Towney, J., Bruder, G., Tenke, C., Leite, P., DeCaria, C.,
Friedman, D., and Hollander, E. 1993. Event-related
potential and clinical correlates of neurodysfunction in
obsessive-compulsive disorder. *Psychiatry Res.* **42**:167–81.

Weilburg, J.B., Mesulam, M.-M., Weintraub, S., Buonanno, F.,
Jenike, M., and Stakes, J.W. 1989. Focal striatal
abnormalities in a patient with obsessive-compulsive
disorder. *Arch. Neurol.* **46**: 233–5.

Winslow, J.T. and Insel, T.R. 1990. Neurobiology of obsessive
compulsive disorder: a possible role for serotonin. *J. Clin.
Psychol.* **51**:27–31.

16

Schizophrenia: a critique from the developmental psychopathology perspective

CHRIS HOLLIS AND ERIC TAYLOR

INTRODUCTION

At first sight, the idea that schizophrenia is a developmental disorder presents something of a paradox. The prototypic "developmental" disorders such as autism, attention deficit/hyperactivity disorder (ADHD) and developmental language disorder (DLD) all begin in infancy or early childhood and can be understood as delayed or deviant development in the neuropsychological processes underlying social cognition, attention or language development. In contrast, schizophrenia, as defined by Diagnostic and Statistical Manual (DSM)-IV and International Classification of Diseases (ICD)-10, is a disorder with onset typically in late adolescence and early adult life, and its core symptoms of delusions and hallucinations appear to lie outside the normal processes of neuropsychological development.

Over the last decade there has been increasing support for a neurodevelopmental model of schizophrenia (Weinberger 1987; Murray and Lewis 1987). There are two main lines of evidence that have been used to support a neurodevelopmental model. First, studies of brain morphology (Jakob and Beckmann 1986) and findings from neuroimaging (Andreasen et al. 1990) have demonstrated structural brain anomalies in schizophrenics that are compatible with aberrant neurodevelopment rather than neurodegeneration. The second line of evidence is more indirect, and relates to findings that suggest abnormal early development in schizophrenia. These include premorbid social and cognitive impairments (Foerster et al. 1991; Jones et al. 1993), obstetric complications (Lewis and Murray 1987) and minor physical anomalies

(Gualtieri et al. 1982; Guy et al. 1983). According to Weinberger's neurodevelopmental model (Weinberger 1987), the primary cause of schizophrenia is a static lesion occurring during fetal brain development. During childhood, this lesion is relatively "silent", giving rise only to subtle behavioural symptoms. In adolescence, or early adult life, however, the lesion interacts with the process of normal brain maturation to manifest itself in the form of psychotic symptoms.

In Weinberger's "early" neurodevelopmental model, the critical neuropathological events in schizophrenia occur in fetal or early postnatal brain development, and premorbid impairments are therefore viewed as age-dependent manifestations of underlying brain pathology. The onset in adolescence or adulthood is attributed to *normal* processes of brain maturation including myelination of the corticolimbic circuits (Benes 1989). A different neurodevelopmental formulation (the "late" model) is presented by Feinberg (1983) who proposed that the key neuropathological events occur as a result of *abnormal* brain development during adolescence characterized by either excessive or insufficient synaptic elimination leading to aberrant neural connectivity. This implies that premorbid abnormalities in early childhood are nonspecific risk factors rather than manifestations of an underlying schizophrenic neuropathology. Both these theories suppose that there is a direct and specific expression of the eventual brain pathology as schizophrenic disorder. A third viewpoint, which we will develop further in this chapter, yields an account of neurodevelopmental schizophrenia in which early brain pathology acts as a risk factor rather than a sufficient cause, so that its effects can only be understood in the light of the individual's later exposure to other risk and protective factors.

The success of any particular neurodevelopmental model will be judged by its ability to answer three key questions in the developmental puzzle of schizophrenia. First, it should account for the typical onset of the disorder in adolescence and early adult life, whereas most developmental disorders begin in early childhood. Second, it should resolve the question of whether premorbid abnormalities in schizophrenia are best understood as precursors or nonspecific risk factors. Third, it should explain the variability in the age at onset, in particular the cause of "atypical" very early onset schizophrenia in childhood.

Our plan in this chapter is to use the perspective of developmental psychopathology (Stroufe and Rutter 1984; Rutter 1988) to explore the developmental puzzle of schizophrenia and to critically examine the rival claims of the "early", "late" and "risk" neurodevelopmental models of schizophrenia. Developmental psychopathology does not constitute a single theory, rather it represents the bringing together of a number of disparate approaches and theoretical concepts to the study of psychopathology over the lifespan. We will outline here some of the key ideas of developmental psychopathology which we will refer to during the chapter. First, the study of normal development informs the study of psychopathological conditions and vice versa. An excellent example is how knowledge of "theory of mind" deficits in autism informs our understanding of normal social and cognitive development in infancy. Similarly, our understanding of attentional problems in ADHD has increased our knowledge of the normal development of attention and impulse control in children. Second, rather than development being predetermined or "canalized", individuals are viewed as developing along flexible trajectories which can be influenced at any point in the lifespan, to either increase or reduce the risk of disorder. Third, the concept of heterotypic continuity is used to refer to differing age-dependent manifestations of the same underlying phenomenon or disorder. This is contrasted with the idea of homotypic continuity, where disorders present in a similar way at different ages. Fourth, age at onset is regarded as a variable of key interest because factors influencing timing of onset may provide important clues to the primary causes of the disorder. Finally,

psychopathological disorders are not seen to emerge from the unfolding of a disease process; rather they are seen to arise out of a dynamic, transactional relationship between the developing capacities of the individual and the changing demands of the environment. Disorder may then arise at a point in development when the gap between an individual's capacities and the demands of the environment exceed a critical threshold.

In the following sections we will first turn to childhood-onset schizophrenia, drawing on the concepts of heterotopy and homotopy to consider its similarities and differences from schizophrenia in adult life. In addition, we will attempt to identify causes of the very early onset, and thereby address the broader question of what causes variability in the age at onset of schizophrenia. Next, we will review the evidence for preschizophrenic abnormalities from clinical follow-back, "high-risk" and birth cohort studies. The status of these abnormalities as either precursors, risk factors or epiphenomena will be discussed. In the final section, we will describe how the approach of developmental psychology, considering interactions between deficits in the development of cognition and other stresses, could provide important insights into the links between aberrant brain development and the onset of schizophrenic symptomatology. We conclude by outlining future directions for research, and highlight the potential value of closer collaboration between developmental research in schizophrenia and other developmental disorders.

CHILDHOOD-ONSET SCHIZOPHRENIA

The onset of schizophrenia in childhood was noted in the descriptions of the illness by both Kraepelin (1919) and Bleuler (1911). Until recently schizophrenia research has largely ignored the small, but significant, proportion of cases that begin in childhood and early adolescence. Murray and Lewis (1987) commented that a problem "stems from the parochialism of those of us working in adult psychiatry for whom patients and so by implication their illnesses, begin at or beyond adolescence . . .". It is interesting to note that the bulk of schizophrenia research has excluded childhood-onset cases, perhaps reflecting more accurately the boundaries of professional disciplines rather than natural cut-offs between different types of disorders. In recent years, however, there has been a renaissance of research interest in childhood-onset schizophrenia which has come about for several reasons. First, since the advent of DSM-III, the same diagnostic criteria have been applied to schizophrenia regardless of the age of onset. This diagnostic uniformity can potentially mask developmental differences, but it has been valuable in facilitating comparisons between childhood and adult-onset schizophrenia. Second, the emergence of a neurodevelopmental model of schizophrenia has focused attention on early-onset cases because they may represent a more severe and etiologically homogeneous form of the disorder, in which etiological risk factors may be more easily discernable.

Historical background

Kraepelin (1919) found that 3.5% of cases of dementia praecox had onsets before the age of 10 years, with a further 2.7% of cases developing between 10 and 15 years. He also remarked that these cases frequently had an insidious onset. In 1906, De Sanctis described a group of young children who exhibited catatonia, stereotypies, negativism, mannerisms, echolalia, and emotional blunting (De Sanctis 1906). De Sanctis viewed this condition as an early onset form of Kraepelin's dementia praecox, and coined the term "dementia praecoccissima".

During this century there has been a shifting debate about how best to categorize schizophrenia in childhood. The expansion and contraction of the concept of schizophrenia in childhood has closely mirrored a similar debate in adult psychiatry. Following the contribution of Kraepelin and De Sanctis, until the early 1930s, schizophrenia in children and adults was seen as essentially the same disorder with a broadly similar presentation. In the 1930s, however, coinciding with the emergence of child psychiatry as a separate discipline, a "unitary" view of childhood psychoses was proposed which included present day concepts of autism, schizophrenia, schizotypal, and borderline personality disorder (Potter 1933; Fish and Rivito 1979). This broad definition of schizophrenia dominated research and clinical practice from the 1940s to the 1970s, and was endorsed by DSM-II and

ICD-8 which grouped all childhood-onset psychoses, including autism, under the category of "childhood schizophrenia". This "unitary" view of childhood psychoses began to be challenged in the 1970s, following the landmark studies of Kolvin (1971) and Rutter (1972) who demonstrated that autism and childhood-onset schizophrenia could be distinguished in terms of age at onset, phenomenology, and family history. This led to the differentiation of adult-type schizophrenia with childhood onset from autism and other psychoses. The use of adult criteria for schizophrenia in cases with childhood onset was endorsed in DSM-III and ICD-9 and has been maintained in DSM-IV and ICD-10. It can be seen that the shifting conception of schizophrenia in childhood reflects a constant tension between the ideas of heterotypic continuity (age-dependent variations in symptomatology) and homotypic continuity (a definition based on phenotypic resemblance with the adult disorder).

This section addresses two key questions concerning the status of childhood-onset schizophrenia. First, there is the issue of whether continuity exists between childhood and adult-onset schizophrenia, or whether they are phenocopies with distinct etiologies. Second, if there is evidence of continuity, what factors account for the "atypical" onset of schizophrenia in childhood? Is it that childhood-onset cases lie at an extreme end of a continuum of liability, and hence are associated with greater severity, poorer outcome, and a greater loading of etiological risk factors? Or does some other factor, such as extreme psychosocial stress, result in an atypically early onset? Throughout this section, childhood-onset schizophrenia will refer to cases meeting DSM-IV and ICD-10 diagnostic criteria for schizophrenia with onsets of 16 years or younger. Clearly this is an arbitrary cut-off, but it includes those subjects usually excluded from adult-onset studies. Where studies refer specifically to younger samples, their ages will be specified.

Diagnostic studies and phenomenology

There is now good evidence that schizophrenia can be diagnosed using adult criteria in children as young as 7 years of age (Green et al. 1984; Russell et al. 1989; Werry 1992). Several issues concerning such early diagnosis need to be borne in mind. First, phenomenological comparisons between child and adult-onset patients using the same diagnostic criteria contain an inherent circularity which could mask true developmental differences. Second, age-specific factors will restrict the possibility of making a phenomenological diagnosis in very young children. For example, distinguishing true delusions and hallucinations from childhood fantasies can present diagnostic dilemmas. Similarly, the interpretation of thought disorder will be affected by the level of the child's language and cognitive development. Finally, the concurrent and predictive validity of the diagnosis in childhood need to be established to exclude the possibility that childhood-onset cases are not simply phenocopies with a different etiology and course.

There have been surprisingly few direct comparisons between clinical features in childhood and adult-onset schizophrenia. Werry et al. (1994) reported that their sample of adolescent-onset schizophrenics was characterized by fewer well-formed systematized delusions, fewer auditory hallucinations, and more undifferentiated subtypes when compared with the published rates for adult schizophrenia. In a study of the age at onset of DSM-IIIR schizophrenia subtypes, Beratis et al. (1994) found that in a sample of first episode schizophrenics, the disorganized subtype had a mean age at onset of 16.7 years (standard deviation 2.5), compared with 22.9 years (standard deviation 5.5) for the undifferentiated subtype and 29.9 years (standard deviation 9.4) for the paranoid subtype. While all subtypes can occur in childhood, there appears to be a relative predominance of disorganized and undifferentiated cases and fewer paranoid cases when compared with adult samples. In a recent study of schizophrenic phenomenology in cases with onset under 12 years of age, Asarnow et al. (1994a) reported hallucinations in 90% of cases, with approximately 50% describing visual hallucinations and 14% tactile or olfactory hallucinations. Recent studies also support Kraepelin's observation that most cases of childhood-onset schizophrenia present with a slow, insidious onset (Green et al. 1984; Asarnow and Ben-Meir 1988).

Studies of childhood-onset schizophrenia have also raised the issue of comorbidity (Gordon et al. 1994). Comorbid conditions can include ADHD, conduct disorder, major depressive disorder, and various developmental disorders, including childhood-onset pervasive developmental disorder. Usually, a hierarchical approach

is adopted with schizophrenia being the primary diagnosis. Relatively little is known about how comorbidity effects the correlates, course and outcome of childhood-onset schizophrenia.

Premorbid development

Children with schizophrenia tend to have relatively poor levels of premorbid adjustment. Asarnow and Ben-Meir (1988) in their University of California, Los Angeles (UCLA) sample, found that children with schizophrenia and schizotypal personality disorder differed from depressed children in having poorer peer relationships, lower levels of scholastic achievement, poorer school adaptation and fewer interests. Watkins et al. (1988), using the same UCLA sample, found that over 70% of children with onsets under the age of 10 years had significant language and motor impairments in infancy. Over one-third of children had a history of autistic symptoms and 17% met criteria for either autism or childhood-onset pervasive developmental disorder before the onset of schizophrenia. Hollis (1995) dichotomized childhood-onset schizophrenics into onsets of 7–13 years and 14–17 years and found that developmental impairments, in particular language impairments, were more common in the younger (7–13 years) onset group. In this study, approximately 20% of the younger onset group would have been diagnosed as having atypical or childhood-onset pervasive developmental disorder before their psychosis. While there is no evidence to suggest that autism and schizophrenia are etiologically related disorders, these studies do indicate that autistic symptoms are associated with an earlier onset of schizophrenia in children. Although Kolvin (1971) found it relatively straightforward to distinguish autism with onset less than 36 months from late childhood-onset schizophrenia, there were a small number of children between the ages of 7 and 11 years where the diagnostic distinction between late-onset autism and childhood-onset schizophrenia proved to be very difficult.

Genetic risk factors

If there is a continuum of transmitted liability for schizophrenia, then as with other disorders of multifactorial origin, early-onset cases of schizophrenia may be associated with a greater genetic loading (Childs and Scriber

1986). Pulver *et al.* (1990) found an increased morbid risk of schizophrenia in relatives of male probands under the age of 17 years. Meanwhile, Sham *et al.* (1994) found an increased morbid risk in females under age 21 years compared with males or later-onset females. While both these studies suggest an inverse relationship between age at onset and transmitted liability, albeit with different sex specific effects and age cut-offs, it would be dangerous to extrapolate these age trends to a younger, childhood-onset, population. Unfortunately, there is a dearth of genetic studies of childhood-onset schizophrenia that have used adequate methodology. Those studies which do exist suggest a higher morbid risk of schizophrenia among relatives of childhood-onset schizophrenics compared with the risk in relatives of adult-onset probands. In the only major twin study of childhood-onset schizophrenia, Kallman and Roth (1956) reported an uncorrected monozygotic (MZ) concordance rate of 88.2% and a dizygotic (DZ) concordance rate of 22.9%. Adult-onset schizophrenia clustered in the families of childhood-onset probands providing support for a similar genetic etiology.

Kendler *et al.* (1987) reviewed the evidence for a genetic influence on age at onset in schizophrenia. While they concluded that there was no strong evidence for an association between age at onset and familial morbid risk (this review appeared before the studies of Pulver *et al.* 1990 and Sham *et al.* 1994), they suggested that the high correlation between age at onset in concordant MZ twins compared with concordant siblings provided good evidence that the timing of onset was under genetic control. An alternative explanation of this finding is that the correlation in age at onset results from the influence of shared environment. This explanation was refuted by Crow and Done (1986), who found that concordant sibling pairs had their onsets at a similar age, not at a similar time. Furthermore, Gottesman and Shields (1972) reported that concordant MZ twins living apart had a *higher* correlation in age at onset than those living together.

One possible genetic mechanism to explain the variability in the age at onset of schizophrenia is the pattern of inheritance called genetic anticipation. The genetic basis of neuropsychiatric disorders including Huntington's disease and fragile X syndrome has been found to be due to the progressive expansion over generations of a tri-

nucleotide (triplet) repeat sequence in a gene (Ross *et al.* 1993). In these disorders, onset becomes progressively younger with each generation, and severity increases in line with the size of the expanding triplet repeat. Ross *et al.* (1993) have speculated that a similar mechanism may occur in schizophrenia. If this were the case, then within multiply affected pedigrees, childhood-onset cases would be expected to be the most severely affected and the age at onset should decrease across successive generations of the pedigree. So far, there has been one report of genetic anticipation in schizophrenia (Basset and Honer 1994). Subjects under the age of 15 years were excluded from this study, however, so the hypothesis that genetic anticipation may account for childhood-onset schizophrenia remains untested.

Structural brain changes

Neuroimaging studies are relatively rare in childhood-onset schizophrenia, and those studies that exist tend to be based on adolescent-onset patients with findings similar to those found in adult schizophrenics. Schultz *et al.* (1983) reported enlarged ventricles (increased ventricular-brain ratios – VBRs) in computerized tomography (CT) scans of a group of teenage schizophrenic patients (mean age 16.5 years) when compared with normal controls and non-schizophrenic patients. Hendren *et al.* (1991), in a study of magnetic resonance imaging (MRI) changes in child psychiatric patients aged 7–14 years, found an increased rate of abnormalities (qualitative observations rather than volumetric measures) in schizophrenia spectrum disorders and pervasive developmental disorders compared with other conditions. The schizophrenia spectrum cases were distinctive in having left more than right (L>R) asymmetries of the frontal horns of the lateral ventricles. Gordon *et al.* (1994) in an MRI study of childhood-onset schizophrenia, found significant enlargement of the left frontal ventricular horn and reduced total brain volume compared with age matched normal controls.

These findings suggest continuity with the results of structural imaging studies in adult-onset patients (Johnstone *et al.* 1989; Andreasen *et al.* 1990). It is important to remember that while ventricular enlargement is associated with early onset, poor outcome and poor premorbid adjustment (Johnstone *et al.* 1989; De Lisi *et al.*

1991), it is neither a necessary nor specific feature of schizophrenia. For example, in autism, there is also evidence of ventricular enlargement on MRI scanning, which suggests developmental atrophy in adjacent limbic and associated frontal structures (Gaffney *et al.* 1989).

Pregnancy and birth complications

Adult schizophrenic patients have been reported as having an excess of obstetric complications compared with normal controls and other psychiatric patients (McNeil and Kaij 1978; Lewis and Murray 1987). In addition, schizophrenic patients with a history of OCs develop their illness on average 5 years earlier than those without such a history (Lewis *et al.* 1989). If OCs were associated with earlier onset of schizophrenia, then we might expect childhood-onset schizophrenics to have higher rates of OCs than comparison adult-onset samples. Unfortunately, we are aware of only one study that has systematically examined adverse perinatal events in teenage psychotics (Gillberg *et al.* 1986). As the majority of the subjects had an onset between the ages of 16–18 years, this study relates to a rather older group than that encompassed by our definition of childhood-onset schizophrenia. The authors reported a small, but significantly increased, rate of "suboptimal" perinatal events in psychotic adolescents compared with controls, but there was no difference in the rates of OCs between schizophrenic and nonschizophrenic psychoses. The lack of comparative studies between childhood and adult-onset schizophrenia makes it impossible, at this stage, to say whether OCs are more common in childhood-onset cases.

Psychosocial risk factors

Another possible explanation for variability in the age at onset of schizophrenia could be differential exposure to psychosocial adversity, such as high levels of parental hostility and criticism ("high EE"). High levels of expressed emotion (EE) among relatives of adult schizophrenics has been shown to be a predictor of psychotic relapse and poor outcome (Leff and Vaughn 1985). Although the role of high EE in precipitating the onset of schizophrenia has not been established, it is theoretically plausible that high EE might act to "bring forward" the onset of the disorder in a vulnerable individual. Goldstein

(1987) reported that parental EE measures of criticism and over involvement taken during adolescence were associated with an increased risk of schizophrenia spectrum disorders in young adulthood. A causal link was not proven, and the association may reflect either an expression of some common underlying trait or a parental response to premorbid disturbance in the preschizophrenic adolescent. More direct comparisons between the parents of adult and childhood-onset schizophrenics fail to support the hypothesis of higher parental EE in childhood-onset cases. Asarnow *et al.* (1994a) used the Five Minute Speech Sample to measure parental EE in childhood-onset schizophrenics and found no significant differences between rates of high EE in parents of subjects and normal controls. Overall, there seems to be little evidence to suggest that the onset of schizophrenia in childhood can be explained by exposure to higher levels of parental criticism and hostility than that experienced by adult-onset patients. Indeed, it appears that, on average, the parents of childhood-onset schizophrenics generally express *lower* levels of criticism and hostility than parents of adult-onset patients due to a greater tendency to attribute their childrens' behaviour to an "illness" which is beyond their control (Hooley 1987).

While the concept of EE is a measure of intrafamilial communication which is not specific to any particular psychiatric disorder, the quality of communication referred to as "communication deviance" (Singer and Wynne 1965) was developed to tap patterns of communication specific to schizophrenia. Communication deviance was constructed as an interpersonal measure of thought disorder and attentional disturbance and has been found to occur in higher levels in the parents of schizophrenic adults compared with parents of adults with other disorders or normal controls. Asarnow *et al.* (1988) reported similar findings, with higher rates of communication deviance among parents of childhood-onset schizophrenics and schizotypal disorders compared with parents of children with depressive disorders. Furthermore, schizophrenic and schizotypal children from families with the highest levels of communication deviance showed the most severe attentional impairments as indicated by the distractibility factor on the Wechsler Intelligence Scale for Children – Revised (WISC-R). During communication tasks, these children exhibited thought disorder and attentional drift. In summary, it appears that communication deviance is found in a proportion of families with both childhood and adult-onset schizophrenia. This finding supports the idea of continuity between childhood and adult-onset schizophrenia. While communication deviance is unlikely to be of etiological significance, it may well be a manifestation of a shared familial impairment in attention and information processing.

Psychophysiological and neuropsychological markers

There is good evidence that children with schizophrenia show some of the same difficulties with attention and information processing that have been identified in adult schizophrenia. Asarnow et al. (1991) and Asarnow and Sherman (1984) have demonstrated that children with schizophrenia have impairments on the span of apprehension task (a target stimulus has to be identified from an array of other figures when displayed for 50 ms). Performance on the task deteriorates markedly when increasing demands are made on information processing capacity (e.g., increasing the number of letters in the display from three to ten). Furthermore, when analyzing event-related potentials on the span of apprehension task, both children and adults with schizophrenia, compared with age matched controls, produce less negative endogenous activity measured between 100 and 300 ms after the stimulus. This finding indicates a deficit in the allocation of attentional resources to a stimulus (Strandburg et al. 1994). On measures of autonomic arousal, childhood-onset schizophrenics, like adult schizophrenics, show high basal autonomic activity and less autonomic responsivity than controls (Gordon et al. 1994). Abnormalities in smooth pursuit eye movements (SPEM) have been found in adolescent schizophrenics (mean age 14.5 years) which suggests continuity with the finding of abnormal SPEM in adult schizophrenics (Iacono and Koenig 1983). Children with schizophrenia also show similar impairments to adult patients on tests of frontal lobe executive function such as the Wisconsin Card Sorting Test (WCST) (Asarnow et al. 1994b).

Adult outcome of childhood-onset schizophrenia

An important test of the validity of the diagnosis of schizophrenia in childhood is to examine the continuity of the disorder over time. Furthermore, if childhood-onset schizophrenia lies on an extreme of a continuum of liability, then as a more severe form of the disorder, we would expect a particularly poor outcome. Unfortunately, there have been relatively few follow-up studies of childhood-onset schizophrenia, and of these, several have been restricted to adolescent-onset cases.

Werry et al. (1991) followed 59 psychotic patients (mean age at index admission 13.9 years) over a period ranging from 1 to 16 years. They found a striking lack of diagnostic continuity. From 54 cases of schizophrenia diagnosed at first admission, at follow-up, 13 had bipolar disorder, seven schizoaffective disorder and two other psychoses. This left 33 cases (61%) of the original schizophrenics who showed diagnostic continuity. The outcome of the group diagnosed as schizophrenic at follow-up was very poor, with an average general adaptive functioning (GAF) score of 40, and a mortality rate of 15%. Out of those initially diagnosed as schizophrenic, diagnostic continuity was predicted by insidious onset, poor premorbid function, and the absence of prominent affective symptoms. Positive psychotic symptoms did not differentiate between schizophrenic cases and those with a psychotic mood disorder. Werry et al. (1991) restricted their analysis of outcome to cases where the diagnosis was validated at follow-up: clearly, a method which contains an inherent circularity. A similar finding of very poor outcome in schizophrenic adolescents (based on all patients first diagnosed as schizophrenic) was reported by Cawthron et al. (1994). Unfortunately, the authors managed to follow-up less than 50% of their index sample of 19 Research Diagnostic Criteria (RDC) schizophrenics. Hence, these results may be subject to an ascertainment bias caused by the difficulty in tracing better functioning schizophrenic cases who were no longer in contact with mental health services. Comparisons with adult-onset follow-up studies require considerable caution given differences in measures, the small size of adolescent samples and potential ascertainment bias. The evidence available suggests that schizophrenia with onset in early adolescence tends to run a chronic course with a very poor outcome. This resembles the finding of poor outcome in schizophrenia with an adult onset under 25 years of age (Murray et al. 1988).

If there is an age-related continuum of liability for schizophrenia, we would expect the worst outcome to be in preadolescent-onset cases. We are aware of only two follow-up studies of preadolescent-onset patients. Eggers (1978) reported on a follow-up of 57 patients aged 7–13 years with a diagnosis of "childhood schizophrenia" made before the introduction of DSM-III and ICD-9 criteria in childhood. Although his results suggest a somewhat better prognosis, with 50% showing some form of improvement, the lack of operational diagnostic criteria make these findings difficult to interpret. Asarnow *et al.* (1994a) reported a recent follow-up study of childhood-onset schizophrenia using DSM-IIIR criteria (age range at onset 6–11.3 years). They found diagnostic continuity in 61% of index schizophrenic cases over a 2–7 year follow-up period, with 56% showing improvement in functioning, and the remainder minimal improvement or a deteriorating course. Somewhat surprisingly, 28% of the sample were classified as having a good outcome, based on a global adjustment scale (GAS) score of 60 or over. The variability of outcome in this young-onset sample suggests the possibility of considerable etiological heterogeneity in schizophrenia with onsets below the age of 11 or 12 years. Variability in outcome may also result from the inclusion of phenocopies and the effect of comorbidity. A category of "multi dimensionally impaired" (MDI) children has been invoked (Gordon *et al.* 1994) to describe those children who meet DSM-IIIR and DSM-IV criteria for schizophrenia and are characterized by mood lability, social ineptness, fleeting hallucinations under stress and odd thinking, particularly if language disorder is present. These children do not seem to exhibit the social withdrawal and negative prodromal symptoms characteristic of schizophrenia with onset in adolescence and early adult life.

SUMMARY

Does childhood-onset schizophrenia lie on a continuum with adult schizophrenia?

Using a definition of childhood-onset schizophrenia based on phenotypic resemblance with adult schizophrenia, there appears to be evidence of continuity of psychophysiological and neuropsychological measures, family history, premorbid impairments and structural brain abnormalities, and clinical course. There is also evidence of age-dependent variations from adult schizophrenia (heterotopy), with childhood-onset being characterized by a more insidious onset, disorganized behaviour, hallucinations in different modalities and a paucity of systematized or persecutory delusions. In addition, there is frequent comorbidity with ADHD, developmental disorders, and autistic symptoms. The variability in outcome of childhood-onset schizophrenia is broadly similar to that seen in young adults and does not suggest that childhood-onset cases have greater etiological homogeneity. Overall, the findings support the view of diagnostic continuity with some age-dependent variations in presentation. Meanwhile, there is rather greater uncertainty about the status of schizophrenia in preadolescent children. The results are eagerly awaited of current research initiatives (Gordon *et al.* 1994) which aim to refine the concept of schizophrenia in this age group.

What factors determine the 'atypical' childhood-onset of schizophrenia?

We raised two possible explanations for childhood onset. The first was that childhood onset cases lie at an extreme on a continuum of liability for schizophrenia, with the highest loading of etiological risk factors. The evidence from family genetic studies suggests that familial morbid risk is higher in adolescent-onset schizophrenics, although further studies with larger very early-onset samples are needed to confirm this. In line with the idea of increased liability, the outcome of childhood-onset schizophrenia is generally poor, although an unexpected finding is that preadolescent-onset cases may have a slightly better outcome than those with onset in adolescence. Various explanations include the possibility that the continuum of liability does not extend to the preadolescent cases, or that they are phenocopies with a different etiology, or that the effects of schizophrenia are buffered by prolonged family support. The overall impression is that the age of onset of schizophrenia is under strong genetic control, although this does not exclude the possibility of interactions with environmental risk factors.

A second explanation for "atypical" childhood-onset is the possibility that onset is "brought forward" by excessive psychosocial stress. If anything, the evidence points in the opposite direction, and suggests that the parents of childhood-onset schizophrenics are *less* likely than parents of adult patients to express criticism and hostility. This finding suggests that both patterns of family interaction and the interventions required may well be different in families where the onset of schizophrenia is in childhood rather than in adult life. As we will discuss later, the most significant psychosocial stressors for children at risk for schizophrenia may be peer relations and scholastic demands, which exert their effect from outside the family.

PRESCHIZOPHRENIA: PRECURSORS, RISK FACTORS OR EPIPHENOMENA?

The observation that some schizophrenics have premorbid abnormalities in personality and social relations has been noted since the earliest descriptions of the condition. Kretschmer (1921) described a form of "risk" model, where the premorbid personality was not seen as a direct precursor of schizophrenia, but as something that, when placed under sufficient stress, increased the probability of developing the disorder. On the other hand, Kraepelin (1919) saw early premorbid personality as a precursor, i.e., a subtle early manifestation of an underlying schizophrenic neuropathology. Although the analysis of premorbid impairments in schizophrenia has broadened in recent years to include more direct markers of central nervous system (CNS) development such as IQ, attention, information processing, and developmental milestones, the debate over whether they constitute specific precursors or nonspecific risk factors for schizophrenia continues.

Precursors are defined as behaviours or symptoms which almost invariably precede the onset of the disorder. They are also assumed to be "endogenous" to the disorder, i.e., expressions of the underlying pathological process at an earlier developmental stage. Epiphenomena are symptoms or behaviours which are associated with the disorder because they share some common cause e.g., minor physical anomalies (MPAs) may be associated with schizophrenia and other developmental disorders if fetal ectodermal development is affected at the same time as neurodevelopment. Epiphenomena such as MPAs are nonspecific correlates and can have no causal link to the onset of schizophrenia. Finally, risk factors are defined as symptoms or stressors which increase the risk of the disorder occurring but are not a manifestation of the disorder. Do the studies of preschizophrenia help us to define the status of these early abnormalities?

Retrospective and "follow-back" studies of clinical samples

Retrospective studies of clinical samples have suggested that adult schizophrenics had poorer scholastic achievement in childhood (Jones *et al.* 1993) and lower childhood IQ than controls (Offord and Cross 1971; Offord 1974). Using retrospective maternal recall of childhood behaviour, Foerster *et al.* (1991) found that social impairments and scholastic difficulties between the ages of 8 and 11 years are more common in male schizophrenics even when the controls are patients with an affective psychosis. In follow-back studies of adult schizophrenic patients who had previously attended a child psychiatry department, Jones *et al.*(1993), found that childhood IQ was low compared with those who developed other disorders as adults. Zeitlin (1986) and Ambelas (1992) used similar follow-back methods, and found preschizophrenic children had higher rates of developmental and personality problems than controls. Walker and Lewine (1990), Walker *et al.* (1993, 1994) have drawn on the home movies made by parents in early childhood. Compared with their normal siblings, the preschizophrenic children showed more atypical emotional expressions and subtle abnormalities in motor development (e.g., unusual left sided hand postures) in the first 2 years of life.

These abnormalities occurred so long before the onset of psychosis that it would be hard to see them simply as the early stage of illness. They are not simply the presence of any type of psychiatric difficulty: neurodevelopmental and personality problems are over represented in comparison with symptoms of other clinic-referred patients. Yet there is nothing to suggest that there is anything very specific about the abnormalities found; they are common problems and sound as though they should increase the risks for many adult disorders. On the other hand, the subtlety of description, that would be needed to capture a specific abnormality such as a thought disturbance, is unlikely to be forthcoming from routinely gathered childhood records.

Another difficulty in retrospective analyses of premorbid abnormalities is that the predictive significance of links between premorbid symptoms and schizophrenia can be overestimated, because such an approach does not take into account the prevalence of the disorder. A hypothetical numerical example illustrates this point. If in a case-control study of adult-onset schizophrenia, poor peer relationships at age 7 years were found in 30% of cases and 10% of controls, this would produce an approximate odds ratio or relative risk of 3 (the odds of schizophrenia were three times greater in those with poor peer relationships). If the prevalence of schizophrenia were 1% in the population, only about one out of every 30 children with poor peer relations would go on to develop schizophrenia, and in this group the absolute lifetime risk for schizophrenia would be approximately 3% compared with 1% in the whole population (a risk attributable to poor peer relations of 2%). This illustrates how important the prevalence is in considering links between antecedents and disorders. Hence, looking forward from childhood to adulthood the link between poor peer relations and schizophrenia looks less impressive than when looking backward from cases of adult schizophrenia.

"High risk" studies

There have been over 20 separate high-risk studies established since the early 1950s. The majority are "genetic high-risk", based on the strategy of following the development of children borne to one or more schizophrenic parent. These children are then compared with children of normal parents and those with other psychiatric disorders. The ultimate goal has been to identify antecedents of schizophrenia in the high-risk groups; however, because of the relatively low number of cases who have actually developed schizophrenia, the majority of comparisons have been between "high" and "low" risk groups rather than between preschizophrenics and controls.

Asarnow (1988) used a developmental perspective to organize these studies into five age periods: conception to infancy, early childhood, middle childhood, adolescence, and early adulthood. In the first period, there is evidence from several studies of increased rates of OCs in schizo-

phrenic mothers. These mothers were more likely than controls to show poor maternal competence, and it may be this factor, rather than genetic risk per se, that is responsible for the link between maternal disorder and OCs (Goodman 1987). The main problems reported during the first year of life point to poor motor and sensorimotor performance, such as an uneven pattern of motor and skeletal development (Fish 1987). In early childhood (ages 2–4 years) abnormalities in gross and fine motor performance are reported in schizophrenic children (Walker et al. 1993, 1994). These children are also those at greatest risk of having received poor antenatal care and inadequate mother–infant interaction (Goodman 1987). By middle childhood, high-risk children are more likely to be described as schizoid (i.e., emotionally flat, withdrawn, passive, irritable), and these features combined with poor motor functioning are associated with families who have the highest genetic loading for schizophrenia (Hanson et al. 1976). At this age, attention and information processing deficits are found, and they predict a psychiatric disorder in young adult life (Erlenmeyer-Kimling and Cornblatt 1987); but they correlate with poor neuromotor performance and lower IQ so their specificity is not established.

In adolescence, there is even greater evidence of impairment in high-risk children. Worland et al. (1984) reported lower IQ scores for children of schizophrenic and bipolar parents than those from nonpsychotic parents during adolescence but not during middle childhood. Children of schizophrenic parents had the lowest IQ correlations between the two age periods, suggesting less continuity, and perhaps some relative decline in intellectual functioning as they enter adolescence. Evidence of social dysfunction can also be found in high-risk samples during mid-childhood and adolescence. Many of these social impairments are found in other clinical populations and are not specific to schizophrenia. Parnas et al. (1982) described two dimensions, poor affective control (easily upset, disturbing class by unusual behaviour) and difficulty making friends, which were identified by teachers and discriminated high-risk adolescents who developed schizophrenia from those who did not.

In short, longitudinal study of the offspring of people with schizophrenia has reiterated the frequency of neurodevelopmental problems but has not yet been able to test mechanisms. The prediction of schizophrenia might show that neurodevelopmental problems are a specific vulnerability rather than a nonspecific risk; but that stage has not yet been reached. Clearer hypotheses will be needed about the proposed pathogenesis.

An alternative "high-risk" strategy is to follow-up children who possess an implicated risk factor. Cohort studies such as these should be able to show the developmental impact; but a precise definition of the risk factor would greatly increase their value. One example is the follow-up of children who presented obstetric complications at birth – a group reviewed by Taylor (1991). They are at risk for a range of disorders; although they have not yet reached an age where the risk for schizophrenia specifically can be assessed, they do show cognitive impairment and anxiety in childhood and adolescence. Interpretation is still limited by the ambiguity of this finding. Obstetric complications are also markers to a range of social adversities, and are more common in children with inherited disorders of the brain. A more exact definition of the hypothesized risk is therefore needed. Another high-risk strategy is exemplified by Rutter and Mawhood's (1991) follow-up of a group of boys with pure receptive language disorder into their early twenties. Three out of 25 cases had developed a schizophreniform psychosis by late adolescence. The majority of their subjects were socially isolated as young adults and had deficits in social cognition. While this study requires replication with a larger sample, the results suggest that deficits in language comprehension and social cognition may be candidates for the developmental processes involved in the pathogenesis of schizophrenia.

Birth cohort studies

The main strength of birth cohort studies is that they provide a window on the early development of a representative group of schizophrenics drawn from an epidemiological population, with observations free of retrospective observer bias. Their drawback is that they were not set up specifically to study schizophrenia, hence the measurements in childhood tend to be rather crude, and unlike the high-risk studies they do not target putative biobehavioural markers of schizophrenia.

Two cohort studies confirm the presence of childhood social and cognitive impairments before the onset of adult schizophrenia. These will not be considered further here as they are discussed in detail in Chapter 9 by Jones and Done.

In all of these types of studies, we have noted two characteristic features of premorbid abnormalities. First, there is a lack of specificity or positive predictive value for morphological brain abnormalities, OCs, MPAs, developmental delays and premorbid social and cognitive impairments. Second, premorbid abnormalities that occur longer before the onset of the disorder appear less likely to satisfy criteria as precursors of schizophrenia. This argues against an "early" neurodevelopmental model in which there is the unfolding of a static neuropathological lesion. If the idea of premorbid impairments as precursors of schizophrenia were to be maintained then one could still invoke a "stage model", where schizophrenia was preceded by an invariable sequence of developmental stages, each with its age-specific manifestations (e.g., neuromotor difficulties in infancy, attentional problems in mid-childhood and social/cognitive impairments in late childhood and early adolescence). The key difference from a deterministic neurodevelopmental model would be that each stage acted as a filter with only a proportion of cases moving on to the next stage. Stage theories in developmental psychopathology have important properties, in particular their ability to account for the age at onset distributions of disorders (Pickles 1993). Unfortunately, data on age-dependent premorbid impairments comes largely from cross-sectional analyses of high-risk studies, and there is relatively little data on longitudinal, within-individual preschizophrenic development. Research has not yet found any specific pattern or developmental progression of preschizophrenic symptoms; but the work so far would not necessarily have detected such a pattern. Furthermore, when continuous (as opposed to categorical) premorbid variables such as IQ are studied (Jones et al. 1994), the results suggest a linear trend in risk for schizophrenia associated with IQ across the whole population. Hence, it seems that when the analysis shifts from categorical to continuous measures such as IQ, premorbid impairments appear to act as independent risk factors rather than specific precursors.

A developmental psychopathology perspective offers a probabilistic, rather than a deterministic, view of the development of schizophrenia. The idea that premorbid impairments are manifestations of a primary causal lesion occurring during fetal neurodevelopment appears difficult to sustain. An alternative neurodevelopmental model proposes that a variety of independent risk factors (and protective factors) acting over the course of child and adolescent development act to increase or decrease the probability of developing schizophrenia. Other premorbid impairments may be epiphenomena which, as non-specific correlates, play no causal role in the development of schizophrenia. Finally, the evidence for premorbid impairments as precursors is strongest for those that arise proximal to the onset of schizophrenia in early adolescence, such as affective instability, social withdrawal, and relative cognitive decline. To understand more about the developmental processes leading to the onset of schizophrenia, it may be necessary to shift our attention from distal processes (fetal neurodevelopment) to proximal processes (social-, cognitive- and neuro-development in late childhood and adolescence).

THE DEVELOPMENTAL PSYCHOPATHOLOGY OF SCHIZOPHRENIA

We have argued that the clinical disorder of schizophrenia can be detected in children and is generally similar to that seen in adults. The preschizophrenic abnormalities seen in children seem, in the light of present knowledge, to be rather nonspecific and of a type often seen in other forms of deviant development. It therefore seems that the neurodevelopmental abnormalities of preschizophrenia are of a rather different nature to schizophrenia itself. They cannot be seen as simply the presentation of schizophrenia in an immature organism (heterotypic continuity), as the immature evidently can develop the full clinical syndrome. Rather, they seem likely to represent a risk factor.

Developmental psychopathology brings the contrasting concepts of risk and disorder to bear on this complex situation. It highlights the importance of finding answers to questions about the ways in which risk and protective factors interact to produce disorder. In this section we consider some issues that follow from this approach: the importance of a variety of changes in cognitive and neurobiological development, the interaction of biological and psychosocial risks during childhood and adolescence, and the implications of continuum and categorical models of neurodevelopmental dysfunction.

Many other developmental disorders, such as autism, ADHD and DLD, are thought to have primary deficits mainly at a cognitive or neuropsychological level. Brain dysfunction is thought to lead to altered understanding and hence to the symptoms of deficit. In autism, for example, early social deficits are now understood in terms of a failure in infancy to develop the normal cognitive abilities of social imitation and recognition of other peoples' mental states – referred to as the child's "theory of mind" (Baron-Cohen et al. 1985). Similarly, in ADHD the characteristic phenomena of overactivity, impulsivity, and distractibility are usually attributed to a primary deficit in the development of cognitive process involved in the inhibition of inappropriate responses (Barkley 1994). Other explanations are possible: Sonuga-Barke et al. (1992a, 1992b) have argued that the "impairment" is rather a matter of aversion to delay and therefore an avoidance of test situations involving delay. In either event, however, a resultant failure of response suppression is a good explanation both of test impairment and of the behavioral changes that constitute the diagnosis. In schizophrenia, our understanding of developmental neuropsychology, and its relationship to psychopathology is less well established.

Executive function and social cognition
It is well recognized that schizophrenic patients manifest a range of cognitive deficits. While basic sensorimotor skills, associative memory and simple language abilities tend to be preserved (Mesulam 1990), deficits are most marked on tasks which require focused and sustained attention, flexible switching of cognitive set, high information processing speed and suppression of prepotent responses. These diverse processes have been integrated under the cognitive domain of "executive functions" which are presumed to be mediated by the prefrontal cortical system. Executive function skills are necessary to generate and execute goal-directed behavior, especially in

novel situations. Goal orientated actions require that information in the form of plans and expectations are held "on-line" in working memory, and flexibly changed in response to feedback. Much of social behaviour and social development would appear to depend on these capacities as they involve integration of multiple sources of information, appreciation of others mental states, inhibition of inappropriate, prepotent responses and rapid shifting of attention.

In order to examine the possible etiological role of executive function deficits in schizophrenia we need to address the following questions. First, how well do executive function deficits explain the symptoms of schizophrenia? Second, how could an executive function deficit explain the timing of onset of schizophrenia? Third, what is the relationship between executive function and developmental brain mechanisms? Fourth, what evidence is there that developmental impairments in executive function are a primary deficit in schizophrenia, rather than a nonspecific correlate of the disorder?

Executive function and psychopathology

There is growing evidence of associations between particular dimensions of schizophrenic symptoms and poor performance on tests designed to measure frontal lobe executive functions. For example, negative features such as poverty of speech and flattened affect, are associated with errors of omission and perseveration on verbal fluency and vigilance tasks. On the same tasks, disorganized features, such as incoherent speech and incongruous affect, are associated with inappropriate responses (errors of commission) (Frith et al. 1991). Meanwhile, positive symptoms, such as hallucinations and delusions, appear not to be associated with any specific deficit on frontal lobe tasks. Liddle et al. (1992) studied the relationship between mental state and resting regional cerebral blood flow (rCBF) in schizophrenic patients. They found associations between psychomotor poverty and reduced rCBF in the dorsolateral prefrontal cortex (DLPFC), disorganized features and reduced rCBF in the right ventrolateral prefrontal cortex, and reality distortion (hallucinations and delusions) and increased rCBF in the parahippocampal region of the left temporal lobe. Weinberger et al. (1986) found that schizophrenic patients when performing the

Wisconsin Card Sorting Test (WCST; which tests the ability to flexibly switch mental set) failed to show the expected activation of the DLPFC. This result was not the result of poor performance on the test, because Huntington's disease patients who also perform poorly on the WCST show normal activation of the DLPFC.

Poor performance on frontal lobe tasks is most clearly associated with negative and disorganized symptoms of psychosis, while hallucinations and delusions have been linked with temporal lobe function. The deficits on neuropsychological tests and the associated symptoms may reflect a breakdown of connections between integrated brain systems rather than the result of a focal brain lesion. Patients with negative features have a specific problem with willed actions, i.e., those actions where the required response is not fully specified by the context. Word generation is an example of such a task, and in normal subjects this task results in a reciprocal increase in activity in the DLPFC and reduction of activity in the superior temporal cortex. In schizophrenic subjects, the increase in activity in the DLPFC is not associated with a reciprocal decrease in the superior temporal cortex on the left (Friston et al. 1995). Hence, it is possible that in schizophrenia, because of disconnections between cortical areas, tasks that place a heavy demand on executive functions may result in unusual patterns of temporal lobe function and associated positive psychotic symptoms. Mlakar et al. (1994) have described a cognitive defect in "self-monitoring", resulting in a breakdown in the ability of a schizophrenic patient to distinguish the origins of his own thoughts or actions from those of others. This loss of "meta-cognitive" or executive capacities may result from a loss of normal connectivity between the prefrontal cortex and other brain regions.

In addition to executive function deficits, there is increasing evidence that people with schizophrenia have deficits in aspects of social cognition that require sophisticated judgments about other people's mental states. While social cognition is unlikely to be entirely independent from executive function, capacities such as emotional perception (faces and intonation) and perception of pragmatics are not usually included in tests of executive function. The ability to attribute mental states to others has been referred to as a "theory of mind" and has been extensively studied in autism. The problems of social cognition encountered in schizophrenia appear both to be much more subtle than in autism and to have a later onset. In schizophrenia, deficits can occur in the understanding of irony, humour and vocal intonations. This can lead to severe difficulties in understanding subtle, context dependent, changes in the meaning of communication. Hence, it is possible to see how such deficits could result in both social handicaps and symptoms such as delusions of reference or persecution as faulty inferences are drawn about other peoples' mental states.

Executive functions and the timing of onset of schizophrenia

Any cognitive theory of schizophrenia would need to be able to explain the timing of onset of the disorder which usually emerges during adolescence and early adulthood. Deficits in executive function and social cognition could be the developmental abnormality predisposing to schizophrenia, as they result in a failure to develop the social skills that normally emerge in early adolescence. This developmental period is associated with a rapid growth in abstract analytical skills, together with a development in the sophisticated social and communication abilities that form the basis of mature social relationships. It is during this period of development (approximately age 8–15 years) that preschizophrenic social impairments become most clearly apparent (Parnas et al. 1982; Done et al. 1994), and preschizophrenics show a relative decline in cognitive abilities (Worland et al. 1984; Jones et al. 1994).

In this view, the onset of psychosis would depend on an interaction between social and cognitive capacities and the demands of the environment. During adolescence, increasing academic and social demands may act as stressors on the preschizophrenic subject. The greater the impairment in social cognition, the earlier the age that a liability threshold will be passed and symptoms will emerge. This developmental model would predict that more severe negative symptoms and social impairments will be found in earlier onset cases, but that these impairments will be independent of the duration of illness, i.e., they will be manifest at first onset (Frith et al. 1991). According to this model, early developmental impairments resulting in cognitive or specific language deficits,

would act as nonspecific, independent, risk factors (not precursors) that increase the liability for schizophrenia and may reduce the age at onset.

Links between cognitive and brain development

Brain development is characterized by initial overproduction of synapses, followed by synaptic elimination which occurs well into adolescence. During the first 2 years of life there is a rapid growth in synaptic connections in the brain. In childhood, and particularly early adolescence, remodeling takes place with progressive pruning and elimination of synapses (Huttenlocher 1979; Purves and Litchman 1980).

Aberrant or excessive synaptic elimination during adolescence may effect the development of executive functions and social cognition as a result of abnormal connectivity between the prefrontal cortex and the hippocampus, amygdala and cingulate gyrus (Hoffman and McGlashan 1994). Synaptic breakdown products include cell membrane phospholipids which can be measured using magnetic resonance spectroscopy (MRS).

Pettegrew et al. (1991) used ^{31}P MRS in first episode, nonmedicated, schizophrenics and found reduced phosphomonoester (PME) resonance and increased phosphodiester (PDE) resonance in the prefrontal cortex. Although preliminary, these results are compatible with reduced synthesis and increased breakdown of connective processes in the prefrontal cortex. A similar finding of reduced PME and increased PDE resonance has been reported in autistic adults, although they showed increased prefrontal metabolic activity, which was not seen in schizophrenic subjects (Pettegrew et al. 1991). It is possible that excessive synaptic elimination is not specific to schizophrenia, but its timing may have important implications for the development of executive functions in late childhood and adolescence.

Specificity of cognitive risk factors

The emergence of hypotheses about the nature of cognitive dysfunction in schizophrenia will make it possible to test whether it is necessary or sufficient for the development of the disorder. An executive function deficit might be a primary deficit in schizophrenia, or a nonspecific correlate of other more fundamental processes. To be considered a primary deficit, it should be specific for the disorder, persistent over time, and show causal precedence (emerging before the onset of other symptoms).

Deficits in executive function have been found in other developmental disorders, including autism (Hughes and Russell 1993) and ADHD (Pennington *et al.* 1993). A more detailed comparison is required of the similarities and differences in executive function deficits in schizophrenia and in disorders such as autism and ADHD. Comparisons are needed between schizophrenics and IQ matched high-functioning autistics in order to ascertain which deficits of executive function and social cognition, if any, are specific to each disorder. Schizophrenic subjects would be expected to pass simple "theory of mind" tasks, but to fail on more complex tasks, requiring appreciation of humour, irony or intonation in order to decode mental states. They should differ from those with autism on measures of abnormal eye movements, which appear both to be a trait marker in schizophrenia and to correlate in normal subjects with the development of the prefrontal cortex.

Comparisons between schizophrenia and developmental language disorders should also be helpful in view of the possibility that language impairment (possibly receptive language disorder) may be part of the etiology of thought disorder and auditory hallucinations. In studies of ADHD children (Welsh *et al.* 1991), deficits have been found in executive function measures that tap planning ability (Tower of Hanoi), flexibility of strategies (WCST), and impulse control (Matching Familiar Figures Test and Continuous Performance Test). There is considerable overlap between the type of executive function deficits seen in ADHD (errors of commission, with failure to inhibit responses) and the errors in schizophrenics associated with the "disorganization syndrome" (incoherent speech and inappropriate affect) (Frith *et al.* 1991). Both structural (Hynd *et al.* 1991) and functional brain imaging (Lou *et al.* 1984) have suggested abnormalities in the right frontal lobe in ADHD, which correlates both with measures of sustained attention and the functional localization of the "disorganization syndrome" in schizophrenia (Liddle *et al.* 1992). Circumstantial evidence suggests that there may be a selective attention impairment in schizophrenia that is not parallelled by anything found in ADHD (Taylor 1995). Direct comparisons should now be fruitful.

A further criterion for establishing whether an executive function deficit is primary in schizophrenia involves demonstrating that it preceded and predicts the onset of the disorder. Longitudinal high-risk studies are needed which study executive function and social cognition in the siblings of probands as they enter the risk period for schizophrenia. A longitudinal twin study design would be valuable to measure behavioural-genetic correlation of phenotypes (e.g., developmental risk factors and schizophrenia). Previous studies have suffered because they have not set out to test specific hypotheses about the nature of cognitive problems which may lead to the development of schizophrenia. In summary, although executive function deficits in schizophrenia are compatible with the premorbid impairments, timing of onset and symptomatology of the disorder, further research is required to establish whether or not they constitute a neuropsychological primary deficit in schizophrenia.

Interactions between biological and psychosocial factors

Psychosocial disturbance alone is unlikely to account for the variability in the age at onset of schizophrenia (see earlier). Results from the Finnish Family Adoptive Study (Tienari *et al.* 1987) suggest that there may be an interaction between genetic and psychosocial risk factors. The authors reported significantly higher rates of schizophrenic and psychotic disorders in biological children of schizophrenic mothers reared in disturbed as opposed to healthy adoptive families. Meanwhile, an adverse adoptive environment did not increase the risk of schizophrenia in offspring of normal parents. In the Copenhagen High-Risk Study, Mednick *et al.* (1987) reported that children of schizophrenic parents who developed schizophrenia had poorer relationships with their mothers and fathers than did those high-risk children who were either not mentally ill or developed other psychiatric disorders. Taken together, these results suggest that social adversity may increase the risk of schizophrenia, but only in subjects with a sufficient underlying genetic liability.

In the birth cohort study reported by Jones *et al.* (1994) the mothers of preschizophrenic children were almost six times more likely than mothers of controls to be rated by health visitors when their children were aged 4 years as deficient in parenting skills and in their understanding of their child. While this finding appears to support the association between poor parental care and schizophrenia in a genetic high-risk sample (Tienari *et al.* 1987), the result may reflect deviant attributes of the child, the mother or both.

The interactions between biological risk and psychosocial stressors may be of several types, and their precise form will have implications for the types of intervention that would be relevant. The simplest is the long-known finding that life events are commoner, in the 3 weeks before admission, than for a group of nonschizophrenic controls (Brown and Birley 1968). This was the case even for "independent" life events that could scarcely be the result of illness (Brown *et al.* 1972). They acted to bring forward the onset of illness rather than as a sufficient cause.

Preschizophrenic abnormalities of cognition may do more than alter the reaction of the individual to a stressor. Individual differences of constitutional origin can determine the likelihood of exposure to environmental risks. The best established psychosocial influence on schizophrenia is that of high expressed emotion (E.E.) on the frequency of relapse; therapeutic reduction of expressed emotion reduces relapse, so the influence is probably causal (Leff *et al.* 1982, Goldstein 1987); however, high EE is not specific in its effects. It is also linked to the outcome of depression in childhood and of hyperactivity (Hibbs *et al.* 1991; Taylor *et al.* in press). Furthermore, EE is reduced when a child's disorder is reduced by medication, so the causal influences go both ways (Schachar *et al.* 1987).

What seems to emerge is a set of developmental pathways in which cognitive abnormalities in the child may lead to altered relationships with other family members and peers, and increase vulnerability to increasing educational demands. These factors may then, in turn, magnify cognitive and social deficits and increase the likelihood of transition into an acute disorder. Longitudinal studies should examine whether this chain of transactional events provides a better account of the development of the disorder than does the notion of a direct expression of a neuropsychological deficit.

Cognitive abnormality in preschizophrenic children could be either a qualitative deviation from normal development, or an extreme position on a continuum that can be attributed to the operation of the same factors that determine the normal range of variation. The abnormality could be unique to schizophrenia, or shared in many disorders of development. It could be that the way that non-specific factors come together is crucial. The developmental psychopathology approach does not answer the questions yet, just draws attention to their importance.

CONCLUSIONS – DIRECTIONS FOR FUTURE RESEARCH

The aim of this chapter has been to examine the status of schizophrenia as a neurodevelopmental disorder from the perspective of developmental psychopathology. We began by considering whether there was continuity between schizophrenia in childhood and in adults. Overall, the available evidence supports the continuity of schizophrenia into childhood and the use of adult diagnostic criteria. The problems of potential phenocopies and comorbid states, together with immature cognitive and language abilities, make preadolescent diagnosis particularly problematic. Unfortunately, there are no satisfactory direct comparisons between childhood and adult schizophrenia. Indirect evidence suggests that childhood onset cases tend to have more severe premorbid impairments, more insidious onset and present with more disorganised subtypes and have a poor outcome. Specifically, there is a need to test the hypothesis that childhood-onset cases lie on a continuum of liability with a greater loading of risk factors (genetic and/or environmental) than adult-onset cases.

We then turned to evaluate the meaning of preschizophrenic childhood abnormalities. There appears to be relatively little evidence to suggest that these childhood abnormalities are the manifestations of a primary causal lesion arising in fetal development. In contrast, the evidence suggests that most childhood abnormalities in schizophrenia are non-specific, independent, risk factors which act to increase the vulnerability of an individual to key neurodevelopmental, cognitive and social changes which occur during late childhood and adolescence. The evidence for preschizophrenic abnormalities as precursors is strongest for those that arise proximal to the onset of the disorder in late childhood and early adolescence, such as affective changes, social withdrawal and relative cognitive decline.

In the final section, we explored how developmental psychopathology may help us to understand the complex transactions between brain development, cognitive development, changing psychosocial demands and the timing of onset of psychiatric symptoms. Many of the symptoms in schizophrenia can be understood in terms of a deficit in frontal lobe executive functions that coincide with a failure to develop "higher-level" social cognition. A failure to cope with the increasing complexity of social and cognitive demands could lead to the onset of psychotic symptoms. The greater the loading of pre-existing developmental risk, the earlier that the psychotic process will occur for any given genetic risk. These deficits in social cognition and executive function may be paralleled at a neurobiological level by excessive synaptic elimination resulting in loss of normal developing connectivity between brain regions. We suggest that the timing of aberrant neurodevelopment may be later than has previously been considered in the "early" neurodevelopmental models of schizophrenia, which have focused largely on fetal neurodevelopment. A shift of attention to the relatively neglected area of neuropsychological and neurobiological development in adolescence is needed.

Any cognitive theory of schizophrenia is faced by a problem of discriminant validity, given the claims of links between many disorders and abnormalities of executive function. Hence, we suggest that schizophrenics and high-risk subjects should be compared on a range of measures of executive function and social cognition with other developmental disorders, such as high-functioning autism, ADHD and developmental language disorders.

If more precise and predictive statements are to be made about the developmental etiology of schizophrenia, then schizophrenia research should focus more on comparisons with the "prototypic" developmental disorders of childhood. An exciting future lies ahead, which promises to abandon the parochial distinction between child and adult psychiatric disorders. A way forward is to integrate research into developmental disorders across the life span, and provide new insights into both normal development and psychopathology.

ACKNOWLEDGMENT

During the preparation of this chapter Dr Chris Hollis was supported by a Medical Research Council (MRC) Training Fellowship.

REFERENCES

Ambelas, A. 1992. Preschizophrenics: adding to the evidence, sharpening the focus. *Br. J. Psychiatry* **160**:401–4.

Andreasen, N., Ehrhardt, J.C., Swazye, V.W., Alliger, R.J., Yuh, W.T.L., Cohen, G., and Ziebell, S. 1990. Magnetic resonance imaging of the brain in schizophrenia. *Arch. Gen. Psychiatry* **47**:35–44.

Asarnow, J.R., 1988. Children at risk for schizophrenia: converging lines of evidence. *Schizophr. Bull.* **14**:613–31.

Asarnow, J.R. and Ben-Meir, S. 1988. Children with schizophrenia spectrum and depressive disorders: a comparative study of premorbid adjustment, onset pattern and severity of impairment. *J. Child Psychol. Psychiatry* **29**:477–88.

Asarnow, J.R., Goldstein, M.J., and Ben-Meir, S. 1988. Parental communication deviance in childhood onset schizophrenia spectrum and depressive disorders. *J. Child Psychol. Psychiatry* **29**:825–38.

Asarnow, R., Granholm, E., and Sherman, T. 1991. Span of apprehension in schizophrenia. In *Handbook of schizophrenia, vol 5. Neuropsychology, psychophysiology and information processing*, ed. S.R. Steinhauer, J.H. Gruzelier and J. Zubin, pp. 335–70. Amsterdam: Elsevier.

Asarnow, R. and Sherman, T. 1984. Studies of visual information processing in schizophrenic children. *Child Dev.* **55**:249–61.

Asarnow, J.R., Thompson, M.C., and Goldstein, M.J. 1994a. Childhood-onset schizophrenia: a follow-up study. *Schizophr. Bull.* **20**:599–617.

Asarnow, J.R., Thompson, M.C., Hamilton, E.B., Goldstein, M.J., and Guthrie, D. 1994b. Family expressed emotion, childhood onset depression, and childhood onset schizophrenic spectrum disorders: is expressed emotion a non-specific correlate of psychopathology or a specific risk factor for depression? *J. Abn. Psychol.* **22**:129–46.

Barkley, R.A. 1994. Impaired delayed responding: a unified theory of ADHD. In: *Disruptive behavior disorders in childhood*, D.K. Ruth ed. New York: Plenum Press.

Baron-Cohen, S., Leslie, A.M., and Frith, U. 1985. Does the autistic child have a "theory of mind"? *Cognition* **21**:37–46.

Bassett, A.S. and Honer, W.G. 1994. Evidence for anticipation in schizophrenia. *Am. J. Hum. Genet.* **54**:864–70.

Benes, F.M. 1989. Myelination of cortical-hippocampal relays during late adolescence. *Schizophr. Bull.* **15**:585–93.

Beratis, S., Gabriel, J., and Hoidas, S. 1994. Age at onset in subtypes of schizophrenic disorders. *Schizophr. Bull.* **20**:287–96.

Bleuler, E. 1911. *Dementia praecox order Gruppe der Schizophrenien*. In Handbuch der Psychiatrie, special part, fasc. 4, ed. G. Ashaffenburg. Vienna: Deuticke.

Brown, G.W. and Birley, J.T.L. 1968. Cases and life changes and the onset of schizophrenia. *J. Health Social Behav.* **9**:203.

Brown, G.W., Birley, J.T.L., and Wing, J.K. 1972. Influence of family life on the course of schizophrenic disorders: a replication. *Br. J. Psychiatry* **121**:241–58.

Cawthron, P., James, A., Dell, J., and Seagroatt, V. 1994. Adolescent onset psychosis: A clinical and outcome study. *J. Child Psychol. Psychiatry* **35**:1321–32.

Childs, B. and Scriber, C. 1986. Age at onset and cause of disease. *Perspect. Biol. Med.* **29**:437–60.

Crow, T.J. and Done, D.J. 1986. Age at onset of schizophrenia in siblings: a test of the contagion hypothesis. *Psychiatry Res.* **18**:107–17.

De Lisi, L.E., Hoff, L.A., Schwartz, J.E., Shields, G.W., Halthore, S.W., Gupta, S.M., Henn, F.A., and Anand, A.K. 1991. Brain morphology in first-episode schizophrenic-like psychotic patients: a qualitative magnetic resonance imaging study. *Biol. Psychiatry* **29**:159–75.

De Sanctis, S. 1906. On some varieties of dementia praecox. In *Rivista Sperimentale di Freniatria e Medicina Legale delle Alienazioni Mentale*, ed. J.G. Howell, pp. 141–65. (Translated by M.L. Osbourn.) New York: Brunner Mazel.

Done, J.D., Crow, T.J., Johnstone, E.C., and Sacker, A. 1994. Childhood antecedents of schizophrenia and affective illness: social adjustment at ages 7 and 11. *Br. Med. J.* **309**:699–703.

Eggers, C. 1978. Course and prognosis in childhood schizophrenia. *J. Autism Child. Schizophr.* **8**:21–36.

Erlenmeyer-Kimling, L. and Cornblatt, B. 1987. The New York High Risk Project: a follow-up report. *Schizophr. Bull.* **13**:451–61.

Feinberg, I. 1983. Schizophrenia: caused by a fault in programmed synaptic elimination during adolescence? *J. Psychiatr. Res.* **17**: 319–44.

Fish, B. 1987. Infant predictors of the longitudinal course of schizophrenic development. *Schizophr. Bull.* **13**:395–409.

Fish, B. and Rivito, E.R. 1979. Psychoses of childhood. In *Basic handbook of child psychiatry, Vol. 2*, ed. J.D. Noshpitz, pp. 249–304. New York: Basic Books.

Foerster, A., Lewis, S., Owen, M., and Murray, R.M. 1991. Pre-morbid adjustment and personality in psychosis. *Br. J. Psychiatry* **158**:171–6.

Friston, K.J., Herold, S., Fletcher, P., Silbersweig, D., Dolan, R.J., Liddle, P.S., Frackowiak, R.S.J., and Frith, C.D. 1995. Abnormal frontotemporal interaction in schizophrenia. In *Biology of schizophrenia and affective disorders*, ed. S.J. Watson. New York: Raven Press.

Frith, C.D., Leary, J., Cahill, C., and Johnstone, E.C. 1991. Disabilities and circumstances of schizophrenic patients: a follow-up study. IV. Performance on psychological tests: clinical and demographic correlates of the results of these tests. *Br. J. Psychiatry* **159**:26–39.

Gaffney, G.R., Kuperman, S., Tsia, L.Y., and Minchin, S. 1989. Forebrain structure in autism. *J. Am. Acad. Child Adol. Psychiatry* **28**:534–7.

Gillberg, C., Wahlstrom, J., Forsman, A., Hellgren, L., and Gillberg, I.C. 1986. Teenage psychoses: epidemiology, classification and reduced optimality in the pre-, peri-, and neonatal periods. *J. Child Psychol. Psychiatry* **27**:87–98.

Goldstein, M.J. 1987. The UCLA High Risk Project. *Schizophr. Bull.* **13**:505–14.

Goodman, S.H. 1987. Emory University Project on Children of Disturbed Parents. *Schizophr. Bull.* **13**:411–23.

Gordon, C.T., Frazier, J.A., McKenna, K. Giedd, J., Zametkin, A., Zahn, T, Hommer, D, Hong, W., Kaysen, D., Albus, K.E., and Rapoport, J.L. 1994. Childhood-onset schizophrenia: a NIMH study in progress. *Schizophr. Bull.* **20**:697–712.

Gottesman, I.I. and Shields, J. 1972. *Schizophrenia and genetics: a twin study vantage point*. Orlando: Academic Press.

Green, W., Campbell, M., Hardesty, A., Grega, D., Padron-Gayol, M., Shell, J., and Erlenmeyer-Kimling, L. 1984. A comparison of schizophrenic and autistic children. *J. Am. Acad. Child Psychiatry* **23**:399–409.

Gualtieri, C.T., Adams, A., and Chen, C.D. 1982. Minor physical abnormalities in alcoholic and schizophrenic adults and hyperactive and autistic children. *Am. J. Psychiatry* **139**:640–3.

Guy, J.D., Majorski, L.V., Wallace, C.J., and Guy, M.P. 1983. The incidence of minor physical anomolies in adult schizophrenics. *Schizophr. Bull.* **9**:571–82.

Hanson, D.R., Gottesman, I.I., and Heston, L.L. 1976. Some possible childhood indicators of adult schizophrenia inferred from children of schizophrenics. *Br. J. Psychiatry* **129**:142–54.

Hendren, R.L., Hodde-Vargas, M.S., Vargas, L.A., Orrison, W.W., and Dell, L. 1991. Magnetic resonance imaging of severely disturbed children: a preliminary study. *J. Am. Acad. Child and Adol. Psychiatry* **30**:466–70.

Hibbs, E.D., Hamburger, S.D., Lenane, M., Rapoport, J.L., Kreusi, M.J.P., Keysor, C.S., and Goldstein, M.J. 1991. Determinants of expressed emotion in families of disturbed and normal children. *J. Child Psychol. Psychiatry* **32**:757–70.

Hoffman, R.E. and McGlashan, T.H. 1994. Cortical connectivity, autonomous networks and schizophrenia. *Schizophr. Bull.* **20**:257–61.

Hollis, C. 1995. Child and adolescent (juvenile onset) schizophrenia: a case control study of premorbid developmental impairments. *Br. J. Psychiatry* **166**:489–95.

Hooley, J.M. 1987. The nature and origins of expressed emotion. In *Understanding major mental disorder: the contribution of family interaction research*, ed. K. Hahlweg and M.J. Goldstein, pp. 176–194. New York: Family Process.

Hughes, C. and Russell, J. 1993. Autistic children's difficulty with mental disengagement with an object: its implications for theories of autism. *Dev. Psychol.* **29**:498–510.

Huttenlocher, P.R. 1979. Synaptic density in human prefrontal cortex: developmental changes and effects of aging. *Brain Res.* **163**:195–205.

Hynd, G.W., Semrud-Clikeman, M., Lorys, A.R., Norey, E.S., and Eliopulas, D. 1991. Brain morphology in developmental dyslexia and attention deficit disorder/hyperactivity. *Arch. Neurol.* **47**:919–26.

Iacono, W.G. and Koenig, W.G.R. 1983. Features that distinguish smooth pursuit eye tracking performance in schizophrenic, affective disordered and normal individuals. *J. Abnor. Psychology* **92**:29–41.

Jacob, H. and Beckman, H. 1986. Prenatal developmental disturbances in the limbic allocortex in schizophrenics. *J. Neur. Transm.*, **65**:303–26.

Johnstone, E.C., Owens, D.G.C., Colter, N., and Crow, T.J. 1989. The spectrum of structural changes in the brain in schizophrenia: age at onset as a predictor of clinical and cognitive impairments and their cerebral correlates. *Psychol. Med.* **19**:91–103.

Jones, P.B., Guth, C., Lewis, S.M., and Murray, R.M. 1993. Low intelligence and poor educational achievement precede early onset schizophrenic psychosis. In *The neuropsychology of schizophrenia*, ed. A.S. David and J. Cutting. Lawrence Erlbaum: Hove, UK.

Jones, P., Rogers, B., Murray, R., and Marmot, M. 1994. Child development risk factors for adult schizophrenia in the British 1946 birth cohort. *Lancet* **344**:1398–402.

Kallman, F.J. and Roth, B. 1956. Genetic aspects of preadolescent schizophrenia. *Am. J. Psychiatry* **112**:599–606.

Kendler, K.S., Tsuang, M.T., and Hays, P. 1987. Age at onset in schizophrenia: a familial perspective. *Arch. Gen. Psychiatry* **44**:881–90.

Kolvin, I. 1971. Studies in the childhood psychoses: I. Diagnostic criteria and classification. *Br. J. Psychiatry* **118**:381–84.

Kraepelin, E. 1919. *Dementia praecox* (R. Barclay, Trans.). Edinburgh: Livingstone.

Kretschmer, E. 1921. *Physique and character* (Trans. 1936). London: Kegan Paul.

Leff, J., Kuipers, L., Berkowitz, R., Eberlein-Vries, R., and Sturgeon, D. 1982. A controlled trial of social intervention in the families of schizophrenic patients. *Br. J. Psychiatry* **141**:121–34.

Leff, J. and Vaughn, C. 1985. *Expressed emotion in families: its significance for mental illness*. London: Guilford Press.

Lewis, S.W. and Murray, R.M. 1987. Obstetric complications, neurodevelopmental deviance and risk of schizophrenia. *J. Psychiatri. Res.* **21**:414–21.

Lewis, S.W., Murray, R.M., and Owen, M.J. 1989. Obstetric complications in schizophrenia: methodology and mechanisms. In *Schizophrenia: scientific progress*, ed. S.C. Schultz and C.A. Tamminga, pp. 56–9. New York: Oxford University Press.

Lou, H.C., Hendriksen, L., and Bruhn, P. 1984. Focal cerebral hypoperfusion and/or attention deficit disorder. *Arch. Neurology* **41**:825–9.

Liddle, P.F., Friston, K.J., Frith, C.D., Hirsch, S.R., Jones, T., and Frackowiak, R.S.J. 1992. Patterns of cerebral blood flow in schizophrenia. *Br. J. Psychiatry* **160**:179–86.

McNeil, T.F. and Kaij, L. 1978. Obstetric factors in the development of schizophrenia. In *The nature of schizophrenia*, L.C. Wynne, R.L. Cromwell and S. Matthysse, pp. 401–29. New York: John Wiley.

Mednick, S., Parnas, J., and Schulsinger, F. 1987. The Copenhagen High-Risk Project, 1962–86. *Schizophr. Bulletin* **13**:485–95.

Mesulam, M. 1990. Schizophrenia and the brain. *New Engl. J. Med.* **322**: 842–5.

Mlakar, J., Jensterle, J., and Frith, C.D. 1994. Central monitoring deficiency and schizophrenic symptoms. *Psychol. Med.* **24**:557–64.

Murray, R.M. and Lewis, S.W. 1987. Is schizophrenia a neurodevelopmental disorder? *Br. Med. J.* **295**:681–2.

Murray, R.M., Lewis, S.W., Owen, M.J., and Foerster, A. 1988. The neurodevelopmental origins of dementia praecox. In *Schizophrenia: the major issues*, ed. P. McGuffin and P. Bebbington, pp. 90–107. London: Heinmann.

Offord, D. 1974. School performance of adult schizophrenics, their siblings and age mates. *Br. J. Psychiatry* **125**:12–19.

Offord, D.R. and Cross, L.A. 1971. Adult schizophrenia with scholastic failure and low IQ in childhood. *Arch. Gen. Psychiatry* **24**:431–5.

Parnas, J., Schulsinger, F., Schulsinger, H., Mednick, S. and Teasdale, T. 1982. Behavioural precursors of schizophrenia spectrum. *Arch. Gen. Psychiatry* **39**:658–64.

Pennington, B.F., Groisser, D., and Welsh, M.C. 1993. Contrasting deficits in attention deficit hyperactivity disorder versus reading disability. *Dev. Psychol.* **29**:511–23.

Pettegrew, J.W., Keshavan, M.S., Panchalingam, K., Strychor, S., Kaplan, D.B., Tretta, M.G., and Allen, M. 1991. Alterations in brian high energy phosphate and membrane phospholipid metabolism in first episode, drug naive schizophrenics. A pilot study of the dorsal prefrontal cortex by in vivo Phosphorous 31 nuclear magnetic resonance spectroscopy. *Arch. Gen. Psychiatry* **48**:563–8.

Pickles, A. 1993. Stages, precursors and causes in development. In *Precursors and causes in development and psychopathology*, ed. D.F. Hay and A. Angold, pp. 23–50. Chichester: John Wiley.

Potter, H.W. 1933. Schizophrenia in children. *Am. J. Psychiatry* **12**:1253–70.

Pulver, A., Brown, C.H., Wolyniec, P., McGrath, J., Alder, T.D., Carpenter, T., and Childs, B. 1990. Schizophrenia: age at onset, gender and familial risk. *Acta Psychiatr. Scand.* **82**:344–51.

Purves, D.L. and Lichtman, J.W. 1980. Elimination of synapses in the developing nervous system. *Science* **210**:153–7.

Ross, C.A., McInnis, M.G., Margolis, R.L., and Li, S.H. 1993. Genes with triplet repeats: candidate mediators of neuropsychiatric disorders. *Trends in Neuroscience* **16**:254–60.

Russell, A.T., Bott, L., and Sammons, C. 1989. The phenomena of schizophrenia occurring in childhood. *J. Am. Acad. Child Adol. Psychiatry* **28**:399–407.

Rutter, M. 1972. Childhood schizophrenia reconsidered. *J. Autism Child. Schizophr.* **2**:315–407.

Rutter, M. 1988. Epidemiological approaches to developmental psychopathology. *Arch. Gen. Psychiatry* **45**:486–95.

Rutter, M. and Mawhood, L. 1991. The long term psychosocial sequelae of specific developmental disorders of speech and language. In *Biological risk factors for psychosocial disorders*, ed. M. Rutter and P. Casaer, pp. 233–59. Cambridge: Cambridge University Press.

Schachar, R., Taylor, R., Wieselberg, M., Thorley, G., and Rutter, M. 1987. Changes in family function and relationships in children who respond to methylphenidate. *J. Am. Acad. Child Adol. Psychiatry* **26**:728–32.

Schultz, S.C., Koller, M.M., Kishore, P.R., Hamer, R.M., Gehl, J.J., and Friedel, R.D. 1983. Ventricular enlargement in teenage patients with schizophrenia spectrum disorder. *Am. J. Psychiatry* **140**:1592–95.

Sham, P.C., Jones, P.B., Russell, A., Gilvarry, K., Bebbington, P., Lewis, S., Toone, B., and Murray, R.M. 1994. Age at onset, sex, and familial psychiatric morbidity in schizophrenia: Camberwell Collaborative Psychosis Study. *Br. J. Psychiatry* **165**:466–73.

Singer, M.T. and Wynne, L.C. 1965. Thought disorder and family relations of schizophrenics. IV. results and implications. *Arch. Gen. Psychiatry* **12**:201–9.

Sonuga-Barke, E.J.S, Taylor, E., and Heptinstall, E. 1992a. Hyperactivity and delay aversion: II. The effects of self versus externally imposed stimulus presentation periods on memory. *J. Child Psychol. Psychiatry* **33**:399–410.

Sonuga-Barke, E.J.S., Taylor, E., Sembi, S., and Smith, J. 1992b. Hyperactivity and delay aversion: I. The effect of delay on choice. *J. Child Psychol. Psychiatry* **33**:387–98.

Strandberg, R.J., Marsh, J.T., Brown, W.S., Asarnow, R.F., and Guthrie, D. 1994. Information processing deficits across childhood and adult onset schizophrenia. *Schizophr. Bull.* **20**:685–96.

Stroufe, L.A. and Rutter, M. 1984. The domain of developmental psychopathology. *Child Devel.* **83**:173–89.

Taylor, E. 1991. Developmental neuropsychiatry. *Ann. Res. Rev., J. Child Psychol. Psychiatry* **32**.3–47.

Taylor, E. 1995. Dysfunctions of attention. Developmental psychopathology *vol. 2. Risk, disorder and adaption*, ed. D.J. Cicchetti and D. Cohen, pp. 243–73. New York: John Wiley.

Taylor, E., Chadwick, O., Heptinstall, E. and Danckaerts, M. Hyperactivity and conduct disorder as risk factors for adolescent development. *J. Am. Acad. Child and Adol. Psychiatry* (in press).

Tienari, P., Sori, I., Lahti, I., Naarala, M., Wahlberg, K.-E., Ronko, T., Maring, J., and Wynne, L.L. 1987. Genetic and psychosocial factors in schizophrenia: the Finnish Adoptive Family Study. *Schizophr. Bull.* **13**:477–84.

Walker, E.F., Grimes, K.E., Davis, D.M., and Smith, A. 1993. Childhood precursors of schizophrenia: facial expression of emotion. *Am. J. Psychiatry* **150**:1654–60.

Walker, E. and Lewine, R.J. 1990. Prediction of adult onset schizophrenia from childhood home movies. *Am. J. Psychiatry* **147**: 1052–56.

Walker, E.F., Savoie, T., and Davis, D. 1994. Neuromotor precursors of schizophrenia. *Schizophr. Bull.* **20**:441–51.

Watkins, J.M., Asarnow, R.F., and Tanguay, P. 1988. Symptom development in childhood onset schizophrenia. *J. Child Psychol. Psychiatry* **29**:865–978.

Welsh, M.C., Pennington, B.F., and Groisser, D.B. 1991. A normative-developmental study of executive function: a window on prefrontal function in children? *Devel. Neuropsychol.* **7**:131–9.

Weinberger, D.R. 1987. Implications of normal brain development for the pathogenesis of schizophrenia. *Arch. Gen. Psychiatry* **44**: 660–9.

Weinberger, D.R., Berman, K.F., and Zec, R.F. 1986. Physiologic dysfunction of the dorsolateral prefrontal cortex in schizophrenia. 1. Regional cerebral blood flow evidence. *Arch. Gen. Psychiatry* **43**:114–24.

Werry, J.S. 1992. Child and adolescent (early onset) schizophrenia. A review in light of DSM-IIIR. *J. Autism Devel. Disorders* **22**:601 24.

Werry, J.S., McClellan, J.M., Andrews, L.K., and Ham, M. 1994. Clinical features and outcome of child and adolescent onset schizophrenia. *Schizophr. Bull.* **20**:619–30.

Werry, J.S., McClellan, J.M., and Chard, L. 1991. Childhood and adolescent schizophrenia, bipolar and schizoaffective disorders: a clinical and outcome study. *J. Am. Acad. Child Adol. Psychiatry* **30**:457–65.

Worland, J., Edenhart-Pepe, R., Weeks, D.G., and Koren, P.M. 1984. Cognitive evaluation of children at risk: IQ, differentiation and egocentricity. In *Children at risk for schizophrenia: a longitudinal perspective*, ed. N.F. Watt, E.J. Anthony *et al.*, pp. 148–59. New York: Cambridge University Press.

Zeitlin, H. 1986. *The natural history of psychiatric disorder in children.* Institute of Psychiatry Maudsley Monograph, 29 Oxford: Oxford University Press.

SECTION III

Integrative models

17 Schizophrenia as an emergent disorder of late brain maturation

IRWIN FEINBERG

INTRODUCTION

This chapter consists of two sections. In Part I, I summarize arguments and evidence that support the hypothesis that schizophrenia results from abnormalities in late brain maturational processes. In Part 2, I comment on several current issues in schizophrenia research: whether abnormalities of schizophrenic thinking derive from impairments of simpler cognitive functions; whether schizophrenic "deficits" are necessarily irreversible; and where the anatomical "locus" of the brain abnormality in schizophrenia might be. I conclude by re-emphasizing the importance of basic research in human brain maturation for understanding mental illness.

SCHIZOPHRENIA AS AN EMERGENT DISORDER OF LATE BRAIN MATURATIONAL EVENTS

In the early 1980s, I put forward a new kind of ontogenetic neurodevelopmental model for the etiology of schizophrenia (Feinberg 1982a, 1982b). It differed from the long-standing, prenatal or perinatal model of Fish (1957) for example, in several respects. First, it explicitly recognized that extensive maturational changes in the physiology and function of the human brain take place over the second decade of life. Second, it argued that the mechanism producing these brain changes was the late elimination of cortical synapses found by Huttenlocher (1979), noting that this synaptic elimination could be viewed as the final ontogenetic expression of the broad developmental strategy of initial overproduction and subsequent pruning of neural elements. Third, it suggested that such

pervasive neuronal rearrangements might sometimes go awry, causing schizophrenia. In this context, I noted that the onset of schizophrenia during or shortly after the second decade of life was an important but, at that time, almost entirely neglected clue to its etiology.

Although these papers occasioned little interest initially, the past decade has witnessed increasing discussion of the issues they raised. The concept of schizophrenia as a neurodevelopmental illness has taken hold, although "neurodevelopmental" is used with a wide range of meanings. Age of onset is now acknowledged to be an important clue to the etiology of schizophrenia and other mental disorders. There is developing recognition that the brain changes dynamically throughout life and that the changes over the second decade, while more subtle than those of the early postnatal years, are none the less substantial and may be particularly important for the etiology of mental illness. Empirical investigation of late brain changes in humans has become a significant area of psychiatric research. The body of relevant data is already too extensive to review here; however, several important contributions appear elsewhere in this volume. I now briefly review my arguments for the late neurodevelopmental model.

Argument 1: a major reorganization of the human brain takes place during the second decade of life

Ontogeny of sleep EEG

My interest in the issue of late maturational changes in the human brain was prompted by observations of sleep electroencephalogram (EEG) ontogenesis. It had long been apparent that deep (stage 4) sleep undergoes a massive decline over the second decade of life (Agnew *et al.* 1967; Feinberg *et al.* 1967; Feinberg and Carlson 1968;

Feinberg 1974; Williams *et al.* 1974). To appreciate the relevance of this finding to the discussion that follows, it is necessary that I briefly describe the EEG characteristics of stage 4 (deep) sleep, its possible role in brain homeostasis, and the neuronal mechanisms believed to generate the high amplitude, slow (delta) waves that characterize this sleep stage.

Stage 4 sleep is a visually-rated stage of nonrapid eye movement (NREM) sleep characterized by abundant, high amplitude, delta waves. The EEG of NREM stages 3 and 2 is qualitatively similar to that of stage 4, but contains progressively fewer high amplitude waves. Early on, my colleagues and I noted that the decline in stage 4 EEG across childhood and in old age might be related to diminishing brain plasticity (Feinberg *et al.* 1967). This inference played an important role in the formulation of the original homeostatic model of delta sleep. According to this model, it is NREM sleep (EEG stages 2–4) that reverses the neuronal effects of plastic brain activities during waking (Feinberg 1974). The intensity of the reversal (homeostatic) processes is proportional to the density of high amplitude delta waves. Delta EEG declines in amplitude and density across sleep (i.e., stages 3 and 4 are replaced by stage 2) as the "substrate" that accumulated during waking is consumed; therefore, as the intensity of plastic waking brain activity diminishes between childhood and the end of adolescence, less substrate for sleep homeostasis would be produced and the amount of stage 4 would decline.

To understand the potential relation of synaptic density to EEG waves, it is useful to know that EEG waves are generated by slow (graded) changes in membrane potential that occur synchronously in large assemblies of cortical neurons and dendrites. Under this view, waves of higher amplitude could be produced by an increase in the number of neurons whose potential is changing in synchrony and/or by an increase in the magnitude of the average potential change/neuron. With this background in sleep physiology, I next describe how observations of sleep ontogenesis stimulated a broader investigation of late brain maturation.

In 1977, Carlson, Hibi and I (Feinberg *et al.* 1977) measured the amplitude of NREM delta waves across age (see Fig. 17.1). We reported a "rapid and striking growth of

delta amplitude during the first years of life" and proposed that this was "an electrophysiological correlate of the vastly increased connections within the cortex associated with postnatal maturation and development" (Feinberg, 1977:94) described in the Conel (1939–63) atlases. In accordance with the mechanisms of EEG generation described above, greater connectivity would permit synchronous change in larger populations of neurons. In addition to the growth of delta wave amplitude during the first years of life, however, we observed a dramatic and puzzling amplitude decline across adolescence. We noted that the "biophysical bases for such changes (over adolescence) are entirely unknown".

Two years later, Huttenlocher (1979) described morphological changes in the human cortex that offered a biophysical explanation for the changes in sleep EEG across adolescence, and for other late maturational brain changes as well. Using quantitative electron microscopy, Huttenlocher showed that, in addition to the expected growth in synaptic density during the early years of life, there occurred an equally large decline across the second decade. Moreover, the shape of Huttenlocher's ontogenetic curve for cortical synaptic density resembled that of the age curve for delta wave amplitude (see later). We were inspired by the neuroanatomical support provided by Huttenlocher's data to investigate and summarize evidence that the brain might be changing in important ways across adolescence.[1]

Ontogeny of cerebral metabolic rate (nitrous oxide method)

One particularly interesting piece of physiological evidence was a substantial decline in cerebral metabolic rate ($CMRO_2$) between the ages of 10 and 20 years. This study, by Kennedy and Sokoloff in 1957 (1957), used the Kety-Schmidt (nitrous oxide) method which gives an average metabolic rate for the whole brain, including both gray and white matter. $CMRO_2$ measured with nitrous oxide was found to be 25% lower in young adults than in 5–10 year-

---

[1] It is perhaps of historical interest to note that, in the early 1980s, there was an extensive literature on brain development in the first few years of life and a substantial literature on senescent brain changes, but very little in between.

old children. This difference is as great as that between the senile and the normal elderly brain. Since the number of children studied by Kennedy and coworkers was small, we suggested that "It would be of great interest to have more extensive measures (of cerebral metabolic rate) . . . especially between the ages of 10 and 20 years". We pointed out that such data could be obtained with positron emission tomography (PET), which is less invasive than the nitrous oxide method, and which can measure regional as well as whole brain $CMRO_2$ (Feinberg 1982–83).

It was not long afterward that Chugani and colleagues (1987) reported their pioneering PET study of the ontogenesis of human cortical metabolic rate (CMR). They found the decline in *cortical* metabolic rate (CMR) across adolescence was much greater (as would be expected) than that found with the nitrous oxide method for whole brain. Of further interest was that the ontogenetic curve for CMR strikingly resembled the published curves for delta wave amplitude and synaptic density, a relation that we later explored statistically (see later).

Other developmental changes suggesting late maturational brain reorganization

A review of data on lesion recovery, evoked potential latencies, and cognitive development also pointed to the possibility that the human brain undergoes a widespread reorganization in the second decade of life. While these reports were not sufficiently systematic to permit construction of age curves, they agreed in showing robust differences between the prepubertal child and the young adult. With regard to lesion recovery, it had long been evident to clinicians that children have a far greater capacity to recover from aphasia-causing lesions than adults. In a careful review, Satz and Bullard-Bates (1981) concluded that there was little doubt that the prepubertal brain has a greater capacity than that of the adult to recover from aphasia-causing lesions, even though the precise age at which this plasticity is lost is uncertain. On a personal note I might mention the case of a 10-year-old child I treated. This boy was totally aphasic after a head injury suffered in a horseback riding accident; his reaction to this disability was of such animal-like fury that he needed care in a locked adult psychiatric ward. One year later he left that ward, speaking almost perfectly and restored to the polite and

pleasant disposition that characterized him before his injury. It is instructive to consider that, had his accident occurred a few years later, the normal maturational brain changes of adolescence would probably have prevented this recovery, leaving him permanently aphasic.

Evidence that the latency of event-related EEG potentials declines across adolescence was of special interest because a change in EEG wave *latency* might involve maturational brain changes different from those that reduce sleep EEG *amplitude*. Of particular interest was an early report by Courchesne (1977) who found that the latency of the P300 wave in 6–8-year-old children averaged 702 ms, compared with 402 ms in a group that ranged in age from 23–35 years. These findings gain interest because the P300 wave depends on *cognitive* processing of an attended, infrequent stimulus, i.e., it is not an obligatory response (like the early and mid-latency evoked potential EEG waves) or an endogenous physiological pattern (like sleep EEG).

More speculatively, I suggested that the emergence of adult cognitive "power" at the end of the second decade of life was not only the incremental result of continued learning but that it involved maturational (programmed) brain changes as well. I proposed that "sheer analytic power at the end of adolescence is at its highest point in the lifespan" and that the emergence of this "power" might require substantial changes in the "neuronal substrate of thought" (Feinberg 1982–83:323) in addition to the incremental growth of cognitive structures through learning.

Age-dependent changes in neurotransmitter responses

My 1982/83 paper did not review the literature on changes in receptor density with maturation and aging, which was already extensive. Here, I wish to note that the response to drugs may change *qualitatively* as well as quantitatively with maturation. Thus, in the past decade it has been found that noncompetitive *N*-methyl-D-aspartate (NMDA) channel blockers (PCP, ketamine, dizocilpine) can produce vacuoles in the posterior cingulate cortex when administered to rats (Olney *et al.* 1989). This response is absent under 20 days of age (Fix *et al.* 1993). This age dependence has been adduced to support the "PCP model" of psychosis.

A second example of a maturational change in drug

response is more directly relevant to schizophrenia. While anecdotal, it is strongly supported by clinical evidence but has received little or no discussion. We have known since the observations of Connell (1958) that amphetamine and similar drugs can produce a clinical syndrome that is sometimes indistinguishable from classical paranoid schizophrenia. Paranoid disorders infrequently occur in response to small doses of amphetamine-like drugs given for brief periods. Their incidence increases to substantial levels with chronic use of high doses. These drug responses, while still inconsistent and unpredictable, probably represent the best pharmacological model of schizophrenia.

Paranoid reactions are rare in the hundreds of thousands of young patients with attention-deficit, hyperactivity disorder (ADHD) who currently are receiving long-term, high-dose treatment with methylphenidate. These reactions were equally rare when dextro-amphetamine was the drug of choice. Some years ago I argued that the cognitive improvement following amphetamine treatment of children with attention deficit disorder should *not* be considered paradoxical (Small *et al.* 1971). What *is* paradoxical is the near-total absence of paranoid psychosis in ADHD patients.

The ADHD example suggests that maturational brain changes over the second decade of life can foster schizophrenic reactions, even in normal individuals. The age-dependence of the vacuolization response to NMDA open channel blockers shows that neurotoxicity is affected by postnatal brain development. These observations indicate that systematic study of behavioral drug response as a function of brain maturation could provide basic science data relevant to the late developmental model of mental illness.

Argument 2: synaptic elimination can explain many late maturational brain changes

Overproduction and constructive regression of neural elements: a general strategy for constructing nervous systems

Fifteen years ago, developmental neurobiologists were beginning to recognize that an initial overproduction of neural elements, and subsequent refinement on the basis of functional activity, was a pervasive theme in the development of nervous systems. First recognized in the "programmed cell death" of embryonic development, it later became apparent that less drastic structural refinements (axonal and synaptic elimination) occurred perinatally. The neurons (or neuronal processes) that survive are those that compete successfully for some trophic or sustaining factor. This developmental strategy reduces the amount of genetic information required to construct a nervous system because it becomes unnecessary to specify the precise connections and geometric relations of billions of neurons. Instead, general genetic programs can be provided that allow the final morphological outcome to be decided by successful competitive neuronal interactions.

The model I proposed in 1982–83 posited that the steep decline in synaptic density across the second decade of life observed by Huttenlocher was a final manifestation of this grand developmental strategy of overproduction and regression. It hypothesized that "the human brain develops virtually all potentially useful interconnections in the first years of life as it cannot be specified which connections will be required for successful adaptation. The excess connections impose substantial costs on biology and information-processing efficiency. At the end of childhood, when the kinds of neuronal connections required for adaptation have been selected by the individual's interactions with his environment, little-used connections are eliminated" (Feinberg 1982–83). (In this statement, "little-used" is not meant literally but rather represents "noncompetitive".) It is important to note that several pioneers in developmental neurobiology speculated that variations in the outcome of neuronal competition might lead to variations in complex behaviors and also that less mortal forms of neuronal combat play significant adaptive roles throughout life (Huttenlocher 1979; Hamburger and Oppenheimer 1982; Chaudhari and Hahn 1983; Purves 1988). These investigators were largely unaware that evidence already existed for late, widespread ontogenetic changes in the human brain.

Regressive changes (synaptic elimination) as an explanatory mechanism for late changes in brain function and physiology

Synaptic pruning provides a relatively straightforward explanation for several of the late brain changes discussed above. For others, so little is known about the underlying processes that an explanation in these terms verges on the metaphorical. Here, I first discuss the maturational changes that appear most directly explainable by late synaptic pruning: the declines across age in delta wave amplitude, brain metabolic rate and the ability to recover from brain lesions.

I noted above that the amplitude of EEG waves depends upon synchronous membrane changes in large assemblies of cortical neurons and dendrites. Greater interconnections among neurons, therefore, would permit larger populations of cells to change potential in synchrony. Therefore, the amplitude increase during infancy, and the amplitude decrease over adolescence, could result from the rise and fall in synaptic density reported by Huttenlocher. The number of neurons that can change potential in synchrony could be proportional to synaptic density.

The *duration* of deep (delta) sleep (i.e., the total number of delta waves) declines markedly across adolescence and this change requires some additional explanation. We interpreted this decline in the context of the homeostatic model of delta sleep (Feinberg 1974) outlined above. If delta sleep reverses the neuronal consequences of plastic brain activities during waking, and this reversal occurs most intensely during deep (stage 4) sleep, the amount of deep sleep should decline as the intensity of plastic brain activity diminishes across adolescence, as fewer new circuits are being constructed.

The steep increase in cortical metabolic rate during infancy, and its decline across adolescence, are also consistent with parallel changes in synaptic density and brain plasticity. Increased brain connectivity could involve larger neuronal populations in a given behavioral or cognitive operation, increasing overall cortical energy consumption. In addition, compared with the adult, the child's more plastic brain is processing information and constructing new neuronal circuits more intensively; metabolic rate should be proportional to this functional activity. A third factor, pointed out by Chugani *et al.* (1987) in interpreting their PET data, is that greater synaptic connectivity creates greater membrane surface area that requires more energy for its maintenance.

It also seems reasonable to expect that functional recovery from brain lesions would be greater with higher levels of synaptic density in the child's brain. More connections would provide more alternative pathways (as Huttenlocher observed) permitting signals to bypass damaged areas and allowing intact structures to substitute for impaired systems.

The age decline in latency of the P300 evoked-potential wave might also result from decreased synaptic connectivity. With fewer branch points, information might be processed more efficiently. The P300 experimental paradigm (counting or attending to an infrequently occurring stimulus) is so simple that it seems unlikely that the actual cognitive operations would be different in children and adults. It seemed "more likely that its (the P300) longer latency in children results from some anatomical difference" (Feinberg 1982–83:325).

Perhaps the most speculative element in my theoretical essay was that the emergence of adult cognitive power toward the end of the second decade of life depends importantly on brain maturation as well as on continued environmental stimulation and learning. This interpretation might be startling in view of the intuitive assumption "the largest possible neuronal networks are required for the most complex neuronal activity". It seemed to me, however, that this intuitive assumption might be wrong, and that there could be situations in nature, as well as in art, where "less is more". The decline in fantasy and imagination, which often accompanies the growth in logical thinking, could also be related to reduced brain connectivity, as could the age-related declines in eidetic imagery and synesthesiae. The possibility that late brain changes play an important role in cognitive development has also been recognized by others (Goldman-Rakic 1987).

Argument 3: schizophrenia might be caused by an error in late maturational brain changes

There is a growing assumption that all patients who develop schizophrenia in adolescence exhibit behavioral abnormalities during childhood. This question can be confounded to some degree by issues of acute versus insidious onset discussed later. My experience, and that of most clinicians, is that cases of typical schizophrenia can emerge in late adolescence in individuals whose premorbid adjustment and intelligence were not only normal but exceptional. It may be that the late developmental model will only apply to such individuals; their number is hardly insignificant and, in human terms, they are among our most tragic and poignant patients.

I prefaced my 1982/83 essay by noting that "schizophrenia" was mentioned in the singular for convenience but that I did not wish to imply that it was a homogeneous entity with a single etiology. It seems certain that at least some cases of what is now diagnosed as schizophrenia will prove to have an etiology different from others. But it remains conjectural whether the great majority of patients diagnosed as schizophrenic share a syndrome that has many independent causes (e.g., pneumonia) or suffer from a disease with a single etiology but protean manifestations (e.g., syphilis or tuberculosis). Just as syphilis can produce pathological effects in many different systems of the body, so might schizophrenia be capable of inducing pathology in many different systems of the mind (brain).

To return to our model: it seemed at least a priori reasonable that the extensive brain changes occurring during the second decade of life might sometimes go awry and cause schizophrenia. Defects in synaptic elimination might particularly disrupt the integration of computing modules or circuits that themselves function normally. Such a disintegration is at the heart of Eugene Bleuler's conceptualization of schizophrenia. Here I would add that the enormous evolutionary growth of the human cerebral cortex may have posed challenges to integrative mechanisms that were not always successfully met. If so, schizophrenia might be a peculiarly human disorder, a disease that is literally *sui generis*.

If, in fact, schizophrenia is due to faulty neuronal integration resulting from errors in synaptic pruning, we still have no basis for deciding whether the fault results from elimination of "too few, too many or the wrong" synapses. One could readily create computer or other models in which any of these errors would produce symptoms of schizophrenia.

Further evidence supporting interrelated late maturational brain changes: parallel ontogenetic curves for cortical metabolic rate (CMR), NREM delta wave amplitude (DA) and synaptic density (SD).

When Chugani *et al.* (1987) published their PET data for ontogenetic changes in cortical metabolic rate, we were

Table 17.1. *Comparison of gamma distribution model and best polynomial*

	Order of best polynomial	Fraction of explained sum of squares*	
		Polynomial	Gamma
Delta amplitude	3	0.676	0.670
Frontal cortex (CMR)	3	0.868	0.862
Synaptic density	4	0.841	0.925
Synaptic density^2	4	0.857	0.913

Notes:
*$1-$(residual sum of squares)/(total sum of squares), which is equal to R^2 in a linear regression. None of the differences between gamma distribution and polynomial fits approached statistical significance. (Reprinted from Feinberg *et al.* 1990b.)

struck by the similarity of the shape of the CMR curve to those of DA and SD. All three curves rise sharply after birth to a maximum level in childhood. Each curve then declines more gradually, with most of the decline occurring in the second decade of life. These patterns appeared consistent with that of gamma distributions. In collaboration with Chugani and Thode, March and I performed analyses to determine whether all three curves would fit this statistical model (Feinberg *et al.* 1990b). Our initial examination of the data suggested that a power of SD would provide a better fit than the raw SD values, so we included SD^2 in our statistical tests.

Figure 17.1 illustrates the fit of individual gamma models to the raw data points for: (1) SD, (2) SD^2, (3) CMR, and (4) DA. Table 17.1 shows that the amount of variance explained by the gamma distributions is as great as that accounted for by the best-fitting ad hoc polynomial. These findings support the view that the three sets of data share a fundamentally similar age pattern.

In an attempt to explain how such curves might be produced, my colleagues and I proposed a model of neuronal development. The model is highly speculative because very little is known of the cell biology of neuronal ontogenesis. Even if entirely incorrect, this speculation would be useful if it directs attention to a pattern of brain changes which, although massive, still receives little attention.

Fig. 17.1. Individual gamma distribution models (curves) fitted to the raw data (scatter grams) for (a) synaptic density; (b) synaptic density squared; (c) cortical metabolic rate; and (d) NREM delta wave amplitude. Only data available for each variable from birth to age 30 years were used. The curves for synaptic density peak earlier (3.2 years) than those for delta amplitude (7.4 years) and frontal cortex metabolic rate (6.1 years). (Reprinted from Feinberg *et al.* 1990b.)

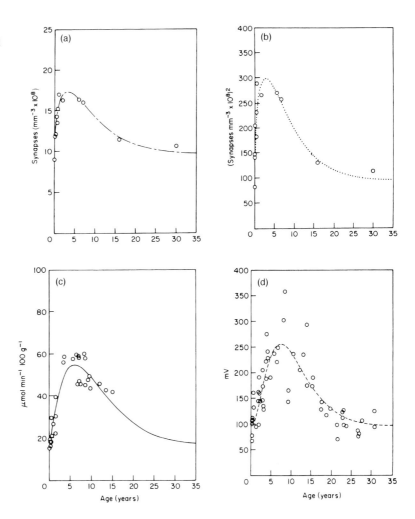

Our model proposes that the postnatal maturation of human cortex consists of three general stages. The first is a proliferative stage (PS) which is triggered by birth and lasts for about 3 years. The PS is characterized by the explosive growth of dendritic and axonal processes described by Conel (1939–63), and the exuberant growth of synapses described by Huttenlocher. This model assumes that the PS is genetically programmed and that its proliferating connections are somewhat promiscuous, being determined by chemical affinities and relatively superficial interactions rather than by seriously meaningful relationships. The outcome of the PS is an extremely

high level of neural connectivity that provides the conditions necessary for the competitive and other neuronal interactions that construct complex and enduring circuits during the organizational state (OS) that follows.

At some point after birth, a given neuron leaves the proliferative state and enters a second, transient state which we call the OS. Entry into this state, which might last minutes to years, could be induced by gene expression that is triggered by a particular temporal interaction with other neurons. While in this growth or OS, neurons are highly plastic, metabolically active and have many synapses. On leaving the OS, neurons enter the committed state (CS). In the CS, they have fewer (but more intricate) synapses, lower metabolic rates and a reduced potential for making new connections. Once a neuron leaves the OS, it cannot return to it, perhaps because the state is also terminated by the one-time expression of a gene or by the action of a trophic factor. At that point the neuron is "committed". One of the curiosities of contemporary neurobiological research is how little is known of the cellular changes a cortical neuron undergoes when it enters the CS and is impressed, more or less irrevocably, into a specific circuit.

This hypothetical mechanism could be modeled quantitatively to produce the ontogenetic gamma curves shown in Fig. 17.1. For example, the gamma distribution could arise statistically as the proportion of neurons which are in the transient OS at each age, if we assume that neurons enter the OS after several occurrences of some stimulus (or stimulus combination) that is widely, but sparsely distributed in the cortex (i.e., is distributed approximately randomly, from a macroscopic perspective). Thus, the number of neurons entering the OS increases rapidly during the PS, as a consequence both of increased connectivity and the increasing number of neurons that have received the necessary pattern of stimulation. These highly active, plastic, densely connected OS neurons account for the rising limb of the gamma curves. As an increasing number of neurons pass through the OS into the CS, the number of OS neurons declines, accounting for the fall in CMR, SD and DA across adolescence.

The formation of ocular dominance columns in the first years of life, and their organization, within a critical period, into circuits that subserve binocular vision, is one example that might fit this model; other functional circuits would develop over different time frames. In general terms, we propose that the gamma curves represent the changing proportions of "uncommitted" and "committed" neurons.[2] These neurons probably differ in many ways other than metabolic rate and synaptic arrangement. Finally, there may be a group of neurons that are meant to

remain permanently in the OS. These might be the neurons that establish the transient structures used in problem solving, the "temporary arrangements" that are "swept clean" by sleep (Jackson 1958).

I mentioned earlier the possibility that faulty synaptic pruning could result in disordered neural integration that would produce impaired integration of mental functions that, phenomenologically, characterizes schizophrenia. Our extended model suggests a related abnormality that might contribute to the late development to mental illness. Some circuits may contain neurons that fail to leave the OS at the appropriate stage. These highly active neurons might disrupt integration through more intense and less modulated activity, rather than solely because of deviant connections. Such hyperactive neurons might be tamed by therapeutic agents that have a nonspecific dampening effect, such as the depolarization blockade produced by neuroleptics (Grace and Bunney 1986).

In our model, the OS is terminated by intrinsic neuronal events but it is also possible that some external influence, such as a noncentral nervous system (CNS) hormone, plays a role in terminating the OS. Since the steep declines of DA, SD and CMR take place over adolescence, the sex hormones are obvious candidates; however, the curves for all three brain variables start to decline before puberty (by at about ages 8–10 years). Another possible endocrine candidate for involvement in late regressive processes are adrenal androgens. A surge in adrenal androgen secretion (whose functional role remains largely unknown) begins in both sexes at about age 6 years. The levels of these hormones then steadily increase until a plateau is reached at about age 16 years (Reiter et al. 1977). Thus, the age curve for adrenal androgen concentration rises during the period that the gamma curves shows their highest rates of decline. If such a non-CNS agent plays a role in synaptic elimination or other late regressive processes, it could obviously not be selective. Instead, it might raise the threshold for synaptic survival "across the board", so that only the more effective connections are retained. Having reviewed our ideas on schizophrenia as an emergent disorder of late brain maturation, and our speculations on what sorts of neuronal changes might be involved, I turn now to a brief comparison of late versus early neurodevelopmental models. The early neuro-

---

[2] I recognize that neuronal commitment is not absolute in the mature brain, even for the relatively hard-wired cortical neurons in primary receptive fields (Sur and Cowey 1995).

developmental model may seem less speculative but that is only because it is more familiar.

Late versus early neurodevelopmental models of schizophrenia

For a scholarly and critical comparison of early and late developmental models of schizophrenia, the reader should consult Pogue-Geile (1991) and Chapter 10, which present a thoughtful definition of developmental illness and a review of the best available data on age of onset. Briefly, the late developmental model I proposed in 1982/83 contrasts sharply with the long-standing model of Fish and more recent models, which hold that the brain abnormality of schizophrenia is present from birth onward. Pogue-Geile notes that a more recent, third kind of neurodevelopmental model (Randall 1980; Weinberger 1986; Murray *et al.* 1988; Benes 1989) postulates that "an individual's risk for schizophrenia is primarily fixed at an early age (by a prenatal or perinatal lesion) and that normal developmental processes that occur during young adulthood for everyone serve only to time the onset of obvious clinical symptoms" (Pogue-Geile 1991:278). The "normal developmental processes" adduced in these models are, typically, a subset of those I discussed in 1982/83 (see Weinberger 1986).

Pogue-Geile's 1991 analysis led him to conclude that the evidence put forward for a prenatal or perinatal brain insult as etiologic in schizophrenia could be interpreted instead as supporting a nonspecific vulnerability. Under this interpretation, "without the presence of the late-onset, schizophrenia-specific developmental genetic abnormalities, the early-occurring environmental insults would not increase one's risk for schizophrenia". For a further discussion of the strengths and weaknesses of the two kinds of model, the reader should consult Pogue-Geile's work.

One distinction that may be useful to consider is that, if the brain defect of schizophrenia emerges during the second decade of life in a previously normal individual, this emergence might not simply depend on the penetrance of late-expressed abnormal genes. There can be no reasonable doubt that genetic factors contribute importantly to cases of schizophrenia and the likeliest mode of transmission is polygenic. It is of interest, however, to consider an additional possibility: that genetic factors are themselves nonspecific and act only to increase the probability that an error will occur in late regressive/constructive neuronal maturation. This error might emerge sporadically with a certain stochastic frequency (e.g., approximately 1%) in the absence of genetic predisposition. This interpretation would be consistent with the fact that the great majority of individuals who develop schizophrenia do *not* have a first degree relative with the disease. It could help explain why the diminished fertility of schizophrenics has not reduced the incidence of schizophrenia, and why this incidence is roughly the same throughout the world.

Quite obviously, schizophrenia is not the only behavioral abnormality that is absent in early life and emerges in the course of development. The same is true for other major psychiatric syndromes as well as for many normal personality characteristics; we have suggested elsewhere (Feinberg *et al.* 1990b) that the maturational abnormality underlying bipolar illness might be more "quantitative" and that underlying schizophrenia more "qualitative". Again, many if not most of these behavior patterns have some genetic contribution but this contribution could also represent a nonspecific diathesis. For example, it seems less likely that the brain of an obsessive-compulsive has an "obsessive-compulsive lesion" at birth that is unmasked by development than that this disorder emerges as a result of intrinsic maturational processes that produce an extreme result.

As Pogue-Geile points out, one of the limitations of the late maturational model is that it is not readily testable. Neither can one test, at this time, a distinction between the late emergence of psychopathology due to the expression of abnormal late genes as opposed to psychopathology resulting from faulty implementation of normal, late genetic instructions. My goal in this discussion is simply to expand the range of conceptual possibilities for explaining the postpubertal of mental disorders.

Abnormal corollary discharge in the motor mechanisms of thought: an integrative defect that could produce many symptoms of schizophrenia

Corollary discharge (efference copy or feed-forward systems) is a mechanism of CNS integration through which sensory and motor systems are "informed" that a motor command has been issued. Neural activity in these systems is then modified to adjust for the effects (e.g., sensory stimulation) of the motor operation (Evarts 1971). These corollary discharges enable the organism to distinguish sensory experiences resulting from its own actions (reafferents) from those produced by the environment, and thus are fundamental to establishing the recognition of "self".

Such feed-forward systems might operate in the motor control of thought (Feinberg 1978). The notion that thinking is, in essence, a motor act may seem incongruous; however, Hughlings Jackson, the great 19th century English neurologist, pointed out that, "The nervous states concomitant (correlative) with psychical states are, according to the doctrine of evolution, sensorimotor. The highest centers are, according to this doctrine, only the most complex, etc. and latest developed of a series of centers, every one of which represents impressions, or movements, or both" (Jackson 1958:367). That these notions are not purely hypothetical is shown by observations of Penfield in his classic studies of brain stimulation in conscious subjects. Penfield noted that when stimulating a motor area and inducing an arm movement, the patient would typically report that "you moved my arm" rather than "I moved my arm". Bypassing the corollary discharge system thus results in an "alien" subjective experience, i.e., of being controlled by external forces.

Successful neural adaptations developed in simple operations tend to be conserved across evolution and employed in more complex systems. If thinking is our most complex motor act, it may also depend upon corollary discharge mechanisms that distinguish internally produced conscious events from those resulting from external stimulation. If so, an impairment of the corollary discharge mechanisms of thought could account for some of the most salient and puzzling features of schizophrenia. These obviously would include the schizophrenic's inability to discriminate self-generated thoughts or ideas from those emanating from the environment (e.g., hearing "voices") and associated distortions of body image and consciousness. Impaired corollary discharge would also render comprehensible some of the hypotheses (mind control) the schizophrenic constructs to explain his distorted conscious experience.

We have suggested elsewhere (Feinberg and March 1995) that corollary discharge mechanisms are normally disabled during dreaming. It is this disablement that produces one of the most striking similarities of dreams to psychosis. Thus, the immediate "knowing" of the dreamer (e.g., "When I saw my son I *knew* he was there to tell me he had totaled my car") seems phenomenologically similar to the autochthonous delusion of the schizophrenic: "When I saw the way the pencils were arranged on the desk I *knew* that meant I would be executed". Neither the dreamer when awake nor the schizophrenic when in remission can explain *how* the belief that caused such intense pain was transmitted. It is as though some of the normal steps of consciousness have been skipped or "short-circuited". For a further discussion of the possibility that corollary discharge mechanisms of thinking are impaired in schizophrenia, the reader is referred to the original publication (Feinberg 1978) and also to the work of Frith (1992) who has adopted and further discussed this idea.

REFLECTIONS ON THE PATHOPHYSIOLOGY OF SCHIZOPHRENIA

In the remainder of this chapter, I discuss several issues regarding the phenomenology of schizophrenia and their implications for research. In these comments, I draw on my clinical experience with large numbers of schizophrenic patients. This experience includes the direct administration of a wide variety of psychological tests and the opportunity, now increasingly rare, to make longitudinal observations of patients whom I knew very well.

Neuropsychological abnormalities in schizophrenia

A first step toward advancing knowledge is disencumbering one's self from weak or misleading evidence. Will Rodgers said, "It ain't so much what we *don't* know that gets us into trouble, it's what we *do* know that ain't so."

Much research in the past century has sought to identify a cognitive defect specific to schizophrenia. Although no such defect has ever been demonstrated, the conviction has grown in the past two decades that such defects *must* exist and that the complex mental symptoms of schizophrenia would be derivable from this more elementary cognitive impairment.

The failure to identify a reliable and specific cognitive defect in schizophrenia is not due to want of effort. There have been decades of research and hundreds (if not thousands) of PhD dissertations devoted to this topic. In some ways, sophistication in this research area may have declined over the past 50 years. It is trivial to devise tests in which schizophrenics will perform more poorly than normal controls. Differences in such simple but compelling factors as level of cooperation ensure this result. Half a century ago, Shakow (1946) illustrated the effect of cooperation level in determining the performance of schizophrenics on psychological tests by including ratings of the degree of involvement and cooperation of his subjects. This is admittedly crude, but it seems cruder still to ignore completely the issue of cooperation and motivation in the test performance of schizophrenics. For this reason, I find the use of the Wisconsin Card Sorting Test (WCST) in schizophrenia to be stunningly inappropriate. In this test, one first requires a schizophrenic patient to guess the correct basis (e.g., form or color) for sorting a set of cards. The patient begins to perform systematically on the basis of one or the other criterion and is rewarded for doing so by being told his sortings are correct. Then the patient is doubled-crossed: the criterion is changed and the patient is punished (told he is making errors) for the responses that were previously correct. The unsuitability of this task for patients who have difficulty in trusting their own perceptions and the motivation of those about them ought to be self-evident. The notion that the brain response to such deception would be limited to a small computing module in the cortex is truly remarkable.

The assumption has grown in recent years that, because schizophrenia is a condition of disordered brain function, there *necessarily* exist impairments in elementary cognitive operations such as are readily demonstrable in patients with "organic" brain disease. As one extreme example, the Newsletter of a major neuroscience research program recently claimed that acutely ill schizophrenic patients show a cognitive profile "characterized by severe impairment in memory and learning"; after being stabilized on neuroleptics, these patients still showed "severe

impairment" in these capacities proving that "learning and memory are primary characteristics (*sic*) of the disease, not secondary results of neuroleptic medication or advanced disease state".

I have not yet seen the evidence for this remarkable claim. If it is correct, it directly contradicts Eugen Bleuler's criteria for schizophrenia. To diagnose schizophrenia, Bleuler required: (1) that certain fundamental (invariant) symptoms be present; and (2) that "simple" brain functions (e.g., memory) be *intact* in the presence of these fundamental symptoms (E. Bleuler 1952). (Of course, today we would not consider memory a "simple" function.) If the findings reported in the Newsletter are correct, we have been using the wrong criteria to diagnose schizophrenia for a century! I suspect that a less earth-shaking explanation will emerge. The conclusion that schizophrenic patients have impaired memory was probably reached by investigators who did not themselves carry out the testing, and thus could not know the extent to which poor performance resulted from lack of cooperation, motivation and trust.

At this time, there exists no convincing evidence that delusions, auditory hallucinations, peculiarities of judgment or even formal thought disorder are caused by or consistently associated with specific impairments of logic, abstraction ability, stimulus barrier or any "simpler" cognitive operation. This is *not* to say that schizophrenics have normal cognition. They clearly do not. The phenomenology of schizophrenia suggests that its cognitive abnormalities will be found at the level of those unknown, complex processes that determine belief, the perception of self and consciousness and not at "lower" levels of cognition.

Prognostic significance of "acute" versus "insidious" onset: a possible confound of duration of illness?

There is an extensive literature indicating that an acute as opposed to an insidious onset of schizophrenia is a favorable prognostic sign. There is also strong evidence that the longer schizophrenic symptoms persist, the less likely that remission will occur. The possibility that these two variables are confounded has not been recognized. Thus, if two individuals develop schizophrenia, one insidiously and the other acutely, it is probable that the patient with acute symptoms will be diagnosed earlier than the patient with insidious symptoms. Indeed, some of these latter patients may remit without ever being diagnosed. For this reason alone, remissions in acute-onset patients could be observed more frequently than in insidious-onset patients. In addition, the fact that insidious-onset patients have been ill longer than acute-onset patients at the time of diagnosis might render their prognosis worse. This issue bears on the good-premorbid-poor premorbid dichotomy and is relevant to one of the questions raised above: whether schizophrenia emerges de novo in adolescence or is necessarily preceded by aberrant behavior stigmatic of the illness.

Can recovery from schizophrenia occur?

Many biological models, particularly those based on CNS defects that emerge during embryonic or perinatal periods, assume that recovery from schizophrenia is not possible. This assumption is not a necessary corollary of these models but it is a common view among their proponents. (The notion that schizophrenia is an irreversible condition is often attributed to Kraepelin rather than Bleuler. This is wrong. Kraepelin explicitly stated that: ". . . the possibility cannot in the present state of our knowledge be disputed that a certain number of cases of dementia praecox attain to complete and permanent recovery . . ." (Kraepelin 1919:4). In contrast, Eugen Bleuler, in his definition of the disease stated: "By the term 'dementia praecox' or 'schizophrenia' we designate a group of psychoses whose course is at times chronic, at times marked by intermittent attacks, and which can stop or retrograde at any stage but does not permit a full *restitutio ad integrum*" (Bleuler 1952:9).

My own clinical experience is that some patients can recover from schizophrenia even after suffering typical and severe symptoms (both positive and negative) for years. More importantly, Harding and her colleagues (Harding, *et al.* 1987; Harding and Zahniser 1994) have provided compelling empirical evidence that recovery from severe and apparently chronic schizophrenic illness can occur. Their results are not idiosyncratic; Manfred Bleuler reached similar conclusions on the basis of his personal, intensive longitudinal study of a large schizophrenic cohort (M. Bleuler 1978).

The general neglect of these careful and important studies is a manifestation of the somewhat doctrinaire ideology of much contemporary schizophrenia research. There is often a simple-minded equation of biological causation with irreversibility. This overlooks the common observation that typical schizophrenic symptoms and signs can occur episodically with normal intervening behavior. In many of these cases, the symptoms appear related to clear and definable environmental stress. While some of these patients may suffer from mood disorders that are atypically expressed with schizophrenic symptoms, I doubt that these account for all or even the majority of the cases.

One dramatic example with which I was personally acquainted was that of a woman who had a catatonic episode with mutism, rigidity, and auditory hallucinations in her early twenties when her father died. She recovered, lived a normal life and successfully raised a family. She then had a virtually identical catatonic episode in her early seventies (when I treated her) following the death of her husband. One acknowledges the treacherous nature of anecdotal evidence. It may nevertheless be useful to describe such patients because the fragmentation of psychiatric care in this country now limits severely the clinician's opportunity to make pertinent, long-term clinical observations.

The fact that recovery from schizophrenia is possible has important implications for research, as Harding and her colleagues emphasize. First, with regard to the conceptualization of the illness, it is intuitively more consistent with a functional imbalance of neural systems than with the operation of an implacable, static structural defect. (Of course, such an imbalance could be caused by either an early or a late developmental brain abnormality.) Second, the fact that recovery can occur in patients who for years have manifested what appears to be a "deficit state" challenges the notion that schizophrenic symptoms derive from permanent impairment in simpler cognitive functions, an issue discussed earlier. Third, if schizophrenia *can* be reversible, it further encourages research and offers hope to families that they may not now be receiving.

Locus of the hypothesized integrative defect in schizophrenia

Since the neural mechanisms of belief and consciousness are unknown, one cannot propose with any confidence the neuroanatomical locus of a defect that would produce the schizophrenic's dis-integration of mental functions, his splitting of thought and affect and his peculiarities of belief and perception. With this caveat, I offer the following speculation. First, it seems unlikely that the abnormality of neural processing in schizophrenia lies within the cerebral cortex. It is probable that the human cortex is too redundant and plastic to be disabled by so subtle a defect as occurs in schizophrenia. The fact that gross cortical damage, at *any* age, rarely *if ever* produces schizophrenia has received insufficient attention. The enormous variety of insults to the human brain produced by automotive and other trauma should give pause to those who believe that schizophrenia is caused by a lesion in specific cortical areas. The fact that trauma does not cause schizophrenia could, of course, indicate that the site of the schizophrenic defect lies in a structure whose damage is incompatible with life, a possibility more consistent with a subcortical than cortical locus. More likely, I believe, is that trauma simply does not produce the subtle, qualitatively unique neural aberrations that give rise to schizophrenia. In this latter regard, it is relevant to note that a century of direct neuropathological examination of the brains of schizophrenics has failed to reveal any gross anatomical lesion: cortical or subcortical.

If the schizophrenia defect can be localized to a specific site, I believe it will be found subcortically, in centers that integrate and coordinate neural function. These areas obviously include the basal ganglia and thalamus. Hassler (cited in Evarts 1971) pointed out that an enormous growth of the thalamus accompanies the evolutionary expansion of the cerebral cortex. Yet only one-eighth of the human thalamus serves somatosensory systems. The remaining seven-eighths serve as relay and integrating stations for other systems, presumably including those of the most complex brain functions. Recent magnetic resonance imaging (MRI) findings by Andreasen and colleagues (1994) of anatomical abnormalities in the thalamus of schizophrenics are interesting in this context.

Implications of the late developmental model for future research

Schizophrenia poses a classical dilemma of medical research. It is a common condition that produces severe and prolonged suffering and it has huge economic costs. As with many other such conditions, it has elicited a concerned constituency that demands more research attention. But what should our research strategy be?

I would argue that a frontal assault (analogous to the ill-fated "war on cancer") would be both costly and unsuccessful. We still know virtually nothing of the neural bases of thought and affect and the mechanisms that integrate them into consciousness. In the absence of strong clues, it may be best to pursue more basic studies, choosing areas of research that, according to one's conception of the illness, have a higher than average possibility of being relevant to its etiology. I believe that studies of late brain development and its behavioral/cognitive correlates are currently the strongest candidates in this regard. It is now widely accepted that late changes take place in the human brain and it is an empirical fact that most serious forms of psychopathology emerge after puberty. Investigators of late maturational processes are therefore assured that they are studying real phenomena of potential relevance to mental illness. Moreover, for many of us, late maturational brain processes and nature's strategy of overproduction and refinement of neural elements through competitive interaction are intrinsically fascinating. There are not a great many other opportunities to conduct research in an area of high intellectual interest that also has some reasonable possibility of contributing to the understanding of psychiatric illness.

I noted in my original paper that there is at least one area of applied clinical research for which the late developmental model holds immediate implications: that of high risk studies (Feinberg 1982–83). These studies have traditionally sought evidence for abnormal brain and behavioral function in the early years of life. If the late developmental hypothesis is correct, the abnormalities pertinent to schizophrenia might not emerge before the second decade of life.

Late maturational brain processes can be studied on many levels, from the molecular to the behavioral. I mentioned above the apparent age-dependence of paranoid reactions to amphetamines and neurotoxic responses to glutamate channel blockade. These observations encourage studies of developmental psychopharmacology. This field is itself in an embryonic state and studies in humans and lower primates could prove particularly fruitful.

I conclude by re-emphasizing the potential value of sleep studies. The massive changes in sleep EEG over the second decade of life can be studied inexpensively, noninvasively and objectively. Existing cross-sectional data show that the decline in delta integrated amplitude between the ages of 10 and 20 years is several-fold greater than that produced by normal aging over the next five decades (Feinberg *et al.* 1990a). Separate measurement of wave amplitude and incidence, the components of integrated amplitude, is possible with period-amplitude computer analysis; data already available indicate that maturation and aging exert proportionately greater effects on amplitude. Longitudinal studies that could determine the within-subject trajectory of these sleep EEG changes reliably, using repeated measurements, are now quite feasible. Of course, one cannot predict whether the maturational brain changes of sleep will prove related to the late emergence of psychopathology; however, it is an empirical fact that no aspect of brain physiology changes as much with maturation and aging as does the sleep EEG. This tight link of sleep to age surely holds clues to two most profound problems in neuroscience: the function of sleep and the biology of brain maturation and aging (Feinberg 1976).

ACKNOWLEDGMENTS

This work was supported by the Research Service of the Department of Veterans Affairs. I am indebted to Deborah Harrington, PhD; James Morrison, MD; Michael Pogue-Geile, PhD; and Nicholas Rosenlicht, MD for helpful comments and suggestions.

REFERENCES

Agnew, H.W., Jr, Webb, W.B., and Williams, R.C. 1967. Sleep patterns in late middle age males: an EEG study. *Electroenceph. Clin. Neurophysiol.* 23:168– 71.

Andreasen, N.C., Arndt, S., Swayze II, V., Cizadlo, T., Flaum, M., O'Leary, D., Ehrhardt, J.C., and Yuh, W.T. 1994. Thalamic abnormalities in schizophrenia visualized through magnetic resonance image averaging (see comments). *Science* 266:294–8.

Benes, F.M. 1989. Myelination of cortical-hippocampal relays during late adolescence. *Schizophr. Bull.* 15:585–93.

Bleuler, E. 1952. *Dementia praecox; or, the group of schizophrenias*, New York: International Universities Press.

Bleuler, M. 1978. *The schizophrenic disorders: long-term patient and family studies. Trans. by SM Clemens*, New Haven: Yale University Press.

Chaudhari, N. and Hahn, W.E. 1983. Genetic expression in the developing brain. *Science* 220:924–8.

Chugani, H.T., Phelps, M.E., and Mazziotta, J.C. 1987. Positron emission tomography study of human brain functional development. *Ann. Neurol.* 22: 487–97.

Conel, J.L. 1939–1963. *The post-natal development of the human cerebral cortex*. Cambridge: Harvard University Press.

Connell, P.H. 1958. *Amphetamine psychosis*. London: Oxford University Press.

Courchesne, E. 1977. Event-related brain potentials: comparison between children and adults. *Science* 197:589–92.

Evarts, E.V. 1971. Central control of movement. V. Feedback and corollary discharge: a merging of the concepts. *Neurosci. Res. Program Bull.* 9:86–112.

Feinberg, I. 1974. Changes in sleep cycle patterns with age. *J. Psychiatr. Res.* 10: 283–306.

Feinberg, I. 1976. Functional implications of changes in sleep physiology with age. In *Neurobiology of aging*, ed. S. Gershon and R.D. Terry, pp. 23–41. New York: Raven Press.

Feinberg, I. 1978. Efference copy and corollary discharge: implications for thinking and its disorders. *Schizophr. Bull.* 4:636–40.

Feinberg, I. 1982. Schizophrenia and late maturational brain changes in man. *Psychopharmacol. Bull.* 18:29–31.

Feinberg, I. 1982–83. Schizophrenia: caused by a fault in programmed synaptic elimination during adolescence? *J. Psychiat. Res.* 17:319–34.

Feinberg, I. and Carlson, V.R. 1968. Sleep variables as a function of age in man. *Arch. Gen. Psychiatry* 18:239–50.

Feinberg, I., Hibi, S., and Carlson, V.R. 1977. Changes in EEG amplitude during sleep with age. In *The aging brain and senile dementia*, ed. K. Nandy and I. Sherwin, pp. 86–98. New York: Plenum Press.

Feinberg, I., Koresko, R.L., and Heller, N. 1967. EEG sleep patterns as a function of normal and pathological aging in man. *J. Psychiatr. Res.* **5**:107–44.

Feinberg. I., and March J.D. 1995.Observations on delta homeostasis, the one stimulus model of NREM-REM interaction, and the neurobiological implications of experimental dream studies. *Behav. Brain Res.* **69**: 97–108.

Feinberg, I., March, J.D., Flach, K., Maloney, T., Chern, W.-J., and Travis, F. 1990a. Maturational changes in amplitude, incidence and cyclic pattern of the 0 to 3 Hz (Delta) electroencephalogram of human sleep. *Brain Dysfunction* 3: 183–92.

Feinberg, I., Thode, H.C., Chugani, H.T., and March, J.D. 1990b. Gamma distribution model describes maturational curves for delta wave amplitude, cortical metabolic rate and synaptic density. *J. Theor. Bio.* **142**:149–61.

Fish, B. 1957. The detection of schizophrenia in infancy. *J. Nerv. Ment. Dis.* **125**:1–24.

Fix, A.S., Horn, J.W., Wightman, K.A., Johnson, C.A., Long, G.G., Storts, R.W., Farber, N., Wozniak, D.F., and Olney, J.W. 1993. Neuronal vacuolization and necrosis induced by the noncompetitive *N*-methyl-D-aspartate (NMDA) antagonist MK(+)801 (dizocilpine maleate): a light and electron microscopic evaluation of the rat retrosplenial cortex. *Exp. Neurol.* **133**:204–15.

Frith, C.D. 1992. *The cognitive neuropsychology of schizophrenia*, Hove, UK: Lawrence Erlbaum Associates.

Goldman-Rakic, P.S. 1987. Development of cortical circuitry and cognitive functions. *Child Devel.* **58**:601–22.

Grace, A.A. and Bunney, B.S. 1986. Induction of depolarization block in midbrain dopamine neurons by repeated administration of haloperidol: analysis using in vivo intracellular recording. *J. Pharmacol. Exp. Ther.* **238**:1092–100.

Hamburger, V. and Oppenheimer, R.W. 1982. Naturally occurring neuronal death in vertebrates. *Neurosci. Comment* 1:39–55.

Harding, C.M., Brooks, G.W., Ashikaga, T., Strauss, J.S., and Breier, A. 1987. The Vermont longitudinal study of persons with severe mental illness, II: Long-term outcome of subjects who retrospectively met DSM-III criteria for schizophrenia. *Am. J. Psychiat.* **144**:727–35.

Harding, C.M., and Zahniser, J.H. 1994. Empirical correction of seven myths about schizophrenia with implications for treatment. *Acta Psychiatr. Scand. (Suppl.)* **384**:140–6.

Huttenlocher, P.R. 1979. Synaptic density in human frontal cortex – developmental changes and effects of aging. *Brain Res.* **163**:195–205.

Jackson, J.H. 1958. *Selected writings of John Hughlings Jackson*, ed. James Taylor. New York: Basic Books.

Kennedy, C. and Sokoloff, L. 1957. An adaptation of the nitrous oxide method to the study of the cerebral circulation in children: normal values for cerebral blood flow and cerebral metabolic rate during childhood. *J. Clin. Invest.* **36**: 1130–7.

Kraepelin, E. 1919. *Dementia praecox and paraphrenia*. Edinburgh: Livingstone.

Murray, R.M., Lewis, S.W., Owen, M.J., and Foerster, A. 1988. The neurodevelopmental origins of dementia praecox. In *Schizophrenia: the major issues*, ed. P. Bebbington and P. McGuffin, pp. 90–106. Oxford: Heinemann Medical Books.

Olney, J.W., Labruyere, J., and Price, M.T. 1989. Pathological changes induced in cerebrocortical neurons by phencyclidine and related drugs (see comments). *Science* **244**:1360–2.

Pogue-Geile, M.F. 1991. The development of liability to schizophrenia: early and late developmental models. In *Schizophrenia: a life-course developmental perspective*, ed. E.F. Walker, pp. 277–98. San Diego: Academic Press.

Purves, D. 1988. *Body and brain: a trophic theory of neural connections*. Cambridge: Harvard University Press.

Randall, P.L. 1980. A neuroanatomical theory on the aetiology of schizophrenia. *Med. Hypotheses* 6:645–58.

Reiter, E.O., Fuldauer, V.G., and Root, A.W. 1977. Secretion of the adrenal androgen, dehydroepiandrosterone sulfate, during normal infancy, childhood, and adolescence, and in sick infants, and in children with endocrinologic abnormalities. *J. Pediatr.* **90**:766–70.

Satz, P. and Bullard-Bates, C. 1981. Acquired aphasia in children. In *Acquired aphasia*, ed. M.T. Sarno, pp. 399–426. New York: Academic Press.

Shakow, D. 1946. The nature of deterioration in schizophrenic conditions. *Nervous and Mental Disease Monographs* 70.

Small, A., Hibi, S., and Feinberg, I. 1971. Effects of dextroamphetamine sulfate on EEG sleep patterns of hyperactive children. *Arch. Gen. Psychiatry* **25**:369–80.

Sur, M. and Cowey, A. 1995. Cerebral cortex – function and
    development. *Neuron* **15**:497–505.

Weinberger, D.R. 1986. The pathogenesis of schizophrenia: a
    neurodevelopmental theory. In *Handbook of schizophrenia*,
    ed. H.A. Nasarallah and D.R. Weinberger, pp. 397–406.
    New York: Elsevier.

Williams, R.L., Karacan, I., and Hursch, C.J. 1974.
    *Electroencephalography (EEG) of human sleep: clinical
    applications.* New York: John Wiley.

18

Schizophrenia as a developmental disorder of neural network integrity: the dysplastic net hypothesis

ED T. BULLMORE, PAUL O'CONNELL,
SOPHIA FRANGOU, AND ROBIN M. MURRAY

Two separate theories which attempt to explain different aspects of schizophrenia have recently gained currency. The first, the neurodevelopmental model of pathogenesis (Murray and Lewis 1987; Weinberger 1987; Murray 1994), postulates that deviations in early development establish a neuronal phenotype which predisposes to, or indeed determines, the later onset of schizophrenia. The second theory proposes that schizophrenic symptoms arise from abnormal neuronal connectivity (Frith *et al.* 1995; Gold and Weinberger 1995).

In this chapter, we will suggest that the findings from these two, hitherto separate, lines of enquiry can be integrated into a unitary framework, *the dysplastic net hypothesis*; in essence, this proposes that dysconnectivity of the adult schizophrenic brain is determined by dysplastic fetal brain development. We will examine possible risk factors for dysplastic formation of neurocognitive networks, and consider how the latter is expressed in both the prepsychotic and psychotic phases.

THE REINCARNATION OF DEVELOPMENTAL INSANITY

The modern neurodevelopmental hypothesis of schizophrenia was proposed in the 1980s (Murray *et al.* 1985; Murray & Lewis 1987; Weinberger 1987) largely in ignorance of the fact that similar ideas were common parlance a century and more ago. Hecker (1871) for example, regarded hebephrenia as "a disease which invariably erupts following puberty", mostly in individuals "who have been slightly retarded in their physical and their mental development from early on . . . A certain weakness of intellect, laziness, and inability to do mental work is already noticed in childhood, but this is not as extreme or as noticeable as in idiocy". Similarly, Clouston (1891) applied the terms "adolescent" or "developmental" insanity to a psychotic condition which afflicted adolescents and young adults, particularly males, and in 30% of cases proceeded to "a secondary dementia". Neuropathologists such as Southard (1915) also reported changes in the brains of psychotic patients which they considered were of developmental origin (Lewis 1989).

Unfortunately, Hecker's "hebephrenia" and Clouston's "adolescent" insanity were incorporated into, and later eclipsed by, Kraepelin's wider concept of dementia praecox. Subsequently, Southard's ideas of a developmental pathology for dementia praecox dissolved in the general scepticism as to whether any brain changes existed in schizophrenia at all.

The modern revival of developmental theories of schizophrenia has derived in part from epidemiological studies which confirmed the existence of early behavioral precursors, and hence diminished the credibility of a discrete prodromal phase in the natural history of schizophrenia. Instead, they raised questions concerning the timing and type(s) of event that might initiate the schizophrenic process. If schizophrenia does not begin when psychotic symptoms develop, then when does it begin? The answer to this question must come from a consideration of the brain abnormalities found in schizophrenia in the context of our increased understanding of normal brain development.

When does the brain begin to be abnormal in schizophrenia?

Subtle structural brain abnormalities are frequently present in schizophrenia (Woodruff and Murray 1994). Lateral ventricles, and to a lesser extent third and fourth ventricles, are enlarged from first presentation (Turner *et al.* 1986; DeLisi *et al.* 1992). Post-mortem brains of schizophrenics are lighter by 5–8% and shorter by 4% (Brown *et al.* 1986; Bruton *et al.* 1990). Magnetic resonance imaging (MRI) studies have reported modest (about 5%) but significant deficits in global gray matter volume (e.g., Zipursky *et al.* 1992; Harvey *et al.* 1993). Changes in neuronal density in cortical regions of schizophrenics have been described by Pakkenberg (1987) and Benes *et al.* (1991).

Such findings are generally now interpreted as being developmental rather than degenerative in origin (Akbarian *et al.* 1993a, 1993b; Murray 1994). When in the course of early brain development could aberration give rise to the anatomical abnormalities which are characteristic of the brain in adult schizophrenia? Adverse events occurring during the first half of gestation cause syndromes of gross intellectual impairment and/or cortical malformation. As these are more immediately obvious than the relatively subtle behavioural and brain changes found in schizophrenia (Woodruff and Murray 1994), it is likely therefore that the pathogenic processes that affect the preschizophrenic brain occur later.

What effect should dysplasia during the second half of gestation have on adult brain anatomy?

During the second half of gestation, there is little increase in neuronal numbers, but profound changes in neuronal organization and gross cerebral appearance. Macroscopically, the cerebral surface becomes convoluted, or gyrencephalic, and adult patterns of hemispheric asymmetry are established. From week 16 onwards, the left (L) fissure typically appears longer and straighter than its counterpart on the right (R); by week 31 there is also evident asymmetry in the size of the planum temporale (L>R). The extent to which such lateralized patterns of cerebral organization are expressed during development is

modulated by the factors determining handedness (Kertesz *et al.* 1990) and sex (McGlone 1980), although the precise mechanisms involved are unknown. Geschwind and Galaburda (1985) have suggested that testicular development in the male fetus, leading to increased titers of testosterone, may exaggerate lateralized development in the male brain. Dysplasia during the second half of gestation should therefore produce an abnormal, sex-modulated, pattern of asymmetry in the adult brain.

During this period, afferent axonal projections from thalamus, basal ganglia, and other regions of cortex, invade the cortical plate and compete for synaptic territory. Establishment of connections between neurons occurs; a primary connection between two (or more) neurons may confer on them some protection against later regressive processes such as cell death. Thus, two further predictions can be made about the adult schizophrenic brain: first, major white matter tracts, formed by intra- and inter-hemispheric axonal projection, should be abnormal; second, cortical regions that have not been axonally interconnected in the normal manner may be selectively vulnerable to regressive processes, leading to alterations in the normal pattern of correlations between regional gray matter volumes.

In short, impairment of development in the second half of gestation should result in abnormal patterns of asymmetry, abnormal axon tract formation, and correlational abnormalities in multiple cortical region of interest measurements.

Does the neuroimaging literature concerning schizophrenia confirm our predictions?

Brain asymmetry

In the normal adult brain, the right hemisphere shows a greater extent than the left, anteriorly and superiorly; the left hemisphere is typically greater in extent than the right, posteriorly and inferiorly. The first imaging studies to consider the effect of schizophrenia on cerebral lateralization used computed tomography (CT) scans to measure right and left hemispheric width and/or length. Some reported reversal of the normal pattern in schizophrenics, but not all studies controlled for differences in sex and handedness, and the results were inconsistent (Tsai *et al.* 1983).

Interest was revived by studies showing temporal horn enlargement and temporal lobe volume loss to be more marked on the left side than the right (Crow *et al.* 1989). Subsequently, Bilder *et al.* (1994), using MRI, combined multiple region of interest measurements in a summary descriptor of overall hemispheric asymmetry, or "torque". They confirmed that regional volume asymmetries were affected by sex and handedness; after controlling for these effects, schizophrenics had reduced asymmetry in several brain regions, and were significantly more likely than controls to show reversed asymmetry (or "torque") over all brain regions.

A more recent study has also shown loss of torque in familial schizophrenics (Sharma *et al.* 1996). Similarly, Bullmore *et al.* (1995), who measured radial displacement of the convoluted boundary between white and gray matter in both right and left hemispheres, demonstrated reversed anterior hemispheric asymmetry specifically in male schizophrenics.

Corpus callosum

The corpus callosum is the main white matter tract connecting the cerebral hemispheres, incorporating at least 90% of all interhemispheric axonal projections. Woodruff *et al.* (1995) reviewed published MRI studies of the corpus callosum in schizophrenia. They noted the effects of sex and/or handedness on normal callosal anatomy, and demonstrated in a formal meta-analysis of 11 studies, a significant (4%) reduction in callosal area of schizophrenics compared with controls.

An association between psychosis and dysgenesis of the corpus callosum had previously been pointed out by Lewis *et al.* (1988) and subsequently confirmed by Swayze *et al.* (1990). Cavum septum pellucidum, an anomaly related to the development of the corpus callosum, occurs more frequently than expected in schizophrenia (Lewis and Mezey 1985; Degreef *et al.* 1992). Lewis *et al.* (1988) inferred from these associations that abnormal development of the corpus callosum may predispose to later schizophrenia.

Abnormal correlations between regional cortical volume measurements

Synapse formation in utero has a trophic effect on both pre- and postsynaptic neurons. Furthermore, establish-

ment of a secure axonal connection between two neurons will confer on them both some degree of protection against developmentally later regressive processes. Therefore, the volumes of brain regions (e.g., frontal and temporal) that are normally interconnected by dense and reciprocal axonal projection should be highly (positively) correlated in adulthood. Likewise, if normal axonal connections fail to become established between these regions in utero, the correlation between adult regional brain volumes should be substantially reduced. We therefore predict that statistical analysis of the covariance or correlation structure of multiple regional volume measurements should be abnormal in schizophrenics. Unfortunately, no published study has yet tested this hypothesis.

We conclude that studies showing lack of normal asymmetry, and/or abnormal callosal anatomy in the schizophrenic brain are suggestive of disruption of the development of the brain in the latter part of fetal life. We also predict that when the relevant studies are carried out, schizophrenics will show reduced interregional volume correlations, in particular between frontal and temporal brain regions.

NETWORK MODELS OF PSYCHOTIC AND PREPSYCHOTIC BRAIN FUNCTION

Can network models explain the features of schizophrenia?

"Higher order" mental processes, such as attention, language and memory, cannot be localized to a single brain region. They are most convincingly localized instead to large-scale neurocognitive networks, comprising several spatially distributed, densely interconnected cortical regions. This neural architecture has the capacity to process information in parallel, which is computationally much more efficient than serial or hierarchical processing. These networks may well be the neural substrates for memory, learning, and language functions, as well as directed attention (Mesulam 1990). The overall function of such networks depends not only on the competence of their constituent cortical nodes, but also on the integrity of axonal connections between nodes. For example, localized injury to axonal tracts linking intact Broca's and

Wernicke's areas in the neurocognitive network for language causes a syndrome of linguistic dysfunction conduction aphasia.

Cognitive Deficits

If, as we have hypothesized, axonal projection between cortical regions were compromised in preschizophrenic brain development, then we should expect impairment of cognitive functions that depend on network integrity in the adult schizophrenic. Saykin *et al.* (1994) found evidence for cognitive deficits in first episode, neuroleptic naive, schizophrenic patients; the functions most affected were verbal memory and learning, attention-vigilance, and visuomotor processing, all of which may be subserved by spatially distributed cortical networks for parallel processing. This study adds to the growing evidence of persistent abnormalities of cognition which Gold & Weinberger (1995) concluded are compatible with "a compromise of integrative cortical function".

Negative Signs

Certain negative features of schizophrenia, such as poverty of speech or alogia, may also be explicable in terms of abnormal network integrity. Frith *et al.* (1992) used positron emission tomography (PET) to study regional cerebral blood flow (rCBF) changes in normal subjects performing a verbal fluency (intrinsic word generation) task. They found increased rCBF in left dorsolateral prefrontal and parietal association cortices, left parahippocampal gyrus and anterior cingulate gyrus; and decreased rCBF in bilateral temporal regions. Friston (1994) later used multivariate statistical techniques to compare this pattern of distributed activation with that seen in PET data from schizophrenic subjects performing an identical task. The pattern of strong inverse correlation between frontal and temporal rCBF changes found in normals was absent in schizophrenics. This suggests that neural activity is functionally disconnected between nodes of a word-generating network in schizophrenia.

Positive Signs

Dysconnectivity may thus underlie the negative features of schizophrenia; but what of the positive symptoms? Psychologists have long theorized that auditory hallucina-

tions may represent the sufferer's own inner speech which is incorrectly perceived as coming from an external source (Frith 1992). McGuire *et al.* (1993) tested this theory by examining rCBF in schizophrenic males, using single photon emission tomography (SPET), at the precise moment that they were experiencing auditory hallucinations, and then again in the nonhallucinating state. During hallucinations, there was increased blood flow in left temporofrontal regions including Broca's area, the area normally concerned with word generation.

McGuire *et al.* (1995) went on to study schizophrenics with a history of frequent auditory hallucinations, and a group of normal controls, while they imagined hearing sentences as if spoken to them by another person. Performance of this task was associated with significant rCBF changes in a cortical network including left inferior frontal and middle temporal gyri, and the supplementary motor area (SMA). Normal subjects showed significant activation in all three areas; whereas these schizophrenics showed significant deactivation in the middle temporal gyrus and SMA.

McGuire *et al.* (1995) suggest that areas in the superior temporal lobe which are part of the verbal processing network determine whether speech is intrinsic rather than extrinsic (Friston *et al.* 1995). They postulate that auditory hallucinations result from disintegrated activation of the network of frontal and temporal lobe neurons which is responsible for monitoring and labeling (as self or other) internal speech (Friston *et al.* 1995). Further evidence of a disruption of normal frontotemporal connectivity comes from a study of monozygotic twins discordant for schizophrenia, in which the affected twins had a smaller left hippocampal volume than the unaffected twins; this volume reduction correlated with reduced activation of prefrontal cortex, measured by rCBF during the Wisconsin Card Sorting Test. This suggested to Weinberger *et al.* (1992) that "schizophrenia involves pathology of . . . a widely distributed neocortical–limbic neural network".

Hoffman and McGlashan (1993) have provided a theoretical framework for such theories by using computer simulations of neurocognitive networks in the brain to examine the effects on network function of reduced connectivity between nodes. They found that as connectivity was reduced, the network became functionally fragmented and parts of it showed autonomous or "parasitic" behavior which they considered analogous to the emergence of passivity phenomena or auditory hallucinations from similarly disconnected networks in the schizophrenic brain.

Thus, the cognitive, negative and positive features of schizophrenia can be conceptualized as the functional expression of anatomically abnormal connections between cortical regions constituting neurocognitive networks. The dysplastic net hypothesis postulates that such abnormal network connectivity is determined by dysplastic, sex-modulated axonal projection in the second half of fetal life. Two further predictions of this hypothesis are that: (1) impairment of those cognitive functions dependent on network integrity is expected not only in adult schizophrenics but also in preschizophrenic children; and (2) male/female differences in schizophrenia result from the modulating effects of sex on fetal brain development.

Are the childhood characteristics of pre-schizophrenics compatible with a dysplastic neural network?

In line with the first of the above predictions, there is considerable evidence of cognitive dysfunction in pre-schizophrenic children. Foerster *et al.* (1991) obtained retrospective maternal reports on 115 schizophrenics and 67 patients with affective psychosis; low educational achievement was more common among the former. In an extension of this study, Jones *et al.* (1994a) found that schizophrenic patients had shown poorer scholastic performance, and scored lower on measures of intelligence.

Jones *et al.* (1994a) also studied adult schizophrenics who had previously attended the Maudsley Hospital Children's Department. Lower IQ scores were found in the childhood records of the 50 attendees who later developed schizophrenia compared with a control group of 45 who developed affective disorder. When Russell *et al.* (1995) later compared the childhood IQ scores of 34 of the patients at the time they had attended the child psychiatry department with scores after they had developed schizophrenia, the scores were very similar. This implies that the cognitive dysfunction is a stable characteristic of schizophrenics in both the pre- and postpsychotic phases.

In particular, cognitive dysfunction is reported in those preschizophrenics who go on to develop psychosis in adolescence, a finding which suggests that developmental dysplasia may be especially relevant to early onset schizophrenia. Thus, Hollis (1995) used a matched case control design to compare 61 children and adolescents with schizophrenia who had attended the Maudsley child psychiatric services with 61 nonpsychotic psychiatric controls. The greatest difference was in the more frequent occurrence of language and speech difficulties in the preschizophrenics; disturbance of language was greatest among those who became psychotic before age 14 years.

Cohort Studies

Two large cohort studies indicate that low IQ is a risk factor for subsequent schizophrenia. This was noted by David *et al.* (1995) who obtained IQ scores at age 18 years on inductees to the Swedish army, and then followed up the subjects. Similarly, the British birth cohort study of Jones *et al.* (1994b), described by Jones and Done in Chapter 9, found that the 30 preschizophrenics had lower verbal and nonverbal scores at age 8 years than the remaining 4716 subjects; once again, more speech problems were found in the preschizophrenics. The fact that speech difficulties are a risk factor for later schizophrenia is not surprising given the evidence reviewed above that auditory hallucinations are secondary to dysfunction in language systems.

High Risk Studies

Having established the existence of cognitive abnormalities in preschizophrenic children, it is pertinent to ask if these are genetically determined. As an affected family member remains the strongest risk factor for schizophrenia (Gottesman 1991), an obvious approach is to study the offspring of schizophrenics.

Fish (1977) described an abnormal sequence of cognitive development in seven offspring of schizophrenic mothers who went on to develop schizophrenia, and concluded that the schizophrenic genotype manifests in infants as a heritable neurointegrative defect which she termed pandysmaturation.

Marcus *et al.* (1993) compared the development of school-age children born of schizophrenic parents with that of children of healthy parents or parents with other psychiatric disorders. The offspring of schizophrenics were more likely to show perceptual-cognitive and motoric dysfunction.

These findings provide support for the idea that certain neurointegrative deficits reflect familial vulnerability to schizophrenia and that these deficits are clearly apparent in infancy, and at school age, long before the onset of psychosis.

Are the sex differences in schizophrenia consequent upon sex modulation of dysplastic neural networks?

The second prediction is that the sex differences in schizophrenia should be explicable in terms of differences in prenatal brain development. Males show an earlier age of onset of schizophrenia (Lewine 1988; Castle *et al.* 1993), have more negative symptoms, and a worse outcome (Castle and Murray 1991). Male schizophrenics also exhibit more abnormalities of childhood personality and social adjustment than their female counterparts (Foerster *et al.* 1991). Low IQ, poor school performance and increased "soft" neurological signs were noted more frequently in males than females who later developed schizophrenia (Jones *et al.* 1994a).

The above sex differences have been related to the evidence that ventricular enlargement appears more pronounced in male as opposed to female schizophrenics (see Woodruff and Murray 1994; Lewine *et al.* 1995). Indeed, ventricular enlargement appears to be particularly marked in male nonfamilial cases. Six studies have shown that male nonfamilial patients have larger ventricles than their familial counterparts; no such familial/sporadic difference has been found for females (O'Connell *et al.* 1996). The obvious implication is that some environmental effect is operating particularly on male nonfamilial cases.

As male neonates are more prone to develop lasting neurodevelopmental damage following obstetric adversity, several investigators have suggested that pregnancy and birth complications (PBCs) may be the critical early environmental effect (Cantor-Graae *et al.* 1994; McGrath and Murray 1995). This line of reasoning suggests that the greater vulnerability of males than females to prenatal hazards may contribute to the greater premorbid abnormalities in male than female preschizophrenics, and

the earlier onset of schizophrenia in males. Rifkin *et al.* (1994) found that in male (but not female) schizophrenics, a low birth weight was correlated with poor premorbid function and cognitive ability. Furthermore, Kirov *et al.* (1996) have shown, in a series of 73 schizophrenics, that when one removes those cases who have suffered obstetric complications (predominantly male), the sex difference in age of onset disappears.

Thus, it is clear that the manifestations of schizophrenia are indeed modified by sex. These different characteristics are already detectable in childhood, and may reflect sex-modulated vulnerability to environmental effects operating during the second half of gestation.

DETERMINANTS OF NETWORK DISINTEGRITY

Genetic

There is, of course, long-standing evidence of a genetic contribution to schizophrenia (Kendler and Diehl 1993), evidence which has been reconfirmed in large and sophisticated family (Kendler *et al.* 1993) and adoption studies (Kety *et al.* 1994). If schizophrenia results from dysplastic formation of neurocognitive networks, then one should seek mutations in genes which control the development, and interconnections, of neurons (Jones and Murray 1991).

Candidate genes involved in neurodevelopment are discussed in detail by Vicente and Kennedy in Chapter 3. Here we shall confine ourselves to mentioning the recent finding of increased repeat sequences detected using the repeat expansion dectection (RED) method in schizophrenia, particularly in early onset schizophrenics (Morris *et al.* 1996). This is especially interesting as there is some evidence that schizophrenia in the young is particularly familial (Sham *et al.* 1994), and as we noted earlier, early onset schizophrenics show more language disorder in childhood.

Are the structural brain changes found in schizophrenia genetically determined? Cannon *et al.* (1993) compared CT brain scans in individuals with one or two parents affected with schizophrenia with those of the offspring of normal parents. They found a generalized effect of genetic risk for schizophrenia on brain structures regardless of region, and a linear increase of the cerebrospinal fluid (CSF)–brain ratios with increasing level of genetic risk.

The unaffected siblings of schizophrenics have larger ventricles than unrelated normal controls (Weinberger *et al.* 1981; DeLisi *et al.* 1986). In families multiply affected with schizophrenia, where genetic factors can be assumed to predominate, CT studies have demonstrated increased ventricular volume in both the affected members and their well relatives (Honer *et al.* 1994).

Do the brain abnormalities in such genetically loaded families result from dysplasia in the second half of gestation? If so, one would expect loss of normal brain asymmetry to be particularly evident in familial schizophrenics. Sharma *et al.* (1996) examined this issue in a sample of schizophrenics and their unaffected first degree relatives from multiply affected families. Compared with controls, the normal pattern of frontal and occipital asymmetry was lost in the schizophrenics and in those relatives who, from the patterns of illness in the families, appeared to have transmitted the schizophrenic genotype without being clinically affected themselves. These findings are compatible with the suggestion of Crow *et al.* (1989) that loss of normal brain asymmetry in schizophrenia reflects disturbances in the expression of the gene(s) that controls the development of brain asymmetry, and obviously points to the period of the development of normal asymmetry as the critical period for mutant gene expression.

CT and MRI studies of monozygotic (MZ) twins discordant for schizophrenia have shown ventricular enlargement and reduction in volume of the temporal lobe and anterior hippocampus in the schizophrenic twin compared with his/her unaffected cotwin (Reveley *et al.* 1984; Suddath *et al.* 1990). As MZ twins share all their genes, this argues for either an environmental effect alone or an environmental effect operating on predisposing genes.

Environment

The twin studies indicate that any interpretation of the neuroanatomical findings in schizophrenia must take into account the contribution of environmental factors. What are these, and does their timing support our thesis that a critical aberration of cortico–cortical connections occurs in the second half of gestation?

Four reviews have summarized the literature on pregnancy and birth complications (PBCs) and schizophrenia. McNeil (1995) concluded that seven out of eight studies that examined obstetric records and nine out of 13 studies that relied on maternal recall, found schizophrenics to have an excess of PBCs. Goodman (1988) calculated that PBCs increase an individual's lifetime risk of schizophrenia from 0.6% to about 1.5%, while a meta-analysis carried out by Geddes and Lawrie (1995) also suggested that PBCs doubled the risk. A final review by McGrath and Murray (1995) pointed out the deficiencies in three recent negative studies (Done *et al.* 1991; McCreadie *et al.* 1992; Buka *et al.* 1993).

Some studies suggest that patients with schizophrenia are born lighter than their unaffected siblings (Lane and Albee 1966; Woerner *et al.* 1973) and have a lower mean birth weight than normal controls (Rifkin *et al.* 1994). Moreover, two recent studies have shown that pre-schizophrenics have smaller head circumference at birth even when gestational age is taken into account (McNeil *et al.* 1993; Kunugi *et al.* 1996). As head circumference at birth is largely determined by intrauterine brain growth, this presumably reflects some earlier impairment of normal brain development.

Whether earlier impairment of brain development causes the excess of perinatal complications observed in schizophrenia remains an open question (Goodman 1988). Certainly, a pre-existing neural tube defect can be the cause of perinatal complications (Nelson and Ellenberg 1986). Such impairment of fetal brain development could be due to abnormalities in the genes controlling neurodevelopment but it could also result from adverse environmental events during pregnancy. Wright *et al.* (1995) reported that those preschizophrenics whose mothers had influenza during their second trimester of gestation were of lower birth weight and subject to more perinatal difficulties than schizophrenics whose mothers had no infections during their pregnancy. Could some at least of the excess of PBCs in schizophrenics be secondary to exposure to maternal infection?

The relationship between prenatal exposure to influenza epidemics and later schizophrenia has attracted much recent attention. The majority of, but not all (Crow and Done 1992; Susser *et al.* 1994), studies have shown that those born following epidemics of influenza have an increased risk of schizophrenia (Mednick *et al.* 1988; Barr *et al.* 1990; O'Callaghan *et al.* 1991; McGrath *et al.* 1995). The peak risk for schizophrenia following exposure to influenza appears to be between the fifth and seventh month of gestation (Sham *et al.* 1992; Adams *et al.* 1993; Takei *et al.* 1994; Stober *et al.* 1994). Takei *et al.* (in press) have reported a tentative finding that those schizophrenics who were exposed in their fifth month of gestation during periods of high influenza prevalence show a greater degree of sylvian fissure widening than in those whose mid-gestation occurred during relatively influenza-free periods. If this finding is replicated, it would be an important explanatory link in the hitherto speculative chain linking prenatal exposure to influenza to later schizophrenia.

Many studies have examined the relationship between PBCs and adult brain structure in schizophrenia (for a review see McGrath and Murray 1995) but unfortunately, most have had to rely on maternal recall for the obstetric information. One exception is the study of Cannon *et al.* (1993) which showed that in individuals at high genetic risk for schizophrenia, PBCs predicted increased ventricular size.

Premature babies are susceptible to hypoxic-ischemic damage, and intraventricular and periventricular hemorrhage are common consequences, often with secondary ventricular dilatation. The latter can be detected on cranial ultrasound at birth, and predicts poor psychomotor and neuropsychiatric outcome at 8 years of age (Roth *et al.* 1993; 1994). We have preliminary results from a study of cerebral structure at age 14 years in babies who were born at less than 33 weeks. Radiologists blindly rated two-thirds of their MRI scans as abnormal compared with only 7% of normal gestation control individuals; abnormal thinning of the corpus callosum, ventricular enlargement, and periventricular abnormalities were particularly common. Thus, it is clear that events before or during birth can mimic some of the cerebral structural abnormalities (e.g., abnormalities of the corpus callosum) which are found in schizophrenia, and which we suspect are consequent upon developmental events in the second half of gestation.

Nevertheless, most fetuses exposed to a broad range of PBCs do not develop schizophrenia and most patients with schizophrenia have no history of obvious PBCs. One possibility, congruent with the dysplastic net hypothesis, is that PBCs only increase risk of later schizophrenia when certain critical neuronal circuits are compromised. Persaud *et al.* (unpublished results) have shown that schizophrenics have more white matter hyperintensities than bipolar patients and controls; these were positively associated with a history of PBCs. Neonatal pediatricians report similar perivascular lesions following hypoxic-ischemic damage. One might speculate that such white matter lesions would be particularly likely to lead to disconnectivity of neurocognitive networks.

Thus, developmental epidemiology suggests that pre- and perinatal complications, including exposure to prenatal viral infection and hypoxic-ischemic damage are risk factors for schizophrenia. The timing is congruent with our thesis that the crucial developmental aberration in schizophrenia occurs in the second half of gestation. Neuroimaging studies of schizophrenic patients are also compatible with this thesis, but what is the biochemical mechanism?

Does hypoxic-ischemic damage induce a glutamatergic disruption of network connectivity?

Hypoxia-ischemia is well known to be associated with glutamate release and subsequent excitotoxic neuronal damage. Olney and Farber (1995) point out that "glutamate is an endogenous agent whose excitotoxic wrath can be unleashed in the fetal brain by circumstances as common as ischemia, and (that) ischemia can be induced in the fetal brain by a mechanism as simple as transient compression of the umbilical cord". They also note that prenatal exposure to viral infection can be associated with glutamatergic-mediated excitotoxic damage.

The cortico-cortical projections are largely glutamatergic, and therefore one would predict that glutamatergic damage would impair neurocognitive networks. Indeed, Hoffman and McGlashan (1993) argue that phencyclidine (PCP) induces a schizophrenia-like psychosis by binding to the ion channel site of the *N*-methyl-D-aspartate (NMDA) subtype of glutamate receptors, and thus disrupting cortico-cortical transmission. Abnormalities have been reported in various elements of the glutamatergic system in schizophrenia (for a review see by Olney and Farber 1995). For instance, Deakin *et al.* (1989) found increased density of non-NMDA receptors in orbital frontal cortex (suggesting an excessive glutamatergic innervation of this region), while Kerwin *et al.* (1990) found losses in non-NMDA receptors in the medial temporal lobe. Kerwin and Murray (1992) suggested that these abnormalities might be consequent upon hypoxic-ischemic damage early in life. Thus a developmental imbalance in glutamatergic transmission could underlie the loss of prefrontal-temporal connectivity noted earlier in schizophrenics prone to auditory hallucinations (McGuire *et al.* 1995).

CONCLUSIONS

Bleuler's word, schizophrenia, by definition implies a mental condition characterized by schism, disintegration, or dysconnectivity. As he put it:

> The thousands of associations guiding our thought are interrupted by this disease in an irregular way here and there, sometimes more, sometimes less. The thought processes, as a result, become strange and illogical, and the associations find new paths.
>
> E. BLEULER (1911: p. 14)

Much of the evidence reviewed above, especially from structural and functional neuroimaging studies, suggests that there may be a biological analogue to this long-established psychological observation. In other words, anatomical and physiological connections between brain regions, as well as associations between ideas, may be irregularly interrupted in schizophrenia.

The case is not yet proven decisively, perhaps partly because many neuroanatomical studies of schizophrenia have adopted a "region of interest" methodology which implicitly assumes there is a focal brain lesion. We anticipate that in the future more structural studies will adopt statistical methods better suited to a direct test of anatomical dysconnectivity in schizophrenia. For example, it would be of considerable interest to know whether patterns of covariance or correlation between multiple regional measures of brain volume are abnormal in schizophrenia (as we have postulated). We also predict that there will be increasing interest in multivariate analysis of functional neuroimaging data, both to corroborate the existing PET findings of fronto-temporal dysconnectivity, and to explore the functional integrity of other neurocognitive networks likely to be involved in schizophrenic psychopathology.

The question at the heart of this chapter, however, is whether dysconnectivity in schizophrenics can be explained by dysplastic brain development in utero. We have argued that the neurodevelopmental processes most likely to determine adult patterns of cortico-cortical connectivity occur in the second half of normal gestation, for it is at this stage of pregnancy that exuberant axonal projections first invade the cortical plate and compete for synaptic territory. It is also during the second half of pregnancy that sex-modulated patterns of cerebral asymmetry become macroscopically evident. If brain development is indeed disordered at this stage in pregnancy, one would expect to find abnormal patterns of cerebral asymmetry in adult schizophrenics, a modulating effect of sex on abnormal brain structure and function, and psychological deficits compatible with impaired neurocognitive network function in childhood. All of these expectations have been reviewed, and largely upheld, in the light of the existing literature.

Many questions remain before the dysplastic net hypothesis can be regarded as proven. In particular, what etiological agents are responsible for the pathogenetic process we have proposed? One possibility is abnormality of the gene(s) normally controlling brain development in the second half of pregnancy; such a genetic mechanism is supported by evidence of abnormal cerebral asymmetry in the relatives of schizophrenics. It is also clear from studies of monozygotic twins discordant for schizophrenia that aberrant genes cannot entirely account for all cases of schizophrenia. Diverse environmental risks in pregnancy, including hypoxia-ischemia and viral infection, might induce cortico-cortical dysconnectivity by the "final common pathway" of glutamatergic excitotoxicity.

ACKNOWLEDGMENTS

The research described in this chapter has been supported by the Medical Research Council, Wellcome Trust, and the Stanley Foundation.

REFERENCES

Adams, W., Kendell, R.E., Hare, E.H., and Munk-Jorgensen, P. 1993. Epidemiological evidence that maternal influenza contributes to the aetiology of schizophrenia. An analysis of Scottish, English, and Danish data. *Br. J. Psychiatry* **163**:522–34.

Akbarian, S., Bunney, W.E., Potkin, S.G., Wigal, S.B., Hagman, J.O., Sandman, C.A., and Jones, E.G. 1993a. Altered distribution of nicotinamide-adenosine dinucleotide phosphate-diaphorase cells in frontal lobe of schizophrenics implies disturbances of cortical development. *Arch. Gen. Psychiatry* **50**:169–77.

Akbarian, S., Vinuela, A., Kim, J.J., Potkin, S.G., Bunney, W.E., and Jones, E.G. 1993b. Distorted distribution of nicotinamide-adenosine dinucleotide phosphate-diaphorase neurones in temporal lobe of schizophrenics implies anomalous cortical development. *Arch. Gen. Psychiatry* **50**:178–87.

Barr, C.E., Mednick, S.A., and Munk-Jorgensen. P. 1990. Exposure to influenza epidemics during gestation and adult schizophrenia. A 40–year study. *Arch. Gen. Psychiatry* **47**:869–74.

Benes, F.M., McSparren, J., Bird, E.D., San Giovanni, J.P., and Vincent, S. L. 1991. Deficits in small interneurons in prefrontal and cingulate cortices of schizophrenic and schizoaffective patients. *Arch. Gen. Psychiatry* **48**:996–1001.

Bilder, R. M., Wu, H., Bogerts, B., Degreef, G., Ashtari, M., Alvir, J.M.J., Snyder, P. J. and Lieberman, J.A. 1994. Absence of regional hemispheric volume asymmetries in first episode schizophrenia. *Am. J. Psychiatry* **151**:1437–47.

Bleuler, E. 1911. Dementia praecox or the group of schizophrenias (trans.(1950) J. Zimkins). London: George Allen & Unwin.

Brown, R., Colter, N., Corsellis, J.A.N., Crow, T.J., Frith, C.D., Jagoes, R., Johnstone, E.C., and Marsh, L. 1986. Postmortem evidence of structural brain changes in schizophrenia: differences in brain weight, temporal horn area, and parahippocampal gyrus compared with affective disorder. *Arch. Gen. Psychiatry* **43**:36–42.

Bruton, C.J., Crow, T.J., Frith, C.D., Johnstone, E.C., Owens, D.G.C., and Roberts, G.W. 1990. Schizophrenia and the brain: a prospective clinico-neuropathological study. *Psychol. Med.* **20**:285–304.

Buka, S.L., Tsuang, M.T., and Lipsitt, L.P. 1993. Pregnancy/delivery complications and psychiatric diagnosis. A prospective study. *Arch. Gen. Psychiatry* **50**:151–6.

Bullmore, E. T., Brammer, M. J., Harvey, I., Murray, R., and Ron, M. 1995. Cerebral hemispheric asymmetry revisited: effects of gender, handedness and schizophrenia measured by radius of gyration in magnetic resonance images. *Psychol. Med.* **25**:349–63.

Cantor-Graee, E., McNeil, T.F., Nordstrom, L. G., and Rosenlund, T. 1994. Obstetric complications and their relationship to other etiological risk factors in schizophrenia. A case control study. *J. Nerv. Ment. Dis.* **182**:645–50.

Castle, D.J. and Murray, R.M. 1991. The neurodevelopmental basis of sex differences in schizophrenia. *Psychol. Med.* **21**:565–75.

Castle, D.J., Wessely, S., and Murray, R.M. 1993. Sex and schizophrenia: effects of diagnostic stringency, and associations with premorbid variables. *Br. J. Psychiatry* **162**:658–64.

Cannon, T.D., Mednick, S.A., Parnas, J., Schuksinger, F., Preastholm, J., and Vestergaad, A. 1993. Developmental brain abnormalities in the offspring of schizophrenic mothers. *Arch. Gen. Psychiatry* **47**:622–32.

Clouston, T.S. 1891. *The neuroses of development*. Edinburgh: Oliver and Boyd.

Clouston, T.S. 1892. *Clinical lectures on mental diseases*, 3rd edn. London: Churchill.

Crow, T.J., Ball, J., Bloom, S.R., Brown, R., Bruton, C.J., Colter, N., Frith, C.D., Johnstone, E.C., Owens, D.G., and Roberts, G.W. 1989. Schizophrenia as an anomaly of cerebral asymmetry. A post-mortem study and a proposal concerning the genetic basis of the disease. *Arch. Gen. Psychiatry* **46**:1145–50.

Crow, T.J. and Done, D.J. 1992. Prenatal exposure to influenza does not cause schizophrenia. *Br. J. Psychiatry* **161**:390–3.

David, A.S., Malmberg, G., Lewis, L., Brandt, P., and Allebeck 1995. Premorbid psychological performance as a risk factor for schizophrenia. *Schizophr. Res.* **15**:114.

Deakin J.F.W., Slater P., Simpson M.D.C., Guilchrist, A.C., Skan, W.J., Royston, W.J., Reyonlds, G.P., and Cross, A.J. 1989. Frontal cortical and left temporal glutamatergic dysfunction in schizophrenia. *J. Neurochem.* **52**:1781–86.

Degreef, G., Bogerts, B., Falkai, P., Greve, B., Lantos, G., Ashtari, M., and Liebermann, J. 1992. Increased prevalence of cavum septum pellucidum in magnetic resonance scans and post-mortem brains of schizophrenic patients. *Psychiatry Res.* **45**:1–13.

DeLisi, L.E., Goldin, L.R., Hamovit. J.R., Maxwell, M.E., Kurtz. D., and Gershon, E.S., 1986. A family study of the association of increased ventricular size with schizophrenia. *Arch. Gen. Psychiatry* **43**:148–5.

DeLisi, L.E., Stritzke, P., Riordan, H., Holan, V., Boccio, A., Kushner M., McClelland, J., Van Eylo, O., and Anand, A. 1992. The timing of brain morphological changes in schizophrenia and their relationship to clinical outcome. *Biol. Psychiatry* **31**:241–54.

Done, D.J., Johnstone, E.C., Frith, C.D., Golding, J., Shepherd, P.M., and Crow, T.J. 1991. Complications of pregnancy and delivery in relation to psychosis in adult life. *Br. Med. J.* **302**:1576–80.

Fish, B. 1977. Neurobiologic antecedents of schizophrenia in children. *Arch. Gen. Psychiatry* **34**:1297–313.

Foerster, A., Lewis, S.W., Owen, M.J., and Murray, R.M. 1991. Premorbid personality and psychosis: effects of sex and diagnosis. *Br. J. Psychiatry* **158**:171–6.

Friston, K. J. 1994. Functional and effective connectivity in neuroimaging: a synthesis. *Hum. Brain Mapping* **2**:56–78.

Friston, K.J., Herold, S., Fletcher, P., Cahill, C., Dolan, R.J., Liddle, P.F., Frackowiak, R.S.J., and Frith, C.D. 1995. Abnormal fronto-temporal interactions in schizophrenia. In *Biology of schizophrenia and affective disorder*, ed. S.J. Watson, New York: Raven Press, (In Press).

Frith, C.D. 1992. *The cognitive neuropsychology of schizophrenia.* Hove, Sussex: Lawrence Erlbaum.

Frith, C. D., Friston, K. J., Liddle, P. F., and Frackowiak, R.S.J. 1989. A PET study of word finding. *Neuropsychologia* **28**:1137–48.

Frith, C.D., Heorld, S., Silbersweig, D., Fletcher, P., Cahill, C., Dolan, R.J., Frackowiack, R.S.J., and Liddle, P.F. 1995. Regional activity in chronic schizophrenic patients during performance of a verbal fluency task. *Br. J. Psychiatry* **167**:343–9.

Geschwind, N. and Galaburda, A. M. 1985. Cerebral lateralisation. Biological mechanisms, associations, and pathology. *Arch. Neurol.* **42**:428–59.

Gold, J. M. and Weinberger, D. R. 1995. Cognitive deficits and the neurobiology of schizophrenia. *Curr. Opin. Neurobiol.* **5**:225–30.

Gottesman I. I. 1991. *Schizophrenia genesis: the origins of madness.* New York: W.H. Freeman.

Goodman, R. 1988. Are complications of pregnancy and birth causes of schizophrenia? *Dev. Med. Child Neurol.* **30**:391–5.

Geddes, J.R. and Lawrie, S.M. 1995. Obstetric complications and schizophrenia: a metanalysis. *Br. J. Psychiatry* **167**:786–93.

Harvey, I., Ron, M.A., Du Boulay, G., Wicks, D., Lewis, S.A., and Murray, R.M. 1993. Reduction in cortical volume in schizophrenia on magnetic resonance imaging. *Psychol. Med.* **23**:591–604.

Hecker, E. 1871. Die Hebephrenie. *Virchows Archiv.* [A] **52**:394–429.

Hoffman, R.R. and McGlashan, T.H.1993. Parallel distributed processing and the emergence of schizophrenic symptoms. *Schizophr. Bull.* **19**:257–61.

Hollis, C. 1995. Child and adolescent (juvenile onset) schizophrenia. A case control study of premorbid developmental impairments. *Br. J. Psychiatry* **166**:489–95.

Honer, W.G., Bassett, A.S., Smith, G.N., Lapointe, J.S., and Falkai, P. 1994. Temporal lobe abnormalities in multigenerational families with schizophrenia. *Biol. Psychiatry* **36**:737–43.

Jones, P., Guth, C., Lewis, S., and Murray, R. 1994a. In *The neuropsychology of schizophrenia*, ed. A. David, and J. Cutting, pp. 131–144. Hove. UK: Lawerence Erlbaum.

Jones P.B. and Murray R.M. 1991. The genetics of schizophrenia is the genetics of neurodevelopment. *Br. J. Psychiatry* **158**:615–23.

Jones, P., Rodgers, B., Murray, R., and Marmot, M. 1994b. Child developmental risk factors for adult schizophrenia in the British 1946 birth cohort. *Lancet* **344**:1398–402.

Kendler, K.S. and Diehl, S.R. 1993. The genetics of schizophrenia: a current, genetic-epidemiologic perspective. *Schizophr. Bull.* **19**:261–85.

Kendler, K.S., McGuire, M., Gruenberg, A.M., O'Hare, A., Spellman, M., and Walsh, D. 1993. The Roscommon Family Study. I. Methods, diagnosis of probands, and risk of schizophrenia in relatives. *Arch. Gen. Psychiatry* **50**:527–40.

Kertesz, A., Polk, M., Black, S. E., and Howell, J. 1990. Sex, handedness, and the morphometry of cerebral asymmetries on magnetic resonance imaging. *Brain Res.* **530**:40–8.

Kerwin, R. and Murray, R.M. 1992. A developmental perspective on the pathology and neurochemistry of the temporal lobe in schizophrenia. *Schizophr. Res.* 7:1–12.

Kerwin, R.W., Patel, S. and Meldrum, B. S. 1990. Autoradiographic localisation of the glutamate receptor system in control and schizophrenic post-mortem hippocampal formation. *Neuroscience* **39**:25–32.

Kety, S.S., Wender, P.H., Jacobsen, B., Ingraham, L.J., Jansson, L., Faber, B., and Kinney, D.K. 1994. Mental illness in the biological and adoptive relatives of schizophrenic adoptees. Replication of the Copenhagen Study in the rest of Denmark. *Arch. Gen. Psychiatry* **51**:442–55.

Kirov, G., Jones, P., Harvey, I., Lewis, S.W., Toone, B., Sham, P., and Murray, R.M. 1996. Do obstetric complications cause gender differences in schizophrenia? *Schizophr. Res.* **20**:117–24.

Kunugi, H., Takie, N., Murray, R.M., and Nanko, S. 1996. Body weight and head circumference at birth in schizophrenia. *Schizophr. Res.* **20**:165–70.

Lane, E.A. and Albee,G.W. 1966. Comparitive birth weight of schizophrenics and their siblings. *J. Psychiatry* **64**:277–81.

Lewis, S.W. 1989. Congenital risk factors for schizophrenia (editorial). *Psychol. Med.* **19**: 5–13.

Lewis, S.W. and Mezey, C. 1985. Clinical correlates of septum pellucidum cavities: an unusual association with psychosis. *Psychol. Med.* **15**:1–12.

Lewis, S.W, Reveley, M.A, David, A.S, and Ron, M.A. 1988. Agenesis of the corpus callosum and schizophrenia: a case report. *Psychol. Med.* **18**:341–7.

Lewine, R.R.J. 1988. Gender and schizophrenia. In: *Handbook of schizophrenia*, vol. 3, ed. H.A. Nasrallah, pp. 379–397, Amsterdam: Elsevier.

Lewine R.R., Hudgins, P., Brown, F., Caudle, J., and Risch. S.C.1995. Differences in qualitative brain morphology findings in schizophrenia, major depression, bipolar disorder, and normal volunteers. *Schizophr. Res.* **15**:253–9.

Mednick S.A., Machon R.A., Huttunen M.O., and Bonett D. 1988. Adult schizophrenia following prenatal exposure to an influenza epidemic. *Arch. Gen. Psychiatry* **45**:189–92.

Mesulam, M.M. 1990. Large-scale neurocognitive networks and distributed processing for attention, language, and memory. *Ann. Neurol.* **28**:597–613.

McGlone, J. 1980. Sex differences in human brain asymmetry: a critical survey. *Behav. Brain Sci.* 3:215–63.

McCreadie, R.G., Hall, D.J., Berry, I.J., Robertson, L.J., Ewing, J.I., and Geals, M.F., 1992.The Nithsdale schizophrenia surveys. X: Obstetric complications, family history and abnormal movements. *Br. J. Psychiatry* **160**:799–805.

McGrath, J., Castle, D., and Murray, R.M. 1995. How can we judge whether or not prenatal exposure to influenza causes schizophrenia. In *Neural development and schizophrenia. Theory and research*, ed. S.A. Mednick and J.M. Hollister, pp. 203–214. New York: Plenum Press.

McGrath, J. and Murray, R.M. 1995. Risk factors for schizophrenia, from conception to birth. In *Schizophrenia*, ed. S. Hirsch, and D. Weinberger, Oxford: Blackwell. pp. 187–205.

McGuire, P.K., Shah, G.M.S., and Murray, R.M. 1993. Increased blood flow in Broca's area during auditory hallucinations in schizophrenia. *Lancet* **342**:703–6.

McGuire, P.K., Silbersweig, D.A., Wright, I., Murray, R.M., David, A.S., Frackowiak, R.S.J., and Frith, C.D. 1995. Abnormal monitoring of inner speech: a physiological basis for auditory hallucinations. *Lancet* **346**:596–600.

McNeil, T.F. 1995. Perinatal risk factors and schizophrenia: selective review and methodological concerns. *Epidemiol. Rev.* **17**:107–12.

McNeil, T.F., Cantor-Graae, E., and Cardenal, S. 1993. Prenatal cerebral development in individuals at genetic risk for psychosis: head size at birth in offspring of women with schizophrenia. *Schizophr. Res.* **10**:1–5.

McNeil, T.F., Cantor-Graae, E., Nordstrom, L.G., Rosenlund, T. 1993. Head circumference in "preschizophrenic" and control neonates. *Br. J. Psychiatry* **162**:517–23.

Marcus J., Hans S.L., Auerbach J.G., and Auerbach A.G. 1993. Children at risk for schizophrenia: The Jerusalem Infant Development Study. II. Neurobehavioural deficits at school-age. *Arch. Gen. Psychiatry* **50**:797–809.

Morris, A.G., Gaitonde, E., McKenna, P.J., Mollon, J.D., and Hunt, D.M. 1996. Associations of CAG repeat expansions with clinical features of schizophrenia. *Schizophr. Res.* **18**:168 (abstract).

Murray, R.M. 1994. Neurodevelopmental schizophrenia: the rediscovery of dementia praecox. *Br. J. Psychiatry* **165**:6–12.

Murray R.M. and Lewis S.W. 1987. Is schizophrenia a neurodevelopmental disorder? *Br. Med. J.* **295**:681–82.

Murray, R.M., Lewis, S., and Reveley, A.M., 1985. Towards an aetiological classification of schizophrenia. *Lancet* **i** 1023–6.

Nelson, K.B. and Ellenberg, J.H. 1986. Antecedents of cerebral palsy. Multivariate analysis of risk. *New Engl. J. Med.* **315**:81–6.

O'Callaghan, E., Sham, P., Takei, N., Glover, G., and Murray, R.M. 1991. Schizophrenia after prenatal exposure to 1957 A2 influenza epidemic. *Lancet* **1**:1248–50.

O'Connell, P., Woodruff, P.W.R., Wright, I., Jones, P., and Murray, R.M. 1996. Developmental insanity or dementia praecox: was the wrong concept adopted? *Schizophr. Res.* (in press).

Olney, J.W. and Farber, N.B. 1995. Glutamate receptor dysfunction and schizophrenia. *Arch. Gen. Psychiatry* **52**:998–1007.

Pakkenberg, B. 1987. Post mortem study of chronic schizophrenic brains. *Br. J. Psychiatry* **151**:744–52.

Reveley, A.M., Reveley, M.A., and Murray, R.M. 1984. Cerebral ventricular enlargement in non-genetic schizophrenia: a controlled twin study. *Br. J. Psychiatry* **144**:89–93.

Rifkin L., Lewis S., Jones P., Toone B., and Murray R. 1994. Schizophrenic patients of low birth weight show poor premorbid function and cognitive impairment in adult life. *Br. J. Psychiatry* **165**:357–62.

Roth, S.C., Baudin, J., McCormick, D.C., Edwards, A.D., Townsend, J., Stewart, A.L., and Reynolds, E.O. 1993. Relation between ultrasound appearance of the brain of very preterm infants and neurodevelopmental impairment at eight years. *Dev. Med. Child Neurol.* **35**:755–68.

Roth, S.C., Baudin, J., Pezzani-Goldsmith, M., Townsend, J., Reynolds, E.O., and Stewart, A.L. 1994. Relation between neurodevelopmental status of very preterm infants at one and eight years. *Dev. Med. Child Neurol.* **36**:1049–62.

Russell A.J., Munro J., Jones P.B., Hemsley D.H., and Murray R.M. 1995. A longitudinal follow-up of IQ in a sample of adult schizophrenics who presented to psychiatric services during childhood and adolescence. *Schizophr. Res.* **15**:132–33.

Saykin, A.J., Shtasel, D.L., Gur, R.E., Kester, D.B., Mozley, L.H., Stafiniak, P., and Gur, R.C. 1994. Neuropsychological deficits in neuroleptic naive patients with first-episode schizophrenia. *Arch. Gen. Psychiatry* **51**:124–31.

Sham, P., Jones, P., Russell, A., Gilvarry, K., Pebbington, P.,

Lewis, S., Toone, B., and Murray, R.M. 1994. Age at onset, sex and familial psychiatric morbidity in schizophrenia. Report from the Camberwell Collaborative Psychosis Study. *Br. J. Psychiatry* **165**:466–77.

Sham, P., O'Callaghan, E., Takei, N., Murray, G., Hare, E., and Murray, R. 1992. Schizophrenic births following influenza epidemics:1939–60. *Br. J. Psychiatry* **160**:461–6.

Sharma, T., Lewis, S., Barta, P., Sigmundsson, T., Lancaster, E., Gurling, H., Pearlson, G., and Murray, R.M. 1996. Loss of cerebral asymmetry in familial schizophrenia: a volumetric MRI study using unbiased stereology. *Schizophr. Res.* **18**:184.

Southard, E.E. 1915. On the topographical distribution of cortex lesions and anomalies in dementia praecox, with some account of their functional significance. *Am. J. Insanity* **71**:603–71.

Stober, G., Franzek, E., and Beckmann, H. 1994. Pregnancy infections in mothers of chronic schizophrenic patients. The significance of differential nosology. *Nervenarzt* **65**:175–82.

Suddath, R.L., Christison, G.W., Torrey, E.F., Casanova, M.F., and Weinberger, D.R. 1990. Anatomical abnormalities in the brains of monozygotic twins discordant for schizophrenia. Published erratum appears in *N. Engl. J. Med.* **31**:1616.

Susser, E., Lin, S.P., Brown, A.S., Lumey, L.H., and Erlenmeyer-Kimling, L.1994. No relation between risk of schizophrenia and prenatal exposure to influenza in Holland. *Am. J. Psychiatry* **151**:922–4.

Swayze, W., Andreasen, N.C., Erhardt, J.C., Yuh, W.T.C., Allinger, R.J. and Cohen, G.A. 1990. Development abnormalities of the corpus callosum in schizophrenia: an MRI study. *Arch. Neurol.* **47**:805–8.

Takei, N., Lewis, S., Jones, P., Harvey, I. and Murray, R.M. Prenatal exposure to influenza and increased CSF spaces in schizophrenia. *Schizophr. Bull.* (in press).

Takei, N., Sham, P., O'Callaghan, E., Glover, G., and Murray, R. M. 1994. Prenatal exposure to influenza and the development of schizophrenia: is the effect confined to females? *Am. J. Psychiatry* **151**:117–19.

Tsai, L. Y., Nasrallah, H. A., and Jacoby, C. G. 1983. Hemispheric asymmetries on computed tomographic scans in schizophrenia and mania. *Arch. Gen. Psychiatry* **40**:1286–9.

Turner, S.W., Toone, B.K., and Brett-Jones, J.R. 1986. Computerised tomographic scan changes in early schizophrenia. *Psychol. Med.* **16**:219–25.

Weinberger, D. R. 1987. Implications of normal brain development for the pathogenesis of schizophrenia. *Arch. Gen. Psychiatry* **44**:660–9.

Weinberger, D. R., Berman K. F., Suddath, R., and Torrey, E.F. 1992. Evidence of dysfunction of a prefrontal-limbic network in schizophrenia: a magnetic resonance imaging and regional cerebral blood flow study of discordant monozygotic twins. *Am. J. Psychiatry* **149**:890–7.

Weinberger, D.R., DeLisi, L.E., Neophytides, A.N., and Wyatt, R.J. 1981. Familial aspects of CT abnormalities in chronic schizophrenic patients. *Psychiatry Res.* **4**:65–71.

Woerner, M.G., Pollack, M., and Klein, D.F.1973. Pregnancy and birth complications in psychiatric patients: a comparison of schizophrenic and personality disorder patients with their siblings. *Acta Psychiatr. Scand.* **49**:712–21.

Woodruff, P.W.R., McManus I.C., and David, A.S. 1995. Meta-analysis of corpus callosum size in schizophrenia. *J. Neurol., Neurosurg. Psychiatry* **58**:457–61.

Woodruff, P.W.R. and Murray, R.M. 1994. The aetiology of brain abnormalities in schizophrenia. In: *Schizophrenia: exploring the spectrum of psychosis*, ed. R. Ancill, pp. 95–144, Chichester: John Wiley.

Wright, P., Takei, N., Rifkin, L., and Murray, R.M.1995. Maternal influenza, obstetric complications and schizophrenia. *Am. J. Psychiatry* **152**:1714–20.

Zipursky, R.B., Lim, K.O., Sullivan, E.V., Brown, B.W., and Pfefferbaum, A. 1992. Widespread cerebral gray matter volume deficits in schizophrenia. *Arch. Gen. Psychiatry* **49**:195–205.

19 Neurodevelopment and schizophrenia: quo vadis?

MATCHERI S. KESHAVAN

We praise the "lifetime of study," but in dozens of cases, in every field, what was needed was not a lifetime but rather a few short months or weeks of analytic inductive inference . . . We speak piously of taking measurements and making small studies that will "add another brick to the temple of science". Most such bricks just lie around the brickyard.
Platt 1964

NEURODEVELOPMENTAL MODELS OF SCHIZOPHRENIA

Recent years have witnessed an impressive expanse of new information pertaining to the neurodevelopmental pathogenesis of schizophrenia. Not surprisingly, this has led to a search for models, i.e., hypotheses and constructs that serve to organize large and complex data sets and generate specific predictions. Several, often conflicting, neurodevelopmental models of this illness have been proposed, a fairly good sampling of which appear in this book. Debate has focused on *whether* neurodevelopment is abnormal in schizophrenia, *when* the proposed deviations may occur, *which* neural networks may be affected, and finally *what* might be the nature of such defective development. In this chapter, I attempt to build potential bridges between the varied arguments proposed in these chapters, as well as by others not represented in this volume, and will offer some further speculations toward an integrated model. I propose that the schizophrenic syndrome results from a cascade effect of a possibly genetically mediated derailment in early and late maturational processes of brain development interacting with adverse humoral and psychosocial factors which occur later during adolescence and early adulthood. Finally, I will review the testable predictions generated by these models, and critically evaluate research strategies that will potentially further our under-

standing of the neurodevelopmental pathogenesis of schizophrenia.

Is schizophrenia a neurodevelopmental disorder?
Several reasons have been advanced to support the view that schizophrenia is a neurodevelopmental disorder: the typical onset of this disorder in adolescence, the occurrence of structural and neurofunctional abnormalities at the onset of the illness, and the fact that these abnormalities do not appear to progress with time in most cases (Murray and Lewis 1987; Weinberger 1987,1995). Further support has been provided by epidemiological studies showing premorbid intellectual deficits dating back to early development (Jones *et al.* 1994; Done *et al.* 1994), and neuropathological studies showing altered cerebral cytoarchitecture indicative of a developmental rather than acquired encephalopathy. The limited number of these neuropathological studies, the relatively small sample sizes, and the potential confounds of neuroleptic treatments makes these post-mortem findings tentative, and in need of replication. Furthermore, aspects of illness suggesting neurodevelopmental deviation may not apply to all individuals suffering from this syndrome, and some authors have argued for neurodevelopmental and non-neurodevelopmental subtypes of the disorder (e.g., Murray *et al.* 1992), and even neurodegenerative subtypes of the disorder (DeLisi *et al.* 1995).

When did the defect in neurodevelopment occur?

Early neurodevelopmental models

Several models of the pathophysiology of schizophrenia (Murray and Lewis 1987; Weinberger 1987), are based on the view that the proposed brain abnormalities in this disorder stem primarily from one or other causal factors early in development, intra or perinatally, perhaps during the second half of gestation. In these *early* neurodevelopmental models (Murray and Lewis 1987; Weinberger 1987), a fixed lesion from early life interacts with normal neurodevelopment occurring later. Post-mortem studies suggest aberrant cortical cytoarchitecture indicative of possible errors in the early developmental phenomena of neural genesis or migration (for a review see Weinberger 1995). This view is also supported by recent findings using magnetic resonance spectroscopy (MRS), which offers a noninvasive in vivo approach to investigating chemistry proton (^{1}H) or phosphorus (^{31}P) containing metabolites (for a review see Keshavan *et al.* 1991; also see Pettegrew *et al.* in Chapter 6). The *N*-acetyl aspartate (NAA) signal from ^{1}H MRS, a mainly intraneuronal metabolite, is considered to be a marker of neuronal viability and is consistently reduced in disorders associated with neuronal loss (Birken and Oldendorf 1989). NAA is reduced in the temporal cortex in first-episode as well as chronic schizophrenia, and in children at risk for this disorder (Keshavan and Pettegrew in press). Thus, an early developmental dysmaturation may occur in at least some schizophrenic patients.

Late neurodevelopmental models

The typical adolescent onset of schizophrenic illness as well as a lack of definitive data pointing to early neurodevelopmental abnormalities or risk factors in many cases of schizophrenia have prompted the alternative view that the pathophysiology of this disorder has its onset in postnatal life. Based on the data that indicate substantial changes in brain biology during adolescence, as reviewed previously, Feinberg (1982–83) proposed that schizophrenia may result from an abnormality in periadolescent synaptic pruning. The question, however, of whether too much, too little, or the wrong synapses being pruned, was left open. Recent neuropathological studies indicate a reduction in the synapse-rich neuropil and a consequent increase in cortical neuron density (Selemon *et al.* 1995); reduction in expression of synaptophysin, a synaptic marker (Eastwood and Harrison 1995); and density of dendritic spines (Glanz and Lewis 1994). Thus, there may be a reduction of cortical synapse density in schizophrenia.

Several in vivo neurobiological measures, which undergo marked changes in adolescence, may indirectly reflect changes in synapse density. During adolescence, substantial reductions are seen in delta sleep, which represent the summed postsynaptic potentials in large assemblies of cortical and subcortical axons and dendrites (Feinberg 1982/83); periadolescent reductions are also seen in membrane synthesis (see Pettegrew *et al.* in Chapter 6), cortical gray matter volume (Jerningan and Tallal 1990) and prefrontal metabolism (see Chugani and Chugani in Chapter 7). In schizophrenia, similar, but more pronounced decrements are seen, relative to healthy controls, in delta sleep (Keshavan *et al.* 1990), membrane synthesis (Pettegrew *et al.* 1991), gray matter volume (Zipursky *et al.* 1992), and prefrontal metabolism (Andreasen *et al.* 1992). Taken together, it appears that an exaggeration of the normative process of synaptic pruning occurs in schizophrenia, at least in the prefrontal cortex (Keshavan *et al.* 1994).

An alternative " late" model has been proposed by Benes (1989). She has argued that a defect in myelination of key corticolimbic pathways could be related to the development of schizophrenia. As discussed earlier, myelination continues into early adulthood and may occur in the mid-life as well. Males have a delay in myelination during adolescence and their earlier illness onset may be related to this.

Early–late interaction

How can we integrate these apparently contrasting models? Synaptic proliferation and development of connectivity is dependent on survival of neurons which is target dependent. Early errors in neuronal migration and/or differentiation could lead to elimination of certain needed networks resulting in reduced synaptic proliferation. This "low baseline" combined with postnatal regressive processes of synaptic elimination could, in effect, cause a *reduced* synapse density due to exaggerated loss of certain needed neuronal connections. Neuronal damage early in development could also lead to an abnormal persistence of anomalous connections. There is evidence that persistence of nonfunctional neuronal networks beyond a certain critical period could lead to a failure of their being pruned out (Janowsky and Finlay 1986; Goodman 1989; and van Ooyan *et al.* 1995). Alternatively, schizophrenia may be associated with maladaptive reinnervation in response to brain damage (Stevens 1992). This view is supported by observations that brain damage can provoke regenerative collateral axonal sprouting, and synaptic reorganization even in adult mammalian brain. This model would predict an *increased* synaptic density. The above phenomena may not be mutually exclusive and may occur in different circuits. In other words, early brain injury could result in a dyspruned neural connectivity, i.e., loss of some neuronal connections that would normally have been retained, and a compensatory retention and/or proliferation of some other connections that would have normally been pruned out. Thus, in schizophrenia, early developmental lesions could lead to a reduced connectivity in certain brain regions (i.e., the prefrontal cortex) perhaps leading to negative symptoms, and a persistent synaptic expansion in certain projection sites of these brain structures, such as the cingulate and temporolimbic cortex and ventral striatum, possibly leading to positive symptoms.

Where is the neurodevelopmental deficit?

Early literature in schizophrenia focused on generalized abnormalities such as ventriculomegaly and cortical atrophy. Subsequent literature mostly devolved on abnormal structure and functioning of one or other discrete brain structures in schizophrenia, and most commonly the temporal and prefrontal cortex were implicated (the "Lesion Models"). More recently, there is increasing support for the view that schizophrenia may be associated with abnormalities in multiple interconnected cortical and subcortical regions.

Our understanding of the neural circuitry models of schizophrenia have been considerably influenced by recent work showing the existence of multiple functionally segregated circuits involving cortico–subcortical feedback loops (Alexander *et al.* 1986). These include five circuits based

on the primary cortical region involved: the motor, oculomotor, dorsolateral prefrontal, lateral orbito-frontal, and cingulate. The dorsolateral circuit mediates "executive" functions (planning and "working memory"); anterior cingulate mediates motivation, and lateral orbitofrontal circuit mediates context-appropriate behavioral responses. These circuits have been considered to be more likely involved in schizophrenia as the salient features of this illness include impairments in executive function, apathy and disinhibition, respectively. Weinberger (1987) and Goldman-Rakic (1994) have implicated the dorsolateral PFC and related circuits based on the prominent impairment of "executive" functions of this brain region in schizophrenia. Swerdlow and Koob (1987) have proposed an abnormality in cortico-striato pallido-thalamic circuits. Walker *et al.* (1993) has argued for a similar model based on her observations of motoric abnormalities antedating schizophrenic illness. Deakin (1994) has argued that the basolateral circuit is abnormal in schizophrenia based on disruption in context-appropriate social behavior. The anterior cingulate circuit has also been blamed, based on motivational impairments in this disorder (Benes *et al.* 1991).

It may be seen that while there is general agreement that the neuropathology and neuropsychological features of schizophrenia are not easily explained by classical "lesion" models (Bilder 1996), the precise circuits attributed vary widely. Evidence supports more complex models that accommodate defects in multiple circuits, each of which may relate to a specific domain of psychopathology. Both negative and positive symptoms could result from abnormal connectivity. On the one hand, negative symptoms such as deficits in willed action could result from reduced functioning in frontostriatal circuits. Such abnormalities in connectivity could result from excessive axonal/dendritic pruning in certain neural circuits, such as in the PFC, as proposed previously (Hoffman and McGlashan 1993; Keshavan *et al.* 1994). Anomalous persistence of certain other circuits, on the other hand, could lead to "parasitic foci" that become autonomous, causing "alien" subjective symptoms referred to as positive symptoms (see Feinberg in Chapter 17). Frith (1995) has recently offered a similar conceptualization. Thus, a dysregulated process of "blooming and pruning" during the postnatal period could lead to a network dysplasia (see Bullmore *et al.* in Chapter 18) or dysmodularity (David 1994) that may mediate the expression of the diverse symptoms in schizophrenia.

What is the nature of the developmental abnormality?

Both post-mortem and neuroimaging research in the past decade have led to a rekindling of interest in the neuropathology of schizophrenia, and have yielded some converging findings. Notable neuropathological findings include: (1) a lack of gliosis supporting a neurodevelopmental, rather than an acquired pathogenesis; and (2) an indication of altered cytoarchitecture, which suggests a defect in the formation of the cortical plate (Jakob and Beckmann 1986; Akbarian *et al.* 1993). The neuropathological observations have been variously postulated to support hypothesized defects in one or other stage of brain development. Structural neuroimaging findings suggest ventriculomegaly and decreased cortical volume, particularly pronounced in gray matter (see Lewis in Chapter 12) reductions in corpus collosal size and loss of cerebral asymmetry (see Bullmore *et al.* in Chapter 18). Functional imaging studies have indicated reduced prefrontal metabolism (Andreasen *et al.* 1992; see Pettegrew *et al.* in Chapter 6).

At a neurochemical level the major explanatory hypothesis over the last two decades has been the dopamine theory. New insights have recently emerged into the pathophysiology of schizophrenia from research into the role of the excitatory neurotransmitter, glutamate, originally proposed by Kim and Kornhuber (Kim *et al.* 1980). Dysfunction of this system may explain the neurodevelopmental mediation of this illness, as well as both the positive and negative symptoms, and the adolescent onset of this disorder (Coyle 1996). This system is of particular interest in relation to the proposed deviations in postnatal brain development in schizophrenia, because the periadolescent reductions in synapse density appear to mainly involve the glutamatergic neurons. A glutamatergic hypofunction could therefore underlie abnormal synaptic pruning. Until recently, however, it has not been possible to directly investigate glutamate in the central nervous system (CNS) in vivo and noninvasively. The recent finding (Stanley *et al.* 1995) of reduced glutamate in PFC of first-episode schizophrenic patients using proton MRS is therefore exciting and needs to be replicated.

TOWARD AN INTEGRATION

The premise often held by several theorists proposing the pathophysiological models of schizophrenia has been that there is a "final common pathophysiological pathway" to which several etiological roads lead. There is increasingly the perception, however, that there may be heterogeneity at both etiological and pathophysiological levels in schizophrenia.

Several environmental influences could potentially be implicated in the pathogenesis of "early" neurodevelopmental impairment in schizophrenia, but only a small percentage of cases may be linked to these insults, and none is likely to represent either a necessary or sufficient cause of the schizophrenic illness. On the other hand, the role of genetic factors is undoubted, although it is unlikely that a single gene accounts for a majority of cases of schizophrenia. It is more likely that vulnerability to schizophrenia is caused by an interaction of multiple genetic and environmental factors affecting early brain development. The timing of onset of the clinical manifestations of the disorder may on the other hand be determined by late brain maturational processes, peripubertal neuroendocrine changes, as well as the levels of psychosocial stresses.

THE JOURNEY FROM MODELS TO FACTS

The central tasks that need to be pursued in our efforts to advance the neurodevelopmental models include: first the characterization of the premorbid deficits in this disorder, and second the nature of the developmental neuropathology. I summarize here the two crucial issues of *whom* to study, and *what* measures to investigate in order to address the above questions.

Which populations to study

The possibility that developmental abnormalities may predate the manifestations of the clinical features of the

Fig. 19.1 Schematic diagram representing an integrated model of the etiology and pathophysiology of schizophrenia.

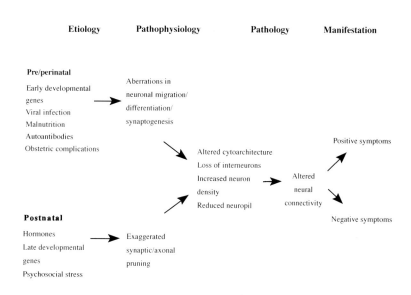

illness by several years has lead to several strategies of investigating such potential precursors. These include studies of preschizophrenia subjects, early-onset schizophrenia patients and subjects with known neurodevelopmental disorders that bear resemblance to schizophrenia in one or other manner.

Preschizophrenia subjects

High-risk strategies

Studies of subjects deemed to be at risk for schizophrenia have been an important area of inquiry in schizophrenia research. In the genetic high-risk strategy, risk is defined by having a higher than normal genetic loading for schizophrenia. Several studies of offspring of schizophrenics have appeared in the literature. These studies indicated that some individuals with genetic risk show early evidence of increased liability to schizophrenia. These "first generation" high-risk studies were, however, limited by the lack of explicit diagnostic criteria, the use of psychiatric control groups, i.e., offspring of parents with nonschizophrenic disorders; and the use of biobehavioral measures of uncertain significance. Not surprisingly, the findings were highly variable across studies, and lacked specificity (for a review see Gooding and Iacono 1995).

As the majority of schizophrenic patients do not have an affected parent, sibling or co-twin, an alternative is to use one or other putative biobehavioral marker(s) of schizophrenia to define risk. The literature is replete with a large variety of measures used in diverse settings; both population-based and clinic-based samples have been used. Some studies have used personality characteristics such as schizotypy, neurobehavioral markers such as Smooth Pursuit Eye Movement (SPEM) dysfunction and attentional deviance, and psychometric indices of deviation, e.g., high scores on perceptual aberration scales and MMPI; others have used psychophysiological measures such as skin conductance (for a review see Gooding and Iacono 1995). One of the problems with these strategies is the question of whether the populations they selected are representative of schizophrenia in general or whether they represent a group of individuals with the given marker who may or may not have this schizophrenic diathesis. Thus, several false positives and false negatives could result, leading in effect to a reduction in statistical power.

Birth cohort studies

Longitudinal studies of general population samples are among the best approaches to investigating the developmental antecedents of schizophrenia. In the UK two birth cohort studies have been published, the Medical Research Council National Survey of Health and Development of

1946 and the National Child Development Study of 1958 (see Jones and Done in Chapter 9). The Jones *et al.* study (1994), in which the participants have lived through most of the age of risk, showed that children destined to develop schizophrenia could be differentiated on the basis of motor and cognitive dysfunction throughout childhood. Birth cohort studies have the advantage of yielding an unbiased estimate of the at risk population, and are valuable in identifying potential etiological factors pertinent to the illlness; however, the information available is often inadequate to address the specific questions relating to pathophysiology.

Follow-back studies

Follow-back studies examine precursors of adult-onset psychopathology by examining medical or scholastic records of individuals with known outcome in adulthood. The main advantage of this approach is that a representative sample of the patient population is obtained. The information thus collected suffers from recall bias, however, and is often inadequate to address the specific questions. An innovative version of this strategy is the Archival–Observational Approach developed by Walker and colleagues (Walker *et al.* 1993). These investigators collected old home movies from families of schizophrenic patients. Children who subsequently developed schizophrenia were distinguished by subtle but significant neuromotor abnormalities compared with their unaffected siblings. These provocative findings support the view that dysmaturation of motor systems may occur in the future schizophrenic patient even in early childhood.

Studies of childhood-onset schizophrenia

A developmental approach to the study of schizophrenia would suggest that the investigation of patients with onset of the illness close to the "sensitive" periods of development, such as the peripubertal period, is likely to be particularly instructive. Earlier onset cases may reflect a form of illness with a greater genetic loading, male preponderance, and possibly a greater contribution by neurodevelopmental pathology (Murray *et al.* 1992). Empirical studies of childhood-onset schizophrenia, however, are plagued by its very low incidence, lack of clarity in phenomenological descriptions of this disorder, and the uncertainty in the use of adult diagnostic criteria (see Hollis and Taylor in Chapter 16). A

careful phenomenological study and neurobiological investigation of this disorder is likely to illuminate important aspects of the pathophysiology of schizophrenia.

Analogies with other neurodevelopmental disorders

Examination of the neurodevelopmental paradigms of schizophrenia is likely to benefit from comparison of this disorder with other disorders whose neurodevelopmental origins are well established. An example of this is cerebral palsy. Cerebral palsy is similar to schizophrenia in terms of the importance of familial and prenatal and perinatal factors, male predominance in severity, possible secular trends of decline, in incidence, and age-dependent variations in clinical picture (see Lewis in Chapter 12). Weinberger (1987) has drawn a parallel between schizophrenia and metachromatic leukodystrophy (MLD), a white matter disease disrupting intracortical connectivity postulated to underlie schizophrenia. Interestingly, when MLD presents during adolescence, the main clinical manifestation is schizophreniform. Other neurodevelopmental disorders that may potentially illuminate schizophrenia include attention deficit disorder and autism (see Hollis and Taylor in Chapter 16). These observations highlight the importance of cross-fertilization between researchers investigating different neurodevelopmental disorders. The comorbidity of developmental disorders among schizophrenic patients should also be investigated further.

In summary, studies of preschizophrenic subjects using birth cohort as well as the high-risk strategies provide valuable information pertaining to disordered development in schizophrenia. These studies are expensive, and the pathophysiological insights derived by them are limited to the information obtained at the onset of the studies, which are determined by the state of knowledge at that time. The follow-back studies, on the other hand, suffer from the disadvantage of recall bias. One way to enhance the power of genetic and psychobiological high-risk strategies is to combine them, rather than use either approach alone. Thus, one can select the subject initially for the presence of an affected relative, and then include only those who show one or other psychobiological markers, such as SPEM impairment, attentional deviation, or ERP abnormality. Such an "enriched genetic-psychobiological high-risk strategy" is likely to have more statistical power to detect differences from controls, and can therefore be used to conduct the newer "second generation" high-risk studies involving more expensive neurobiological studies. Studies of early-onset schizophrenia provides the opportunity of examining the illness at the critical developmental period of early adolescence; examination of schizophrenia, like disorders of known neurodevelopmental origin, can shed light on schizophrenia by analogy. Thus, each of the above approaches to examining the neurodevelopmental pathology have their unique advantages, and are complementary to each other.

Which neurobiological measures to investigate?

Progress in schizophrenia research as in other developmental disorders has often resulted from the limitations in definitive assessments of brain function as well as the frequent use of exploratory, rather than hypothesis-driven research. Formulation of alternative models which lead to testable predictions is important to avoid over attachment to any one theory (Carpenter *et al.* 1993). The newer developmental models allow formulation of alternative hypotheses that are testable, and the newer in vivo imaging techniques make it feasible to examine several such hypotheses. The following caveats should be borne in mind in hypothesis testing: first, hypotheses chosen must be decisive, i.e., where negative results are as important as positive results in theory modification, and lead to the decision for the next experiment (Platt 1964). Second, the chosen putative neurodevelopmental indicator(s) of schizophrenia need to be demonstrated to have a significant association both with the schizophrenia diathesis as well as with brain maturation. Third, where possible, one should look for converging evidence from use of multiple neurobiological approaches to enhance confidence in findings, positive or negative (Carpenter *et al.* 1993).

Several testable hypotheses can be generated from the various neurodevelopmental models of schizophrenia (e.g., early versus late), which can potentially be tested in subjects at high risk for schizophrenia. For example, in in vivo anatomical studies, the *early* model would predict that subjects at high risk for schizophrenia have reduced cranial size, and reductions in both gray and white matter volumes (because of loss of both neurons and axons). On the other hand, the *late* pruning models which do not invoke an early

lesion predict a prominent gray matter volume reduction without changes in cranial size or white matter volume. In vivo neurochemical studies, using ^{1}H MRS would show NAA reductions if an early lesion had resulted in neuronal loss; a late developmental deviation in dendritic pruning would on the other hand predict mainly alterations in membrane turnover without alterations in NAA. The *interactional* models would predict NAA reductions in certain brain regions (e.g., PFC) and NAA increases in certain other regions such as temporal–limbic cortex which suggests increased synapse density. Investigation of such questions is now made possible by the advent of several new in vivo approaches to examine neuroanatomical, metabolic, and physiological changes during neurodevelopment. It is now possible to image and map myeloarchitectonic features of cerebral cortex in the living human using magnetic resonance imaging (MRI; Clark *et al.* 1992). Using Blood Oxygenation Level Dependent (BOLD), Contrast Functional Magnetic Resonance Imaging (fMRI) (Belleveau *et al.* 1991), it has now become possible to study regional brain activation during human development (Born *et al.* 1996). The development of neural networks as well as the changes in neural plasticity can thus be monitored noninvasively. It is also possible to conduct in vivo MRS studies prospectively from early in development to track metabolic changes (Keshavan *et al.* 1991; Keshavan and Pettegrew in press). The use of high field magnets (3–4 Tesla) provide an opportunity to conduct fine-grained MRS investigations of brain metabolites relevant to brain maturational processes, such as glutamate, glutamine and gamma amino butyric acid (Keshavan and Pettegrew in press). Newer, sophisticated power spectral analytic approaches can provide accurate estimates of physiological markers of brain development, such as delta sleep, and have been used to investigate early brain development (Ktonas *et al.* 1995).

In designing studies of abnormal brain maturation processes in schizophrenia, it is also important to keep in mind the fact that certain periods during development may be particularly sensitive to the impact of adverse biological or environmental influences. Such "sensitive" periods include the fetal, neonatal, and early childhood periods as well as adolescence. The period of late postnatal development is unique in this regard, as it involves an experience-dependent reorganization of neural structures. Neurobiological

Table 19.1. *Examples of testable predictions from the neurodevelopmental models of schizophrenia*

	Early neurodevelopmental model	Late excessive synaptic pruning model	Early–late interaction models
MRI volumetric studies	Decreased cranial volume, loss of gray and white matter	Normal cranial volume; reduced gray matter volume	Decreased cranial volume, loss of gray and white matter
Proton and ^{31}P MRS studies	Reduced cortical NAA; normal PME levels	Normal NAA levels; reduced PME levels	Reduced NAA as well as reduced PME levels in PFC; maybe increased PME levels in temporo-limbic cortex
Neuropathology studies	Reduced cell numbers; altered cell location and cytoarchitecture	Reduced synapse density, increased cortical neuron density; normal cell location and cytoarchitecture	Reduced neuron numbers as well as synapse density in PFC; possibly increased synapse density in certain other brain region such as temporolimbic cortex, altered cell location and cytoarchitecture
Clinical and neurobehavioral studies	Neurofunctional deficits in the majority of subjects from early childhood onwards	Neurofunctional deficits begin mostly around early adolescence	Neurofunctional deficits begin in early childhood and are exaggerated around adolescence

Notes:
NAA: *N*-acetyl aspartate; PFC: prefrontal cortex; PME: phosphomonoesters.

phenomena that undergo major changes during such critical periods (e.g., delta sleep, membrane synthesis, and cortical gray matter structure) are therefore likely to yield valuable insights into the pathophysiology of this disorder. It is important to ensure, however, that the variables being examined have temporally stabilized because of the enormous influence of age on several biological parameters of interest.

CONCLUSIONS AND FUTURE DIRECTIONS

While several shots have been heard in our attempts to trace the culprit(s) causing schizophrenia, it may be safe to

say that the "smoking gun" is yet to be found. It is reasonable, however, to conclude that disordered brain development mediates the pathogenesis of at least a subgroup of patients with the schizophrenia syndrome. The emergence of psychopathology in adolescence is best explained by an interaction between early neurodevelopmental lesions and a disruption in late postnatal brain maturational processes; genetic factors and environmental variables, both biological and psychosocial, may be involved in mediating the emergent developmental neuropathology. The net result of such a complex interplay of causative factors may be a multinodal network dysplasia in critical cortical–subcortical systems, with the clinical expression of the disorder varying with the particular networks predominantly involved. The available facts about this illness therefore fit best with a model that accommodates both etiological and pathophysiological heterogeneity.

Efforts to further investigate the neurodevelopmental hypotheses of schizophrenia should be a major priority in psychiatric research. The following questions need to be addressed to confirm the neurodevelopmental origins in schizophrenia (in a manner analogous to the Koch's postulates in medicine). (1) Are there brain abnormalities in schizophrenia that unambiguously point to derailment in one or other neurodevelopmental process? This issue can be resolved by establishing the validity of cytoarchitectural findings of neurodevelopmental abnormalities by carefully designed neuropathological studies. (2) Can such pathology be demonstrated in the individuals at or close to the time periods when the brain is undergoing the developmental changes proposed to be abnormal in the disorder? The question can best be addressed by examining the hypothesized neurobiological abnormalities in preschizophrenic subjects (e.g., "high risk" relatives) using state of the art neuroimaging and electrophysiological techniques. Also needed are hypothesis-driven longitudinal and cross-longitudinal studies of preschizophrenic children focusing on the critical "sensitive" periods of brain development. (3) Do putative etiological factors predictably cause the observed developmental neuropathology? This question will benefit from cross-disciplinary studies which examine relations between etiological factors (e.g., viruses, genetic factors), neuropathology (e.g., reduced synapse density, cellular disarray), and phenomenology (e.g., positive and negative syndromes). Using in vitro expression systems and animal models (e.g., the hippocampal lesion model; Lipska and Weinberger 1994), it may also be possible to directly examine the causal link between potential etiological factors and the neuropathological changes.

Recent advances in developmental neurobiology and neuroscience make it reasonable to expect a paradigm shift in research on schizophrenia. What is needed is an increasing dialogue between developmental neurobiologists and clinical researchers to characterize both vulnerability as well as protective factors mediating emergent psychopathology; studies should focus on the roles of nature as well as nurture. Finally, such research needs to be tied to our efforts to develop better approaches to early detection and intervention.

REFERENCES

Akbarian, S., Bunney, W.E., Potkin, S.G., Wigal, S.B., Hagman, J.O., and Sandman, C.A. 1993. Altered distribution of nicotamide-adenine dinucleotide phosphate-diaphorase cells in frontal lobe of schizophrenics implies disturbances of cortical development. *Arch. Gen. Psychiatry* 50:169–77.

Alexander, G.E., DeLong, M.R., and Strick, P.L. 1986. Parallel organization of functionally segregated circuits linking basal ganglia and cortex. *Annu. Rev. Neurosci.* 9:357–81.

Andreasen, N.C., Rezzi, K., Alliger, R., Swayze, I.I., Falum, M., Kirchenr, P., Cohen, G., and O'Leary, D.S. 1992. Hypofrontality in neuroleptic-naive patients and in patients with chronic schizophrenia, *Arch. Gen. Psychiatry* 49:943.

Belleveau, J.W., Kennedy, J.N., McKinstry, R.C., Buchbinder, B.R., Weissleoff, R.M., Cohen, M.S., Verea, J.M., Brady, T.J., and Rosen, B.R. 1991. Functional mapping of the human visual cortex by magnetic resonance imaging. *Science* 254:716–18.

Benes, F.M. 1989. Myelination of corticalhippocampal relays during later adolescence. *Schizophr. Bull.* 15:585–93.

Benes, F.M., McSparran, J., Bird, E.D., SanGiovanni, J.P., and Vincent, S.L. 1991. Deficits in small interneurons in prefrontal and cingulate cortices of schizophrenic and schizoaffective patients. *Arch. Gen. Psychiatry* 48:990–1001.

Bilder, R. 1996. Neuropsychology and neurophysiology in schizophrenia. *Cur. Opin. Psychiatry* 9:57–62.

Birken, D.L. and Oldendorf, W.H. 1989. *N*-acetyl-L-aspartic acid: a literature review of a compound prominent in ^{1}H-NMR spectroscopic studies of brain. *Neurosci. Biobehav. Rev.* 13:23–31.

Born, P., Rostrup, E., Leth, H., Peitersen, B., and Lou, H.C. 1996. Changes of visually induced cortical activation patterns during development. *Lancet* 347:543–4.

Carpenter, W. T., Buchanan, R. W., Kirkpatrick, B., Tamming, C., and Wood, F. 1993. Strong inference, theory testing, and the neuroanatomy of schizophrenia. *Arch. Gen. Psychiatry* 50:825–31.

Clark, V.P., Courchesne, E., and Grafe, M. 1992. In vivo myeloarchitecture analysis of human striate and extrastriate cortex using magnetic resonance imaging. *Cerebral Cortex* 2:417–24.

Coyle, J. T. 1996. The glutamatergic dysfunction hypothesis for schizophrenia. *Harvard Rev. Psychiatry* **3**: 241–53.

David, A.S. 1994. Dysmodularity: a neurocognitive model for schizophrenia. *Schizophr. Bull.* **19**:109–40.

Deakin, J.F.W. 1994. Neuropsychological implications of brain changes in schizophrenia: an overview. *Psychopathology* **27**:251–4.

DeLisi, L.E. 1995. A prospective follow-up study of brain morphology and cognition in first-episode schizophrenic patients: preliminary findings. *Biol. Psychiatry* **38**:349–60.

Done, D.J., Crow, T.J., Johnstone, E.C., and Sacker, A. 1994. Childhood antecedents of schizophrenia and affective illness: social adjustment at ages 7 and 11. *Br. Med. J.* **309**:699–703.

Eastwood, S.L. and Harrison, P.J. 1995. Decreased synaptophysin in the medial temporal lobe in schizophrenia demonstrated using Immunoautoradiography. *Neuroscience* **69**:339–43.

Feinberg I. 1982/1983. Schizophrenia: caused by a fault in programmed synaptic elimination during adolescence? *J. Psychiatry Res.* **17**:319.

Frith, C. 1995. Functional imaging and cognitive abnormalities. *Lancet* **1995**:615–20.

Glantz, L.A., and Lewis, D.A. 1994. Decreased synaptophysin immunoreactivity in prefrontal cortex of schizophrenia. *Biol. Psychiatry* **35**:717 (abstract).

Goldman-Rakic, P.S. 1994. Working memory dysfunction in schizophrenia. *J. Neuropsychiatr. Clin. Neurosci.* **6**:348–57.

Gooding, D.C. and Iacono, W.G. 1995. Schizophrenia through the lens of a developmental psychopathology perspective. In *Developmental psychopathology*, vol. 2, ed. D., Cicchetti, and D.J. Cohen, pp. 535–580. New York: John Wiley.

Goodman, R. 1989. Neuronal misconnections and psychiatric disorder. Is there a link? *Br. J. Psychiatry* **154**:292–9.

Hoffman, R.E. and McGlashan, T.H. 1993. Parallel distributed processing and the emergence of schizophrenic symptoms. *Schizophr. Bull.* **19**:119–40.

Huttenlocher, P.R. 1979. Synaptic density in human frontal cortex. Developmental changes and effects of aging. *Brain Res.* **163**:195.

Jakob, H. and Beckmann, H. 1986. Prenatal developmental disturbances in the limbic allocortex in schizophrenics. *J. Neurol. Transm.* **65**:303.

Janowsky, J.S. and Finlay, B.L. 1986. The outcome of brain damage: the file of normal neuronal loss and retraction. *Dev. Med. Child Neurol.* 375–89.

Jernigan, T.L. and Tallal, P. 1990. Late childhood changes in brain morphology observable with MRI. *Dev. Med. Child Neurol.* **32**:379–85.

Jones, P., Rodgers, B., Murray,R., and Marmot, M. 1994. Child developmental risk factors for adult schizophrenia in the British 1946 birth cohort. *Lancet* **344**:1398–402.

Keshavan, M.S., Anderson, S., and Pettegrew, J.W. 1994. Is schizophrenia due to excessive synaptic pruning in the prefrontal cortex? *J. Psychiat. Res.* **28**:239.

Keshavan, M.S., Kapur, S., and Pettegrew, J.W. 1991. Magnetic resonance spectroscopy: potential, pitfalls and promise. *Am. J. Psychiatry* **148**:976–85.

Keshavan, M.S. and Pettegrew, J.W. Magnetic resonance spectroscopy in schizophrenia and psychotic disorders. In *Brain imaging in clinical psychiatry*. ed. K.R.R. Krishnan, New York: Marcel-Dekker (in press).

Keshavan, M.S., Reynolds, C.F., Kupfer, D.J. 1990. Electroencephalographic sleep in schizophrenia: a critical review. *Comprehen. Psychiatry* **30**:34–47.

Keshavan, M.S. and Schooler, N.R. 1992. First episode studies in schizophrenia: criteria and characterization. *Schizophr. Bull.* **18**:491.

Kim, J.S., Kornhuber, H., Schid-Burgk, W., and Holzmuller, B. 1980. Low cerebrospinal fluid glutamate in schizophrenic patients and a new hypothesis on schizophrenia. *Neurosci. Lett.* **20**:379.

Ktonas, P.Y., Fagioli, I., and Salzuralo, P. 1995. Delta (0.5–1.5 Hz) and sigma (1.5–15.5 Hz) EEG power dynamics throughout quiet sleep in infants. *Electroencephalogr. Clin. Neurophysiol.* **95**:90–6.

Lipska, B.K. and Weinberger, D.R. 1994. Behavioral effects of subchronic treatment with haloperidol or clozapine in rats with neonatal excitotoxic hippocampal damage. *Neuropsychoparmacology* **10**:199–205.

Murray, R.M. and Lewis, S.W. 1987. Is schizophrenia a neurodevelopmental disorder? *Br. Med. J.* **295**:681.

Murray, R.M., O'Callaghan, E., Castle, D.J., and Lewis, S.W. 1992. A neurodevelopmental approach to the classification of schizophrenia. *Schizophr. Bull.* **18**:319.

Platt, J.R. 1964. Strong inference. *Science* **146**:347–53.

Pettegrew, J.W., Keshavan, M.S., Panchalingam, K., Trychor, S., Kaplan, D.B., Tretta, M.G., and Allen, M. 1991.

Alterations in brain high-energy phosphate and phospholipid metabolism in first episode, drug-naive schizophrenia. A pilot study of the dorsal prefrontal cortex by in vivo ^{31}P NMR spectroscopy. *Arch. Gen. Psychiatry* **48**:563.

Selemon, L.D., Rajkowska, G., and Goldman-Rakic, P.S. 1995. Abnormally high neuronal density in the schizophrenic cortex. *Arch. Gen. Psychiatry* **52**:805–18.

Stanley, J.F., Drost, D.J., Williamson, P.C., and Carr, T.J. 1995. In vivo proton MRS study of glutamate and schizophrenia. In *NMR spectroscopy in psychiatric brain disorders*, ed. H. A. Nasrallah and J. W. Pettegrew, p. 21. Washington, DC: American Psychiatric Press.

Stevens, J.R. 1992. Abnormal reinnervation as a basis for schizophrenia: a hypothesis. *Arch. Gen. Psychiatry* **49**:238–43.

Swerdlow, N.R. and Koob, G.F. 1987. Dopamine, schizophrenia, mania, and depression: toward a unified hypothesis of cortico–striato–pallidothalamic function. *Beh. Brain Sci.* **10**:197–245.

Van Ooyen, A., van Pelt, J., and Corner, M.A. 1995. Implications of activity dependent neurite outgrowth for neuronal morphology and network development. *J. Theoret. Biol.* **172**:63–82.

Walker, E., Grimes, K., Davis, D., and Smith, A. 1993. Childhood precursors of schizophrenia: facial expressions of emotion. *Am. J. Psychiatry* **150**:1654–60.

Weinberger, D.R. 1987. Implications of normal brain development for the pathogenesis of schizophrenia. *Arch. Gen. Psychiatry* **44**:660–7.

Weinberger, D.R. 1995. From neuropathology to neurodevelopment. *Lancet* **346**:552–7.

Zipursky, R.B., Lim, K.O., Sullivan, E.V., Brown, B.W., and Pfefferbaum, A. 1992. Widespread grey matter volume deficits in schizophrenia. *Arch. Gen. Psychiatry* **49**:195–205.

Index